The
Sail Magazine
Book of
Sailing

The Sail Magazine Book of Sailing

PETER JOHNSON

ALFRED A. KNOPF · NEW YORK · 1989

A DORLING KINDERSLEY BOOK

PROJECT EDITOR·SIMON ADAMS
EDITORS·SALLY MACEACHERN
·LINDA MARTIN
ART EDITOR·MARK RICHARDS
DESIGNERS·MARTYN FOOTE
·THOMAS KEENES
PICTURE EDITOR·ANGELA MURPHY
MANAGING EDITOR·VICKY DAVENPORT

THIS IS A BORZOI BOOK
PUBLISHED BY ALFRED A. KNOPF, INC.

Library of Congress Cataloging-in-Publication Data

Johnson, Peter.
   The sail magazine book of sailing / Peter Johnson. — 1st ed.
     p.   cm.
   ISBN 0-394-57457-5
   1. Sailboat racing — History.   2. Sailing — History.   I. Title.
   GV826.J64   1989   89-2531
   797.1'4 — dc19   CIP

Typeset by MFK Typesetting Ltd, Hitchin, Hertfordshire, UK
Color reproduction by Bright Arts, Hong Kong
Printed and bound in Spain by Graficromo SA, Cordoba

First American Edition

Author's Note

Unless otherwise stated, a mile is always a nautical mile (1.85 km, 1.15 statute miles).

When detailing the length of a boat in the text, 'length' or 'long' refers to its overall length; the abbreviation LOA is sometimes used. LWL means length on load waterline, as designed or generally accepted. A technically exact LWL is difficult to measure and varies with the load.

Although meters are used as the primary unit throughout this book, the dimensions of many classes and the rules on sizes of boats were, and still are, often stated in feet. When these ratings and names are mentioned, they are quoted in the unit in which they were drawn up: thus an imperial-measure equivalent is inappropriate for the 12-Meter class, while the International 14 is a 14-ft dinghy for which no metric equivalent is required.

Title page – 1987 Admiral's Cup race; pp 8-9 – a Dutch yacht of the States-General and a boier, from an etching by Rudolf Backhuizen, mid-17th century; pp 26-7 – H.W. Tilman's Mischief in the Antarctic; pp 58-9 – Hitchhiker, a member of the 1985 Australian Admiral's Cup team; pp 138-9 – Australia II, 1983 winner of the America's Cup; pp 158-9 – the start of a race at the 1987 International 14 World Championships, Inawashiro, Japan; pp 190-1 – Tornados rounding a mark in the 1984 Olympic Games, Long Beach, California; pp 210-11 – Dutch Regenboog one-design keelboats; pp 300-1 – the port of Hvar, Yugoslavia.

Introduction

$\mathcal{T}$he renowned sailor and yacht designer Uffa Fox once remarked that people spend huge sums of money to enjoy the discomforts of the sea. Today, that remark is more relevant than ever, even if many people would disagree about the nature of those discomforts. All over the world, ingenuity, time and, of course, money are spent in the design, building and sailing of boats, the prime objective being the pursuit of pleasure. In days gone by, sailing boats were employed for transport, commerce, fishing or war. We are fortunate that now we can enjoy them purely for sport, an immense attraction in this mechanical and electronic age.

The Sail Magazine Book of Sailing documents this sport in its continuing variety. Facts, records and stories concerning the growth, development and current state of sailing are described and illustrated. Instruction, criticism and opinion are avoided throughout, although all sailors can undoubtedly learn from the successes and failures of past yachtsmen and their boats.

It is this historical aspect that is emphasized at the beginning of the book, for the structure and practices of sailing are not particularly consistent or rational, having derived from the various attempts to organize and develop the sport – at first on a local, and then a national level. Thus today's offshore and dinghy racing involves many hundreds of individual boat classes, some unique to particular places or countries, yet the rules of racing are truly international.

The more relaxed pastime of cruising under sail is not forgotten. In recent years, many more sailors have undertaken cruises of various kinds than have raced, but such voyages have been markedly less well recorded. The focus is, therefore, on the well-documented pioneers and those who have led the way by outstanding feats.

Even in ocean racing, the best-remembered scenes are not necessarily those illustrated and recorded in the pages of this book. For when land is out of sight and the sun is about to touch the western horizon but, on some occasions, the cockpit is dry, I recall the words of Joshua Slocum, "As for myself, the wonderful sea charmed me from the first." It has had this effect on me too, and has been a stimulating incentive to research and to present, with the help of many others, this record of sailing the seas.

Contents

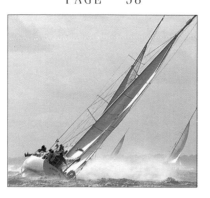

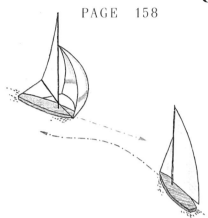

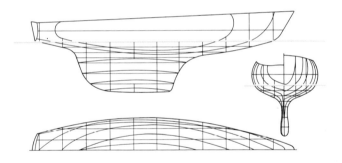
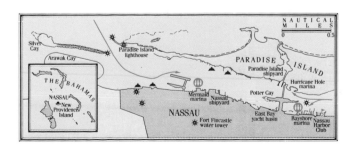

Chapter 1

The Origins of Yachting

For most of the period in which ships were reliant on sail, the idea of travelling on the sea for pleasure was incredible. Dr Samuel Johnson remarked in 1759 that "No man will be a sailor who has contrivance enough to get himself into jail; for being in a ship is being in a jail, with the chance of being drowned..." Yet in older literature of the sea, it is suggested that when the weather and wind were fair, or the ship was in the tropics, such a life had much to recommend it. A number of factors needed to exist before sailing for pleasure – or yachting – could take place. There had to be a wealthy society containing people who could afford the time to sail for pleasure and the money to employ a crew; a knowledge of shipbuilding; and sheltered waters protected from pirates. Such a combination of circumstances arose in the Netherlands in the late 16th century.

THE FIRST YACHTS

The words 'yacht' and 'yachting' come from the Dutch word *jaghen*, meaning to hunt, chase or pursue, suggesting speed, whether on land or sea. In 1599 a Dutch-Latin dictionary published in Antwerp described a *jaght schip* and a *jaght* (or *joghte*) as a light and swift vessel of war, commerce or pleasure. By this date the word 'yacht' was familiar in both England and France as describing the small but fast ships that accompanied the Dutch navy and that were used to carry dispatches, government officials and officers on errands.

It should come as no surprise that yachting originated in the Netherlands, for in the 16th and 17th centuries it was the world's major maritime power. Officially recognized as an independent nation in 1648, the Netherlands was enjoying a golden age. Its substantial mercantile economy was the most prosperous in Europe, based on maritime trade and commerce throughout Europe and round Africa to India and the Far East. Many of its wealthy citizens had prospered in the herring industry, their boats dominated

A New Sport *Housed in the Nederlands Scheepvaart Museum in Amsterdam is this early-17th century drawing by S. Savery showing a small and attractive sailing boat containing a group of people relaxing, eating and drinking, evidently enjoying a day out. It is one of the earliest pictures of people yachting.*

the North Sea fishing industry, and its many seaports boasted a large company of boat designers, builders and sailmakers.

This flourishing economy supported a large number of people intimately connected with the sea who could afford to commission and buy boats to use for convenience and occasional leisure. A small sailing vessel in the numerous protected inland waters of the Netherlands was at many times of the year a more pleasant conveyance than a swaying carriage on a potholed road.

At first yachting took place on sheltered, inland waters, for apart from the high casualty rate for all sailing ships due to bad weather or rough seas, there was also the ever-present possibility of encountering pirates. It was not until the early 19th century that the seas around Europe became free of pirates.

On 17 June 1640, for example, the sailing ship *Elizabeth*, returning from the English colony of Virginia with a crew of 30 commanded by Captain Doves, met three Turkish ships off the Lizard Point on England's south coast. *Elizabeth* tried to make to the shore, but the Turkish boats surrounded and attacked it. The captain

Bezan *Presented by the Dutch to the English king Charles II in 1661, Bezan was a typical yacht of the period, with a single mast on which is hoisted a sprit carrying a loose-footed mainsail. The painting is by the contemporary Dutch painter Barent Cornelisz Kleenknecht.*

and several of the crew were killed, but as the Turks scrambled on board, hoping to seize the crew as slaves, they were shot at by "a passenger with a musket". One of the Turks who was shot was then beheaded, his body thrown over one side of the ship while his head went over the other. The Turks withdrew in search of easier prey, leaving *Elizabeth* to continue the voyage.

On the way up the English Channel *Elizabeth* encountered a further 11 damaged and abandoned ships, previous victims of the Turks who had captured their crews and shipped them off to slavery. Faced with incidents like these, it is not surprising that sailing remained a coastal or inland water sport.

AN AMUSING PASTIME

Although these early ships had occasionally been used purely for pleasure, their main purpose was for transport or communication. To find the first example of

The Russian Visitor *The Russian czar Peter the Great toured Western Europe in 1697-8. He studied industrial techniques, including shipbuilding, and hired craftsmen to work in Russia. In this painting by Abram Storck, he is shown on board a highly decorated yacht (on the left) taking part in a mock battle staged by the Dutch in in 1697 on what is now the Ijsselmeer. The other vessels are a mixture of yachts and working boats.*

sailing for pleasure, one must look to the English king, Charles II.

After he was driven into semi-exile on the Channel Island of Jersey at the height of the English Civil War in 1646, the-then Prince of Wales used to amuse himself by sailing a small boat out of one of the island's harbors. In exile in the Netherlands after the execution of his father, Charles I, in 1649, Charles learned the Dutch custom of travelling by water. On his restoration to the throne in 1660, he undertook the first part of his journey home by yacht, from Breda to Delft. A contemporary account of that voyage stated that "the yacht on board of which the king sailed had been built for himself by the Prince of Orange, but now belongs to the Board of Admiralty of Rotterdam. The king found his yacht so comfortable,

that he remarked, while discoursing with the Deputies, that he might order one of the same style, so soon as he should arrive in England, to use in the River Thames."

A few months after his return to London, Charles was presented with a yacht recently built in Rotterdam for the Dutch East India Company. It was called *Mary*, was 15.8m (52ft) long and 5.8m (19ft) wide, and had a draft of 3m (10ft). It also sported 10 cannons and had a crew of 20. Although originally rigged as a sloop with a sprit for the mainsail in the Dutch tradition, *Mary* was rerigged during a refit in 1662 with the gaff rig commonly used in England. But apart from that, there were very few differences in design between *Mary* and other small vessels used for commerce or trade. Yachts tended to have a superior standard of finish and equipment: a contemporary observer noted that *Mary* "had the interior of the cabins decorated and gilded, while some of the best artists have been engaged in making beautiful paintings and sculptures with which to embellish the vessel, within and without."

Mary arrived in the River Thames from the Netherlands in August 1660, and so

Peter Pett *Son of Phineas Pett, shipbuilder during the reign of Elizabeth I, Peter Pett designed and built* Anne, *one of the first yachts to be built in England, for the Duke of York in 1660. His brother Christopher and his cousin Phineas built yachts for Charles II.*

eager was the king to see his new boat that the diarist Samuel Pepys "found the king gone this morning by five of the clock to see a Dutch pleasure boat below bridge." The arrival of the yacht created quite a stir, and immediately the shipbuilders Peter and Christopher Pett began thinking how to design and build a similar or better version of *Mary*. Pepys and Peter Pett went on board *Mary* in November, noting that it "is one of the finest things that ever I saw for neatness and room in so small a vessel. Mr. Pett is to make out to outdo this for the honor of the country, which, I fear, he will scarce better."

So it was that the decision was made to build two yachts in England, the first ever of this previously unique Dutch breed of sailing vessel. Christopher Pett built *Catherine* for Charles II, named after the king's bride-to-be Catherine of Braganza. The yacht was 16.7 m (55 ft) long overall, with a beam of 5.8 m (19 ft) and a weight of 94 tons. Peter Pett modelled a very similar vessel for the king's brother, the Duke of York, called *Anne* after the duke's wife, slightly longer than *Catherine* and weighing 100 tons. Both vessels drew 2.1 m (7 ft). The rig on each yacht was single masted,

The royal yacht Mary, *built by Phineas Pett for Charles II in 1677.*

with two headsails, a gaff mainsail and a square topsail over it.

A year later, in 1661, another yacht, *Bezan*, 16.5 m (54 ft) in overall length, arrived from Holland. With *Mary*, there was thus a fleet of four yachts in England. Samuel Pepys escorted his wife and some friends and "showed them the King's and Duke's yachts and we had great pleasure in seeing all four yachts, Viz. these two and two Dutch ones."

This nascent yacht fleet gave birth to the first recorded yacht race. Sailing vessels often used to race each other to be

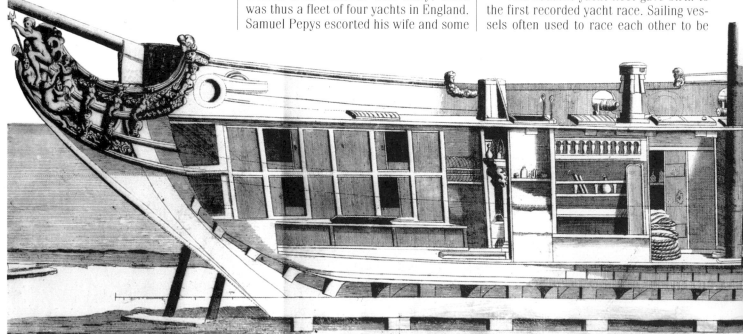

first back to port with their cargo, but this was the first time two yachts had raced each other for sport. The king was aboard *Catherine*, the duke on *Anne*.

The first leg of the course was down river from Greenwich to Gravesend. With an east wind blowing into the estuary, the yachts were sailing into the wind. Probably they could not sail much closer than 70° to the wind – a modern ocean racer can point at 38° – but the ebb tide helped them and *Anne* proved itself better at sailing to windward. The diarist John Evelyn recorded the event:

"I sailed this morning with His Majesty in one of his yachts (or pleasure boats), vessels not known among us till the Dutch East India Company presented that curious piece to the King; being very excellent sailing vessels. It was on a wager between his other new pleasure boat, built frigate-like, and one of the Duke of York's; the wager £100, the race from Greenwich to Gravesend and back. The King lost it going, the wind being contrary, but saved stakes on returning. There were divers noble persons and lords on board, His Majesty sometimes steering himself. His barge and kitchen boat attended." Frigate-like, according to one source, meant lower free-board; in other words, *Catherine* was more flush decked than the original *Mary*.

THE GROWING FLEET

Altogether 26 yachts were built in England between 1661 and 1683 by a small group of builders, notably the Pett brothers. These yachts were an improvement on the Dutch ones to suit the deeper and more exposed British waters, and fixed keels were substituted for Dutch leeboards. The shortest of the new yachts was 9.5m (31ft), the longest 23m (74ft), although even the smallest carried four guns. Little is on record of their activities, but they would probably have been used for conveying royalty, government officials, naval officers and dispatches. Some of them might even have had informal races.

Samuel Pepys took several voyages on these yachts. On 1 October 1663 he was on board *Bezan* visiting the Royal Navy. "We breakfasted betimes and some to the fleet about two o'clock in the afternoon, having a fine day and fine wind. My Lord received us mightily kindly.... After supper on board the *Bezan*, and there to cards for a while, and then to read and so to sleep. But Lord! The mirth which it caused me to be waked in the night by their snoring round me; I did laugh till I was ready to burst, and waked one who could not a good

while tell where he was that he heard one laugh so, till he recollected himself, and I told him what it was at, and so to sleep again, they still snoring.

"October 2. We having sailed all night (and I did wonder how they in the dark could find the way), we got by morning to Gillingham." On November 2, "intending to have gone this night in a ketch, down to the fleet, they persuaded me not to go till morning, it being a horrible dark and windy night." The next day they sailed out to the fleet, then "I took the *Bezan* back with me, taking great pleasure of learning the seamans' great pleasure of singing, when they sound the depths."

◆◆◆

Royal Yacht *A cross-section of a royal yacht built for Charles II in 1693. The fast lines, decorative finish and comfortable accommodation emphasize its purpose for pleasure sailing.*

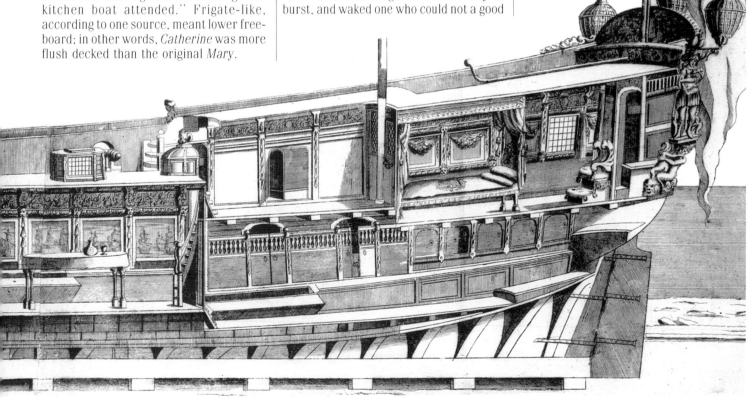

THE EIGHTEENTH CENTURY

In 1754 the English novelist and dramatist Henry Fielding remarked, while sailing down the Thames past Greenwich on his way to Portugal, on "the deplorable want of taste in our enjoyments which we show by almost totally neglecting the pursuit of what seems to me the highest degree of amusement. This is the sailing ourselves of little vessels of our own contrived only for our ease and accommodation. This amusement, I confess, if enjoyed in any perfection, would be of the expensive kind; but such expense would not exceed the reach of a moderate fortune

◆◆◆

Charlotte *Launched in 1749 as* Royal Caroline, *after the wife of George II, this royal yacht was renamed* Charlotte *in 1761 in honor of George III's bride, Princess Charlotte of Mecklenburg-Strelitz. In this contemporary painting, the royal yacht, shown in the center festooned with flags and accompanied by an escort of warships and other, smaller yachts, is depicted leaving the German port of Stade to bring the princess back to England for her wedding. The 232-ton* Charlotte *remained in its capacity as a royal yacht until 1803.*

and would fall very short of the prices which are daily paid for pleasures of a far inferior rate."

That Fielding was aware of yachting (and its cost) is beyond doubt, but obviously at the time of his writing, the sport was not flourishing, at least on the lower Thames, as it once had. This was partly due to the lengthy periods of warfare that existed between the major European powers throughout the 18th century, but, as before, the threat of pirates and the vagaries of the sea discouraged many from this potentially hazardous sport.

Fielding was a much-published writer, so his words are readily available to us. Otherwise we have to guess at the state of yachting during the 18th century from the occasional reports that appeared in various newspapers and magazines. *The Gentleman's Magazine* of 1773 reported that on 26 September 1773, "Earl Ferrer, an admiral in the British Royal Navy, arrived at Deptford in his yacht from a cruise of about three weeks, which he took in order

to make a trial of his new method of constructing ships. ... They say she is not only a surprisingly fast sailer, but also carried her sail remarkably well and has every good quality ... and more particularly in a large head sea." Ferrer's yacht beat up the Thames against the spring ebb "which was never done before, nor can be done by any other vessel."

Another newspaper reported on 5 July 1783 that "yesterday night, the Duke of Richmond set sail in his new yacht for France. He is accompanied by his brother, Lord George Lennox, Lady Louisa Lennox, the Misses Lennox and Captain Berkeley." A few years earlier, when the American War of Independence was in progress, the duke had sailed his yacht flying the American colors through some of the British fleet at Spithead, in order to show his sympathy with the revolutionary cause and his opposition to the policies of George III and his government. This spectacle was observed by the king himself on board a naval vessel.

THE ROYAL YACHTS

The English royal yachts of the 18th century were not the sporty personal boats of Charles II; rather they were more like small ships. Under naval command, they were often used for official duties such as reviewing the fleet. *Royal Caroline*, built at Deptford in 1749 was 22 m (72 ft) along the keel with a beam of 7.5 m (24 ft 7 in) and a tonnage of 232 tons. Though termed a ketch, it had three masts and squaresails. Among its voyages was a trip to Germany to collect Princess Charlotte of Mecklenburg-Strelitz who was to be George III's bride.

At the end of the century a larger replacement, *Royal Sovereign*, was built weighing 350 tons, and it in turn was followed by further royal yachts, none of which had much to do with yachting in the recreational sense. As today, the royal yachts were used for official business and for royal holidays, sometimes attending sailing regattas or rallies.

The last royal yacht to make use of sail, *Royal George*, was built in 1817, but it was replaced in 1843 by the first *Victoria and Albert*, a paddle-steamer. The replacement of sail by steam followed a particularly slow voyage under sail with the queen on board from London to Scotland in 1842.

A PLEASURE PORT

During the 18th century spas like Bath and Cheltenham had developed as inland resorts for those who could afford to find time for leisure. Coastal resorts such as Scarborough and later Brighthelmstone, now known as Brighton, became popular too as the healthy benefits of sea air were recognized. In the later part of the century the small, south-coast town of Cowes, on the Isle of Wight, joined them in popularity. Its sheltered position facing the mainland away from the open sea, and thus any possible attack from a foreign fleet, made it a popular resort.

River Sailing Union, *a sloop-rigged yacht, belonging to Mr. Baptist May, is depicted in this engraving from a painting of 1751. It is sailing opposite his house at Hammersmith on the River Thames above London.*

The local people encouraged this development of their town, for when the country was at peace the naval ships no longer needed provisioning from the town's stores, and the local inhabitants were no longer hired as boatmen and pilots. They thus welcomed the chance to entertain any visitors on boating trips and show off their boating skills at town regattas in which local workboats tried to match each other for speed. The combination of an excellent anchorage for the private vessels of the aristocracy, a pleasant resort for their families and friends, and a pool of skilled, coastal seamen always available, served the town well and guaranteed its place among favored sailing resorts.

EARLY RALLIES AND RACES

Of all the yachting activities that took place in the 18th century, the most famous are those of the Water Club of Cork, in the south-west of Ireland. The exact year of its founding is not known, but records and paintings in the club's possession date it back to at least 1720. However a series of elaborate rules drawn up for the fortnightly meetings that took place from April to September include the instruction that "no admiral do bring more than two dozen of wine to his treat, for it has always been deemed a breach of the ancient rules and constitution of this club." Such a statement suggests a much earlier date for the club's foundation. By these same rules, the club was limited to 25 members, elected its admiral annually and had its headquarters on Haulbowline Island in Cork Harbor.

THE CHASE

The meetings of the Water Club were either formal dinners or what would now be called rallies. Contemporary paintings show the club sailing gaff-rigged, bluff-bowed cutters about 12 m (40 ft) long of a type then in use by pilots and revenue officers. These yachts used to engage in maneuvers under the command of the admiral, who used signal guns and flags. The nearest they probably got to racing was a "chase. When the admiral will have ... a single boat to chase ... he will hoist a pendant and fire as many guns from the side a boat is distanced from him."

◆◆◆

The Water Club of Cork *Dating back to at least 1720, the Water Club can lay claim to be the world's first yacht club. In this drawing, the club fleet is shown putting to sea.*

Hardly a race, although it does sound similar to the kind of chase given when smugglers and privateers were pursued by coastguards or the navy.

An eyewitness account of the Water Club occurs in *A Tour through Ireland*, published in London in 1748. "I shall now acquaint your lordships with a ceremony they have at Cork. It is somewhat like that of the Doge of Venice wedding at sea. A set of worthy gentlemen ... proceed a few leagues out to sea once a year in a number of small vessels, which for painting and golding exceed the King's yacht at Greenwich and Deptford. Their admiral, who is elected annually, and hoists his flag on board his little vessel, leads the van and receives the honors of the flag. The rest of the fleet fall in their proper stations and keep their line in the same number as the King's ships. This fleet ... forms one of the most agreeable and splendid sights your lordships can conceive."

The Water Club prospered until 1765, but thereafter there are no more records, and activities must at some point have ceased. In 1806 the Marquess of Thomond and others met to try to revive the club, but its activities were restricted to encouraging competition among the fishing and rowing boats of Cork Harbor, to which they gave prizes. By 1821 the club was all but extinct, prompting some of the surviving members to combine with another recently formed local club, the Little Monkstown. In 1828 the joint club adopted the title Cork Yacht Club, receiving a royal imprimatur in 1830.

Despite this somewhat broken record, the Royal Cork Yacht Club can lay claim to be the world's oldest club, and in the 1980s can boast an extremely active organization covering all forms of yacht racing and cruising.

Intriguingly a Russian record suggests that in 1717 Peter the Great made available over 100 vessels to encourage "a taste for navigation, to spread nautical knowledge and to give service men and their children a taste for the sea." The claim to this being the world's first yacht club is based on the craft having their own flag and the title of Flotilla of the Neva, the river that flows through what was then the new capital city of St. Petersburg, now Leningrad. This club however sounds more like a group of naval training ships for young people than a proper yacht club.

ROYAL RACES

In England in 1749, the Prince of Wales, later George III, presented a cup to be raced for by "twelve yachts or pleasure boats" from Greenwich in London to the Nore lightship in the Thames estuary and back again, evidence enough to dispute Fielding's assertion that yachting did not take place on the river. The *Gentleman's Magazine* of August 1749 reported in connection with the race that "the river seemed overspread with sailing yachts, galleys and small boats."

There are no known records of similar events taking place for many years,

but personal diaries show that some richer people had a small boat on the river that they used for recreation or for taking short journeys. There must have been enough of these small yachts by the summer of 1775 to enthuse the Duke of Cumberland, brother of George III, to give "a silver cup to be sailed for on Thursday 11 July, from Westminster Bridge to Putney Bridge and back by pleasure sailing boats from two to five tons burthen, and constantly lying above London Bridge." Twenty boats entered; unfortunately information about the race is sparse, although we do know that it was won by *Aurora*, owned by "Mr. Parks, late of Ludgate Hill", and that second place was taken by *Fly*, owner unknown.

The Duke of Cumberland gave a prize every year until 1782 for a similar event that took place on an identical course, and contestants soon came to form the Cumberland Sailing Society, of which members were reported to "have come to a resolution to be dressed in aquatic uniforms." This club thus became the first yacht club in England.

Its organization is shown by the ceremonies at the end of each race for the duke's cup. The captains (the owners of the yachts) waited in skiffs and only boarded their yachts when the Duke of Cumberland appeared in his gilded barge and boarded the commodore of the fleet's yacht. The victorious owner was then summoned to the commodore's yacht and was introduced to the duke, who filled the cup with claret, drank the health of the winner and presented the cup. The whole fleet then sailed to Mr. Smith's tea gardens at the southern end of Vauxhall Bridge. In time these gardens came to be known as the Cumberland Gardens, and Mr. Smith was for five years commodore of the club.

Some club members undoubtedly possessed larger sea-going yachts, as substantiated by the fact that a yacht owned by Thomas Taylor, who succeeded Mr. Smith as commodore, went aground off Margate in the Thames estuary, while another member's yacht was apparently chased into Calais by an American privateer.

In later years reports give us glimpses of further races. The *Morning Chronicle* of 19 July 1786 reported that "there was an attempt of foul play against the winner, *Prince of Wales*, by other boats getting in

The Cumberland Sailing Society *Formed in 1775, the fleet was the first yacht club in England. It took its name from the Duke of Cumberland, who presented a cup for a race to be held on the Thames. In this painting by an unknown artist, the fleet is shown racing above London Bridge in 1782.*

her way, but she got clear by a liberal use of handspike." On 23 July 1795, *The Times* noted that "*Mercury*, leading, got foul of *Vixen*. The captain of *Vixen* cut away the rigging of *Mercury* and fairly dismantled her, *Mermaid* winning the cup."

A main characteristic of yachting has always been participants' interest in design and construction, and the best kind of boat to buy or sail. The members of the Cumberland Sailing Society met these criteria, as shown in a report on a match race in the July 1796 issue of the *Sporting Magazine*. One of the boats, "*Atlanta*, belonging to a gentleman at Vauxhall, and built by Hodges upon a plan intended to unite the qualities of a long vessel as well as a wide one, which is in this miniature of a cutter most successfully accomplished, her bottom being so formed that in light air she is a mere slip and when it blows hard she seems to possess uncommon power to carry sail."

THE NINETEENTH CENTURY

The ending of the Napoleonic Wars in 1815 ushered in a period of prolonged peace between the major European powers that was to last, almost without interruption, for the rest of the century. British naval supremacy throughout the world ensured that the seas were free of pirates, and so at last it became possible to sail offshore without being attacked. Coupled with rising prosperity due to the industrial revolution, conditions were ideal for the expansion of such leisure pursuits as yachting among the richer members of society.

On 1 June 1815 a group of English gentlemen met at the Thatched House Tavern, St. James's Street, London, for one of the most memorable meetings in yachting history. Under the presidency of Lord Grantham, they decided to form a club to consist of men who were interested in sailing yachts on salt water. Those who were present, and others who had expressed interest, 42 in total, decided on an entry fee of three guineas, and for future members the ownership of a yacht of at least 10

◆◆◆

On the Waterfront *With the establishment of the Royal Yacht Squadron in 1815, Cowes became the major yachting center in Britain. This contemporary print by Robert Cruikshank shows members of Cowes society on the esplanade: the print reputedly includes caricatures of Squadron members.*

tons. It was resolved "that the club be called The Yacht Club". It was the first time that the expression had been used for any organization.

Although formed in London, the club had already established links with the town of Cowes on the Isle of Wight. Prior to the club's formation, the 42 initial members – all but 19 titled members of the aristocracy – had met regularly in Cowes during August, and now decided to formalize the association with an annual dinner to be held at a hotel in East Cowes on 24 August. Thanks to their interest, the town enhanced its reputation as a popular resort for yachting members of the gentry.

ROYAL APPROVAL

Although formed as a yacht club, the club was in many ways no different from the many London gentlemen's clubs such as the Athanaeum and Whites. Its members originally had no intention of meeting more than a few times each year, mainly for social reasons, in Cowes and London. However the club soon expanded well beyond these limited horizons.

On 15 September 1817, a special meeting was called at East Cowes during which the following letter was read out: "Sir, The Prince Regent desires to be a member of The Yacht Club and you are to consider this

as an official notification of His Royal Highness's desire. I have the honor to be, sir, Your obedient humble servant, – Charles Paget."

The prince was immediately elected member, and the following spring two other royal princes joined. From then on the club became more conscious of its position. In 1818 a club uniform was designed and the qualification of yacht size became 20 tons minimum. In 1820, when the Prince Regent became George IV, the title of the club was changed to the Royal Yacht Club, and in 1824 it acquired the lease of a clubhouse on the Cowes sea front and appointed its first commodore, the Earl of Yarborough.

Although there had been informal races between members of the club, the first official race was not held until 10 August 1826 for "vessels belonging to the Royal Yacht Club of any rig or tonnage for a gold cup of the value of £100; to start at 9.30 am precisely off Cowes Castle." The annual regatta ball was on the same evening, the dinner the following day, a Friday, and "a splendid display of fireworks on the same night at the Parade, West Cowes." Apart from the years of the two world wars, organized racing, and fireworks on Friday night, have taken place in early August at Cowes ever since.

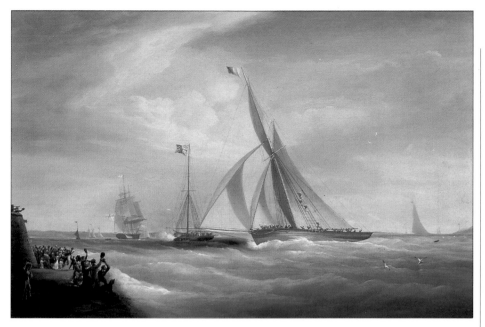

The cutter Alarm *wins the Royal Yacht Squadron's King's Cup in 1831.*

A further development in the club's history took place in July 1833 with a letter from Lord Belfast to the-then secretary of the club. "Sir, I have it in command from His Majesty [since 1830, William IV] to acquaint you, for the information of the Commodore and the officers of the Royal Yacht Club, that as a mark of His Majesty's gracious approval of an institution of such national utility, it is his gracious wish and pleasure that it shall be henceforth known and styled 'The Royal Yacht Squadron' of which His Majesty is graciously pleased to consider himself the head." By this time the burgee or pennant of the club had been fixed as a red cross on white with a crown on the intersection, and the ensign as the White Ensign of the Royal Navy.

The name and two flags of the Royal Yacht Squadron remain unchanged to this day. Although both the Royal Cork Yacht Club and the Royal Thames Yacht Club have older ancestry, they do have some gaps in their history. This means that the Squadron is the oldest yacht club with unbroken service in the world, and the first to be founded as a yacht club in anything like the modern sense. Its founders had no idea that they were setting a precedent for the thousands of yacht and sailing clubs that exist today throughout the world.

Away from Cowes the Cumberland Sailing Society continued to flourish on the Thames. By 1823, in honor of the coronation of George IV, its name had been changed to the Coronation Society. However that year's race produced a dispute, as a result of which the committee ordered it to be resailed. A number of members would have none of this and, on 14 August 1823, broke away to found the Thames Yacht Club, holding their first race on 9 September. Deprived of its most active members, the Coronation Sailing Society faded into oblivion by about 1827, while the Thames Yacht Club received the royal imprimatur in 1830 when

●◆●

A Yacht Regatta *In early regattas, yachts started the race from their moorings or from anchor. This painting by H. Forrest shows the start of a regatta at the Royal Dart YC, southern England, in 1868.*

Yachts from the Royal Thames Yacht Club racing at Cowes in 1844.

its patron, the Duke of Clarence, was crowned William IV.

INTERNATIONAL GROWTH

In the same year the club at Cork became the Royal Cork Yacht Club, bringing the number of royally endorsed clubs to three. Thus by the 1830s yachting was becoming an organized and increasingly popular sport, with many similarities to its appearance today: there were clubs, owners and races; the advent of steam ships gave sailing an added novelty; and finally there were sets of rules established by clubs and regatta committees that, although initially all different, were slowly consolidated first locally, then nationally and eventually internationally.

Not surprisingly this consolidation first took place in Britain where clubs emerged in imitation of the three royal ones. Although few of them started out with royal imprimaturs or with the same name as they bear today, a number of clubs sprang up after 1815: The Royal Dee was founded in late 1815; the Royal Northern (on the Clyde in Scotland) in 1824; the Royal Western at Plymouth in 1827; the Royal Gibraltar, the first colonial club, in 1829; the Royal Irish in 1831; the Royal Southern in 1837; and the Royal London, the Royal St. George in Ireland, and the Royal Hobart Regatta Association in Tasmania, Australia, all in 1838.

How far yachting had come in Britain from the early years of the century, when we have to look for odd clues as to its existence in occasional newspaper reports or old handbills, is borne out by the existence of a small book called *The Yachtsman's Annual and General Register*, published in 1845. The register lists two regatta associations, at Weymouth and Teignmouth, and 12 clubs.

The entry for the Royal Yacht Squadron shows that it had 160 members and 100 vessels, most of which weighed between 50 and 120 tons, although one schooner weighed in at 393 tons, while other craft were as light as 30 tons. The Royal Thames Yacht Club had 150 rather smaller yachts, but together they show that by the middle of the century the British yachting fleet was considerable.

The world's first yacht club outside the British empire was founded in Sweden in 1830. It is thought that Lord Bloomfield, a member of the Royal Yacht Squadron, spoke of the squadron's activities when he was in Sweden as British ambassador. Six gentlemen heard him and, meeting one evening in May 1830, decided to form the Segel Sallskapet (The Yacht Club). The statutes of the club were drawn up in 1833, having first been approved by the Swedish crown prince, and the club changed its name to the Svenska Segel Sallskapet (The Swedish Yacht Club, SSS). The royal (kungelig) imprimatur followed a few years later and the club became the Royal Swedish Yacht Club (the Kungelig Svenska Segel Sallskapet, the KSSS).

THE WORLD OF YACHTING

Although the first yacht clubs were formed in the British Isles, it was not long before other countries started to form their own clubs. The first outside Britain was in the British colony of Gibraltar, the first outside the British empire, in Sweden. Soon almost every country in the world where yachts were sailed had formed clubs.

1829 ROYAL GIBRALTAR YC
1830 KUNGELIG SVENSKA SEGEL SALLSKAPET, ROYAL SWEDISH YC
1838 SOCIÉTÉ DES RÉGATES DU HAVRE, FRANCE
1838 ROYAL HOBART REGATTA ASSOCIATION, AUSTRALIA
1844 NEW YORK YC, USA
1844 ROYAL BERMUDA YC
1846 ROYAL BOMBAY YC, INDIA
1847 ROYAL NETHERLANDS YC
1847 ROYAL YACHT CLUB DE OOSTENDE, BELGIUM
1851 ROYAL YACHT CLUB DE BELGIQUE
1852 ROYAL CANADIAN YC
1857 BROOKLYN YC, USA
1857 ROYAL HALIFAX YC, CANADA
1857 ROYAL MAAS YC, NETHERLANDS
1858 CERCLE DE LA VOILE DE PARIS, FRANCE
1858 ROYAL NATAL YC
1859 SOUTHERN YC, NEW ORLEANS, USA
1864 LONG ISLAND YC, USA
1865 ROYAL PERTH YC, AUSTRALIA
1865 BOSTON YC, USA
1866 ROYAL DANISH YC
1867 ROYAL PRINCE ALFRED YC, AUSTRALIA
1867 YACHT CLUB DE FRANCE
1867 SAN FRANCISCO YC, USA
1869 ROYAL SYDNEY YACHT SQUADRON, AUSTRALIA
1869 NORDDEUTSCHER REGATTA VEREIN, HAMBURG, GERMANY
1870 EASTERN YC, BOSTON, USA
1871 ROYAL NEW ZEALAND YACHT SQUADRON
1871 SEAWANHAKA YC, NEW YORK, USA
1879 YACHT CLUB ITALIANO
1887 MARINE REGATTA VEREIN KIEL, GERMANY, NOW KIEL YC

IN AMERICA

With the expansion of the American colonies in the 18th century, maritime traffic increased. Fast sailing vessels were developed for coastal transport, for it was often speedier and more convenient to sail from Boston to New York than attempt the journey by land. But throughout the century it was rare for Americans to sail for pleasure. An exception was Colonel Lewis Morris, who at the start of the century built a small sloop called *Fancy*, purely for recreation. It is depicted in the 1717 print of New York Harbor shown below (*Fancy* is second from the right) sailing to windward with two headsails and a mainsail on a short gaff. Its length was about 10.7 m (35 ft). The contemporary *Memorial History of New York* says that "the peaceful waters of the Sound gave fine harbor and safe opportunity for sailing."

The first American yacht recorded in the 19th century was a 22-ton sloop, *Jefferson*, built in 1801 for George Crowninshield of Salem, Massachusetts. Crowninshield was a merchant with his own ships, and built the *Jefferson* for his personal use and as a training ship for his sons and associates. The sloop was then commissioned as a privateer in the war of 1812 against the British, and in 1815 was eventually sold

New York Harbor in 1717, as depicted by William Burgis.

Cleopatra's Barge *Launched in 1816, the sumptuously appointed* Cleopatra's Barge *attracted large crowds at every port it visited on its cruise around the Mediterranean in 1817. In this contemporary print she is shown in the harbor at Genoa, Italy.*

for fishing. His next yacht was considerably larger, a 191-ton yacht, 25 m (83 ft) on the waterline and drawing 3.5 m (11 ft 6 in), that was modelled on his trading vessels. Named *Cleopatra's Barge*, it cost the-then immense sum of $50,000 and was furnished like a sumptuous country house, containing "elegant settees with velvet cushions, chairs with paintings upon them, mirrors, buffets loaded with plate of every name, the best glass and porcelain..." It sported the latest deck gear: "the best patent horizontal windlass, a rudder fixed to move with great ease and safety upon a new patent device", and was equipped with numerous light-weather sails.

In the summer of 1817, owner and yacht set off for the Mediterranean. They visited Gibraltar, Tangier, Majorca, Barcelona – where 8,000 people who had never seen an American or a yacht before visited it in one day – Marseilles, Genoa and Leghorn. On its return to America, Crowninshield planned a cruise the following year to northern Europe and the Baltic, but he died on board in November 1817. The yacht was subsequently sold to a commercial concern which resold it in 1820 to King Kamehameha of Hawaii, who paid for it in sandalwood. His men soon wrecked the boat, and the hulk finished up on a beach on Honolulu.

In the 1820s, a Bostonian, Benjamin Cutler Clark, was to be seen sailing around Boston Harbor in a small yacht, *Mary*. In 1832, he ordered *Mermaid*, an 11-ton schooner said to be the first decked yacht in Boston. In due course Clark sold this boat, indicating that there must have been a market for second-hand yachts, and bought *Raven*, which he sailed in the area for 20 years. In 1845 *Raven* was reported sailing off Nahant, north of Boston, in a race promoted by hotel-owner Paran Stevens, in which it beat a yacht called *Cygnet*.

The honor of being the first yacht club in the United States is sometimes credited to the Boston Boat Club (no connection with the present Boston Yacht Club) founded in 1834. Like the early days at Cowes, informal boating and shoreside pursuits brought together a group of enthusiasts in a club. Perhaps they were more than a group of mutual owners, for they raised $2,000 to buy the 14-m (46-ft) schooner *Dream*. The vessel was used for day sailing, short-range cruising, picnics and gambling parties. With the success of this boat, the club then purchased the 16-m (52-ft) schooner *Breeze*. For several years both boats were a feature of Boston Harbor, but in 1837 there was a recession in the US, the boats were disposed of and the club faded from the records.

As in England, the formation of a club like the Boston Boat Club by men of some influence and an interest in salt-water sailing was needed to stimulate the sport of yachting as we understand it today. Colonel John Stevens was treasurer of New Jersey during the American Revolution. He had three sons and in later years enjoyed sailing with them on the lower Hudson River. He and his family were also involved in the development of early steamers and railroads. One of the sons was the founder of the Stevens Institute of Technology, where nearly a century later America's Cup models were tank-tested, while the eldest son, John Cox Stevens, built a series of boats from 1809, testing different designs and techniques. Some of these boats were far from small, measuring up to 28 m (91 ft) long.

THE NEW YORK YACHT CLUB

On 30 July 1844, nine men met in the cabin on John Cox Stevens' current yacht, the 15.5-m (51-ft) schooner *Gimcrack*, moored off the Battery in New York Harbor. They decided to form the New York Yacht Club, and Stevens was chosen as commodore. A committee was appointed to draw up a set

John Cox Stevens, first commodore of the NYYC.

The New York Yacht Club Clubhouse *The original site of the NYYC clubhouse was at the Elysian Fields, Weehawken, New Jersey, where it was constructed in 1845. As Weehawken became increasingly urbanized, the building was first moved in 1904 to Glen Cove, Long Island, and then in 1949 to Mystic Seaport, Connecticut.*

of rules, and a decision made to hold a club cruise from New York to Newport, Rhode Island. This took place in early August 1844, and was completed by *Gimcrack* and seven other similar yachts. As the club grew larger it built a clubhouse at the Elysian Fields, Weehawken, New Jersey.

The first formal race in American waters was held by the NYYC in July 1845. It took the fleet through the New York Narrows, around a buoy in the Lower Bay and back again. In another such race, Stevens was defeated; he decided to replace *Gimcrack* with a faster boat. His new boat was a sloop, the 33.5-m (110-ft) *Maria*, equipped with a large gaff mainsail and a centerboard, and for some years this was the fastest yacht in the NYYC fleet. For these races, the club devised a handicap rule, allowing 45 seconds per mile of the course for each ton under the existing US Custom House Tonnage formula.

These pleasant summers in which members of the club cruised and raced against each other in the waters around New York, rather as the titled gentlemen were doing off Cowes, might have continued to pass without note, were it not for a letter received from England in 1850 by one of the founding members of the NYYC, George Schuyler. Its invitation to send a New York pilot boat to race in English waters was the first step in the series of events that led to the establishment of the America's Cup (see pp 140-1).

The eventual dispatch of the newly launched *America* to Britain in 1851 marks the start of a new era in yachting history, one which, for better or worse, saw the end of the essentially clubby boating atmosphere that until then had been the essence of the sport. The era of international yacht racing was beginning.

◆◆◆

A New York Yacht Club Regatta *Yachts line up at the start of the NYYC regatta in 1869 in the Narrows off Staten Island. By this date events of this type were a regular fixture.*

THE CHRONOLOGY OF SAILING

THE SEVENTEENTH CENTURY

Early 17th century: Yachts built in the Netherlands: sailed at festivals and by wealthy citizens.

1660: Charles II receives gift of yacht *Mary* from the Dutch.

1661: First yacht race (England) from Greenwich to Gravesend and back, between Charles II and the Duke of York.

THE EIGHTEENTH CENTURY

1720: Records date The Water Club of Cork, Ireland, to this year, making it the world's first yacht club.

1775: Cumberland Fleet races on the Thames.

THE NINETEENTH CENTURY

1815: The Yacht Club formed to race at Cowes.

1820: The Yacht Club becomes The Royal Yacht Club.

1826: Yachts first race for a cup at Cowes Regatta.

1829: Royal Gibraltar Yacht Club founded, the first yacht club outside Britain.

1830: Royal Swedish Yacht Club founded, the first yacht club outside the British Empire.

1833: The Royal Yacht Club renamed The Royal Yacht Squadron.

1838: The Société des Régates du Havre, France, and the Royal Hobart Regatta Association, Australia, founded.

1844: New York Yacht Club formed.

1845: First formal race in American waters held off New York.

1850: Richard Tyrrell McMullen (UK) starts cruising in *Leo.*

1851: *America* wins the Hundred Guinea Cup at Cowes, later regarded as the first America's Cup race.

1856: Lord Dufferin (UK) cruises the Arctic in *Foam.*

1866: First eastbound transatlantic race.

1870: *City of Ragusa* crosses Atlantic from east to west.

1870: First defense of the America's Cup.

1876: Yacht Racing Association (UK) formed.

1876: First eastbound single-handed crossing of the Atlantic by Alfred Johnson (USA).

1876: *Sunbeam* sets off on cruise around the world.

1880: Cruising Club (UK) formed.

1882: First Kiel Week.

1883: Bernard Gilboy (USA) makes first single-handed crossing of the Pacific Ocean.

1886: Tonnage rating abolished in Britain.

1887: World's first one-design class: Dublin Bay Water Wags.

1887: Frank Knight cruises in the Baltic.

1893: Nine big racing cutters launched in Britain and US, more than ever before or since.

1895: Production begins on the Solent One-Design, the first British one-design class.

1895: First race for the Seawanhaka Cup.

1896: First race for the Canada's Cup.

1897: America's first one-design, the A Scow, built.

1898: Joshua Slocum (USA) completes the first single-handed voyage around the world.

1898: Inaugural Chicago-Mackinac Race.

1898: La Coupe de France first competed for.

1899: First race for the One Ton Cup.

THE TWENTIETH CENTURY

1900: Sailing introduced as a sport in the Olympic Games.

1903: Universal Rule adopted by New York Yacht Club.

1903: *Reliance*, the biggest cutter ever built, is launched to defend the America's Cup.

1904: First offshore race for amateur small boats: Brooklyn to Marblehead.

1905: *Atlantic* sets transatlantic speed record from west to east that lasts for 75 years.

1906: First Transpacific (Transpac) Race.

1906: New York to Bermuda Race first sailed.

1906: Roald Amundsen (Norway) is first to sail through Northwest Passage in *Gjoa.*

1906: International Rule drawn up.

1907: International Yacht Racing Union (IYRU) formed.

1908: Cruising Association (UK) formed.

1909: Clyde Cruising Club (UK) formed.

1911: First Star class one-design keelboat built.

1919: Rules drawn up for 14-ft dinghy in Britain; becomes International 14 in 1928.

1920: Last America's Cup race using time allowances.

1921: First British-American Cup raced for in 6-Meters.

1922: Cruising Club of America formed.

1923: First Bermuda Race from New London, Connecticut to Bermuda, organized by the Cruising Club of America.

1925: North American Yacht Racing Union (NAYRU) formed.

1925: Ocean Racing Club (UK) (later the Royal Ocean Racing Club) is formed.

1925: Harry Pidgeon (USA) becomes the second man to circumnavigate the world single-handed.

1925: Seven boats cross the line for the first Fastnet Race.

1925: First circumnavigation south of Cape of Good Hope and Cape Horn by Conor O'Brien (Ireland) in *Saoirse.*

1926: The Little Ship Club (UK) formed.

1927: Genoa sail makes first appearance at a 6-Meter regatta in Genoa, Italy.

1929: Irish Cruising Club formed.

1930: Last America's Cup Challenge by Sir Thomas Lipton (UK) and first year of J-class.

1930: First Trans-Tasman Race.

1930: Swiftsure Lightship Classic inaugurated.

1931: Bill Robinson (USA) and Etera (Tahiti) become first two-handed crew to circumnavigate the world.

1931: RORC Rule introduced.

1932: CCA Rule introduced.

1932: The Star one-design keelboat makes its first appearance in the Olympic Games.

1934: Al Hansen (Norway) becomes the first lone sailor to round Cape Horn from east to west.

1937: Last year of the J-class in America's Cup.

1937: America's Cup defender *Ranger* experiments with sails of rayon, the first time artificial fiber is used for sails.

1939: First Marblehead to Halifax Race.

1941: Southern Ocean Racing Conference series first held.

1945: Inaugural Sydney to Hobart Race.

1946: First Newport Beach to Ensenada Race, now the world's biggest offshore race.

1947: Colored, nylon spinnakers first appear.

1947: Glenans Organization (France) formed.

1947: First Buenos Aires to Rio de Janeiro Race.

1948: Vernon Nicholson sets up boat charterers in Antigua for tropical cruising.

1948: Paul Elvström (Denmark) wins the first of his four consecutive Olympic gold medals.

1952: North American Yacht Racing Union joins International Yacht Racing Union; one code of racing rules is used worldwide from 1958.

1953: Anne Davison (UK) becomes the first woman to cross the Atlantic single-handed.

1953: *Favona* wins the Fastnet Race, the smallest boat to do so.

1953: First Giraglia Race.

1954: Ocean Cruising Club (UK) formed.

1954: Dacron sails win Star World Championships; dacron gradually replaces cotton.

1956: First Auckland to Suva Race.

1957: Annapolis to Newport Race first sailed.

1957: Crew of *Tzu Hang* survive pitchpoling off Cape Horn.

1957: First Admiral's Cup series of races starts new inshore/offshore series concept.

1958: First America's Cup series since 1937, held in 12-Meter boats to internationally agreed rules.

1959: Fastnet Race entries exceed 50 boats.

1960: The first OSTAR – the first westbound single-handed transatlantic race.

1961: First Little America's Cup match race for catamarans.

1962: Australia's first challenge for America's Cup.

1965: Fastnet Race entries exceed 100 boats.

1965: Congressional Cup match – racing series first held at Long Beach, California.

1965: First modern One Ton Cup series for boats with RORC rating of 22 ft or under.

1966: Inaugural Half Ton Cup series of races.

1966: Two-Handed Around Britain and Ireland Race first sailed.

1967: First series held for Quarter Ton and Two Ton cups.

1967: Southern Cross Trophy series first held.

1968: International Offshore Rule is introduced throughout the world, replacing separate British and American rules.

1969: Completion of first single-handed, non-stop world circumnavigation by Bernard Moitessier (France).

1969: First single-handed, non-stop race around the world won by Robin Knox-Johnston (UK).

1969: Windsurfers first sailed.

1969: First Middle Sea Race.

1970: Robert Griffith and family (NZ) set off on the first cruise around Antarctica.

1970: Robin Lee Graham (USA) becomes the youngest person to circumnavigate the world single-handed, having set out on his voyage in 1965 aged 16.

1971: Fastnet Race entries exceed 200.

1972: Olympic Games competed for without any formula class.

1972: David Lewis (UK) begins first single-handed cruise to Antarctica.

1973: First Whitbread Race around the world starts.

1974: Three-Quarter Ton Cup series of races first held.

1974: *Williwaw*, skippered by Willy de Roos (Belgium), is the first small boat to sail through the Northwest Passage.

1978: Krystyna Chojnowsja-Liskiewwicz (Poland) becomes the first woman to sail around the world single-handed.

1978: Sardinia Cup first competed for by teams of ocean racers.

1978: First series of races held for Mini Ton Cup.

1978: Hawaii International Ocean Racing Series first held.

1978: First Women's World Championship in dinghies.

1978: Route du Rhum from St. Malo to Guadeloupe first raced.

1978: First Tour de France à la Voile.

1979: Fastnet Race with 303 starters – the biggest entry ever – hit by a severe storm; 15 persons killed.

1980: Olympic boycott by some sailing nations.

1980: *Paul Ricard*, skippered by Eric Tabarly (France), breaks transatlantic record set by *Atlantic*.

1980: Satellite navigation sets first produced for boats.

1980: La Baule to Dakar Race first sailed.

1981: First westbound two-handed transatlantic race.

1982: Jon Sanders (Australia) sails twice around the world without stopping.

1982: Kevlar introduced for sails.

1982: First BOC Challenge Around-Alone Race starts.

1983: The US loses the America's Cup to Australia.

1984: Sailboards first used in Olympic Games.

1984: One Ton rating increased to 30.5 ft IOR; Two Ton rating is scrapped.

1984: Advertising allowed on boats under IYRU rulings.

1985: John Gore-Grimes (Ireland) is the first yachtsman to make an inshore passage from Scoresby Sound down the east coast of Greenland.

1986: Pascal Maka (France) sets sailing speed record of 38.86 knots over $\frac{1}{2}$ km on a sailboard.

1987: The US regains America's Cup.

1988: First women-only class (470 dinghies) in Olympic Games, making a record eight classes.

1988: Jon Sanders (Australia) completes first single-handed circumnavigation of the world three times without stopping.

1988: America's Cup disputes result in series reverting to conditions of original 'Deed of Gift'.

1988: *Jet Services V*, sailed by Serge Madec (France) and crew, crosses Atlantic west to east in 7 days 21 hr 35 min, averaging 15.27 knots; the fastest-ever ocean crossing under sail.

1988: *Fleury Michon IX*, sailed single-handed by Philippe Poupon (France), sets record for east-west Atlantic crossing – 10 days 9 hr 15 min.

1988: Kay Cottee (Australia) becomes first woman to circumnavigate the world non-stop.

1988: Eric Beale (UK) raises new sailing speed record to 40.33 knots.

Chapter 2

Cruising

···

*B*ecause a race creates a story and there is always a winner, it is racing that makes the news and sets the records. But many sailors do not want to participate in the cut and thrust of racing; for them, sailing is a more leisurely, though none the less exciting and demanding, activity. What they do is cruise.

Those who take their boats on cruising voyages have inevitably gathered knowledge and confidence from an intrepid, often engagingly eccentric, band of pioneers, some of whom have written of their adventures. From accounts such as these, erratic though they may be, it is possible to present a history of cruising, although inevitably it is impossible to recount details of every single voyage that has been undertaken.

THE FIRST CRUISES

With the spread of yachting to England in the reign of Charles II, London lawyer Roger North wrote of what were undoubtedly cruising ventures in the Thames Estuary. He explored the river while living aboard his own seagoing cutter of between 10-15 tons, and his accounts convey a delight in the sport with which any modern cruising sailor can readily identify.

Unfortunately, it is the case that cruising is generally less well documented than racing. Unless there was somebody aboard who kept a journal that was subsequently published as a book, or unless the cruise undertaken was a stunt so remarkable that it was reported in the newspapers of the day, the achievements of the earliest pioneers of small-boat cruising go largely unsung. Even today, extensive and remarkable voyages are unreported, unless the sailors concerned write of their adventures or win one of the few cruising prizes available. However, this lack of written evidence does not mean that no such voyages took place.

Well before the growth of yacht clubs in the 19th century, individuals set off on prolonged cruises, although they were restricted to territorial waters for fear of meeting pirates further afield. As early as the late 18th century, 'pleasure boats' were cruising, notably in the waters of the Hebrides. In such areas, as Dr. Johnson and Boswell discovered during their

RICHARD TURRELL McMULLEN

Richard McMullen (1830-1891), was one of the most influential Victorian pioneers of cruising. Not only did he considerably raise the standard of amateur seamanship, his writings admirably articulated the ethos of cruising.

Intolerant of weakness and errors of judgment in others, McMullen was sufficiently humble to admit his own errors. From his book, *Down Channel*, (1869), we learn that he almost sank *Leo* on its first voyage, and on another occasion, a flapping sail hit him in the face, a sharp sisterhook catching his eye. It was nearly a month before "it could take its turn of duty and be properly considered a weather eye."

famous tour in 1773, privately owned craft were often the best means of transport, and at times they fulfilled the role of cruising boat. A specific account of cruising as such comes from the log kept by Robert Harvey, the squire of Malin in northern Ireland. In 1814, he cruised his 30-ton cutter *Rambler* to the Hebrides, and he mentioned meeting other pleasure craft similarly engaged in Tobermory.

In 1815, a founder member of the Royal Yacht Squadron, Sir William Curtis, sailed to St. Petersburg, now Leningrad, in his

76-ton cutter, *Rebecca Maria*, while in 1816, Lord Craven was sighted off Bordeaux, France, in his square-rigged, 325-ton yacht, *Louisa*. In 1817, George Crowninshield cruised in his 190-ton brigantine yacht, *Cleopatra's Barge*, which was considered extremely elegant in its day (see pp 21-2). The 150-ton *Falcon* was often sailed by its owner, Lord Yarborough, down to the west of France and Spain to pick up wines, and a report in 1828 noted that Lord Belfast had damaged the mast of his cutter, also called *Louisa*, off the Dutch coast. Together with the voyage of *Cleopatra's Barge*, it meant that within the first quarter of the 19th century, the Baltic and the Mediterranean had already made their mark as desirable cruising destinations. It would appear that the waters immediately north of Cape Horn also had their appeal. The 40-ton American sloop *Hero*, owned by Benjamin Pendleton, was sailing in the waters near Cape Horn as early as 1821, but little is known over and above this one tantalizing fact.

However, these early cruises were taking place in boats that were no different in size to small warships, with professional crews to man them, and with small cannon and personal side arms for protection. For the first documented cruise in a small boat as understood today, it is necessary to look to 1850.

Lord Yarborough's 150-ton Falcon *(center).*

Orion, *in which McMullen sailed over 5,000 miles.*

RICHARD TURRELL McMULLEN

Richard Turrell McMullen, the quintessential middle-class Victorian stockbroker, began his serious cruising in the tiny cutter, *Leo*, just 6.1m (20ft) long and weighing only 3 tons. He had it fitted out as a miniature seagoing yacht, and with one 16-year-old paid hand as crew, he sailed 8,222 miles on the waters between the Thames and Land's End between 1850 and 1857. During the course of 1863, he sailed right around Britain in *Sirius*, a 9.8-m (32-ft) gaff cutter.

His next boat, the 12.8-m (42-ft) *Orion*, built in 1865, required several hands to crew it. However, as a natural seaman, he felt strongly that the amateur seaman should know and understand every aspect of his boat. He was therefore determined to discover by practice and experience: "In this manner, getting into scrapes and out of them, I learned more of practical sailing in a few months than I should have learnt in several years if I had a hired man to take the lead in everything." *Orion* was converted to a yawl in 1877, and McMullen was able to dismiss his crew; he claimed they were lazy and smoked too much. His sailing theories were expounded in his book, *Down Channel*, published in 1869. It was full of sage advice, including perhaps the greatest of all truths of seamanship – that in bad weather, it is the shore, not the water, that holds danger for an efficient, small craft. McMullen's natural gift of expression has made *Down Channel* one of the classic books about cruising, and it has remained constantly in print. He was able to impart his own overwhelming interest and love for this pastime to all his readers.

Richard Turrell McMullen died alone in mid-Channel at the age of 61, while at the helm of his 8.2-m (27-ft) yawl *Perseus* in June 1891. An acquaintance of his remarked that "He was a little man, but a terrible worker. Everything had to be done as perfectly as possible, irrespective of bad weather or previous fatigue." *The Field* magazine published an obituary in which it was said: "Mr. McMullen was unlike any other yachtsman we ever met: we have known men just as fond of the sea as he was, but never anyone who regarded it with such reverential interest. Yachting and yacht racing in the ordinary sense of the terms had no charms for him."

A FLEET CRUISE

A cruise by a fleet of yachts in the US was inaugurated in 1854. The New York Yacht Club cruise was a summer mixture of passage races, harbor exploration and decidedly energetic socializing by most of its members, and the same event continues to thrive today. Yet even in its earliest days, some members argued that this kind of organized proceeding was at variance with the true character of cruising. At about the same time, the publication in Scotland in 1858 of Hugh Miller's *Cruise of The Betsy* is evidence to suggest that the magical cruising ground of the Hebrides continued to be a fertile development area for this form of sailing.

FIRST TO THE ARCTIC

From Lord Dufferin's *Letters from High Latitudes*, we learn of the cruise of the schooner *Foam*, from England to Iceland, Jan Mayen Island, Spitsbergen and Norway in 1856. It is a book that continues to inspire those who sail to the Arctic today. Subsequently, Dufferin was to achieve additional sailing fame with his pioneering of single-handed cruising in the Mediterranean with the ingenious little yawl, *Lady Hermione*.

Lord Dufferin is thought of as the man who led the way to the Arctic, but in fact, six years before him, W.T. Potts' 100-ton cutter *Caprice* had cruised from Dublin Bay to Iceland and Norway. Although *Foam* went much further north on its cruise, it is evident from *Caprice*'s privately circulated log that cruising boats in Icelandic waters were not unknown prior to 1850.

Arctic Explorer *The schooner* Foam, *in which Lord Dufferin cruised Icelandic and Norwegian waters in 1856.*

EARLY PIONEER CRUISES

There was a variety of boats that made cruises in the pioneering days of the 19th century. In 1865, a London barrister, John Macgregor, built a 4.6-m (15-ft) long sailing canoe in which he cruised alone along the inland waterways of Europe, venturing over to Denmark, Sweden and Norway in 1866. The following year he launched a 6.4-m (21-ft) version with iron ballast, in which he made short sea crossings and cruised the coasts of England and France, as well as sailing up the Seine to Paris.

His books about these exploits, *The Voyage alone in the Yawl Rob Roy* and *A Thousand Miles in the Rob Roy Canoe*, attracted much attention and encouraged many imitators. One of these was Edward Empson Middleton, who circumnavigated England by passing through the Clyde-Forth Canal in the middle of Scotland in his 7-m (23-ft) yawl *Kate* in 1869. Most nights he found safe anchorage off the shore or harbor – no mean feat in the days before satisfactory pilot guides.

Macgregor's canoe rides the rollers at Ostend.

FIRST AROUND THE WORLD

It is to Joshua Slocum that the first voyage around the world is usually attributed; he completed his single-handed circumnavigation in 1898, aboard the 10.1-m (36-ft) yacht *Spray*, (see p 35). However, the first yacht circumnavigation is generally accepted to have been by Lord Brassey's 51.9-m (170-ft), three-masted auxiliary schooner, *Sunbeam*. Brassey left Cowes on the Isle of Wight on 6 July 1876 for a voyage that took in many ports of call on the route down through the Atlantic, through the Magellan Strait,

Lord Brassey at the wheel of Sunbeam. *Inset: Sunbeam, 1893.*

The City of Ragusa *sailed across the Atlantic from east to west in 1870.*

across the Pacific to Japan, across the Indian Ocean to the Red Sea, through the Suez Canal and then through the Mediterranean back home again in May 1887.

Sunbeam was a 531-tonner, built with steel frames and wood planking and carrying a 350 hp steam engine that consumed 4 tons of coal a day when in use. The yacht was manned by 32 crew, including a ladies' maid, and could berth 11 people, including a doctor.

Brassey was a lifelong sailing enthusiast as well as being a railway tycoon, MP and member of the Royal Yacht Squadron. He began his amateur seafaring with the little 8-ton cutter *Spray of the Ocean* in 1854, and gradually progressed through boats of increasing sizes – 14 in all – in which he sailed a total of 228,682 miles.

SHORT-HANDED VOYAGES

In 1857, a two-handed, west-to-east crossing of the Atlantic was made by a 13.1-m (43-ft) ketch, *Charter Oak*, helmed by C.R. Webb. As the prevailing winds in the North Atlantic are westerly, it is not surprising that this was the obvious direction for the first short-handed passage. However, in 1870, John C. Buckley (USA) and Nicolas Primoraz (Austria) sailed from east to west in the 6.10-m (20-ft) converted lifeboat, *City of Ragusa*. The yawl-rigged craft, with topsail and bowsprit, took 84 days from Cork, Ireland, to Boston, Massachusetts.

A feat that attracted considerable attention from the press of the day was the west-to-east crossing of the Atlantic by a two-handed crew in a boat of less than 9.1m (30ft). *Red, White and Blue*, with an overall length of 7.8m (26ft), was an iron, ship-rigged (square sails on three masts) lifeboat sailed by William Hudson and Frank E. Fitch (USA). They left New York on 9 July 1866 and arrived at Deal, England, 35 days later. After the voyage, the boat was exhibited in Paris and London.

The first single-handed crossing of the Atlantic was accomplished by another American, Alfred Johnson, in 1876, the centenary of the American Revolution. He crossed from Gloucester, Massachusetts to Abercastle, Wales, in 64 days in his 6.1-m (20-ft) flush-decked sailing dory, *Centennial*.

VICTORIAN NAVIGATION

Navigation for boats or ships changed little throughout the 19th century, indeed until the advent of radio aids in the middle of the next century. "Lead, log and lookout ..." was a major motto, implying taking early soundings with a lead and line to avoid hitting the shore, and consulting the distance run on a patent log. If these precautions failed, there was always the lookout.

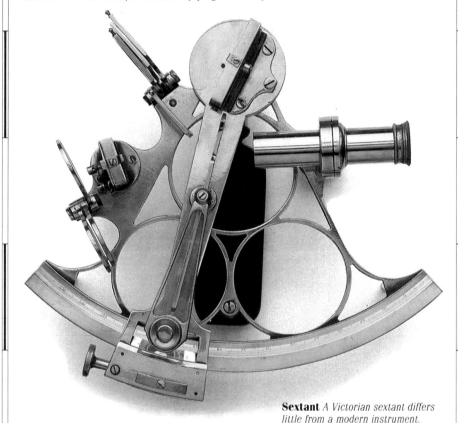

Sextant *A Victorian sextant differs little from a modern instrument. Celestial sights played an important part in position finding; for these a chronometer was essential, but such readings were difficult in a small boat. Methods of calculating position from the sextant sight were complex.*

Compass *A magnetic steering compass was held in gimbals to keep it horizontal. Though 90 degrees in each quadrant are around the edge, steering was by traditional points of the compass of which there were 32. They did not represent an exact number of degrees, but enabled the helmsman to read a conspicuous point.*

THE ROYAL CRUISING CLUB

The year 1880 saw a development of great interest to cruising sailors. Arthur Underhill, a young lawyer from the Midlands of England, decided that there should be a club devoted solely to cruising, as opposed to racing. Together with eight of his friends, he formed the Cruising Club during a meeting at his law chambers in London in December 1880. The first commodore was the Rev. A van Straubenzee; Arthur Underhill became the first vice-commodore. In subsequent years, the Club became rather exclusive, membership being by invitation only. In the Club's early days, the sport as practiced by the members developed as the boats they acquired became more sophisticated with their increasing personal affluence. During much of the 1880's, an extensive part of club activity consisted of river and canal cruising in canoes and other open craft.

However, during the late-1880's, the emphasis was increasingly on sea cruising and the Cruising Club decided to publish charts for private circulation among the members. These charts did much to establish the Club as an authority on cruising. Each year from 1882, the Club has published a journal with accounts of some of the cruises that members have undertaken throughout the world, and in 1896, a Georgian silver rose bowl was purchased, which subsequently became the coveted prize for the best cruise of the year, the Challenge Cup. The Club presents a number of cups for distinguished cruises

Sir Arthur Underhill at the wheel of Wulfruna.

of various kinds in which exceptional seamanship, navigation and pilotage are shown.

The Cruising Club became the Royal Cruising Club in 1902, while its founder was eventually knighted.

RCC CUPS

The Royal Cruising Club presents a series of cups:

The Challenge Cup: This silver rose bowl was first presented in 1896 and is the most prestigious of the RCC cups. It is the world's oldest award on a regular basis for the best cruise of the year. However, the award is open only to members of the Royal Cruising Club and membership is strictly limited.

The Romola Cup: Awarded for the best cruise which was not considered suitable for the main award. Perhaps it might be of low mileage, but of particular significance because of the pilotage involved, or the new ground discovered.

The Founder's Cup: Awarded for the best 'short' cruise of the year.

The Claymore Cup: Awarded, like the Romola Cup, as a runner-up, being for the best short cruise, which was not, however, eligible for the Founder's Cup.

The Cruising Club Journal of 1900

THE OCEAN CRUISING CLUB

A unique club, and one with considerable attraction to a wide range of cruising sailors, came into being in 1954. Its founder, Humphrey Barton, was an offshore sailor and a partner in a leading design firm in Britain, Laurent Giles and Partners. One of Barton's early long cruises was from England to New York in the Giles-designed, 7.6-m (25-ft) sloop *Vertue* in 1951. He subsequently made more than 20 Atlantic crossings, as well as many other voyages, mostly in his boat *Rose Rambler*.

With the increasing appeal of ocean cruising, Barton felt that existing cruising clubs were rather too exclusive. In order to qualify for membership of the Royal Ocean Racing Club, for example, it was necessary to have competed in the Fastnet Race, and a degree of exclusivity was guaranteed for the Royal Cruising Club as membership was by invitation only. He therefore established the Ocean Cruising Club in 1954; the only qualification required for membership was the completion of an open-water passage of at least 1,000 miles, non-stop, in a boat of not more than 21.3 m (70 ft).

The OCC membership totals about 1,100, and is open to sailors of all nationalities; the Club's flying fish burgee is seen world-wide. Owing to the scattered membership, activities are obviously limited, but the OCC has staged several rallies in the Azores, involving a 'pursuit race' from varying destinations. Each boat is given a time to leave its port of departure and races to be the first at the Azores finishing line.

In recent years, the OCC has lifted its ban on professional sailors (delivery skippers, sponsored racers, etc.); there is no longer any 'amateur' distinction.

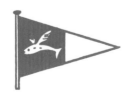

As with all cruising awards, unlike the clear-cut result of a race, the criteria involved in allocating these cups are interpreted by a panel of judges. Perhaps for this reason, these awards receive little general publicity. The RCC's annual publication compensates for this by publishing accounts of a number of cruises, including those which were not awarded trophies.

The first winner of the Challenge Cup was Dr. Howard Sinclair of Belfast for a cruise from Belfast Lough clockwise around Ireland in the 4-ton cutter *Brenda*, in which he sailed 1,079 miles in 33 days.

OTHER CHALLENGE CUP WINNERS

It was Dr. Sinclair who won the Challenge Cup the following year as well, this time for a 16-day cruise from Belfast Lough, through the Pentland Firth and home via the Caledonian Canal in his newly acquired 8-ton cutter *Saiph*. By 1898 he had changed boats again, and won the Cup for a third time for a cruise to the Hebrides in his 10-ton cutter *Yucca*.

In 1899, the Challenge Cup was won by R. Barrington Baker with the 38-ton cutter *Inyoni*. With an amateur crew, *Inyoni* cruised to Kiel for the regattas there, before cruising home to the Solent. It was a mixture of offshore racing and cruising which was later to prove an attractive combination to many.

More recent notable winners have included Crispin Rushworth-Lund in 1984 for an extensive cruise in Labrador waters in *Heptarchy*, a ferrocement variant of the famous Dyarchy design (see p 46); John Gore-Grimes in 1985 for his cruise in Greenland waters in *Shardana* (see p 51); and in 1986 and 1987, Willie Ker for cruises in the North Atlantic and the Arctic in *Assent* (see p 51).

EARLY CRUISING GUIDES

The publication of information specifically for cruising boats was fundamental to the development of cruising. During the late 19th century, the writer and cruising man Frank Cowper was one of its most influential exponents.

Cowper had been cruising extensively from 1877 onward and much of his research for *Sailing Tours* – published

Inyoni, in which Barrington Baker combined offshore racing and cruising in the late 19th century.

between 1892 and 1895 – was undertaken in the hefty 14.6-m (48-ft) cutter, *Lady Harvey*, a fishing lugger from Dover that had been converted into a yacht by the addition of a counter stern and roomy cabins. The five volumes of *Sailing Tours*, in which he described the creeks and harbors of the British coast, the east coast of Ireland and the northern French coast, did much to encourage cruising.

Another pioneer of cruising, the professional journalist, Frank Knight, appealed to the more humble sailors who could not afford to build new boats. In his books he extolled the virtues of converting ships' lifeboats and fishing boats; a low deckhead was perfectly acceptable to him: "If one wishes to assume an erect position, one can always go on deck," he remarked!

In 1880, Knight left Southampton in the 28-ton yawl *Falcon* on his way to South America. He and his small crew were away for nearly two years and the story of their cruise up the Plate and Parana rivers was told in his book, *The Cruise of the Falcon*.

However, the book that really captured the public's imagination was *The Falcon on the Baltic*, the account of his 1887 cruise in a converted lifeboat through the shallow waters of the Netherlands and Germany,

and then on into the Baltic. Harwich to Goeree, immediately opposite on the Dutch coast, was the only part of the journey on the open sea. From Goeree, Knight sailed to Rotterdam and then on to Amsterdam by river and canal. From Amsterdam, *Falcon* crossed the Zuiderzee, which was then open to the North Sea, calling on the island of Urk. From Urk, his route skirted the Dutch and German Frisian Islands. The Kiel Canal had not yet been built, so he sailed through the River Eider and along the local canal that joined it to Kiel. Then followed a Baltic cruise through the Little Belt and the islands of Denmark until his arrival in Copenhagen.

Falcon on the Baltic

THE RIDDLE OF THE SANDS

Knight's approach to cruising had many followers, one of whom was Erskine Childers, a young clerk in the House of Commons and a member of the Cruising Club. Following the example and advice of Knight, Childers purchased a converted lifeboat, *Vixen*, in Dover on 1 August 1897. *Vixen* was 9.1m (30ft) LOA, with 2.1m (7ft) beam and 0.8m (2ft 9in) draft with the centerboard up.

On 10 August, having taken extended leave from the House, he left Dover, timing his voyage to coincide with Parliament's long summer recess. His intention was to head westward down the French coast, but he changed course to the Dutch coast as a result of adverse westerly winds. Like Knight, Childers sailed via the Zuiderzee, eventually arriving at the Dutch town of Nieuwediep, close to Texel on the first of

Erskine Childers at the helm of Vixen *(above).*

the Frisian Islands. The first German port of call for *Vixen* was Norderney, which was not reached until toward the end of September. Stretching into early October with its shortening days, Childers explored the waterways inside the German Frisian Islands. During this time he did not see any other boats; few made such cruises, even in the summer. He continued to cruise throughout the fall, following Knight's tracks through the River Eider and its canal connecting it to Kiel, and into some of the Danish islands. However, unlike Knight, Childers then turned back south into the Frisian Islands, sailing among them until, on 13 December, he sailed to the Dutch port of Terschelling where he laid *Vixen* up.

The following April, Erskine Childers and a paid hand from Burnham-on-Crouch returned to the Netherlands to sail *Vixen* back to Dover. In 1901, Childers joined a syndicate that intended to buy a larger boat, and he sold *Vixen*, renamed *Dulcibella*, in 1899, to a Mr. George Newbury who converted it into a houseboat.

His novel, *The Riddle of the Sands*, published in 1903, was concerned with the problem of national defense, and was based on his notion that the rapidly expanding German empire could utilize the many remote inlets of the Frisian coast to hide a fleet of flat-bottomed barges to assist in the invasion of England across the North Sea. Once this book was published, no longer was it necessary for the enthusiasts of this eccentric form of sailing to rationalize their pleasure. The joy of sailing in intriguing waters in an odd little boat – "the gay pursuit of a perilous quest" – was fully expounded.

The Riddle of the Sands was made into a film in 1978, by which time the growth of sailing had greatly increased the general public's awarenesss of cruising.

The specialized pleasure of cruising the creeks has developed steadily over the years, and the tradition inspired by Knight, Childers and others continues today, kept alive by such writers as Francis B. Cooke and Maurice Griffiths.

The Riddle of the Sands *It was during Childers' voyage among the Frisian Islands in* Vixen *that he was inspired to write his classic novel.*

SAILING ALONE AROUND THE WORLD

Perhaps the greatest boost to the cause of cruising in the 19th century was Captain Joshua Slocum's epic single-handed voyage around the world.

Slocum, an American sea captain, was already 51 years old when he began his world cruise in 1895. His boat, *Spray*, was a beamy 18th-century oysterman that he had first seen propped up in a field and covered with canvas. During the course of 1893, he completely rebuilt it, using white pasture oak. It was 11.2 m (36 ft 9 in) LOA, with 4.3 m (14 ft 2 in) beam and 1.2 m (4 ft) draft. "Her lines were supposed to be those of a North Sea fisherman." However, Slocum added a foot of freeboard to the original model. Slocum was amply rewarded by *Spray*'s performance; its self-steering properties, coupled with its easy motion and good turn of speed when conditions suited, were ideal.

Slocum set sail from Boston, Massachusetts, at the end of April 1895, crossing the Atlantic, via the Azores, to Gibraltar. He then sailed back across the south Atlantic to Brazil, sailed down the South American coast, spending Christmas 1895 in Buenos Aires, and entered the Pacific through the Strait of Magellan; for anybody to round the Horn in a boat of *Spray*'s size would have been risky in the extreme. He spent some time in Australia before sailing across the Indian Ocean to Cape Town where he spent Christmas

JOSHUA SLOCUM

Joshua Slocum (1844-1909), was the first person to sail around the world single-handed. His boat, *Spray*, was a rebuilt vessel of 18th-century origin and his voyage during 1895-8 was one of the most remarkable feats ever to be accomplished by a lone sailor. In 1900, Slocum published his account of that voyage in a book called *Sailing Alone Around the World*. From the day it appeared, this book, which has remained in print almost continuously, has been a classic source of inspiration to sailing men and women, and is undoubtedly one of the finest sea stories of all.

1897. He crossed the Atlantic for a third time, via St. Helena and Ascension Island, and completed the last part of his voyage, up the north coast of South America back to Rhode Island, arriving on 27 June 1898. He was 54 when he completed the voyage.

After his return he continued to sail *Spray* on long cruises such as to the West Indies and back. In 1909, he set out single-handed from Bristol, Rhode Island, for the Orinoco, but was never seen again. He is believed to have been run down by a steamer, probably when fast asleep below.

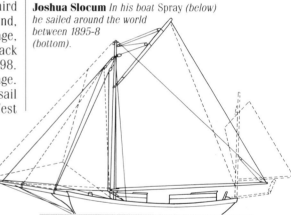

Joshua Slocum *In his boat* Spray *(below) he sailed around the world between 1895-8 (bottom).*

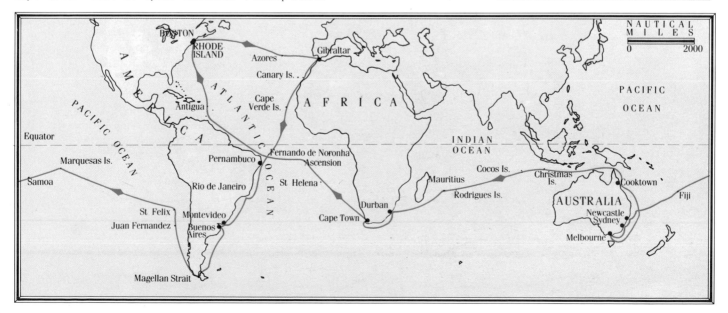

THE EARLY 20TH CENTURY

In the years immediately following the voyage of *Spray*, the encouragement of cruising and offshore sailing in America was largely due to a remarkable sailing journalist, Captain Thomas Fleming Day.

The crusading proprietor and editor of the magazine *Rudder*, a leading American boating magazine until it ceased publication in 1977, Day was concerned that in the early part of the 20th century the majority of boating people were neither determined racing men nor dedicated cruisers; they enjoyed the world of boats, the pleasure of the occasional sail, but had no real structure to their activity.

Day arranged for a series of easy-to-build cruiser designs to be published in his magazine in the hope of enticing new blood into the sport. There were three designs of slightly differing dimensions – the Seabird, Naiad and Seagoer. Hundreds of each were built, and it was in a Seabird that Harry Pidgeon (USA) made a world circumnavigation in 1921-5. Day's next initiative was to instigate a series of offshore races to demonstrate the seagoing power of these little craft. In 1904, he organized a race from Brooklyn to Marblehead, but the best known of these offshore races was the Bermuda Race, first run in 1906 from Gravesend Bay, New York,

Captain Thomas Fleming Day
Determined to encourage cruising, Day published a series of easy-to-build cruiser designs in his boating magazine. Rudder.

to Bermuda (see pp120-2). However, cruising was not forgotten in the Day scheme of things; in 1911, he sailed one of his *Rudder* designs, the 7.7-m (25-ft) Seabird class, from Providence, Rhode Island, across the Atlantic to Gibraltar and on to Naples, with a crew of two. There are many versions of Seabird class boats sailing the seas of the world today.

THE CRUISING ASSOCIATION

Two more useful organizations specifically for the cruising sailor were founded in Britain during the early 20th century.

A completely new club, the Cruising Association, was formed in 1908. This remains extremely active today, and differs from the Royal Cruising Club considerably in that it has unlimited membership and aims to provide special facilities for all cruising sailors. These include a handbook of sailing directions for British ports, including Ireland and north and west France; a list of recommended boatmen at

Seabird *One of three designs promoted by Day. Hundreds of each were built, and versions of the Seabird class are still sailed today.*

various ports; the publication of harbor plans; the presentation of annual challenge cups; and a London headquarters with an extensive nautical library, one of the finest in the world. The Cruising Association has more than 5,000 members today, with local groups throughout Britain and individual members world-wide.

CLAUD WORTH

One of the prime instigators of the Cruising Association was Claud Worth, who was also a distinguished member of the Royal Cruising Club. In 1887, Worth had met McMullen, who encouraged him at a time when seagoing in small boats was still thought of as foolhardy. Over the years Worth became regarded as almost the leading authority on sailing, with an intimate knowledge of seamanship and cruising. At a time when design was developing more slowly for cruisers than for racers, his two books, *Yacht Cruising* (1910) and *Yacht Navigation and Voyaging* (1927) were profoundly influential.

CLYDE CRUISING CLUB

The second significant cruising event at this time was the establishment of the Clyde Cruising Club in 1909. In Scotland, where cruising and passage racing had long been flourishing in excellent sailing waters, the early years of this century saw a growing need for an organization specifically devoted to the needs of cruising people. In 1909, a small number of yachtsmen met at Rothesay, chaired by H. Donald Mathieson. This initial meeting was followed by a larger meeting in Glasgow and the appointment of a committee to draw up a set of rules. On 10 November, the rules were adopted and the CCC came into being. The objects of the Club were promoted as being "to encourage cruising and foster the social side of sailing."

The influence of the CCC on sailing, cruising, and also offshore racing, has been steady and consistent. Today it is involved in far more activities than are usual for a yacht club; it includes junior training and dinghy sailing; the running of offshore races; cruising awards and the organization of cruising meets. The CCC was also a pioneer in the introduction of yachtmaster qualifications.

Claud Worth

In addition to this, the Clyde Cruising Club is responsible for the publication of seven volumes of immensely detailed sailing directions for the whole of the west coast of Scotland, Orkneys and Shetlands. The ways in and out of the many anchorages; where to anchor and moor; and available facilities are detailed, with accompanying sketch charts. This information enables sailors unfamiliar with these waters to sail virtually anywhere in the islands and inlets of this coast.

Until recently, volumes carried the seamanlike and charming notice: "Owners of motor yachts and auxiliaries should bear in mind that these directions are written primarily for sailing craft and that, under power, little difficulty will be experienced in making any of the anchorages." Today a pure sailing craft is rare.

A typical entry for one of the many distant anchorages, Loch Scathvaig, reads: "The principal danger is the terrific squalls for which this place is noted . . . a fall of rock at the back of the Loch shows up white from a long way off . . . Stores — none. Water — at burn (stream). Steamer calls once a week in summer."

The 75th anniversary of the Clyde Cruising Club in 1984 attracted a huge fleet from both sides of the Atlantic for a celebratory fleet cruise in the Hebrides and on the west coast of Scotland. This included the world's largest sunflower raft — 191 boats — in Loch Sunart.

CRUISING ASSOCIATION CUPS

These cups are open to members of the Association only, and the criteria employed in deciding the winners have changed over the years, reflecting the changes of attitude and ideas within cruising circles. At one time, the cups were awarded for reasonably major feats, but in many cases, those who now embark on long voyages do not return for several years, and do not always inform the Association of their achievements when they do. The current qualifications are therefore of a somewhat more 'domestic' nature than in the past.

Hanson Cup: Awarded for the best log of any cruise. Routes in recent years include Salvador to Annapolis; Florida to Falmouth; Lymington to Scandinavia; Ullapool to the Faeroes, West Indies to England.

Love Cup: Presented by John Love, first president of the Association, in 1911 for the best log of a short cruise.

Dugon Cup: Awarded for a cruise in any vessel under 8.5m (28ft) LOA.

Dolphin Cup: Awarded for a photographic log.

Dingle Cup: Awarded for a log by a person under 16 years of age.

Brittain Cup: Awarded for information on pilotage and work on sailing directions. This is sometimes awarded to contributors to the Cruising Association Handbook, which covers most parts of the European coastline.

The Hanson Cup

POST-WAR ACTIVITY

After the end of World War I in 1918, some cruising sailors sought to escape the post-war gloom in Europe. The South Seas became a popular venue with cruising enthusiasts; the many charms of the Pacific islands had been enthusiastically expounded by the writings of both Herman Melville and Robert Louis Stevenson and, of course, Joshua Slocum.

One such enthusiast was Ralph Stock, an Englishman who, during the war, had found his 'dream ship' in Devon. *Oeger* was a 1908 lifeboat that had been converted into a yacht, and the designer was Colin Archer, a Norwegian of Scottish descent who played a major role in the development of Norway's maritime history. Not only did Archer design ships for polar explorers such as Nansen and Amundsen, he also improved the design and construction of the pilot boats, fishing and life-saving vessels of his country. In the light of findings in recent years, there is no doubt at all that Archer's basic concept was extremely sound. He is, perhaps, best known for his *Redningsskoites*, the distinctive double-ended sailing rescue boats that he evolved for working off the exposed Norwegian coast.

In 1919, Ralph Stock set out with his sister Mabel, and one friend, on a voyage from Brixham, Devon, to the Pacific Tonga Islands, stopping at Vigo and the Canary Islands, then passing through the Panama Canal and on to the Marquesas, Tahiti, the Savage Islands and Tonga.

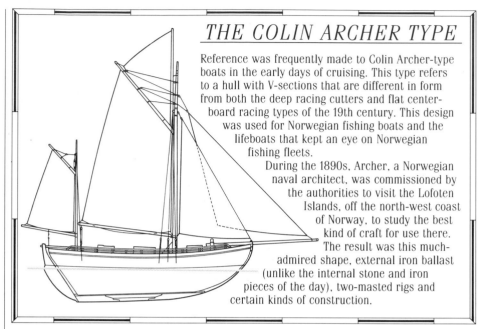

THE COLIN ARCHER TYPE

Reference was frequently made to Colin Archer-type boats in the early days of cruising. This type refers to a hull with V-sections that are different in form from both the deep racing cutters and flat center-board racing types of the 19th century. This design was used for Norwegian fishing boats and the lifeboats that kept an eye on Norwegian fishing fleets.

During the 1890s, Archer, a Norwegian naval architect, was commissioned by the authorities to visit the Lofoten Islands, off the north-west coast of Norway, to study the best kind of craft for use there. The result was this much-admired shape, external iron ballast (unlike the internal stone and iron pieces of the day), two-masted rigs and certain kinds of construction.

Stock's cruise was a cruise in the true sense of the word, and not just a case of port-hopping. It was quite different from the single-handed epic cruises that had gone before him, and appealed to the less eccentric and more leisurely cruising sailors. On his return to England, Stock wrote of his voyage in a book, *The Cruise of the Dream Ship*. His boat *Oeger* was sold to a persistent purchaser before Stock and his companions reached Australia and so it therefore fell to another voyage the next year to become the first post-war cruise around the world.

George Mulhauser, a member of the Royal Cruising Club since 1913, was a former naval officer who found shore life too dull. He bought the 40-year-old, 36-ton yawl *Amaryllis* and in September 1920, left Plymouth with a small crew. He returned to England three years later, having sailed 31,159 miles around the world, on a route that took in the Panama and Suez canals. However, as with many circumnavigators since, he had great difficulty in finding suitable crew and exhausted himself working the heavy boat with little assistance. He died within just a few weeks of completing the venture.

There was a considerable amount of sailing activity in post-war France too. In 1923, the Frenchman, Alain Gerbault, circumnavigated in the 10.1-m (36-ft) ex-racing cutter, *Firecrest*, and experienced an exceptionally stormy crossing of the Atlantic. He sailed single-handed against the prevailing winds from east to west, and then sailed by way of the Panama Canal to the South Seas where he spent considerable time. The voyage took 6 years, 3 months, and he returned to France in July 1929.

———— ◆◆◆ ————

Amaryllis *In 1920, George Mulhauser and a small crew left Plymouth in Amaryllis. He returned three years later, having sailed 31,159 miles, but died shortly after of exhaustion.*

THE GREAT CAPES

The Royal Cruising Club's Challenge Cup was awarded to the same man in three successive years for skippering the first circumnavigation south of the Great Capes, Good Hope and Horn. In June 1923, Conor O'Brien left Ireland with a small crew in his 12.8-m (42-ft) gaff ketch *Saoirse* and returned on 20 June 1925. O'Brien's vessel, which he designed himself, was based on the design of an Arklow fishing boat of the 1860s, although it was built in Baltimore, West Cork in 1922.

It is worthy of note that Slocum's pioneering *Spray* was a rebuilt vessel of 18th-century origins and, indeed, Robin Knox-Johnston's cruising 'first' in 1969 was achieved in a Colin Archer-influenced ketch, *Suhaili*. These three important pioneering voyages in cruising's history were made in boats that were almost 'primitive' in style.

HARRY PIDGEON AND BILL ROBINSON

In 1925, the third Blue Water Medal (see p 41) was awarded to the remarkable Harry Pidgeon, a quiet American who built his own 10.4-m (34-ft) yawl *Islander* to one of Tom Day's Seabird designs. He sailed around the world single-handed via the Panama Canal on a 4-year voyage between 1921 and 1925 and became the second man to circumnavigate the world single-handed. He made a second circumnavigation between 1932 and 1937, also in

William Albert Robinson *Robinson and his crew, Etera, became the first two-man crew to circumnavigate the world. The voyage took three years and won Robinson the 1931 Blue Water Medal.*

Saoirse *Conor O'Brien won the Challenge Cup in three successive years for his voyage in* Saoirse *south of Capes Horn and Good Hope.*

Islander, and was the first man to have circumnavigated alone twice.

In 1928, Pidgeon entered the Bermuda Race in *Islander*. Also taking part was another enthusiast of world cruising, William Albert Robinson (USA), who was using the race as the first and introductory leg of his world cruise. His boat was the bermudan-rigged ketch *Svaap*, 9.9m (32ft 6in), designed by the well-known American designer, John G. Alden. Ironically, it was *Islander*, with its traditional gaff rig that reached Bermuda first. However, Robinson and his crew of one, Etera, a Tahitian, went on to become the first two-man crew to circumnavigate. The three-year cruise took them through the South Seas to Singapore, via Sri Lanka, the Red Sea, the Mediterranean, Gibraltar, the Canaries and back to New York. On his return in 1931, Robinson was awarded the Blue Water Medal for that year. Robinson subsequently spent much of his life in the Pacific Islands.

THE LITTLE SHIP CLUB

The year 1926 saw the founding of yet another yacht club. A meeting of 27 yachtsmen in the Old Ship Tavern, Charing Cross, London, resulted in the formation of The Little Ship Club.

The instigator of this club was Robert Gibbon, and its first President was the-then commodore of the RCC, Claud Worth. The objectives of the club were stated as being: "The furtherance of knowledge of seamanship and navigation of small craft and interchange of ideas at social gatherings." Meetings and instruction classes were introduced, a library started, and women admitted as members in 1927.

The Little Ship Club was at its peak in the 1930s, when it pioneered systematic instruction for sailors, mostly those who worked in central London or the City. In pursuance of this, an imposing club house was built in the 1950s.

In more recent years, the promotion of instruction by the national authority (RYA Yachtmaster qualifications) has tended to eclipse the club's original role. These days, The Little Ship Club is more of a forum for people working in London to socialize and to attend lectures and discussions on cruising.

THE BLUE WATER MEDAL

The exciting atmosphere of the 1920s was reflected in the energy put into various seaborne activities. Few were more energetic than William Washburne Nutting, an American with little practical knowledge of the sea, but with great enthusiasm for the notion of voyaging in small craft.

In 1920, he hurriedly constructed the 13.8-m (45-ft), William Atkin-designed ketch *Typhoon*. Although not untypical of American cruising boats of the period, *Typhoon* was not specially suitable for ocean cruising. Its displacement was heavy, some of this weight being made up of loose inside ballast, which turned out to be extremely dangerous at sea on at least one occasion. The bows were fine and the stern was broad. The rig was that of a ketch with a gaff mainsail and a gaff mizzen, and it had a bowsprit. Nutting and Atkin sailed *Typhoon* from Nova Scotia to Cowes, ostensibly to report the Harmsworth Cup powerboat race in Nutting's capacity as managing editor of the magazine *Motor Boat*.

While in England, Nutting also took the opportunity to make the acquaintance of those involved in cruising and sea-going craft. In Cowes, he met with Claud Worth, the-then vice-commodore of the Royal Cruising Club. Nutting, the epitome of youthful American enthusiasm, could not fail to be even further enthused by Worth's account of the RCC's activities, and sailed back to America (his crew

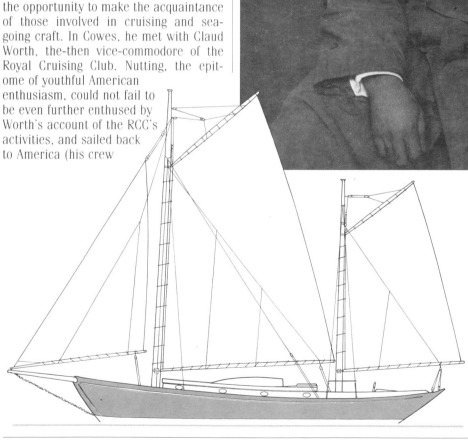

William Washburne Nutting *'Typhoon Bill' Nutting, founder of the Cruising Club of America. In 1921, Nutting sailed to Cowes in* Typhoon *(left), where he made the acquaintance of Claud Worth, vice-commodore of the RCC.*

including two extra Englishmen, one of whom was the young Uffa Fox) with a burning ambition to emulate the example of the RCC in America.

THE CRUISING CLUB OF AMERICA

It was at a restaurant called Beefsteak John's in Greenwich Village, New York, that Nutting met with his friends to discuss the formation of a club. On 15 May 1922, the Cruising Club of America was formally

Alain Gerbault on board Firecrest

commissioned. It had a nine-man board of governors, several specialist sub-committees, and it began with 36 charter members, who included Thomas Fleming Day and Herbert L. Stone, editor of *Yachting* magazine and a figure of considerable influence, as well as Gilbert Grosvenor of the *National Geographic Magazine*.

The new club developed rapidly, and by 1924 had a busy program, including the running of Tom Day's Bermuda Race. Tragically, in that same year, 'Typhoon Bill' Nutting was lost at sea, travelling from Norway to Iceland, Greenland and on toward Canada and the US in the 12.8-m (42-ft) Colin Archer cutter, *Lief Eiriksson*. The boat went missing on the leg from Greenland to Labrador; weather conditions were bad and there was the ever-present possibility of ice. The *Lief Eiriksson* and its crew were lost without trace. Although a tragic loss both to the Cruising Club of America and the development of cruising as a whole, Bill Nutting has left a lasting memorial in the CCA and the Blue Water Medal, the world's top award for offshore sailing and cruising.

THE BLUE WATER MEDAL

The original proposal for the CCA's Blue Water Medal was put forward by Henry A. Wise Wood on 27 February 1923. It was to be awarded "for the year's most meritorious example of seamanship, the recipient to be selected from among the amateurs of all nations." The Medal proved difficult to award fairly; in some

The 1940 Blue Water Medal

years there were several outstanding achievements, and in others there was none. There was then, and still is, the problem of how to define 'amateur.' The problems were in evidence from the Blue Water Medal's inauguration; the somewhat eccentric lone French sailor, Alain Gerbault, was the first winner for his 100-day voyage from France to New York in the narrow, old cutter *Firecrest*. It was a slow voyage, riddled with equipment failure, and much of Gerbault's 'meritorious seamanship' stemmed from his having to put right things that should not have gone wrong in the first place. However, Gerbault learned from his mistakes, and went on with *Firecrest* to become France's first circumnavigator and the third man in the world to get around single-handed. The awards committee benefited from this experience too, and the allocation of the Blue Water Medal today is undertaken with great deliberation.

The roll call of those who have been awarded the Blue Water Medal since 1923 provides a unique insight into the development of deep-sea sailing in small craft.

BLUE WATER MEDAL WINNERS

Islander

Jolie Brise

	BOAT	SKIPPER	NAT.	
1923	FIRECREST	ALAIN GERBAULT	FR.	*Left Gibraltar 7 June 1923. Arrived Fort Totten, Long Island, 100 days later. Nonstop. Single-handed. Dixon Kemp-designed 11.9-m (39-ft) British cutter.*
1924	SHANGHAI	AXEL INGWERSEN	DEN.	*Left Shanghai 20 February 1923. Arrived Denmark via Cape of Good Hope May 1924. Crew of three. Double-ended 14.3-m (47-ft) ketch.*
1925	ISLANDER	HARRY PIDGEON	USA	*First ever circumnavigation from Los Angeles to Los Angeles via Cape of Good Hope and Panama Canal. Left 18 November 1921. Arrived 31 October 1925. Single-handed. 10.4-m (34-ft) Seabird yawl.*
1926	JOLIE BRISE	E.G. MARTIN	UK	*Double transatlantic crossing, including Bermuda Race. Left Falmouth, England 3 April 1926. Arrived Plymouth, England 27 July 1926. Le Havre 17-m (56-ft) pilot cutter.*
1927	PRIMROSE IV	FREDERICK AMES	USA	*15.2-m (50-ft) Alden schooner sailed to England for 1926 Fastnet Race. Medal awarded for the return passage from Portsmouth, via Iceland, Labrador, Cape Breton Island, 58 days to Newport, Rhode Island.*
1928	SEVEN BELLS	THOMAS COOKE	USA	*Eastbound transatlantic passage. Left Branford, Connecticut 5 July 1928. Arrived Falmouth 31 July 1928. Roue-designed 17-m (56-ft) ketch.*
1929	POSTSCRIPT	F. SLADE DALE	USA	*4,000-mile West Indies cruise with crew of two, from and to Barnegat Bay, New Jersey. 7-m (23-ft) cutter.*
1930	CARLSARK	CARL WEAGENT	USA	*13,000-mile cruise from Ithaca, New York to Ithaca, Greece and return New York. Left 20 June 1929. Completed 30 May 1930. 14-m (46-ft) ketch.*
1931	SVAAP	WILLIAM ROBINSON	USA	*Left New London, Connecticut, 23 June 1928 in Bermuda Race. Circumnavigated via Panama and Suez canals with crew of just two. Arrived New York 24 September 1931. 9.9-m (32-ft 6-in) Alden ketch.*
1932	JOLIE BRISE	ROBERT SOMERSET	UK	*Awarded for seamanship and courage in rescuing all but one of 11-man crew of schooner Adriana in 1932 Bermuda Race.*
1933	DORADE	ROD STEPHENS	USA	*Three-month, 8,000-mile transatlantic crossing from New York to Norway and back, including victory in Fastnet Race. 15.9-m (52-ft 3-in) Stephens-designed yawl returned home from England by northern route in 26 days.*
1934	MAY L	W.B. REESE	UK	*Left England Fall 1933. Arrived Nassau January 1934. Single-handed. Small double-ended ketch.*
1935	—	CHARLES TILLINGHAST	USA	*For seamanship in trying to save three crew of the Hamrah and for bringing disabled and short-handed ketch into Sydney Harbor.*
1936	ARIELLE	MARIN-MARIE	FR.	*Single-handed transatlantic crossing in 12.9-m (42-ft 7-in) motorboat. 23 July 1936 - 10 August 1936. Two self-steering devices.*

	BOAT	SKIPPER	NAT.	
1937	DUCKLING	CHARLES ATWATER	USA	New York to Reykjavik, Iceland to Newport, via Trepassey, Newfoundland. 19 June 1937 - 26 August 1937. 11.4-m (37-ft 6-in) Mower cutter.
1937	IGDRASIL	ROGER STROUT	USA	Circumnavigation with wife in Spray-type cutter, finally rigged as yawl, via Panama Canal and Cape of Good Hope. June 1934 - May 1937.
1938	CAPLIN	ROBERT GRAHAM	UK	Bantry Bay, Ireland to Funchal and Bermuda with daughter. 20 April 1938-27 June 1938, then to West Indies. 10.7-m (35-ft) yawl.
1939	IRIS	JOHN MARTUCCI	USA	11,000-mile cruise New York to Naples and return, which included non-stop, 35-day run from Tanger to Bermuda during World War II. 10.9-m (36-ft) MacGregor yawl.
1940	—	BRITISH YACHTSMEN AT DUNKERQUE	UK	Awarded to British yachtsmen, alive and dead, who had helped in evacuation of British Expeditionary Force, June 1940.
1941	ORION	ROBERT NEILSON	USA	Left Honolulu 5 June 1941. Arrived San Pedro, California 15 July 1941. Crew of one. Orion subsequently continued through Panama Canal to Tampa, Florida, 7,978 miles. 9-m (30-ft) auxiliary ketch.
1947	GAUCHO	ERNESTO URIBURU	ARG.	Buenos Aires, through Mediterranean to Suez Canal, then to New York, following Columbus' route from Palos, Spain to San Salvador. 15.2-m (50-ft) ketch.
1950	LANG SYNE	WILLIAM & PHYLLIS CROWE	USA	Honolulu to New England, via Cape Horn. Spring 1948-Spring 1950. 11.8-m (39-ft), Block Island-type, double-ended schooner.
1952	STORNOWAY	ALFRED PETERSEN	USA	Circumnavigation from and to New York via Panama and Suez canals. June 1948-August 1952. Single-handed. 10-m (33-ft) double-ended cutter.
1953	OMOO	L.G. VAN DE WIELE	BEL.	Circumnavigation with wife plus one other crew member. Nice, France to Zeebrugge, Belgium via Panama Canal and Cape of Good Hope. 7 July 1951 - 2 August 1953. Steel 13.7-m (45-ft), gaff-rigged ketch.
1954	VIKING	STEN & BRITA HOLMDAHL	SWE.	Circumnavigation by Panama Canal and Cape of Good Hope from Marstrand back to Gothenburg, Sweden. 17 June 1952 - 22 June 1954. Double-ended 10-m (33-ft) ketch converted from fishing boat.
1955	WANDERER III	ERIC & SUSAN HISCOCK	UK	Circumnavigation via Panama Canal and Cape of Good Hope. 24 July 1952 - 13 July 1955. 9.1-m (30-ft) Giles-designed cutter.
1956	MISCHIEF	H.W. TILMAN	UK	20,000-mile voyage from Britain through Strait of Magellan, up west coast of South America, through Panama Canal back to England. 6 July 1955 - 10 July 1956.
1956	—	CARLETON MITCHELL	USA	"For his meritorious ocean passages, his sterling seamanship and his advancement of the sport by counsel and example."

Dorade

Captain Lockwood, USN, presents Medal to British yachtsmen, 1941.

John Guzzwell

Eric Tabarly

	BOAT	SKIPPER	NAT.	
1957	LANDFALL II	WILLIAM HOLCOMB	USA	*Circumnavigation from San Francisco, via Suez and Panama canals, with trips to South America, Britain, North Africa and New York. 18 September 1953 - 15 September 1957. 14.1-m (46-ft 6-in) schooner.*
1958	LES QUATRE VENTS	MARCEL BARDIAUX	FR.	*Circumnavigation west-about around Cape Horn and Cape of Good Hope from Ouistreham, France to Arcachon, France. Single-handed. 24 May 1950 - 25 July 1958. Home-built 9.3-m (30-ft 9-in) sloop.*
1959	TREKKA	JOHN GUZZWELL	CAN.	*Circumnavigation from Victoria BC, to Victoria, via Cape of Good Hope and Panama Canal. Single-handed. 10 September 1955 - 10 September 1959. 6.3-m (20-ft 10-in), home-built yawl.*
1959	LEHG I LEHG II SIRIO	VITO DUMAS	ARG.	*Global circumnavigation in Lehg II, 1942-3. Other single-handed voyages in Lehg I, 1931-2; Lehg II, 1945-7; Sirio, 1955.*
1960	GIPSY MOTH III	FRANCIS CHICHESTER	UK	*Won first OSTAR race, east to west, in 1960. Plymouth, England to Newport, Rhode Island.*
1961	SEACREST	PAUL SHELDON	USA	*Extensive cruises along coasts of Nova Scotia, Newfoundland and Labrador.*
1962	ADIOS	THOMAS STEELE	USA	*Two circumnavigations – one in 1950-5, other in 1957-63. 9.8-m (32-ft) ketch.*
1964	PEN DUICK II	ERIC TABARLY	FR.	*Won second OSTAR race.*
1965	DELIGHT	WRIGHT BRITTON	USA	*New York to Greenland and return with wife, Patricia, as crew.*
1966	JOSHUA	BERNARD MOITESSIER	FR.	*Mooréa Island, South Pacific, around Cape Horn to Alicante, Spain, with wife, Françoise, as crew. 12.5-m (41-ft) steel ketch.*
1967	GIPSY MOTH IV	FRANCIS CHICHESTER	UK	*29,630-mile circumnavigation via Cape of Good Hope and Cape Horn. Single-handed. Stopped only in Sydney, Australia.*
1968	LIVELY LADY	ALEC ROSE	UK	*Circumnavigation stopping only at Melbourne, Australia and Bluff, New Zealand. Single-handed. Left Portsmouth, England 16 July 1967. Arrived Portsmouth 4 July 1968.*
1970	CARINA	RICHARD NYE	USA	*Meritorious cruising and ocean racing.*
1970	ELSIE	FRANK CASPER	USA	*Extensive single-handed cruising, including a circumnavigation and frequent transatlantic crossings.*
1971	WHISPER	HAL ROTH	USA	*18,538-mile cruise around Pacific basin from San Francisco. Sailed new route, never taken before by cruising sailboat. Wife, Margaret, as crew.*
1972	AWAHNEE II	ROBERT L. GRIFFITH	USA	*Three circumnavigations with wife and son. First in Uffa Fox-designed cutter, Awahnee I, east to west around Cape Horn and Cape of Good Hope. Second in Awahnee II, eastward via Capes and Japan. Third circumnavigation in Awahnee II, 12,800-mile cruise around Antarctic.*

	BOAT	SKIPPER	NAT.	
1973	TZU HANG	MILES & BERYL SMEETON	CAN.	*Seamanship and outstanding cruising. The Smeetons cruised to almost all parts of globe during 1955-1970.*
1974	ANGANTYR	JAMES CRAWFORD	USA	*Over 20 years cruising, many single-handed passages or with family in specially developed cutter, Angantyr. Also circumnavigated in 1959 in Alden schooner, Dirigo.*
1975	GALWAY BLAZER	BILL KING	UK	*Circumnavigation south of Capes in lug-rigged, light-displacement schooner, 12.8-m (42-ft), despite being rolled and holed by white shark.*
1976	REINDEER	E. NEWBOLD SMITH	USA	*Cruise to Spitsbergen and Greenland in Swan 43.*
1977	TORGUS	GOSTA ERIKENSEN	FIN.	*Driven ashore in Philippines typhoon. Succeeded in refloating ketch and completing cruise home to the Baltic.*
1978	ROSE RAMBLER	HUMPHREY BARTON	UK	*Founder of Ocean Cruising Club. Completed 20 transatlantic passages, most in Giles-designed sloop Rose Rambler.*
1979	FOREIGN AFFAIR	BILL & MARY BLACK	USA	*4-year circumnavigation in 13.7-m (45-ft) boat, including detailed cruising in remote areas of South America.*
1980	WILLIWAW	WILLY DE ROOS	BEL.	*First cruising yachtsman to cross Northwest Passage, he eventually completed circuit of Americas and a circumnavigation.*
1982	—	DAVID LEWIS	NZ	*Cruised Greenland Sea 1963. First circumnavigation in multihull 1964-7. First single-handed circuit cruise of Antarctica 1972-4. Cruised Antarctica 1977-8. Extensive study of Polynesian navigation methods in Pacific cruises.*
1983	SHARDANA	JOHN GORE-GRIMES	IRE.	*"Extraordinary, well-executed and purposeful cruising in high latitudes." Notable for use of standard Nicholson 31 for exploratory voyages. Later became first cruising yachtsman to make inshore passage from Scoresby Sound, Greenland, southwards.*
1984	NORTHERN LIGHT	ROLFE BJELKE & DEBORAH SHAPIRO	SWE.	*Circumnavigation around Cape Horn 1977-81. Extensive cruising in 12.2-m (40-ft) ketch in Arctic and Antarctic waters, June 1982 - June 1984.*
1985	GLOBE STAR	MARVIN CREAMER	USA	*Two transatlantic crossings and circumnavigation without instruments. December 1982-May 1984.*
1986	PALAWAN	TOM WATSON JR	USA	*More than 15 years extensive, well-planned, carefully executed expeditions. 1986 cruise from Newfoundland to Churchill, Manitoba, on western Hudson Bay.*
1987	TOTORORE	GERRY CLARK	NZ	*3½-year circumnavigation in home-built, 10-m (33-ft) cutter to study bird life along Antarctic convergence.*
1988	WAR BABY	WARREN BROWN	BER.	*For a series of cruises in 19.2-m (63-ft) cutter, including to Spitsbergen and the Antarctic Peninsula, taking in the Galapagos, the Patagonian Channels and Cape Horn.*

Lively Lady

David Lewis

THE THIRTIES AND FORTIES

Fortunately for the advancement of cruising, the economic depression of the early 1930s did not have an entirely negative effect. Indeed, faced by a bleak economic future, many young people, particularly in America, felt that they should travel for a few years, and ocean voyaging seemed a very attractive prospect.

A design that was particularly popular for this purpose was the 9.1-m (30-ft) Tahiti Ketch, a gaff-rigged vessel designed in 1924 by John G. Hanna of Florida. The concept of this boat – yet another variant on the well-proven Colin Archer theme – was that it could be built for $1,000 using local material and home labor. The number of plans sold to blue-water dreamers ran into many thousand, although only a hundred or so actually reached the sea.

By the time the Tahitis were roaming the high seas, their rigs may already have looked old-fashioned, the bermuda rig gaining in popularity all the time. However, many splendid cruises were still being achieved at this time in gaff-rigged craft, notably by former pilot cutters.

THE PILOT CUTTERS

The most famous of all pilot cutters is the *Jolie Brise*, a handsome 17-m (56-ft) boat built in 1913 for the Le Havre pilot service, and winner of the Blue Water Medal in 1926 and 1932 in the ownership of George Martin and Bobby Somerset respectively. It also won the first Fastnet Race in 1925.

The most numerous as cruising boats were the Bristol Channel cutters, a number of which still sail today. An early example was Roger Pinckney's *Dyarchy*, a 12.5-m (41-ft) boat built in Bristol in 1901, which distinguished itself under the RCC's burgee during the 1920s and 1930s. In 1939, it was replaced by a new *Dyarchy*, a 14.3-m (47-ft) boat designed by Jack Laurent Giles and built in Sweden. Setting a so-called advanced gaff rig, it proved a splendid cruising boat, and although the hull shape was much developed from the basic pilot cutter type, there were some marked resemblances to the original nevertheless.

This moderate-to-heavy displacement hull type has greatly influenced other cruising designs. One example is the Giles-designed, 7.7-m (25-ft) *Vertue*, which had remarkable success, including several circumnavigations and other voyages that would have been remarkable in any boat, and which were especially notable for a craft of this size.

MORE 'FIRSTS'

The 1930s saw not only an increasing sophistication in design and equipment, but also a number of single-handed 'firsts'. In 1934, the Norwegian Al Hansen, became the first lone sailor to round Cape Horn from east to west against the prevailing winds. The same year saw a retired British naval commander, R.D. Graham, battling east to west single-handed across the North Atlantic, from Ireland to Newfoundland. His vessel was the little 7-ton gaff cutter *Emanuel*, built by its designer, A. Anderson. The account of this cruise was told by Commander Graham in a book, *Rough Passage*. Graham was awarded the RCC Challenge Cup in 1934 for this voyage.

Commander Graham subsequently won the Blue Water Medal in 1938 for his cruise across the Atlantic to the Caribbean in the 10.7-m (35-ft) yawl, *Caplin*. At the time that R.D. Graham won the RCC Challenge Cup in 1934, Claud Worth was the vice-commodore of the RCC. Worth's account of why the Cup was awarded to Commander Graham provides an insight into the care with which the RCC awarded its prestigious Cup.

"*Emanuel* is a 7-ton cutter without auxiliary power. Commander Graham planned to sail from Falmouth to Newfoundland. After a fruitless search for a companion he decided to sail alone rather than give up the venture.

"On May 19, *Emanuel* left Falmouth and three days later arrived in Baltimore, Cork, after a rather rough passage. Already running gear had begun carrying

The Giles-designed Dyarchy, *a successor to the Bristol Channel pilot cutter design.*

R.D. Graham aboard Emanuel

away, which it continued to do at intervals throughout the voyage. Commander Graham tells us that he started with his old gear in order to save the new rope for the Newfoundland coast – a rather dangerous economy, and the frequent repairs must have been exhausting for a lone hand. On 26 May, *Emanuel* took her departure from Mizen Head and the Bull Rock. When possible the vessel was made to steer herself with the helm lashed. Being single-handed greatly increases the risk of such a voyage. Once, while the yacht was running with helm lashed and the owner asleep, there arose a strong wind and big sea, and a wave crest washed on board, waking him in time to see that the yacht was running too fast for safety. The mainsail was furled and two warps towed astern and she drove to the N.W. safely at about 2 to 3 knots. Crossing the Labrador current the air was bitterly cold, there was much fog, and icebergs were seen. St John's, Newfoundland, was reached on June 19. After a few days' rest Commander Graham cruised on the Labrador coast, where he nearly came to grief owing to the jib sheet carrying away.

"The news that *Emanuel* had been sailed single-handed from England to Newfoundland at first caused some misgiving. The Club is for the encouragement of good seamanship and legitimate enterprise, but

recklessness is not regarded with favor. But Commander Graham had proved himself and his vessel in cruises to Spain, the Faroe Islands, and elsewhere. I am satisfied that, having failed to find a companion, he was justified in sailing alone if he wished to do so, and that the voyage was undertaken with adequate knowledge and solely for the love of adventure at sea. It was a remarkable achievement, quite different from a similar voyage in the warm and steady trade-wind zone. The winds were mostly fair and of moderate strength. This was due partly to good luck but more to good judgement in keeping well to the northward. When cyclonic wind systems are driving eastwards across the N. Atlantic, they cause fresh or strong westerly winds in the right-hand semicircle, where the speed of progression is added to the speed of rotation. Further north, in the left-hand semicircle, winds would tend to be easterly, and moderate in force, for the speed of progression would be deducted. Sixty years ago, Captain Beachey, in his book, *Navigation of the Atlantic Ocean*, laid it down that the further north a ship's starting point from Europe the better her chance of fair winds to the Grand Bank."

THE YANKEE STORY

One of the most remarkable cruising careers of the 20th century began in the 1930s when the American couple Irving and Electa Johnson made their first voyage around the world in the former German North Sea pilot schooner, *Yankee*, 28 m (92 ft). Their source of inspiration was another American, Warwick Tompkins, who cruised extensively in a similar vessel called *Wander Bird*.

However, *Wander Bird* never completed a circumnavigation, whereas the intrepid Johnsons made no less than seven circuits between 1933 and 1958 in the original *Yankee* and its steel-built, brigantine-rigged successor, also called *Yankee*. This phase of their cruising career completed, they commissioned Sparkman and Stephens to design yet another *Yankee*, this time a shoal-draft, 15-m (50-ft) ketch with two centerboards. The steel boat was built in the Netherlands, and cruised virtually all of Europe's waterways in addition to many other coasts and rivers, including the Nile.

Yankee *The former pilot schooner* Yankee *in which the Johnsons cruised around the world.*

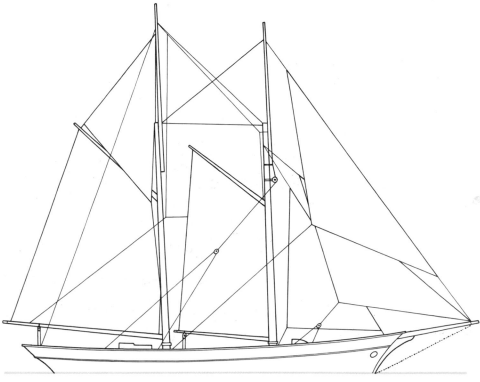

FRENCH SUCCESS

It was during this decade that fresh sailing blood emerged in France, a country that up until this time had been represented solely by the idolized Alain Gerbault.

In 1933, the marine artist, Marin-Marie, sailed his double-ended cutter *Winnibelle* – a slimmed-down version of a Colin Archer boat – from France to New York. In 1936, he made the crossing in the other direction, single-handed as before, but this time in the 12.8-m (42-ft) motor-cruiser *Arielle*, for which he had developed vanes for self-steering; he had worked with twin headsails during his passage across in *Winnibelle*. Steering vanes were later to play a vital role in the development of short-handed sailing.

On 10 August 1936, 12 days after *Arielle* had completed its voyage, a retired sea captain, Louis Bernicot, sailed single-handed from the Gironde on France's Biscay coast, around the world via the Strait of Magellan, the South Sea islands, and the Cape of Good Hope, in his newly built, double-ended, 12.5-m (41-ft) gaff sloop, *Anahita*. He returned home on 30 May 1938.

A.G.H. MACPHERSON

The British yachtsman, A.G.H. Macpherson was a true cruiser, as opposed to a voyager; many long-distance sailors tended not to visit many ports, whereas Macpherson avidly explored every nook and cranny everywhere he went.

He was fortunate in that his infectious enthusiasm for cruising inspired Sir James Caird to finance the building of his two cruising boats. Both were called *Driac* (Caird spelt backward). The first, in which he began cruising in 1930, was a 12.2-m (40-ft) boat designed by Charles Nicholson; the second was smaller, a 9.8-m (32-ft) boat, designed by Sidney Graham and built in 1932, although still with a bermudan cutter rig. Crewed by one paid hand, *Driac II* had sailed 45,000 miles by the time its skipper 'swallowed the anchor' and retired in 1938. An excellent example of a state-of-the-art cruising boat of its time, *Driac II* had cruised north to Iceland, north-east to Leningrad, down to the southern tip of Africa, west to Mexico and east to Indonesia.

Macpherson was arguably the greatest cruising man of the 1930s, and was several-times winner of the RCC Challenge Cup in a seagoing career taken up late in life. The adventures of this fine seaman are told in the book, *The Macpherson Voyages*.

A.G.H. Macpherson *Perhaps the greatest true small-boat cruising man of the 1930s, Angus Macpherson took up his seagoing career late in life. His association with Sir James Caird resulted in* Driac I *(seen above) and* Driac II, *in which Macpherson cruised extensively until his retirement in 1938.*

VITO DUMAS

Argentina was one corner of the world where World War II was not raging, and it was from here that one of the most remarkable voyages so far achieved began on 27 June 1942.

Vito Dumas was an Argentinian who in 1931 sailed single-handed from France to Buenos Aires in an 8-Meter, a racing boat considered unsuitable for ocean crossing. In 1933 he commissioned the local designer Manuel Campos to draw up a 9.8-m (32-ft) seagoing ketch along Colin Archer lines. It was in this craft, *Lehg II*, that he became one of South America's leading offshore sailors. However, he was forced to sell the boat due to financial pressures.

In 1942, a group of loyal friends provided Dumas with the money to buy back *Lehg II* and to equip it for a lone voyage around the world. He set off from Buenos Aires in an easterly direction, across the Atlantic to Cape Town – the only route he could take due to many seas being blocked off by wartime activities. Conditions were atrocious, and the passage from Cape Town to Wellington, New Zealand took 104 days. From there, Dumas sailed to Valparaiso, Chile. Though now back in neutral South America, he still needed to round Cape Horn to return home, which for some reason he did in June, mid-winter! In very rough seas he rounded the Horn, and on 7 July 1943, *Lehg II* arrived at Mar del Plata, having completed the first lone voyage south of the great capes.

THE GLENANS SAILING SCHOOL

World War II inevitably brought an abrupt halt to sailing for pleasure. However, the ending of the war saw a resumption of cruising activities world-wide. Inspired by cruising adventures of recent years, some veterans of the French resistance decided to form a sailing school. In 1947, in the Îles de Glenans off the coast of southern Brittany, Philippe Viannay and some of his compatriots created the Glenans Organization, the aims of which were to teach seamanship in all weather and waters. Although many years later there are a number of successful sailing schools, these are invariably places where students are taught to sail dinghies, with perhaps the opportunity to steer a slightly larger vessel in sheltered waters. However, because it is necessary to sail straight out to the open sea from most French harbors, Glenans students were often taken out to the open sea in ex-ocean racers and taught seamanship in all weathers – an ability which is completely taken for granted today.

By the early 1960s, the first of the influential Glenans Sailing Manuals had been published, and fleet activity was expanding rapidly. As well as the acquisition of the 13-Meter cutter *Glenan*, the organization was able to build up a fleet of Mousquetaires, attractively simple, 6.4-m (21-ft) cruising sloops that were designed by Jean-Jacques Herbulot for coastal cruising but which proved themselves able to complete some notable offshore passages.

Glenans has nine bases in three countries, France, Ireland and Greece, and in excess of 13,000 members. The organization possesses a total fleet of more than 600 boats, ranging from dinghies up to the Glenans flagship, a First 42 sloop designed in Argentina and built in France. However, tradition is maintained by the sailing of older craft, thereby continuing the original Glenans spirit.

Glenans Mousquetaire *One of the fleet of Glenans Mousquetaires originally designed for coastal cruising, but which have proved capable of completing some notable offshore passages.*

THE LAST FRONTIERS

In more recent years, the only seas left for the true pioneer to explore were those of the Arctic; it was still a largely unexplored area, despite the voyages of a small number of cruising boats earlier.

From 1955 onwards, it was the memorable mountaineer-turned-sailor, H.W. Tilman (UK), (see p107), who did much to open up the last frontiers. Cruising in three different Bristol Channel pilot cutters, Bill Tilman was very much the individualist. Though born in 1898, and therefore approaching 60, he made a considerable number of voyages from 1955 onward to remote places, including the Arctic and Antarctic, with a crew of young, able-bodied men. On arrival at a suitable place, they disembarked in order to go mountaineering, often in snow and ice. Of the three pilot cutters used for these voyages, *Mischief*, *Seabreeze* and *Baroque*, all between 13.8-15.2 m (45-50 ft), two were lost on cruises. The first, *Mischief*,

The indefatigable H.W. Tilman

was lost in 1968 off Jan Mayen Island, Iceland, when under tow. The second, *Seabreeze*, foundered and sank south of Angmagssalik, Greenland in 1972. In 1955-6, Tilman took *Mischief* to the coasts of South America and the Strait of Magellan in the Cape Horn region. In 1963, the voyage was to the bleak shores of Baffin Bay, and in 1967, Punta Arenas and the South Shetlands.

This is the only boat known to have inspired official geographical names – Mont de Mischief on Île de Possession, Îles Crozet; Cap Mischief on Île de Kerguelen; Mount Mischief on Baffin Island. Tilman was awarded the Blue Water Medal in 1956, and became the first winner of the Royal Cruising Club's newly instituted Goldsmith Exploration Award in 1964. He was awarded it again in 1974.

In 1980, Tilman, who was by then 82 years old, and his crew disappeared without trace on a voyage in a converted tug to South America and the Antarctic.

THE NORTHWEST PASSAGE

The Northwest Passage, north of Canada and Alaska, had long proved to be a stumbling block for even the most adventurous

Polar cruising *Above: Mischief, one of Tilman's pilot cutters. Below: Gore-Grimes' Nicholson 31 fiberglass sloop, Shardana.*

sailors. Many ships and men had been lost in the ice before the Norwegian sailor, Amundsen, finally made it after two winters in the ice. His breakthrough came in 1906 in the 47-ton *Gjoa*.

However, it is significant that *Gjoa*, even though it was basically a sailing cutter, was equipped with a small auxiliary engine that enabled it to make progress at times of calm when the paths through the ice were not closed off by wind.

The first breakthrough by a sailboat was in 1974 by the Belgian Willy de Roos in his 18-ton steel ketch *Williwaw*; he had already completed a circumnavigation south of the Capes in the same boat, designed by his fellow countryman, Louis van de Wiele, whose *Omoo* had become the first steel boat to circumnavigate the world in 1953. Willy de Roos' spectacular voyage through the Northwest Passage was completed in just one season, and mostly single-handed, and he continued his cruising with a circuit of the Americas. In recognition of his remarkable voyages, de Roos won the RCC's Seamanship Medal for 1977, and was the Blue Water Medal winner for 1980.

Good, modern design in action: Assent *sailed to within 850 miles of the North Pole.*

By the beginning of this decade, cruises in high latitudes were becoming regular occurrences, and in response to this, the RCC introduced the Tilman Medal in honor of the great sailor. The first winner of this new trophy was the Irish skipper John Gore-Grimes for a cruise to Spitsbergen. He was also the recipient of the Blue Water Medal in 1983 for his series of "extraordinary, well-executed and purposeful cruises in Arctic waters". This way of life obviously suited Gore-Grimes, for in 1985 he became the first yachtsman ever to make the inshore passage from Scoresby Sound down the heavily iced east coast of Greenland.

The most remarkable feature of Gore-Grimes' voyaging is that it was all undertaken in a standard Nicholson 31 fiberglass sloop, *Shardana*, proving conclusively that a sound modern boat can cope with ice if properly handled.

This theory is given additional credence by the voyage made by RCC member Willie Ker in 1987. Ker took his Contessa 32, *Assent*, into the waters west of Greenland; *Assent* is a standard version of one of today's most popular cruising boats, yet it got within 850 miles of the North Pole, covering nearly 8,000 miles from its home port of Plymouth. This voyage reflected great credit not only on the skipper and his crew, but also on the quality of good modern design and understandably swept the boards in awards; Willie Ker received the RCC Challenge Cup, the Goldsmith Exploration Award and the Tilman Medal.

ANTARCTICA

The first cruise specifically around Antarctica began on 22 December 1970. New Zealander Dr. Robert Lyle Griffith and his family set off in an Uffa Fox-designed cutter *Awahnee II*, a 16.2-m (53-ft) ferrocement boat that became the first boat in this material to complete the circuit. In true

exploration style, *Awahnee II* and its crew discovered uncharted islands, and returned to home port after 111 days and some very rough sailing. Bob Griffith and his family were awarded the Blue Water Medal for 1972.

The first single-handed cruise to Antarctica was made by a veteran of the first single-handed Transatlantic Race of 1960, Dr. David Lewis. He had subsequently become the first skipper to circumnavigate in a multihull, a feat he achieved in 1964-67. Lewis had also sailed around the Polynesian islands, but in 1972, he heeded the call of the south and made a two-year journey around the coast of Antarctica in his 9.1-m (30-ft) steel cutter *Icebird*.

He left Sydney, Australia, on 19 October 1972, and Oban, on the south coast of New Zealand, on 2 November. Most of the voyage was between the 60th parallel and the farthest north pack-ice. Although midsummer, the weather was bitterly cold and there were almost continual gales. On 29 November, Lewis was in hurricane force winds of 70 knots and experiencing the worst conditions he had ever known. "The whole sea was white ... these are not seas, I thought, they are snowy mountains." *Icebird* was knocked down by one of these gigantic rollers and the mast was smashed. Eventually, Lewis set a short jury-rig mast, but was knocked down again. He managed to sail 2,500 miles to

the US Palmer Station on Anvers Island, Antarctica, at a rate of 41 miles per day, arriving 29 January 1973. This is the fastest rate known for such a small craft under jury rig, and says much for the strength of wind, resulting current, and the determination of Lewis.

From Palmer Station, Lewis set sail again after repairs in November 1973 and continued around the frozen continent. However, *Icebird* was dismasted yet again, and sailed 1,500 miles to Cape Town under a further jury rig, arriving there on 20 March 1974.

One of the most striking voyages in Antarctic waters was completed in 1987 when Gerry Clark returned to New Zealand having spent 3½ years cruising around the continent in his home-built, steel, 10-m (33-ft) cutter *Totorore*. His objective was of a scientific nature – the study of bird life along the Antarctic convergence. Clark was the 1987 recipient of the Blue Water Medal for this expedition.

The Antarctic is a particularly productive area for cruises with a scientific objective. One of today's best-known cruising boats, the 15-m (49-ft) steel ketch *Damien II*, has made Antarctica its home

Gerry Clark aboard Totorore

waters, having spent one winter and several summers in the region. *Damien II* has access to shallow inlets through having a lifting keel, and earns its living by taking scientific researchers into the area. This scientific theme recurs with ever increasing frequency.

NORTHERN LIGHT

The winners of the 1984 Blue Water Medal made some of the most remarkable voyages in recent years. Rolf Bjelke (Sweden) and Deborah Shapiro (USA) made a two-handed voyage to the Arctic and Antarctic in their boat *Northern Light*, calling at places in between. The 12-m (39-ft 6-in) steel ketch was of the same design as *Joshua*, designed by Jean Knocker and built in France. During their trip, Bjelke and Shapiro took many outstanding photographs, published in due course in their book, *Northern Light*. These photographs were taken in all weathers in some truly isolated places and at great risk to the crew. In June 1982, they sailed from the west coast of Sweden north to Svalbard in the Barents Sea until they could make no further progress in the pack-ice. Weaving between icebergs, they sailed down the

Northern Light *Above: Rolf Bjelke and Deborah Shapiro made some remarkable voyages in their steel ketch,* Northern Light.

Arctic and Antarctic waters
Right: Northern Light *left Sweden in June 1982 and completed her voyage at Boston, Massachusetts, June 1984.*

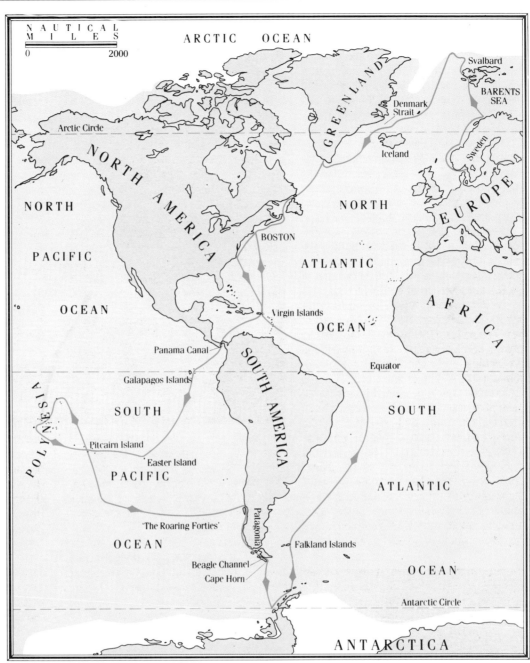

Denmark Strait between Greenland and Iceland to the southern fiords of Greenland.

After a stop at home in Boston, Massachusetts, they continued via the Panama Canal to Easter Island and Pitcairn. Both these islands are isolated and have no anchorage for a deep-draft boat, making landing sometimes impossible. At both places, one crew member went ashore to take photographs, leaving the other to anchor at sea or sail up and down. It was an unnerving time, but "worth it". During September 1983, they cruised around the Polynesian islands and then sailed south via the Roaring Forties and Patagonian Channels of Chile, through the Beagle Channel and past Cape Horn southward to Antarctica where they arrived in January 1984. From here, *Northern Light* began the 8,000-mile journey home to Boston, via the Falkland and Virgin Islands, arriving in June 1984.

The following is an extract from the log: "We paid constant attention to the boat over the 24,000 miles we covered to get here from Sweden. *Northern Light* is as sealed as a steel drum; she will take a pitch pole, a knock-down or a capsize without flooding the interior. The only difference between her and a washing machine is that the washing machine keeps its water inside. To avoid personal injury in heavy weather, we have secured or stowed everything heavy or sharp. Our living area is stark; the homey atmosphere is gone. Only soft clothing remains on the shelves. Lockers or floorboards are bolted or screwed shut. It is preferable to being killed by a flying canned chicken."

THE EXTENT OF OCEAN VOYAGING

Although many voyages and passages of all kinds continue to go unrecorded, it is possible to make some assessment as to the number of world circumnavigations made in sailing boats. The best authority estimates that in 1988, at any given moment, there were about 1,000 boats making extended passages – defined as sailing in deep water, away from the continental shelf of their own countries. The number is thought to increase during vacation periods, especially in the Pacific.

There are many possible ways of circumnavigating the world: via both the Panama Canal and Suez Canal, or either one of them; past the American continent via the Northwest Passage or Strait of Magellan;

via Cape Horn and all, or some, of the five great southern capes – Cape Horn itself; Cape of Good Hope, South Africa; Cape Leeuwin, southwest Australia; South East Cape, Tasmania; South West Cape, Stewart Island, New Zealand; and all in either an easterly or westerly direction. The fact that up until 1937, only five single-handed circumnavigations and five crewed ones (large, professional vessels of over 18.3 m, 60 ft, not included), had been recorded illustrates just how relatively recent such cruises are. A sailor who did much to popularize ocean sailing through his extensive voyages with his wife, Susan, and his prolific writing, was Eric Hiscock (UK). In 1955, he and Susan returned home from a

three-year voyage around the world in the Giles-designed, 9.14-m (30-ft) *Wanderer III*. In that year, he became the first recipient of the annual British Yachtsman of the Year award. In the late 1960s, the Hiscocks built a steel ketch, *Wanderer IV*, in Holland to a Van de Meer design. They then voyaged to New Zealand, where the boat was based. The Hiscocks' third full circumnavigation was from New Zealand and back via South Africa, England, the Panama Canal and Tahiti. It took two-and-a-half years, covered 31,895 miles and was completed in September 1976. Hiscock was awarded an MBE in 1985.

The number of sailboat circumnavigations up to mid-1988 is approximately 450 (plus or minus five per cent), although it is impossible to be completely accurate. There were 155 single-handed circumnavigations, including multihulls; 125 crewed boats below 15.5 m (50 ft); 90 crewed boats above 15.5 m, and 50 crewed multihull categories.

OTHER CATEGORIES

The majority of around-the-world cruises are made by stopping at a number of ports, and in some cases staying at those ports for extended periods. However, there are those who choose to sail around the world 'non-stop'. This means no outside assistance of any kind is received and no harbor moorings can be made: anchoring in a bay is, however, normal racing practice, and would not disqualify the crew. The non-stop sailor may also heave-to at sea.

Up until mid-1988, 14 sailors had made the single-handed circumnavigation non-stop. One of these was a woman, Kay Cottee (Australia). The first person to have achieved this was Bernard Moitessier (France) in *Joshua*, who crossed his outward track west of the Cape of Good Hope on 12 March 1969. Robin Knox-Johnston was the first to make such a voyage and return to his home port.

There was a notable circumnavigation in 1965, although it was not non-stop. Robin Lee Graham (USA) left San Pedro, California, on 27 July 1965, aged 16, and sailed by way of Honolulu; Polynesia; Darwin, northern Australia; Mauritius in the Indian Ocean; Cape Town, South Africa; across the Atlantic to the West Indies;

Eric and Susan Hiscock in Wanderer III

through the Panama Canal and on up the west coast of North America, arriving at Los Angeles on 30 April 1970 – after sailing 30,600 miles. Graham thereby became the youngest person ever to circumnavigate the world single-handedly.

He sailed two boats: the first, *Dove*, was a production fiberglass sloop of 7.3 m (24 ft). Graham sold it in the West Indies and bought a 9.8-m (32-ft) fiberglass sloop, *The Return of the Dove*. A full feature film was made of Graham's circumnavigation, the only one of which a film (as opposed to a documentary) has ever been made.

ATLANTIC CROSSINGS

The approximate figure for single-handed crossings of the Atlantic up to mid-1988 is estimated at 1,200 (plus or minus 10 per cent). The vast majority of these were after 1945, before which time about 60 single-handed crossings had been made. The first woman to cross the Atlantic was Anne Davison (UK), who left Plymouth, England in May 1952 in her 7-m (23-ft) sloop, *Felicity Ann*, and reached Miami, Florida, in August 1953, later sailing on to New York.

PACIFIC CROSSINGS

Here the definition is less easy, due to the nature of the vast ocean and the main islands between which boats can sail. Few single-handed sailors have sailed from continent to continent, or even to or from major islands such as Japan or the Philippines. However, it is estimated that 800 lone sailors have crossed the Pacific Ocean non-stop.

SMALL CRAFT

At the extremity of offshore sailing limits are those who have crossed oceans in very small boats indeed. Of these, the 1.79-m (5-ft 10½-in) *Toniky-Nou*, in which Eric Peters crossed the Atlantic from east to west, will be extremely hard to beat!

In the case of *Giltspur*, Tom McClean stated that he wished to beat the existing 'smallest' recorded west-to-east crossing by Bill Dunlop (USA), who had crossed in a 2.762-m (9-ft ¾-in) boat which was smaller than McClean's first *Giltspur* at 2.97 m (9 ft 9 in). The second *Giltspur*, at 2.369 m (7 ft 9¼ in) appears to be the smallest vessel to have crossed the North Atlantic west to east by the northern route. In 1986, Sergio Testa's boat *Acrohc Australis*, 3.6 m (11 ft 10 in), became the smallest vessel to cross the South Atlantic.

TRANSATLANTIC SMALL BOAT VOYAGES

	BOAT	LOA	SKIPPER	NAT.	ROUTE	TIME days hr min	
1964-5	SJØ ÄG	3.66 m (12 ft)	JOHN RIDING	UK	PLYMOUTH-AZORES-BERMUDA-NEWPORT	67 — — (Azores-Bermuda)	Continued via Panama Canal to San Diego
1966	NONOALCA	3.66 m (12 ft)	BILL VERITY	IRE.	FORT LAUDERDALE-TRALEE, IRELAND	66 — —	Followed route home said to have been taken by Brendan the Navigator, AD554
1968	APRIL FOOL	1.8256 m (5 ft 11⅞ in)	HUGO VIHLEN	USA	CASABLANCA-MIAMI	84 — —	—
1979	YANKEE GIRL	3.05 m (10 ft)	GERRY SPIESS	USA	NORFOLK, VIRGINIA-FALMOUTH, ENGLAND	54 — —	Outboard carried
1981-2	SODIM (SAILBOARD)	2.75 m (9 ft)	CHRISTIAN MARTY	FR.	DAKAR-KOUROU, FRENCH GUIANA	37 16 14	Slept and ate on board. Food etc. supplied by 12 crew aboard 22-m (72-ft) boat Assiduous
1982	GILTSPUR	2.97 m (9 ft 9 in)	TOM McCLEAN	UK	ST. JOHN'S, NEWFOUNDLAND-FALMOUTH, ENGLAND	50 18 28	Outboard carried
1982	WIND'S WILL	2.762 m (9 ft 0¾ in)	BILL DUNLOP	USA	PORTLAND, MAINE-FALMOUTH, ENGLAND	76 16 20	No outboard
1982-3	TONIKY-NOU	1.79 m (5 ft 10½ in)	ERIC PETERS	UK	LAS PALMAS - POINTE-À-PITRE, GUADELOUPE	46 — —	No outboard
1982-3	GOD'S TEAR	2.717 m (8 ft 11 in)	WAYNE DICKINSON	USA	POINT ALLERTON-ARANMORE, IRELAND	142 — —	No supplies from passing shipping. No outboard carried
1983	GILTSPUR	2.369 m (7 ft 9¼ in)	TOM McCLEAN	UK	ST. JOHN'S, NEWFOUNDLAND-OPORTO, PORTUGAL	61 10 —	LOA questioned. Unconfirmed as "smallest". Outboard carried
1986	ACROHC AUSTRALIS	3.6 m (11 ft 10 in)	SERGIO TESTA	AUS.	CAPE TOWN-PORT NATAL, BRAZIL	20 — — (Ascension to Port Natal, Brazil)	Broke journey in St. Helena and Ascension Island

WOMEN SAILORS

Four women have sailed around the world single-handed, and three of them made the journey in 1977. The first to set out was Krystyna Chojnowska-Liskiewwicz (Poland) in *Mazurek*, 9.5m (31ft 3in). She sailed west via the Panama Canal from Las Palmas, and crossed her outward track in March 1978. Meanwhile, Naomi James (NZ born, British resident) sailed from Dartmouth, England in *Express Crusader*, 16.2m (53ft), around the five great southern capes, crossing her outward track several weeks after Chojnowska-Liskiewwicz. Brigitte Oudry (France) also circumnavigated south of three of the capes in *Gea*, 10.5m (34ft 4in) during 1977-8.

The first woman to sail around the world non-stop was Kay Cottee (Australia) in the 11.5-m (38-ft) *Blackmore's First Lady*, which arrived back in Sydney on 5 June 1988 after sailing 25,000 miles in 189 days.

Naomi James

The Smeeton family

SURVIVAL AT SEA

In 1957, there was an incident at sea that was to pave the way for future survival. It involved the 14-m (46-ft) cruising ketch *Tzu Hang*; on 14 February 1957, on a voyage from Melbourne for Cape Horn and on to England, the boat was knocked down and pitchpoled by a huge sea, which swept away the rudder, both masts, all the rigging and all the deck structure, leaving a gaping chasm in the deck. The crew of three, Brigadier Miles Smeeton, his wife Beryl, and John Guzzwell, set to work, determined to survive in the sinking boat. Covering up the holes with canvas, a task made even more difficult by the gale conditions of the Roaring Forties, and making a jury rig, they reached a Chilean port after six weeks.

Nine months later, without John Guzzwell and after a major refit, the intrepid couple set off again, but encountered a severe gale some 300 miles away from the Horn. To obviate the possibility of pitchpoling again, they decided to lie a-hull, but a great sea knocked them down and the rig was swept away for a second time. Somehow they managed to patch up the boat sufficiently to reach Valparaiso in Chile.

The significance of these two incidents was to prove that boats could suffer knockdown and survive, and in many future cases, precautions were taken. As a result, many knock-downs were survived without any great harm befalling the crew.

TWICE, THEN THREE TIMES AROUND

The late 1970s and 1980s proved a fruitful period for the energetic and determined sailor, Jonathan W. Sanders (Australia), the impressive culmination of which was his single-handed triple circumnavigation during 1986-8.

However, prior to this, Jon Sanders had been extremely active. In 1973, he took delivery of a 10.4-m (34-ft) sloop designed by Sparkman and Stephens, *Perie Banou*. It was a standard hull built in Fremantle, but the mold had been obtained in England after production there had ceased on this S&S 34.

By 1980, Sanders had sailed 70,000 miles in this boat, 15,000 of them single-handed; among his many single-handed passages were cruises from Rio de Janeiro to the British Virgin Islands and from Hobart to Fremantle. Crewed, he sailed her via the Suez Canal and Mediterranean to England, after which he raced home via the Cape. He also sailed around the world via the Indian Ocean, Panama Canal and the south of Australia to Fremantle.

All this was invaluable preparation for *Perie Banou*'s next cruise. On 6 September 1981, Sanders left Fremantle to complete a unique, single-handed, double circumnavigation. He sailed *Perie Banou* south of New Zealand, around Cape Horn and then to Plymouth, England, where he took on supplies and mail without stopping in port, or mooring. He proceeded south around the Cape, south of Tasmania and New Zealand again, south of Cape Horn, the Cape of Good Hope and back to Fremantle on 29 October 1982. During this voyage, *Perie Banou* was knocked down several times and once it was turned upside down.

Undeterred, Sanders began to plan his next, even more ambitious, cruise – a triple circumnavigation, and this time there would be no taking on of supplies or outside assistance of any kind. The only contact with the rest of the world, apart from radio, would be newspapers dropped on board and an exchange of mail off Fremantle on completion of the first rounding. A new boat was purchased and converted; the 14-m (46-ft) *Parry Endeavour* (sponsored by the Parry Corporation) was a masthead sloop of foam-sandwich construction, with separate rudder and full skeg. Designed by Phil Curran (Australia) in 1979, it was considerably strengthened internally for the journey ahead of her, and a new, heavy-duty mast with duplicated rigging was fitted.

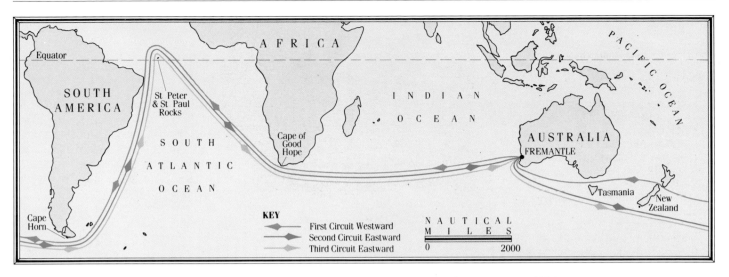

Jon Sanders' 71,000-mile route for his single-handed triple circumnavigation which took 657 days.

Jon Sanders left Fremantle on 25 May 1986 and sailed east (against the prevailing wind), via the Cape of Good Hope and toward the equator where he rounded St. Peter and St. Paul Rocks in mid-Atlantic, 54 miles north of the equator. He then sailed south of Cape Horn, through Cook Strait (New Zealand), through Bass Strait between Australia and Tasmania, turned around off Fremantle and began the second leg of his journey on 31 January 1987.

On this second leg, Sanders went south of Tasmania, Stewart Island (New Zealand), Cape Horn, round St. Peter and St. Paul Rocks and the Cape of Good Hope, arriving off Fremantle on 15 September 1987.

The third circumnavigation followed exactly the same route, and *Parry Endeavour* arrived back in Fremantle on 13 March 1988.

There were several alarming incidents during this cruise: *Parry Endeavour* struck a squid-fishing boat off the Falkland Islands which broke the forestay, loosened other rigging and bent the mast. For most of the voyage, all instruments had failed and there was no speed and distance log. For the last five months there was no HF radio, except for very short range; however, Sanders' position was known via Argos automatic transmitter. His own celestial sights were obtained using a digital watch which was always on GMT. This triple circumnavigation surpassed all previous exploits in cruising and voyaging, and it is unlikely that any race will ever be run three times round the world without stopping.

THE SHAPE OF THINGS TO COME

With the breakthrough in Antarctica, the only remaining frontier for cruising boats under sail is the Northeast Passage north of the USSR. However, even in the best of summers, ships sailing this briefly-accessible route often require the service of ice-breakers, so the chances of a boat getting through are somewhat questionable.

The political situation also has to be taken into account. It is only in the latter part of this decade that boats have once more been permitted to cruise to Leningrad. However, one of the more recent voyagers, Roger Foxall, an Irishman who sailed to Leningrad in 1987, was surprised by the level of Russian sailing activity. It may well be that it will be a Soviet cruising boat that breaks this final frontier.

While there may be little left in the way of geographical barriers, there will always be psychological barriers of various kinds to be broken. After a number of his 'gadgets' broke down during extensive cruising, the American yachtsman Marvin Creamer became intrigued by the possibility of sailing without today's vast array of instruments. From December 1982 to May 1984, he made two transatlantic crossings and a circumnavigation without any instruments whatsoever, not even a clock or compass, in the steel-built Goderich 35 cutter *Globe Star*. This feat was not regarded as merely a stunt; he was subsequently awarded the 1985 Blue Water Medal for his experiment.

Escapades such as these would surely have seemed foolhardy to even the most adventurous of the pioneering cruising sailors, but there is no doubt that the intrepid voyages of yesterday are commonplace today, with new barriers being broken all the time.

Although cruising people draw on the lessons learned by those who race, they certainly do not wait to follow their lead. Indeed, it is often the other way around. For example, the frequency with which boats now cross the Atlantic by the trade wind route, in all seasons, encouraged the instigation of the Atlantic Rally for Cruisers (ARC) in 1986, sailed from Las Palmas to Barbados (see p86). The fearless spirit of cruising sailors must also have been instrumental in inspiring Colonel H.G. 'Blondie' Hasler to push for a single-handed transatlantic race, OSTAR, sailed from Plymouth, England, to Rhode Island, Newport (see pp86-90). These two events are, however, very different; the ARC is sailed in mainly fair winds, with people of all ages, including children, taking part. OSTAR on the other hand, attracts many entrants, but remains a struggle against the elements which cause regular accidents and retirements.

However, the crew of a racing boat go to the starting line knowing the exact course that has been mapped out for that particular event. The cruising boat and its crew set their own agenda, having chosen it from a vast array of possible routes that leave very little of the world's seas unexplored.

Chapter 3

Offshore Racing

*O*ffshore racing has increased mas-
sively in popularity since 1945, with offshore events representing the ultimate in
competitive sailing. The fascination of the
ocean racer sailing through all weathers
and waters has stimulated many people,
previously uninterested in the sport, to
participate. New races have been organized throughout the world as the sport has
developed from short-distance races for
fully crewed conventional boats to mara-
thon around-the-world and single-handed
races in specially designed racing
machines. Yet it has not always been
this way; when the sport first started
there was active hostility from those who
considered it unwise and unnecessary.

AN INTRODUCTION TO OFFSHORE RACING

As the origins of racing were on inland waters and estuaries, it is hardly surprising that racing in the open seas and oceans, as we know it today, was a late development. By the middle of the 19th century, people were cruising far afield in large-sized boats, joined by a few brave sailors, usually regarded as eccentrics, in much smaller craft. Organized racing under sail was an occupation to be undertaken on summer days, in sight of land, and with courses designed to finish at least by late afternoon.

Offshore racing and ocean racing are broad terms, but they can be taken to mean races where the boats are not in direct control or sight of the race committee, but continue on the course 24 hours a day until they have completed it. They have written sailing instructions that take them to a finish line where they are timed in. No one checks that they have rounded the marks in the right order, if at all, or whether they obeyed the rules at sea.

It follows from this that offshore ocean racers must be designed, built and crewed to stay at sea in all conditions. Such strictures are not required for inshore racers, which can be open to the sea, lightly built and sparred, and without electrical systems or plumbing.

◆◆◆

The Kaiser's Race *Seven of the 11 entrants cross the start line in the 1905 Transatlantic Race – a race sponsored by the German kaiser. This was only the fourth race ever across the Atlantic, and one of the few offshore races of the time. Atlantic, the eventual winner, is third from right.*

The relatively recent arrival of ocean racing is demonstrated by the Whitbread Around-the-World Race (see pp 80-3), held every four years since 1973. Ten years or so previously, no sailor would have believed that such a race could succeed, especially on such a regular basis. It would have been greeted with cries of 'stunt!', but today the race engages the best designers, the most advanced building techniques, sailors of the highest competence, and has a record of achievement not previously envisaged possible for any race, inshore or offshore. As a result, offshore racing attracts financing by commercial sponsors and other organizations.

Size and length of boat do not by themselves define offshore racing. A boat can be as small as a Quarter Tonner at 7.6 m (25 ft), although most are bigger. The minimum for the Fastnet Race is 21-ft IOR rating, which is about 8.5 m (28 ft) LOA, while the minimum for the Whitbread Race is a rating giving a boat an overall length of 15.2 m (50 ft). There is also a limit to the largest size: since IOR ratings above 70 ft are not scored, this is the upper limit for most long-distance races, resulting in boats of about 24 m (80 ft) LOA. In practice, many offshore races have the bulk of entries between 11 m and 18 m (35 ft and 60 ft); such a size of boat is found sailing on offshore courses the world over.

The length of a course is less important than its nature. However, a race of less than about 60 miles is hardly offshore. Over this length, a course that is exposed

and out of immediate range of the race committee could be said to be offshore. Numerous local races under 100 miles take place, often known as 'overnight' races. Anything over 150 miles is usually an offshore or ocean race; 350 to 650 miles unquestionably constitutes an offshore race, and such distances are sailed on the Fastnet, Skaw, Newport-Bermuda, Sydney-Hobart and many other classic races.

Offshore racing has its own controlling body, the ORC (see pp 64-5) organized by the limited number of countries where ocean racing takes place. The rules are international and cover rating, safety, fixtures and fittings and so on, while each country has its own national and sometimes local additions and amendments.

TENTATIVE BEGINNINGS

Like many a 'first' in yacht racing, the first ocean race was the result of a wager, made between four wealthy men over a New York dinner table in October 1866. The businessmen concerned argued about the relative merits of their yachts, and the race, from Sandy Hook, New York, across the North Atlantic to the Needles off the Isle of Wight, England, was the first ocean race, and the first transatlantic race, in history.

The details of this transatlantic race, and its three successors, in 1870, 1887 and 1905, can be found in the pages concerned with transatlantic racing (pp 84-91). All the boats in these races were large vessels more akin to the sailing ships that traded all-year-around and that had just a few

Atlantic *Winner of the 1905 Transatlantic Race, the three-masted schooner* Atlantic *was a typical offshore racer of its time, a large and complex boat manned by an all-professional crew.*

years earlier comprised the world's navies. They were manned by professional crews and owned by wealthy men, for whom they were as often as not status symbols. It was not until the 1920s that smaller craft, crewed by amateurs, made their appearance in ocean racing.

The other remarkable feature about these early races was how few and far between they were. There were only four transatlantic races held between 1866 and 1905; a single race around Britain took place in 1887; an annual race from Dover in England to the German North Sea island

of Helgoland was first sailed in 1892; the first Canada's Cup match took place in 1896; and the first Chicago-Mackinac Race was sailed in 1898. But apart from these races, offshore racing at the end of the 19th century was a rare activity.

Those offshore races that were being organized and sailed in this period were often private challenges or restricted to members of a club only. Publicly announced races of any sort were a rarity, hence *America*'s difficulty in finding a race to enter at Cowes in 1851. One exception was the series of races from Newport, Rhode Island, to New York and back, held for several years after 1858. These races were for a cup donated by James Gordon Bennett Jr., and were open to boats of around 80 tons. Yet anyone sighting this racing fleet would hardly distinguish the yachts from other coastal craft making all possible speed, and the crew might in their next job be crewing a square rigger with cargo along the same route.

Whatever the status of the race, early offshore ocean racing was not considered to be 'real racing', and commentators such as Brooke Heckstall-Smith were antagonistic toward the sport (see right). This attitude lasted well into the 1950s and 1960s, for the International Yacht Racing Union left offshore racing well alone. In reply, the ocean-racing clubs such as the CCA and the RORC took little notice of the traditional type of inshore racing around fixed marks. It took many years before this ambivalent attitude was overcome.

OCEAN RACING – NEVER!

Years before ocean racing was regularly established, arguments for and against it rumbled on. Brooke Heckstall-Smith, a leading British writer on yacht racing, was strongly against it. In the *Yacht Racing Calendar and Review* of 1903, he questioned the wisdom of the sport:

"A good many years have passed since the question of a sailing match across the Atlantic Ocean has been seriously considered, and, although a few enthusiasts appear to be prepared to encourage a contest of this kind, there is no reason to believe this form of racing will ever commend itself to experienced yachtsmen.... There is no reason why ocean racing, especially when conducted without proper rules and restrictions, should have any beneficial influence upon the design of yachts, nor encourage in any way a healthy and seaworthy type of vessel. There is, moreover, only one way of testing the relative merits of yachts, namely, to race them over a fair course of moderate length, properly marked out with stationary marks, as is done in the contests for the America's Cup and other well-managed races. All other systems of yacht racing, from a sportsman's point of view, are worthless.

"... Many of us are wont to regard the German Emperor's Cup race from Dover to Helgoland, a distance of 300 miles, as too long a course. How much greater the danger of sailing 3,000 miles across the Atlantic? It does not follow that because three and thirty years ago, the schooners *Cambria* and *Dauntless* sailed the race without mishap, similar good fortune would attend modern racers.... Yacht racing and cracking on sail in broad daylight is capital fun, and does not incur more risk than many other manly sports and pastimes in which country gentlemen indulge; but the owner who encourages his crew to court disaster by 'carrying on' in mid-ocean is not only wilfully endangering the lives of his men, but acting in a spirit directly contrary to the first principles of seamanship."

THE BIRTH OF MODERN OFFSHORE RACING

The first offshore race on the east coast of America took place in 1904, at the instigation of Thomas Fleming Day, the respected editor of the American sailing magazine *Rudder*. Six boats sailed from Brooklyn, New York, north-east to Marblehead, Massachusetts, while 12 sailed the next year in a slightly longer race from Brooklyn south-west to Hampton Roads, Virginia. The important thing about these two races was that the competing boats were no bigger than 11m (35ft) LOA, and they were manned by owners and amateurs who normally cruised in their boats, rather than raced. This was quite unlike the all-professional, large sailing vessels that took part in the world's first ocean races across the North Atlantic in the late 19th century.

In 1906, Day proposed a more adventurous race, a 660-mile ocean course from Brooklyn, south-east to the British island colony of Bermuda. Three boats sailed this race, which was run annually until 1910, although never with large entries. When no entries were received for the planned 1911 race, this event collapsed, and was not revived until 1923.

After the end of World War I, a small number of amateur-owned boats under 15m (50ft) were making long ocean voyages, and by 1922 there were enough enthusiasts to form the Cruising Club of America. It was this club that, despite its membership of cruising sailors, resurrected the race to Bermuda in 1923. Twenty-two boats competed that year, but only 14 started in 1924: for some reason there was certainly no rush to get into ocean racing. The race was held again in 1926 and was well established by 1928.

The full story of the Bermuda Race can be read on pp 120-2, but at this point it is sufficient to state that it was a significant and unique-enough event to be noticed by a group of British sailors, one of whom, the author Weston Martyr, remarked in an article in a British sailing magazine that there was no British equivalent. As a result of his intervention, that equivalent, the Fastnet Race, was first sailed in 1925, and since then has become.established as one of the world's classic ocean races.

INTERNATIONAL GROWTH

The Bermuda and the Fastnet races have remained the two most important, regularly sailed, offshore races up to the present day. Together with the Transpac Race, first sailed across the Pacific in 1906 – which, though being for large boats in sub-tropical and inevitably downwind conditions, is a rather different kind of race –

❖❖❖

The Bermuda Race *First sailed annually from 1906 to 1910, the race from an American east-coast port to Bermuda was resurrected in 1923 and has been run regularly ever since, its start fixed at Newport in 1936. The format of the race was copied by the Fastnet, and for many years, these two races dominated offshore racing. The photograph below shows the start of the 1923 race, when 22 boats came to the starting line.*

Jolie Brise, *winner of the first Fastnet Race.*

these three races dominated ocean racing until the start of World War II.

After the war, numerous other offshore races were established. The Southern Ocean Racing Conference started its Winter Circuit in 1941, but it did not become a regular event until 1947, while the Sydney-Hobart Race was first sailed in 1945. They were soon joined by many other races, but unlike those first events in America and Britain, these were instituted at a time when there were precedents to follow, a framework within which to work, experience on which to base offshore competitions, and, most importantly, an agreed upon set of rules.

THE RORC

Not only did the Bermuda Race spawn the Fastnet Race, it was also indirectly responsible for the formation of the Royal Ocean Racing Club. These two institutions have remained the core of offshore racing in Britain and throughout Europe.

The Ocean Racing Club (later to become the Royal Ocean Racing Club in 1931) was formed in August 1925, by the owners of the boats that competed in the first Fastnet Race that year, at a dinner held at the Royal Western Yacht Club, Plymouth, to celebrate the conclusion of the race. Its object was "to provide annually one ocean race of not less than 600 miles in length." Unlike in the US, where the Cruising Club of America organizes the Newport-Bermuda Race, the British Royal Cruising Club wanted no part in the Fastnet Race, and one of its leading members, the cruising authority Claud Worth, expressed strong doubts about the wisdom of a 'public ocean race' (as opposed to a private wager).

Ever since its foundation, the RORC has specialized in the techniques of offshore racing to the exclusion of all other types of sailing. Thus races of various lengths and courses have been run by the club year after year, both in British and European waters. In the Mediterranean, it has organized the Middle Sea Race, and in the Far East, the China Sea Race. In true English style, its members – who must each qualify by sailing a Fastnet or other offshore race – set up a clubhouse in London. The first address, established in February 1936, was at 2 Pall Mall Place, London, but this was destroyed by a bomb in November 1940. A new clubhouse was opened by the exiled king of Norway in July 1942, at 19 St. James's Place, London, and the club has been there ever since, used by a membership from all over the world.

Up to 1927, the ORC, as it then was, only ran the Fastnet Race; in 1928 it began the annual Channel Race from Cowes to a mark off the French coast and back. By 1933 it was running 5 races, by 1938, 10. Forty years later the number of races run annually has settled to around 14 to 17.

THE ORGANIZATION OF OFFSHORE RACING

Although the International Yacht Racing Union (see pp160-1) is yacht racing's world governing body, offshore racing has its own autonomous authority recognized by the IYRU but acting independently of it. The Offshore Racing Council (ORC) – which shares its London headquarters with the RORC – remains separate from the IYRU for two reasons. The first is that ocean racing remains an expensive sport engaged in by those few, rich countries where there is freedom of the seas and where back-up facilities exist for offshore boats. The IYRU, on the other hand, has numerous member nations, whose nationals sail only the small boats of the Olympic classes and other dinghies and dayboats. It would not be appropriate for these countries to have a say in offshore racing, the traditions of which are confined to English-speaking countries, Europe, South America and Japan.

There is a second, associated, historical, reason. The rating rule that the ORC was formed to administer was simply evolved from bringing together the British RORC and the American CCA rules in the period 1967-9. Therefore, the people who had been running the rules in these two countries continued to run the new organization independently of any existing international body such as the IYRU.

MERGING THE RULES

As previously detailed, the growth of ocean racing was uneven and national, rather than international, in organization. Such a piecemeal development created problems when boats of different countries met to race against each other, for they varied considerably according to where they were built. For instance, from about 1935 until 1969, those built in America were designed to the rules of the Cruising Club of America, those in Britain to the rules of the Royal Ocean Racing Club. Although some compatability was possible by altering the sail plan, a boat visiting another country and sailing under another rule was denied much chance of success.

By the late 1950s, the amount of ocean-racing activity outside the US and Britain was growing, but in numbers of boats and races, it remained very small. But growing it was, and to rely on the two

different 'Anglo-Saxon' domestic rules seemed lacking in logic to European sailors. Therefore, at a meeting of German and other offshore racers in June 1961 in Bremen, Germany, a request was made for the creation of a single, uniform, international rating rule for ocean-racing boats. Since the leading offshore sailors and designers knew each other well, it was not hard for the various interests to get together. They formed an Offshore Rules Coordinating Committee, a title that said nothing about creating a single rule. However, three developments sped matters in that direction.

First, in the early 1960s, the IYRU began to consider the possibility of an

offshore ocean-racing class sailing in the Olympic Games. They asked Olin Stephens, the American yacht designer – who among other positions was an adviser to the IYRU – to see if the two ocean-racing rules could not be united for this purpose.

Second, in 1962, the last race was held in the 6-Meter class for the One Ton Cup.

— ••• —

IOR Boats *The introduction of the IOR in 1971 led to a rush to measure boats to the new rule. Numbers rose quickly so that by 1977, there were over 10,500 IOR-rated boats worldwide. However, in recent years, the rule has created 'grand prix' racing machines rather than all-purpose boats, leading to a sharp downturn in numbers. The graph below shows the numbers of IOR craft worldwide and in five selected countries.*

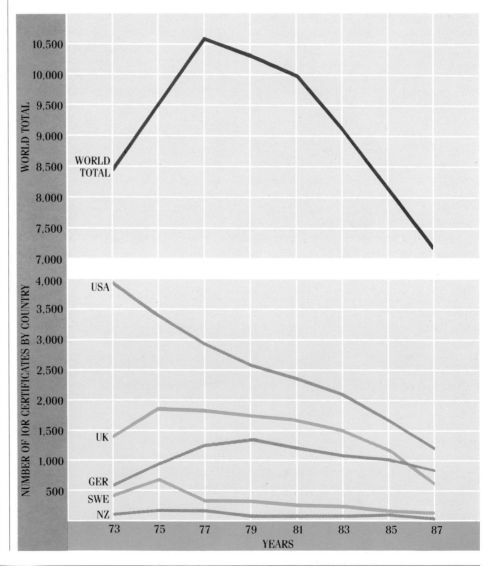

Jean Peytel, a leading member of Le Cercle de la Voile de Paris, owners of the One Ton Cup, felt that the dying 6-Meter class could no longer support the One Ton races, and suggested a short series of offshore and inshore races by ocean-racing boats rating 22 ft RORC. The novelty of this was that there would be no time allowance: the boats only had to be on, or below, the required rating to enter, and would then race without handicap; the first boat home won the race. This of course had been done in the meter classes but it was new to ocean racing.

Third, the most successful designers to the RORC rule for European owners in this period were from the New York firm of Sparkman and Stephens. This firm also designed many boats under the CCA rule, placing it, and its leading designer Olin Stephens, at the center of both rules.

Of these three developments, the proposed offshore Olympic class came to nothing, but it served as a useful spur to international interest in an international rating rule. In 1967, the Offshore Rules Coordinating Committee formed an 'international technical committee' to join the two rules together. Chaired by Olin Stephens, the six-member committee included Dick Carter, an American who also designed to the RORC rule and who had won both the One Ton Cup and the Fastnet Race in his own designs; David Fayle, the British chief measurer, and Robin Glover, both RORC measurers; Gustav Plym, a Swedish yacht designer and ocean-racing skipper; and E. Van de Stadt, an experienced Dutch yacht designer. In November 1968, the draft of a new rule was approved by the coordinating committee: International Offshore Rule Mark I took full effect on 1 January 1971.

To govern this new rule, a group of interested ocean racers from various countries founded the international Offshore Rating Council – in deference to the IYRU, the ORC did not have 'international' in its title, which it later changed in wording from Rating to Racing. The CCA and the RORC both agreed to give up their own rating rules and run their races under the new common rule. Other clubs soon followed their example, and abandoned their own rules in favor of the IOR.

Inevitably there was a rush to measure yachts to the IOR, which meant creating an administration to arrange uniform measurement and certification, promulgate amendments and so on. This remains the function of the ORC. New boats were designed to the new rule, which inevitably outdated existing boats designed to the old rules. Now that there was a single rule, international events became more popular and the competition stiffer.

The new rule also affected yacht design, for slowly but surely the IOR has created more specialized boats. By the late 1980s, the consensus was that the IOR (by this time Mark III) was for what had become known as 'grand prix' boats; these ensured top-flight racing competition but were a far cry from those offshore racing boats that existed when the IOR was first created. Those were boats that could both cruise and race and accommodate their crews; the late 1980s produced pure racing machines only to the same rule.

THE ORC'S STRUCTURE

The countries that comprise the ORC are those where ocean-racing boats are to be found. They are Argentina, Australia, Austria, Belgium, Brazil, Britain, Canada, France, Germany, Hong Kong, Ireland, Italy, Japan, Portugal, the Netherlands, New Zealand, Scandinavia, Spain, Switzerland and the US. From these countries are drawn members of committees that run various aspects of the ORC's work, the names of which indicate the areas of control exercised by the ORC.

International Technical This is the original committee that made the rule. It meets frequently, amending the IOR and investigating the problems of fair rating under the rule. Such problems are often highly technical and most of the committee are practicing designers. It has had four chairmen since 1969: Olin Stephens (USA), 1969-73 and 1976-9; Peter Johnson (UK), 1973-6; Gary Mull (USA), 1979-87; Nicola Sironi (Italy), 1987-.

Measurement It is no good having a complex formula if boats are not measured to it accurately and uniformly all over the world. A chief measurer heads a team of certified measurers in the user countries.

Level-rating Classes The rules for these are in the province of the ORC, and are in fact the only classes as such controlled by the committee. For these five classes – One, Three-Quarter, Half, Quarter and Mini Tons – there exist rules for the equipment and size of the boats in addition to the IOR rule itself. The committee also makes the arrangements for the annual Ton Cup championships.

Special Regulations This committee ensures that boats racing offshore comply with "special regulations governing minimum equipment and accommodation standards", in other words, safety rules for boats at sea. But these rules are more than just safety rules, for without them boats would take risks in search of speed.

An ocean racer must have both regular and emergency equipment on board. Regular equipment might be "navigation lights, to be shown as required, mounted so that they will not be masked by sails or the heeling of the yacht." An example of emergency equipment, carried by every boat that sails under these rules, is a "horseshoe-type life buoy marked with the boat's name and with self-reflecting tape, equipped with a drogue and self-igniting light within reach of the helmsmen and ready for instant use."

The rules are amended with ratification by the ORC from year to year; there are also varying national definitions and extras enforced by respective governments. Scales exist within the equipment rules for races of different lengths and type: race organizers select the category that fits their race.

Rules Compliance This committee has become necessary because of the difficulty of enforcing the complex rules of offshore racing. Because of the isolated nature of racing at sea, ocean racing has to be self-policing. Rule infringements are normally dealt with after a protest from another boat in the same way as the right-of-way rules when racing. In major regattas, there are now rigorous inspections for special regulations and ratings, but after that the sailors are not supposed to change anything. In some races, there can be a snap inspection at the finish line, but it means qualified people and suitable boats need to be available to carry out this task; it is not, therefore, undertaken often.

MEASURING A BOAT

Under any modern rule of measurement, there are a number of features on a boat that are principally assessed. The figures that result are then inserted by means of a computer program into a complex formula to determine the final rating. Displacement, that is total weight, is seldom measured directly by weighing, although that is possible, but is discovered by such roundabout means as measuring the depth of the hull in the water at certain points. Similarly, sail area is conventionally found by measuring along the spars and deck, and then limiting the sails to within those parameters.

Measurement Points *Many parts of a boat are measured to determine its rating. Among the main measurements taken are the following:*
1 *The mainsail is treated as a triangle,* **P** *and* **E** *being fixed by marks on the spars. The extra area in the luff of the mainsail is not measured, but the curve is limited.*
2 *To determine the foretriangle – that is the area between the mast, forestay and deck –* **I** *and* **J** *are measured. Genoas, jibs and spinnakers are then limited by reference to those two dimensions.*
3 *Neither overall nor waterline length are measured. Instead, several measurements are taken of the girth and elsewhere and, by a series of complex formulae, a 'measured length' is arrived at.*
4 *Freeboard* **F** *is penalized if unduly low.*
5 *If displacement is not measured directly, depth measurements are taken.*
6 *Draft is penalized if excessively deep.*
7 *Actual surface area, including shapes and sizes of keel and rudder, is never measured because of the difficulties involved.*
8 *Allowance is made in the rating for the weight of the engine and the type and diameter of the propeller.*
9 *Maximum beam is a major factor in determining the rating.*
10 *Stability is assessed by inclining the boat across a small angle.*

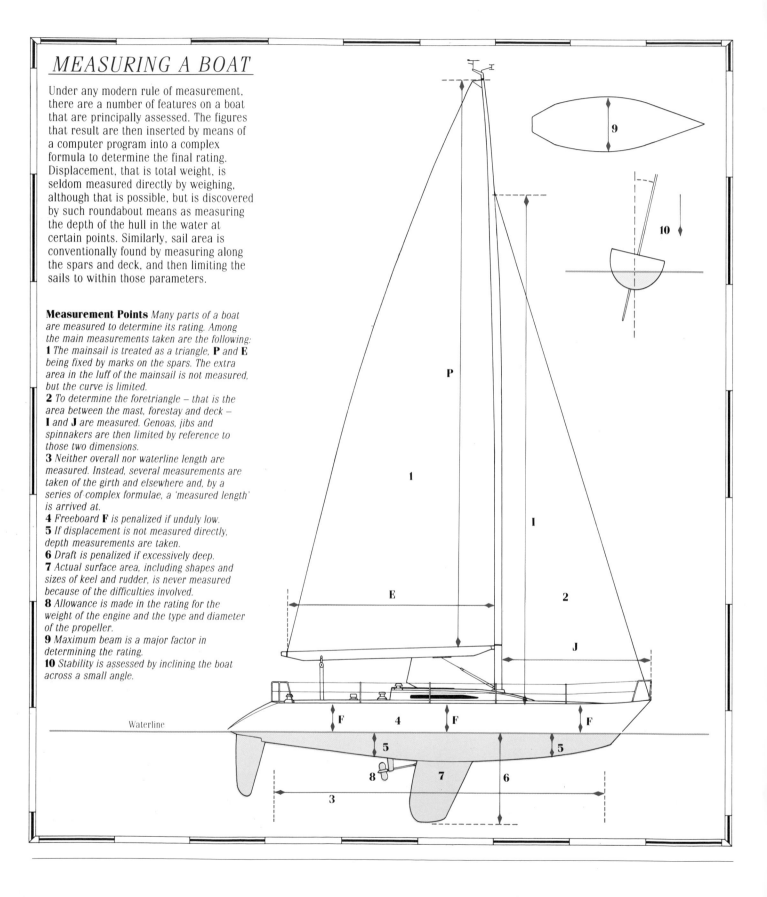

RATING RULES

Although the IOR, as amended from year to year, remains the rule to which boats have to be measured to compete in many major races, racing at all levels also takes place under a number of different rating rules, handicap systems and time allowances. While the list that follows names some of these, there is nothing to stop a club inventing its own time-allowance system. Indeed this often happens locally, where all boats are well known and the club handicapper can put a time-allowance figure on each one.

The trouble arises when an unknown boat arrives to race; maybe it is given a figure that penalizes it unduly. It is this often-repeated situation that demands a regional or a national handicap system. One might think that it is better to have one system for, say, all cruiser-racers, but once it becomes international, all the pressures of high-level winning and top-flight design are loaded on to it. Therefore, these national and regional variations serve a useful purpose and give enjoyable and fair racing to those that make use of them.

VARIATIONS TO THE IOR

There are various additional formulas that give older boats what is called a Mark IIIA rating, thus allowing a retrospective advantage for those boats not designed to the very latest version of the IOR. All boats are dated on their rating certificates with a hull date and the date of the design; these are used to introduce a sliding scale of allowances.

Not so much a variation, but rather a fair procedure, is the use of standard hull measurements. Production boats are measured, so that an agreed hull measurement is found for the standard hull out of the mold. This avoids irritating differences between similar boats due to measurement discrepancies, and makes the rating procedure itself slightly less costly.

A further variation to IOR is the application of age allowances to the ratings of older boats. This system is not part of the rule but is applied by national authorities. The RORC system is to give an age allowance in the form of a slightly improved time allowance for boats when their design date becomes greater than five years.

IMS

The International Measurement System (IMS) is the second rule controlled by the Offshore Racing Council, and officially dates from 1986. In practice, it is the up-dated American Measurement Handicap System (MHS) by another name. This system has operated satisfactorily in the US for a number of years, although not on any wide scale. During the course of 1988, it was experimented with and used to some extent outside the US.

Using computerized measuring machines that read the hull shape of a boat, this system avoids the distortions that occur because the IOR uses only measuring points. However, it is an expensive process. The IMS is unusual in that it was invented at the Massachusetts Institute of Technology, funded by a grant to search for a new offshore handicap rule. Rather than evolving from or imitating existing and tried systems, the research sought to invent a 'velocity prediction program', which means that the IMS tries to give an optimum speed for each boat on different points of sailing and in different wind speeds. The theory is that the winning boat is the one that sails best to its predicted performance for the conditions. Reports however are sparse on this mode of handicapping, and many race committees in the US simply use one set of time allowances for the IMS rather than choose from the many that are available.

PHRF

The Performance Handicap Racing Fleet (PHRF) is the giant among handicap systems, and is a prime example of time allowances based solely on performance and not on measurement. There are over 20,000 boats in 115 fleets using the system in the US, and it is also used in New Zealand.

Although the rule attempts to give a handicap rating, it is really a time allowance allotted in seconds per mile: in other words it is a time-on-distance system. The allowance is given against the speed potential of the boat, based on observations of previous racing experiences. Obviously this is easiest for stock or production boats where the PHRF is already known, for the main problem with performance systems is in allocating a rating for a one-off or a new production design. Since that design must resemble another class in some way, a rough estimate can be arrived at and then modified, as its performance becomes apparent, by

Hull Measurement *When measuring a boat hull under the IMS or IOR, the measurements are calculated using a laser beam fired from a computerized measuring instrument. At the point at which the laser beam hits the hull, the measurer places a pointer, attached to which is a reeled line fed out from the instrument. The length of the line to the pointer is calculated by the computer, thus giving the exact measurement. For these hull measurements, the boat is brought ashore and levelled: it is not a cheap procedure.*

CALCULATING A HANDICAP

A handicap such as the PHRF is expressed in seconds per mile. The lower the handicap number, the faster the boat is assumed to go. If a boat's handicap number is decreased, the boat is penalized; if the number is increased, the boat gains an advantage.

To take an actual example: if Boat A has a time allowance of 150 seconds per mile and Boat B, a slower boat, one of 198 seconds per mile, and they are both sailing on a 15-mile course, then the time Boat A gives to Boat B is found by subtracting 150 from 198 and multiplying the remainder by 15, giving an answer of 720 seconds, or 12 minutes. This is the time allowance that Boat B has over Boat A. Therefore, if it finishes less than 12 minutes behind Boat A, Boat B will win. In practice, each boat in a race is given a corrected time, and therefore a place in the final results, by multiplying the distance of the race by the individual time allowance and subtracting that from the elapsed time it took to sail the course.

For a boat to have the base handicap of its class or type, it is assumed that the boat is standard in at least the following respects: the spinnaker pole is equal to J, the base length of the jib; the maximum width of the spinnaker is equal to 180% of the spinnaker pole length; the maximum length of the spinnaker is equal to 95% of the length of the jibstay; the genoa's area is limited by insuring that the LP, that is the diagonal width of the genoa, is not more than 150% of J; the boat is in racing condition; the boat has a folding or feathering propeller or a retractable outboard motor; and, finally, that the hull is unmodified.

Thus allowances are not given for extra cruising equipment such as a big dinghy cover, steps up the mast or dinghy davits, nor for three-bladed propellers. But if there are 'fast' modifications, such as an extra-long spinnaker pole or a stripped-out interior, then a higher rating will be allotted, for the boat is no longer at base handicap.

the United States Yacht Racing Union, the controlling body.

Base handicaps, of which the PHRF is one, assume that the boat is not modified or 'souped-up' in any way. Thus the PHRF makes no allowance for good or bad sails, a clean and polished bottom or, of course, crewing and sailing tactics. These are meant to be the race winning factors, not part of the design. Unlike the IMS, but like almost all other rules, there is a single handicap figure for all weathers. There therefore exists the possibility of one boat doing well in, say, a beat in strong winds ('her weather') while an opponent is more likely to win when there is a lot of close reaching in lighter winds. The PHRF may thus be administered to the satisfaction of some competitors and not others, but it does have the potential for becoming ever-more accurate. Its importance is that, unlike a measurement rule, it can never be outdesigned, since the time allowances are given on the basis of the boat's actual results on the water.

This does not mean that dimensions are not used to help in the first assessment of a new boat or in checking against a similar production boat. IOR and MORC (Midget Ocean Racing Club) certificates may be used to make an assessment, especially of dimensions of individual items shown on them, and they are essential in making helpful comparisons between different boats.

Such is the success of the PHRF that there are now divisions in many ocean racing events, and major regattas and race weeks throughout the US, including Block Island Week and Florida's Suncoast Race Week. For regular weekend and weekday evening races, PHRF is very often the dominant handicap system.

COURSE CROISIÈRE AU HANDICAP

Like the PHRF, this is a system used in France for standard production boats. Each boat has a Groupe de Handicap: a table shows what this means in terms of a time-correction factor (time-on-time) and a time-on-distance figure. There are restrictions on the dimensions and number of sails if boats are to be eligible for racing, and rules for equipment and modification.

PORTSMOUTH YARDSTICK SYSTEM

Perhaps the original performance rating system, this method was first organized for dinghy classes where each boat complied strictly with the class rules. It has been extended to cruiser-racer classes in Britain and was also used in several areas of the US before the advent of PHRF. It has suffered from idiosyncratic administration and a complex time-allowance system.

The way the system works is that boats are checked locally for performance and the results are then sent to the national authority – in Britain the Royal Yachting Association – so that a handicap can be arrived at. There are two different grades of Portsmouth Numbers, which are the handicap figures of this system.

The Primary Yardstick is a well-attested number published centrally, while the Secondary Yardstick has less rigidity, allowing a club more freedom to vary it for a particular race. The numbers are a "measurement of performance over a common but unspecified distance", but because the higher the number, the slower the boat is expected to go, the Yardstick has always been slightly obscure by using such a system. As with the PHRF and the Course Croisière au Handicap, there is a base handicap for cruiser-racers, and guides for changes in sail plan, extra equipment and other modifications that might affect the handicap rating.

ECHO

This Irish handicapping method, under the authority of the Irish Yachting Association (ECHO was originally the East Coast Handicapping Organization), is a performance-based system. Time allowances are allocated directly to each boat, but again class norms are a basis. They are in the form of three-figure TCFs, that is a time-correction factor that is multiplied by the elapsed time to give the corrected time, in effect a time-on-time system. The compact and essentially localized nature of Irish sailing means that it is possible for tight control to be exercised over the entire system, which has a carefully laid down series of arrangements for revision and adjustments of TCFs.

CHS

The Channel Handicap System (CHS) was introduced in 1983 as an alternative to the IOR by the Royal Ocean Racing Club and the Union Nationale pour la Course au Large. It is different from all the other rules in that it is a secret measurement rule, designed to prevent existing boats becoming outclassed by new designs exploiting the rating rules. The two authorities can alter the formula and its emphasis – by adding new factors, dropping others and adjusting the scale of time allowances – to take account of inequities shown up in results. The latter is possible because, like most other rules, the time allowance is built in to the rating, which is issued as a TCF (time-correction factor). However, unlike other rules, each individual boat must have a certificate issued centrally with the TCF shown; it is not enough for the boat to belong to a class. It must have an owner, a name and an approved sail number, and the certificate only lasts one year. Thus a tight control is kept over the CHS fleet, and the ratings can, and do, change from year to year for any or every boat.

The owner measures his own boat and submits a form, or measurements are taken from an IOR certificate. As with other rules there are norms for size of spinnaker, its pole, largest headsails, and adjustment for specials like wing keels, double centerboards and extra big rigs. Exotic and very light displacement materials, including Kevlar sails, are fairly heavily penalized, and IOR boats that gain rating advantage by adding extra bulk to measurement points do not get any help under this system.

The CHS certificate, issued by computer, shows a number of details of the boat, including length, displacement, sail dimensions, rigging and headstay detail, spreaders and checkstays (a clue here to one of the secret factors), and design year (another clue, to age allowance); the owner signs an acceptance of these particulars. The fee for a CHS measurement is about twice that of a PHRF one, because each boat is individual. However, it is still around one-twelfth the cost of the infinitely more complex and time-consuming IOR measurement.

OTHER NATIONAL RULES

Other rules used in various countries are as follows: Dansk Handicap; Cruiser-Racing Class of Belgium; Nederlandse Kruiser Klasse (NKK); Handicap Formula Rio and the Conventional Handicap Rules of Brazil; La Formula del Rating Sud Americana, used in Chile and other South American countries; and such measurement rules as those of the Midget Ocean Racing Club and the Junior Offshore Group of Australia, both of which are for small offshore racers. Scandicap is a well-established rule used in the Baltic on many boats.

RULE COMPLIANCE

Sailboat racing has no referees or umpires, and it is obviously not possible to blow a whistle to stop the race. Thus, from the earliest races, redress has been obtained by filing a protest, receiving a hearing along the lines of a court, complete with witnesses, statements and evidence, and then being given a verdict by the protest committee. This usually results in the disqualification of one of the boats involved or in the dismissal of the protest. The alleged foul cannot be dealt with unless someone actually protests.

If there is a collision, those involved are not allowed to collaborate or cover-up the incident: a boat must either retire or one or both must protest. If another boat racing, or a race committee member, sees an incident when neither boat involved does anything about it, that third party can protest both the others.

At the end of a hearing, if the committee does not disqualify a boat or dismiss the protest, it may award a percentage or a place penalty instead. There are many paragraphs in the racing rules about how a protest shall be made, but it has to be remembered that protesting is a normal part of sailboat racing.

The deliberate flouting of rules by carrying sails that have not been measured, or ballast that is brought aboard when not on a boat's certificate, is a quite different problem from the cut and thrust of racing, when everyone does their best to stick within the rules, but falls foul of them in the heat of the moment. This deliberate flouting is most likely to occur in offshore racing, when boats are away from the race committee and the shore and not closely in sight of each other. In all ordinary racing events, movable ballast is not permitted, but there is a temptation for crew to pile sails not in use, tool boxes and other heavy items, on to the windward side of the boat to give extra power: such movements are illegal. Water, too, can only be used for its primary purposes, which are drinking, cooking and washing. However, in the past, there have been instances of crews bringing aboard fresh 'drinking' water in cans, loading it on the windward side when sailing to windward and then pumping it out when sailing downwind, when the weight is not required.

Such incidents are not easy to police. Traditionally, clubs and committees have relied on the numbers on board – out of nine or so crew, it is unlikely that all would conspire to break the rules. There are also pre-race inspections, and further inspections once a boat has finished, but it remains impracticable to have an inspector on board during a race.

The rules on ballast and weights are quite clear and are in the text of the IOR, as well as other rules; including the racing rules distributed by the IYRU. Disputes about weights have occurred at intervals from the time of Lord Dunraven's complaints in 1895 during the America's Cup (see pp 144-5), and will always need rulings to meet possible variations in the future.

Many rules have evolved over a long period of time as the following extracts show. The Royal Thames Yacht Club rules for the 1865 season stated that " any yacht having been disabled by foul sailing on the part of any yacht, or having valid cause of complaint, shall hoist the club ensign as a signal of protest, which signal shall be answered by the Commodore firing a gun." This is not unlike the IYRU rules for the period 1985-8, which state that "An intention to protest an infringement of the rules occurring during a race shall be signified by the protesting yacht conspicuously displaying a flag. Code flag B is always acceptable, irrespective of any other provision in the sailing instructions. ... The flag shall be displayed until the yacht finishes, or ... until acknowledged by the race committee..."

THE FINANCE OF SAILING

Commercial backing for racing is in direct contradiction to the essence of the sport: the pursuit of pleasure rather than trade or commerce, in specially built private craft, unsullied by any financial concern or motive. Yet commerce is now a major force in modern racing, lending its name and its money to both boats and races, especially the prestigious offshore events. The irony of this is that while sailing is an expensive sport that often requires outside financial support, the richest and most successful businessmen, who sail the larger boats, are the last people to need or want such backing. It is not surprising, therefore, that it is often these people who spearhead any moves to ban commercialism from sailing.

Professionalism, sponsorship and advertising have been controversial in the world of sailboat racing for many years. Of these, the first is probably the most reasonably straightforward case.

PROFESSIONALISM

In its racing rules, the IYRU defines an amateur as a "yachtsman who engages in yacht racing as a pastime, as distinguished from a means of a livelihood or part-time compensation. No yachtsman shall lose amateur status by reason of his livelihood being derived from designing or constructing yachts, yacht parts, sails or accessories; or from similar professions associated with the sport; or solely from the maintenance (but not the *racing*) of yachts." As a result of this definition there are few who admit to being professional sailors. Yet sailmaking firms, for example, often have highly skilled helmsmen and sailmakers on their staffs; these men go aboard boats that have been recently supplied with new sails, their objective being to win races for the owner. The prospect of their presence gives him the incentive to buy those particular sails in the first place, and subsequently, good results promote the sails. However, although these expert sailors would consider themselves technical advisers on the sails, the fact is that they were taken on by the sailmaking firm in part because of their racing skills.

The old type of yacht hand is now almost extinct, but today would certainly be considered a professional in that he is paid for crewing on the boat. Many offshore racers over a certain size have one or more young men employed to look after and maintain the vessel, as well as sail with it in races, although this does not usually apply to the helmsman. If they are paid for 'maintenance', as mentioned in the IYRU rule, they are still considered to be amateurs. But there is the problem of top helmsmen who are enlisted aboard the crack racers and who are paid cash to try to bring these boats success. This is a gray area in that such deals are confidential. In theory such people could not compete in the Ton Cups, where the rule states that "every member of the crew of all competing yachts shall be amateur, as defined by the IYRU."

Yet another case is the single-handed, long-distance sailor, competing for a record or in a race, whose whole voyage is paid for by the sponsor. Was he or she paid, or was the money just for the boat and expenses while the competitor actually sailed for nothing? Such distinctions become important in the Olympic Games, where International Olympic Committee Rules apply. These rules are extensive and are similar to other sports, so those sailing an Olympic campaign must take care to keep within the boundaries.

SPONSORSHIP

Sponsorship for racing events is commonplace and does not cause any special difficulty. The facilities, promotion and press arrangements are paid for by the firm, whose name may well be coupled

with the race. If well handled, all competitors benefit from this arrangement. Quite different is the commercial sponsorship of individual boats. If some are sponsored and some are privately financed, there is always the accusation of unfair advantage. Other objections include the accompanying pressure to put commercial interest before seamanship, and the existence of high budgets, which has the undesirable effect of eventually driving the limited-budget amateur out of the sport or at least out of that particular class or competition.

ADVERTISING

Advertising is the outlet for professionalism and sponsorship and is the most controversial of these three related topics. Until a revision of the IYRU racing rules in

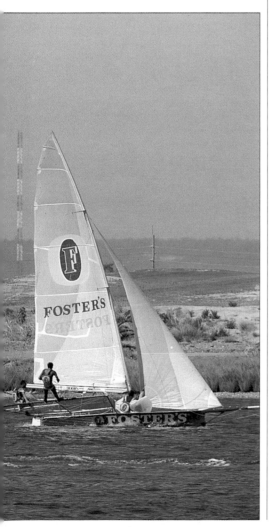

Advertising on Boats *The racing rules lay down strict controls on the amount of advertising boats are allowed to display. Two notable exceptions to the rule are the Sydney Harbor 18-ft skiffs (left), whose sails and hulls are wholly given over to advertising, and sponsored boats, which can fly a special spinnaker bearing the sponsor's logo after the race has finished, when the rules no longer apply (as with the boat above).*

1984, there was a deterrent to sponsorship in that no advertising was allowed on hulls or on crew clothing. There remain strict controls on advertising, although there has been considerable interest in the new race categories. What this does is to allow some advertising, so long as a national authority gives special permission for the event and it conforms in size, style and other features. Otherwise, boats cannot carry any advertising, other than such things as manufacturer's trade marks on hulls, sails and spars. This is why boats are not covered in the slogans and logos seen on power boats and racing cars. However with the movement toward more corporate sponsorship, there will probably be a trend in this direction – particularly at major racing events.

There are various precedents for this, notably the Sydney Harbor 18-ft skiffs, the sails of which are wholly given over to commercial advertising. Sponsored boats may have a special spinnaker with the commercial logo or design upon it: this sail cannot be used when racing but can be flown for photographic or promotional purposes after finishing a race.

There are other instances when the races are simply outside the rules of the IYRU: typically, heavily promoted, single-handed transocean races will undoubtedly have boats with commercial names and all manner of logos. As these races are relatively infrequent, and as they cross national frontiers and have a mixture of nationalities in the entry, there is little that any one national authority can do, or, for that matter, really wants to do about this situation.

This lack of authority gives a clue as to the ultimate solution to the problems posed by professionalism, sponsorship and advertising. It lies with the class of boat. The class could decide what rules its own boats require on these matters. Some would accept individual sponsorship and every kind of promotion and advertisement, while others would decide to enforce absolute amateurism and would forbid sponsorship in all its many forms. Individual sailors would then have the choice as to which one of these classes, or the many variations in between, they would like to compete in.

OFFSHORE BOATS

When the IOR was introduced in 1968, it was envisaged that any boat with a rating, which also complied with the various offshore rulings, could race anywhere in the world and compete with a potentially equal chance of success. However, it has not worked out like that; different kinds of boat have evolved for several levels of racing. All can still use the IOR or one of the other rules (see pp 67-9).

'GRAND PRIX' RACER

This unofficial name was borrowed from motor racing and its meaning is clear enough. It refers to a boat that is after a major prize, such as one of the Ton Cups or one of the big ocean races such as the Transpac or the Sydney-Hobart.

The cost of one of these boats is huge, and has to be measured in terms of a campaign. The cost includes design, building, sails, equipment and the cost of measurement, as well as replacement sails of exotic materials, new spars to replace those broken during the season, haul-outs and bottom polishing, delivery or shipping to events, entry fees and running costs during each event. The crew may well be paid, and the helmsman and/or skipper can command a high salary.

A 'grand prix' racer is designed to the latest ideas on the IOR and is not expected to perform well for more than about two seasons. Accommodation is to the minimum required by the rules, and the crew live ashore when in harbor. The quest for minimum weight, especially at the extremities of the bow, stern and rig is obsessive, and the construction will be hi-tech, with a hull of foam-filled plastic, titanium fittings, and carbon fiber spars. If the boat is intended for a long race, such as a transatlantic or around-the-world event, then it will have stronger fittings and more suitable crew accommodation.

LEVEL RATER

The origin and development of the level-rating classes are discussed on the following pages, but at this point it is necessary to note that the most recent level raters are in fact 'grand prix' boats. But even more fuss has to be made of a 'grand prix' level rater than an average 'grand prix' boat, in that it has to achieve its rating exactly; much time and money can be spent on altering trim and rig to attain this accuracy. As a result of this fine tuning, level raters are responsive to crew weight, are easily steered by tiller rather than wheel, and use gear that is comparatively lightweight in seagoing terms.

There are older level raters that fit the cruiser-racer category more, which can race with similar boats in more local level-rating contests. In particular, there are a number of boats at around 27.5ft which until 1984 was the One Ton level. These boats are about 11.6 m (38 ft) LOA, and give good sailing offshore without having to compete against current level raters. In Europe in particular, before one of the Ton Cups is held, there is usually a surge of building to that rating in the area. After the championship is over, a number of boats of the class remain to sail against each other in regular racing until they gradually disperse. The cycle then occurs again at another Ton Cup level.

OFFSHORE CRUISER-RACER

A little below 'grand prix' level is a wide range of fast and competent offshore boats. They may have been specially built but are more likely to be production boats built to a recent racing design, with accommodation more suitable for cruising. Their rig is optimized for racing and they have a plentiful sail wardrobe, full electronics and a deck layout designed for racing competition. But this layout is not unsuited to cruising, and the boat can be sold as a cruising boat when its racing days are over. The boats can sail to the IOR, but also to other handicap systems. Also in this category are yesterday's 'grand prix' boats, which can no longer compete with the latest boats. However, more and more IOR top-class boats cannot be converted for any other use because of the racing specifications of their design.

ONE-DESIGN FOR OFFSHORE

One way of racing offshore without buying a new boat every year is to sail a one-design. One-designs can enter the same regular races, but cannot be outclassed with changes unless these are authorized by their own owners' committee. It seems an ideal arrangement: the problem is that to get a worthwhile race, a boat and crew must find a sufficient number of its own class competing. The races in which they take part will also be decided ahead by the class committee.

The choice of one-design is difficult for an offshore owner, who may find that the class fades rapidly or no longer engages in the type of racing most preferred. If the boat does not do well, it cannot be altered by its owner, but its second-hand value is at least predictable, without the big losses involved in disposing of 'grand prix' boats. In a successful class, there is tremendously close sailing, and more than the average associated social activities.

CLUB RACER

This is a term reserved for a boat with offshore capacity, but which in fact races locally without any pretensions to a high standard. Typical races might be for a couple of hours in the bay on a Saturday afternoon with occasional passage races to another port over a distance of about 25 miles. The races are organized by local clubs and standards vary considerably between localities. There is plenty of fun and competition at club level, without which other more publicized kinds of sailing would not exist. There are also many very skilled sailors who do not aspire to higher competition as they are not prepared to give up the amount of time that such dedication takes. The boats sailed at this level do not look very different from cruiser-racers, but they may not be so fully equipped with ocean racing equipment, new sails and electronic aids.

NON-RULE RACER

There are some potentially fast and exotic boats that cannot be rated under the IOR because of certain features it either bans or penalizes so much that their ratings are unacceptably high. Keels with wings are one such feature, ultra-light displacement another. If the owners of such boats wish to race, then they must find a club that has a usable handicap system allowing for such features. It is likely that they will not fare well under most handicap systems, if only because the organizers of races cannot afford to outclass the mass of their more conventional fleet.

LEVEL-RATING RACING

One of the most influential developments in modern ocean racing has been the establishment of level-rating or 'Ton Cup' racing. This simple system of racing without a time allowance has had a profound impact on the sport.

From the earliest days of offshore racing, time allowances had always been employed. Originally this was because the entries were existing cruising boats that required allowances to insure fair racing against each other. More recently, boats have been designed and built to suit various rating rules; when measured they were given a rating. If this was a lower figure than a potential competitor, it gave a better time allowance. For many years, all important races were sailed on a time allowance with ratings spread fairly evenly across all sizes of boat, which were grouped by size as 'classes'. This made it possible to buy or build a boat to suit a particular rating. For instance, if Class IV was fixed at the band 23ft to 25.4ft (as it was in 1974), then someone wishing to have a boat rating low in Class IV would go for a boat rating at, say, 23.5ft. This system did not apply in the US.

Certain boat sizes were popular because they were eligible for classes or annual races that had particular limits. For many years, 29ft was the lower limit of RORC Class II as well as the lowest limit for entry to the Britannia Cup held during Cowes Week. For a long time, the RORC also had a lower *waterline* limit, regardless of rating, of 24ft (7.3m), and many ocean-racing boats were built close to this minimum size.

THE ONE TON CUP

In the summer of 1964, Le Cercle de la Voile de Paris (CVP), an old club founded in 1858, presented its major trophy for a new series of races to be sailed in 1965. The trophy, known as Le Coupe International du CVP or more commonly the One Ton Cup, was to be awarded to boats rating 22ft or less under the current RORC rating rule, and was to be sailed for without time allowances.

The series was to be held at Le Havre, at the mouth of the Seine, and was to consist of one offshore race of between 200 to 300 miles and two shorter inshore races. Each competing nation could enter a maximum of three boats, but despite this, the event was not a team race: the winner would be the individual boat with the best score in the series.

The major instigator of this series was a leading member of the CVP, Jean Peytel, a French delegate to the IYRU who was involved in discussions concerning the possibility of introducing an ocean-racing class of yachts to the Olympic Games. Part of his plan, therefore, was to show that it was possible to have an ocean-racing class without handicaps, these being unacceptable for Olympic competition.

The Olympic committee never did adopt an ocean-racing class – the main two reasons being the unsuitability of night sailing and the lack of ocean racers in many countries – but the One Ton Cup series was an immediate success, attracting worldwide attention with great interest shown among designers and owners. It has been sailed for every year, with two exceptions, since 1965.

The new class was given rules about its accommodation, which included a specified headroom height in the cabin. There were also requirements about bunks, the galley, chart room, and equipment. For the first year, existing boats were pressed into service, some adapted to meet the necessary 22-ft rating by altering the ballast or sail area.

Such steps were only necessary for the first event; by the time of the second series in 1966, boats were being designed and built especially to fit the rating and the special rules of the cup.

Without time allowances, every effort could now be concentrated into making the boat as fast as possible within the rules. The 'One Ton' ocean racer, sailed by the most professional of crews, thus represents the most technologically advanced kind of ocean racer. The growth of the specialist, racing, 'grand prix' boat since the early 1970s is in great measure due to the One Ton Cup.

A SUCCESSFUL FORMULA

The success of the One Ton Cup soon insured that it was not long before the idea spread to other sizes of offshore boats. Hardly had the first One Ton Cup been

THE ONE TON CUP

The One Ton Cup is one of sailing's most impressive trophies. It is 902mm (2ft 9in) high and 655mm (2ft 2in) between handles, and was originally chiselled from 10kg (22lbs) of solid silver. It was commissioned from a Paris silversmith, Robert Linzeler, by a syndicate that had successfully raced the yacht *Esterel* at Cannes in 1898. When they sold the boat later that year to Baron Edmund de Rothschild, they used the proceeds to commission the cup which they then presented to Le Cercle de la Voile de Paris for a new international challenge race to be sailed by yachts rating at One Ton under the-then current French tonnage rules. This rating was a simple rule of sail area, length and beam, and produced a partly decked boat of low freeboard and large sail area, ideal for sailing in protected waters.

The first race for the One Ton Cup took place in 1899 on the River Seine at Meulan, near Paris, between a French and a British yacht. Until 1903 the races were held between a single yacht each from France and Britain, with Italy competing once; twice it was sailed at Cowes. In 1906 the series resumed, and the cup was continuously raced for in the new International 6-Meter class until 1962, excepting the war years of 1914-18 and 1939-45. By this time, the series had been expanded to allow several boats to participate: nine boats competed for the trophy in 1930 when it was held in Sweden. However, by 1962, it was apparent that interest in 6-Meter racing was waning, and the cup was uncontested until its transformation into the contemporary One Ton Cup in 1965.

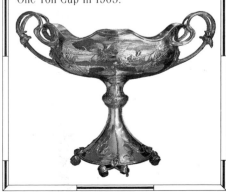

sailed than the Société Régates Rochelaise, France, announced a similar contest at La Rochelle for boats of 18-ft RORC rating, roughly 8.8-9.8 m (29-32 ft) LOA. Known as the Half Ton Cup, or more accurately the Lord Granard Cup, it was won by a single boat each year, with a prize for the winning team of three boats per nation. In 1967, the first race was sailed, also at La Rochelle, for the Quarter Ton Cup for boats of 15-ft rating, about 7.9 m (26 ft) LOA.

In due course the demand arose for a boat right at the bottom of the IOR scale. In 1975 and the years immediately following, several groups in Britain and France promoted a class at about 16-ft IOR rating (7 m, 23 ft, LOA) and built a few boats of this size before any international agreement was established. An Eighth Ton Cup for such boats was sailed in Britain, with boats from France, the Netherlands and the home country. However, by 1978, agreement was reached on a Mini Ton Cup at a 16-ft rating: because the boats were so small, its five races were held inshore and in daylight, the longest lasting about 12 hours.

A Micro Ton class also exists, but this is not an offshore ocean racer. At 5.5 m (18 ft) LOA, it is really a large dinghy with a set of rules that give young amateur designers a chance of trying out their ideas cheaply, with the guarantee that races will be held for such boats to compete in. The rules were originated by the French sailing magazine *Bateaux*.

Further up the scale, a new class was inserted between the Half Ton and the One Ton when the One Ton boats turned out to be larger than the originators had envisaged. The United States Yacht Racing Union gave this class, measuring in at about 10.5 m (34 ft) LOA, a trophy known as the Three-Quarter Ton Cup.

At the top of the scale, a few large yachts sailed to a 28-ft RORC rating in Italy for a series that became known as the Two Ton Cup.

— ◆◆◆ —

One Ton Cup Winner *The Danish ocean racer* Andelstanken *sailing to victory in the 1986 One Ton Cup, held in Palma, Spain. All its nine-man crew are sitting on the windward side in order to add power to the boat as it sails upwind.*

Quarter Ton Cup Winner McDonald's, *Danish winner of the Quarter Ton Cup in 1987 and 1988.*

◆ ◆ ◆

CHANGING THE RULES

As the rating rules have changed, so too have the rating limits of the various Ton Cup classes. When the RORC rating rules were abandoned in favor of the International Offshore Rule (IOR) in 1969, the ratings for the four Ton Cups then in existence were adapted so as to allow the same-sized boats as before to compete. When the total changeover to the IOR took place in 1971, alterations to the rating figures again proved necessary.

The Two Ton Cup rating was reduced in 1974 to bring it into line with the Canada's Cup rating. But despite this change, the size and the cost of such boats meant that the class was not well supported, and it was suspended after 1981. When no One Tonners turned up for their annual championship in Brighton, England, in 1982, the opportunity was seized to rearrange the ratings at the top of the scale. The old One Ton rating was scrapped, the Two Ton rating abolished, and a new One Ton rating, close to the old Two Ton rating, established for the 1984 series at La Trinité-sur-Mer, France. This new rating also matched the smaller boats allowed to sail in the biennial Admiral's Cup.

Soon after the changeover from the RORC rule to the IOR, the French clubs that had previously administered the

ONE TON CUP			TWO TON CUP		
	VENUE	BOAT	NATIONALITY	VENUE	BOAT	NATIONALITY
1965	LE HAVRE, FRANCE	DIANA	DENMARK	—	—	—
1966	COPENHAGEN, DENMARK	TINA	USA	—	—	—
1967	LE HAVRE, FRANCE	OPTIMIST	GERMANY	GENOA, ITALY	AIRELA	ITALY
1968	HELGOLAND, GERMANY	OPTIMIST	GERMANY	GENOA, ITALY	LA MELORIA	ITALY
1969	HELGOLAND, GERMANY	RAINBOW	NZ	—	—	—
1970	—	—	—	—	—	—
1971	AUCKLAND, NZ	STORMY PETREL	AUSTRALIA	GENOA, ITALY	VILLANELLA	ITALY
1972	SYDNEY, AUSTRALIA	WAI-ANIWA	NZ	GENOA, ITALY	LOWRA	ITALY
1973	PORTO CERVO, ITALY	YDRA	ITALY	—	—	—
1974	TORQUAY, ENGLAND	GUMBOOTS	UK	SAN REMO, ITALY	AGGRESSIVE	USA
1975	NEWPORT, RI, USA	PIED PIPER	USA	DETROIT, USA	RICOCHET	USA
1976	MARSEILLE, FRANCE	RESOLUTE SALMON	USA	KIEL, GERMANY	WILLIWAW	GERMANY
1977	AUCKLAND, NZ	THE RED LION	NZ	—	—	—
1978	FLENSBURG, GERMANY	TILSALG	GERMANY	RIO DE JANEIRO, BRAZIL	IORANA	USA
1979	NEWPORT, RI, USA	PENDRAGON	USA	POOLE, ENGLAND	GITANA VII	FRANCE
1980	NAPLES, ITALY	FILO DA TORCERE	ITALY	—	—	—
1981	CORK, IRELAND	JUSTINE III	IRELAND	PORTO CERVO, ITALY	HITCHHIKER	AUSTRALIA
1982	—	—	—	*The Two Ton Cup was suspended after 1981 and the One Ton*		
1983	RIO DE JANEIRO, BRAZIL	LINDA	ITALY	*Cup rating was increased in 1984 to 30.5 ft IOR.*		
1984	LA TRINITÉ-SUR-MER, FRANCE	PASSION 2	FRANCE	—	—	—
1985	POOLE, ENGLAND	JADE	UK	—	—	—
1986	PALMA, SPAIN	ANDELSTANKEN	DENMARK	—	—	—
1987	KIEL, GERMANY	FRAM X	NORWAY	—	—	—
1988	SAN FRANCISCO, USA	PROPAGANDA	NZ	—	—	—

CHANGES IN RATINGS

	TWO TON	ONE TON	THREE-QUARTER TON	HALF TON	QUARTER TON	MINI TON
1965	—	22 ft RORC	—	—	—	—
1966	—		—	18 ft RORC	—	—
1967	28 ft RORC		—		15 ft RORC	—
1971	33 ft IOR	27.5 ft IOR	—	21.7 ft IOR	18 ft IOR	—
1974	32 ft IOR		24.5 ft IOR			—
1978						16 ft IOR
1979				22 ft IOR	18.5 ft IOR	16.5 ft IOR
1981	*Suspended*					
1984		30.5 ft IOR				

One Ton   Three-Quarter Ton   Half Ton   Quarter Ton   Mini Ton

different series handed over responsibility to the international Offshore Racing Council. The ORC now makes the rules for the races and decides where they will be held each year. This replaces the earlier system whereby the winner was allowed to defend the cup in his own waters, producing a repetition of some venues in the early years. Once the Ton Cups moved over to the IOR, the US was able to compete fully, since the IOR was in use in America; until then only a few enthusiasts willing to build boats to a foreign, RORC, rule had attended the events.

THE TON CUP FORMAT

After an initial four days for inspection and measurement, the races for each class occupy between six and nine days. For all the events, day 5 is an Olympic-type course; day 6, a long offshore race; day 9 or 10, another Olympic-type course; day 10 or 11, a short offshore race; and finally day 12 or 13, the last Olympic-type course. The Mini Ton Cup has the same scheme of races in a slightly different order.

The length of the offshore races is planned to be appropriate to the size of boat. The mileage is such that for the One Tonners, the long offshore course lasts about 54 hours, covering two nights at sea, while the inshore race lasts about 27 hours with one night at sea. The Quarter Ton races last about 24 hours and 18 hours respectively, while the races for the Mini Tonners are all in daylight. The Olympic-type course distances are specified to vary from 27 miles for the One Tonners to 14 miles for the Mini Tonners, about six hours sailing time depending on the wind.

With all the cups, the principal award goes to a single boat, with limits to the total entry and each country's entry. If entries are likely to be small, this last limit can be expanded. Crew numbers are limited to nine for the One Ton, six for the Three-Quarter Ton, five for the Half Ton, four for the Quarter Ton and three for the Mini Ton. At least half the crew, including the owner, charterer or borrower, must be of the same nationality as that under

THREE-QUARTER TON CUP

	VENUE	BOAT	NATIONALITY
1966	—	—	—
1967	—	—	—
1968	—	—	—
1969	—	—	—
1970	—	—	—
1971	—	—	—
1972	—	—	—
1973	—	—	—
1974	MIAMI, USA	SWAMP FIRE	USA
1975	HANKO, FINLAND	SOLENT SARACEN	UK
1976	PLYMOUTH, ENGLAND	FINN FIRE II	FINLAND
1977	LA ROCHELLE, FRANCE	JOE LOUIS	FRANCE
1978	VICTORIA BC, CANADA	PENDRAGON	USA
1979	HUNDESTED, DENMARK	REGNBAGEN	SWEDEN
1980	LA TRINITÉ-SUR-MER, FRANCE	MALIGAWA	FRANCE
1981	HELSINKI, FINLAND	SOLDIER BLUE	DENMARK
1982	DENIA, SPAIN	LILLE DU	DENMARK
1983	TRIESTE, ITALY	BOTTA DRITTA 3	ITALY
1984	KIEL, GERMANY	POSITRON	GERMANY
1985	MARSTRAND, SWEDEN	GREEN PIELE 85	DENMARK
1986	TORQUAY, ENGLAND	INDULGENCE	UK
1987	NIEUWPOORT, BELGIUM	JELFI X	NETH.
1988	LIVORNO, ITALY	OKYALOS IV	GREECE

HALF TON CUP

	VENUE	BOAT	NATIONALITY
1966	LA ROCHELLE, FRANCE	RAKI	FRANCE
1967	LA ROCHELLE, FRANCE	SAFARI	FRANCE
1968	LA ROCHELLE, FRANCE	DAME D'IROISE	FRANCE
1969	SANDHAMN, SWEDEN	SCAMPI	SWEDEN
1970	SANDHAMN, SWEDEN	SCAMPI	SWEDEN
1971	PORTSMOUTH, ENGLAND	SCAMPI III	SWEDEN
1972	MARSTRAND, SWEDEN	BES	DENMARK
1973	HUNDESTED, DENMARK	IMPENSABLE	FRANCE
1974	LA ROCHELLE, FRANCE	NORTH STAR	GERMANY
1975	CHICAGO, USA	FOXY LADY	AUSTRALIA
1976	TRIESTE, ITALY	SILVER SHAMROCK	IRELAND
1977	SYDNEY, AUSTRALIA	GUNBOAT RANGIRIRI	NZ
1978	POOLE, ENGLAND	WAVERIDER	NZ
1979	SCHEVENINGEN, NETH.	WAVERIDER	NZ
1980	SANDHAMN, SWEDEN	AR BIGOUDEN	FRANCE
1981	POOLE, ENGLAND	KING ONE	FRANCE
1982	PIRAEUS, GREECE	ATALANTI II	GREECE
1983	HANKO, FINLAND	FREELANCE	FRANCE
1984	TROON, SCOTLAND	C	FRANCE
1985	PORTO ERCOLE, ITALY	ANTHEOR	FRANCE
1986	HELSINKI, FINLAND	C	FRANCE
1987	LA ROCHELLE, FRANCE	R. CHARTEAU VIDEO	FRANCE
1988	POOLE, ENGLAND	SKIP. ELF AQUITAINE	FRANCE

which the boat is entered, and the crew has to stay the same throughout the series, unless circumstances such as illness or injury occur, in which case special permission for substitution has to be obtained from the international jury present throughout the series.

The rules specify adequate space and headroom inside the boat, as well as the number of bunks, and the existence of a galley, chart table, emergency equipment and other standard items. These rules prevent the use of special crew for different weathers and courses, and stop the removing of equipment in the pursuit of speed. The number of sails is strictly limited for each class.

Intentionally, competitors have stretched the rules to the limit while juries and sailing committees have plugged any holes in the rules and attempted to deal strictly with competitors who infringe them. Several days are allocated to inspecting boats before each series and checking that the rating certificates match the dimensional limits; if sails are too large, they are cut down to size. The whole question of what weight may be taken out of the boat for the race or moved about during the race is one of the most complex areas of the rules, and the one which most concerns every race committee.

ONE TON HISTORY

The One Ton and other level-rating classes have attracted the top names in ocean racing, for the testing format and high standards of racing mean that success in these annual championships is among the top sailing accolades.

The first One Ton Cup race in 1965 attracted 14 boats, from eight countries, with existing ratings that qualified them for inclusion. As new boats were designed to fit the RORC rating rules used by the One Ton Cup, entrants grew to a record 34 boats in 1974. By this time an increasing number of professional skippers and sailors were involved in the series. American designs triumphed in the first four series. The ORC chose the locations of the series from 1973 onward, but it remained noticeable how often the winning boat came from the host country; such is the advantage of sailing on familiar waters.

Throughout the 1970s, the boats were becoming lighter and faster. American designs again predominated, winning from 1973 to 1976, but after a further win in 1979, interest waned in 1980, reducing the fleet to 14 boats.

With the merging of the One and Two Ton Cups in time for the 1984 season, interest in the event revived, with 1974's record entry of 34 boats being equalled at Kiel in 1987. European-designed boats have dominated in recent years with boats that are now the same size as those used in the Admiral's Cup. This has given owners more incentive to build new boats and has enhanced the 'grand prix' aspect of the series even more. However, the increasing specialization of design and the cost of building and campaigning a new boat has restricted the field to a relatively few wealthy people and, in recent years, to commercial sponsors.

Gone are the days of the all-around owner who wanted a boat to race and cruise in, and who then eventually sold it for cruising or club racing when it became outdated. Today's One Tonner is a highly developed racing machine that gives close competition when sailed against others of her class, but at a considerable cost to her owner and with rapid obsolescence in design and speed.

QUARTER TON CUP / MINI TON CUP

	VENUE	BOAT	NATIONALITY	VENUE	BOAT	NATIONALITY
1966	—	—	—	—	—	—
1967	LA ROCHELLE, FRANCE	DEFENDER	BELGIUM	—	—	—
1968	BRESKENS, NETH.	PIRHANA	NETH.	—	—	—
1969	BRESKENS, NETH.	LISTANG	GERMANY	—	—	—
1970	TRAVEMÜNDE, GERMANY	FLEUR D'ECUME	FRANCE	—	—	—
1971	LA ROCHELLE, FRANCE	ECUME DE MER	FRANCE	—	—	—
1972	LA ROCHELLE, FRANCE	PETITE FLEUR	FRANCE	—	—	—
1973	WEYMOUTH, ENGLAND	EYGTHENE	USA	—	—	—
1974	MALMO, SWEDEN	ACCENT	SWEDEN	—	—	—
1975	LE HAVRE, FRANCE	45 SOUTH	NZ	—	—	—
1976	CORPUS CHRISTI, USA	MAGIC BUS	NZ	—	—	—
1977	HELSINKI, FINLAND	MANZANITA	SPAIN	—	—	—
1978	SAJIMA, JAPAN	MAGICIAN V	JAPAN	PORTO ERCOLE, ITALY	WAHOO	AUSTRIA
1979	SAN REMO, ITALY	BULLIT	FRANCE	ESTARTIT, SPAIN	WAHOO	ITALY
1980	PANMURE, NZ	BULLIT	FRANCE	EDINBURGH, SCOTLAND	MR BILLS DOG	USA
1981	MARSEILLE, FRANCE	LAYCDON PROTIS	FRANCE	LAKE CONSTANCE, SWITZ.	GULLISARA	ITALY
1982	MELBOURNE, AUSTRALIA	QUARTERMASTER	AUSTRALIA	MARSTRAND, SWEDEN	GULLISARA	ITALY
1983	—	—	—	ST. RAPHAËL, FRANCE	KHINISPRI	GERMANY
1984	NIEUWPOORT, BELGIUM	COMTE DE FLANDRES	FRANCE	CORFU, GREECE	LIGULE	ITALY
1985	AJACCIO, FRANCE	ROYAL FLUSH	SOUTH AFRICA	HANKO, FINLAND	CREOLA	ITALY
1986	COPENHAGEN, DENMARK	COMTE DE FLANDRES	AUSTRALIA	LAKE GARDA, ITALY	WITCHIE	NORWAY
1987	CROSSHAVEN, IRELAND	McDONALD'S	DENMARK	MEDEMBLIK, NETH.	MANNAGGIA	ITALY
1988	TRAVEMÜNDE, GERMANY	McDONALD'S	DENMARK	VARBERG, SWEDEN	FOR SALE	NORWAY

SINGLE-HANDED RACES AROUND THE WORLD

Ocean races around the world are a relatively recent development, a logical outcome of the steadily increasing dependability and speed of ocean racers. Although there have been single-handed circumnavigations of the world since Joshua Slocum's voyage of 1895-8, these earlier passages were relatively unhurried cruises. The success of OSTAR after its inception in 1960, and the circumnavigation by Francis Chichester in 1967, led yachtsmen to think of the possibility of racing around the world single-handed, with or without a stop.

The opportunity for such a race arose in early 1968 when five sailors were preparing to sail single-handed around the world without a stop. The British *Sunday Times* newspaper sponsored a race for them, attracting a further four entries. Starting from a British port of their choice on their own chosen date between June and October 1968, the nine entrants had to sail via the two great southern capes of Good Hope and Cape Horn back to the same port, without stopping. The prizes offered were the Golden Globe trophy for the first boat home and £5,000 ($7,500) for the fastest passage.

◆◆◆

Single-handed Races Around the World *There have been three such races around the world:*
1 *The record-setting Golden Globe Race, sailed in 1968-9 without stopping.*
2 *The BOC Challenge Around-Alone Race, sailed in 1982-3 and 1986-7 with three stops.*

Suhaili, *winner of the 1968-9 Golden Globe Race.*

GOLDEN GLOBE RACE 1968-9
WINNER · *SUHAILI*
HELMSMAN · ROBIN KNOX-JOHNSTON (UK)
TIME · 313 days
COURSE · FALMOUTH-CAPE OF GOOD HOPE-CAPE HORN-FALMOUTH
STARTERS · 9

For all concerned, the Golden Globe Race was one of the most unfortunate to have ever been held. The winner – Robin Knox-Johnston (UK) – was the only man to complete the course, and at the age of 30 achieved a double first: the first man to circumnavigate the world without stopping, and the first man to circumnavigate it single-handed without stopping. He left Falmouth, England in his four-year-old bermudan ketch *Suhaili* (9.9 m, 32 ft 5 in LOA) on 14 June 1968, returning on 22 April 1969, 313 days later.

Of the eight others, six – Chay Blyth, Donald Crowhurst, Commander Bill King and John Ridgway (all UK), Louis Fougeron (France) and Alex Carozzo (Italy) – never got beyond the Cape of Good Hope. Donald Crowhurst, aboard his trimaran *Teignmouth Electron* sent back false signals from the South Atlantic so that it was thought he was making good progress around the world. His boat was discovered abandoned and it is assumed he had committed suicide, presumably by throwing himself overboard.

Nigel Tetley in *Victress*, sailed around the world and was on the final leg when, 800 miles off Spain; his trimaran began to break up and he was rescued.

The final entrant did sail around the world but did not return to Britain to complete the course. Bernard Moitessier (France) left Plymouth on 22 August 1968 on board *Joshua*, but after rounding Cape Horn in February 1969, he decided to sail on around the world for a second time. He passed the south of Australia again before putting into Tahiti. He had been at sea 301 days and had logged 37,455 miles.

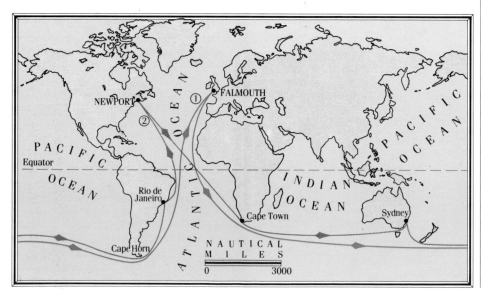

FIRST BOC CHALLENGE AROUND-ALONE RACE 1982-3

WINNER · *CRÉDIT AGRICOLE*	
HELMSMAN · PHILIPPE JEANTÔT (FRANCE)	
TIME · 159 days 2 hr 26 min	
COURSE · NEWPORT-CAPE TOWN-SYDNEY-RIO DE JANEIRO-NEWPORT	
STARTERS · 17	

After the fiasco of the Golden Globe Race, no further organized single-handed races around the world were contemplated. However the success of the fully crewed Whitbread races (see pp 80-3) and various individual single-handed cruising feats once again raised the issue. An American, David White, began to work on the idea from his base at Newport, Rhode Island, in 1979. A sponsor was found in BOC, the British Oxygen Company, much of whose business is in the US. The planning of the race was meticulous; the course was from Newport, via the Capes of Good Hope and Horn, back to Newport, the first race of its type to start and finish in the US.

Seventeen boats drawn from eight countries started the race on 28 August 1982. The first leg was 7,100 miles to Cape Town; the second, 6,900-mile leg started on 13 November 1982 and finished at Sydney; the third, 8,250-mile leg started on 16 January 1983 and finished at Rio de Janeiro; the final, 5,300-mile leg home started on 10 April 1983. The winner was the French entrant Philippe Jeantôt sailing *Crédit Agricole*, whose total elapsed time was 159 days, 2 hr, 26 min.

Only 10 of the 17 starters finished the course. Of the remainder, two retired from the first leg, four from the second leg and one from the third. Four of these seven pulled out with mechanical failures, particularly of the self-steering gear.

The other three met rather different fates. *Gipsy Moth V*, owned by Francis Chichester's son Giles and sailed by Desmond Hampton (UK), was wrecked when it ran on to Gabo Island off southeast Australia when the skipper was asleep. The British boat, *Lady Pepperell*, sailed by Tony Lush, pitchpoled and began to sink on the second leg, and was rescued by Francis Stokes (USA) in *Moonshine*. The third boat to run into difficulties, the French *Skoiern III*, sailed by Jacques de Roux, pitchpoled and began to sink on the third leg. In a rescue coordinated by world-wide shortwave radio, Richard Broadhead (UK) in *Perseverance* was directed from over 300 miles away in order to rescue de Roux in heavy seas and 30-knot winds. Broadhead later won awards in Britain and France for this feat.

◆◆◆

Philippe Jeantôt *Winner of the first BOC Challenge Around-Alone Race in 1982-3, sailing* Crédit Agricole, *the French sailor Philippe Jeantôt won the second race in 1986-7 on board* Crédit Agricole III.

SECOND BOC CHALLENGE AROUND-ALONE RACE 1986-7

WINNER · *CRÉDIT AGRICOLE III*	
HELMSMAN · PHILIPPE JEANTÔT (FRANCE)	
TIME · 134 days 5 hr 23 min	
COURSE · NEWPORT-CAPE TOWN-SYDNEY-RIO DE JANEIRO-NEWPORT	
STARTERS · 25	

Twenty-five boats with lone sailors drawn from 10 countries lined up at Newport on 30 August 1986 for the start of the second BOC, and third single-handed race around the world. Three boats were involved in collisions on the starting line, one with a spectator boat, causing two of the entries to return for repairs and subsequent late start. Five days after the start, *Air Force*, sailed by the American Dick Cross, hit a submerged object and sank, the skipper being rescued from his life-raft.

Sailing the same legs as the first race, 19 boats reached Cape Town and all of them started the second leg on 15 November 1986. The fleet then met extreme weather conditions with winds of 65 knots and huge seas. *Skoiern IV*, sailed by Jacques de Roux, who had already been rescued in the first race, was observed in the vicinity of Gabo Island on no set course. There was no sign of de Roux, who was presumed to have fallen or been washed overboard; all the safety gear and harnesses were unused.

Of the 18 boats that finished the second leg, all but one started the third on 18 January 1987. Soon after the start, *Joseph Young*, sailed by the Canadian John Hughes, was dismasted, but the skipper rigged a jury rig and sailed toward Chile. However winds were light, so he decided to continue the course around Cape Horn, sailing a total of 4,400 miles to the Falkland Islands. There the boat was rerigged and he rejoined the race.

The final leg saw 15 starters on the line at Rio de Janeiro on 11 April 1987, with *Joseph Young* starting late after the others had left. All the boats completed the course back to Newport. As with the first race, the winner was the French yachtsman Philippe Jeantôt, sailing *Crédit Agricole III*. He was the winner of the first and third legs, runner-up on the second leg and third on the final leg.

FULLY CREWED RACES AROUND THE WORLD

Despite the failure of the single-handed Golden Globe race, which ended in 1969, the idea of races around the world continued to excite interest. Ocean Publications, a London-based magazine and promotions firm that published several boating magazines, floated the idea again in 1972, to considerable enthusiasm. They looked for an organization that could handle such an event: the British Royal Naval Sailing Association fit the bill, with some assistance from the British navy. Financial sponsorship came from Whitbread & Co Ltd, a British brewery.

The course of the Whitbread Race was to start and finish at Portsmouth, England, and follow the usual route round the Capes of Good Hope and the Horn. As a reaction against the extreme duration of the Golden Globe course, there were to be stops at Cape Town, Sydney and Rio de Janeiro. Multihulls were banned, the boats had to

rate between 30 ft and 70 ft IOR and comply with ORC regulations. The most important difference between this race and the Golden Globe was the requirement that the crew had to number at least five, and there was no restriction on changing crews at any time.

Prior to the race, there was much talk about the inadvisability of racing around the notorious Cape Horn, which had acquired a fearsome reputation with the sailing ships of past centuries. In 1898 Joshua Slocum took *Spray* through the Strait of Magellan on his round-the-world voyage, and most circumnavigations followed suit or went through the Panama Canal. When Conor O'Brien took his 12.8-m (42-ft) *Saoirse* round the world in 1923-5, he passed 100 miles off the Cape, such was the dubious windward ability of his boat. It was only in 1967 when Francis Chichester rounded close to the Horn in *Gipsy*

Moth IV that it began to lose its mystique. It was therefore decided to allow the Whitbread entrants to sail around close in sight of the Horn.

◆◆◆

Racing Around the World *The first four Whitbread Races and the FT Clipper Race have all gone eastbound around the world, utilizing the prevailing winds. Because the FT Clipper Race was staged to beat a record established in 1869 from London to Sydney, it followed that course without stopping. However, the Whitbread races had three stops – in Cape Town, either Sydney or Auckland, and in a South American port.*

The 1989-90 Whitbread Race broke with this tradition by stopping five times, avoiding a controversial stop in South Africa, and attracting wider attention by visiting Western Australia and the US. The course legs were first to Punta del Este in Uruguay (6,281 miles), then to Fremantle in Western Australia (7,658 miles), Auckland in New Zealand (3,434 miles), Punta del Este again (6,255 miles), then to Fort Lauderdale in Florida (5,475 miles) before returning to Portsmouth (3,837 miles), a total distance of 32,940 miles.

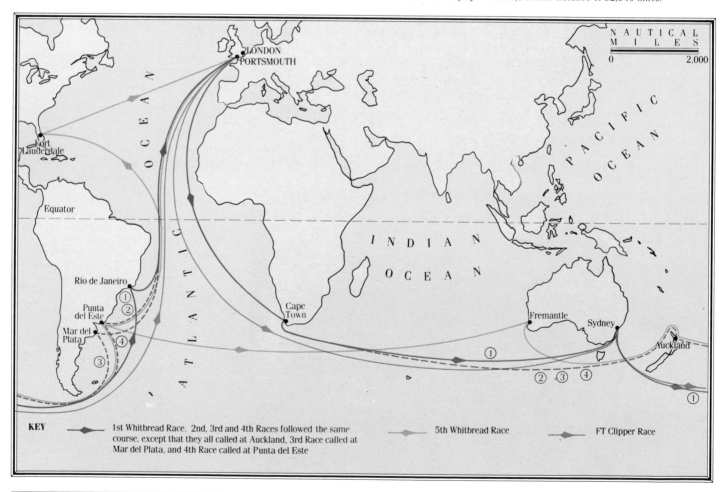

KEY ◆ 1st Whitbread Race. 2nd, 3rd and 4th Races followed the same course, except that they all called at Auckland, 3rd Race called at Mar del Plata, and 4th Race called at Punta del Este   ◆ 5th Whitbread Race   ◆ FT Clipper Race

FIRST WHITBREAD RACE 1973-4

WINNER · *SAYULA II*

SKIPPER · RAMON CARLIN (MEXICO)

BEST TIME · 144 days 10 hr

COURSE · PORTSMOUTH-CAPE TOWN-SYDNEY-
RIO DE JANEIRO-PORTSMOUTH

STARTERS · 17

The 27,120 mile race started on 8 September 1973, and was the longest race for fully crewed boats that had yet been attempted. Apart from the Golden Globe course, the third leg from Sydney to Rio de Janeiro was the longest-ever single leg on a course, both facts an indication of the tremendous advance in seaworthiness in ocean-going craft that had been achieved during the 50 years since the first modern ocean race.

the Bermuda Race of 1923 from New London, Connecticut to Bermuda.

The race itself was marred by the loss of two Englishmen and one Frenchman overboard – the only such casualties in the first four Whitbread races. The best elapsed time of the race was by *Great Britain II*, skippered by Chay Blyth (UK), with a time of 144 days, 10 hr, but the overall winner was *Sayula II*, a production Swan 65 measuring 19.6 m (64 ft 6 in) LOA, designed by Sparkman and Stephens of New York, built by Nautor Ky of Finland, and owned by Ramon Carlin of Mexico. With its crew of Americans, Britons and Mexicans, *Sayula II* had the best corrected time under the IOR and a special time allowance system used for this race.

FT CLIPPER RACE 1975-6

WINNER · *GREAT BRITAIN II*

SKIPPER · COMBINED BRITISH SERVICES CREW

TIME · FIRST LEG – 67 days 5 hr

SECOND LEG – 66 days 22 hr

COURSE · LONDON-SYDNEY-LONDON

STARTERS · 4

Between the first and second Whitbread races, a one-off race occurred with an interesting origin. In the days when clipper ships carrying cargo sailed from Britain to its colony in Australia, speed was of the essence. The fastest time between London and Sydney via the Cape of Good Hope – 13,650 miles – was 69 days, accomplished by the Aberdeen-registered *Patriarch* in 1869. The idea of staging a race to beat this time was suggested, as with the Whitbread races, by Ocean Publications, who attracted the London *Financial Times* newspaper as sponsors. The start and finish of the race was to be Sheerness, downstream from London in the Thames Estuary, but unusually there was to be only one stop during the race, at Sydney. Thus the race was to have two long legs, a considerable ordeal for many boats and, in the event, despite considerable advance interest, only four boats started the race, with one more joining at Sydney for the return, 12,730-mile leg via Cape Horn.

The four boats that started on 31 August 1975 were the 23.5-m (77-ft) *Great Britain II*, sailed by a joint British military services crew; the Italian *CSeRBII Busnelli* (20 m, 65 ft 6 in), skipper, D.M. di Malingri; the Dutch *The Great Escape* (16.8 m, 55 ft), skipper, Henk Huisman; and the French *Kriter II* (22.2 m, 73 ft), helmed by O. de Kersauson. They were joined on the home leg by the Australian *Anaconda* (24.4 m, 80 ft), owned by Josko Grubic. *Great Britain II* was first home on both legs, as well as having the best overall elapsed time and corrected time using IOR rating. Its outward time of just over 67 days narrowly beat the clipper record of 69 days.

7208

Sayula II *Although the British entry* Great Britain II *had the best elapsed time in the first Whitbread Race of 1973-4, the boat with the best corrected time, and thus the overall winner, was the Mexican entry* Sayula II, *owned and skippered by Ramon Carlin and sailed by an international crew.*

SECOND WHITBREAD RACE 1977-8

WINNER · *FLYER*	
SKIPPER · CORNELIS VAN RIETSCHOTEN (NETH.)	
BEST TIME · 134 days 12 hr	
COURSE · PORTSMOUTH-CAPE TOWN-AUCKLAND-RIO DE JANEIRO-PORTSMOUTH	
STARTERS · 15	

The second Whitbread race followed the successful formula of the first, with only one change of stopping point, substituting Auckland for Sydney. After the loss of three lives in the first race, stringent rules on life lines and safety harnesses were instituted to ensure that crew members were secured to the vessels in bad weather. The minimum size of boat eligible for entry was set at 33 ft IOR, in effect a vessel of about 15 m (50 ft).

For the second time, *Great Britain II*, skippered by Rob James on this occasion, had the best elapsed time of 134 days 12 hr, but the 19.9-m (65-ft 2-in) *Flyer*, owned and skippered by Cornelis van Rietschoten, with the second best time in the fleet of 136 days 5 hr, was some 15 days better on corrected time, being 4 m (13 ft) shorter. It was designed by Sparkman and Stephens specially for the race, and meticulous sea trials, including a tune-up sail across the Atlantic and back, followed the April 1977 launch by Dutch builders.

Cornelis van Rietschoten *Winner of the second Whitbread Race in 1977-8 on corrected time in* Flyer, *and winner of the third Whitbread Race in 1981-2 on both corrected and actual time in a new* Flyer, *Cornelis van Rietschoten is one of the world's most successful ocean racing campaigners.*

Flyer *Winner of the 1981-2 Whitbread Race.* Flyer *was designed specially for the race.*

THIRD WHITBREAD RACE 1981-2

WINNER · *FLYER (II)*	
SKIPPER · CORNELIS VAN RIETSCHOTEN (NETH.)	
BEST TIME · 120 days 6 hr	
COURSE · PORTSMOUTH-CAPE TOWN-AUCKLAND-MAR DEL PLATA-PORTSMOUTH	
STARTERS · 29˙	

In this third race, the Argentinian port of Mar del Plata was substituted for Rio de Janeiro. *Flyer*, the second boat of that name, achieved the goal of its owner and skipper Cornelis van Rietschoten in winning both on corrected and actual time.

The new *Flyer* was bigger than its predecessor at 23.2 m (76 ft), and was designed by the Argentinian German Frers and built by Wolter Huisman in the Netherlands. *Flyer* was extremely well-prepared for the race, but others were not as ready: of the record 29 starters, only 20 finished. Four were dismasted, three of them on the first leg. One of these was *Ceramco New Zealand*, skippered by the New Zealander Peter Blake. With a temporary mast and a jury rig, it managed to sail 200 miles a day to Cape Town, where it was last to finish. With a new rig, it then won the next leg to its home country. Both *Ceramco* and the French *Charles Heidsieck III*, as well as *Flyer*, beat the previous around-the-world records and were respectively second and third to finish.

FOURTH WHITBREAD RACE 1985-6

WINNER · *L'ESPRIT D'EQUIPE*	
SKIPPER · LIONEL PAEAN (FR.)	
BEST TIME · 117 days 14 hr	
COURSE · PORTSMOUTH-CAPE TOWN-AUCKLAND-PUNTA DEL ESTE-PORTSMOUTH	
STARTERS · 15	

Following the Falklands war, and because the race was run by the Royal Naval Sailing Association, the South American port of call was again changed, this time from Mar del Plata to the Uruguayan port of Punta del Este. The number of starters was down to 15, reflecting the increasing specialization and the high cost of ocean racers designed for this race, and the necessity for commercial sponsorship. A high proportion of the starters were maxi-raters, with only one boat less than 16.8 m (55 ft) long. Two boats were dismasted, one on the first leg and one on the third, but there were no crew casualties and only one boat failed to complete the course.

The first boat to finish was *UBS Switzerland*, a 24.3-m (79-ft 8-in) boat built in Switzerland to a Bruce Farr (NZ) design in plastics and then flown to the sea by aircraft. Skippered by Pierre Fehlmann, its time was a course record. Second home was the French boat *Côte d'Or*, the biggest entrant at 25.3 m (83 ft) LOA. It was skippered by Eric Tabarly, who had sailed in all the Whitbread races. However, the winner, *L'Esprit d'Equipe* was not a maxi-rater like these two and was smaller than any of the other three winners. It was also the first winner from France, although many distinguished French boats had competed in the four races. At 17.6 m (57 ft 9 in) LOA, with a light displacement and a fractional rig – by this date the fashion for racing boats – it was designed by Philippe Briand and built in France. Its size was kept deliberately moderate so that the stores would not be excessively heavy and the small crew of eight could drive the boat at its maximum.

◆◆◆

1985-6 Whitbread Race UBS Switzerland *(above) was the first boat home in the 1985-6 Whitbread Race and broke the record time for the race. The overall winner on corrected time was the French boat* L'Esprit d'Equipe *(below).*

TRANSATLANTIC RACING

At a New York dinner party in October 1866, the tobacco heir Pierre Lorillard declared that his 32-m (105-ft) centerboard schooner *Vesta* was the fastest yacht afloat. George and Franklin Osgood, owners of the 32.3-m (106-ft) *Fleetwing* disputed this, and waged $30,000 against him. James Gordon Bennett Jr., the newspaper tycoon and owner of the 32.6-m (107-ft) *Henrietta*, added a further bet of the same sum; $90,000 was now at stake. In order to prove their rival claims, the three agreed to race their three yachts across the Atlantic; the start was to be off Sandy Hook, New York, and the date, 11 December, when Atlantic gales are prevalent and the hours of darkness long.

With an agreement that only working sails, small sails and working topsails be carried, the three 200-ton schooners set out, and encountered bad weather that swept six men off the deck of *Fleetwing*. The race was closely fought. *Vesta* led at the Scilly Isles but lost out to *Henrietta* as they sailed up the English Channel. *Henrietta* crossed the finish line at the Needles at 15.45 on Christmas Day, while *Fleetwing* came in second, 40 minutes ahead of *Vesta* which lost its way in the dark. The first transatlantic race between fully crewed yachts was over.

THE PATTERN OF RACES

Only two more fully crewed races across the Atlantic took place before 1900, in 1870 and 1887; one was held in 1905 and 15 have occurred since 1928, although always on an irregular basis. The first single-handed race did not take place until 1960. This was sailed westbound, in contrast to the fully crewed races, all but one of which were sailed eastbound from either an American port, or occasionally Bermuda, to a suitable European destination such as Bergen in Norway, Marstrand in Sweden, the Skaw in Denmark, Plymouth or Cowes in Britain, Cork in Ireland or La Coruña in Spain.

An exception to this usual pattern of eastward-bound races was the second fully crewed transatlantic race held in July 1870 when two schooners, the British *Cambria* (33 m, 108 ft) and the American *Dauntless* (37.8 m, 124 ft) raced westward from Daunt Rock, Ireland, to Sandy Hook at the entrance to New York Bay.

Dorade, winner of the 1931 Transatlantic Race.

Cambria was on its way to contest the America's Cup (see p142), and beat *Dauntless* over the 3,000-mile course by 1 hr 43 min. It won a set of silverware then valued at £250, but later failed to win the America's Cup race itself.

WEST TO EAST

The third transatlantic race, reverting to an eastbound course, was not held until March 1887 – when the winds were strong and the water at its coldest – and once again took the form of a wager between two wealthy New York industrialists who owned what were virtually small ships with an all-professional crew. The 40.5-m (133-ft) *Coronet*, owned by Rufus T. Bush, crossed from New York to Cork, Ireland, in 14 days 19 hr. 30 hours in front of *Dauntless*, owned by the son of the Colt revolver's inventor, Caldwell H. Colt, who actually sailed the race on board his yacht.

The first transatlantic race of the 20th century was held in 1905 from Sandy Hook, New York to the Lizard Point, the most southerly point of England, a distance of 2,925 miles. The race was for a gold cup presented by Kaiser Wilhelm II and was promoted by the German Imperial Yacht Club, which drew up a set of rules that included having propellers removed from their shafts and lashed on deck. Eleven yachts from Britain, Germany and the USA were started on 17 May 1905 by a cannon

fired by the German naval attaché to the USA. The majority of them were big schooners, although the square-rigged *Sunbeam* of Lord Brassey was among their number. The German cruiser *Pfeil* was stationed off the Lizard Point to time in the yachts; the 56.4-m (185-ft) *Atlantic* – owned by the American, Wilson Marshall, skippered by the America's Cup helm, Charlie Barr, and designed by William Gardner of New York, whose office also designed the Star class – crossed the line first after 12 days 4 hr 1 min, an average speed of 10.02 knots. This time set the record for the fastest passage across the Atlantic in either direction: it was not to be bettered until 1980, 75 years later.

Since that record-setting race, west-to-east races have been held in the summers of 1928, 1931, 1935, 1936, 1950, 1951, 1952, 1955, 1956, 1957, 1963, 1966, 1968 and 1969, with the last race occurring in 1975. These fully crewed eastbound races faded in popularity in the face of competition from the single-handed and two-handed transatlantic races and from such bigger events as the Whitbread Round-the-World Race. Smaller ocean racers find the Ton Cups and the various inshore and offshore races more challenging.

Of that long list of races held since 1928, a number have certain important features. The 1931 race from Newport, Rhode Island, to Plymouth, England, was won by the-then unknown brothers Olin and Rod Stephens. Sailing their own design *Dorade*, they went on to win the Fastnet Race that same year.

By the time of the next race in 1935, the two brothers were established in the New York yacht design firm of Sparkman and Stephens. Their latest design, the 16.5-m (54-ft) *Stormy Weather*, owned by the American Philip Le Boutillier, won the race with Rod Stephens aboard. It also won the Fastnet that same year, the first SORC series in 1941, and proved its longevity by competing in the 1987 Fastnet.

After the interruption of the war, the first transatlantic race for 14 years was held in 1950, starting in Bermuda after the completion of the Bermuda Race. The size of the competing boats had diminished considerably, and the winner, the British boat *Cohoe*, owned by K. Adlard Coles, was only 9.8 m (32 ft) long.

The 1952 race, again started from Bermuda after the Bermuda Race, perpetuated this trend, the winning boat *Samuel Pepys*, owned by the Royal Naval Sailing Association and helmed by Erroll Bruce, measuring only 9.5 m (31 ft).

By the 1966 race, held to celebrate the centenary of the KDY, the Royal Danish Yacht Club, the length of the competing boats was increasing. Forty-two boats — the biggest entry ever for an eastbound race — sailed the race from Bermuda to The Skaw, Denmark. The winner was *Ondine* (17.4 m, 57 ft), owned by the American, Sumner A. Long.

Another record was established in 1969. The maxi-rater *Kialoa II*, (22.3 m, 73 ft), owned by John B. Kilroy (USA),

Transatlantic Races *Nine major series of races have been held across the North Atlantic Ocean in both directions.*

1 *Fully crewed eastbound races have been held from an American port or Bermuda to a variety of European destinations. The first race in 1866, shown here, went from New York to the Needles off the Isle of Wight, England. The last such race was in 1975.*

2 *Fully crewed westbound race from Falmouth, England, via Las Palmas to Antigua, West Indies.*

3 *The ARC, a fully crewed westbound race from Las Palmas to Barbados, West Indies.*

4 *OSTAR, single-handed westbound race from Plymouth, England, to Newport, Rhode Island.*

5 *Single-handed westbound Route du Rhum from St Malo, Brittany, to Guadeloupe.*

6 *Two-handed Le Transat en Double from Lorient, Brittany, around Bermuda and back.*

7 *Two-handed southbound race from La Baule in Brittany to Dakar in Senegal, West Africa.*

8 *Two-handed westbound race from Plymouth to Newport.*

9 *Two-handed race from Quebec, Canada, to St Malo, the only eastbound race now in existence.*

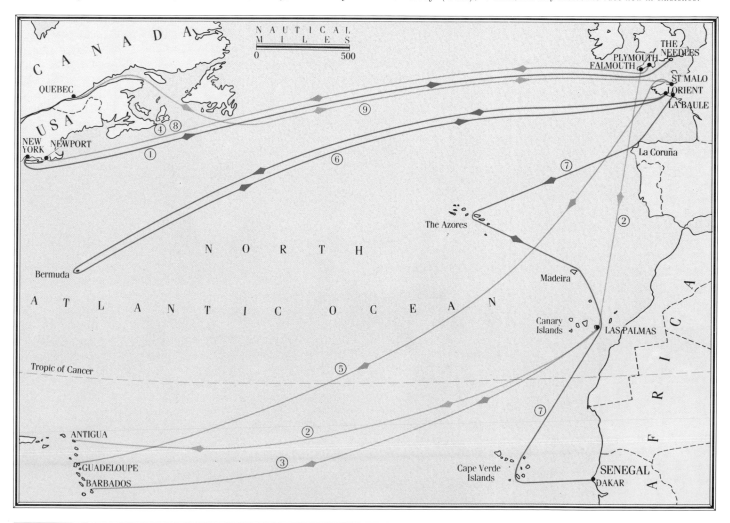

completed the course from Newport, Rhode Island, to Cork, Ireland, for the celebration of the 250th anniversary of the Royal Cork Yacht Club, in 12 days 5 hr 43 min. It was the fastest passage since *Atlantic*'s in 1905, but the record itself remained unbroken.

EAST TO WEST

Apart from the second transatlantic race of 1870, no westbound race was contemplated for years, for there was little incentive to race across the North Atlantic to windward against the prevailing winds. To insure fair winds, it is necessary to take the trade wind route from Europe via the Canary Islands to a finish in the Caribbean, the race taking place after October to avoid the hurricane season.

Such a race did not occur until 1981, when the Royal Ocean Racing Club held a race from Falmouth, England, starting in November and stopping at Las Palmas on Gran Canaria in the Canary Islands, with a restart aimed at finishing at Antigua in mid-December. A feeder race was run from Barcelona in Spain to Las Palmas. The winner was the 13.1-m (43-ft) British boat *Stormbird*, owned by Richard Matthews, which sailed the Canaries-Antigua leg of 2,800 miles in 16 days 7 min at an average speed of 7.16 knots. The same race was held again in 1985, when *Colt International*, a Swan 61, completed the second leg in 15 days 9 hr 23 min at an average speed of 7.58 knots.

In 1987 this RORC race was combined with a race for cruising boats called the Atlantic Rally for Cruisers (ARC), sailed from Las Palmas to Barbados. The first ARC race started on 29 November 1986 with 209 starters, a record number for any transatlantic race. The size of the boats varied from 7.3 m to 18.9 m (24 ft to 62 ft) and most of the designs were production cruisers and cruiser-racers, including multihulls, rather than specially designed ocean racers. There were numerous prizes for all classes and sizes of boats; the handicap winner was *Molla III* (9.1 m, 30 ft), owned by Kari Hynninen of Sweden, while the best time was by the 16.5-m (54-ft) trimaran *Running Cloud*, sailed by the American Larry Pollock, in 13 days 22 hr 4 min averaging 8.1 knots.

SHORT-HANDED TRANSATLANTIC RACES

By the mid-1970s, fully crewed races had largely given way to single-handed or two-handed events. The last fully crewed west to east race occurred in 1975, while short-handed races continue to be run into the 1980s. Most public attention is now focused on the short-handed races, all but one of which (Quebec-St. Malo) are westbound; these are invariably sponsored, attract considerable publicity, and include, or are solely for, multihulls.

The main short-handed races are the single-handed Route du Rhum from St. Malo in Brittany, France, to Guadeloupe in the West Indies; the two-handed Transat en Double from Lorient in Brittany to Bermuda and back without stopping; the two-handed multihull race from La Baule in Brittany along a zig-zag course to Dakar in Senegal, West Africa; the two-handed transatlantic race from Plymouth, England to Newport, Rhode Island; the two-handed race from Quebec, Canada, to St. Malo, Brittany, the only short-handed eastbound race; and, the first to have been run and still the most important, the single-handed transatlantic race from Plymouth to Newport, for many years known as OSTAR.

OSTAR/C-STAR

The British sailor, Colonel H.G. 'Blondie' Hasler, had become disenchanted with the high cost and big crews required for the

latest ocean racers. In 1957 he therefore proposed a race across the Atlantic against the prevailing wind, the only rule being that each boat must be sailed by only one person. Hasler himself proposed to sail a 7.6-m (25-ft) junk-rigged Folkboat, *Jester*, which could be trimmed, reefed and unreefed from a central hatch. He imagined that this was the type of economic and easily handled vessel which would turn out to be sailed in the event.

Hasler managed to get sponsorship for his scheme from the *Observer* newspaper in London, whose involvement gave the race – held every four years – the name of the Observer Single-Handed Transatlantic Race, or OSTAR. The newspaper remained involved until 1984; the 1988 race being sponsored by the Carlsberg brewing firm.

Gipsy Moth III *(above)*

The 1988 race was rather awkwardly known as C-STAR; future commercial sponsors might change the actual name again. Throughout its history the race has been organized and started by the Royal Western Yacht Club of Plymouth. The American end of the race has been organized by the Ida Lewis Yacht Club of Newport, Rhode Island. Thus was born OSTAR, the first such event of its type.

The first race in 1960 had five entries, four from Britain and one from France. The winning boat, *Gipsy Moth III*, sailed by Francis Chichester, completed the race in 40 days 12 hr. Hasler finished in second place eight days later, and the last-placed French boat, *Cap Horn*, sailed by Jean Lacombe, crossed the finishing line 34 days later – the longest crossing in the race's history. At 12.2 m (40 ft), Chichester's boat was thought by many to be too big for one man to sail safely, but as the race grew in popularity and starters increased to a record 125 in 1976, so too did the size of boat.

Far from breeding small, cheap family-type boats for ocean racing, this race has encouraged the development of such craft as the three-masted staysail schooner *Vendredi Treize* (39 m, 128 ft), helmed by Jean Yves-Terlain (Fr) in 1972, and the even bigger 71.9-m (236-ft) four-masted *Club Méditerranée* sailed in 1976 by Alain Colas (Fr), both of which came second in their respective races. Such vast boats led to considerable doubts about the ability of one person to sail such racing machines single-handed, doubts shared by the organizers who, in 1976, placed a limit on entries for the 1980 race of 17 m (56 ft) LOA and a total entry of 110. The size limit was later increased to 19.8 m (65 ft) and then decreased to 18.3 m (60 ft). This upper size limit was unpopular with some entrants, especially the heavily sponsored French multihulls, and thus has been a contributing factor to the creation of a variety of events run from France in which

Club Méditerranée *Measuring 71.9 m (236 ft), this four-masted monohull was sailed single-handed across the Atlantic by the French sailor Alain Colas in the 1976 OSTAR Race. Difficult for one person to control, it had to stop off for a couple of days in St John's, Newfoundland, for repairs and came a close second.*

boats up to 25.9 m (85 ft) have been permitted to enter.

Over the years the format of OSTAR has changed in various minor ways, with the exact number of permitted starters varying, and classes being divided by size to allow prizes for different winners. But the major prize remains for the first boat to finish, with the result that the favorites to win are invariably those built near to the maximum 18.3-m (60-ft) length. Monohulls won in 1960, 1964, 1968 and 1976, with trimarans winning in 1972, 1980, 1984 and 1988 and increasingly taking the major places in more recent races. Their involvement in the race has led to the time taken for the crossing falling from the 40 days 12 hr 30 min taken by Chichester in 1960 to the 10 days 9 hr 15 min taken by the winning boat *Fleury Michon IX*, sailed by Philippe Poupon in 1988.

French interest and ascendancy in the race was started by Eric Tabarly, who first sailed the race in 1964. There has always been a strong French, or more accurately Breton, tradition of short-handed cruising, but from Tabarly has flowed the recent domination by Frenchmen of short-handed racing and record breaking; in the 1980s this has been in multihulls. In the 1964 OSTAR, in which few multihulls took part, Tabarly sailed the 13.4-m (44-ft) ketch *Pen Duick II*, built to his own design and looking rather like the RORC racers of the time. His ambition was "to beat the English", which he most certainly did, the runner-up, Francis Chichester, taking two and a half days longer in *Gipsy Moth III*. Tabarly returned to France a hero, and was decorated personally by President de Gaulle. Since then Tabarly has sailed all the great ocean courses, and has trained and inspired many successors. It is difficult to see how this would have begun without the existence of OSTAR.

Eric Tabarly entered again in 1968 in the 20.4-m (67-ft) trimaran *Pen Duick IV*, but the boat hit a small freighter at 15 knots when he was below brewing coffee, and he was forced to retire with serious

Multihull Dominance *French multihulls have dominated the OSTAR races since Alain Colas won the event with a trimaran in 1972. A group of four trimarans are shown starting the 1988 race.*

Fleury Michon IX *set the record for a single-handed westbound crossing of the Atlantic in 1988.*

damage. After repairs he set out again, but was again forced to retire, this time with steering trouble. In heavy weather on this race, 16 of the 35 starters retired, and the winner, the 17.1-m (56-ft) *Sir Thomas Lipton*, was a conventional monohull, albeit one specially designed by Robert Clark

for its skipper, Geoffrey Williams. The French sailors came back in 1972 with ample preparation. A well-tested *Pen Duick IV*, a monohull sailed by Alain Colas, took the first prize, and French boats followed in second, third, sixth and eighth places. Since then, with very few

exceptions, Frenchmen have led the fleet, taking the first two places in 1976 – Tabarly winning in the multihull *Pen Duick VI* with Colas second in the giant monohull *Club Méditerranée* – and the first three places in 1984 and 1988.

The 1988 race was remarkable for its high speeds. The usual string of eastbound Atlantic depressions were absent for the leading boats, and there was an undue amount of reaching with the wind, which suited the big multihulls. Not only did *Fleury Michon IX* beat the east-to-west record with a time of 10 days 9 hr 15 min, but so did the first 10 boats to finish, most of which were French multihulls carrying sponsored names. The seventh-placed finisher, Florence Arthaud, recorded the fastest time for a single-handed woman in the race, sailing the 18.3-m (60-ft) multihull *Groupe Pierre Ier*. The leading monohull was the 12th-placed *UAP 1992*, sailed by Jean-Yves Terlain. Once again, multihulls proved superior.

The entries for OSTAR have risen steadily from five in the first race to 125 in 1976, settling down to just below 100

OSTAR/C-STAR

	PLACE	BOAT	TYPE	SKIPPER	NATIONALITY	TIME days hr min			Av. SPEED IN KNOTS	STARTERS/ FINISHERS
1960	1	GIPSY MOTH III	MONOHULL	FRANCIS CHICHESTER	UK	40	12	30	3.09	5/5
	2	JESTER	MONOHULL	BLONDIE HASLER	UK	48	12	02		
	3	CARDINAL VERTUE	MONOHULL	DAVID LEWIS	UK	55	00	50		
1964	1	PEN DUICK II	MONOHULL	ERIC TABARLY	FRANCE	27	03	56	4.38	15/14
	2	GIPSY MOTH III	MONOHULL	FRANCIS CHICHESTER	UK	29	23	57		
	3	AKKA	MONOHULL	VAL HOWELLS	UK	32	18	08		
1968	1	SIR THOMAS LIPTON	MONOHULL	GEOFFREY WILLIAMS	UK	25	20	33	4.60	35/19
	2	VOORTREKKER	MONOHULL	BRUCE DALLING	SOUTH AFRICA	26	13	42		
	3	CHEERS	PROA	TOM FOLLETT	USA	27	00	13		
1972	1	PEN DUICK IV	TRIMARAN	ALAIN COLAS	FRANCE	20	13	15	5.80	55/40
	2	VENDREDI TREIZE	MONOHULL	JEAN-YVES TERLAIN	FRANCE	21	05	14		
	3	CAP 33	TRIMARAN	JEAN-MARIE VIDAL	FRANCE	25	05	40		
1976	1	PEN DUICK VI	MONOHULL	ERIC TABARLY	FRANCE	23	20	12	5.24	125/73
	2	CLUB MÉDITERRANÉE	MONOHULL	ALAIN COLAS	FRANCE	24	03	36		
	3	THE THIRD TURTLE	TRIMARAN	MIKE BIRCH	CANADA	24	20	39		
1980	1	MOXIE	TRIMARAN	PHIL WELD	USA	17	23	12	6.96	92/72
	2	THREE LEGS OF MAN III	TRIMARAN	NICK KEIG	UK	18	06	04		
	3	JEANS FOSTER	TRIMARAN	PHILIP STEGGALL	USA	18	06	45		
1984	1	UMUPRO JARDIN V	TRIMARAN	YVON FAUCONNIER	FRANCE	16	06	00	7.69	92/64
	2	FLEURY MICHON VI	TRIMARAN	PHILIPPE POUPON	FRANCE	16	12	25		
	3	ELF AQUITAINE II	CATAMARAN	MARC PAJOT	FRANCE	16	12	48		
1988	1	FLEURY MICHON IX	TRIMARAN	PHILIPPE POUPON	FRANCE	10	09	15	11.23	95/72
	2	LAITERIE MONT ST MICHEL	TRIMARAN	OLIVIER MOUSSY	FRANCE	11	04	17		
	3	LADA POCH II	TRIMARAN	LOÏC PEYRON	FRANCE	11	09	02		

since 1980. Many of the starters have failed to finish the course – 52 out of 125 in 1976 – even though all entrants are experienced sailors who have completed an arduous qualifying sail offshore in their entered boat before the race, and many have sailed in previous OSTARS and other long-distance races. However, such is the challenge of the OSTAR course that the race retains its position as one of the world's major offshore races.

ROUTE DU RHUM

The major, and first-to-be-organized, French single-handed race, the Route du Rhum, starts in the Brittany port of St. Malo in November – when the weather can be bad and the nights are long – and finishes 3,700 miles away in the French West Indian island of Guadeloupe, which is

where the rum in the title of the race can be found. The first race was run in 1978, a direct result of the length restriction placed by the British organizers on OSTAR.

For the first Route du Rhum race there was no such restriction, but it now stipulates a maximum 25.9-m (85-ft) length. There are large cash prizes for the winners and heavy sponsorship of many competitors, an area of racing sponsorship in which France leads the field.

Owing to the bad weather in the northern latitudes at this time of year, each race has seen many retirements in its early stages, and is a great test for all involved. Two famous French sailors, both with many single-handed and other successes to their name, have been lost in this race, both sailing multihulls. In the first race, the 1972 OSTAR winner, Alain Colas

Olympus Photo *The Canadian helmsman Mike Birch was the first winner of the Route du Rhum race from St. Malo in Brittany to Guadeloupe in the West Indies in this 17.1-m (56-ft) trimaran.*

disappeared without trace from his trimaran *Manureva*, formerly *Pen Duick IV*, while Loïc Caradec was lost when his catamaran *Royale II* capsized in the 1986 race.

The first race was remarkable for the fact that *Kriter V*, a 21.3-m (70-ft) monohull sailed by Michel Malinovski of France, finished only 98 seconds behind the multihull winner *Olympus Photo*. In the second race, the 18.3-m (60-ft) proa *Rosierès* capsized and sank only 20 minutes after the start of the race.

With so many fast multihulls gathered at Guadeloupe, attempts have been made after the race to hold speed trials. Such

ROUTE DU RHUM

	BOAT	TYPE	SKIPPER	NATIONALITY	TIME days hr min	Av. SPEED IN KNOTS	STARTERS
1978	OLYMPUS PHOTO	TRIMARAN	MIKE BIRCH	CANADA	23 06 57	6.2	39
1982	ELF AQUITAINE	TRIMARAN	MARC PAJOT	FRANCE	18 01 38	8.53	55
1986	FLEURY MICHON VIII	TRIMARAN	PHILIPPE POUPON	FRANCE	14 15 57	10.51	33

Royale II *Raced by the French duo of Loïc Caradec and Olivier Déspaigne, this 25.9-m (85-ft) trimaran won the second two-handed transatlantic race in 1986, setting a course record.*

◆◆◆

trials do in fact require complex organization, and despite the trade winds, the speeds made by the big boats over short distances have not looked impressive in comparison to those achieved by boards and those craft which have been specially designed for speed records.

LE TRANSAT EN DOUBLE

First sailed in 1979, this arduous, quadrennial 5,780-mile, two-handed race is run from Lorient in Brittany around Bermuda and back without stopping. The majority of the entrants – 40 in the first race – are sponsored French multihulls near the maximum length limit of 25.9 m (86 ft). The first race was notable in that the second-placed boat – *Paul Ricard II*, helmed by Eric Tabarly and Marc Pajot – finished only five minutes behind the first-placed *Kriter V*, a monohull helmed by

Michel Malinovski and Pierre Lenormand, after 34 days 6 hr 31 min of sailing.

Held again in 1983, 45 multihulls and 9 monohulls entered the race; the winner – the 20.1-m (66-ft) catamaran *Charente Maritime* helmed by Pierre Follenfant and Jean-Francois Fountaine – completed the course in only 22 days 9 hr 1 min, at an average speed of 10.8 knots, setting a course record.

LA BAULE TO DAKAR

Although not strictly a transatlantic race, the two-handed race from La Baule in Brittany to Dakar in Senegal, West Africa takes in much of the eastern Atlantic as it wends its zig-zag way via the north-west coast of Spain, the Azores, Madeira, Las Palmas and the Cape Verde islands, a total of 3,200 miles. First held in 1980 for all types of boat, and then again in 1983, the race had by 1987 become exclusively a multihull event for craft between 15.2 m and 22.9 m (50 ft and 75 ft). Most of the entries are French, for whom this is one of the major, offshore, multihull races. The

best time achieved is by Loïc Peyron and Jacques Delorme in the 22.9-m (75-ft) trimaran *Lada Poch II* in October 1987, which completed the course in 11 days 9 hr 19 min at an average speed of 12.8 knots.

TWO-HANDED TRANSATLANTIC RACE

Like the OSTAR, the two-handed transatlantic race is started at Plymouth by the Royal Western YC and is finished at Newport by the Ida Lewis YC. It takes the same course as OSTAR, and has the same sponsors. The race arose out of opposition in some quarters to the single-handed race on the grounds of safety of the competitors. When OSTAR was fully subscribed in 1980, the two-handed race was announced for 1981. It had the attraction over its single-handed partner of a upper limit of 25.9 m (85 ft) LOA, with a maximum entry of 135 boats.

The first race saw 76 starters and was won by the 19.8-m (65-ft) trimaran *Brittany Ferries*, sailed by the British Chay Blyth and Rob James in 14 days 13 hr 54 min at an average speed of 8.57 knots. Despite the high length limit, most of the entries were below 15 m (50 ft); several teams were husband/wife or man/woman and many of the entrants were competing just for the fun of it.

The second race was held in 1986 when 64 boats entered. It was won by the French pair of Loïc Caradec and Olivier Déspaigne, sailing the 25.9-m (85-ft) trimaran *Royale II* across in 13 days 6 hr 12 min at an average speed of 9.43 knots, and setting a course record.

TWO-HANDED WEST TO EAST

The only eastbound, two-handed, transatlantic race still in existence, the French-organized Quebec, Canada, to St. Malo, Brittany race celebrates the connection between France and its former empire in North America. The first race was held in 1984 and attracted 49 starters. The upper limit of 25.9 m (85 ft) attracts some powerful multihulls. The maxi-rated trimaran *Royale II*, sailed by Loïc Caradec and Olivier Déspaigne, won the first race. In 1988, *Jet Services V* (Serge Madec) won the race in 7 days 21 hr 35 min at an average speed of 15.27 knots.

THE FASTNET RACE

The establishment of the Fastnet Race in 1925 makes it the oldest, regular, ocean-racing event in European waters. Until 1931, it was sailed each summer, but a low number of entries meant that it became a biennial event in odd years from 1933 onwards, with a pause between 1939 and 1947 for the duration of the war. It alternates with the Bermuda Race on which it was modelled, and which in the early days was the only comparable race in the world. Today the Fastnet has to compete with many other similar races across the world, but it is still considered to be one of the world's premier ocean races. Since 1957 its importance has been increased by its inclusion as one of the qualifying races in the Admiral's Cup, the international three-boat team race organized by the Royal Ocean Racing Club from Cowes (see pp 98-101).

The race has its origin in articles written by the author Weston Martyr in the British sailing press. He had competed in two Bermuda Races and remarked in his report concerning the race that there was no British equivalent. Early in 1925, Martyr and a few others got the blessing of the Yacht Racing Association to organize a race started by the Royal Victoria Yacht Club at Ryde, Isle of Wight, leaving the island to starboard, then down the English Channel and out across the open Atlantic to the Fastnet Rock off the south-west coast of Ireland, rounding it to starboard and returning to a finish organized by the Royal Western Yacht Club at Plymouth. There was talk of the race rounding the Tuskar Rock further to the east off County Wexford and almost due north of the Isles of Scilly, but it was decided that there must be 'ocean' in the course, and that it should be closely equal in length to the 630-mile Bermuda Race, at around 600 miles – the Fastnet course is 605 miles in length.

Seven boats, all British, came to the line on 15 August 1925 for what turned out to be a light-weather race. First home, and winner on corrected time, was the 17-m (56-ft) *Jolie Brise*, a one-time gaff-cutter and Le Havre pilot boat converted to a yacht and owned by George Martin. It took no less than 4½ days to reach the Fastnet Rock, rounding it at 19.50 on 19 August.

The turning point: the Fastnet Rock, off Ireland's south-west coast.

The wind increased for the leg back to Plymouth and it finished two days later in a little under 6½ days – a very slow speed by modern standards. Two boats retired, one of them close to the finish line inside Plymouth Sound, owing to light wind and a foul tide; the other four successfully completed the course.

THE COURSE

The route itself is a considerable attraction to many of the entrants, even though some consider that it is not really an ocean race at all, since much of it is along a coast. But that coastline is often inhospitable, with strong tides and a series of headlands and obstacles to sail around. The weather is always unpredictable in the long term and only a little better forecast in the short term, and there is always a good chance of a long beat to windward for much of the course, strangely a condition not always found on many of the world's better-known ocean-racing courses.

The course has varied from the first few races when it started at Ryde and left the Isle of Wight to starboard. In 1935, the race started at Yarmouth on the west of the island and went out past the Needles

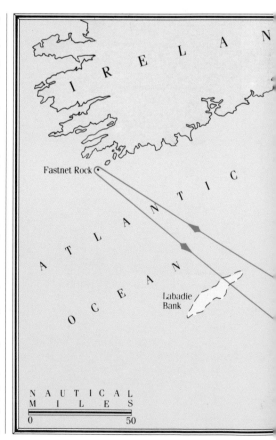

into the English Channel, leaving the island to port. In 1937 and 1939, the start was once again at Ryde, while in 1947, the Royal Navy helped to start the race off Portsmouth, on the mainland facing Ryde, these three races once again leaving the island to starboard. In 1949, the start was finally fixed on the Royal Yacht Squadron's line at Cowes, with the fleet sailing westward down the Solent and out past the Needles, the island on their port side.

On the outward journey to the Fastnet Rock, the Isles of Scilly have always been left to either side. The rock was rounded to starboard in the first race, then either way from 1926 to 1973, and then to port since 1975. On the return journey, the Isles of Scilly must be left to the north, that is to port. The finish line is at the western end of the breakwater at the entrance to Plymouth Sound. The only exception to this was in 1933, when the race finished by sailing back up the English Channel, rounding the Nab Tower and up the Solent to Cowes, a distance of 720 miles.

THE START

The Fastnet Race is started from the long Royal Yacht Squadron line, as used in Cowes Week, which stretches across the main shipping channel in the Solent. There is little discipline on the line, which is crowded with spectator boats and the many other racing crews waiting their turn to start their own races. Once across the line, the fleet usually beats into the prevailing south-west wind down the Solent, the start timed so as to catch the ebb tide. At this stage the fleet is engaged in close tacking to try to stay in the strongest part of the stream. In some years the wind direction is from the east, which causes the start to be a reach or a run, the boats breaking out spinnakers as they cross the line.

The first test after the start comes at the exit from the Solent, where tide and wind conflict in the Needles channel: to the south are the Needles rocks, to the north the dangerous Shingles shoal, on which several boats have grounded. Once clear of this narrow channel, the fleet stands out into the relatively unobstructed waters of the English Channel.

OUTWARD BOUND

Almost alone among ocean races, the Fastnet Race has to negotiate major obstacles – three headlands along the south coast of England. Portland Bill, where the tidal race can run up to seven knots, can be reached from the start line 48 miles away before the tide turns, if the wind is right. Mostly, however, the boats arrive at the headland when the tide is turning against them. They can then either pass well to seaward or try to sail through the narrow stretch of water close in to the end of the Bill and inside the tidal race.

Another 60 miles on, and the exposed headland of Start Point has to be negotiated. Here the tides are less extreme, but in bad weather the seas can be especially rough, leading to many retirements. A further 60 miles on is the Lizard Point, the southernmost point of the British Isles and

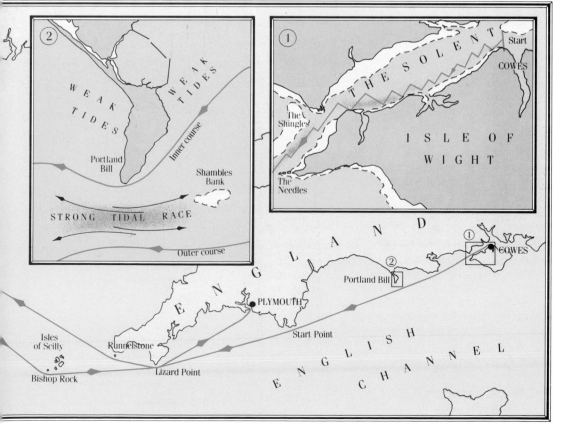

The Course *The 605-mile Fastnet Race course takes the fleet across the start line at Cowes, down the Solent and out into the English Channel. Once around the Lizard Point and the Runnelstone, the boats have a 170-mile leg to the Fastnet Rock, off the south-west coast of Ireland. Rounding it to port, they return and pass to the south of the Bishop Rock and head for the finish at Plymouth.*

On their outward journey to the rock, the fleet encounters several major obstacles, including the Solent itself, Portland Bill, Start Point and Lizard Point.

1 *From Cowes, the fleet sails down the Solent with the ebb tide. If the wind is from the south-west, the boats have to tack constantly to stay in the strongest part of the tide. At the mouth of the Solent, the fleet passes through the narrow channel between the Shingles shoal to the north and the Needles rocks to the south.*

2 *A second major obstacle occurs at Portland Bill. If the tide is against them, the boats have to stay in the weakest part of the tidal flow, sailing either close in under the headland or well out to sea, avoiding the strong tidal race.*

the third obstacle on the course. Its rock-strewn extremity has claimed several competitors trying to keep out of the foul tide, but if the tide is fair, up to five knots can be added to boat speed. As some boats round before the tide turns on these three headlands, and others just miss the same tide, gaps open out in the fleet and advantages are taken which may hold for the rest of the race.

From the Lizard Point, the boats sail 17 miles across Mounts Bay to the Runnelstone, south of Land's End, and then leave behind the sheltered coastline as they sail directly north-west to the Fastnet Rock, a distance of 170 miles in open water. If the wind is west or just north of west, the fleet will be on the wind and will have to tack to reach the rock. The rock stands out clearly from the Irish coast and is easily recognized; slower boats will see the leaders returning after rounding.

HOMEWARD BOUND

The homeward course crosses the Labadie Bank, an underwater shoal over which the sea's depth is reduced from 60 to 35 fathoms (110 to 64 m). This causes the water to become confused and turbulent in heavy weather. Once over this, the fleet continues to the Bishop Rock lighthouse, the south-west extremity of the Isles of Scilly, which it leaves to port. From there it is a straight course back into the English Channel to the Lizard Point, which again can be a tidal gate in light-wind years.

In the days when such hyperbolic aids as Decca or Loran were unavailable to navigators and subsequently forbidden by RORC rules, landfalls were difficult. Approaching the Bishop Rock after the long sail back from Fastnet could be a problem in difficult weather, while the course from the Lizard to Plymouth had few lights at night to guide incoming boats – ships would make for the offshore Eddystone lighthouse and then steer north-east into Plymouth, unlike boats.

There are many tales of risky approaches to Plymouth after a Fastnet Race, for the boats have to round Rame Head and then Penlee Point before crossing the finish line at the western end of the harbor breakwater. Once over the line, the boats sail into the shelter of Plymouth

Sound and into one of the marinas; before these were built, the fleet was accommodated in Millbay Dock, a ship basin.

THE RACE ITSELF

Ever since its inception, the Fastnet Race has been the principal race of the Royal Ocean Racing Club, founded after the first race in 1925 (see p 63). Any person completing the course is eligible to apply for membership of the RORC. Since 1957, crews competing for the Admiral's Cup have sailed the Fastnet as the most important of their qualifying races.

The Start *A 35-knot wind batters the start of the 1985 Fastnet Race as the boats beat down the Solent from the start line at Cowes at the beginning of the 605-mile classic race.*

Boats sailed in the race have varied enormously over the years. The main change is that overall size has gradually reduced. Until 1939, the minimum size was 10.7 m (35 ft) LWL, reduced in 1947 to 9.1 m (30 ft). In 1953 the minimum size was reduced again to 7.3 m (24 ft) LWL, where it remained until the introduction of the IOR for the 1971 race, when the minimum

The 1987 Winner *The Mike Peacock-owned* Juno *won the Fastnet Race in 1987. A member of that year's British Admiral's Cup team, her victory helped the British team into second place.*

◆◆◆

rating became 21ft IOR – in effect a minimum length of about 9.1m (30ft). The maximum stood at 60-ft RORC rating until 1969, when it was increased to 70ft IOR, about 25m (80ft) LOA.

There is no one type of boat suitable for the Fastnet Race, for the weather is so unpredictable on the course as to make all entrants potential winners. Thus the type of boats sailing each year is determined by the rating rule and ocean-racing design in general. The winner can make a name for the designer, although this is now less true with the larger number of comparable races worldwide. In the 32 races to 1987, American designs have won 15 times, 10 with Sparkman and Stephens designs.

RECORDS AND ENTRANTS

As boat speed has increased over the years with lighter boats and faster rigs, Fastnet skippers no longer expect to take the week allowed for by the first entrants in the race. Unless the weather is extreme – either very windy or very calm – the bulk of the fleet takes close to 4½ days at an average speed of about 5½ knots.

The course record was set in 1939 at 3 days 20hr 58min by the 25.9-m (85-ft) German yacht *Nordwind*, and stood until 1965 when Baron Edmund de Rothschild's 27.6-m (90-ft 5-in) *Gitana IV* completed the course in 3 days 9hr 40min. The current record is held by the 24.4-m (80-ft) American yacht *Nirvana*, owned by Marvin Green, which in the 1985 race sailed the course in 2 days 12hr 41min at an average speed of 9.97 knots.

By modern standards the race only engaged a handful of enthusiasts until 1957, the first year in which the Admiral's Cup was sailed. After then the entries increased rapidly until the disastrous race of 1979, when over 300 boats sailed through a Force 12 hurricane (see over). Subsequently there was a drop to 244, caused not only by the caution of competitors but also by the introduction of tighter safety qualifications for entry. By 1987, the fleet was down to 187, the lowest since 1969. However, this decrease has to be considered in the context of far smaller entries for such other major events as the Bermuda and Sydney-Hobart races.

The Fastnet entries are divided into five classes by rating, and there are prizes for places in each class as well as the overall winner, with many additional prizes for boats with different qualifications and nationalities. Those boats competing in the Admiral's Cup also stand to win further cup prizes.

FASTNET WEATHER

Mention the Fastnet Race to anybody on the quayside, and they will associate it with rough weather. Over the years, however, there have been many light-weather races, notably in 1933 and 1937, when some boats took over seven days to finish the course.

As the light-weather performance of boats has improved over the years, overall race times have shortened, but light winds can still cause problems, as they did in the 1969, 1973, 1975, 1977, 1981 and

1987 races. In 1981, all the smaller boats caught up the becalmed fleet ahead of them; the winning boat, *Mordicus*, was the smallest-rated boat in the fleet. In 1987, a similar event occurred, although the fastest boats managed to finish before the last calm set in.

Light weather is more prevalent on the Fastnet Race than on the Bermuda or Sydney-Hobart races, and usually seems to occur along the Cornish coast as the boats approach the finish. Whatever their size, boats bunch up with the tide in the struggle to find wind, which seriously affects the final results.

The reputation for heavy weather and gales arose in the 1930s and was later confirmed by the disastrous race of 1979, when 15 crew lost their lives in storm-force winds. In the early races the boats were poor at beating to windward and tactics were not so well understood as they are now. Boats therefore took large tacks down the English Channel; in contrast a

modern boat will work the tidal changes along the shore, point closer and sail faster. Between 1925 and 1930, this lack of seaworthiness resulted in only 31 of the 61 starters finishing the course. In 1927, strong to gale-force winds blew almost continuously and only 2 of the 14 starters finished. In 1929, there was a blow near the Rock itself; in 1930, a gale lasted for nearly the whole race; while in 1931, one crew member was swept off the stern of a boat in heavy weather on the Labadie Bank and was drowned.

In the post-war years, 1949 saw a severe gale, and the 1951 race started in a gale off Cowes: of the 29 starters, 13 retired. The 1957 race was sailed through

---•••---

Carina *Winner of the Fastnet Race in 1955, the American-owned* Carina *survived the stormy 1957 race to win for the second time. Its skipper, Richard Nye, remarked to the tired crew at the finish, after they had bailed out water the whole way around the course, "OK boys, you can let the damn boat sink!"*

another strong gale for almost its entire duration, and of the 42 starters, only 12 finished. The heavy weather continued in 1961 when a storm center passed over some of the fleet, at first becalming them and then restarting violently with a sudden Force 9 gale.

In many of these gales, boats had been able to retire by taking shelter on the way down the English Channel, but a prime contribution to the 1979 disaster was that the winds had been generally light in the first part of the race. The weather was considered to be 'suspicious', but in modern ocean racing a crew sails on and takes the weather as it comes.

The gale force winds struck the largest fleet ever to start a Fastnet Race, 303 boats, as they were strung out between Land's End and the Fastnet Rock. By the early hours of Tuesday 14 August, 60 hours into the race, a westerly gale had reached velocities of over 64 knots – hurricane Force 12 – and for long periods was blowing at between 48 and 55 knots, Force 10. The seas were very steep and breaking, more so after the wind veered from south-south-west to north of west and was at an angle to the breaking waves. Ted Turner, the eventual race winner in his 16.8-m (55-ft) sloop *Tenacious*, said that he had never seen such seas, despite sailing thousands of miles in many waters of the world. The worst seas were before daybreak on Tuesday morning; by the afternoon the wind had blown itself out and began to moderate and was down to a steady Force 4 by the evening.

THE LESSONS LEARNED

Certain features of the 1979 storm are prominent, not least the vast rescue operation involving ships, helicopters and aircraft that was mounted to help the numerous boats in distress. Many boats were blown over to the horizontal while a third of the fleet was inverted at least once. Only five boats sank, although 19 others were abandoned and subsequently recovered. Of the 15 people lost, none went down with a boat: most were either swept overboard or died of exposure when their liferafts failed; one was trapped under a capsized boat which later righted itself; and one was lost when climbing on

to a rescue ship. Despite all this, 85 boats completed the course, although only 13 of these were in Classes III, IV and V, that is below about 11.9 m (39 ft) overall length.

A report was commissioned by the Royal Ocean Racing Club and the Royal Yachting Association to consider the events of the race and suggest what steps might be taken to avoid a repetition of the disaster. It was recognized that the light-weather races of the 1970s had generated some complacency in design and fitting out. Certain materials were found to be unsuitable for rudder construction, for example, and personal security harnesses came in for strong criticism, not least because 51 boats had a crew member overboard at least once; in most cases they were quickly recovered.

In order to prevent some of the accidents happening again, the report recommended that liferafts be redesigned, that cabin entrances be lockable from inside or out, and that heavy equipment, such as stoves, anchors and batteries stored below, be fixed securely so that they could not break adrift and cause serious injury. The RORC also took care in future races to check which boats started each race, for it had proved extremely difficult to be sure exactly how many boats were at sea during the 1979 race, and just which ones they were.

After the gales of 1979, 1981 was a light-weather race and 1983 a moderate year, both involving fleets well down in numbers from 1979. Two gales with winds up to 50 knots swept the 1985 race, the first blow being in the English Channel. Sixty per cent of the fleet retired, but no outside assistance was required, except in the case of the maxi-rater *Drum*, owned by the British rock singer Simon LeBon. *Drum*'s keel snapped, causing her to capsize. This occurred near the shore, and although the crew were at first trapped in the hull, naval helicopters and divers rescued all hands.

From 1983, the ban on hyperbolic aids giving an instant position read-out was lifted by the RORC. From then on, every Fastnet boat potentially knew exactly where it was, an invaluable and essential aid in rough weather.

The 1979 winner Tenacious *battling through the storm that struck this Fastnet Race.*

THE FASTNET RACE

	BOAT	OWNER	NATIONALITY	STARTERS
1925	JOLIE BRISE	E.G. MARTIN	UK	7
1926	ILEX	ROYAL ENGINEERS YC	UK	9
1927	TALLY HO	LORD STALBRIDGE	UK	14
1928	NINA	PAUL HAMMOND	USA	12
1929	JOLIE BRISE	ROBERT SOMERSET	UK	10
1930	JOLIE BRISE	ROBERT SOMERSET	UK	9
1931	DORADE	ROD STEPHENS	USA	17
1933	DORADE	ROD & OLIN STEPHENS	USA	6
1935	STORMY WEATHER	P. LE BOUTILLIER	USA	17
1937	ZEEAREND	C. BRUYNZEEL	NETHERLANDS	29
1939	BLOODHOUND	ISAAC BELL	UK	26
1947	MYTH OF MALHAM	J.H. ILLINGWORTH	UK	25
1949	MYTH OF MALHAM	J.H. ILLINGWORTH	UK	29
1951	YEOMAN	OWEN AISHER	UK	29
1953	FAVONA	MICHAEL NEWTON	UK	40
1955	CARINA	RICHARD NYE	USA	47
1957	CARINA	RICHARD NYE	USA	42
1959	ANITRA	S. HANSEN	SWEDEN	58
1961	ZWERVER	W. VAN DER VORM	NETHERLANDS	95
1963	CLARION OF WIGHT	D. BOYER & D. MILLER	UK	98
1965	RABBIT	R.E. CARTER	USA	151
1967	PEN DUICK III	ERIC TABARLY	FRANCE	170
1969	RED ROOSTER	R.E. CARTER	USA	186
1971	RAGAMUFFIN	S. FISCHER	AUSTRALIA	222
1973	SAGA	E. LORENTZEN	BRAZIL	293
1975	GOLDEN DELICIOUS	P. NICHOLSON	UK	288
1977	IMP	DAVE ALLEN	USA	284
1979	TENACIOUS	TED TURNER	USA	303
1981	MORDICUS	C. CAILLÈRE	BELGIUM	244
1983	CONDOR	BOB BELL	BERMUDA	222
1985	PANDA	PETER WHIPP	UK	243
1987	JUNO	MIKE PEACOCK	UK	187

THE ADMIRAL'S CUP

The Admiral's Cup is pre-eminent among ocean racing fixtures for three main reasons. First, when established in 1957, it was the first of the now widely imitated inshore-offshore type series for national three-boat teams. Second, it contains the Fastnet Race – one of the world's premier ocean races – as a qualifying event (see pp 92-7). Third, the combination of the Fastnet Race with five other races, a mixture of inshore and offshore events, constitute a varied and challenging series of races for all the competitors.

Between 1977 and 1987, the Admiral's Cup consisted of five races. These were the 200-mile Channel Race across the English Channel and back to Cowes, the home port of the cup; two Olympic courses in the open waters of nearby Christchurch Bay, where tides are weak and courses can be set away from the influences of the shoreline; a third inshore race around buoys in the Solent; and the concluding Fastnet Race. From 1989 a further 40-mile inshore race, in the eastern Solent, was added, giving a total of six races. With inspections before the racing, crews need to devote three weeks to the event. In practice they come to Cowes earlier and sail a number of races to familiarize themselves with the local conditions.

The series is run with exemplary efficiency by the Royal Ocean Racing Club and takes place between mid-July and mid-August each odd-numbered year.

Competitors cross the start line at the beginning of the fourth race of the 1987 Admiral's Cup.

The Admiral's Cup

ORIGINS

Since *America* came to the Solent in 1851 for the first America's Cup race, there has been a long tradition of American boats competing against the best the British could offer in their home waters. American boats had won five of the pre-war Fastnet races and had made a considerable impact on British sailboat racing.

In order to attract renewed American interest in racing in British waters after the enforced pause of the war years, a group of British sailors recommended in 1951, the centenary of the first America's Cup race, that King George VI present a new cup to attract American sailors to visit Cowes. The Britannia Cup was to be sailed for on the Tuesday of Cowes Week, the annual weekly regatta held at Cowes in early August (see pp172-3). The New York Yacht Club joined in by presenting an equally important trophy – the New York Yacht Club Cup – to be sailed for on the Thursday. Both cups are perpetual rather than challenge cups, and return to Cowes each year to be competed for again.

However, some leading members of the RORC went further, for to them ocean racing, rather than inshore racing, was the more worthwhile event. In 1956 Sir Myles Wyatt, Admiral of the RORC, John Illingworth, twice Fastnet winner and originator of the Sydney-Hobart Race, with Peter

Green, Geoffrey Pattison and Selwyn Slater, all keen offshore racers, announced the inauguration of the Admiral's Cup. This cup would be competed for biennially in odd-numbered years between three-boat teams from Britain and America. A simple points system would decide the winning team using the Fastnet Race, the Channel Race, the Britannia Cup and the New York Yacht Club Cup as qualifying events. All boats were to be between 9.1m and 18.3m (30ft and 60ft) LWL.

The first series, held in July and August 1957, took place between the American team of *Carina II*, *Figaro* and *White Mist* and the British team of *Jocasta*, *Myth of Malham* and *Uomie*, owned respectively by four of the donors of the new cup, Illingworth and Green, Pattison, and Slater.

It was customary in those days for British navigators to sail on foreign boats, a job Francis Chichester did on *Figaro*. However *Figaro* failed to arrive in time for the Channel Race and the American team was put at a big disadvantage. Balance was restored by the retirement of the British *Uomie* from the heavy-weather Fastnet Race. The eventual result was very close, with the British eventually winning by only two points.

In 1959 no American boats were available, so their representatives agreed that other nations might compete for the cup. Dutch and French teams were therefore invited, with the British team beating the Dutch into second place with the French team third. In 1961 the Americans returned and won the cup against British, Dutch, French and Swedish teams. The international standing of the Admiral's Cup was now confirmed.

EVOLUTION OF THE CUP

Between 1957 and the present day, ocean racing has undergone a considerable technological revolution and international competition has become far more intense. These changes have been particularly apparent in the Admiral's Cup. The format of the cup races has also changed, for as the cup has become more competitive, and entries increased, races for Admiral's Cup boats have been separated from Cowes Week races, in which many other boats would join the cup fleet.

1959: Regulations are tightened up for safety and equipment. Before this the rules merely stated that "it is contrary to the spirit of ocean racing to save weight by sailing without equipment normally carried while cruising."

1963: British owners begin to order designs specifically for the cup races from the distinguished New York design firm of Sparkman and Stephens. *Clarion* is the first such boat.

1965: The first Australian team arrives; they win at their second attempt in 1967.

1969: For the first time an American boat, *Red Rooster*, owned and designed by Dick Carter, is designed to the RORC rule rather than to rules in use in the US. It is involved in a controversy over its finishing time in the Fastnet Race, which was then timed by a lighthouse watchman at Plymouth. Thereafter the RORC puts its own timekeepers on duty. For the first time the cup entry reaches double figures – 11 teams – and stays there.

1971: The IOR is used for the first time for rating the boats. Since this rule has also been adopted for use in America, American owners are now much happier to build to the rating rule of the races. International rules for safety and equipment are introduced for the first time.

1973: For the first time, a non-English speaking team – Germany – wins the cup. All three of the boats are American-designed, two by Sparkman and Stephens, one by Dick Carter. After the races, one of the team, *Saudade*, a 13.1-m (43-ft) boat rating at only 34.6 ft, is remeasured when under new ownership and found to rate much higher. The rating limits for all competing boats are now between 29 ft and 45 ft IOR. The Britannia Cup and NYYC Cup Races are replaced as qualifying races by two inshore races, exclusive to Admiral's Cup boats, held in the Solent on the first Monday and Wednesday of the competition. Thus the Admiral's Cup is divorced from Cowes Week races.

1975, 1977, 1979: Nineteen teams take part, the highest number ever. The numbers decline slightly in the 1980s.

1977: A third inshore race is added to the

Irish Independent *Sponsored by a national newspaper,* Irish Independent *was a member of the 1987 Irish Admiral's Cup team. It had the best performance of any of the Admiral's Cup boats in the Fastnet Race that year, but as a sponsored boat was ineligible to win the race itself.*

Beating to Windward Diva, *a member of the winning German team, beats to windward at the start of the 1985 Fastnet Race, one of the qualifying races in the Admiral's Cup. In windy conditions such as these, the crew have to balance the boat when sailing upwind by sitting on the windward side, often for hours at a time. All the Admiral's Cup races, both the short inshore and long offshore races, include long windward legs.*

series to take place before the crowded Cowes Week begins. Admiral's Cup boats now have their own starts in the Channel and Fastnet races. The rating band is narrowed to between 30ft and 42ft IOR.

1979: The popularity of Sparkman and Stephens-designed boats begins to wane. Twenty boats are designed by Doug Peterson (US) and 16 by Ron Holland (NZ). In the disastrous Fastnet Race, only 42 out of the 57 cup boats finish. Australia wins in these extreme conditions.

1981: One third of the starters rate under 31ft IOR because they reckon the advantage lies with the smaller boats. Britain wins by a substantial margin for the 8th (and to date final) time in 16 events. One of the British team, *Victory*, owned by Peter

de Savary, is later involved in a rating scandal when its rating rises by 1.4ft. However, this would not have affected the overall British result. Two boats are disqualified for not carrying the required number of their own nationals.

1983: It is announced that from 1984 the level rating for the One Ton Cup is to be 30.5ft IOR. This means that Admiral's Cup boats and One Ton boats now become roughly synonymous. This brings about a considerable increase in competitive pressure as more boats are designed to sail in both events.

1985: The rating band is narrowed to between 30ft and 40ft IOR. Admiral's Cup crews are obliged to report their positions in the Fastnet Race by radio to help with media coverage of the race.

1987: One Austrian boat is disqualified for gross infringement of the rules by moving water ballast while racing. The British team is also accused of irregularities, but is cleared after a lengthy formal inquiry.

1989: A fourth inshore race of 40 miles, sailed in the eastern Solent, is added to the series.

THE CUP TODAY

The Admiral's Cup has developed considerably from the first race in 1957 when six boats in two teams lined up at the start. Today's Admiral's Cup usually has between 10 and 18 national teams, made up of the finest and fastest boats afloat. A fully equipped media center serves accredited journalists, while TV and video companies film the entire proceedings. The Admiral's Cup is one of the world's major ocean racing events, and has been organized to perfection by the RORC.

To obviate the possibility of rating scandals, boats report four days before the first race and are scrupulously measured and rechecked. To avoid the three-boat team all being at the smallest and favored end of the rating band, the total ratings must add up to at least 95ft; in effect this means that there can be two small boats rating around 30.5ft, but the third must rate at about 35ft, giving each team at least one big boat.

As costs rise for new boats, pricing them out of the reach of all but a very few rich individuals, sponsors are becoming

more involved in the financing of individual boats and teams. In 1987, the Australian team sailed in three boats named *Swan Premium I, II* and *III* respectively, while it is reputed that one of the British team's boats had incurred a bill of just over £1m ($1.7m) for planning, design, building, fitting out, buying extra equipment, sailing early trials abroad, hiring and paying a crew and campaigning. The growth of sponsorship and advertising is permitted but carefully regulated. The event itself has for a number of years been sponsored by the French champagne company G.H. Mumm & Co, giving the series the title of the Champagne Mumm Admiral's Cup.

THE ADMIRAL'S CUP

	1st	2nd	3rd	No. OF TEAMS
1957	UK	USA	—	2
1959	UK	NETHERLANDS	FRANCE	3
1961	USA	UK	NETHERLANDS	5
1963	UK	USA	SWEDEN	6
1965	UK	AUSTRALIA	NETHERLANDS	8
1967	AUSTRALIA	UK	USA	9
1969	USA	AUSTRALIA	UK	11
1971	UK	USA	AUSTRALIA	17
1973	GERMANY	AUSTRALIA	UK	16
1975	UK	GERMANY	USA	19
1977	UK	USA	HONG KONG	19
1979	AUSTRALIA	USA	= HONG KONG/ITALY	19
1981	UK	USA	GERMANY	16
1983	GERMANY	ITALY	USA	15
1985	GERMANY	UK	NZ	18
1987	NZ	UK	AUSTRALIA	14

WORLD CHAMPIONSHIPS

There are no true world championships in ocean racing, but various awards have been offered internationally.

In 1968 the St. Petersburg Yacht Club, Florida, nominated 18 established, international races over a three-year period in which a boat had to enter seven to qualify. The first series was won in 1972 by *American Eagle*, owned by Ted Turner, the second in 1975 by *Aura*, owned by Wally Stenhouse, the third in 1978 by *Kialoa III*, owned by Jim Kilroy.

The format was then changed to the best three out of five races over a two-year period: the Bermuda, Fastnet, St. Petersburg-Fort Lauderdale, Sydney-Hobart and Transpac races. The winner in 1980 was *Acadia*, owned by Burt Keenan. With the addition of the Round Hawaii Race, *Scaramouche*, owned by Chuck Kirsch won the 1982 series.

In 1981 a different type of award was introduced, for national teams of three boats between 30ft and 40ft IOR. The Champagne Mumm World Cup is competed for over three years; the qualifying events are the Southern Cross series in the first year, the Kenwood Cup and the Sardinia Cup in the second, and the SORC and the Admiral's Cup in the third. Teams must enter three events to qualify. The 1981-3 championship was won by the USA, the 1983-5 by New Zealand, and the 1985-7 by Britain and New Zealand.

RACES AROUND THE BRITISH ISLES

A voyage around the British Isles has always had an enormous appeal to British sailors, and in recent years various races have taken place. It is possible to sail around England, Wales and southern Scotland only by passing through the Caledonian Canal that bisects Scotland, thus avoiding the wilder Atlantic coast of the west of Scotland. For racing however, the preferred route is outside all the islands of Great Britain and Ireland, a distance of about 1,900 miles, depending on exactly which of the more outlying islands are rounded.

In 1887, the year of Queen Victoria's Golden Jubilee, the Royal Thames Yacht Club announced a £1,000 prize for a race around Britain and Ireland, starting at Southend in the Thames Estuary. Eleven yachts entered, all very large in the manner of the time, ranging from the 255-ton schooner *Selene* down to the 40-ton cutter *Sleuthound*. The Prince of Wales entered his 191-ton schooner *Aline*, although he did not actually sail on it, restricting himself to firing the starting gun on 14 June. The yachts went up the east coast of Britain and around Britain and Ireland in an anti-clockwise direction. Five retired, five finished on 27 and 28 June, and one finished a few days later after being becalmed. The winner was Sir Richard Sutton's 80-ton cutter *Genesta*, the 1885 challenger for the America's Cup.

TWO-HANDED RACING

Despite the success of the 1887 race, it was not repeated, and no further races around the British Isles were attempted until the 1960s. Then, following the success of the OSTAR single-handed transatlantic races in 1960 and 1964, Blondie Hasler, their instigator, suggested a new race to be run around Britain and Ireland, with a crew of two on each boat.

The first such race was held in 1966, with succeeding races every four years until 1982, then a three-year gap to 1985

with the next race reverting to a four-year cycle in 1989. The winner is the first boat to finish, and as there are no rating rules, the race is usually won by a multihull. Entrants are limited to a maximum 25.9 m (85 ft), a minimum 7.6 m (25 ft) LOA. Within these limits there are seven classes by size, so there are plenty of prizes for the smaller boats.

The race, organized by the Royal Western Yacht Club of England – the same club that organizes the transatlantic races – starts and finishes at Plymouth. The course goes clockwise around Ireland and Britain, with compulsory stops at the end of each leg. The first leg to Crosshaven in Ireland is 230 miles long, the second to Castlebay in the Outer Hebrides is 460 miles, the third rounding St. Kilda to Lerwick in the Shetland Isles is 420 miles, the third to Lowestoft in East Anglia, the easternmost port in England, is 470 miles,

---

Around Britain Races *There are two main races around the British Isles:*
1 *The two-handed race starting and finishing at Plymouth, held every four years from 1966 to 1982, and then again in 1985.*
2 *The fully crewed British Islands Race starting and finishing in the Solent, held in 1976 and 1980.*

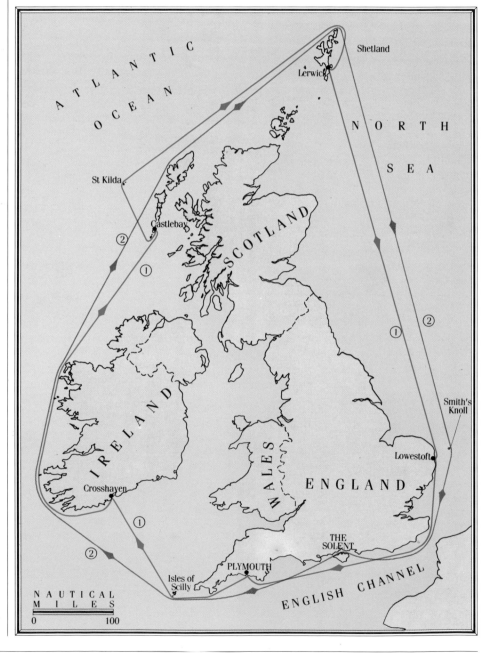

while the homeward leg back to Plymouth is 305 miles. The boats must stop for 48 hours at each port and then leave; the leaders arrive back at Plymouth many days before the smallest boats. Self-steering devices can be used, and crews are allowed 'muscle power': there are instances of boats being rowed for long periods in a calm, a practice outlawed in ordinary racing.

Although there are now a number of two-handed races, including such short-distance courses as an annual race around the Isle of Wight, the two-handed race around Britain and Ireland was for a long time the only one of its type. The first race in 1966 had 16 starters, and was won by the 12.8-m (42-ft) trimaran *Toria*, designed and sailed by Derek Kelsall with Martin Minter-Kemp, in a time of 11 days 17 hr 23 min. By 1982 that time had been reduced to 8 days 15 hr 3 min, an average speed of 9.4 knots, by the winning tri-maran *Colt Cars GB*. As the numbers rose to a record entry of 100 boats in 1982, a limit of 100 entries was introduced for future events. Many of the smaller boats take part merely to complete the circum-navigation, without any chance of winning.

Apricot, the winner of the 1985 two-handed race around Britain and Ireland.

TWO-HANDED AROUND BRITAIN AND IRELAND RACE

	BOAT	TYPE	CREW	TIME days	hr	min	ENTRANTS
1966	TORIA	TRIMARAN	DEREK KELSALL & MARTIN MINTER-KEMP	11	17	23	16
1970	OCEAN SPIRIT	MONOHULL	ROBIN KNOX-JOHNSTON & LESLIE WILLIAMS	12	08	10	25
1974	BRITISH OXYGEN	CATAMARAN	ROBIN KNOX-JOHNSTON & GERRY BOXALL	10	04	26	61
1978	GREAT BRITAIN IV	TRIMARAN	CHAY BLYTH & ROB JAMES	9	07	33	74
1982	COLT CARS GB	TRIMARAN	ROB JAMES & NAOMI JAMES	8	15	03	100
1985	APRICOT	TRIMARAN	TONY BULLIMORE & NIGEL IRENS	9	07	33	74

FULLY CREWED RACES

In June 1976, the RORC ran a fully crewed race which it called the British Islands Race. The race gave the entrants the option of stopping or sailing the course non-stop. This meant that entries in each section were modest, and conditions quite different for various boats. The race began in the Solent, then clockwise to Crookhaven in Ireland, inside St. Kilda to Stornoway in the Outer Hebrides, around the Shetland Islands to Blyth in Northumberland, and back to the finish at the Nab tower in the Solent. As with the two-handed race, those in the stopping race had to stop in each port for 48 hours.

Whereas the non-stop race had 25 entries, only eight boats entered the stopping race, which was not a great success. As a result, the 1980 race was non-stop for all competitors, starting and finishing in the Solent with a clockwise course around the west of Ireland, inside St. Kilda's, around the Shetland Islands and outside Smith's Knoll light vessel in the North Sea. The course record is held by the 1976 non-stop winner, *More Opposition*, skippered by Robin Knox-Johnston, who completed the course in 11 days 8 hr 43 min at an average speed of 6.8 knots.

THE BRITISH ISLANDS RACE

	BOAT	TYPE	HELM	ENTRANTS
1976 non-stop	MORE OPPOSITION	MONOHULL	ROBIN KNOX-JOHNSTON (UK)	25
1976 stopping	ELECTRON II	MONOHULL	ROYAL NAVY (UK)	8
1980	CHICA TICA II	MONOHULL	C.M. BALESTRA (ITALY)	13

BRITAIN

The British racing calendar is largely condensed into the period between the beginning of May and the end of September. Outside of these months, the nights become long and the possibility of severe gales, persistent fog, and cold conditions with very cold water, make organized racing inadvisable. Short-duration races close to shore are however possible from October to December on days when conditions are amenable.

Within these five summer months a large number of races occur. They vary from long, day events, perhaps taking as little as 5 hours or as much as 12, depending on the weather and the course set, to 'holiday' races taking four or five days. There are also the occasional 'specials', like the fully crewed British Islands Race. Probably the best supported, however, are the 'overnight' events, which cover a mileage of about 100 miles at an average speed of 5 knots, therefore lasting 20 hours or so. If the race starts on a Friday evening, it can end in a port across the English Channel, the North Sea or the Irish Sea early the next afternoon, allowing for time ashore and a leisurely sail back during the weekend.

It will be seen that clubs join together in suitable regions to run an offshore series over several months; because of the concentration of boats and clubs, the central south coast of England has a somewhat different organization. The Royal Ocean Racing Club, the Junior Offshore Group and local clubs' coordinate their program through the Solent Cruising and Racing Association. In this area there is sometimes an embarrassment of clashing fixtures for a given class of boat, both offshore and inshore; the result is that the numbers of starters in these races varies considerably from year to year. For the offshore racer, the RORC runs a series of distance races (see table), the JOG runs races of the same style but for smaller boats and of a shorter duration, and individual clubs run their own program of regular day or overnight events. All such events are open to all comers and not restricted to club members.

Most British races return to their starting base, but some finish in another, often foreign, port, allowing time for the boats to return home at the end of the race. A typical course from a south-coast port will take the fleet across the Channel to a French port. In most regions these races will have been organized by one of ten associations or clubs; the Royal Ocean Racing Club organizes races across the whole country, while the other nine are regional in coverage. The most popular areas in which offshore racers are based, and in which most racing therefore takes place, are the South Coast, East Anglia and the Thames Estuary to the east of the country, and the Clyde Estuary on the west coast of Scotland.

RORC RACES

The main organizing body of offshore races in Britain is the Royal Ocean Racing Club. As well as the Fastnet Race, the Admiral's Cup and the British Islands Race, the RORC organizes a regular series of weekend and longer races, most of which sail out of south-coast ports. Frequently held in collaboration with the local clubs, these races are usually over 200 miles or more, the intention being to leave shorter courses to other clubs.

The main RORC races are the North Sea Race, invariably held early in the year, between Harwich and a Dutch port such as Scheveningen; the Irish Sea Race from a Welsh port like Abersoch or Pwllheli to Howth or Dun Laoghaire near Dublin; the Blue Water Trophy, starting in the Clyde and finishing anywhere from Brittany to the Orkneys; the Morgan Cup Race, a midsummer race in the Channel, usually from the Solent round a buoy in Torbay and back; the Cowes to St. Malo, Brittany, Race, held at the beginning of the French holiday period in early July and thus

BRITISH OFFSHORE RACING ORGANIZATIONS

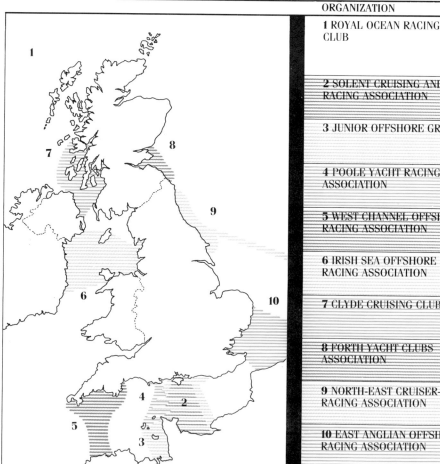

	ORGANIZATION
	1 ROYAL OCEAN RACING CLUB
	2 SOLENT CRUISING AND RACING ASSOCIATION
	3 JUNIOR OFFSHORE GROUP
	4 POOLE YACHT RACING ASSOCIATION
	5 WEST CHANNEL OFFSHORE RACING ASSOCIATION
	6 IRISH SEA OFFSHORE RACING ASSOCIATION
	7 CLYDE CRUISING CLUB
	8 FORTH YACHT CLUBS ASSOCIATION
	9 NORTH-EAST CRUISER-RACING ASSOCIATION
	10 EAST ANGLIAN OFFSHORE RACING ASSOCIATION

attracting a large entry; and the Channel Race, held on the first weekend of Cowes Week in early August. In recent years the course for this race has varied considerably, although for many years it was a 225-mile triangle between the English and French coasts. It was first sailed in 1928 as a race for those boats which were ineligible to enter the Fastnet Race because of their small size.

In addition to those races, the RORC also organizes a series of 'holiday' races from south-coast ports to la Trinité-sur-Mer or La Rochelle in France, Cork in Ireland or Bayona in Spain, among other places, and three or more triangular courses in the English Channel, starting and finishing in the Solent.

Each year, continuity is provided in the RORC races by awarding points to find seasonal champions in each class, and also a boat of the year, arrived at by using a formula involving points and corrected time in races. The interest of other clubs in RORC races is maintained by competing boats nominating, at the beginning of the year, a club (other than the RORC itself) to which their points are allocated. A club trophy – the Martin Illingworth Trophy – is awarded to the club with the best points.

JUNIOR OFFSHORE GROUP

Created in 1950 when the RORC specified a minimum of 24 ft (7.3 m) LWL for its races, the Junior Offshore Group existed to run similar but shorter races to those of the RORC for boats of between 4.9 m and 7.3 m (16 ft and 24 ft) LWL, using the-then RORC rating rule. Not very well supported at the outset, it grew in popularity during the 1970s with the rise of the Half Ton and smaller Ton Cups, and is now strongly supported on the south coast of England where it holds some 14 races a year – varying in length from 35 to 150 miles, with most at about 80 miles. The current JOG rule limits entries to boats rating from 16 ft to 28 ft IOR (boats between roughly 6 m and 12 m, 20 ft and 40 ft LOA).

SOUTH COAST

The south coast of England is the most popular sailing area in Britain; it is well-served by natural harbors and river estuaries, all within easy reach of London and other major cities in the region. As well as the RORC and JOG, the Solent Cruising and Racing Association, the Poole Yacht Racing Association and the West Channel Offshore Racing Association each organizes a regular series of races, in addition to the many individual clubs that hold races. Typical of these is the Cowes to

AREA COVERED	CLASSES ELIGIBLE	TYPE OF PROGRAM	MAIN EVENTS	Av. STARTERS
Britain and overseas	IOR; CHS; level rating; OODS	18 races, mostly over 200 miles	Admiral's Cup; Blue Water Trophy; British Islands Race; Channel Race; Cowes-St. Malo Race; Fastnet Race; Irish Sea Race; Morgan Cup Race; North Sea Race.	60
Solent outwards and across the Channel	IOR; CHS; OODS	More than 50 events by 20 clubs	Round-The-Island Race	—
English Channel	IOR rated 16-28 ft; CHS below 10.4 m (34 ft) LWL	14 races, 35-166 miles	—	40
Solent to Weymouth and across the Channel	Local handicap – 3 divisions	6 races, coastal and offshore	Poole-St. Vaast Race	30
The Exe to Lands End	IOR; CHS	15 races by 8 clubs	Tops'l Trophy	35
North-west England, Wales, Isle of Man and Ireland, east and south	IOR; level rating	7 races, including 1 with RORC	ISORA Race Week	40
Clyde Estuary, west of Scotland and north Irish Sea	Local CCC handicap; CHS; OODS	20 offshore and passage races	Scottish Week	50
Forth Estuary from Tay to Holy Isle	Portsmouth yardstick	4 coastal races	Bell Rock Race	10
Amble to Bridlington	Local handicap – 3 divisions; level rating	10 coastal races	North Sea-Netherlands Race	40
Lowestoft to Ramsgate and North Sea	IOR; CHS	13 to 15 races, average 50 miles	East Anglian Week	30

Around the Island *The annual race around the Isle of Wight has for more than 50 years attracted the biggest number of starters in any British race. Here the fleet rounds the distinctive landmark of the Needles on the western end of the island.*

◆◆◆

Deauville Race, held annually every spring on a public holiday without interruption since 1965, and organized jointly by the JOG and the Royal Southern, Royal London and Deauville Yacht Clubs. It usually attracts about 130 starters, British and French.

The most popular race in the region, and the one that draws the greatest number of starters each year in Britain, is the Round-The-Island Race, run by the Island Sailing Club of Cowes. All classes of cruiser-racer and multihull, and some day-racers, can enter. The course is 50 miles around the Isle of Wight, starting and finishing at Cowes and leaving the island to port. First held in 1931, it soon became the best-supported race in Europe, attracting 80 entries in 1939, which at that time was a record for any race held in Europe. The number of starters has continued to increase, reaching a peak in 1988, when 1,536 boats came to the line.

EAST ANGLIA

The buoyage and marks of the southern North Sea and the Thames Estuary provide plenty of marks for racing from the ports of East Anglia. Each club in the East Anglian Offshore Racing Association holds one or more races each season. As the average length of these races is 50 miles, this means that they can be completed in daylight. There are also some longer courses held overnight, some finishing in the Netherlands.

Traditionally the East Anglian coast has been a breeding ground for the most skilled sailors in Britain; once men from here were fishermen in the winter months and professional hands on the big cutters – the J-class boats and their predecessors – in the summer. Then the region was a center for the first RORC boats built by some of the best builders of wooden yachts in the country, and it remains today an area of first-class offshore racing. At the end of each season, around the end of August, all sizes of boats – from ocean racers down to small dinghies – meet at Burnham-on-Crouch for a week's inshore racing, the Burnham Week.

SCOTLAND

In northern waters, around 56° north, the summer is shorter but the days are longer. This means that most races in this region are held in June and July. The scenery is among the most impressive in the British Isles; deep inlets give much protected water, often welcome in the rapidly changeable weather. Long periods of settled weather with high pressure also occur at times during the summer months.

The Clyde Cruising Club, despite its name, organizes up to 20 races each year,

Racing in the Clyde *About 20 races a year are organized by the Clyde Cruising Club in and around the Clyde Estuary in the west of Scotland. An average of 50 boats compete in each race, held in some of the most dramatically beautiful scenery in the entire British Isles.*

◆◆◆

varying from 10 or so miles – in effect short races before rallies or 'musters' – to longer offshore races of 200 miles or more. Such races are the 85-mile Inverkip in the Clyde Estuary to Belfast Lough in Ireland; Inverkip around the Isle of Mull in the Inner Hebrides to Crinan on the west coast, a distance of 110 miles; and feeder races to Tobermory on Mull for a major meet. Scottish Week is held at Tarbert in the Clyde Estuary at the end of May, with feeder races from Gourock in the Upper Clyde (130 miles), Dun Laoghaire in Ireland (170 miles) and Bangor in North Wales (100 miles), followed by short off-shore and Olympic course races. The CCC has its own handicap system that it uses in addition to the IOR system.

THREE PEAKS RACE

Devised by the mountaineer and sailor, Bill Tilman, this unique race was first held in 1977 and has been organized annually ever since. It is one of the strangest races in the world, for it involves stops at three ports on the west coast of Britain, at each of which two members of the crew ascend a nearby mountain and then return to the boat before recommencing the race. The ports tend to be shallow, drying out at low tide; for this reason multihulls or other shallow-draft craft are favored.

After starting at Barmouth in mid-Wales, the entrants sail 62 miles to Caernarfon, from where Snowdon – Wales' highest mountain at 1,085 m (3,560 ft) – is scaled in a 39-km (24-mile) round-trip. From Barmouth the boats sail 92 miles to Ravenglass, from where Scafell Pike, at 978 m (3,210 ft) England's highest hill, is climbed, involving a journey of 51 km (32 miles). The final leg is 235 miles to Fort William in Scotland. Once in port, two crew members set off on the 28-km (17½-mile) round-trip to Ben Nevis – at 1,343 m (4,406 ft), Scotland's and Britain's highest mountain. The first crew back from this climb wins the race.

◆◆◆

The Three Peaks Race *The combination of sailing and mountain climbing (shown on the map to the right) attracts crews from such organizations as the Royal Marines, the police and other public services. Below are two competitors running for the winning line in Fort William, Scotland.*

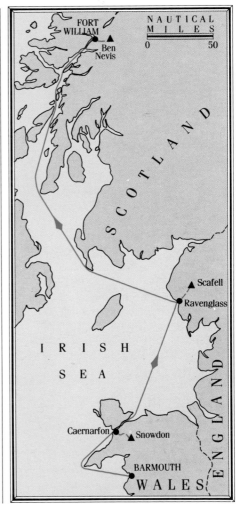

WESTERN EUROPE

As well as numerous short-distance races organized from ports in Britain, France, Ireland, Portugal and Spain, there exist a number of long-distance races of an arduous nature. The most famous of these – the Fastnet and the two around-Britain races – have already been covered on preceding pages, as have the numerous, shorter offshore races from Britain.

AZORES AND BACK RACE

Known as the AZAB, this race follows a 1,300-mile course from Falmouth in the south-west of Britain to Ponta Delgada in the Azores, returning via the same route after a 10-day break, making a total voyage of 2,600 miles. Although the boats sail towards the weather pattern known as the 'Azores High', there is the likelihood of gale-force winds from the Atlantic at some stage of the course. Originally organized for boats below 12 m (40 ft), it now allows boats up to 24 m (80 ft) to enter. As only single-handed or two-handed crews can enter this ocean race, it serves as a training and qualifying run for the single-handed transatlantic race (see pp 86–90) and is thus held in the preceding year to that race, once every four years.

COURSE EN SOLITAIRE DU FIGARO

Known by a variety of names as the sponsors have changed, the single-handed Figaro race has been sailed in the Bay of Biscay since 1970. It is special in that all boats are Half Tonners, with potentially equal speed; obviously such a race can only be run where there are enough boats of the same type, as is the case on the

◆◆◆

Western European Races *Among the major races held in Western European waters are:*
1 The short-handed 2,600-mile Azores and Back Race from Falmouth, England, to Ponta Delgada, Azores, and back, held once every four years.
2 The single-handed Course en Solitaire du Figaro, held annually in the Bay of Biscay.
3 The Tour de France à la Voile, an annual, fully crewed, stopping race around the coast of France, involving the transport of the competitors by land from Arcachon in the Bay of Biscay to Cap d'Agde in the Mediterranean.
4 The Course de l'Europe, a fully crewed multihull race around the west coast of Europe from Scheveningen in the Netherlands, via the north of Scotland and the west of Spain, to San Remo in Italy. The course varies each race.

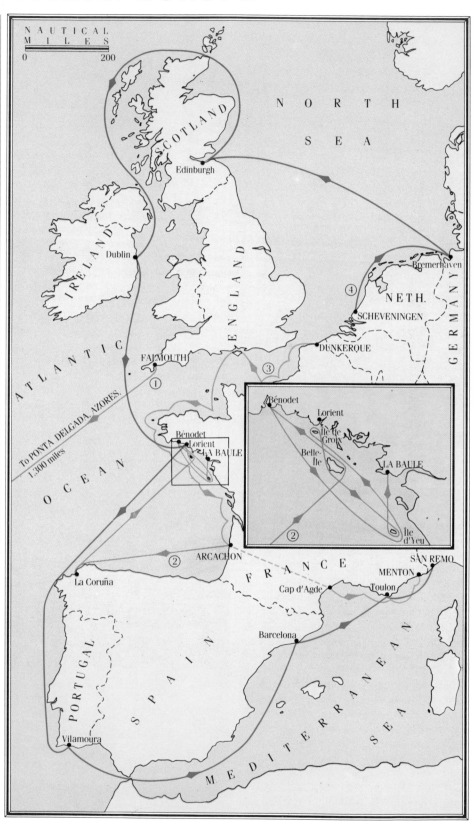

Atlantic coast of France. An average entry of 25 or 30 boats sails a course that varies from year to year. A typical course over 1,110 miles starts at Arcachon in southwest France and goes to La Coruña in Spain, 300 miles away. From there the boats sail 390 miles via Belle Île to Bénodet in Brittany, followed by a figure-of-eight course around Île d'Yeu and Île de Groix to finish at La Baule.

Around France *One of the major features of the annual Tour de France à la Voile is that all the boats in the race are identical, and are all financed by sponsors who advertise themselves on the many flags the boats fly when in port, as well as on their spinnakers. In addition, the sponsors provide a great fair of trailers and displays at each of the many ports visited.*

TOUR DE FRANCE A LA VOILE

The Tour de France is a long-established cycle race around France noted for its high degree of commercialism; its 1,300-mile sailing equivalent is equally commercial, and draws between 30 and 40 fully crewed boats from French coastal towns, from which each boat draws its name. Numerous sponsors finance each entry, and there is no restriction on advertising on spinnakers or on the many flags the boats can fly when in port.

Held each July, the fleet starts at a northern port, often Dunkerque, and then calls at more than 20 towns, which vary each year, with a race between each. At each port a vast fair of displays and exhibits is provided by the many sponsors.

Two features make this race unique. First, the boats are all strict one-design, cruiser-racers of around 11 m (35 ft), thus giving excellent racing; and second, when the boats arrive at Arcachon, the southernmost stop in the Bay of Biscay, all are taken on trucks across to the French Mediterranean coast for the last half-dozen legs of the course from Cap d'Agde eastward to Menton. Entries have been received from California and Britain, but the overwhelming number are French. For the first race in 1978, Ecume de Mer class boats were used, with a new class in 1979 and 1982. Since 1984 the 10.9-m (36-ft) Selection class has been chosen.

COURSE DE L'EUROPE

First held in 1985 and then again in 1987, this 3,500-mile course is for fully crewed multihulls between 18.3 m and 24.4 m (60 ft and 80 ft). In 1987, the race started on 12 July at Scheveningen in the Netherlands, went north to Bremerhaven in Germany, thence to Edinburgh in Scotland, around the north of Scotland and down through the Irish Sea to Dublin in Ireland, south to Lorient in Brittany, Villamoura on the southern coast of Portugal, through the Straits of Gibraltar to Barcelona in Spain, Toulon in France and then to a finish at San Remo in Italy on 15 August. Because the entrants must all be large multihulls, the majority have been French, as have the two winners, *Crédit Agricole II*, helmed by Philippe Jeantôt in 1985, and *Jet Services V* helmed by Daniel Gilard in 1987.

THE MEDITERRANEAN

If the traditional ocean race such as the Bermuda or the Fastnet no longer has the singularity it once possessed in offshore racing – some of its thunder having been stolen by the long-distance, short-handed, heavily sponsored events – more conventional ocean racing crews have found international team series to be increasingly attractive. The Admiral's Cup is the main one of these; its mixture of inshore and offshore races has been emulated by the Southern Cross, the Onion Patch and the various Ton Cups. The Sardinia Cup has adopted this formula too, and is now one of the leading team-race events in the world.

THE SARDINIA CUP

The Sardinia Cup series is based at Porto Cervo on the Costa Smeralda in Sardinia: what was originally just a small fishing haven has now been developed into a major international yacht center with money from a syndicate headed by the Aga

The Sardinia Cup *Many of the races for this biennial international team event take the boats close in to the rocky Sardinian shore.*

Pinta *A member of the winning German team in the Sardinia Cup in 1984.* Pinta *helped the team to second place in 1986. Here it is seen surfing downwind on a spinnaker run.*

Khan. The series began in 1978 with rules taken from the Admiral's Cup; 12 national teams of three boats competed in the first event. The races are held biennially in even years in September, that is alternating with the Admiral's Cup. The weather is usually calm but a Mistral may well bring 48 hours of 40-knot winds.

The series consists of a short offshore race; the 145-mile Asinara Race from Porto Cervo to a mark off the island of Asinara and back; two Olympic-course races of about 25 miles each; a long offshore race through the Straits of Bonifaco between Sardinia and Corsica, then northwest to the Île de Porquerolles near Hyères on the French Riviera, and then back to Porto Cervo, a total distance of about 300 miles; and a final 28-mile coastal race. The Yacht Club Costa Smeralda, which runs the series, is a very expensive, exclusive modern club; a factor which, for top racers, is one of the main attractions of the Sardinia Cup.

THE SARDINIA CUP

	1st	2nd	3rd	No. OF TEAMS
1978	ITALY	USA	BELGIUM	12
1980	USA	ITALY	GERMANY	15
1982	ITALY	USA	BELGIUM	19
1984	GERMANY	ITALY	IRELAND	16
1986	UK	GERMANY	SPAIN	12
1988	GERMANY	ITALY	BAVARIA	7

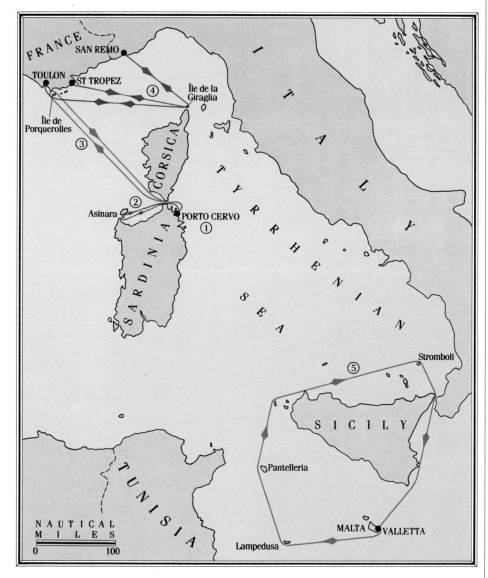

The Mediterranean *The major offshore events in the western Mediterranean are:*
1 The Sardinia Cup, a biennial international team race. Its four inshore races are held off Porto Cervo, on the Costa Smeralda.
2 The 145-mile Asinara Race from Porto Cervo to a mark off the island of Asinara and back, part of the Sardinia Cup.
3 A 300-mile race from Porto Cervo to the Île de

Porquerolles on the French Riviera and back, part of the Sardinia Cup.
4 The Giraglia Race, starting and finishing at either St Tropez, San Remo or Toulon, via Île de la Giraglia off the north coast of Corsica, a distance of about 250 miles.
5 The 612-mile Middle Sea Race, starting and finishing at Valletta in Malta, and circumnavigating Sicily and a number of other islands.

GIRAGLIA RACE

Generally regarded as the Mediterranean equivalent of the Fastnet or the Bermuda race, this lengthy race was first held in 1953 after a meeting attended by leading sailors from France and Italy, with representatives of the Yacht Club de France and Yacht Club Italiano. The organization follows the usual fully crewed, ocean-racing rules of the IOR and the race is held annually in July.

The start and finish vary, being from St Tropez or Toulon in France via Île de la Giraglia off the north of Corsica to San Remo in Italy; in some years this route is reversed. The total length is about 250 miles. The record time for the course is held by the 20-m (66-ft) sloop *Benbow*, owned by S. Recchi of Italy, which completed the course in 27 hr 30 min in 1975. Although an established tradition, this race is less prestigious now because of the multiplicity of offshore sponsored events, in France in particular, and it has failed to attract entries outside France, Italy and other Mediterranean nations.

MIDDLE SEA RACE

Started in 1969 by two Englishmen residing in Malta, Jimmy White and Alan Green (later to be secretary of the RORC), this race takes place in early October, when the offshore season in northwest Europe is over. Partly for that reason, the race has attracted several famous participants, but political problems, notably strikes in the island's boatyards, have made Malta a less than satisfactory venue, and entries have declined since the 1970s. The race is organized by the Valletta Yacht Club with the assistance of the RORC.

It starts in Malta and then heads clockwise around the islands of Lampedusa and Pantelleria with their dramatic, sheer cliffs, along the north side of Sicily to the volcanic island of Stromboli, and thence back through the Straits of Messina – guarded either side by the legendary Scylla and Charybdis – to the home port of Valletta in Malta, a total distance of 612 miles. The course record is held by the 14.9-m (49-ft) American yacht *Aura*, owned by Wally Stenhouse, which completed the course in 89 hr 56 min in 1973 at an average speed of 6.8 knots.

GERMANY AND THE BALTIC

German offshore races are traditionally focused on week-long events, but the majority of German ocean crews have made their name abroad in such events as the Admiral's and Sardinia cups because of the limited and sometimes inhospitable German coastline. However, the Baltic Sea gives scope for a number of interesting courses, and is tideless with many sheltered harbors that provide refuge from the occasionally bad summer weather. A number of races in the region are organized from the various Scandinavian countries. The North Sea is completely different, with an exposed, strongly tidal coastline and difficult seas in the estuaries of the Weser and the Elbe. The island of Helgoland is a tax-free area and is a popular offshore destination away from the outlying sandbanks of the mainland. In the early days of the RORC, annual races were

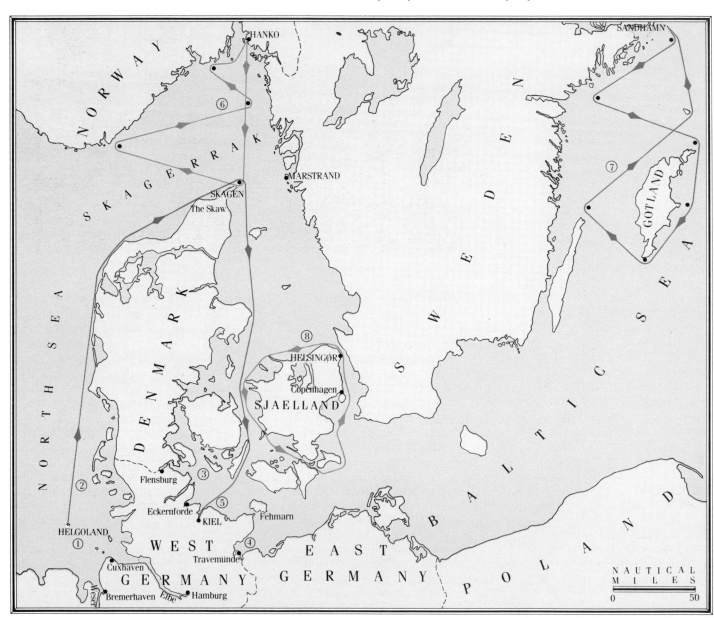

Germany and the Baltic *Among the major races and events sailed on the North German coast and in the Baltic are the following:*
1 *North Sea Week, an annual event of four short offshore races from German ports.*
2 *The biennial, 500-mile Skagen Race, sailed from Helgoland around the north of Denmark to Kiel.*

3 *Flensburg Week, an annual event containing three inshore races and one overnight race of about 100 miles.*
4 *Travemünde Week, an annual event composed of inshore events and a longer, overnight race.*
5 *Kiel Week, an annual event containing both inshore and longer offshore races.*

6 *The annual Skaw Race around the Skagerrak, the 350-mile course changing from year to year.*
7 *The annual Gotland Runt, a 415-mile race from Sandhamn in Sweden around the island of Gotland, off the east coast of Sweden.*
8 *The annual Sjaelland Rundt, a 235-mile race around the Danish island of Sjaelland.*

held to and from Helgoland and the British east-coast port of Burnham.

Every year in May, a North Sea Week is held, making it suitable for Admiral's Cup trials when appropriate. Open to all IOR classes, it is based on Helgoland and was founded in 1922 by clubs from Bremen and Hamburg. During the week, races are held from Hamburg to Cuxhaven (60 miles), Cuxhaven to Helgoland (50 miles), Bremerhaven to Helgoland (50 miles), and a lengthy around-Helgoland race of 60 miles. Every other year, Germany's longest ocean race, the Skagen, takes the fleet 500 miles from Helgoland via Skagen on the northernmost tip of Denmark to the port of Kiel in the Baltic.

GERMAN BALTIC RACES

There are two, well-established, week-long regattas held by German clubs in the Baltic. Flensburg Week in the western Baltic occurs each year in mid-September. Founded in the 1920s by the Flensburger Segel Club, the week includes three inshore events and one overnight race of about 100 miles. Travemünde Week is based in the bay of that name, which is virtually on the border with East Germany. Dating from 1892, the week is mainly for inshore classes, but with an overnight race for IOR and local handicap classes, including Scandicap.

The main regatta in the Baltic is Kiel Week (see pp170-1). It features offshore classes with inshore Olympic-type and triangular courses in Kiel Bay. There are also three offshore races: Kiel to Eckernforde, a port in the next estuary, 40 miles north; a return race from Eckernforde to Kiel; and the 150-mile race from Kiel to the island of Fehmarn.

THE SKAW

Among the many ocean races held each summer in the Baltic, the annual Skaw Race is the most demanding. It is organized by the Royal Danish (KDY), the Royal Norwegian (KNS) and the Royal Gothenburg (GKSS) yacht clubs, and is also listed by the RORC. Each year, one of the three organizing clubs starts the race from either Skagen on the Skaw peninsula of Denmark, from which the race takes its name, Hanko in Norway or Marstrand in

The 1986 Sjaelland Rundt fleet passes under the Farø Bridge.

Sweden. The triangular course takes the boats around the Skagerrak – the stretch of water between the three countries – around the Skagen Rev no. 1 buoy off the Skaw and a number of other marks to give the race its full 350-mile length. The actual route varies according to which club is organizing the race in that year; when the race was first run in 1953, it was only 240 miles long. This race has been run every year except 1955, 1959 and 1961.

GOTLAND RUNT

This annual race often attracts an entry of at least 400 in its circumnavigation of the 70-mile-long island of Gotland off the east coast of Sweden. The race is organized by the Royal Swedish Yacht Club (KSSS) and starts and finishes its 415-mile course at Sandhamn, taking in a number of marks to achieve a figure-of-eight course around Gotland. The course record is held by the 24.4-m (80-ft) *Nirvana*, owned by the American, Marvin Green, which in 1987 completed the course in 52 hr 15 min at an average speed of 7.9 knots.

The Gotland Runt originated in the 1930s, when cruisers and big racers sailed

from Sandhamn to Visby on Gotland. In 1937 and 1939, boats from several countries rounded Gotland, starting and finishing at Visby. Since 1946 the race has been run annually, and the course has varied several times, as have the rating rules used; by the late 1980s, the fleet consisted of those rated IOR and those on Danish Handicap, DH, a system widely used in Norway and Sweden as well as Denmark.

SJAELLAND RUNDT

This annual race was first started in 1947 by the Helsingør Amateur Sailing Club, although informal races round Sjaelland had been run in 1893, 1926 and 1935. Not quite an offshore race, this counterclockwise course around the principal island of Denmark, on which Copenhagen is situated, attracts all kinds of boats from ocean racers to daysailers. The distance is about 235 miles, and the main feature of the race is the sheer number of competitors it attracts. On 21 June 1984, 2,072 boats started at Helsingør – the largest number of starters for any race in the world. Entries throughout the 1980s have varied between 1,500 and 1,800 each year.

THE SYDNEY-HOBART RACE

Since its inception in 1945, the Sydney-Hobart Race has become Australia's most important ocean race and, along with the Bermuda and Fastnet races, one of the three major offshore races in the world. It has been sailed every year since 1945 and has grown in size from nine entrants to well over 100 in the late-1970s – a record 212 boats crossed the start line in 1985. Despite competition from similar events elsewhere, this classic offshore race has maintained its pre-eminent status in world ocean racing.

The race was originated by Captain John Illingworth RN, who had raced successfully in Britain in the late 1930s. He found himself in 1945, at the conclusion of the war in the Pacific, dismantling a naval base built for the British in New South Wales. He bought a locally designed and built boat, the 10.7-m (35-ft) *Rani*, to sail when not working; when asked to join a 630-mile Christmas cruise from Sydney,

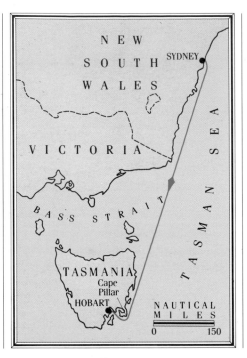

New South Wales, to Hobart, Tasmania, he replied that he would do so if it could be a race. Accordingly a race was organized to start on 26 December 1945 – Boxing Day – and nine boats came to the start line in Sydney Harbor.

Rani had a pleasant sail down the New South Wales coast but later met a 'Southerly Buster' which blew up to Force 9. It lost touch with its fellow competitors and officials on shore began to fear for its safety, for it had not been sighted for some hours. However, as the weather calmed down, *Rani* sailed unannounced up the

––– •••

The Sydney-Hobart Race *After the boats leave Sydney Harbor, they head south along the New South Wales coast and then out across the Tasman Sea until they make landfall midway down the east coast of Tasmania. Once around Cape Pillar on the south-east of the island, the fleet heads west into Storm Bay and up the River Derwent to the finish at the island's capital of Hobart. The length of the course is 630 miles.*

Sovereign, *winner of the 1987 Sydney-Hobart Race.*

River Derwent into Hobart to discover that it had won the race.

Gales such as this are common in the Bass Strait between Australia and Tasmania, giving the race a tough reputation. In 1977, 58 of the 129 starters, and in 1984, 105 of the 152 starters, were forced to retire in a severe gale.

After the boats leave the sheltered New South Wales shore, they cross the Bass Strait and next make landfall about midway down the east coast of Tasmania, a rocky coastline rising to 300 m (1,000 ft)

in places and where fog is not uncommon. Rounding Cape Pillar on the south-east of the island, they turn west into Storm Bay for the final seven miles up the River Derwent, to finish off the foreshore of Hobart. This final leg of the course is often windless, and many places can change in these last few miles, especially if the tide is ebbing.

The race itself, always starting on Boxing Day, is open to all sizes of IOR boat down to a half tonner. It is run by the Cruising Yacht Club of Australia from its

Congested Start *The classic Sydney-Hobart Race starts in Sydney's crowded harbor. Once over the start line, boats competing in the race often have to tack out through a mass of spectator boats, there to watch the spectacle. Once clear of the harbor, the fleet turns south toward Hobart.*

⋯

headquarters in Rushcutters Bay, Sydney, as is the biennial team race, the Southern Cross series, of which it has formed a part since 1967 (see p116). The course record has stood since 1975 at 2 days 14 hr 33 min, an average of 10.1 knots, achieved by the 24.1-m (79-ft) *Kialoa III*, helmed by the American John Kilroy. Several famous sailors have won the race, including in 1969 the-then leader of the opposition and soon-to-be prime minister of Great Britain, Edward Heath, who won with the Sparkman and Stephens-designed *Morning Cloud*; and Ted Turner, the America's Cup defending helmsman in 1977, who sailed the converted 12-Meter *American Eagle* to victory in 1972. But other than Illingworth, Heath, Turner, Kilroy and four others, the remaining 35 winners up to 1987 have been Australian, including five-times winners Trygve and Magnus Halvorsen, who had competed in 26 races by 1976. The Sydney-Hobart Race appears to favor local knowledge.

THE SYDNEY–HOBART RACE

	BOAT	OWNER	NATIONALITY	STARTERS
1945	RANI	J.H. ILLINGWORTH	UK	9
1946	CHRISTINA	J.R. BULL	AUSTRALIA	19
1947	WESTWARD	G.D. GIBSON	AUSTRALIA	26
1948	WESTWARD	G.D. GIBSON	AUSTRALIA	18
1949	TRADE WINDS	M.E. DAVEY	AUSTRALIA	15
1950	NERIDA	C.P. HASELGROVE	AUSTRALIA	16
1951	STRUEN MARIE	T. WILLIAMSON	AUSTRALIA	14
1952	INGRID	J.S. TAYLOR	AUSTRALIA	17
1953	PIPPLE	R.C. HOBSON	AUSTRALIA	24
1954	SOLVEIG	T. & M. HALVORSEN	AUSTRALIA	17
1955	MOONBI	H.S. EVANS	AUSTRALIA	17
1956	SOLO	V. MEYER	AUSTRALIA	28
1957	ANITRA	T. & M. HALVORSEN	AUSTRALIA	20
1958	SIANDRA	G.P. NEWLAND	AUSTRALIA	22
1959	CHERANA	R.T. WILLIAMS	AUSTRALIA	30
1960	SIANDRA	G.P. NEWLAND	AUSTRALIA	32
1961	RIVAL	A. BURGIN & N. RUNDLE	AUSTRALIA	35
1962	SOLO	V. MEYER	AUSTRALIA	42
1963	FREYA	T. & M. HALVORSEN	AUSTRALIA	44
1964	FREYA	T. & M. HALVORSEN	AUSTRALIA	38
1965	FREYA	T. & M. HALVORSEN	AUSTRALIA	53
1966	CADENCE	H.S. MASON	AUSTRALIA	46
1967	RAINBOW II	C. BOUZAID	NZ	67
1968	KOOMOOLOO	D. O'NEIL	AUSTRALIA	67
1969	MORNING CLOUD	E. HEATH	UK	79
1970	PACHA	R. CRICHTON-BROWN	AUSTRALIA	61
1971	PATHFINDER	B. WILSON	NZ	79
1972	AMERICAN EAGLE	TED TURNER	USA	79
1973	CEIL II	W. TURNBULL	HONG KONG	92
1974	LOVE & WAR	P. KURTS	AUSTRALIA	63
1975	RAMPAGE	P. PACKER	AUSTRALIA	102
1976	PICCOLO	J. PICKLES	AUSTRALIA	85
1977	KIALOA III	J.B. KILROY	USA	129
1978	LOVE & WAR	P. KURTS	AUSTRALIA	108
1979	SCREW LOOSE	R.J. CUMMING	AUSTRALIA	147
1980	CERAMCO NZ	N.Z. AROUND THE WORLD COMM.	NZ	102
1981	ZEUS II	J.R. DUNSTAN	AUSTRALIA	159
1982	SCALLYWAG	R.E. JOHNSTON	AUSTRALIA	118
1983	CHALLENGE III	L. ABRAHAMS	AUSTRALIA	173
1984	INDIAN PACIFIC	J. EYLES & G. HEUCHMER	AUSTRALIA	152
1985	SAXACIOUS	G. APPLEBY	AUSTRALIA	212
1986	EX-TENSION	A. DUNN	AUSTRALIA	121
1987	SOVEREIGN	B. LEWIS	AUSTRALIA	158

THE SOUTHERN CROSS TROPHY

Just as the British Admiral's Cup post-dates the Fastnet Race but includes it in its series of races, so too does the Southern Cross Trophy with the Sydney-Hobart Race. Modelled on the Admiral's Cup, the Southern Cross team-race event was first sailed in 1967 and has since been held every other year in December, following on four months later from the Admiral's Cup itself. It is organized by the Cruising Yacht Club of Australia from its headquarters in Sydney.

The three-boat teams enter from a number of countries, but for geographical reasons they have been limited to relatively few: a joint Australian team, as well as individual teams from its six states and the Australian Capital Territory; the EC; Hong Kong; Japan; New Zealand, and teams from its two islands; Papua New Guinea; UK; and the US.

Numbers of teams entering the series have varied considerably. In 1987, 11 teams entered, but six of those were from Australian states, one from Australia itself, and only four – Hong Kong, New Zealand, Papua New Guinea and the USA – from other countries. Australia won the series, the first time she had entered a national team in her own right.

The series includes the two 30-mile inshore events with starts and finishes inside Sydney Harbor; a 180-mile offshore race along the New South Wales coast taking in two offshore islands; and concludes with the Sydney-Hobart Race – a four-race series that is testing for the competitors with its mix of inshore and offshore races in a variety of conditions.

THE SOUTHERN CROSS TROPHY

1967	NZ
1969	NEW SOUTH WALES
1971	NZ
1973	UK
1975	NZ
1977	NZ
1979	NEW SOUTH WALES
1981	NEW SOUTH WALES
1983	NZ
1985	UK
1987	AUSTRALIA

AUSTRALIAN OFFSHORE RACES

Owing to the country's vast size and the scarcity of anchorages on a coastline that often does not lend itself to sailing, offshore racing in Australia is usually a lengthy affair. The courses are between the main sailing centers, and from those centers to such places as Ambon and Bali in Indonesia, Lord Howe Island, Noumea in New Caledonia, and Port Moresby and Samarai in Papua New Guinea. In addition, there are numerous short events that go into the open sea, around a few marks, and then return to port.

With the growth of sponsorship in Australian sailing, new events are promoted every year, including an around-Australia race. However, while some of these events may become regular fixtures, others fall by the wayside as sponsors change from year to year and competitors lose interest in the event. The map below therefore details only those events that have become firmly established in the annual calendar of ocean races.

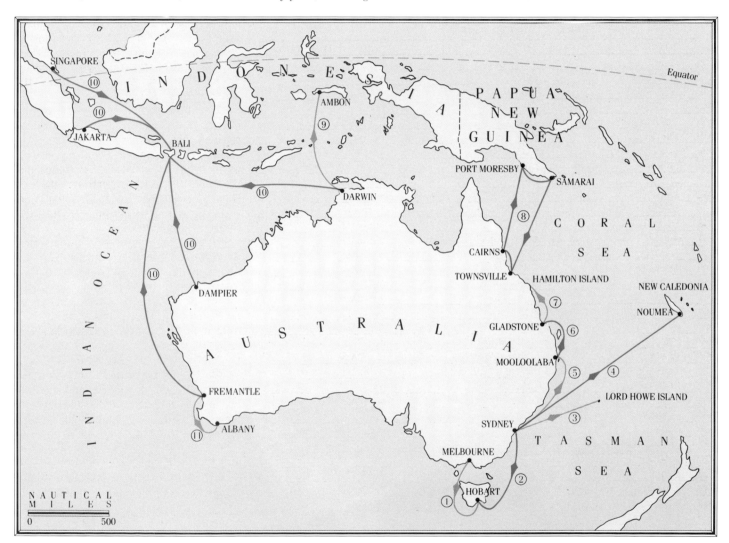

The Major Races

1 *Melbourne to Hobart – 420 miles. Classes – IOR, CHS; held annually in February.*
2 *Sydney to Hobart – 630 miles. Classes – IOR; held annually in December.*
3 *Sydney to Lord Howe Island – 450 miles. Classes – IOR; held annually in February.*
4 *Sydney to Noumea, New Caledonia – 1,058 miles. Classes – handicap for short-handed crews; held every 3 to 4 years.*
5 *Sydney to Mooloolaba – 460 miles. Classes – IOR, local handicap; held annually in March.*

6 *Brisbane to Gladstone – 380 miles. Classes – IOR, local handicap, multihull; held annually in March.*
7 *Gladstone to Hamilton Island – 220 miles. Classes – IOR, local handicap, multihull; held annually in March or April.*
8 *Coral Sea series – four races: Townsville to Cairns; Cairns to Port Moresby in Papua New Guinea; Port Moresby to Samarai; Samarai to Townsville – a total of 1,435 miles. Classes – IOR, local handicap, multihull; held biennially in mid-summer.*

9 *Darwin to Ambon, Indonesia – 600 miles. Classes – IOR, local handicap, multihull; held biennially in April.*
10 *Races to Bali, Indonesia – Darwin to Bali – 940 miles; Dampier to Bali – 700 miles; Fremantle to Bali – 1,475 miles; Jakarta, Indonesia to Bali – 535 miles; Singapore to Bali – 880 miles. Classes – IOR, local handicap; held biennially in May, with race starts arranged to enable all boats to arrive at about the same time in Bali.*
11 *Fremantle to Albany – 325 miles. Classes – IOR, local handicap; held annually in March.*

NEW ZEALAND

The first recognized offshore race from New Zealand took place in 1930 when an Australian sailor from Melbourne, Frank Bennell, sailed his 12.8-m (42-ft) ketch *Oimara* to Wellington and challenged local sailors to race him back across the Tasman Sea to Australia. Finding that nobody was interested, he sailed on to Auckland where his challenge was taken up by Erling Tambs, an enthusiast of long-distance cruising.

A few days before the scheduled start on 14 March, Bennell and Tambs were joined by Allan Leonard, sailing his gaff cutter *Rangi* (9.3m, 30ft 6 in), a fishing vessel for 14 years before being converted to a yacht. What was to be a private race was given official status by the presentation of the silver Trans-Tasman Cup by the Akarana (now Royal) Yacht Club. After a race that ran into southerly gales and then extended periods of calm, *Oimara* finished first in Sydney after 11 days 20 hr

at an average speed of 3.9 knots, while Tambs' boat *Teddy* won on corrected time. *Rangi* took nearly 20 days to complete the 1,275-mile course, having first made a landfall 272 miles south of Sydney.

Six more trans-Tasman races were held between 1934 and 1961, after which date the race stopped, for other than in 1951 and 1952, the event had never attracted large numbers of entrants. Racing the same distance to Suva in Fiji (see next page) was more appealing to local sailors. The heavy cruising boats that had

taken part in the early trans-Tasman races were being replaced by smaller, short-distance, RORC-rule racers.

An attempt was made in 1967 to revive trans-Tasman racing when a single-handed race was run on a more northerly route from New Plymouth to Mooloolaba in Queensland, Australia, a distance of 1,145 miles. The race was won by a 12.2-m (40-ft) trimaran *Rebel*, sailed by Marvin Glenn from the US. Local sailor Bill Belcha won the second race in 1974 in a single-hulled sloop *Raha* (7.3 m, 23 ft 11 in).

FULLY CREWED TRANS-TASMAN RACES

	ROUTE	DISTANCE	BOAT	OWNER	NATIONALITY
1930	AUCKLAND–SYDNEY	1,275 miles	OIMARA	FRANK BENNELL	AUSTRALIA
1934	AUCKLAND–MELBOURNE	1,435 miles	TE RAPUNGA	G. DIBBERN	GERMANY
1938	AUCKLAND–HOBART	1,347 miles	NO FINISHERS	–	–
1948	AUCKLAND–SYDNEY	1,275 miles	PEER GYNT	T. & M. HALVORSEN	AUSTRALIA
1951	AUCKLAND–SYDNEY	1,275 miles	SOLVEIG	T. & M. HALVORSEN	AUSTRALIA
1952	HOBART–AUCKLAND	1,347 miles	LADYBIRD	B. WOOLACOTT	NZ
1961	HOBART–AUCKLAND	1,347 miles	NORLA	T. & M. HALVORSEN	AUSTRALIA

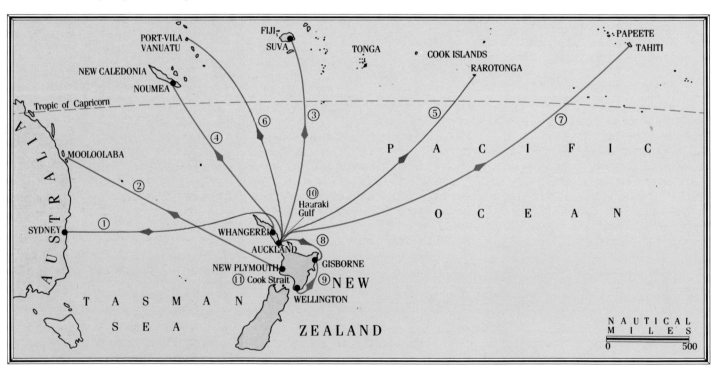

New Zealand *There are 11 major inshore and offshore races held in New Zealand:*
1 *The fully crewed Trans-Tasman Race, sailed in 1930 from Auckland to Sydney, Australia, a distance of 1,275 miles. Six other races between 1934 and 1961 crossed the Tasman Sea in both directions.*
2 *The single-handed Trans-Tasman Race, sailed in 1967 between New Plymouth and Mooloolaba in*

Queensland, Australia, a distance of 1,145 miles. A second race took place in 1974.
3 *The biennial 1,100-mile race from Auckland to Suva, Fiji.*
4 *The 780-mile race from Whangerei to Noumea, New Caledonia.*
5 *The 1,700-mile race from Auckland to Rarotonga in the Cook Islands.*

6 *The 850-mile race from Auckland to Port-Vila in Vanuatu.*
7 *The 2,200-mile race from Auckland to Papeete in Tahiti.*
8 *The 320-mile race from Auckland to Gisborne.*
9 *The 280-mile race from Wellington to Gisborne.*
10 *The annual Balokovic Cup in Hauraki Gulf.*
11 *The biennial 17-mile race across the Cook Strait.*

The 1987 Auckland - Suva Race gets off to a colorful start in Waitemata Harbor.

AUCKLAND-SUVA RACE

The most important regular event in the New Zealand ocean-racing calendar is the 1,100-mile race from Auckland to Suva, Fiji, inaugurated in 1956. Now held biennially in odd-numbered years, it had a somewhat erratic start, with 10 years passing between the first and second races. The first race attracted 13 entries but interest grew so much that 30 started the second race in 1966 and 110 started in 1977. Recently, entries have declined to around 30. Originally sailed to the RORC rule, the IOR was adopted in 1977 with a PHRF class added in 1979; in 1979, 1981 and 1985, one boat has won both classes. The course record was set by John Dacey's 12.5-m (41-ft) *Urban Cowboy* in 1985, which completed the course in 5 days 8 hr 53 min. Since 1977, the race has had two finishes; one at Suva, and one on the other side of Viti Levu island at Lautoka.

OTHER OFFSHORE RACES

In the years when the Auckland-Suva race is not held, occasional races are run from Auckland and other New Zealand ports to destinations in the Pacific. The two major ones are the quadrennial 780-mile race from Whangerei to Noumea in New Caledonia, first sailed in 1964, and the 1,700-mile race from Auckland to Rarotonga in the Cook Islands, first sailed in 1974. Races are also sailed from Auckland to Port-Vila on Vanuatu, a distance of 850 miles, and to Papeete on Tahiti, a distance of 2,200 miles.

Shorter offshore races are also held between home ports, such as the 320-mile Auckland to Gisborne and the 280-mile Wellington to Gisborne races. The annual Balkovic Cup in the Hauraki Gulf is a popular race for top ocean racers and other offshore boats, while the short 17-mile race across the Cook Strait between North and South Islands, held in odd years, is particularly renowned for the tough sailing encountered on the windy, disturbed waters of the strait.

AUCKLAND-SUVA RACE

	BOAT		OWNER	STARTERS
1956	WANDERER		TOM BUCHANAN	13
1966	ROULETTE		FRED ANDREWS	30
1969	CASTANET		LYN CARMICHAEL	27
1973	WHISPERS II		GEOFF STAGG	78
1977	COUNTRY BOY		CLYDE COLSON	110
1979	KISHMUL		R. TAPPER & L. SMITH	52
1981	TINKER		BRUCE USSHER	7
1983	(IOR)	COVELL	DOUG McKEE	47
	(PHRF)	IN SHA'ALLAH	BRUCE ODGERS	
1985	URBAN COWBOY		JOHN DACEY	33
1987	(IOR)	DICTATOR	B. & B. PETERSON	26
	(PRHF)	FOREIGN EXCHANGE	DAVID NATHAN	

THE AMERICAN EAST COAST

The editor of the American sailing magazine *Rudder*, Thomas Fleming Day, was an active sailor who used his influential position to campaign for ocean racing. In 1904 he managed to get six boats, one of them his own 25-ft yawl, *Sea Bird*, to start in a race from Brooklyn in New York, around Long Island and Cape Cod, to Marblehead, Massachusetts, a distance of about 240 miles. *Sea Bird* came in last. The next year twice as many boats took part in a slightly longer race from Brooklyn southward to Hampton Roads, Virginia, and this time, Day finished first.

In 1906, Day announced the race that he had always had in mind, a 660-mile ocean race from Gravesend Bay in Brooklyn, south-east to the British island colony of Bermuda. Sir Thomas Lipton, five-times British challenger for the America's Cup, presented a $500 cup for the race. On 26 May 1906, three local boats came to the line: Day's 11.6-m (38-ft) yawl *Tamerlane*, Richard Floyd's 12.2-m (40-ft) yawl *Lila*, and George Robinson's 8.5-m (28-ft) sloop *Gauntlet*. Six hours after the start *Lila* was dismasted in a squall and escorted back to Gravesend Bay, Brooklyn, by *Tamerlane*, who set out again for Bermuda two days later. However, luck was with *Lila's* rescuer; *Gauntlet* had met a storm while crossing the Gulf Stream

and run-off for 48 hours. *Tamerlane* was thus able to make up for lost time and, crossing the Gulf Stream in better weather, finished first on the afternoon of 3 June. *Lila* set out again with a repaired mast, but turned back after meeting renewed bad weather.

The arrival of the two American boats was much hailed in Bermuda. The island's government had passed a special decree allowing them to sail into Bermudan waters without picking up pilots, as usually required for a visiting ship. In addition, the Royal Bermuda Yacht Club and the Hamilton Dinghy Club (now the Royal Hamilton Amateur Dinghy Club) hosted a series of local races to mark the occasion in which both *Gauntlet* and *Tamerlane* were invited to take part.

Despite the discouraging start to the race, the determined Day continued to promote it through his magazine: 12 boats came to the starting line in Gravesend Bay for the next Bermuda Race in 1907, including a totally overhauled *Lila*. There were two classes, *Lila* winning the smaller class, the 26-m (85-ft) schooner *Dervish*, owned by Harry Morss, the larger. In order to attract more entries for future races, larger boats with professional crew were allowed to enter. However, only five boats started from Marblehead in 1908 and five again from Gravesend Bay in 1909, while in 1910 only two large schooners crossed the start line in Gravesend Bay. The race collapsed in 1911, when there were no entries at all. Strangely enough, there was a series of highly successful motor boat races from New York to Bermuda in these years, the last being in 1913.

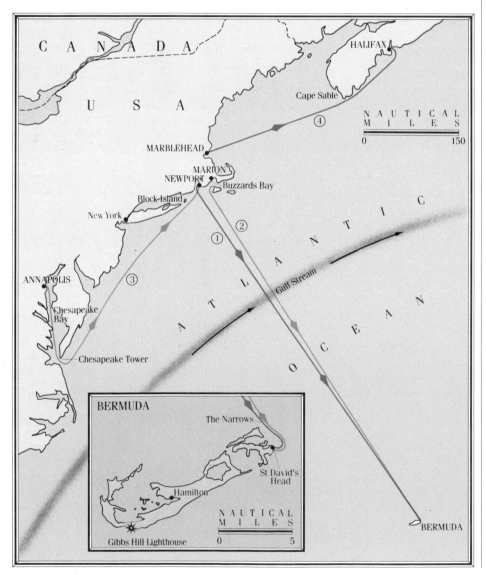

● ● ●

The American East Coast *Four of the major offshore races sailed on the East Coast of America:*
1 *The biennial, 635-mile race from Newport, Rhode Island, to Bermuda, originally established by Thomas Fleming Day and now administered by the Cruising Club of America.*
2 *The biennial, 640-mile race from Marion, Massachusetts, to Bermuda, essentially for cruising boats without big crews.*
3 *The biennial, 473-mile race from Annapolis, Maryland, to Newport – a major East Coast race, alternating with the Bermuda Race.*
4 *The biennial 363-mile race from Marblehead, Massachusetts, to the Canadian port of Halifax, Nova Scotia.*

THE BERMUDA RACE

When the Cruising Club of America was formed in 1922, its primary function was to provide a club for cruising sailors. But some of its members also liked to race, one such member being Herbert L. Stone, editor of *Yachting* magazine. He planned a race from New London, Connecticut, to Bermuda. Twenty-two boats came to the line on 12 June 1923; they started out in fine weather but encountered a blow in the vicinity of the Gulf Stream, the fine weather returning at the end of the race.

The race was proclaimed a success, yet in 1924 only four of the 1923 competitors came to the line, accompanied by 10 first-time entrants. The CCA did not hold another race until 1926, when 16 boats started. In 1925, the Fastnet Race had been sailed for the first time, in direct imitation of the Bermuda Race, and its first winner, *Jolie Brise*, sailed in the 1926 Bermuda Race. By 1928 the Bermuda Race was well established: 24 boats started that year and all but one finished. Thereafter the race has been held every other year, excepting the war years of 1941-5, and has alternated with the Fastnet Race. After starting every race since 1923 in New London – apart from 1932 when the race started from Montauk on the eastern end of Long Island – the start was finally fixed in 1936 at Newport, Rhode Island, shortening the course slightly to 635 miles.

One of the factors that has always influenced the character of this race is that the course is totally in the open Atlantic, out of sight of land, making it quite different from the Fastnet or the Sydney-Hobart races. The course is a direct one from Brenton Reef Tower off Newport to St David's Head on the east side of the Onion Patch, the sailors' name for the islands of Bermuda. These number over 300, including rocks and reefs, and are 22 miles long and low lying, making it difficult for sailors to locate them. In order to finish on the east side of the main island, the boats have to sail around several offshore buoys. Experienced navigators can identify a number of landmarks to guide them to the finish, such as North Rock, the 18.3-m (60-ft) tower on the northern coral bank, and the 107.9-m (354-ft) Gibbs Hill lighthouse.

For these reasons, boats in the Bermuda Race have been ahead of those in most other events in their employment of radio navigation aids. Use was made of radio beacons – the Gibbs Hill lighthouse had a beacon with a range of 120 miles – until their replacement in the 1960s by Loran and now satellite navigation. Such aids are now employed in every ocean race in the world as a matter of course, but because of the nature of its route and the availability of suitable navigational equipment in the US, the Bermuda Race has led the way in this field.

One of the major features of the course is the Gulf Stream, which meanders across it. Today, satellite photographs are available before the start of the race to help navigators locate the stream, but traditionally they had to take the sea temperature every half hour. The Gulf Stream at 27°C (81°F) is 5°C (9°F) warmer in its center than the surrounding ocean, and

Finisterre *One of the most successful ocean racers of all times, the 11.8-m (38-ft 8-in) Sparkman & Stephens-designed* Finisterre, *owned by Carleton Mitchell, won the Bermuda Race an unprecedented three-times running, in 1956, 1958 and 1960.*

◆◆◆

everyone attempts to stay in its strongest part for at least some of the race.

Another factor that influences the character of this race is that it has always been organized by the Cruising Club of America. The CCA remains foremost a club for cruising sailors and its members tend to be very concerned with the proper use of good seamanship. The only race it organizes is the Bermuda Race, with an occasional transatlantic race in the past, and its approach is a little different from most clubs which run races elsewhere in the US or in Europe.

For each race, an organizing committee is appointed that revises the rules and sets the conduct for the next race, based

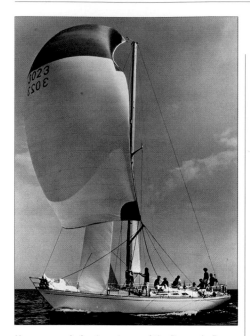

Noryema, only foreign winner of the Bermuda Race.

◆◆◆

on the club's experience with the preceding one. Thus the rating rule has tended to be changed to disadvantage the type of boat that has just won, and the safety and equipment rules have usually been considerable. Traditionally there has been a dislike of the more extreme type of racing boat. The CCA's own rating rule was used from 1934, and the club set its own conditions for entry, but after the introduction of the IOR, combining the CCA rule with that of the RORC, there was dissatisfaction from the club with the design of boat this internationally controlled rule produced. Since 1978, therefore, equal status has been given to the newly introduced MHS rule. In 1980, there was no IOR class at all, but the club reintroduced it in 1982, following protests by many American and other competitors.

Entries to the race are "by invitation", and boats under about 10.7 m (35 ft) are excluded. Numbers are limited to about 160, the actual figure varying from race to race. In 1988, there were 20 IOR and 99 IMS (previously MHS) starters. Yet the availability of so many other events means that the Bermuda Race is much less popular than it once was.

The Bermuda Race has only once been won by a non-American boat: in 1972, the British *Noryema*, owned by Ron Amey, won, although the Australian *Bumblebee IV* had the fastest elapsed time in 1980, but failed to win on handicap. The course record is held by *Nirvana* (24.4 m, 80 ft), owned by Marvin Green of the US, who finished the course in 1982 in 2 days 14 hr 29 min at an average speed of 10.2 knots.

In 1964, the organizers ran an inshore-offshore series equivalent to the Admiral's Cup – the Onion Patch Trophy. For geographical reasons, the number of nations able to produce three-boat teams for the Bermuda Race, a short offshore race, usually from Long Island Sound to Newport, and two inshore races, has been somewhat limited, but Argentina, Australia, Brazil, Canada, the UK and the USA have all competed. The latter country has won on every occasion other than in 1966, when a British team won.

THE BERMUDA RACE

	BOAT	OWNER	STARTERS
1906	TAMERLANE	FRANK MAIER	3
1907	(LARGE CLASS) DERVISH	HARRY MORSS	12
	(SMALL CLASS) LILA	RICHARD D. FLOYD	
1908	(LARGE CLASS) DERVISH	HARRY MORSS	5
	(SMALL CLASS) VENONA	E.J. BLISS	
1909	MARGARET	GEO S. RUNK	5
1910	VAGRANT	H.S. VANDERBILT	2
1923	MALABAR IV	JOHN G. ALDEN	22
1924	MEMORY	R.N. BAVIER	14
1926	MALABAR VII	JOHN G. ALDEN	16
1928	RUGOSA II	RUSSELL GRINNELL	25
1930	MALAY	R.W. FERRIS	42
1932	MALABAR X	R.I. GAVE & JOHN G. ALDEN	27
1934	EDLU	R.J. SCHAEFER	29
1936	KIRAWAN	R.P. BARUCH	44
1938	BARUNA	HENRY C. TAYLOR	38
1946	GESTURE	A.H. FULLER	31
1948	BARUNA	HENRY C. TAYLOR	36
1950	ARGYLL	WILLIAM T. MOORE	59
1952	CARINA	RICHARD NYE	58
1954	MALAY	D.D. STROHMEIER	77
1956	FINISTERRE	CARLETON MITCHELL	89
1958	FINISTERRE	CARLETON MITCHELL	111
1960	FINISTERRE	CARLETON MITCHELL	131
1962	NINA	DeCOURSEY FALES	131
1964	BURGOO	MILTON ERNSTOF	143
1966	THUNDERBIRD	T.V. LEARSON	167
1968	ROBIN	F.E. HOOD	152
1970	CARINA	RICHARD NYE	152
1972	NORYEMA	R.W. AMEY	178
1974	SCARAMOUCHE	C.E. KIRSCH	166
1976	RUNNING TIDE	A.G. VANMETRE & A.G. VANMETRE JR.	150
1978	(MHS) BABE	A.C. GAY	72
	(IOR) ACADIA	B.H. KEENAN	89
1980	HOLGER DANSKE	J. WILSON	160
1982	(MHS) BRIGADOON III	R.W. NORTON	102
	(IOR) CARINA	RICHARD NYE	77
1984	(MHS) PAMIR	FRANCIS H. CURREN JR.	79
	(IOR) MERRY THOUGHT	JACK KING	73
1986	(IMS) PURITAN	DONALD ROBINSON	82
	(IOR) SILVER STAR	DAVID CLARK	42
1988	(IMS) CANNONBALL	CHARLES ROBERTSON	99
	(IOR) CONGERE	BEVIN KOEPPEL	20

Nirvana, holder of the course record for the Bermuda Race, set in 1982.

MARION-BERMUDA CRUISING BOAT RACE

Every odd-numbered year since 1977, a rival race to the Bermuda Race sets out from Marion, Massachusetts, on the north side of the renowned cruising area of Buzzard's Bay. Organized by the Beverly Yacht Club in Marion, the Blue Water Sailing Club and the Royal Hamilton Amateur Dinghy Club, this 640-mile race was designed for cruising boats without big crews. The handicapping system used is unique for this race.

Entry numbers have varied in this race, from 104 in 1977 to 143 in both 1981 and 1987. The course record is held by the 17.4-m (57-ft) sloop *Runaway*, owned by the American Paul D'Arcy, who completed the course in 3 days 8 hr 47 min at an average speed of 7.9 knots. This record was achieved in winds of between 15 and 20 knots, but in some years the weather has been quite different: in 1981 one quarter of the fleet retired in 45-knot winds and one boat sank, the crew being taken off to safety, while in 1985 one boat was abandoned, another dismasted and many retired in repeated thunderstorms. There is no guarantee of good weather in any race to Bermuda.

Included in the rules for the race are a number of stipulations that are intended to ensure that boats are essentially cruisers and not tuned-up racers. All boats must be between 9.75 m and 18.3 m (32 ft and 60 ft) and each must carry certification that it is not primarily designed for racing. There are restrictions on the number and type of sails, no spinnakers are allowed, and no sails can contain Kevlar or certain hi-tech fibers. Every boat must carry 10 gallons of water per person and sufficient fuel for 200 miles, it must carry a dinghy or tender on board, and is allowed wind vanes and powerless self-steering devices. Celestial navigation, as opposed to Loran or other electronic aids, is encouraged. Finally, the race committee neither organizes nor sanctions races back to the US because of the cruising nature of the race. These stipulations are not unlike those the Cruising Club of America sets for the Bermuda Race, but almost all of them are the opposite of most conventional races, including all those using the IOR.

ANNAPOLIS-NEWPORT RACE

This major East Coast classic race is run in June every odd-numbered year, thus alternating with the Bermuda Race. Before World War II, a series of races was held between New London, Connecticut, and various ports in Chesapeake Bay, Maryland. Between 1947 and 1953, the course was between Newport, Rhode Island, and the Chesapeake Bay port of Annapolis, while in 1955 it reverted to starting from New London. Since 1957, the course has been reversed, from Annapolis to Newport, a distance of 473 miles.

Until 1985, the race was organized by the New York Yacht Club, as well as clubs each end, but it is now run by the Annapolis Yacht Club, the Ida Lewis Yacht Club in Newport, and the US Naval Academy Sailing Squadron.

Annapolis is 130 miles from the open ocean in the upper reaches of the immense estuary of Chesapeake Bay, an area that suffers from a variety of adverse conditions: calms, variable winds, strong tidal streams and shallow water. Once free of this bay, the boats head out to sea, rounding Chesapeake Tower before turning north-east and sailing parallel with the coast, although well offshore. They therefore cross the shipping lanes in and out of New York and other East Coast ports before rounding Block Island and turning north to finish at Castle Rock Light or another finish line close to Newport.

As with other major races, the time allowances in this race were to various rules in the early days, before the CCA rating was settled on from 1947 to 1969. The IOR was then used until 1981, when the race had IOR and MHS classes. The course record was achieved in 1987, when the 21.3-m (70-ft) *Starlight Express*, owned by Bruce Eissner, USA, finished the course in 2 days 5 hr 35 min at an average speed of 8.8 knots.

ANNAPOLIS-NEWPORT RACE

	BOAT	OWNER	STARTERS
1957	HARRIER	J-M. BONTECOU	48
1959	CAPER	H. IRVING PRATT	71
1961	REINDEER	E.NEWBOLD SMITH	86
1963	DYNA	CLAYTON EWING	88
1965	DYNA	CLAYTON EWING	93
1967	LANCETINA	JUAN CAMELOO	91
1969	AMERICAN EAGLE	TED TURNER	84
1971	SORCERY	JAMES BALDWIN	91
1973	EQUATION	JACK POTTER	80
1975	SALTY GOOSE	ROBERT DIRECKTOR	85
1977	JACKKNIFE	JACK GREENBERG	67
1979	TENACIOUS	TED TURNER	77
1981	(IOR) IMPASSE	WILLIAM PACKER	74
	(MHS) MANDATE	MORGAN BAKER	
1983	ESPRIT	P. VAN ARSDALE	72
1985	(IOR) SILVER STAR	DAVID CLARK	55
	(MHS) INVICTUS	BERL BERNARD	
1987	STARLIGHT EXPRESS	BRUCE EISSNER	69

MARBLEHEAD-HALIFAX RACE

	BOAT	OWNER	STARTERS
1939	TIOGA TOO	HARRY E. NOYES	13
1947	TICONDEROGA	ALLAN P. CARLISLE	N/A
1949	VALKYRIE	JOHN MacDONALD	N/A
1951	CARINA	RICHARD NYE	N/A
1953	SALMAGAL II	A.B. HOMER	N/A
1955	MALAY	D.D. STROHMEIER	N/A
1957	GALLIARD	E. NEWBOLD SMITH	N/A
1959	MAGIC CARPET	PETER RICHMOND	N/A
1961	ROBIN TOO II	FRED E. HOOD	N/A
1963	DIABLO	J.M. ROBINSON	N/A
1965	HUNTRESS	MORTON H. ENGEL	N/A
1967	NINA	USMM ACADEMY	N/A
1969	SUMMERTIME	IRWIN W. TYSON	N/A
1971	ROBIN	FRED E. HOOD	N/A
1973	LA FORZA DEL DESTINO	NORMAN RABEN	N/A
1975	LA FORZA DEL DESTINO	NORMAN RABEN	N/A
1977	MADCAP	CHARLES M. LEIGHTON	63
1979	(IOR) RECLUTA	WALTER E. HANSON	54
	(MHS) SONNET	JANES D. DROWN	22
1981	(IOR) RECLUTA	WALTER E. HANSON	33
1983	(IOR) MORNING STAR	C. ULMER	35
	(PHRF) DEJA-VU	J. HEARL	35
	(MHS) ALACRITY	G. CLOWERS	19
1985	(IOR) BLUE YANKEE	R. TOWSE	21
	(PHRF) ALDEBARAN	B. KOETHER	39
	(MHS) VIVA	R. SEAMANS	19
1987	(IOR) RAMPAGE	R. RICHMOND	20
	(PHRF) ROGUE	E. DOLE	28
	(IMS) NIGHT TRAIN	C. McNEELY	35

MARBLEHEAD-HALIFAX RACE

The Eastern Yacht Club of Marblehead, Massachusetts, one of the oldest yacht clubs on the American East Coast, first ran a 363-mile race from Marblehead to Halifax, Nova Scotia, in 1905, in which five American boats started. Between the wars, there were several races from various American ports to Halifax, organized by different clubs. However, the race in its current format was first sailed by 13 boats in 1939 and was revived after the war in 1947. Sailed biennially in odd-numbered years, the race is started by the Eastern Yacht Club and finished by the Royal Nova Scotia Yacht Squadron in Halifax, and is currently for IOR, IMS and PHRF classes.

As Halifax is approximately 45° north, the race enters a more temperate weather zone than other American East Coast races, with fog a probability. Because of the shape of the Gulf of Maine, the straight-line course from Marblehead to Cape Sable on the south-west tip of Nova Scotia – which is rounded before heading up the coast to the finish – takes the boats about 90 miles from any land at the furthest position. The record for the course was established in 1979 by the 20.1-m (66-ft) *Circus Maximus*, skippered by John McNamara, USA, who completed the course in 1 day 11 hr 35 min at an average speed of 10.1 knots.

◆◆◆

Circus Maximus *The record time for the 363-mile race from Marblehead to Halifax was set in 1979 by Circus Maximus.*

THE GREAT LAKES

The three major offshore races on the Great Lakes are the Chicago-Mackinac (pronounced "Mackinaw"), Port Huron-Mackinac and Chicago-Sarnia races. Of these, the former, which is over 333 miles, is considered the premier event. It is remarkable for being one of the oldest offshore races in the world, and is the most continuous, since unlike almost all other existing offshore races, it did not stop during World War II.

The Chicago Yacht Club was founded in 1875 and organized the first race from Chicago to the finish line off Mackinaw City in the Strait of Mackinac in 1898. It was won by the sloop *Vanenna*, owned by W.R. Crawford. The race was not held again until 1904, after which it was run annually until 1916. After a five-year lapse, it was restarted in 1921 and has been sailed every year since. Numerous rating rules and divisions of classes have been used in the history of the race; in the late 1980s IOR and IMS classes competed.

The course record for the Mackinac Race was established in 1911 by the 30.5-m (100-ft) schooner *Amorita*, which completed the course in 1 day 7 hr 14 min. This time held for 76 years until it was finally beaten in 1987 by *Pied Piper*, a 21.3-m (70-ft) Santa Cruz 70 owned by the American ocean racer Dick Jennings. With the 15- to 30-knot wind blowing from astern, and then drawing ahead as it moderated, the conditions were perfect for a fast sail; *Pied Piper* sailed at up to 18 knots at an average speed of 12.9 knots and completed the course in 1 day 1 hr 50 min. Many of the other 299 IOR and 89 IMS boats also achieved record times.

LAKE HURON RACES

The 259-mile Port Huron-Mackinac Race is held every year, alternating each year between starting either before or after the Chicago-Mackinac Race. In the years when the race from Port Huron is sailed first, many of the boats then cruise down to Chicago to join in the race back to Mackinaw City. When the race takes place after the Chicago-Mackinac race, the latter race is restarted at Mackinaw City and continues through Lake Huron to Sarnia, a port adjoining Port Huron but on the Canadian side of the St. Clair waterway that connects lakes Huron and Erie. The aggregate distance for this biennial Chicago-Sarnia race is 631 miles; when it is completed, some boats sail the short distance from Sarnia to Port Huron for the start of the Port Huron-Mackinac Race.

All three races in the Great Lakes require considerable local knowledge of topography and weather: the winds are light more often than not, yet severe gales are not unknown and have caused numerous retirements on occasions. Participation from other than American or Canadian crews is predictably minimal, but owners from other parts of the US find the prestige of the races worth the effort of bringing a boat to Chicago or Port Huron.

The Great Lakes *There are three major races in the Great Lakes:*
1 *The annual 333-mile Chicago-Mackinac Race.*
2 *The annual 259-mile Port Huron-Mackinac Race.*
3 *The biennial 631-mile Chicago-Sarnia Race. This race is in two legs: the first leg is the Chicago-Mackinac Race, the second, after a rest, continues to Sarnia.*

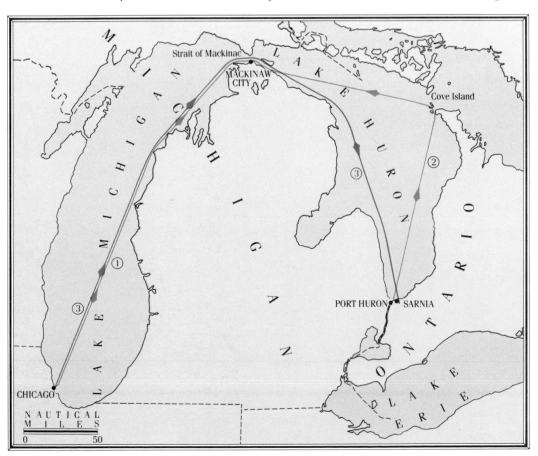

THE SORC

Offshore racing has been well established in Florida since the 1920s, with the Lipton Cup, competed for off Miami, first sailed in 1928, and the Miami-Nassau Race started in 1934. In February 1941, several Florida clubs decided to combine their existing events to make a new series to be known as the 'Winter Circuit', or just the 'circuit', held when the rest of the country was in the grip of winter in order to attract a good turnout.

The first series was won jointly by *Gulf Stream* and *Stormy Weather*, the latter having won both the 1935 transatlantic and Fastnet races. Under various owners, she won the Miami-Nassau Race in the series five times running, and won the whole circuit again in 1948.

This new series was interrupted by the entry of the US into World War II in December 1941, and was not resumed until 1947. It has been held every year since, usually spread over weekends in February and March. The clubs that hold the races have since 1961 officially formed SORC, the Southern Ocean Racing Conference.

At present, clubs that comprise the SORC are the Biscayne Bay YC, Coral Reef YC (Miami), Lauderdale YC, Miami YC and St. Petersburg YC, all in Florida, and Nassau YC in the Bahamas. Each club runs its races in its own waters.

Although the contributing races have changed over the years, a typical year sees a 50-mile triangular course off St. Petersburg; a 400-mile offshore race from St. Petersburg to Fort Lauderdale; a 132-mile triangular ocean race out of Miami; a 40-mile triangular course for the Lipton Cup from Miami; a 176-mile offshore race from Miami to Nassau in the Bahamas; and a 35-mile course off the harbor at Nassau for the Nassau Cup.

Since 1970, the circuit has been run using the IOR with the fleet divided into a number of classes by rating, usually six, running from A to F. Such has been its success that in the 1960s and 1970s, it attracted the very top ocean-racing boats in the US. As it was early in the season, the latest designs that scored well in the circuit were hailed as the ultimate in design, at least for that year. Yet despite some impressive international entries that have won individual events, the overall winner has always been American.

For some years, the circuit was used to select the American Admiral's Cup team, but the trials for this event are now held later in the year off Newport, Rhode Island, on the grounds that the circuit does not provide conditions that are similar to those found in Admiral's Cup waters.

PREMIER EVENT

Although not directly comparable with the Bermuda Race, the standing of the circuit insured that it replaced that race as the premier American ocean-racing event. This change has been accentuated by the frequent alteration of rules for the Bermuda Race. The number of starters in the circuit has increased annually, reaching a record 135 in 1973, since when it has gradually decreased; competition from the top boats, manned by full-time professional crews and sailmakers, has discouraged production boats, and even good, all-around, boats from entering. By 1987 the fleet was down to 37 IOR boats and an additional 22 boats sailing under the IMS rule introduced that year. In 1988, there was a collapse in entries and the future of the series came into question.

Since the circuit has been very much a designers' and innovators' event, there have been some controversial boats and winners over the years. Carleton Mitchell has been the only skipper to win three times, sailing beamy, heavy, centerboard

The SORC *The contributing races to the SORC circuit have changed over the years, but in a typical year the following races are sailed:*
1 *A 50-mile race on a triangular course off St. Petersburg.*
2 *A 400-mile offshore race from St. Petersburg round Key West to Fort Lauderdale.*
3 *A 132-mile ocean triangle race sailing out of Miami.*
4 *The Lipton Cup race, sailed over a 40-mile triangular course off Miami.*
5 *A 176-mile offshore race from Miami around Great Isaac Island and Great Stirrup Cay to Nassau in the Bahamas.*
6 *The Nassau Cup race, a 35-mile triangular course around marks off Nassau Harbor.*

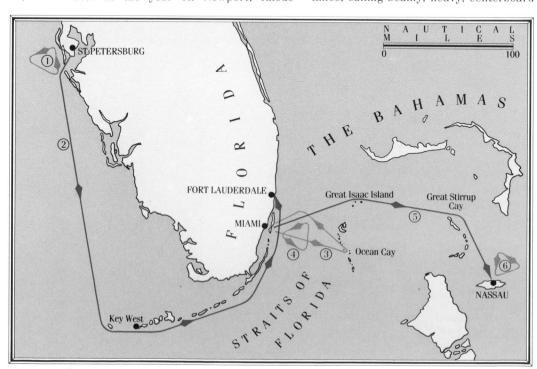

Abracadabra *The 12.8-m (42-ft) Abracadabra sails to victory in the 1986 SORC.*

❖❖❖

boats that benefited under the Cruising Club of America (CCA) rule then in use; in 1952 and 1953, he sailed the 17.5-m (57-ft 6-in) *Caribbee* to victory, winning the circuit again in 1956 in the 11.8-m (38-ft 8-in) *Finisterre*. In 1954 and 1955, the very light displacement *Hoot Mon* (11.9 m, 39 ft), resembling a Star class boat and crewed by Star sailors, beat the CCA rule. Shortly after the introduction of the IOR in 1970, the low-rating, cat-rigged, 11.6-m (38-ft) ketch *Cascade*, with two masts and no headsails, won three of the races and its class, but not quite the series. The first fiberglass boat to win the circuit was the 12.2-m (40-ft) *Paper Tiger* in 1961. *Conquistador*'s victory in 1964 proved important, for this Cal 40, designed by Bill Lapworth, had its rudder separate from the fin keel. Its win, and victories by boats with a similar rudder and keel configuration in major races later in the season, spelt the end of the long keel with a rudder on its after end for all racing boats, whatever the rating rule.

Controversy entered the circuit in 1981 when the leading boats were remeasured to the IOR after racing, prior to leaving for the Admiral's Cup. *Williwaw* and *Acadia* were both found to rate a foot more than stated, while the winner, *Louisiana Crude*, was disqualified when found to have been incorrectly measured, although this was disputed by the owner. *Williwaw*'s owner was banned from racing for two years after one of his crew admitted filling the bilge with water to depress the bow and decrease the rating. Lawsuits were then filed as the findings were disputed.

In 1982, the British boat *Victory of Burnham* was found to have been sailing with a rating over a foot too low. In the subsequent inquiry, the boat having been disqualified, the owner, Peter de Savary, and designer, Ed Dubois, were exonerated.

THE SORC

	BOAT	OWNER	STARTERS
1941	= STORMY WEATHER	WILLIAM LABROT	N/A
	= GULF STREAM	DUDLEY SHARP	
1947	CICLON	A. GOMEZ-MENA & M. BUSTAMENTE	N/A
1948	STORMY WEATHER	FRED TEMPLE	N/A
1949	TINY TEAL	PALMER LANGDON & RICHARD BERTRAM	N/A
1950	WINDIGO	WALTER GUBELMAN	N/A
1951	BELLE OF THE WEST	WILL ERWIN	N/A
1952	CARIBBEE	CARLETON MITCHELL	N/A
1953	CARIBEEE	CARLETON MITCHELL	N/A
1954	HOOT MON	BROWN, PIRIE & ULMER	N/A
1955	HOOT MON	BROWN, PIRIE & ULMER	N/A
1956	FINISTERRE	CARLETON MITCHELL	N/A
1957	CRIOLLO	LUIS VIDANA	N/A
1958	ÇA VA	J.W. HERSHEY & ROBERT MOSBACHER JR.	N/A
1959	CALLOOH	JACK BROWN & BUS MOSBACHER JR.	N/A
1960	SOLUTION	THOR RAMSING	N/A
1961	PAPER TIGER	JACK POWELL	43
1962	PAPER TIGER	JACK POWELL	35
1963	DOUBLOON	JOE BYARS	45
1964	CONQUISTADOR	FULLER E. CALLAWAY III	30
1965	FIGARO IV	WILLIAM SNAITH	51
1966	VAMP X	TED TURNER	74
1967	GUINEVÈRE	GEO MOFFETT	74
1968	RED JACKET	PERRY CONNOLLY	88
1969	SALTY TIGER	JACK POWELL & WALLY FRANK	99
1970	AMERICAN EAGLE	TED TURNER	92
1971	RUNNING TIDE	JAKOB ISBRANDTSEN	98
1972	CONDOR	HILL BLACKETT	110
1973	MUÑEQUITA	JACK VALLEY & CLICK SHRECK	124
1974	ROBIN TOO II	TED HOOD	111
1975	STINGER	DENNIS CONNER	91
1976	RATTLER	JOHN KIRK	77
1977	IMP	DAVE ALLEN	75
1978	WILLIWAW	SEYMORE SINETT	81
1979	WILLIWAW	SEYMORE SINETT	67
1980	ACADIA	BURT KEENAN	64
1981	INTUITION	PAT MULLOY	73
1982	RETALIATION	DAVE FENIX, DENNIS CONNER & TOM WHIDDEN	73
1983	SCARLETT O'HARA	M. WINGATE & C. CORLETT	80
1984	DIVA	BERNARD BEILKEN	70
1985	SMILES	CHARLIE SCOTT	71
1986	ABRACADABRA	JIM ANDREWS & LARRY LEMAK	51
1987	(IOR) SPRINT	JOHN STEVENS	37
	(IMS) REGARDLESS	BOB LYNDS	22
1988	(IOR) LA POSTE	DANIEL MALLE	6
	(IMS) MY FAIR LADY	RAY DEMIERE	10

THE CANADA'S CUP

Ishkareen *(left) and* Venture II *competing for the Canada's Cup in 1954.*

One of the oldest match-racing events in the world, the Canada's Cup was first competed for in 1896 and has been held 16 times since, each match between an American and a Canadian boat. Unlike the America's Cup, the series has never been one-sided: Canada has won 7 times, the US 10 times.

The races are always held at a site on the Great Lakes, the cup holder's club hosting the event. Until 1975, the competing Canadian club was the Royal Canadian Yacht Club, but since then the Royal Hamilton Yacht Club has also competed; both these clubs are in Toronto. Yacht clubs in Chicago, Rochester, Cleveland, and Detroit have represented America.

ORIGINS

The contest began with a challenge in 1895 when the commodore of the Lincoln Park Yacht Club of Chicago, Charles Berriman, sought a boat of the Royal Canadian Yacht Club to race against his new boat, the 19.2-m (63-ft) *Vencedor*. The RCYC syndicate, headed by Aemilius Jarvis, commissioned a design from the Scottish designer William Fife; the 17.4-m (57-ft) *Canada* defeated the larger *Vencedor* in two straight races off Toronto, sailed under the American Seawanhaka rating rule and a time-allowance system. It won a trophy in the shape of an elaborate cup supported by a lion and an eagle, donated by the city of Toledo, Ohio.

The Canada's Cup

In 1899, the year of the second match, the cup became known as the Canada's Cup and by deed it was stated that it be held "in trust as a perpetual challenge cup for friendly competition between sailing yachts representing yacht clubs of the two nations bordering the Great Lakes". The wording has a familiar ring: the contest has long been thought of as the 'America's Cup of the Great Lakes'.

RACES AND RATINGS

After the first match, which consisted of the best two races out of three, the nine matches from 1899 to 1954 were decided by the best three races out of five. Since the 1969 match, either the best three out of four or best four out of seven races have been sailed. Until 1969, all the races had been short, inshore races, but for the first time that year, an offshore race of between 150 and 250 miles was introduced to complement the inshore races.

The rating rules in use have changed over the years. For the second match, the boats were limited in size by a 35-ft (10.7-m) girth rule, allowing boats of between 12.8m and 13.4m (42ft and 44ft) LOA to compete. This rule was used again in 1901, but was replaced in 1903 by a rule limiting entries to 40ft (12.2m) LWL,

reduced in the 1905 match to 30ft (9.1m). The 1907 match adopted the Universal Rule, introducing slightly smaller boats, while from 1930 to 1954, the International 8-Meter class was raced. Faced with the virtual demise of 8-Meter racing by the 1960s, ocean racers were sailed in the 1969 and 1972 matches using the Cruising Club of America rule, with the boats rating at 37ft (about 13.7m, 45ft, LOA). From 1975 until 1984, an IOR fixed rating of 32ft – the Two Ton rating measure – was used, changed in 1988 to 30.5ft IOR, the current One Ton rating.

THE COMPETITORS

The first six matches from 1896 to 1907 took place between a variety of different sized boats, with 'big yachts' competing in 1903. While the Americans designed and built their own boats, employing such notable designers as Nathanael Herreshoff in 1907, the Canadians used British designers and, in 1907, builders.

This situation changed little when the International 8-Meter class was used for the four matches of 1930, 1932, 1934 and 1954, the first three of which the US won. As before, the Americans designed and built their own boats, the 1930 winner, *Thisbe*, designed by Clinton Crane, the

1932 and 1934 winner, *Conewago*, by Olin Stephens of Sparkman and Stephens. The Canadian boats however were still all designed in Britain, and the 1932 and 1934 loser, *Invader II*, was built there too.

By the time of the 1954 match, however, there were few 8-Meters left to sail. The Canadian designer George Cuthbertson was sent to Scotland to buy *Ishkareen*, designed by Olin Stephens and built in Sweden. When he arrived he found that it had just been bought by Herbert Wahl of the defending Rochester Yacht Club! The Canadians therefore bought an American boat in Detroit, *Venture II*, designed by E.A. Shuman, which won the series.

With the replacement of the 8-Meter rule by the CCA rule in 1969, the Canada's Cup has been competed for from 1969 by ocean-racing boats. The CCA boats were able to compete in the Bermuda Race and other American offshore events. From 1975 to 1984, the 32-ft IOR rating was intentionally the same as the Two Ton Cup, but there was no wide adoption of this class. The 1988 match was for boats of the One Ton rating of 30.5 ft IOR, giving a boat of about 12.2 m (40 ft): this rating brought the Canada's Cup into line with the Admiral's Cup, as well as the One Ton Cup.

Evergreen, *winner of the Canada's Cup in 1978.*

THE CANADA'S CUP

	WINNER	LOSER	RESULT	RACES	RULE
1898	CANADA (CAN) AEMILIUS JARVIS ROYAL CANADIAN YC	VENCEDOR (USA) J.G. BARBOUR CHICAGO YC	2-0	2 of 3	SEAWANHAKA RULE AND TIME ALLOWANCE
1899	GENESEE (USA) C.G. DAVIS CHICAGO YC	BEAVER (CAN) AEMILIUS JARVIS ROYAL CANADIAN YC	3-0	3 of 5	35-ft GIRTH RULE
1901	INVADER (CAN) AEMILIUS JARVIS ROYAL CANADIAN YC	CADILLAC (USA) W.H. THOMPSON CHICAGO YC	3-1	3 of 5	35-ft GIRTH RULE
1903	IRONDEQUOIT (USA) JAMES BARR & ADDISON HANAN ROCHESTER YC	STRATHCONA (CAN) AEMILIUS JARVIS ROYAL CANADIAN YC	3-2	3 of 5	40-ft WATERLINE
1905	IROQUOIS (USA) L.G. MABBETT ROCHESTER YC	TEMERAIRE (CAN) E.K.M. WEDD ROYAL CANADIAN YC	3-2	3 of 5	30-ft WATERLINE
1907	SENECA (USA) ADDISON HANAN ROCHESTER YC	ADELE (CAN) AEMILIUS JARVIS ROYAL CANADIAN YC	3-0	3 of 5	UNIVERSAL RULE – 27-ft RATING
1930	THISBE (USA) WILLIAM BARROWS ROCHESTER YC	QUEST (CAN) NORMAN GOODERHAM ROYAL CANADIAN YC	3-2	3 of 5	8-METER
1932	CONEWAGO (USA) WILMOT CASTLE ROCHESTER YC	INVADER II (CAN) WALTER WINDEYER ROYAL CANADIAN YC	3-1	3 of 5	8-METER
1934	CONEWAGO (USA) WILMOT CASTLE ROCHESTER YC	INVADER II (CAN) T.K. WADE ROYAL CANADIAN YC	3-0	3 of 5	8-METER
1954	VENTURE II (CAN) DAVID HOWARD ROYAL CANADIAN YC	ISHKAREEN (USA) HOWARD KILTGORD ROCHESTER YC	3-1	3 of 5	8-METER
1969	MANITOU (CAN) PERRY CONNOLLY & GORDON FISHER ROYAL CANADIAN YC	NIAGARA (USA) JOHN LOVETT CLEVELAND YC	4-0	3 of 4	37 ft CCA
1972	DYNAMITE (USA) LLWYD ECCLESTONE BAYVIEW YC	MIRAGE (CAN) GORDON FISHER ROYAL CANADIAN YC	3-2	3 of 4	37 ft CCA
1975	GOLDEN DAZY (USA) DON CRINER BAYVIEW YC	MARAUDER (CAN) DAVID HOWARD ROYAL CANADIAN YC	4-2	4 of 7	32 ft IOR
1978	EVERGREEN (CAN) DON GREEN ROYAL HAMILTON YC	AGAPE (USA) TERRY KOHLER BAYVIEW YC	4-3	4 of 7	32 ft IOR
1981	COUG (CAN) TONY RONZA ROYAL HAMILTON YC	BLACK MAGIC (USA) MIKE THOMPSON BAYVIEW YC	4-0	3 of 4	32 ft IOR
1984	COUG II (CAN) TONY RONZA ROYAL CANADIAN YC	STARS & STRIPES (USA) MIKE THOMPSON BAYVIEW YC	4-0	3 of 4	32 ft IOR
1988	CHALLENGE 88 (USA) JOHN UZNIS BAYVIEW YC	STEADFAST A&T (CAN) FRED SHERRATT ROYAL CANADIAN YC	4-3	4 of 7	30.5 ft IOR

HAWAII

With the trade wind blowing fresh and often strong from the north-east, and the Hawaiian Islands being just inside the tropics at between 19° and 23° north, the Hawaii International Ocean Racing Series has become established as a major one for IOR boats, especially for those at the larger end of the scale. The warm air and water, consistent winds and attractive conditions afloat and ashore have made this series a sought-after event, but unlike most of the traditional offshore races and regattas, it is not near to any world centers of population. It was thus only possible to organize such an event in the last few years, when the larger boats were seawor-

The Hawaii International Ocean Racing Series *This biennial series of races consists of five events:*
1 Three 27-mile Olympic-course races off Waikiki.
2 The Molokai Race, a short offshore race from Waikiki along the north shore of Molokai to a mark off Maui, and then back, a distance of 150 miles.
3 The 775-mile Around-the-State Race.

thy and fast enough to make the long journey to compete and the smaller ones could be shipped.

Three-boat national teams enter this event, but there are also class and overall prizes for individual boats, which must rate between 30ft and 70ft IOR, the maximum IOR rating. Predictably the entries are mainly from the US and from other Pacific Basin countries such as Australia, Japan and New Zealand, but unusually for such an event, more than one national team is allowed to enter: in 1986, for example, there were four American teams and two Japanese teams.

HISTORY OF THE SERIES

The Around-the-State Race began in 1972, a 775-mile ocean race around all the main islands of the Hawaiian group, organized by the Waikiki Yacht Club of Honolulu. This annual race expanded into an international series, thanks to the work of Dick Gooch, a Honolulu resident, who attracted

sponsorship from the airline Pan Am. In 1978 the first Pan Am Clipper Cup series was competed for, with team and individual prizes for the 41 starters from 4 countries. There were five qualifying races: the Around-the-State Race; a medium-length race around Oahu; and three short inshore races around a triangular course off Waikiki. Australia won the team prize against Japan, New Zealand and the US.

In 1980, 64 boats in 11 teams from 6 countries competed in the series, and in 1982, the numbers rose to 80 entries, again from 6 countries. Pan Am continued to sponsor the series in 1984, but because of the administrative workload, the Royal Hawaiian Ocean Racing Club was formed to take over the administration of the series from the Waikiki Yacht Club. A new sponsor, the Kenwood Corporation, took over in 1986 and the series was renamed the Hawaii International Ocean Racing Series; the team race was for a new trophy, the Kenwood Cup.

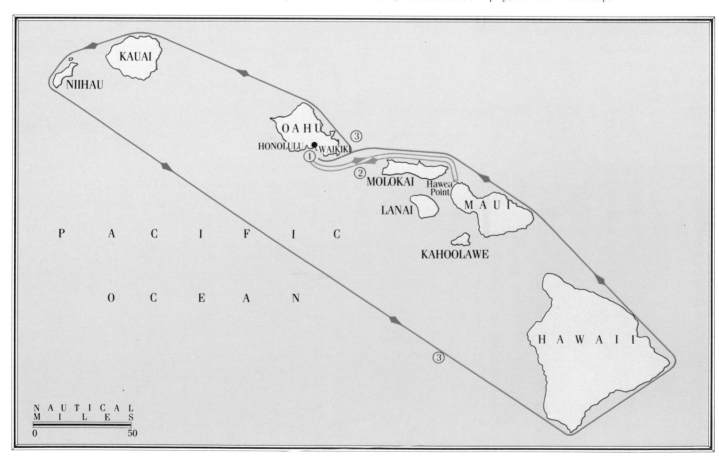

The format of this biennial series, which takes place at the end of July and the beginning of August, now comprises a long and a short offshore race and three Olympic-course races. The first two days consist of two 27-mile Olympic-course 'Ocean Triangles' off Waikiki, with the short offshore race – the 150-mile Molokai race from Waikiki along the north shore of Molokai to a mark near Hawea Point on Maui, and then back – taking place on day three. On day five there is a further ocean triangle race of 27 miles, and the series is finished with the long-distance Around-the-State Race.

Classes are decided after all the entries have been received; a commonly used American procedure that produces roughly equal classes, unlike the European system of using the rating bands as classes into which boats are entered, regardless of numbers. Maxi-class boats, which are regular contenders for line honors, have their own class, and an extra division is available for ultra-light displacement boats if there are at least five of them.

Although the north-east trade wind always blows, there are periods when the boats are struggling in light winds, often caused by wind shadows in the lee of islands. Conversely, thermals caused by the hot land, and the considerable acceleration of the trade wind around headlands and down valleys, can produce periods of strong wind. In 1982, three tropical storms passed close-by the fleet and there were winds of up to 50 knots during some of the races, damaging many boats.

Racing in Hawaii *Races in Hawaii take place against the dramatic backdrop of the islands' mountainous scenery. Here a group of boats are preparing to start a short race inshore.*

The Kenwood Cup

HAWAII INTERNATIONAL OCEAN RACING SERIES

	No. OF BOATS	No. OF COUNTRIES	TEAM WINNER	OVERALL WINNER
1978	41	4	AUSTRALIA	MONIQUE (NZ)
1980	64	6	AUSTRALIA	RAGAMUFFIN (AUS)
1982	80	6	USA	KIALOA (USA)
1984	69	9	USA	BOOMERANG(AUS)
1986	48	5	NZ	CRAZY HORSE (USA)
1988	45	4	AUSTRALIA	BRAVURA (USA)

THE CANADIAN PACIFIC COAST

There are three main races held off Canada's Pacific Coast: the annual Swiftsure Lightship Race, the annual Southern Straits Race, and the biennial Victoria to Maui, Hawaii, Race. Because these races start from Vancouver or Victoria, both ports near the American border, they attract considerable entries from Seattle and other towns on the American north-west coast.

SWIFTSURE LIGHTSHIP CLASSIC

This annual 136-mile offshore race is held every May by the Royal Victoria Yacht Club, founded on Vancouver Island in 1892 and given a royal warrant in 1906. The race was first run in 1930 on the suggestion of Captain Barney Johnson RN, who had taken part in the first Fastnet Race five years earlier. Like so many of these events, the first race was between a few enthusiastic owners, three boats coming to the starting line. The race was sailed again the next year and in 1934, and has

Swiftsure Lightship Classic *The 1984 winner, 20.4-m (67-ft) Hawaiian sloop* Charley, *completed the course in 21 hr 43 min.*

been held every year since 1947, becoming one of the west coast's most prestigious racing events.

The start is at Brotchie Ledge at the entrance to Victoria's inner harbor; from there the boats sail out through the 18-mile-wide, but exposed, Juan de Fuca Strait into the open Pacific Ocean to an anchored naval vessel marking the Swiftsure Bank. Once around the vessel they return to the finish. The bank was named after *HMS Swiftsure*, the ship that had surveyed the shoal here in 1889, and the race was named after the lightship that had marked the shoal until 1961.

The first three races were held under the-then RORC rule; from 1947 to 1970 the CCA rule was used. Since 1971 the IOR rule has been in use, with the addition of a class using the PHRF. The course record was set in 1978 when the 22.25-m (73-ft) ketch *Windward Passage*, one of the greatest ocean racers, completed the course in 20 hr 36 min at an average speed of 6.6 knots.

The Canadian Pacific *There are three major races held off Canada's Pacific Coast:*
1 *The annual 136-mile Swiftsure Lightship Classic from Victoria to a buoy on the Swiftsure Bank and back.*
2 *The annual Southern Straits Race held in the Strait of Georgia, is raced over a course that varies from year to year. A typical long course is 135 miles, a typical short course for smaller boats is 85 miles.*
3 *The biennial 2,308-mile race from Victoria to Maui, Hawaii.*

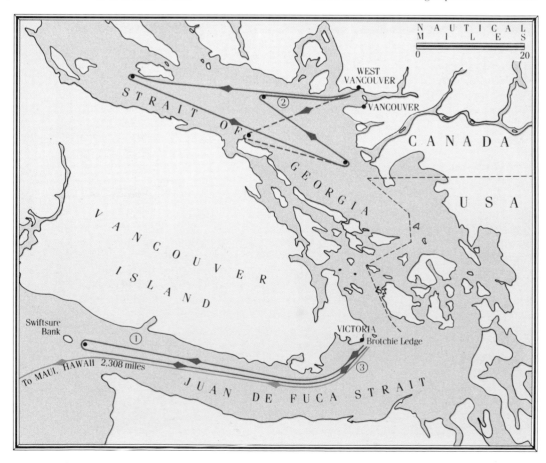

SWIFTSURE LIGHTSHIP CLASSIC

	WINNER	OWNER	ENTRANTS
1975	ELUSIVE	J.E. SPROUSE	103
1976	LADY BUG	ALAN HOLT	91
1977	KANATA	VLAD PLAVSIC	87
1978	SACHEM	BILL BUCHAN	86
1979	PEARCE ARROW	KEN PEARCE	76
1980	LADY BUG	ALAN HOLT	87
1981	HEATHER	FRED RUSWALD	37
1982	PACHENA	JOHN NEWTON	41
1983	SLICK SILVER	DAVID HADDLESTON	34
1984	CHARLEY	BOYD. RATNER & NIEMI	69
1985	COUNTRY STYLE	STEVE MERRIMAN	46
1986	SORCERY	JACOB WOOD	47
1987	SACHEM	BILL BUCHAN	44
1988	SACHEM	BILL BUCHAN	21

SOUTHERN STRAITS RACE

This annual race is held early each season in the Strait of Georgia between Vancouver Island and the mainland. The weather tends to be extremely variable, and the race course changes each year but always begins from a starting line set up by the race organizer, the West Vancouver Yacht Club. A typical route takes the boats on a long triangular course of 135 miles; an 85-mile course for smaller boats is in the form of a figure-of-eight. The average number of starters is 120, with a maximum of 135; classes used are IOR and PHRF.

VICTORIA TO MAUI RACE

Canada's version of the Transpac Race is organized by the Royal Victoria Yacht Club and is run from Victoria to Maui in Hawaii, a distance of 2,308 miles. It has been held in midsummer every even year since 1968, with entries numbering between 20 and 36. Owing to the usually windless 'Pacific High' area of weather which lies across the direct route, the boats often take a more southerly route to pick up the north-east trade winds. The IOR is used, sometimes modified to allow for the nature of the course, and entries must carry both VHF and single sideband radio. The course record was set in 1978 by the 20.4-m (67-ft) American ultra-light displacement boat *Merlin*, owned and designed by Bill Lee, who completed the course in 10 days 2 min at an average speed of 9.6 knots.

Sachem *Bill Buchan's ocean racer has won the Swiftsure twice in a row, in 1987 and 1988. Buchan also won the Classic in 1978 with another boat called* Sachem.

THE AMERICAN WEST COAST

One of the leading regular classic ocean races in the world, the Transpacific, or Transpac Race, is also one of the longest. Starting off from Los Angeles, California, with a short leg southward to the Catalina Buoy, the course is then downwind in the steadily blowing north-east trade winds to the Diamond Head Buoy off Honolulu on the island of Oahu, Hawaii, 2,225 miles away.

Because the course is largely downwind, many boats have been designed to perform well off the wind just for this race, to the exclusion of other characteristics. Normal rating rules and time allowances cannot therefore be used satisfactorily, so although the entrants are all IOR rated, a special time allowance and other factors are applied to the results.

The boats designed for this race are known as ultra-light-displacement boats (ULDBs), or 'sleds', a name that alludes to their main design feature. They are ultralight maxis that not only try to win the Transpac on corrected time, but also to establish a new record. This has not been bettered since 1977, when the 20.4-m (67-ft) ULDB *Merlin*, designed by Bill Lee of the USA, was first to finish in 8 days 11 hr 1 min for an average speed of 11 knots.

The race is run by the Transpacific Yacht Club, formed in 1928, which took over the organization of a race first sailed across the Pacific from San Pedro, California in 1906. Further Transpac races took place in 1908, 1910, 1912, 1923, 1926, 1928, 1930, 1932, 1934, 1936, 1939 and 1941, resuming after the war in 1947, after which date the race has been held biennially in odd-numbered years.

About 60 boats usually enter the race, three-quarters of which are between 13 m and 17 m (42 ft and 55 ft). Other than one or two below that group, the remaining dozen or so are sleds of around 21 m to 21.5 m (68 ft to 70 ft). The maximum entry has never exceeded 80 boats, owing to berthing limitations for larger boats in Honolulu harbor.

TRANSPAC COURSE RECORDS

	BOAT	ELAPSED TIME
1923	MARINER	11 days 14 hr 46 min
1949	MORNING STAR	10 days 10 hr 13 min
1953	MORNING STAR	9 days 15 hr 5 min
1969	BLACKFIN	9 days 10 hr 21 min
1977	MERLIN	8 days 11 hr 1 min

Winner of the 1977 Transpac Race, Merlin *holds the course record.*

CALIFORNIA-MEXICO RACES

A number of races are sailed in the open ocean from southern California to ports in Mexico. Those that go south of Cabo San Lucas enter the tropics.

The most popular of these is the annual Newport Beach-Ensenada Race, a short 130-mile hop across the international frontier, organized by the Newport Ocean Sailing Association. Since its inception in 1946, it has attracted both monohulls and multihulls and has become the biggest offshore race in the world: 573 boats entered in 1973, and numbers have regularly passed 500 since then. The entries are divided into numerous classes and divisions, which have varied from time to time and which have included IOR, PHRF, ULDB and multihull divisions. Over the years the race has acquired a number of nicknames, notably the 'Race to Husong's' and the 'Margarita Derby'.

Newport Beach is also the starting point for a 790-mile race to Cabo San Lucas, the most southerly tip of Baja California. Held every odd-numbered year, this popular race has a big entry and is regarded as a tune-up for the Transpac Race. All classes are IOR and the big sleds turn out for it.

Another long race is the San Diego to Manzanillo Race, which is 1,100 miles in length. It is sometimes called 'the race to Las Hadas', Las Hadas being a famous hotel in Manzanillo. The race was first sailed in 1976, replacing a longer, 1,400-mile race from San Diego to Acapulco sailed for the last time in 1974. The Manzanillo Race is held biennially in even-numbered years.

There are three other races which are also sailed southward from Southern California: the 1,125-mile Marina del Rey to Puerto Vallarta Race, held in odd-numbered years; the 807-mile Long Beach to Cabo San Lucas Race, held every other year since 1965 and organized by the Long Beach Yacht Club; and the biennial 870-mile Los Angeles to Cabo San Lucas Race, first sailed in 1986 and organized by the Los Angeles Yacht Club. This latter race replaced a 999-mile race from Los Angeles to Mazatlan, which had first been sailed in 1961 and then in even-numbered years from 1962 to 1984.

MEXORC

The races from San Diego to Manzanillo and Marina del Rey to Puerto Vallarta act as feeders for the Federación Mexicana de Vela's Mexican Ocean Racing Circuit (MEXORC). The six-race program is held alternately at Manzanillo or Puerto Vallarta. Mexican boats from the Club de Yates de Acapulco sail north to the host port for the regatta, while large numbers of American boats sail south to join them. In this series, the times of starts are not quite so rigidly programed as similar series held elsewhere: if a party is in full swing as the start time approaches, the start is postponed until later.

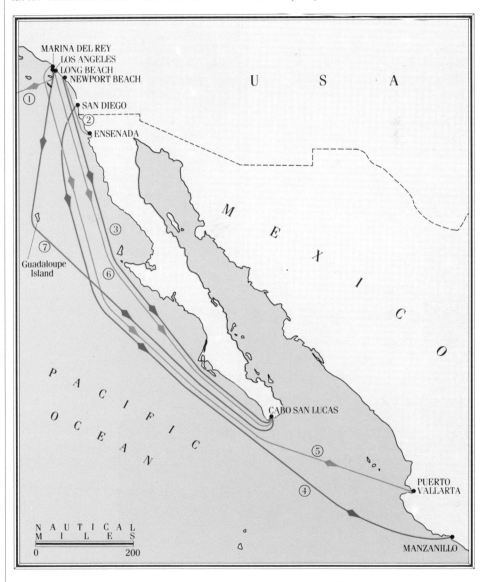

West Coast Races *Among the major races sailed from ports in California on the American West Coast are the following:*
1 *The biennial 2,225-mile Transpac Race from Los Angeles to Honolulu, Hawaii, one of the world's classic ocean races.*
2 *The annual 130-mile race from Newport Beach to Ensenada, Mexico.*
3 *The biennial 790-mile race from Newport Beach to Cabo San Lucas, Mexico.*
4 *The biennial 1,400-mile race from San Diego to Manzanillo, Mexico.*
5 *The biennial 1,125-mile race from Marina del Rey to Puerto Vallarta, Mexico.*
6 *The biennial 807-mile race from Long Beach to Cabo San Lucas, Mexico.*
7 *The biennial 870-mile race from Los Angeles to Cabo San Lucas, Mexico.*

SOUTH AMERICA

There are three main offshore races in South America: the 1,200-mile race from Buenos Aires in Argentina to Rio de Janeiro in Brazil; the 912-mile Mil Millas triangular race from Valparaiso in Chile via Robinson Crusoe Island (364 miles) and Talcahuano (335 miles) back to Algarrobo (213 miles); and a shorter 250-mile race from Buenos Aires down the Argentinian coast to Mar del Plata.

RACES FROM BUENOS AIRES

In 1932, members of the Yacht Club Argentino – an old club founded in 1883 – followed the example set by ocean races in Britain and the US and established an offshore race that ran from Buenos Aires, south along the coast to Mar del Plata, a distance of about 250 miles. It took place each year, with variable entries, until 1946, but since that date it has only been held biennially in even-numbered years, and has been eclipsed in popularity by a far larger race. For in 1947, an Argentinian yachting magazine promoted the idea of a 1,200-mile race from Buenos Aires to Rio de Janeiro in Brazil. Ten boats

The 1959 start of the Buenos Aires – Rio de Janeiro Race

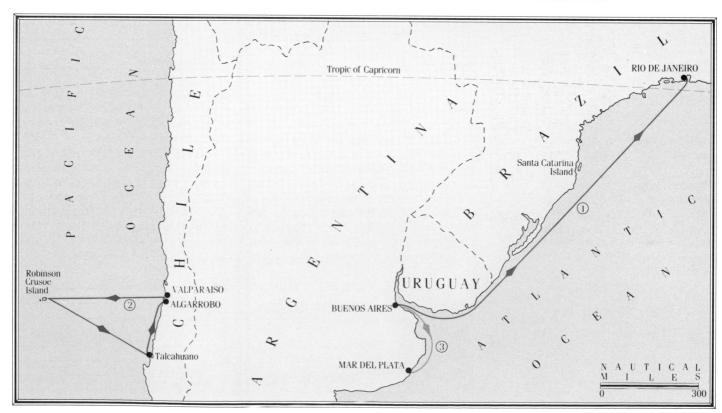

Ondine II *S.A. Long's 22-m (73-ft) Ondine II won the 1968 Buenos Aires – Rio de Janeiro Race.*

South America *There are three major offshore races in South America (see map, left):*
1 The 1,200-mile Buenos Aires-Rio de Janeiro Race, now held biennially in odd-numbered years.
2 The 912-mile Mil Millas Race from Valparaiso to Robinson Crusoe Island, Talcahuano and Algarrobo, held biennially in even-numbered years.
3 The 250-mile Buenos Aires-Mar del Plata Race, sailed in even-numbered years, alternating with the race from Buenos Aires to Rio de Janeiro.

started, eight Argentinian and two Brazilian, and the race was won by the Argentinian boat *Alfard*.

The next race was in 1950, when 31 boats started, including one from Britain and two from Germany, at a time when German boats were still not acceptable at most European regattas. Since then the race has been held in 1953, 1956, 1959, 1962, 1965, 1968, 1971, 1974, 1977, 1979, 1981, 1985 and 1987, in the mid-summer month of January, with between 25 and 39 entries, the latter in 1987. Boats from Chile, Mexico, Uruguay and the US have joined the many entries from Argentina and Brazil. From 1950 to 1971, the race was run under the CCA rating rule and since then has been under the IOR, using the American time-on-distance tables. A cruising class was added in 1979.

The course has been described as three races in one. The first leg is in the shallow estuary of the River Plate with headwinds from the south. Once clear of this, the second, ocean, leg is along the Uruguayan and low-lying southern Brazilian coasts, with a chance of fresh headwinds. Once past Santa Catarina island, the race becomes near tropical with moderate or light winds and an adverse current. Near Rio itself there is frequently calm to upset the finishing order. In 1965, S.A. Long's *Ondine* was the first non-South American boat to win this race; he then went on to win the 1968 race in *Ondine II*. The record for the course is held by *Cisne Branco* (ex-*Ondine IV*), owned by the Brazilian Navy, which completed the course in 4 days 18 hr 53 min in 1987 at an average speed of 10.4 knots.

BUENOS AIRES-RIO DE JANEIRO RACE

	BOAT	OWNER	NATIONALITY	STARTERS
1965	ONDINE	SUMNER A. 'HUEY' LONG	USA	30
1968	ONDINE II	SUMNER A. 'HUEY' LONG	USA	27
1971	PLUFT	I. KLABIN	BRAZIL	28
1974	RECLUTA III	C. CORNA	ARGENTINA	26
1977	WA-WA-TOO	F.N. De ABREU	BRAZIL	38
1979	MADRUGADA	P.P. COUTO	BRAZIL	35
1981	FORTUNA II	M. RIVERO KELLY	ARGENTINA	36
1985	CONGERE	BEVIN KOEPPEL	USA	33
1987	DAPHNE	GERMAN FRERS	ARGENTINA	39

MIL MILLAS RACE

This well-established race is, despite its name of Mil Millas (thousand miles), actually only 912 miles long, and is run by the Club Náutico Oceánico de Chile, based at Valparaiso. It consists of three legs: the first of 364 miles from Valparaiso to Robinson Crusoe Island, the second of 335 miles to Talcahuano on the Chilean coast, and the third of 213 miles northward back to Algarrobo, adjoining Valparaiso. The Club Náutico Oceánico first ran a race to

Robinson Crusoe Island in 1968, and organized the first Mil Millas Race in 1975. Since then six more races have been held at roughly two-year intervals.

The entries for this race, normally held in early February, mainly come from Argentina and Chile, but boats from Australia, Britain, France, Peru and South Africa have also taken part. It uses the IOR to a minimum rating of 20 ft; there is also a class under the regional South American Rating Formula.

MIL MILLAS RACE

	BOAT	SKIPPER	NATIONALITY	ENTRANTS
1975	VIKING II	K. ZONDEK	CHILE	7
1978	RISQUE III	J. BAILAK	ARGENTINA	8
1980	FANTASMA II	H. BOHER	ARGENTINA	13
1982	CONDOR	J.A. MERINO	CHILE	13
1984	BLANCA ESTELA	F. ACOSTA	CHILE	16
1986	RECLUTA	F. ACOSTA	CHILE	17
1988	FANTASMA III	H. BOHER	CHILE	20

Chapter 4

The America's Cup

𝒯he America's Cup is unique in sailing history. Ever since the schooner *America* arrived in English waters in 1851, there has been a public interest in the event not afforded to any other yacht race: the boats have always seemed bigger and more expensive, the personalities of owners, helmsmen and designers larger than life, the controversies more frequent. Yet over the years the races themselves have been far from memorable occasions. They have often been remarkably one-sided: American boats have won 87 out of the 99 races sailed, usually leading from the start, and have retained the cup 27 out of the 28 times it has been competed for. One club, the New York Yacht Club, held the trophy from 1851 to 1983, earning itself a place in record books for the longest unbroken sequence of wins in any sport. It is a record that emphasizes the central theme of the cup: that it has always been a challenge match to determine who has the best design, technology and sailing skills.

1851

In 1850, George Schuyler, one of the founders of the New York Yacht Club, received a letter from England informing him of the first ever 'world fair' to be held in London the following year. It suggested that, as part of the celebrations, a New York pilot boat be sent to race in English waters. These schooner-rigged craft were between 24 m (80 ft) and 30 m (100 ft) long and designed for speed, as the first one to reach an incoming ship got the job of escorting it into port. Rather than send an existing boat, George Schuyler and five other members of the NYYC, including its commodore John Cox Stevens, formed a syndicate to commission George Steers to design a new boat. They chose him for his reputation of designing (or rather modelling, for he always worked with carved blocks of wood) the fastest pilot boats. The new boat was to be called *America*, an indication of the importance attached to her in challenging the longstanding maritime supremacy of Great Britain.

THE CHALLENGE

America was launched on 1 April 1851. It measured 31 m (101 ft, 9 in) LOA, 27.5 m (90 ft 3 in) LWL, had a beam of 6.9 m (22 ft 6 in), a draft of 3.5 m (11 ft 6 in), a sail area of 489 sq m (5,263 sq ft), and a tonnage, according to the measurement of the time, of 170 tons. It cost a total of $20,000. The syndicate took delivery on 18 June and prepared it for the voyage to England. By this time John Cox Stevens had received a welcoming letter from the Earl of Wilton, commodore of the Royal Yacht Squadron, stating in part that "for myself I may be permitted to say that I shall have the great pleasure in extending to your countrymen any civility that lies in my power, and shall be glad to avail myself of any improvements in shipbuilding that the industry and skill of your nation have enabled you to elaborate."

Stevens replied that "should she answer the sanguine expectations of her builder, we propose to avail ourselves of your friendly bidding, to take with a good grace the sound thrashing we are likely to get by venturing our longshore craft on your rough waters..."

However competition, not defeat, was in the mind of Stevens and the rest of the

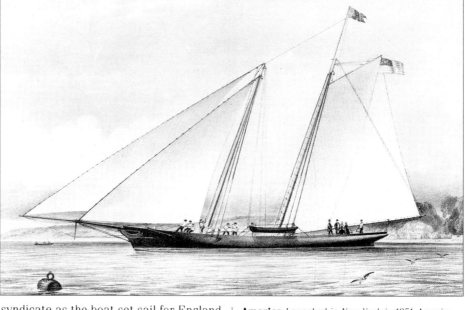

America *Launched in New York in 1851, America (shown here in a contemporary lithograph by E.T. Dolby) first crossed the Atlantic in the same year to compete in what became the first America's Cup race, remaining in Europe until 1862. It was renamed Camilla in 1856. On returning to America, it took part in the Civil War as a blockade runner before being scuttled in Florida. Raised, and returned to its former name, in 1863, it became a naval training ship, and was one of the defenders of the America's Cup in 1870, when it finished fourth. After several refits as a racing yacht, America finished its life in a boatyard in Annapolis, where it was destroyed in a snowstorm in 1945.*

syndicate as the boat set sail for England. Apart from *Cleopatra's Barge* in 1817, no American yacht had crossed the Atlantic before, but *America* made the passage safely in 20 days, arriving in the French port of Le Havre in mid-July. After some refitting, it sailed across the Channel on 31 July, anchoring on its arrival in Spithead. The next morning it began to sail towards Cowes, some five miles away; the British cutter *Laverock* sailed down to accompany it. As they sailed up the Solent, *America*, astern and to leeward of *Laverock*, soon overtook it to windward. In Cowes, the news soon spread that here was a fast boat and an unusual one too.

After its arrival, nothing much happened. Many people visited the schooner and it took members of the RYS for a sail, but there was no regular program of races for *America* to participate in, for at that time races were between individual yachts and usually limited to RYS members only. However one member, G.R. Stephenson, agreed on a £100 wager for a race between *America* and his 100-ton schooner *Titania*. This little-publicized race eventually took place on 28 August, six days after the famous race around the Isle of Wight, and was to the Nab light and back, a distance of about 28 miles. *America* won by 4 min 12 sec; it was however nearly twice the size of its opponent. Other than this race, no challenges were forthcoming, despite

an open challenge by the Americans to race against any British schooner on a course to be selected by the RYS, subject to there being at least six knots of wind.

The RYS therefore invited the Americans to compete in a race "open to all nations" that had already been scheduled for 22 August around the Isle of Wight. This 50-mile course potentially favored local boats with their knowledge of the tricky shoreline and complex tidal streams.

THE RACE

On the morning of the race, *America* and 14 British yachts of various sizes were lined up at anchor, as was the starting method then, ready for the gun at 10 am. The story of the race is well known in sailing mythology. *America* was slow getting up the anchor and was last to start, but in the light westerly wind ran through all the

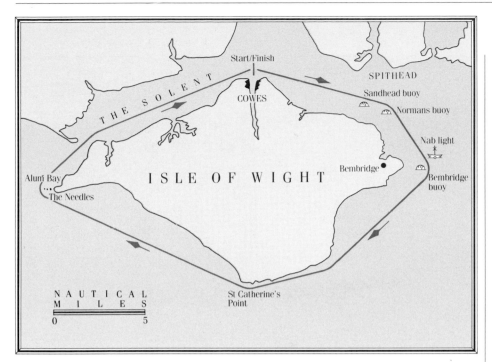

Around the Island *America and its competitors were sent clockwise around the Isle of Wight, starting and finishing at Cowes. In a muddle over the course, the hired English pilot, Robert Underwood, took it inside the Nab light, while some of the other yachts went around it. The Nab Tower, still in use today, was not in place until 1921 and is far to the east of the old Nab light shown here.*

• • •

fleet but four – *Beatrice*, *Volante*, *Arrow* and *Aurora* – by the time it was at the Nomans buoy near the eastern end of the island. A few miles later, *America* overtook the leader, *Volante*, and led the fleet.

Then occurred one of those misunderstandings that bedevil yacht racing. A number of yachts stood on for the Nab light, but *America* continued to sail around the island in the strengthening breeze, increasing its lead immensely. *Arrow*, one of the faster English boats, ran on to rocks east of St. Catherine's Point and lay there for 20 minutes before being towed off by a pleasure steamer. *Alarm*, one of the best British cutters, spent time going to its assistance. Then *Volante*, another fancied cutter, lost its bowsprit in a collision with *Freak* and retired. The only boats now left in with a chance to beat *America* were *Aurora*, *Bacchante*, *Eclipse* and *Brilliant*. *America* found a better breeze further offshore and reached up the south-west of the island toward the Needles, which it rounded at 17.47. In a failing breeze *America* passed Queen Victoria on the royal

yacht *Victoria and Albert* in Alum Bay, and crawled up the Solent towards Cowes, finally crossing the finishing line at 20.37. *Aurora* followed at 20.45, *Bacchante* at 21.30, *Eclipse* at 21.45 and *Brilliant* at 01.20. None of the other 10 yachts finished.

There was a protest that *America* had failed to round the Nab light, but this was quickly withdrawn. Although the printed program called for the rounding of the light, the race card with the names and colors of the yachts demanded only that the yachts sail around the island. That night, while vast crowds watched a firework display in celebration of the race, a cup was presented by the RYS to John Cox Stevens as representative of *America*.

The race itself in tidal waters and light air had not been very significant, but *America* was. It had more speed on all points of sailing and had outshone all the British craft. Its sharp bow and wide beam, simple rig and sail plan, and machine-spun cotton sails that were laced to the boom, all made it closer winded, faster and easier to control than the blunt-bowed, narrow British yachts with their complex rigs and loose-footed linen sails that stretched in the wind. Such was its effect on British yachting that for the 1852 season all the leading sailors had converted their boats to carry rigs similar to that of *America*, and had learned techniques employed by the Americans.

1870-1887

After the establishment of the Deed of Gift for the America's Cup in 1857 (subsequently revised in 1881 and 1887), the ground rules were laid for future races. However, because the event was so new and without precedent – there was no other international sailing competition of any sort at the time – the early races for the cup were haphazard and often chaotic, and usually favored the American defenders. The competitors had to work out the conditions, schedules and rules for themselves without the aid of any international arbitration body; the rating rules varied between America and Britain; the boats were often of widely differing designs and lengths, the American boats were usually centerboarders in contrast to the British keel designs; and the challengers, if British, had to sail across the rough North Atlantic under their own sail and then race in the generally light summer weather off New York. Each race was conducted on a handicap basis, the time allowance accorded each yacht worked out by waterline area (1870), displacement (1871), cubic contents (1876, 1881), and finally length-and-sail-area (1885, 1886, 1887).

◆ ◆ ◆

The Inner Course *Between 1870 and 1887, the America's Cup was sailed on the New York Yacht Club's inner course, the boats starting and finishing in the narrow entrance to New York's busy harbor. The distance of the course was about 38 miles.*

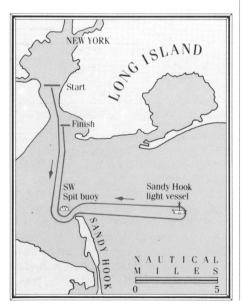

Participants in the first defense of the America's Cup in 1870 round the Sandy Hook light vessel.

1870

MAGIC beat CAMBRIA and 22 others 1-0

CHALLENGER · *CAMBRIA*
LOA · 33 m (108 ft)
DESIGNER · MICHAEL RATSEY
OWNER · JAMES ASHBURY
SKIPPER · J. TANNOCK
CLUB · ROYAL THAMES YC, UK

DEFENDER · *MAGIC*
LOA · 26 m (84 ft)
DESIGNER · R.F. LOPER
OWNER · FRANKLIN OSGOOD
SKIPPER · ANDREW COMSTOCK
CLUB · NYYC, USA

In 1868 the British schooner *Cambria* beat the visiting American yacht *Sappho* in a race around the Isle of Wight. This victory encouraged the owner, James Ashbury, a self-made businessman, so much that he decided to challenge for the America's Cup itself, if only to make a name for himself. After narrowly winning a race across the Atlantic against *Dauntless*, an American yacht owned by the vice-commodore of the NYYC, *Cambria* was favored to win the single race for the cup, to be sailed with 23 American yachts. However victory went to the schooner *Magic*, a centerboarder able to skirt the shoals around the course. *Cambria* came 10th; *America*, original winner of the cup, was fourth.

1871

COLUMBIA and SAPPHO beat LIVONIA 4-1

CHALLENGER · *LIVONIA*
LOA · 39 m (127 ft)
DESIGNER · MICHAEL RATSEY
OWNER · JAMES ASHBURY
SKIPPER · J.R. WOODS
CLUB · ROYAL HARWICH YC, UK

DEFENDER · *COLUMBIA* (3 races)
LOA · 32.9 m (107 ft 10 in)
DESIGNER · J.B. VAN DEUSEN
OWNER · FRANKLIN OSGOOD
SKIPPER · NELSON COMSTOCK
CLUB · NYYC, USA

DEFENDER · *SAPPHO* (2 races)
LOA · 41 m (135 ft)
DESIGNER · C.&R. POILLON
OWNER · COL. W.P. DOUGLAS
SKIPPER · SAM GREENWOOD
CLUB · NYYC, USA

After much argument between James Ashbury, making his second challenge for the cup in *Livonia*, and the NYYC, the club defended the cup with four yachts, choosing the most suitable one for the day's weather in the five-race series. In the third race, *Livonia* defeated *Columbia* after it was partially disabled in heavy weather – the last time an American defender was defeated in a race until 1920. A protest about the course used in the series soured the atmosphere considerably.

1876

MADELEINE beat *COUNTESS OF DUFFERIN* 2-0

CHALLENGER · *COUNTESS OF DUFFERIN*
LOA · 22.7 m (74 ft 7 in)
DESIGNER · ALEXANDER CUTHBERT
OWNERS · MAJOR CHARLES GIFFORD & SYNDICATE
SKIPPER · J.E. ELLSWORTH
CLUB · ROYAL CANADIAN YC, CANADA

DEFENDER · *MADELEINE*
LOA · 32.4 m (106 ft 4 in)
DESIGNER · DAVID KIRBY
OWNER · JOHN S. DICKERSON
SKIPPER · JOSEPHUS WILLIAMS
CLUB · NYYC, USA

The two Canadian challenges in 1876 and 1881 came from clubs on the Great Lakes, where they sailed light-displacement centerboard boats. The challenge of 1876 was the first one in which the Americans agreed to use only one boat in their defense, and to sail a series of the best of three races; it also marked the last time schooners were used. The result, however, was a shoo-in for the defenders, for the Canadian challenger was poorly built and inadequately rigged.

1881

MISCHIEF beat *ATALANTA* 2-0

CHALLENGER · *ATALANTA*
LOA · 21 m (70 ft)
DESIGNER, OWNER & SKIPPER · ALEXANDER CUTHBERT
CLUB · BAY OF QUINTE YC, CANADA

DEFENDER · *MISCHIEF*
LOA · 20.6 m (67 ft 5 in)
DESIGNER · A. CARY SMITH
OWNER · JOSEPH BUSK
SKIPPER · NATHANIEL CLOCK
CLUB · NYYC, USA

For the first time single-masted yachts of around 21 m (70 ft) – not much longer than today's 12-Meter boats – were used in the cup races, and selection heats were used by the defenders to choose their best boat. However the Canadian challenge was ill-prepared against the better-equipped and sailed American boat, and went down to a two-race defeat. The winning margin in the final race of 38 min 54 sec has never been exceeded.

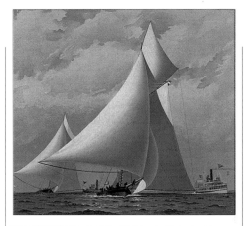

The 1881 Defense Mischief *leads* Atalanta *in one of the races, both yachts sporting flat spinnakers that were gradually replacing the more common square sails. Parachute spinnakers were not introduced until the 1920s.*

❖❖❖

1885

PURITAN beat *GENESTA* 2-0

CHALLENGER · *GENESTA*
LOA · 29.4 m (96 ft 5 in)
DESIGNER · J. BEAVOR-WEBB
OWNER · SIR RICHARD SUTTON
SKIPPER · JOHN CARTER
CLUB · ROYAL YACHT SQUADRON, UK

DEFENDER · *PURITAN*
LOA · 28 m (94 ft)
DESIGNER · EDWARD BURGESS
OWNERS · J. MALCOLM FORBES, GEN. CHARLES J. PAINE & SYNDICATE
SKIPPER · AUBREY J. CROCKER
CLUB · NYYC, USA

In 1884 two simultaneous British challenges by Sir Richard Sutton were made with the request that if the first failed in August 1885, the second be sailed two weeks later. The NYYC was not prepared to accede to this request, with the result that the challenges were put down for successive years.

In 1885 the British boat was *Genesta*, a long, deep and narrow cutter of a design popular in Britain. The American boat was a centerboard sloop designed by Edward Burgess to be a compromise between the larger American schooners popular at the time and the smaller British cutters. Of the three races started, the second was notable for a foul by *Puritan* on *Genesta* that should have led to its retirement. *Genesta* also retired rather than win the race unchallenged, Sutton gaining considerable respect for his action.

1886

MAYFLOWER beat *GALATEA* 2-0

CHALLENGER · *GALATEA*
LOA · 31.3 m (102 ft 7 in)
DESIGNER · J. BEAVOR-WEBB
OWNER · LT WILLIAM HENN RN
SKIPPER · DAN BRADFORD
CLUB · ROYAL NORTHERN YC, UK

DEFENDER · *MAYFLOWER*
LOA · 30 m (100 ft)
DESIGNER · EDWARD BURGESS
OWNER · GEN. CHARLES J. PAINE
SKIPPER · MARTIN STONE
CLUB · NYYC, USA

The 1886 challenger *Galatea*, designed like *Genesta* by J. Beavor-Webb, was more of a cruising boat, on which the owners lived in considerable comfort. The defender, again a compromise design by Edward Burgess, held the cup in two straight races, winning the second race by a margin of 29 min 9 sec. The challenger contested that the winds had been too light and waited at Marblehead until the following spring, when in a 'good breeze' it was again easily defeated.

1887

VOLUNTEER beat *THISTLE* 2-0

CHALLENGER · *THISTLE*
LOA · 33.1 m (108 ft 6 in)
DESIGNER · GEORGE L. WATSON
OWNERS · JAMES BELL & SYNDICATE
SKIPPER · JOHN BARR
CLUB · ROYAL CLYDE YC, UK

DEFENDER · *VOLUNTEER*
LOA · 32.4 m (106 ft 3 in)
DESIGNER · EDWARD BURGESS
OWNER · GEN. CHARLES J. PAINE
SKIPPER · HENRY C. HAFF
CLUB · NYYC, USA

From now on the competition for the cup became more like modern racing; the two boats were actually designed and built to suit the current handicap length-and-sail-area rule. The defender was Burgess' third cup boat while *Thistle* came from the board of the renowned Scottish naval architect George L. Watson. Both cutters, they looked similar and were almost identical in overall and waterline length. *Thistle* however was outclassed in management and handling and lost both races.

1893-1895

The races of 1893 and 1895 took place between two of the so-called 'big yachts' that dominated yacht racing at this time. Expensive to build and maintain, such boats could only be afforded by the richest owners. One such man was the Earl of Dunraven, a larger-than-life character who introduced a new note of acrimony into the proceedings. The controversy surrounding his activities in the 1895 race produced the worst conflict ever seen in cup racing. By this time, however, the rules concerning the cup had become more established. The races were now to be sailed on an open water course beyond New York's crowded harbor; the dimensions of the boats were fixed at no more than 27 m (90 ft) LWL, with a handicapping system based on waterline length and sail area; the challenger had to give information about his boat in advance so that a comparable defender could be built; and the best of five races were to be sailed. As before, however, the challenging boat still had to sail to the races on its own bottom, which meant that it was built more heavily than the defender, and needed to be rerigged with racing spars and canvas on arrival in New York.

◆ ◆ ◆

The Outer Courses *Between 1893 and 1920, the cup races were sailed outside New York's harbor on either a triangular or a windward/leeward course of about 30 miles in length, the first leg of which was always to windward.*

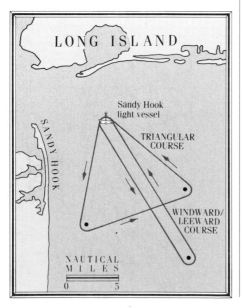

LORD DUNRAVEN

Windham Thomas Wyndham-Quin, fourth Earl of Dunraven, was an Irish peer of energetic and eccentric character. Born in 1842, he played an active part in Irish politics and for a time worked as a war correspondent for the London *Daily Telegraph* during the Franco-Prussian War of 1870-1. A keen steeplechaser, his main love, however, was sailing. He wrote a three-volume book, *Self-instruction in the Practice and Theory of Navigation*, held a Master's Certificate in seamanship, was the joint designer of several yachts, and, at the age of 79, built *Sona*, one of the first diesel-powered yachts. Yet throughout his long life – he died in 1926 at the age of 84 – he was best remembered for his dispute with the NYYC over the 1895 America's Cup.

1893

VIGILANT beat *VALKYRIE II* 3-0

CHALLENGER · *VALKYRIE II*
LOA · 35.7 m (117 ft 3 in)
DESIGNER · GEORGE L. WATSON
OWNER · EARL OF DUNRAVEN
SKIPPER · WILLIAM CRANFIELD
CLUB · ROYAL YACHT SQUADRON, UK

DEFENDER · *VIGILANT*
LOA · 38 m (124 ft)
DESIGNER · NATHANAEL G. HERRESHOFF
OWNERS · C. OLIVER ISELIN & SYNDICATE
SKIPPER · WILLIAM HANSEN
CLUB · NYYC, USA

George Watson once again designed the challenging boat, but the defenders turned to a new designer, Nathanael G. Herreshoff, who over the next six cup series was to stamp his mark on yacht design. Both boats were vast, and both were supreme in their own countries. But when the series started properly, after a first race in which both boats failed to finish due to lack of wind, the defender won three straight races, although the last was by only 40 seconds after *Valkyrie II* had led at the windward mark but lost its lead downwind to the better-sailed *Vigilant*. Despite this close result, the outcome left no doubt as to which boat was the fastest.

1895

DEFENDER beat *VALKYRIE III* 3-0

CHALLENGER · *VALKYRIE III*
LOA · 39 m (129 ft)
DESIGNER · GEORGE L. WATSON
OWNERS · EARL OF DUNRAVEN & SYNDICATE
SKIPPER · WILLIAM CRANFIELD
CLUB · ROYAL YACHT SQUADRON, UK

DEFENDER · *DEFENDER*
LOA · 37 m (123 ft)
DESIGNER · NATHANAEL G. HERRESHOFF
OWNERS · C. OLIVER ISELIN, J.P. MORGAN & WILLIAM K. VANDERBILT
SKIPPER · HENRY C. HAFF
CLUB · NYYC, USA

The 1895 series of races marked the first time that sport contributed adversely to international relations, causing bad feelings between America and Britain. This state of affairs resulted entirely from the activities of Dunraven, making his second challenge for the America's Cup.

Dunraven challenged in *Valkyrie III*, designed as his previous yacht had been by George Watson, while the Americans defended in the Herreshoff-designed *Defender*: both were typical 'big yachts' of their day. The first race was won by the defender, and was promptly followed by a letter from the Earl of Dunraven to the race committee of the NYYC. In it he made two

LONG ISLAND

Sandy Hook light vessel

TRIANGULAR COURSE

WINDWARD/ LEEWARD COURSE

SANDY HOOK

NAUTICAL MILES

0 5

complaints, the first of which was that the spectator fleet had obstructed the starting line and confused the water through which the challenger was sailing. This complaint was justified, but the race committee was largely powerless to prevent spectator boats crowding in on the challenger, an object of greater interest than the defender. It was not until the next challenge for the cup in 1899 that the course was patrolled by the US Navy.

Dunraven's second complaint was that *Defender* had loaded extra ballast after measurement, against the rules. Both yachts were remeasured with the same results, but Dunraven continued to complain about this throughout the series.

As if this was not enough to sour relations, the second race resulted in a collision before the start between the two yachts; *Valkyrie III*'s boom fouled *Defender*'s topmast shroud which led to the cracking of its topmast. *Valkyrie III* continued to sail the course to the finish, without waiting to see what damage it had done or raising a protest flag, and was subsequently disqualified from the race. Dunraven then refused the offer of a resail, and also refused to compete in the third race by retiring shortly after crossing the start line, leaving *Defender* to finish the race alone.

The controversy caused by these events, and the continuing exchange of letters about the ballast of *Defender*, led to a five-day inquiry at the NYYC, starting on 27 December 1895, which Dunraven attended in person. On the committee were the distinguished naval historian Captain A.T. Mahan, the former US ambassador to Britain E.J. Phelps, and officers of the club. Both sides were represented by admiralty lawyers, but after much argument the inquiry found Dunraven's charges to be entirely unfounded. No apology was received from him, and in February 1896 he was expelled from his honorary membership of the NYYC.

◆◆

Pre-start Maneuvers Valkyrie III *leads* Defender *towards the start line in the second race of the 1895 challenge. Thirty seconds later,* Valkyrie III *fouled and partially disabled* Defender *and was disqualified after protest.* Inset: *Captain Haff and the crew of* Defender.

1899-1920

For the five successive series from 1899 to 1930, the NYYC was challenged to defend the America's Cup by Sir Thomas Lipton. He had started life as a grocer's clerk and built up a substantial business based on tea and other products. He was 51 and knew nothing about sailing when he first raced for the cup – in all his challenges he won only two individual races and did much to contribute to the reputation of invincibility held by the NYYC. But his sense of sportsmanship and genial character did much to endear him to the Americans, and he repaired the damage done to the sport by the Earl of Dunraven.

The reasons for NYYC's consistent supremacy in this period were threefold. Firstly, Lipton's motivation was flawed: the owners and syndicates of the NYYC had one object only – to defend the cup – while Lipton wanted to cement friendly relations and promote the sale of tea in the US. It is a measure of his success off the water that Lipton's tea is still the most widely drunk brand in the country. Secondly, the Americans could call on the services of the brilliant Nathanael G. Herreshoff to design their winning boats; and thirdly, the challenging boats still had to sail across the Atlantic while the defenders were preparing in home waters.

The races themselves were all held in the congested waters south of New York and were handicap events: from 1899 to 1903 an increasingly sophisticated length-and-sail-area system was used, to be superseded in 1920 by a new Universal Rule largely invented by Herreshoff.

◆◆◆

Friendly Competition *Although Sir Thomas Lipton challenged for the cup five times, he failed to win it. His sporting approach to the event made him a popular challenger in America, as can be seen in this 1901 cartoon from* The Judge, *which is captioned: "An English proverb illustrated. There is many a slip twixt the CUP and the LIP(ton)."*

Columbia, without a topsail, narrowly leads Shamrock 1 *in the final race of the 1899 series.*

1899

COLUMBIA beat *SHAMROCK I* 3-0
CHALLENGER · *SHAMROCK I*
LOA · 39 m (128 ft)
DESIGNER · WILLIAM FIFE
OWNER · SIR THOMAS LIPTON
SKIPPER · ARCHIE HOGARTH
CLUB · ROYAL ULSTER YC, UK
DEFENDER · *COLUMBIA*
LOA · 40 m (131 ft)
DESIGNER · NATHANAEL G. HERRESHOFF
OWNERS · C. OLIVER ISELIN, J.P. MORGAN & E.D. MORGAN
SKIPPER · CHARLES BARR
CLUB · NYYC, USA

The first challenge from Lipton for the cup was scheduled for October 1899. Lipton commissioned William Fife to design the first of the *Shamrocks* he was to challenge in, but the new boat's preparation for the series was minimal. It had time to sail only a few inconclusive trials against the Prince of Wales' *Britannia* before leaving England on 3 August for the series of races starting in October. The Americans were better prepared, having raced the defender *Columbia* against the 1895 *Defender*. *Shamrock* and *Columbia* were evenly matched in the races, but it was the better handling skills of the Americans that won the day in three straight races.

1901

COLUMBIA beat SHAMROCK II 3-0

CHALLENGER · *SHAMROCK II*
LOA · 42 m (137 ft)
DESIGNER · GEORGE L. WATSON
OWNER · SIR THOMAS LIPTON
SKIPPER · E.A. SYCAMORE
CLUB · ROYAL ULSTER YC, UK
DEFENDER · *COLUMBIA*
LOA · 40 m (131 ft)
DESIGNER · NATHANAEL G. HERRESHOFF
OWNERS · J.P. MORGAN & E.D. MORGAN
SKIPPER · CHARLES BARR
CLUB · NYYC, USA

Controversy entered the 1901 matches when a wealthy speculator from Boston Massachussets, Thomas Lawson, insisted on entering a new boat, *Independence*, for the defender trials. The NYYC refused to let him enter, insisting that he either join their club or lend his boat to a member, neither of which he would do. After considerable correspondence, *Independence* raced informally against the two-year-old *Columbia* and a new boat, *Constitution*. In the event, Lawson's boat turned out to be much slower and it leaked badly.

The Americans sailed *Columbia*, the first boat to defend the cup twice running. It had beaten *Constitution* in the defender trials, and went on to beat *Shamrock II* – the longest cup boat yet – in three straight races. This was not the shoo-in it seemed, for in the last race *Shamrock II* crossed the line two seconds ahead of *Columbia*; however, as it had to give 43 seconds time allowance, it lost on corrected time.

1903

RELIANCE beat SHAMROCK III 3-0

CHALLENGER · *SHAMROCK III*
LOA · 40.9 m (134 ft 4 in)
DESIGNER · WILLIAM FIFE
OWNER · SIR THOMAS LIPTON
SKIPPER · ROBERT WRINGE
CLUB · ROYAL ULSTER YC, UK
DEFENDER · *RELIANCE*
LOA · 43.7 m (143 ft 8 in)
DESIGNER · NATHANAEL G. HERRESHOFF
OWNERS · C. OLIVER ISELIN & SYNDICATE
SKIPPER · CHARLES BARR
CLUB · NYYC, USA

At 43.7 m (143 ft 8 in) LOA with a beam of 7.8 m (25 ft 8 in) and a draft of 6 m (20 ft), the bronze-hulled, lead-keeled *Reliance* was the biggest boat ever to compete in the America's Cup. On its steel mast and wooden topmast, it boasted a sail area of 1,501 sq m (16,160 sq ft), the greatest ever rigged on a single-masted boat: to it is ascribed the origin of the expression 'racing machine'. *Shamrock III*, the challenger, was of a similar size: the two of them were huge, lightly built skimming dishes of an extreme type that needed more than 60 crew to sail them. Equipped with the latest technology, including highly innovative winches, *Reliance* outsailed and outperformed the less advanced *Shamrock III*, which lost two races before losing its way in the fog and failing to finish the third.

1920

RESOLUTE beat SHAMROCK IV 3-2

CHALLENGER · *SHAMROCK IV*
LOA · 33.6 m (110 ft 4 in)
DESIGNER · CHARLES NICHOLSON
OWNER · SIR THOMAS LIPTON
SKIPPER · WILLIAM BURTON
CLUB · ROYAL ULSTER YC, UK
DEFENDER · *RESOLUTE*
LOA · 32.4 m (106 ft 4 in)
DESIGNER · NATHANAEL G. HERRESHOFF
OWNERS · HENRY WALTERS & SYNDICATE
SKIPPER · CHARLES FRANCIS ADAMS
CLUB · NYYC, USA

A 17-year gap occurred between challenges for the cup, caused both by World War I and by the feeling that races should take place in smaller, more manageable boats than those sailed up to 1903. But it was not until 1912 that a new rating system, the Universal Rule, was introduced, limiting boats to a waterline length of 75 ft (22.9 m) and thus restricting excess sail area. Time allowances were still required however, for the ratings of the competing boats were still different.

The first challenge for the cup after the introduction of these new rules was scheduled for September 1914, but war broke out as the British *Shamrock IV* was crossing the Atlantic and it was to spend the war years in storage in Brooklyn, New York. The contest was resumed in 1920, with the Herreshoff-designed *Resolute* defending against a substantially refitted *Shamrock*. The challenger won the first race when the defender had to retire with a broken halyard – the first time a defender had failed to finish a race – and then won the second on sheer boat speed, outsailing the defender on all legs of the triangular course. One more win would lead to the cup returning to Britain. The next race was a dead heat, the only one in cup history, but *Resolute* won on time allowance by seven minutes. The defender then went on to win the next two races and thus hold the cup by the tightest of margins of three races to two.

"I canna win" was Lipton's response. It seemed as if the 'Auld Mug' – Lipton's nickname for the cup – was destined to remain in America forever.

◆◆◆

A Close-run Thing *The Nicholson-designed* Shamrock IV *came within one race of winning the* America's Cup *for Britain in 1920.*

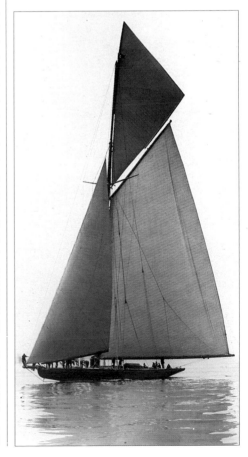

1930-1937

The 1930 America's Cup was the first to be held in bermudan-rigged boats conforming to the American Universal Rule, J-class, which specified a waterline length of between 75 ft (22.9 m) and 87 ft (26.5 m) provided that the rating did not exceed 76 ft. Because the waterline length and sail area were now so closely defined under this rule, races for the America's Cup took place for the first time without any time allowances: the first boat across the line won the race. Two other changes affected the 1930 series: the course was moved away from the congested waters of New York to Newport, Rhode Island, a favorite summer residence for the wealthy; and the number of races in the series was increased from the best of five to the best of seven.

The use of the J-class for the 1930 cup races was agreed to after three months of correspondence by the NYYC and Sir Thomas Lipton, making his fifth and final challenge for the cup at the age of 80. While he had once competed purely as a sporting gesture, he was now obsessive about the event – he let it be widely known that he expected to win in 1930. However, an era in cup racing ended with his sudden death in 1931.

◆ ◆ ◆

The J-class Courses *From 1930 to 1962, either a triangular or a windward/leeward course off Newport, Rhode Island, was used for America's Cup races. Each course was sailed around once, a distance of about 30 miles.*

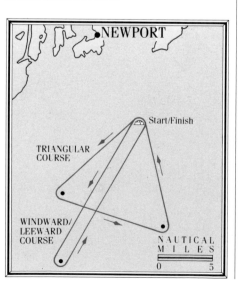

1930

ENTERPRISE beat SHAMROCK V 4-0
CHALLENGER · SHAMROCK V
LOA · 36.3 m (119 ft 1 in)
DESIGNER · CHARLES NICHOLSON
OWNER · SIR THOMAS LIPTON
SKIPPER · NED HEARD
CLUB · ROYAL ULSTER YC, UK
DEFENDER · ENTERPRISE
LOA · 36.8 m (120 ft 9 in)
DESIGNER · W. STARLING BURGESS
OWNERS · WINTHROP ALDRICH & SYNDICATE
SKIPPER · HAROLD VANDERBILT
CLUB · NYYC, USA

The untried British challenger *Shamrock V* was at an immediate disadvantage against *Enterprise*, which had raced and won against three other J-class boats in trials. Steered by Harold 'Mike' Vanderbilt, with an amateur afterguard but a professional crew, it was extremely well prepared and had no difficulty in beating *Shamrock V* in four straight races, the third of which was a shoo-in when the challenger retired with a broken main halyard.

1934

RAINBOW beat ENDEAVOUR 4-2
CHALLENGER · ENDEAVOUR
LOA · 39.6 m (129 ft 8 in)
DESIGNER · CHARLES NICHOLSON
OWNER & SKIPPER · T.O.M. SOPWITH
CLUB · ROYAL YACHT SQUADRON, UK
DEFENDER · RAINBOW
LOA · 38.6 m (126 ft 7 in)
DESIGNER · W. STARLING BURGESS
OWNERS · HAROLD VANDERBILT & SYNDICATE
SKIPPER · HAROLD VANDERBILT
CLUB · NYYC, USA

The British challenges in 1934 and 1937 came from T.O.M. Sopwith, builder of such famous warplanes as the Camel. Charles Nicholson again designed the challenger and Sopwith's chief aviation designer, Frank Murdoch, was consultant on the rig. It was recognized on its arrival in Newport as the most serious British challenger yet.

However, shortly before *Endeavour* left for America, the crew struck for higher wages. Sopwith sacked most of them and replaced them with amateurs. It was to prove a costly decision, for although

experienced, they were not of the same caliber as *Rainbow*'s professional crew.

American fears about *Endeavour* were justified when it won the first two races by 2 min 9 sec and 51 sec respectively. In the third race *Endeavour* was leading with only a close reaching leg to the finish and victory. At this point Harold Vanderbilt, the defending helmsman, handed over the helm to one of his afterguard, Sherman Hoyt, who outmaneuvered *Endeavour* to snatch the lead.

In the fourth race, *Endeavour* protested *Rainbow* (see below), who went on to win the race. Once again Sopwith suffered from the lack of professional advice, for the American racing rules – not to be united with those of Europe until 1958 – called for a protest flag to be hoisted immediately after the incident. The British rules, which Sopwith followed, only required such a flag be flown at the finish of the race. The NYYC followed the American rules and threw out the protest, in despite the fact that the NYYC observer, C.F. Havemeyer, on board *Endeavour* (each boat carried a representative from the other side) had advised Sopwith that carrying a flag at the finish was sufficient, and that this was common practice in American racing.

With the series tied at two races all, there was still much to fight for. *Rainbow* took the fifth race and went in to the sixth needing only one more victory to win the series. *Endeavour* still needed to win two

1934—FOURTH RACE

1 Endeavour *reaches the windward mark ahead of* Rainbow.
2 Rainbow *sails to windward of* Endeavour, *who mistakenly sails too low, and starts to overtake.*
3 *To keep the lead,* Endeavour *luffs* Rainbow, *who keeps straight on.*

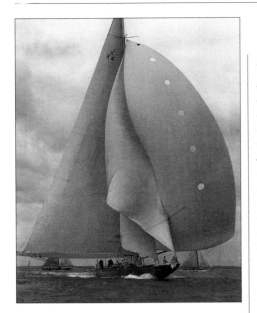

Endeavour *Designed by Charles Nicholson and owned and helmed by T.O.M. Sopwith. Endeavour won the first two races in 1934 and was a faster boat than the defender* Rainbow.

more races to win. The sixth race started with intense pre-start maneuvers that led to protest flags raised on both boats. *Endeavour* eventually got the better of the fight and led over the start line by 48 sec. It held its lead around the first mark but was caught in the strengthening breeze with too much canvas and was overtaken by the defender as it changed sails. *Rainbow* led into the final run, and although pursued by *Endeavour*, maintained its lead and won the race, and the series, by 55 sec. Both starting protests were withdrawn.

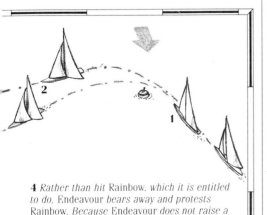

4 *Rather than hit* Rainbow, *which it is entitled to do,* Endeavour *bears away and protests* Rainbow. *Because* Endeavour *does not raise a protest flag immediately, but waits until the end of the race, the protest fails.*
5 Rainbow *sails on to win the race.*

1937

RANGER beat ENDEAVOUR II 4-0
CHALLENGER · *ENDEAVOUR II*
LOA · 41.4 m (135 ft 9 in)
DESIGNER · CHARLES NICHOLSON
OWNER & SKIPPER · T.O.M. SOPWITH
CLUB · ROYAL YACHT SQUADRON, UK
DEFENDER · *RANGER*
LOA · 41.4 m (135 ft 9 in)
DESIGNERS · W. STARLING BURGESS & OLIN J. STEPHENS
OWNER & SKIPPER · HAROLD VANDERBILT
CLUB · NYYC, USA

After his near-miss in 1934, Sopwith challenged again in late 1935, commissioning Charles Nicholson to build *Endeavour II*.

The NYYC requested a delay until 1937, to avoid the presidential election of 1936, and entrusted the defense once again to Harold Vanderbilt. His new boat was *Ranger*, designed by Starling Burgess, assisted by the young Olin Stephens. It was extensively tank-tested against other J-class boats, including the 1934 challenger *Endeavour*, and sported a massive spinnaker of 1,672 sqm (18,000 sqft). To increase sail area the designers worked the maximum sail area possible into the foretriangle measurement, in a way that is done today as a matter of course. With superior tactics, it beat *Endeavour II* in four straight races, two of which were by margins of over 17 minutes.

The American-designed Ranger *is considered to be the greatest J-class boat ever built.*

1958-1964

After the enforced lull in America's Cup racing during World War II, interest revived in the 1950s. However a new, smaller and cheaper class of yacht was required for the competition, for all the American J-class boats had been broken up by 1941 and few British ones remained in a sailable condition. Indeed it was said that there was no more chance of seeing a J-class sailing than a dinosaur grazing.

On 30 July 1956, the NYYC petitioned and later gained agreement from the New York State Court to alter the Deed of Gift to reduce the permitted waterline length to 44ft (13.4m), which allowed the smaller 12-Meter boats to race in the event. The British had been building these boats since 1906, 12 alone in the 1930s, while the Americans had started in 1928, with six launched in the 1930s. Both countries therefore had experience in the class. One further change to the Deed of Gift enabled challengers to ship rather than sail their boats to the race course, while for the first time internationally agreed racing rules were used, replacing the NYYC rules in use until then.

❖❖❖

The 12-Meter Courses *In 1958 and 1962, the competitors either sailed once around a triangular course or twice around a windward/leeward course. From 1964 to 1983 they sailed once around an Olympic-type course, the first leg to windward. Each course was roughly 24 miles long.*

1958

COLUMBIA beat SCEPTRE 4-0

CHALLENGER · *SCEPTRE*
LOA · 21m (68ft 10in)
DESIGNER · DAVID BOYD
OWNERS · HUGH GOODSON & SYNDICATE
SKIPPER · GRAHAM MANN
CLUB · ROYAL YACHT SQUADRON, UK

DEFENDER · *COLUMBIA*
LOA · 21.2m (69ft 7in)
DESIGNER · SPARKMAN & STEPHENS
OWNERS · HENRY SEARS & SYNDICATE
SKIPPER · BRIGGS CUNNINGHAM
CLUB · NYYC, USA

The first post-war challenge came from an RYS syndicate led by Hugh Goodson. He owned an old 12-Meter, *Flica II*, that had been converted to cruising; another pre-war yacht, *Evaine*, that had been laid up since 1939, was bought by Owen Aisher, an active offshore racer, and acted as trial horse for the challenger, the grandly named *Sceptre*. This new 12-Meter was designed by David Boyd of Scotland who previously had had success with the pre-war 6-Meter *Lalage*. However, once launched *Sceptre* had considerable difficulty in beating the aged *Evaine*.

The Americans modelled their challenger, *Columbia*, on *Vim*, the last 12-Meter built before the war. Owned by Harold Vanderbilt, it had come to Britain in 1939

and swept the board in every race. Like *Vim*, *Columbia* was designed by the firm of Sparkman and Stephens. It was a wise choice, for *Columbia* beat two other recently built 12s – *Easterner* and *Weatherly* – and went on to defeat *Sceptre* easily in four straight races. Once again, the challenger had been outdesigned and outsailed by the American defender.

1962

WEATHERLY beat GRETEL 4-1

CHALLENGER · *GRETEL*
LOA · 21.2m (69ft 5in)
DESIGNER · ALAN PAYNE
OWNERS · SIR FRANK PACKER & SYNDICATE
SKIPPER · JOCK STURROCK
CLUB · ROYAL SYDNEY YS, AUSTRALIA

DEFENDER · *WEATHERLY*
LOA · 20.4m (66ft 10in)
DESIGNER · PHILIP RHODES
OWNERS · HENRY MERCER, ARNOLD FRESE & CORNELIUS WALSH
SKIPPER · BUS MOSBACHER
CLUB · NYYC, USA

One advantage of the change in deed concerning the passage of challenging boats to the race course was that it had the effect of allowing countries from all over the world to compete. No longer did a challenging club have to be within sailing distance of Rhode Island.

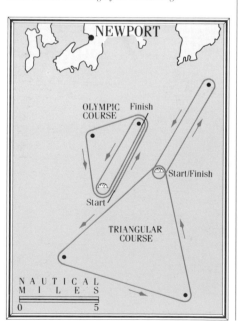

The 1958 defender Columbia *reaches downwind.*

After rounding the final mark behind Weatherly *(left),* Gretel *was quicker hoisting its spinnaker and surfed past to win in the second race in 1962.*

In 1962 Australia challenged for the first time. The challenge came from Sir Frank Packer, a newspaper magnate who used his wealth to build *Gretel* and charter *Vim* as a trial horse. The NYYC assumed that the depth of 12-Meter knowledge in Australia was not that great and only one new 12-Meter, the Ted Hood-designed *Nefertiti*, was built. However an older boat, *Weatherly*, was chosen, and in retrospect it was apparent that as with *Rainbow* in 1934, the 'wrong boat' had been picked. Although it defeated *Gretel* by four races to one, the winning margins were not great. Indeed, the 26-second victory in the fifth race was the closest finish ever in a cup race. The Australians had a fast boat and considerable sailing abilities, but their inexperience in 12-Meter racing handicapped them. Their first challenge proved they were formidable opponents.

1964

CONSTELLATION beat SOVEREIGN 4-0
CHALLENGER · *SOVEREIGN*
LOA · 21 m (69 ft)
DESIGNER · DAVID BOYD
OWNER · TONY BOYDEN
SKIPPER · PETER SCOTT
CLUB · ROYAL THAMES YC, UK
DEFENDER · *CONSTELLATION*
LOA · 20 m (65 ft 5 in)
DESIGNER · SPARKMAN & STEPHENS
OWNERS · WALTER GUBELMAN & SYNDICATE
SKIPPERS · ROBERT BAVIER & ERIC RIDDER
CLUB · NYYC, USA

Britain returned to the fray in 1964 with a challenge from Tony Boyden of the Royal Thames Yacht Club. The challenger, *Sovereign*, was once again designed by David Boyd; in trials against its sistership *Kurrewa V* and the 1958 challenger *Sceptre*, *Sovereign* had considerable difficulty holding the 1958 challenger, which was not considered a good omen for the new boat.

In America, two new boats, *Constellation* and *American Eagle*, were joined by *Columbia*, *Nefertiti* and *Easterner* in the trials. It soon became apparent that the newer boats were in a class completely on their own. *Eagle* pushed *Constellation* hard in the selection trials, with the inevitable result that when the races started against the challenger, *Constellation* was in a perfect state. It beat *Sovereign* in four straight races with the overwhelming margins of 5 min 34 sec, 20 min 24 sec, 6 min 33 sec and 15 min 40 sec respectively. Its lead in the second race was the biggest winning margin since *Mayflower* beat *Galatea* by 29 min 9 sec in 1886.

1967-1980

It was evident after the debacle of 1964, that the main challenge to America's cup supremacy was going to come from the Australians. With its first taste of success in 1962, Australia gained expertise and confidence at every challenge, slowly learning the skills of design and boat handling that were necessary to challenge successfully American domination of the cup.

1967

INTREPID beat DAME PATTIE 4-0
CHALLENGER · DAME PATTIE
LOA · 19.8 m (65 ft 2 in)
DESIGNER · WARWICK HOOD
OWNERS · EMIL CHRISTENSEN & COMMERCIAL SYNDICATE
SKIPPER · JOCK STURROCK
CLUB · ROYAL SYDNEY YS, AUSTRALIA
DEFENDER · INTREPID
LOA · 19.5 m (64 ft)
DESIGNER · SPARKMAN & STEPHENS
OWNER · INTREPID SYNDICATE
SKIPPER · BUS MOSBACHER
CLUB · NYYC, USA

Only one new boat, *Intrepid*, was built by the Americans to defend the cup against the Australians in 1967. Much as *Ranger* had comprehensively beaten *Endeavour II* in 1937 after the close shave of 1934, so *Intrepid* put behind it the strong Australian challenge of 1962 and, helmed by Bus Mosbacher, easily defeated *Dame Pattie* in four straight races.

Intrepid *Designed by the American firm of Sparkman and Stephens, Intrepid successfully defended the cup in 1967 and 1970.*

1970

INTREPID beat GRETEL II 4-1
CHALLENGER · GRETEL II
LOA · 18.9 m (62 ft)
DESIGNER · ALAN PAYNE
OWNER · SIR FRANK PACKER
SKIPPER · JIM HARDY
CLUB · ROYAL SYDNEY YS, AUSTRALIA
DEFENDER · INTREPID
LOA · 19.5 m (64 ft)
DESIGNER · SPARKMAN & STEPHENS
OWNER · INTREPID SYNDICATE
SKIPPER · BILL FICKER
CLUB · NYYC, USA

For the first time, a series of elimination races was held for the right to challenge the Americans. The Australian *Gretel II* easily disposed of *France*, the French challenger, owned and sailed by Baron Bich, and prepared to challenge the aging *Intrepid*, defending the cup for America for the second time.

The cup races themselves were accompanied by acrimony as sharp as anything since the days of the Earl of Dunraven, with the first collision since 1895 and the first protest since 1934. In the first race the Australian skipper, Jim Hardy, protested over an alleged infringement before the starting gun, but his protest was dismissed by the NYYC race committee.

In the second race a collision occurred just after the starting gun (see a sketch of the incident below), causing both boats to protest. *Gretel II* went on to cross the

finish line first but was then disqualified by the race committee, to the dismay of its supporters, after the protest was heard. The international friction was considerable, for many people, misunderstanding the highly technical racing rules, thought the NYYC was not allowing the Australians their rightful win.

Gretel II got its revenge by winning the fourth race by a minute, but the defender took the third and fifth races by less than two minutes each. Once again, a quicker challenger was outwitted by superior American sailing and expertise in a slightly slower boat, showing just how difficult it was for a challenger to actually win the cup.

1974

COURAGEOUS beat SOUTHERN CROSS 4-0
CHALLENGER · SOUTHERN CROSS
LOA · 20.5 m (67 ft 3 in)
DESIGNER · BOB MILLER
OWNER · ALAN BOND
SKIPPER · JOHN CUNEO
CLUB · ROYAL PERTH YC, AUSTRALIA
DEFENDER · COURAGEOUS
LOA · 21 m (66 ft)
DESIGNER · SPARKMAN & STEPHENS
OWNER · COURAGEOUS SYNDICATE
SKIPPER · TED HOOD
CLUB · NYYC, USA

After the controversy about the protest in 1970, an international jury replaced the NYYC race committee, but the 1974 series

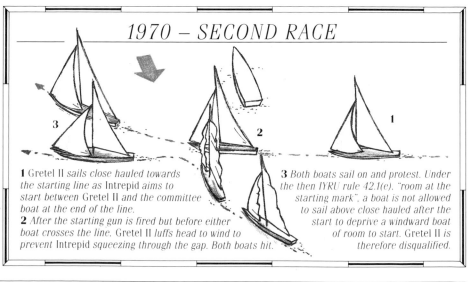

1970 – SECOND RACE

1 *Gretel II sails close hauled towards the starting line as* Intrepid *aims to start between* Gretel II *and the committee boat at the end of the line.*
2 *After the starting gun is fired but before either boat crosses the line,* Gretel II *luffs head to wind to prevent* Intrepid *squeezing through the gap. Both boats hit.*
3 *Both boats sail on and protest. Under the then IYRU rule 42.1(e), "room at the starting mark", a boat is not allowed to sail above close hauled after the start to deprive a windward boat of room to start.* Gretel II *is therefore disqualified.*

Gretel II *The 1970 Australian challenger* Gretel II *powers to windward. The American* Intrepid *defeated it 4-1 in the most acrimonious series of cup races since 1895.*

❖❖❖

of races proved to be a far more placid affair. For the first time it was now permitted to build 12-Meters in aluminum as well as wood, bringing back memories of the steel hulls used in the J-class boats before the war.

Once again selection trials took place between the French, represented by Baron Bich's new *France*, and the Australian *Southern Cross*, owned by Alan Bond and designed by Bob Miller, later to change his name to Ben Lexcen. The Australian craft won the trials easily in four straight races, but then went on to be defeated comfortably by the defender *Courageous*, steered by the sailmaker Ted Hood with Dennis Conner as starting helmsman. Only in the second race did the boats finish within a minute of each other.

1977

COURAGEOUS beat AUSTRALIA 4-0
CHALLENGER · *AUSTRALIA*
LOA · 19.7 m (64 ft 6 in)
DESIGNERS · BEN LEXCEN & JOHAN VALENTIJN
OWNER · ALAN BOND
SKIPPER · NOEL ROBINS
CLUB · SUN CITY YC, AUSTRALIA
DEFENDER · *COURAGEOUS*
LOA · 21 m (66 ft)
DESIGNER · SPARKMAN & STEPHENS
OWNER · KINGS POINT FUND INC
SKIPPER · TED TURNER
CLUB · NYYC, USA

Elimination trials for the right to challenge America took place between France with Baron Bich's *France II*, Sweden with Pelle Pettersson's *Sverige* and Australia with Alan Bond's *Australia*, with the Australian boat easily winning the series. *Australia* was designed by Ben Lexcen and Johan Valentijn, who later took American citizenship and designed 12-Meters for the Americans, including the defender in the 1983 series of races, *Liberty*.

Two new boats were built in America – *Enterprise*, designed by Sparkman and Stephens, and *Independence*, designed by Ted Hood – but it was the heavily modified *Courageous* that won the right to defend the cup. Her helmsman was Ted Turner, the media and baseball mogul, who was also a highly successful ocean-racing helmsman: his sailing record has included winning the Congressional Cup in 1977 and subsequently the notorious Fastnet Race in 1979.

In the first race *Courageous* was out ahead and slightly to the leeward of *Australia* just 10 minutes after the start. The challenger was expected to pick up speed downwind but made no real impression and trailed *Courageous* over the line by 1 min 28 sec. In the second race light wind caused time to run out before either boat could finish the course. The next three races saw the defender winning, the last one by 2 min 25 sec, producing another clean sweep for the NYYC. The two boats had sometimes been close, but Ted Turner and his crew were just a little better in every department, even though their four-year-old boat was up against the latest and most advanced 12-Meter.

1980

FREEDOM beat AUSTRALIA 4-1
CHALLENGER · *AUSTRALIA*
LOA · 19.7 m (64 ft 6 in)
DESIGNERS · BEN LEXCEN & JOHAN VALENTIJN
OWNER · ALAN BOND
SKIPPER · J. HARDY
CLUB · ROYAL PERTH YC, AUSTRALIA
DEFENDER · *FREEDOM*
LOA · 19.3 m (63 ft 6 in)
DESIGNER · SPARKMAN & STEPHENS
OWNER · FR. SCHUYLER FOUNDATION INC.
SKIPPER · DENNIS CONNER
CLUB · NYYC, USA

Well aware of Sir Thomas Lipton's persistent efforts to win the cup, Alan Bond had no hesitation in entering his third challenge in 1980. Once again France challenged with *France III*, Sweden with *Sverige*, and Tony Boyden of Britain returned after 16 years with *Lionheart*. Alan Bond and the Australians campaigned with the refitted and heavily modified *Australia*, the defeated challenger in 1977, and won the elimination trials.

Technologically the most adventurous boat of the trials was the Ian Howlett-designed *Lionheart*. It sported a mast with a flexible top section, allowing it to bend when the boat sailed to windward – a device outlawed after the series ended. The Australians rerigged their boat with a similar mast for the cup races but were up against a strong defender, *Freedom*, the last boat to be designed by Sparkman and Stephens, who had been associated with every defender since 1937. *Freedom* had defeated several strong boats and crews, including the old *Courageous*, losing only 4 out of 40 races in the elimination series.

In the cup races, *Australia* won the second, light-wind race, but lost the other four by small margins. It was a closely fought series, with the Australian attitude lacking the razzmatazz of the earlier challenges. In his professional and serious approach to mounting a campaign to win the cup, Alan Bond was a formidable opponent. He came out of the 1980 series with the belief that he was only a little short of equalling the Americans' skills in 12-Meter construction and racing. Australia now had the technical knowledge to mount a winning campaign.

1983

It will long be argued as to why the New York Yacht Club, holders of the America's Cup for 132 years, should lose it in 1983. There had been close shaves before, and obviously the longest winning stretch in any sport must prove finite. A number of answers present themselves.

THE CHALLENGE

By 1983 many of the traditional disadvantages to the challenger had been eroded. It no longer had to sail to the series across an ocean and, with the internationalization of yachting, could benefit from the advances made in yacht technology in America. Furthermore, several American 12-Meters, but never the winning boat, had been sold to foreign syndicates, enabling them to tune up against proven designs.

The 1983 challenge from Australia also had two further benefits. The first was that it was headed by the experienced Alan Bond, making his fourth attempt to win. The second was that the challenger had to beat six other boats – a record number – before winning the right to challenge. The successful boat – *Australia II*, designed by Ben Lexcen – had beaten the British *Victory 83*, the French *France III*, the Italian *Azzura*, the Canadian *Canada I*, and the Australian *Advance* and *Challenge 12*, in a series of trials that improved its own performance.

THE DEFENSE

In the US, three new boats were built by two syndicates. Freedom 83 syndicate, with Dennis Conner as helmsman, commissioned *Spirit of America* from Sparkman and Stephens (Olin Stephens, though retired, was available as a consultant) and *Magic* from Johan Valentijn. The other, 'people's syndicate,' organized by Gary Jobson and Tom Blackaller, commissioned a new *Defender* from designer Dave Pedrick, and rebuilt the old *Courageous*. In trials held in 1982, none of the three new boats proved a match for the two trial horses, *Courageous* and the 1980 defender, *Freedom*, so Dennis Conner commissioned Valentijn (who was now an American citizen) to build another 12-Meter, *Liberty*. At one point it looked as if *Courageous* was faster than this boat too, but eventually it was *Liberty* that was selected to defend.

THE KEEL

The one factor that markedly differentiated *Australia II* from *Liberty* was the former's wing-shaped keel. The concept of such a keel is simple: under the 12-Meter rule, it pays to lower the center of gravity by keeping the weight of the keel as low as possible. A simple bulb attached to the bottom of the usual fin shape would cause extra resistance through the water, but a wing shape can improve performance, if it is correctly designed. This had always been the elusive factor in such keels, but as a result of some original thinking from designer Ben Lexcen, and with help from the Ship Model Basin at Wageningen in the Netherlands, *Australia II* was fitted with a wing keel.

When it became apparent in June 1983 that *Australia II* had a revolutionary keel, it was too late for its rivals to design and fit the same to their boats. However, one or two of them did try to fit smaller wings, or winglets, without success. The Australian keel itself was kept under wraps and not seen or photographed. It had, however, been officially measured along

◆◆◆

The Keel *By adding wings to either side of the keel,* Australia II *was given an edge on performance over conventional 12-Meters, including the defender* Liberty. *Declared legal under the 12-Meter rule, the winged keel caused considerable controversy throughout the 1983 series.*

with the rest of the boats early in the season by the team of measurers – an American, an Australian and an Englishman, who was the chief measurer of the IYRU. Although allowed, no representative from the NYYC had been present at the measurement, and once satisfied that the boat was proper, the three members of the measurement committee were not obliged to comment further.

The NYYC preferred tougher tactics; its first response to this was to show that wings were illegal under the 12-Meter rule. When this attempt failed, it then tried to show that the keel, with its Dutch tank testing, had been designed by non-Australians, also illegal under the rules. This attempt also failed, so the NYYC had to put the affair known as 'keelgate' behind them and fight it out against the Australians race by race on the water.

1983

AUSTRALIA II beat LIBERTY 4-3
CHALLENGER · *AUSTRALIA II*
LOA · 19.7 m (64 ft 6 in)
DESIGNER · BEN LEXCEN
OWNER · ALAN BOND
SKIPPER · JOHN BERTRAND
CLUB · ROYAL PERTH YC, AUSTRALIA
DEFENDER · *LIBERTY*
LOA · 19.4 m (63 ft 6 in)
DESIGNER · JOHAN VALENTIJN
OWNER · FR. SCHUYLER FOUNDATION INC.
SKIPPER · DENNIS CONNER
CLUB · NYYC, USA

The 1983 series was the most drawn-out series ever held, taking place over 14 days from 13 to 26 September. The best four of seven races counted, and for the first time all seven were sailed. Lack of wind caused one further race to be abandoned and prevented the start of two others. The timetable of that agonizing fortnight reads like this:

Tuesday 13: Lack of wind prevents the start of the race.
Wednesday 14: Liberty wins the first race.
Thursday 15: Liberty wins the second race.
Friday 16: The Australians call for a lay day, as allowed by the rules.
Saturday 17: The time limit expires during a light-wind race in which Liberty trails Australia II. Despite this omen, it still

1983 – FINAL RACE

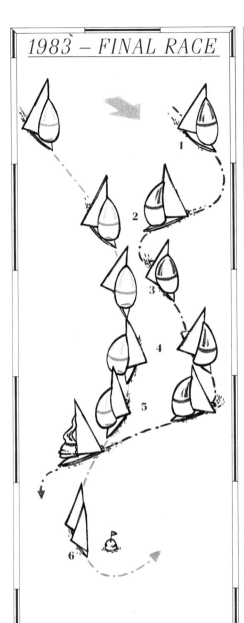

1 Liberty *leads* Australia II *by 52 seconds at the last windward mark and sails off to the port side of the course.*
2 Liberty *gybes onto starboard and closes in on* Australia II.
3 Liberty *gybes again back to port, close to* Australia II.
4 Australia II *gybes onto starboard and picks up more breeze.*
5 *As they meet again,* Australia II *is sailing faster and overtakes* Liberty.
6 Australia II *rounds the leeward mark ahead of* Liberty *and goes on to win the race by 41 seconds, and with it the cup.*

looks as if, five days into the series, America will retain the cup.

Sunday 18: With the light breeze continuing, *Australia II* shows superiority on every leg of the course, especially downwind, and wins by 3 min 14 sec, the best win by a challenger since *Endeavour* beat *Rainbow* by 2 min 9 sec in 1934. The score is now 2-1.

Monday 19: The Americans call for their first lay day.

Tuesday 20: Liberty wins again, bringing its score to 3-1, and needs only one more victory to retain the cup.

Wednesday 21: In a fresher breeze *Liberty* has a rigging failure before the start, which is repaired but then fails again during the race, allowing *Australia II* to win. With the score now at 3-2, the world begins to sense that something historic is happening at Newport.

Thursday 22: The challenger picks up better wind on the course and wins again, levelling the series at 3-3, an unprecedented result. For almost a quarter of a century – since 1958 and the start of 12-Meter racing, challengers had won only three races.

Friday 23: The Australians call for another lay day.

Saturday 24: Lack of wind prevents the start of the race.

Sunday 25: The Americans call for their second lay day.

Monday 26: For the last race in light air, both boats have an equal start and *Liberty* leads around the last windward mark. As described in the sketch to the left, *Australia II* overtakes it and wins the series – and with it the cup – by 4-3.

In the Lead *(above)*
The challenger Australia II *leads the red-hulled* Liberty *downwind in the 1983 cup series.*

Moment of Victory
(left) Alan Bond, owner of Australia II, *shows his jubilation in winning the America's Cup for Australia.*

1987

If there was a shadow of negligence or complacency in the American camp in 1983, there was none at all in evidence for the 1987 America's Cup held in Perth, Western Australia. Having suffered the ignominy of losing the cup for the first time in 132 years, the Americans were determined to regain it this time.

In preparation for the event, the NYYC, traditional defenders of the cup, built three successive boats called *America II*, hoping to emulate the first *America*'s success. Other American clubs followed: the Newport (California) Harbor Yacht Club Eagle syndicate commissioned *Eagle*; the Chicago Yacht Club Heart of America challenge produced *Heart of America*; the St. Francis Yacht Club (San Francisco) Golden Gate challenge built *USA 1* and *USA 2*; and the Yale Corinthian Yacht Club rebuilt the old *Courageous*.

The successful boat, however, came not from the NYYC but from San Diego. The Sail America Syndicate, under the flag of the San Diego Yacht Club, financed Dennis Conner's *Stars and Stripes*. He successfully defeated all the other American boats and those of the five other challenging nations – Canada, France, Italy, New Zealand and the UK – in a lengthy series of races, and won the right to challenge the Australians. This was the chance for Conner to avenge his defeat in 1983.

The 1987 Course *A modified Olympic course was used for the 1987 series, consisting of a windward/leeward leg, a triangle, a second windward/leeward leg, and a final beat. Although the course, at 24 miles, was the same length as that used between 1964-83, there were more legs; each was shorter.*

1987

STARS AND STRIPES beat KOOKABURRA III 4-0

CHALLENGER · *STARS AND STRIPES*
LOA · 19.6 m (64 ft 4 in)
DESIGNERS · DAVID PEDRICK, BRITTON CHANCE & BRUCE NELSON
OWNER · SAIL AMERICA SYNDICATE
SKIPPER · DENNIS CONNER
CLUB · SAN DIEGO YC, USA

DEFENDER · *KOOKABURRA III*
LOA · 20.4 m (66 ft 11 in)
DESIGNERS · JOHN SWARBRICK & IAIN MURRAY
OWNER · TASKFORCE '87 SYNDICATE
SKIPPER · IAIN MURRAY
CLUB · ROYAL PERTH YC, AUSTRALIA

The Royal Perth Yacht Club had chosen its defender, *Kookaburra III*, from trials involving five straight races. Alan Bond, the 1983 cup winner, had built two new boats, *Australia III* and *Australia IV*, while another Australian businessman, Kevin Parry, had built three 12-Meters, *Kookaburra I, II* and *III*. The latter defeated Bond's *Australia IV* in the final challenge round, and went on to race against Conner's *Stars and Stripes*. In the final, *Stars and Stripes* had four straight wins out of the best of seven. On three successive days she beat *Kookaburra III* by 1 min 41 sec, 1 min 10 sec, and 1 min 46 sec. After a day's rest, the Americans regained the cup after a final victory of 1 min 59 sec.

The Cup Winner *The budget for the 1987 America's Cup winner, Stars and Stripes, was estimated at $16 million (£10 million). In order to build the fastest boat possible, three well-known designers were taken on to design Conner's boat. The Americans left nothing to chance in their quest to recapture the cup.*

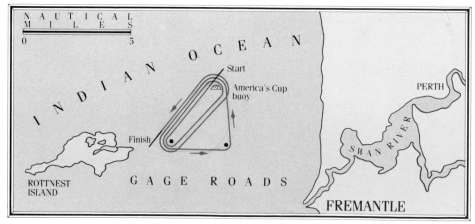

A jubilant Dennis Conner – 1987 Cup winner.

1988

After Fremantle, the Californian port of San Diego became host to the America's Cup. However, the San Diego Yacht Club was slow in acquainting would-be challengers with its intentions. As a result of this delay, Michael Fay, head of a New Zealand syndicate, lodged a challenge that took the Americans by surprise.

Fay challenged with a 27.4-m (90-ft) waterline boat, *New Zealand*, not a conventional 12-Meter as expected. When the Deed of Gift had been amended in 1956 (see p150), lowering the minimum waterline length to accommodate 12-Meter boats, the maximum length had not been changed. The original deed (see p141) had stipulated that boats racing for the cup should not be "more than ninety feet [27.4m] on the waterline, if of one mast."

When the SDYC realized that Fay's challenge was serious, a court action ensued, but Fay's action was declared legal. The defending Sail America Foundation declined to build a similar boat for the defense; in the absence of rules other than those pertaining to the waterline length, they constructed a 18.3-m (60-ft) catamaran, *Stars and Stripes*. Once more, the two parties returned to court, Fay trying to get the multihull declared illegal on the grounds that the two boats were totally dissimilar but the court could find nothing in the deed to prevent such a contest.

◆◆◆

The 1988 Courses *Because no agreement was reached, the event was sailed according to the Deed of Gift. Three races were planned, the best two deciding the winner. The first and third were over a windward/leeward course of 20 miles each leg, the second a triangular course with legs of 13 miles.*

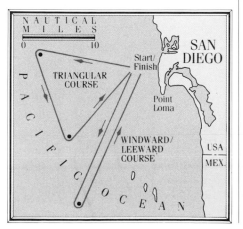

1988
STARS AND STRIPES beat *NEW ZEALAND* 2-0
CHALLENGER · *NEW ZEALAND*
LOA · 37.5 m (123 ft)
DESIGNER · BRUCE FARR
OWNER · MICHAEL FAY & SYNDICATE
SKIPPER · DAVID BARNES
CLUB · MERCURY BAY BOATING CLUB, NZ
DEFENDER · *STARS AND STRIPES*
LOA · 18.3 m (60 ft)
DESIGNERS · BRITTON CHANCE, DAVE HUBBARD,
DUNCAN McLANE, GINO MORELLI,
BRUCE NELSON & BERNARD NIVELT
OWNER · SAIL AMERICA FOUNDATION
SKIPPER · DENNIS CONNER
CLUB · SAN DIEGO YC, USA

The result was to be on the best of three races: under the gaze of the smallest spectator fleet for years, *Stars and Stripes* won the first race by 18 min 15 sec, and the second by 21 min 10 sec. The defenders had won; the last time they had needed to sail so few races was in 1887.

There was subsequently much discussion within interested circles concerning the most suitable boat – to be agreed by all parties – for future America's Cup racing. Since the first defense in 1870, a number of measurement rules have been introduced. After more than 30 years of using the 12-Meter class, a new 22.9-m (75 ft) class has been proposed and is expected to be used for the next America's Cup.

◆◆◆

Ill-matched Pair *The enormous difference in size between the 1988 America's Cup contenders caused much acrimony. The 37.5-m (123-ft) monohull* New Zealand *dwarfs the American 18.3-m (60-ft) catamaran,* Stars and Stripes.

Chapter 5

Inshore Racing

*B*efore the days of offshore and lengthy international races, all regular racing took place around marks close to the shore or on inland waters. Today, such races retain their popularity with the many people who prefer the intensity and close competition enjoyed on inshore courses.

Inshore racing is more closely fought between boats than offshore racing, and includes the championships of hundreds of classes, many international trophy races and regattas, the Olympic Games, the America's Cup, and countless club races and events. For many years, it was argued that the relative merits of boats could only be tested in an inshore race. This is true to a large extent, although the importance of good preparation, sound equipment and, above all, the ability of helmsman and crew, are also major factors. The ever-present element of luck is also of great significance.

THE ORGANIZATION OF WORLD RACING

Today, sailors take it for granted that they can jump on a plane in, say, New York, fly to the south of France, and charter a boat that they can then race according to a set of rules and codes recognized throughout the world. It has not always been so straightforward.

In the early days of yachting, enthusiasts formed themselves into clubs, not just for social reasons but also for the important purpose of drawing up suitable rules under which to race each other. Two kinds of rules were – and are – required in order that racing might take place. The first is a rating, measurement, or one-design rule for the boats; the second is a set of 'right-of-way' rules to deal with what happens when boats overtake, cross each other or collide. The evolution of measurement rules is recounted on pp 284-97, but both in these and in the right-of-way rules, a few clubs over the years have tended to take the lead and write their own rules, which have been adapted and amended by other, newer clubs to suit their own needs.

One of the earliest rules in most clubs was that every boat must carry either its owner or another club member while racing. The point of this rule was that racing depended on a code of honor between club members; races open to outsiders were rare. This rule still applies today, as Rule 21: "Every yacht shall have on board a member of a yacht or sailing club recognized by its national authority to be in charge of the yacht."

The Royal Thames Yacht Club rules of 1866 stated in Rule X: "That a yacht sailing in a match shall have some member of the club to which she belongs on board, who shall be held fully responsible for the vessel being sailed in accordance with the rules..." The same set of rules also stated that: "In sailing to windward, the yacht on the port tack must invariably give way to the yacht on the starboard tack; any yacht disobeying this regulation forfeits all claim to the prize." Today, this rule is simplified to read: "A port tack yacht shall keep clear of a starboard tack yacht." Those same Royal Thames Yacht Club rules also included the measurement proviso in Rule VIII: "That in all matches on the River Thames, schooners to be classed according to Mr. Ackers' scale...")!

The IYRU holds its annual conference in 1987.

NATIONAL UNITY

Before nations could get together to unify some of the rules, they needed a degree of unity between their own clubs. The first attempt in Britain was in 1852, with a proposal for a 'Confederation of Commodores', but this came to nothing. Neither did the suggestion in 1863 for a 'National Yacht Racing Club'. *Hunt's Yachting Magazine* published a draft constitution for a unifying body in 1868 and the Royal Victoria Yacht Club called a meeting, but there was no agreement.

At last, in 1876, the Yacht Racing Association was formed, although it appeared to have a largely personal membership of influential yacht owners, for it was in their, rather than the club's, interests to unify the rules. Some of the leading clubs ignored its existence and continued with their own rules, but when in 1881 the Royal Yacht Squadron joined the YRA, persuaded by the Prince of Wales, later Edward VII – who was both commodore of the RYS and president of the YRA – its success was assured. Thereafter, any club in Britain that wished to run races invariably joined the YRA and used its racing rules. The YRA became the RYA, the Royal Yachting Association, in 1953.

Elsewhere in Europe, unlike in Britain, the primary club has often remained the authority for racing, so that in Sweden, the Royal Swedish Yacht Club, and in France, the Yacht Club de France, combined both roles for many years. Today, although there are always national authorities, the hierarchy in such organizations is often the same as in the major clubs.

In the United States, the sheer size and vast separation of sailing areas meant that it was a long time before a national authority was either desired or formed. Nor has such a body ever had the authoritative role enjoyed by its European counterparts. The first mention of any attempt to set up a national racing organization appeared in 1879, when the New Jersey Yacht Club called for "the formation of a National Yacht Racing Association". The smaller clubs around New York got together in 1883, but, as in Britain, the major clubs kept clear of any such association and the idea did not catch on.

The most promising attempt at unity occurred in 1897, when delegates from as far afield as San Francisco and Canada joined with those from the east coast to form the North American Yacht Racing Union. After its inaugural meeting, two delegates went to England to talk to the YRA about current rules of measurement. Unfortunately, it was these rules that ensured the demise of the NAYRU in its first incarnation, for the YRA recommended the adoption of the length-and-sail-area rule. This rule was tried out on the Great Lakes but was not generally approved, and was abandoned in 1900. Member clubs were advised to retain their own methods of handicapping, although they continued to use the nationally agreed right-of-way rules; these being much the same as individual club rules in any case. In 1903, the New York Yacht Club adopted the Universal Rule and formed a loose conference with those other major clubs that intended to use it. This conference did not cooperate with the NAYRU, which soon became inactive.

In 1925, a new conference was called, this time in the knowledge that all other major sailing nations possessed a national racing association. By this time, there were a number of important American regional racing associations. Largely through the efforts of Clifford D. Mallory, a member of both the New York and Indian Harbor yacht clubs, these associations formed a reorganized NAYRU, to which all American clubs, and associations in Canada and Mexico, eventually belonged. In 1926, Mallory and Clinton Crane of the NAYRU attended an International Yacht Racing Union (see below) meeting in London as observers, and in 1929, the NAYRU adopted the same racing rules, with some small modifications.

The NAYRU did not join the IYRU until 1952; then in 1974, in preparation for the 1976 Olympic Games organized by Canada, Canada formed its own national authority, as did Mexico, leaving the union with the name it has today, the United States Yacht Racing Union (USYRU).

INTERNATIONAL UNITY

The International Yacht Racing Union arose out of the muddle and arguments between the various national authorities over yacht measurement rules that existed at the end of the 19th century. In 1906, the British Yacht Racing Association, in the person of its secretary Brooke Heckstall-Smith, contacted the various sailing authorities, or the most senior clubs, in Europe, and suggested a conference to try to unify the rating rule. The New York Yacht Club was also invited but did not attend. Together, the Europeans agreed a new measurement rule, the first International Rule, in London in April 1906.

In October 1907, the delegates met again in Paris, this time to unify the racing and right-of-way rules. To control both these and the measurement rules, the conference became the International Yacht Racing Union. Its inaugural members were Austria-Hungary, Belgium, Denmark, Finland, France, Germany, Great Britain, Italy, the Netherlands, Norway, Spain, Sweden and Switzerland, and they quickly adopted the IYRU rules as their own: the British did this for the 1908 season and have used the rules, as amended, ever since. The US did not join, having no national authority. Heckstall-Smith became the secretary; members of the first permanent committee were Alfred Benzon (Denmark), Michel le Bret (France), Konrad Brusley (Germany) and R.E. Froude (Britain).

By 1936, the membership had nearly doubled to 24 nations. Heckstall-Smith combining the secretarial role with a similar role at the YRA. By 1988, there were 89 members. The IYRU suspended activities during the two world wars, and re-admitted Germany and Japan in 1951. The USSR joined in 1952, as did the US, the NAYRU having sent observers for a number of years before then.

THE ORGANIZATION OF THE IYRU

Throughout its history, the IYRU headquarters have been in London, initially sharing an office, and an administration, with the RYA, an arrangement that ended in 1974. A chairman was appointed to run each meeting until 1946, when the first president, Major Sir Ralph Gore, was elected; the secretary now is entitled the Secretary-General.

IYRU PRESIDENT
1946-55   Major Sir Ralph Gore (UK)
1955-69   Sir Peter Scott (UK)
1969-86   Dr Beppe Croce (Italy)
1986-   Peter Tallberg (Finland)

IYRU SECRETARY-GENERAL
1907-39   Brooke Heckstall-Smith (UK)
1946-65   Francis Usborne (UK)
1966-86   Nigel Hacking (UK)
1987-   Michael Evans (UK)

To make the volume of business manageable, the Permanent Committee of the IYRU divides the world up into 14 administrative regions, such as North America, Scandinavia, and Southern Europe etc.

In addition there are 11 committees, reflecting the many tasks undertaken by the organization. These committees cover the constitution; class policy and organization; measurement; keelboats; centerboard boats; multihulls; boardsailing; racing rules; youth sailing; women's sailing; and international regulations. Of these, the racing rules and measurement committees have been in existence since the foundation of the IYRU in 1907, while the others have been added as required. The international regulations committee is concerned with national or international rules and laws that might affect yacht racing, and on which the IYRU might wish to exert an influence: such rules have nothing to do with the racing rules. The class policy and organization committee looks after the 40 classes recognized by the IYRU as 'International' classes; these include the original classes built to the International Rule — such as the 6-, 8- and 12-Meters — as well as more recent additions, most of which are one-designs, and four board classes. Two major areas over which the IYRU has no control are ocean racing of all kinds, and rules for cruiser-racers, both of which are handled by the Offshore Racing Council. However, all ocean racers sail to the IYRU racing (right-of-way) rules.

The IYRU meets annually in early November, usually in London, for eight days of conferences for all its committees. The ORC meets separately, but nearby, at the same time. At the conclusion, the IYRU Permanent Committee, or a general assembly of members, confirm or amend the decisions. Apart from the formal meetings, this conference also serves to gather together those who run the world's racing, to exchange views and informally discuss the international status and performance of sailing.

THE RACING RULES

The different rules that apply to inshore racing are the class rules, whether the boat be a one-design or designed to a formula; any time allowance or other handicapping system in operation; and the racing rules, which primarily concern entry specifications, right-of-way, conduct on the water, and protests. Additionally, there will be national prescriptions to the international racing rules; regional or club standing rules for the season; and a set of sailing instructions for the specific race, which can be either quite short or very elaborate, depending on the nature and duration of the race itself.

The racing rules remain the most internationally unified part of the IYRU administration. All over the world, sailing boats use exactly the same rules of racing; any additional instructions and procedures peculiar to individual nations do not affect the basic rules. These rules are fixed for periods of four years at a time and are renewed the year following an Olympic Games. Each time there are amendments and a number of small wording changes, based on experiences in racing from all over the world.

The refinements of the rules over many years is demonstrated by the Royal Cork Yacht Club rule of 1866 (before rules were unified nationally) concerning the rounding of marks. "In rounding a flag boat or buoy used to mark the course, vessels must give each other sufficient room to pass clear of such marks; should the marks be touched by a breach of this rule, the penalty to attach to the vessel which infringed it." One wonders how soon the rule was changed after it was discovered that it failed to say which boat had a duty to keep clear!

By comparison, today's rules on rounding a mark are extensive and have been up-dated many times. They have to deal with: (a) when rules about mark rounding begin to apply, as opposed to other rules along the course; (b) which boat has the right of way and which keeps clear, defined by their position to each other; (c) what happens when the mark is a starting mark; (d) how a boat can exonerate itself if it touches a mark; (e) other, small complexities.

Traditionally, boat racing has no referees, so an infringement of the rules is dealt with by the voluntary retirement of the offending boat. If one competitor thinks that another has infringed a rule, it hoists a red swallowtail flag, which signifies B in the international maritime signal code, and it flies this throughout the race. Once back in dock or on land, it lodges a protest and it is considered by a jury, which has already been appointed for such an eventuality. Protests in boat racing should not, therefore, be considered as something exceptional; they are the ordinary method of rule enforcement.

Although, as previously stated, there are no referees in boat racing, a system of on-course observers has been tried out on suitable inshore courses in recent years, notably in Congressional Cup-type racing where the fleet is not scattered and the turning marks are not far from the committee boat. These observers can hand out instant penalties, but as there are no established or international rules for it, the system remains experimental.

THE REFORM OF THE RULES

When the NAYRU adopted the rules of the IYRU in 1929, it did so with some small modifications. Thus when Europeans raced in American waters, it was necessary for them to check the minor points that were different – as *Endeavour*'s afterguard failed to do in the 1934 America's Cup fourth race (see p148).

But both sets of rules shared the same right-of-way rules, which were based on what happened when non-racing sailing ships met at sea. The basic rule of the sea is that a boat on port – that is one with its mainsail on its starboard side – gives way to one on starboard – that is a boat with its mainsail on its port side. However, for several hundred years, this was overruled when a close-hauled vessel met one running free. The close-hauled vessel had right of way over the one running free, regardless of which tacks they were both

Rounding a Mark *When dinghies approach a mark, the complex rules of rounding come into play to prevent collisions and ascertain which boats have right of way, and which must get out of the way. Helmsmen need to know these rules when racing in order to insure that they are not protested against and possibly disqualified from the race itself.*

on, on the grounds that the old square-rigged ships were entitled to every yard made to windward and a craft bowling downwind could afford the luxury of slightly diverting from its course.

This same principle was applied to yacht racing, but there were two problems. First, it was not always easy to say whether or not a boat was close hauled and therefore had to give way to one running free. Were a boat to bear fractionally away from the wind, then the basic rule of starboard priority over port would apply instead. Second, unlike the old square rigger, a modern boat was actually more maneuverable when under jib and mainsail than running free under spinnaker.

In the 1940s, Harold S. 'Mike' Vanderbilt, twice-defender of the America's Cup, led a movement in the US to reform this rule. He proposed major changes to a number of boat-racing rules, the most radical of which was to abolish the right-of-way rule that a boat running free give way to one close hauled. This he wanted to replace with a rule stating that a boat on starboard tack, on whatever point of sailing, always had priority over one on port. The difference between the two rules was therefore striking.

By 1947, the Europeans decided to give these new rules a trial in selected events, but in America, the Vanderbilt Rules were so popular that the NAYRU adopted them as the norm in January 1948. From that date on, there existed two quite separate right-of-way rules for racing boats on either side of the Atlantic.

Throughout the 1950s, trials took place in Europe, and discussions continued between European sailors and the NAYRU; discussions made easier by the membership of the NAYRU in the IYRU during 1952. Joint committees, under the chairmanship first of Crown Prince Olav of Norway and then of Niels Benzon of Denmark, worked toward a world-wide set of rules. Agreement was eventually reached, and in 1958, the IYRU adopted radically new rules that were based for their right-of-way element on the NAYRU Vanderbilt Rules and which have been used ever since in racing. The right-of-way rule for sailing ships at sea was changed some years later to conform with the new racing rules.

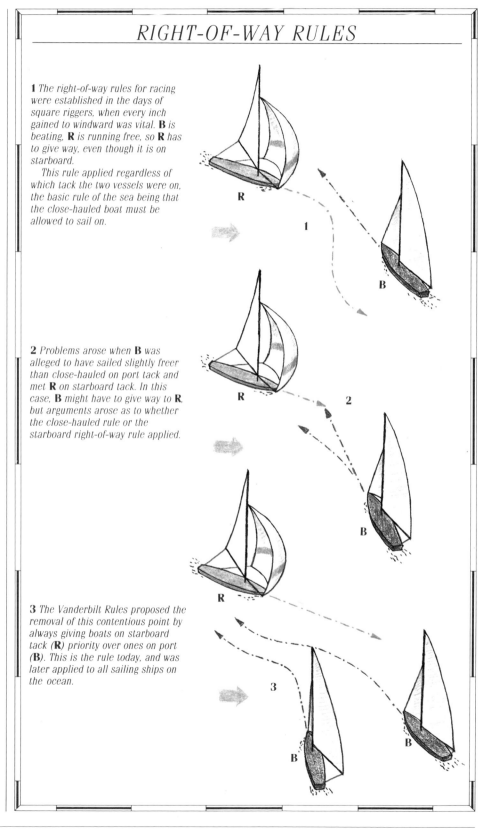

RIGHT-OF-WAY RULES

1 *The right-of-way rules for racing were established in the days of square riggers, when every inch gained to windward was vital. **B** is beating, **R** is running free, so **R** has to give way, even though it is on starboard.*

This rule applied regardless of which tack the two vessels were on, the basic rule of the sea being that the close-hauled boat must be allowed to sail on.

2 *Problems arose when **B** was alleged to have sailed slightly freer than close-hauled on port tack and met **R** on starboard tack. In this case, **B** might have to give way to **R**, but arguments arose as to whether the close-hauled rule or the starboard right-of-way rule applied.*

3 *The Vanderbilt Rules proposed the removal of this contentious point by always giving boats on starboard tack (**R**) priority over ones on port (**B**). This is the rule today, and was later applied to all sailing ships on the ocean.*

THE CAPABILITIES OF RACING BOATS

Although ocean racers can race equally both inshore and offshore, there are many racing boats that are unseaworthy in open waters, yet which can safely race inshore in all but the severest conditions. All types of racing boat, from the largest ocean racer down to the smallest dinghy, have different capabilities, but they can be assessed according to a number of different criteria.

Stability and stiffness Stability is the ultimate ability of a boat to right itself if capsized or knocked down by wind or sea. Stiffness is the power to carry sail and drive forward as the wind increases.
Watertight integrity At its most basic, this is the ability of boats to keep out water, for they are likely to be swept by seas or at least spray. Many types of smaller boat, however, do not need to be sealed, for they

can be bailed out by the crew or empty themselves through self-bailers.
Crew protection This is comprehensive for larger boats with cabins, but minimal or non-existent for keelboats and dinghies.
Safety provisions Some boats need no rescue facilities when racing, except in dire emergencies, while others need constant support. All crews are equipped with personal flotation devices.

KEY	DEEP-SEA OCEAN RACER	LIGHT OCEAN RACER	OFFSHORE MULTIHULL	INSHORE MULTIHULL
Spray and sea / Principal ballast				
STABILITY AND STIFFNESS	Both very high; self-righting if capsized	Both high, but boat needs balancing by crew in strong winds; self-righting if capsized	Inherent stiffness, but can lose stability and flip over	Depends on crew balance
WATERTIGHT INTEGRITY	Total; equipped with heavy, watertight, hatches	Total, but some gear is lightweight and vulnerable in heavy seas	Total; can float upside down	Total; can float upside down
CREW PROTECTION	Bunks; heating; storage space for food, water and medical supplies	Adequate below, but exposed on deck	Bunks; storage space for food and water	Nil
SAFETY PROVISIONS	Own liferaft; crew have harnesses	Own liferaft; crew have harnesses	Own liferaft; crew have harnesses	Rescue boats when racing

KEY	KEELBOAT	HEAVY CENTERBOARD DINGHY	LIGHT CENTERBOARD DINGHY	SAILBOARD
Spray and sea / Principal ballast				
STABILITY AND STIFFNESS	Considerable	Provided by crew weight and boat's inherent stability	Depends entirely on balance of crew	Depends on crew's athleticism, which controls all motion and direction via sail
WATERTIGHT INTEGRITY	Some can sink when knocked down flat	Minimal; equipped with self-bailers, but requires crew to bail out in emergencies	Capsize common in fresh winds; totally watertight, since hull is a sealed unit	Capsize common in fresh winds; totally watertight, since hull is a sealed unit
CREW PROTECTION	Partial protection	Nil	Nil	Nil
SAFETY PROVISIONS	Rescue facilities required in emergencies	Rescue boats when racing	Rescue boats when racing	Rescue boats when racing

RESTRICTED AND FORMULA CLASSES

In a world dominated by one-design classes, there is still considerable interest in the many restricted and formula classes that exist around the world, mainly because they challenge boat designers to produce for the needs of an owner a winning boat within the class rules, using the latest technology.

The IYRU gives international status to a number of restricted classes, such as the A-, B-, C- and D- division catamarans, and the 14-ft International Dinghy, commonly known as the International 14, which is discussed in more detail on the next page. There are four, IYRU-recognized, formula classes: the 12-Meter, used from 1958 until 1987 for the America's Cup; the 8-Meter, of which mainly a few old boats remain; and the 6-Meter, of which a few new boats are built each year. These three are to the International Rule; the fourth is the obsolescent 5.5-Meter class, for 16 years one of the classes in the Olympic Games. For details of the distinction between formula and restricted classes, see pp 212-13; for the history of the various formula classes, see pp 290-2.

Most of the restricted-class dinghies in the world are not recognized as 'International' by the IYRU, and survive and prosper locally rather than nationally or internationally. Four of these classes are worthy of special attention, for they exhibit several peculiar and indeed unique characteristics.

NORFOLK PUNT

The Norfolk Punt is a strange case of an essentially local class which, like most classes in the world, became fixed as a one-design. Uniquely, however, it has since reverted to being a restricted class so that designers can try their hand at improving the class and its performance.

The Punt originated as a gun punt used by wildfowlers in the flat marshlands, lakes and rivers of the Norfolk Broads in eastern England. Early in this century, a number were converted to sail, and later additions to the fleet were built exclusively as sailing boats. As with so many of these early classes, races came from challenges between punts built by different builders, in this case from the many villages in the Norfolk Broads.

In the 1920s, the class gradually became organized, and, by 1930, it was sophisticated enough to have a design commissioned from Uffa Fox, the leading British, racing-dinghy designer of the time. However, it was a local man, Herbert Woods, who designed most of the boats, culminating in a proposed one-design Punt based on his latest ideas in 1939. This was of carvel-wood construction and had a sail area of 16.4 sq m (176 sq ft).

Only a few boats were built to this design before war intervened, and thus when a new design was introduced in 1952, this time in hard-chine construction, it was this one that became the one-design Norfolk Punt. But when Andrew Wolstenholme designed and built a new double-chine boat in 1985, the class meeting held the following year to approve the new one-design decided instead to set the clock back. It made the Punt a restricted class, using modern technology and advanced dinghy design to insure the class' future. One of the first designs to the new rules was built by Phil Morrison, a designer of other restricted-class dinghies in the International 14 and National 12 classes; his design can be seen on p 232.

Norfolk Punt (1952 design)

SHETLAND MAID

The Shetlands are the most northerly of the British Isles, 100 miles north of the Scottish mainland. Every August, in the capital of Lerwick, 80 or so open boats of the Shetland Maid class gather for their annual regatta. There is no concession to economic design or one-design 'fairness' with this class: these boats are rated and have a time allowance of 15 seconds per-mile-per-foot of rating. Either 80 years behind or in front of every other class, they use a formula of waterline length, sail area and displacement.

Under the rules, the 5-m (16-ft 5-in) hull must be double-ended, that is with a pointed bow and stern, and is built of wood in a clinker style or in fiberglass. No centerboards are allowed. One rule states that "ends of stem shall project above the gunwale as in traditional boat's horns".

Away from outside pressures, the Shetland Maid is designed and built by builders who are frequently professionally concerned with the sea, as fishermen, seamen, oil-industry workers or coastguards. These sloops have the rules their owners and builders desire, and a level of competition to their own satisfaction.

Shetland Maid

INTERNATIONAL 14

The '14' has long been the aristocrat among dinghies, a valid description given its long and well-documented history, its quality and expense, and its relatively small numbers at any one time. Yet despite these limitations of cost and numbers, the International 14 class has had an influence on the rest of dinghy racing and design out of all proportion to its popularity.

The international class association comprises fleets in Bermuda, Canada, Japan, South Africa, the US, and its original home, the UK; both the Australian 14-ft Skiff and the New Zealand 14-ft Javelin are 'first cousins' in matters of design and rules. The dinghy originated in Britain, where several, rather similar, 14-ft (4.3-m) dinghies were raced locally; some had a lug sail, others carried a small jib in addition. Among these were the West of England Conference dinghy and the Norfolk dinghy, both undecked. Apparently, there was at least one challenge race between the two.

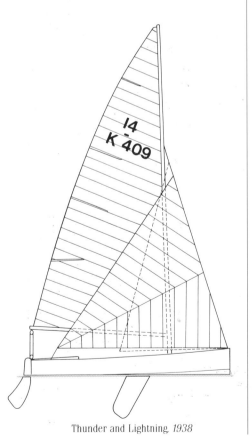

Thunder and Lightning, 1938

Based on the rules of these two dinghies, the YRA published a set of rules for a new national 14-ft class in 1919. The class grew well in the 1920s, and took a big leap forward when the Prince of Wales presented a cup for its annual championship in 1927. The first Prince of Wales Cup race was held at Cowes and attracted 41 starters; it has been competed for every year since, excepting 1940-5. Helmsmen from outside Britain have won it eight times.

In the US, 14-footers carried cat rigs until 1932, before changing over to the more common bermudan rigs. The class gained IYRU International status in 1928 and has always been at the forefront of dinghy design. Uffa Fox designed, built and sailed a string of successful boats, introducing the concept of a planing dinghy, that is one which sails faster in a fresh wind than its hull speed. This principle long ago spread round the world and is still the basis of most racing dinghies today. Later designers with successful boats to their credit include Austin Farrar and Ian Proctor; in recent years success has been spread among a wider range of names.

Year after year, the class rules have been argued over by the owners, and innovations introduced. The trapeze was first tried in 1939 and then briefly banned, but has long since been reintroduced. Although the concept of an open boat with no decks, common among dinghies, has been retained, self-bailers were only allowed after some controversy. In Bermuda, Canada and the US, fiberglass boats were first introduced in the 1960s, while the British continued to use cold-molded wood boats for some time.

Thus developments have tended to get out of step in various countries, leading to prolonged wrangles before all fall back into line. Trapezes are now allowed for both crew and skipper (the class rules restricting the crew to two). Asymmetrical spinnakers and the introduction of fully battened mainsails have been tested in the late 1980s. Annual international team races between three boats from each country act as a major spur to improvements, both within those countries and in the class as a whole.

In the field of design, there are few restrictions, for it is open to any designer to design and build the fastest boat, restricted only by a mere six pages of class rules. Restrictions include the overall length of 14ft (4.3m), a maximum and minimum beam, restrictions on construction to ensure the traditional 'open boat' design, a minimum weight, a set of sail dimensions, and rules concerning buoyancy when swamped.

Some 3,500 14s have been built since 1928, but at any one time, only about 250 are in commission in the world. The class is not the largest in the world by a long way, nor is it the fastest, even for its size, but its position as a classic racing dinghy and design leader is not disputed.

FORMULA 40

Outside the jurisdiction of the IYRU is a restricted class for multihulls, confusingly called the Formula 40. Despite its name, it is not really a formula class in the sailing sense, the word having been borrowed from motor racing.

In this class, length, beam, weight and sail area are limited, with overall length restricted to between 10.6 m-12.2 m (34 ft 8 in-40 ft), the maximum beam of the whole configuration set at 12.2 m (40 ft), and the maximum weight set at 1,800 kg (3,968 lb). But because the class rules only lay down restrictions on maximum size without specifying hull configuration, both catamarans and trimarans can be built. There is no limit to mast height, but the number of sails carried is limited to four – a mainsail, jib and two 'off-wind headsails', that is spinnakers – with a maximum area of the mainsail and jib of 90 sq m (969 sq ft). There are also restrictions of various kinds on hull structure and spars, and bans on techniques such as trapezing and loading water ballast.

What results from all this is an evenly matched, exciting class that has established an international circuit of inshore races: an average season might comprise 10 regattas in Britain, France, Italy, the Netherlands, Spain and the US.

The International 14 *The evolution of this restricted class can be seen by comparing the design of* Thunder and Lightning, *a successful International 14 from 1938 (below left), with that of two recent 14s from 1987 (above). The trapeze was forbidden in 1939, but in a modern 14, both helmsman and crew have trapezes to stabilize the boat. Mainsail shape and batten lengths have changed, as have many items of equipment, but the hull has always remained totally open, with a maximum length of 14 ft (4.3 m).*

The Formula 40 *(right) The rules of this restricted class limit the overall length and beam but do not specify the design of the hull. Thus both catamarans and trimarans can be sailed boat for boat against each other.*

INSHORE ONE-DESIGN CLASSES

All but a few races inshore are sailed in one-design classes. Boat after boat listed in Chapter Seven (pp 210-49) is a one-design, although some notable restricted classes give the opportunity to design and equip a boat as well as race her. For a definition of a one-design class, see p 212.

THE WORLD'S FIRST

The world's first one-design class originated in Dun Laoghaire, Ireland; it was a 4-m (13-ft), clinker-built, double-ender with a 1.5-m (4-ft 10-in) beam, a steel centerboard and a lug sail. The design, by local designer J.E. Doyle, was copied from a Norwegian Praäm dinghy that had come into the possession of a young Irishman living in Shankhill, County Dublin, in 1878. A group of young men formed 'The Water Wag Association' in the harbor of Dun Laoghaire (then called Kingstown) in 1887 and built some 20 of these sailing dinghies. They raced them, according to a near-contemporary source, "at all the local regattas in the neighborhood, the popularity of which is abundantly testified by the number of prizes that are offered for competition as an inducement to the Water Wags to come and sail." The name Water Wags soon became interchangeable between the sailors and their boats.

For reasons that are now forgotten, the design of this earliest one-design class was superseded by a new design in 1900. Designed by Mamie Doyle, daughter of the original designer, the dinghy was 4.3 m (14 ft 3 in) LOA with a wide beam (1.7 m, 5 ft 6 in), a transom stern, a lug mainsail and small jib, and an asymmetrical spinnaker on a long pole. McKeown of Belfast built 12 boats straight away and the dinghy is still sailed today; 23 boats took part in a centenary regatta in June 1987, including two boats built since 1985.

The popularity of the Water Wags was not just a reaction to the cost and continual out-dating of rated boats, but was due largely to the-then novel form of one-design dinghy racing these boats enjoyed. In England, however, the first one-design — the Solent One-Design — arose, it was stated at a meeting of boat owners, directly from the expressed "concern at the ever increasing expenditure attendant on small class racing on the Solent . . . the sport should be conducted in a manner suitable to the means of the majority, and not merely with a view to the encouragement of the few who can afford year after year to build a new boat."

Initially, 10 boats were built in 1895-6 by White Brothers of Itchen Ferry, Southampton, to a design by H.W. White. A fully decked keelboat, the Solent One-Design had a central racing cockpit, a gaff rig and two headsails, one on a bowsprit. The dimensions were 10 m (33 ft) LOA, 2.4 m (7 ft 9 in) beam, 1.5 m (5 ft) draft, and a 69.7 sqm (750 sqft) sail area. At one time, 20 of this class were racing in the Solent, but it became extinct after 1914.

About the same time as the Solent One-Design class started up, in 1896, the Redwing Sailing Club was formed at Bembridge, Isle of Wight. The Redwing class — designed by Charles E. Nicholson and built by Camper and Nicholsons across the Solent on the mainland at Gosport — had a one-design hull, but the owners could rig them any way they wished as long as the sail area did not exceed 18.6 m (200 sqft). The sails, however, had to be red in color. The overall length of the hull was 6.7 m (22 ft) and the beam 1.7 m (5 ft 6 in).

The same designer was commissioned in 1938 by a group of owners to replace the aging boats with a new design in wood of 8.5 m (27 ft 11 in) LOA but still with the same optional sail plan within the same maximum area allowance, and still with the distinctive red color sails. The Bembridge Redwing has recently been built in fiberglass and still races today in the Solent under class rules that have hardly changed since 1938.

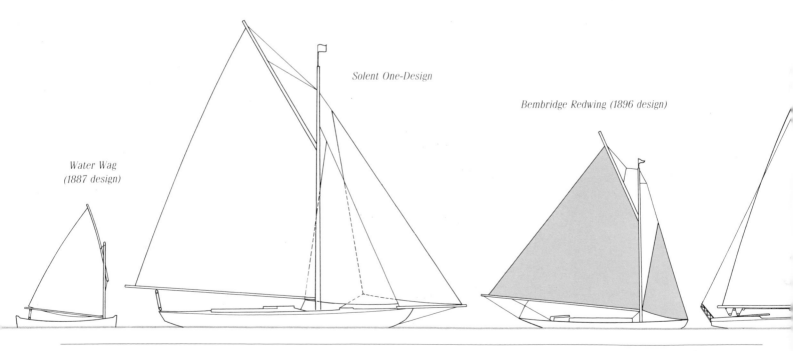

Water Wag
(1887 design)

Solent One-Design

Bembridge Redwing (1896 design)

ONE-DESIGN SURVIVAL

The concept of one-design classes was soon appreciated after the success of the three classes discussed above, and at the turn of the century there existed a number of successful one-design classes in Britain and Ireland. Together with the various restricted classes, there were perhaps as many as 30 in existence at this time. But the oldest one-design class still sailing comes not from the British Isles, where the present Water Wag design dates from 1900, but from America, where the A Scow dates from 1897.

The Inland Yachting Association A Scow was designed and built by John Johnson in 1897. It is a flat-hulled type with an LOA of 11.7 m (38 ft 6 in), a beam of 2.6 m (8 ft 6 in) and a large sail area of 51.7 sqm (557 sqft); it takes a crew of five. Thirty of these craft still sail regularly on the Great Lakes.

In the British Isles, three of the one-design classes still racing date from 1898. The Howth 17, a 17-ft (5.2-m) LWL one-design, had its first race on 4 May 1898 and can claim to be the oldest one-design class still racing in the British Isles as originally designed. There are 15 sailing at Howth, County Dublin, Ireland, still with jackyard topsails. Two boats were built in 1987, but the rest date from before 1913.

The Seabird Half Rater, sailed at Abersoch in Wales and on the River Mersey in England, was designed by Herbert G. Baggs and W. Scott Hayward in 1898; the first boats were built in the next year. It is thus the oldest centerboard class still racing in the British Isles. Its LOA is 6.1m (20ft), its beam 1.8m (6ft), and its weight 1,016 kg (2,240 lb). The hull is decked, has a cockpit and a centerboard. Since its inception, 90 boats have been built and 69 still exist, preserved by its one-design rules and its rugged construction for the conditions it was designed for. This class is interesting since it once had a rating, under the length-and-sail-area rule, of 0.5, hence its name.

The oldest keelboat still sailing in Britain is the Yorkshire One-Design, the hull of which has not altered in design since 1898. Designed by J.S. Helyar of Field and Co. of Itchen Ferry, Southampton, who built the early boats, 6 of the originals built in 1898 are still racing in a fleet of 12 at the Royal Yorkshire Yacht Club in Bridlington in north-east England. The original owners called themselves the Pirate Yacht Club (as with the Water Wags, raffish names seemed to be in vogue then) and agreed on a design, changed only by the adoption of a bermudan, instead of the original gunter, rig in 1971. Yet since its

birth, only 15 boats in total have been built; ironically it is the small numbers, and the local patronage of the class, that have ensured its preservation.

The examples here are only the very oldest one-designs still sailing, but Chapter 7 (pp 210-49) has numerous examples of classes that are 50, 60 or 70 years old. For longevity, it seems that a local affiliation or at least a regional one is desirable, as are like-minded owners who race at club level year after year. There are, of course, many classes that have not survived; often the hulls have simply become unfit for sailing or maybe enthusiasm has waned in favor of national or international classes of a more modern type.

— ••• —

Early One-Design Classes *Four of the world's first one-design classes still race regularly: two, the Water Wag and the Bembridge Redwing, have been succeeded by new designs which remain active; while one, the Solent One-Design, is defunct. All seven one-designs illustrated below originated at the end of the 19th century as a revolt against rating rules, which had been forcing owners into building a new boat to a new design each year if they wished to remain competitive; one-design racing was, therefore, a new concept in racing but one that was to revolutionize the sport. The low freeboard, generally long ends and generous sail area seen here followed the fashion of the time and evolved from measurement rules based mainly on waterline length.*

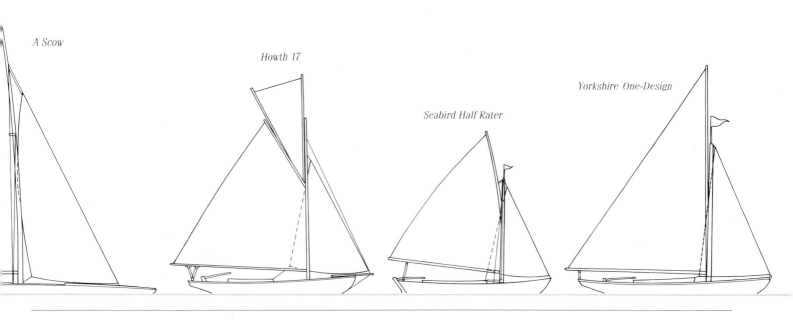

A Scow

Howth 17

Seabird Half Rater

Yorkshire One-Design

MAJOR INSHORE EVENTS

For the owner of an inshore racing boat, the major event in the sailing calendar is the class championship. Depending on the class, this may be a local, state, national, continental, international, junior or inland event; many classes organize all of these events and more each year. In addition to class events, there are hundreds of inshore regattas and numerous handicapped events in which many different classes can compete. Three of the main regattas are at Cowes in Britain, Kiel in Germany, and Block Island in the US.

COWES WEEK

Cowes Week is the longest-running, regular regatta in the world, having been held in early August every year (except during the two world wars) since the first race started at 09.30 on Thursday, 10 August 1826. That first race was for a "Gold Cup of the value of £100", and was held under the flag of the Royal Yacht Club, later the Royal Yacht Squadron. There was another race the next day for prize money only (£30 for first place, £20 for second), a ball on Thursday evening and a dinner and fireworks on Friday evening.

The same traditions still prevail, but since 1946, seven clubs and the town regatta committee participate over a period of nine days. Also traditional is the attendance of members of the royal family, and an extensive social program organized by the various clubs and classes participating in the regatta.

A typical Cowes Week in the 1980s has 20 starts a day for the same number of classes; the number of boats taking part varies each year between 700 and 1,200. Classes include cruiser-racers (to IOR, CHS and other current rules), offshore one-designs and numerous keelboat classes. The classes participating have tended to reflect the sailing activities of the day. Until 1914, the big cutters and schooners raced, while between the wars there were cruiser handicap classes and local one-designs, although the 6-, 8- and 12-Meters attracted the most racing interest. After 1946, ocean-racing classes predominated, especially after the first Admiral's Cup was sailed for in 1957 and the two ocean races that start and finish the week – the Channel and Fastnet races – began to gain in popularity. Because the Fastnet Race is held in odd-numbered years only, another offshore course is sailed in even years to attract ocean-racers to the regatta.

———— ◆◆◆ ————

Cowes Week *A major feature of the annual Cowes Week regatta is the many races held for local, one-design classes. Fleets of X-Boats (shown below) and other classes enjoy close, competitive racing on courses that often bring them right up to the shore line as well as out into the Solent.*

Cowes Week (above) With anywhere up to 1,200 boats taking part in Cowes Week, there is considerable pressure on mooring, berthing and marina space at Cowes.

Kiel Week (below) Held annually every June, Kiel Week attracts ocean-racers, keelboats and dinghies, all sailing in the tideless waters of Kiel Bay and the Baltic Sea.

KIEL WEEK

Kiel Week shares with Cowes both a long tradition and a wide variety of classes. The first regular regatta is considered to have been held on 23 July 1882, when sailing men of the Norddeutscher Regatta Verein in Hamburg gathered enough boats to stage a regatta. Boats came from ports close by in the Baltic as well as from Hamburg and the North Sea; the Kiel Canal had not been built at this stage, so these boats had to sail round the north of Denmark into the Baltic.

In the early 20th century, Kiel Week was promoted by Kaiser Wilhelm II in imitation of Cowes Week, complete with his royal patronage and his own 'big class' boats. The Imperial Yacht Club – the Kaiserlicher Yacht Club – was the main organizer; the name remained until 1937, when all the clubs in the area were forced to merge into the Yachtclub von Deutschland. The regatta was suspended during the war, and was first sailed again in 1945, organized by the occupying British forces.

In 1949, the Kiel Yacht Club took control and the modern Kiel Week was born. By 1987, there were 23 different classes, with participants from 42 nations. The Dragons compete for the Felca-Preis, a major trophy first raced for in 1913. Unlike Cowes, the tideless waters of Kiel Bay attract Olympic and dinghy classes.

BLOCK ISLAND WEEK

Among numerous race weeks across the United States, the distinction of Block Island Race Week is that it is in easy reach of numerous sailing centers between New York and Newport, Rhode Island. Held every odd year since 1971, Block Island Week is organized by the Storm Trysail Club, a club without a fixed clubhouse formed by a group of offshore sailors in 1938. The Race Week is run along European lines as a regular regatta with excellent racing and a strong social element.

The week is largely for cruiser-racers, currently divided into 12 classes under the IOR, IMS and PHRF rules, with up to 300 boats competing. Although the boats may be fewer in number than at Cowes or Kiel, they are on average much larger in size, therefore the number of crews are roughly comparable.

MAJOR INSHORE TROPHIES

Throughout the world, there are a number of inshore trophies that are long-established and of sufficient standing not to be attached to the fortunes of one class.

THE SEAWANHAKA CUP

Started in 1895 by the Seawanhaka Corinthian Yacht Club of Oyster Bay on Long Island, New York, this challenge trophy was one of the earliest attempts to encourage international yacht racing in small, inshore boats. The first challenger, J.A. Brand of the Minima Yacht Club, London, was defeated in his 7.1-m (23-ft 3-in) boat *Spruce IV* by the similarly sized *Ethelwynn*, owned by the defending American yachtsman, W.P. Stephens. The next nine races were all won by Canadian boats, the type of boat being of low freeboard, long overhang and large sail area favored under the rating rule in use for the cup. In 1905, the Universal Rule was adopted for cup racing, and was replaced in 1922 by the International Rule, introducing 6-Meters to the competition. A Scottish boat won in 1922 and 1938, and a Norwegian boat in 1927 and 1928. After the war, 6-Meters were again used, with a change in 1962 to the 5.5-Meter class and then to the Soling class in 1971. The cup was revived in 1987 for 6-Meters, when boats from Australia, Britain, Hong Kong and Sweden challenged the American holders. The winner was *Battlecry*, owned by Eric Maxwell of the RYS, Cowes.

LA COUPE DE FRANCE

The Yacht Club de France established this trophy on 6 January 1891 as a challenge to a single boat built and owned in a foreign

La Coupe de France

♦♦♦

country, in imitation of the America's Cup. No one challenged for the trophy until 1898, when the British boat *Gloria* beat the French boat *Esterel* at Cannes. (It was the proceeds from the sale of *Esterel* that were used to purchase the One Ton Cup.) Both *Gloria* and *Esterel* were 20-tonners under the French tonnage rule; this class was used in three further matches in 1899, 1900 and 1901, before the introduction of 10-tonners in 1902. Since then, a variety of classes have been sailed, notably the 8-Meter class, for which the cup was its most important prize.

THE ENDEAVOUR TROPHY

In a number of countries, a series of races are held to find a 'champion of champions', that is an overall champion drawn from the invited national champions of all the main dinghy classes. In Britain, the representatives of the various classes compete for the Endeavour Trophy, a silver model of the 1934 America's Cup challenger presented by one of her crew, Beecher Moore. The championship is organized by the Royal Corinthian Yacht Club at Burnham-on-Crouch, which provides a fleet of one-design dinghies, usually the Enterprise or more recently the Lark or the GP14. No competitor is allowed to sail his or her own boat, but, despite this, it is felt that the representative from the class being sailed that year does have an advantage in the competition. However, it is more true to say that the continuing success of the Enterprise national champion in winning the Endeavour Trophy has more to do with the fact that the Enterprise class is one of the most competitive dinghy classes in Britain, regularly attracting more than 200 boats to its national championships.

THE BRITISH-AMERICAN CUP

The British-American Cup started life in 1920 at a time when the America's Cup was almost the only international trophy in sailing. Unlike the America's Cup, the rules stated that contests for the cup would be held alternately in America and Britain, and the cup itself was a joint purchase by sailors from both countries. The cup was the idea of Paul Hammond – an American yachtsman who had always worked to improve Anglo-American relations – and was given for the International 6-Meter class, which at that time was exclusively European. The Seawanhaka Corinthian Yacht Club sent a 6-Meter team to race against the British at Cowes in 1921.

From 1922 to 1938, the cup was regularly raced for either at Cowes or Oyster Bay. With the One Ton Cup (see p 73) and the Seawanhaka Cup also sailed in 6-Meters at this time, this class represented the highest skills in inshore racing.

The cup was raced for again in 1949, 1951, 1953 and 1955, but with the decline of the 6-Meter class, it was not competed for again until 1974, when the two clubs competed on the Clyde in the Soling class. With renewed interest by a few sailors in 6-Meters, the class was used again in 1987 for a race off Cowes, Isle of Wight.

LA COUPE DE FRANCE

	CLASS	EVENTS	WINNERS
1898-1901	20-TON, FRENCH RULE	4	UK (4)
1902-10	10-TON, FRENCH RULE	5	FRANCE (3), GERMANY (1), ITALY (1)
1911-14	10-METER, INT. RULE	4	UK (3), FRANCE (1)
1922-38	8-METER, INT. RULE	15	UK (7), NORWAY (4), FRANCE (3), ITALY (1)
1953-67	5.5-METER, IYRU CLASS	11	SWITZERLAND (5), AUSTRALIA (1), FRANCE (1), GERMANY (1), ITALY (1), SWEDEN (1), UK (1)
1984-88	6-METER, INT. RULE	4	SWEDEN (2), SWITZERLAND (2)

British and American 6-metres compete in the 1951 British-American Cup.

THE AUSTRALIAN-AMERICAN CUP

Since 1968, this trophy has been used for match racing in the 6-Meter class between American syndicates from Seattle or San Francisco and individual Australian owners based in Sydney.

AMERICAN NATIONAL TROPHIES

The success rate of American sailors in comparison with those from most other nations is largely due to the high standard of sailing within the US. In order to maintain those standards, national competition is fostered from an early age by a number of major trophies, which sailors of various groups sail for after a series of eliminations at club, local and regional level. Considerable support is given by the 10 area yachting associations that form the body of the USYRU; in many cases these areas contain more racing boats than do individual countries in Europe and elsewhere.

In addition to the many national trophies, there are also three junior trophies. The Sears Cup is for the winning crew, male or female, aged between 13 and 17, chosen on an area basis. Depending on the type of boat used, the crew consists of three or four people. The Bemis Trophy is run on the same basis and age group, but is for a two-handed boat, while the Smythe Trophy is for the junior, single-handed champion. All three run in conjunction.

AMERICAN NATIONAL TROPHIES

	CATEGORY	DATE OF ORIGIN	TYPE OF BOAT	WINNER	TROPHY DETAILS
CLIFFORD D. MALLORY CUP	US men's sailing championship	1952; annual	Keelboat	Individual skipper and crews	Presented by the family of Clifford D. Mallory. First President of the NAYRU, now the USYRU
PRINCE OF WALES BOWL	US match-racing championship	1931; annual since 1965	Cruiser-racer one-design or production boat	Club and crew	Presented by Edward, Prince of Wales, in 1931 to Royal Nova Scotia YC. The Trophy was retired in 1937 but was revived again in 1965 and has been held annually ever since.
GEORGE D.O'DAY TROPHY	US, single-handed sailing championship	1962; annual	Laser or other single-handed centreboard class	Individual representatives	Presented by American sailor George O'Day for this purpose.
MRS. CHARLES FRANCIS ADAMS TROPHY	US women's sailing championship	1924; annual except from 1942-5	Various keelboats with 3 or 4 in crew	Named club and crew	There has been a women's sailing championship since 1924. A perpetual trophy was presented by Mrs. Adams in 1935.

THE CONGRESSIONAL CUP

Match racing, that is a race sailed as a duel, has been in some form a part of yacht racing ever since Charles II first raced against his brother on the River Thames in 1661. A specialized and highly competitive form of match racing was created by a new kind of series held in 1965 at Long Beach, California. The founder of the series, William T. Dalessi of Long Beach Yacht Club, wanted a 'Presidential Cup' to present at the event, but was obliged to settle instead for a cup presented for the event by the US Congress.

Since that first competition, the name Congressional Cup has become synonymous with match racing around the world, for although the America's Cup and Canada's Cup are both match races, both of them emphasize the design of the boats as the winning factor. The Congressional Cup, by using as nearly identical craft as possible, has restored the competitive ethos of matching crew against crew, helmsman against helmsman.

In the first series in 1965, the cruiser-racer Cal 40 class was used, and crews had a free hand in preparing their boats. They were able to use a limitless number of sails and could modify fittings. These rules were soon changed to ensure more uniformity between the boats, but by 1980, it was found that the aging Cal 40s were becoming difficult to keep the same, and a switch was made to the Catalina 38 class, a modern cruiser-racer. A major back-up by the manufacturers and assistance by the race organizers is provided to ensure that the boats are identical in every detail and remain so throughout the series.

MATCH-RACING TACTICS

Because the leading boat has a built-in advantage upwind over its trailing rival, the start is disproportionately important in Congressional Cup racing: this is where the all-important tactics, the excitement, and the protests, occur.

Before the start, the two boats circle each other to be in the best position at the starting gun in accordance with their rights under the racing rules. After the start, the race can become quite tedious, for one boat can often remain ahead for the entire course. In order to prevent this happening as much as possible, the boats sail twice around a windward-leeward course, each leg of which is one and a half miles, giving a total distance of six miles. Thus half the course is beating into the wind, half is running downwind; this insures that any gains made by the leading boat upwind can be challenged by the pursuing boat downwind as it attempts to close the gap between the two by sitting on and stealing the leader's wind.

Tactics in match racing are thus quite different than those in fleet racing, for it is tactics, rather than speed, that win the race. With only one competitor to beat, the leading boat must always cover its pursuer to insure that it remains behind. The result is a closer and more aggressive race than would occur in a large fleet, where concentration on only one other boat might allow third parties the chance to slip past into the lead. In match racing, of course, there are no third parties.

◆◆◆

Match Racing *It is important in match racing to gain and keep an advantage over the other boat before the start. In this picture of a start at the 1988 Congressional Cup series, the boat on the left is slightly ahead and in a favorable position to backwind its opponent and thus take the lead on the first beat.*

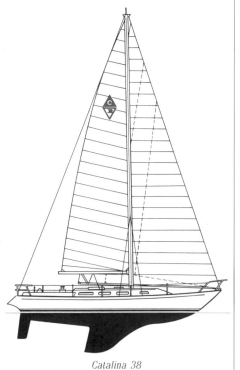

Catalina 38

ORGANIZATION OF MATCH RACING

The format of match racing has changed little since the first Congressional Cup event. Ten identical boats with their helmsmen and crew take part, and are sent off at short intervals round the same course, two by two. The winner is established either in a knock-out tournament or by having the most wins. The event usually spreads over five or six days.

In 1974, a Californian sailor, Bill Green, introduced the Congressional Cup concept to Britain, and a British Congressional Cup was sailed that year. From 1976 onward, the series was organized by the Royal Lymington Yacht Club, which invites leading match-racing helmsmen from all over the world to compete. The first four British match races were sailed in Contessa 32s, but between 1979 to 1984, OOD 34s were used, until these, too, became difficult to keep identical. In 1985, Westerly Fulmars were supplied for the competition by the builders, who also sponsored the event. A fleet from a sailing school was loaned for the competition each year thereafter.

The Congressional Cup

◆◆◆

In the 1980s, the match-racing idea has spread still further, with similar events, financed by commercial sponsorship, starting in Australia, Bermuda, France, Japan, New Zealand and on the east coast of America in New York.

The logical step to this growth occurred in 1988, when the various clubs organizing match races founded a 'World Championship of Match-Race Sailing', with the national winners meeting at one of the clubs for a final, international series to find a world champion.

	USA CONGRESSIONAL CUP		UK CONGRESSIONAL CUP	
	HELMSMAN	NATIONALITY	HELMSMAN	NATIONALITY
1965	GERRY DRISCOLL	USA	—	—
1966	GERRY DRISCOLL	USA	—	—
1967	SCOTT ALLAN	USA	—	—
1968	SCOTT ALLAN	USA	—	—
1969	HENRY SPAGUE III	USA	—	—
1970	ARGYLE CAMPBELL	USA	—	—
1971	TOM PICKARD	USA	—	—
1972	ARGYLE CAMPBELL	USA	—	—
1973	DENNIS CONNER	USA	—	—
1974	BILL FICKER	USA	PETER NICHOLSON	UK
1975	DENNIS CONNER	USA	—	—
1976	DICK DEAVER	USA	PHIL CREBBIN	UK
1977	TED TURNER	USA	PHIL CREBBIN	UK
1978	DICK DEAVER	USA	HAROLD CUDMORE	UK
1979	DENNIS DURGAN	USA	DICK DEAVER	USA
1980	DENNIS DURGAN	USA	HAROLD CUDMORE	UK
1981	ROD DAVIES	NZ	HAROLD CUDMORE	UK
1982	SCOTT PERRY	USA	HAROLD CUDMORE	UK
1983	DAVE PERRY	USA	JOHN BERTRAND	AUS.
1984	DAVE PERRY	USA	HAROLD CUDMORE	UK
1985	ROD DAVIES	NZ	HAROLD CUDMORE	UK
1986	HAROLD CUDMORE	UK	PETER ISLER	USA
1987	EDWARD WARDEN OWEN	UK	PETER GILMOUR	AUS.
1988	PETER GILMOUR	AUS.	PETER GILMOUR	AUS.

LITTLE AMERICA'S CUP

The real name for this trophy is the International Catamaran Challenge Trophy, but the nickname is invariably used. The deed of gift was originated by the Sea Cliff Yacht Club, New York, for a match between C-class catamarans on the lines of the America's Cup. It arose from rival claims for supremacy from American and British catamaran sailors, whose boats had each won 'one-of-a-kind' regattas – comprising one boat from each country to find out which boat was fastest.

The first match in 1961 saw the British *Hellcat* defeat the American *Wildcat* by four races to one. Then, for seven years, it was the America's Cup in reverse, as British defenders fought off challenges from Australia and the US in races held in the Thames Estuary. In 1969, a Danish challenge was successful, and the cup has not returned to Britain since. Denmark lost the trophy to Australia in 1970, and it has alternated between Australia and the US ever since. After the first series of races in the donor's sailing waters at Sea Cliff, the site has always been the home waters of the defending boat.

THE C-CLASS

The C-class is the most highly developed of the four IYRU catamaran divisions, and one of the most advanced classes in existence. In common with the other three international catamaran divisions, but unlike most other classes, it has no minimum weight or sail measurement rules, so the very lightest, exotic, structural materials can be used for the hull, and the sails can follow aircraft and other aerodynamic practice.

In the early years of the Little America's competition, the C-class rig had a fully battened mainsail and a jib hoisted up a traditional mast. The jib was soon dispensed with, and by the late 1960s, the mast had become an integral part of the sail, like the foils on an aircraft wing.

It is this rig that most distinguishes modern C-class boats from any other boat. Although each design differs, a modern rig is made up of a collection of vertical aerofoil sections, in the shape of a wing. The sections are made of Kevlar and carbon fiber around a framework of hi-tech materials. The 'sail' of *The Edge*, which won the 1987 series, contained three foils that could change their direction relative to each other. The top half of the sail could also be moved separately; the whole rig could therefore be shifted around to give optimum drive. Such a rig insured that over the 19.8-mile course, *The Edge* finished in 1 hr 38 min at an average speed of 12.2 knots. This speed is very high when it is considered that there were four windward legs on the course; in other words, its average reaching speed was considerably higher.

The early C-class boats weighed about 360 kg (800 lb), but, by the 1980s, this was reduced to 200 kg (450 lb). The hulls are usually built of wood, but like the most advanced rowing hulls, the wood consists of layers of cold veneer fastened with epoxy resin. The inside of the hull is coated with Kevlar, and a core of either PVC foam or a low density wood such as obeche, similar to balsa, is sandwiched between the wood and the Kevlar. The total effect of all these changes to hull and rig has been to increase the speed of a C-class catamaran by over 25% since 1961.

LITTLE AMERICA'S CUP

	BOAT	WINNER	LOSER
1961	HELLCAT	UK	USA
1962	HELLCAT	UK	USA
1963	HELLCAT II	UK	AUSTRALIA
1964	EMMA HAMILTON	UK	USA
1965	EMMA HAMILTON	UK	AUSTRALIA
1966	LADY HELMSMAN	UK	USA
1967	LADY HELMSMAN	UK	AUSTRALIA
1968	LADY HELMSMAN	UK	USA
1969	OPUS	DENMARK	UK
1970	QUEST III	AUSTRALIA	DENMARK
1972	QUEST III	AUSTRALIA	USA
1974	MISS NYLEX	AUSTRALIA	NZ
1976	AQUARIUS V	USA	AUSTRALIA
1977	PATIENT LADY III	USA	AUSTRALIA
1978	PATIENT LADY III	USA	ITALY
1980	PATIENT LADY V	USA	ITALY
1982	PATIENT LADY V	USA	ITALY
1985	VICTORIA 150	AUSTRALIA	USA
1987	THE EDGE	AUSTRALIA	UK

Evolution of the C-class *Since it was first used in the Little America's Cup in 1961, the C-class catamaran has changed beyond recognition. Its traditional bermudan rig has been replaced with a collection of vertical foils, and its hull weight has been reduced by the use in its construction of cold veneers and Kevlar fibers around a foam or wood core.*

Hellcat, *1961*

Opus, *1969*

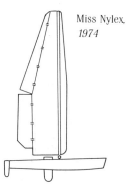

Miss Nylex, *1974*

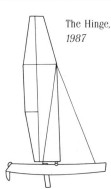

The Hinge, *1987*

The Edge. *Australian winner of the 1987 Little America's Cup.*

IYRU CATAMARAN DIVISIONS

The four IYRU catamaran divisions have the briefest and least restrictive rules of any of the international restricted classes, the effect of which has been to allow the development of extremely advanced and innovative craft. The rules state only that the boats must have twin, symmetrical, parallel hulls, and specify a maximum overall length, and extreme beam, a maximum sail area and crew limits.

Of the four divisions, the A-division is a single-hander and is frequently home-built to a one-off design. There are thus a wide diversity of boats in this class, which tends to attract inventors as well as potential race winners to its regattas. The A-division world championship is attended by about 70 boats each year, but no one design dominates. The B-division is not active for it has, in effect, been frozen as the Tornado class used in the Olympic Games. The C-class has benefited from its use in the Little America's Cup, developing its rig and hull design over the years. The D-division is potentially so exotic that only a handful exist in the world as experimental projects.

THE FOUR DIVISIONS

A-DIVISION
MAX LOA · 5.6 m (18 ft)
MAX BEAM · 2.3 m (7 ft 6½ in)
MAX SAIL AREA · 14 sq m (150 sq ft)
CREW · 1 WITH TRAPEZE

B-DIVISION
MAX LOA · 6.1 m (20 ft)
MAX BEAM · 3.1 m (10 ft)
MAX SAIL AREA · 21.8 sq m (235 sq ft)
CREW · 2 WITH 1 TRAPEZE

C-CLASS
MAX LOA · 7.6 m (25 ft)
MAX BEAM · 4.3 m (14 ft)
MAX SAIL AREA · 27.9 sq m (300 sq ft)
CREW · 2 WITH 1 TRAPEZE

D-DIVISION
MAX LOA · NO LIMIT
MAX BEAM · NO LIMIT
MAX SAIL AREA · 46.5 sq m (500 sq ft)
CREW · 3 WITH 2 TRAPEZES

SPEED UNDER SAIL

Before the 18th century, records of speed under sail are vague because there was no system of measuring them. The time taken for a voyage was obviously known, but the variable winds and different routes added to the uncertainty of how fast the boat had sailed. It is unlikely that any ship ever exceeded 10 knots, and such were the perils of sailing at that time that a safe passage through bad weather and potential enemy waters was more notable than the time taken.

The incentive for speed in sailing vessels came from a number of different sources. During wartime, navies required fast warships to catch up or escape an enemy, while revenue officials needed fast cutters to catch smugglers; in turn, smugglers needed speed to escape them! In commerce, speed was crucial in order that merchant ships could deliver cargoes early to obtain a good price; and pilot boats needed speed, as the first one to board an incoming boat got the commission.

A FAST BOAT

Unlike a racing car that has a potential maximum speed and heads for it straight away, a boat has a range of speeds for unpredictable and different wind speeds and directions. For example, there is the best speed obtainable in heavy winds, and a considerably lower, best speed obtainable in light winds. If the boat is sailing to windward, its speed then is represented by the progress made into the wind, usually known as Vmg – velocity made good – which is a combination of its angle to the wind and its speed through the water.

'Straight-line speed' is not the only quality that enables a boat to go fast. It must be able to sail close to the wind, to tack speedily, and accelerate quickly as the wind increases. So absolute speed is not necessarily sought in a racing boat, more the ability to go faster around a course in varied weather than its opponents. Very often it is not speed as such

♦♦♦

Flying Cloud *On a voyage from New York to San Francisco in the mid-19th century, Flying Cloud, shown here in a contemporary painting by Charles Robert Patterson, was meticulously timed over 24 hours as sailing at an average speed of 15.4 knots. This is one of the few credible speed records from this period.*

that wins a race but boat handling, which may be facilitated by the design actually sacrificing some hull speed. The differences in speed between boats beating each other by one or two places are not detectable on speedometers: it is the speed of one boat relative to another that is important, and whether one boat is gaining or losing on another. Thus the records listed in the following pages are not the whole story, nor are they necessarily the product of boats specially designed to attain any record-breaking speeds.

SPEED RECORDS

There are three types of speed records:
24-hour run Since speed varies over a long passage at sea as wind and sea conditions alter, an average speed can be taken over a 24-hour period. Alternately, shorter periods of an hour or more can be used. Offshore multihulls are the best craft for this type of record attempt.
Passage records These are the times over courses at sea, which may be regular races or courses nominated for the purpose, notably Sandy Hook, New York, to the Lizard Point, England. As with the 24-hour run, multihulls are the best craft.
Half-kilometer run This is the distance chosen for finding the fastest possible speed over a short distance.

24-HOUR RUN

The 24-hour run was a favorite figure used by 19th-century ship owners to promote their clipper ships when cargo was moved by sail, largely because talking about passage times for most voyages sounded so unexciting. A good 24-hour run could only be achieved with the wind almost astern, a point of sailing known as broad reaching and which produces best records. Modern boats will go at maximum speed with the wind abeam; when the wind draws aft and a spinnaker is hoisted, the extra sail area and possibility of surfing can result in higher speeds.

Timing a 24-hour run at sea has always been an unreliable affair. Most of the times recorded were from noon to noon, because sextant observations were taken daily at noon, but observing the meridian altitude depended on locating local noon, which, of course, varies with position. Thus the time between local noons was not exactly 24 hours, nor were the sextant sights likely to be accurate to any more than within two miles, especially when taken in rough weather and poor visibility. Yet these are the conditions when the fastest speeds could occur.

Another method used to time a passage over 24 hours was to use a taffrail log.

In 1987, Fleury Michon VIII *attained the fastest-claimed recorded speed under sail for a 24-hr run.*

These would give the distance through the water, but were not that accurate, for the readings would depend on the height of the waves and the state of the sea's surface. Thus all early sailing ship speeds are more in the nature of claims by masters and ship owners than true speed records.

The best day's run claimed for a sailing ship is 467 miles, achieved by the Black Ball liner *Champion of the Seas* on 11-12 December 1854. This 67-m (221-ft) square-rigged vessel was on passage in the Southern Ocean from Liverpool in England to Melbourne in Australia, and claimed in that 24-hour period to be sailing at an average speed of 19.5 knots. Such a speed is unlikely, considering that for the whole voyage, it was averaging only 8 knots, or 199 miles a day.

The most credible record is that of the 68-m (225-ft) American clipper *Flying Cloud,* on passage from New York to San Francisco via Cape Horn in the mid-19th century. On the 58th day of the voyage as it ran northward up the west coast of South America after rounding Cape Horn, it sailed 374 miles in 24 hr 19 min 4 sec, an average speed of 15.4 knots. This run was carefully calculated by the captain's wife, who apparently had three chronometers and was painstaking in her work.

Whatever the veracity of these figures, they do give an indication of the kind of speeds achieved in the last days of commercial sail. When comparing them with modern boat speeds, it must be remembered that the hulls, spars and sails of today's boats are built of lightweight materials, and that they carry no payload. However well designed they were, sailing ships were fully loaded with cargo doubling their displacement.

Modern boat skippers are always interested in their day's run on any voyage, whether racing or cruising, but when it comes to validating records, the accuracy available falls short of the ideal. For an 'official record', some independent check of position is needed: one current idea is that this could be done by the Argos satellite or a system similar to it. The Argos satellite, devised in France, can locate a boat by means of a monitoring device implanted in its deck and relay that information back to ground. Except in cases of emergency, this monitor is out of the control of the crew. At the time of writing, the errors in the system do not allow a certain 24-hour run to be shown.

The most credible recent record, is that of *Fleury Michon VIII,* a 22.9-m (75-ft) trimaran, in which the French yachtsman Philippe Poupon and a crew of four broke the transatlantic passage record in 1987 (see pp180-1). On 16-17 June, they sailed 517 miles across the mid-Atlantic at an average speed of 21.5 knots. That this speed was attained is confirmed by the average speed of 16.18 knots for the whole passage, and for some of the time, *Fleury Michon VIII* was actually sailing or surfing at between 25 and 30 knots.

24-HOUR RUN

	BOAT	SKIPPER	Av. SPEED IN KNOTS
mid-C19th	FLYING CLOUD	JOSIAH CRESSY	15.4
1984	FORMULE TAG	MIKE BIRCH (UK)	21.35
1987	FLEURY MICHON VIII	PHILIPPE POUPON (FR.)	21.5

PASSAGE RECORDS

Since boats rarely sailed long distances,
there were few recorded passages until
ocean races became established in the
early years of this century. From the first
Bermuda and Fastnet races onward, the
elapsed times have been recorded by the
organizing club and a record kept of the
best time achieved on the course. These
records are detailed for many races in
Chapter Three (pp 58–137). Other than
those achieved by multihulls, in which
speeds of 12 to 16 knots are common, the
average speeds recorded by monohulls
rarely top 10 knots at the most, and are
usually much slower.

It must be remembered that since
almost all races use time allowances, the
development of the best boats was not
along the lines of absolute speed but of
speed for rating. This remains the case
today, with the crack Admiral's Cup boats
designed near the bottom of the rating
band and so theoretically slower than the
potentially fastest Admiral's Cup boat.

A further point is that in one of the
most famous yacht races in history, when
America won the race around the Isle of
Wight in 1851, no time allowance was in
force, and it was thus the fastest boat that
won: since the winds were light throughout
the race, the actual speed attained on that
occasion has never been of interest.

Two factors have combined to change
this situation. The first is the establishment of single- and short-handed races, all
of which are on a 'first-to-finish' basis,
thereby focusing interest on the winner's
time. Boats are therefore designed to be
faster in absolute terms specifically for
these races.

The second factor is the development
of maxi-raters and multihulls. Boats built
to maximum figures under a rating rule are
designed to be first to finish, rather than
win a race under corrected time. They thus
have every chance of breaking the course
record. The whole purpose of multihulls, in
their early days, was to show that they
were faster than monohulls over a course.
This is now taken for granted, but their
speeds and therefore elapsed times are
the most impressive that exist for sailing
boats of any size.

EASTBOUND TRANSATLANTIC RECORDS

The record for sailing fully crewed across
the Atlantic in the fastest direction – that
is west to east with the prevailing winds –
was set in the 1905 Transatlantic Race by
Atlantic (see p 84). Under the control of
skipper Charlie Barr, the 56.4-m (185-ft)
schooner took 12 days 4 hr 1 min to cross
the Atlantic at an average speed of 10.02
knots. She set a record that was to remain
unbeaten for 75 years.

Subsequent, fully crewed, transatlantic races with invariably smaller boats
produced no times to beat that set by
Atlantic, although Jim Kilroy (USA) came
close in 1969 in *Kialoa II*, taking 12 days 5
hr 43 min to cross from Newport, Rhode
Island, to Cork, Ireland (see pp 85–6). But
by the 1970s, the owners of maxis and
other large boats became interested in the
possibility of beating the record.

Atlantic *The 56.4-m (185-ft), three-masted
schooner* Atlantic *won the 1905 Transatlantic Race
in a time of 12 days 4 hr 1 min. This time set a
record that was to last for 75 years.*

◆◆◆

Early in 1980, the *Sunday Times* newspaper of London and *Le Point* newspaper
of Paris offered a $50,000 prize to any
boat that could beat *Atlantic*'s time on the
same Sandy Hook, New York, to the Lizard
Point route. Their interest was aroused by
the unexpected discovery of the derelict,
sunken hull of *Atlantic*, rotting in a dock
in Norfolk, Virginia.

The challenge was quickly taken up by
Eric Tabarly, who sailed the course in his
trimaran *Paul Ricard* in 10 days 5 hr 14
min, averaging 11.93 knots. This new record did not stand for long: successive
French sailors in multihulls have bettered
it with regularity, setting new records in
1981, 1984, 1986, 1987 and 1988. One

Beating the Record *The transatlantic record set by* Atlantic *in 1905 was finally beaten in 1980 by the trimaran* Paul Ricard *(top) sailed by Eric Tabarly. Its time of 10 days 5 hr 14 min has been bettered five times since then, most recently in 1988 by* Jet Services V *(bottom), sailed by Serge Madec.*

---

further attempt on this record was made by Bruno Peyron (France), who sailed single-handed from Sandy Hook to the Lizard Point in April 1987. Sailing a 22.6-m (74-ft) catamaran *Ericsson*, he completed the voyage in 11 days 11 hr 46 min, at an average speed of 10.61 knots, considerably slower than that achieved by all the fully crewed multihulls.

As a measure of comparison, the Cunard liner *QEII* takes approximately five days on its scheduled passage from New York to the south coast of England, while the powerboat record for the same route is held by *Virgin Atlantic Challenger II*, owned and sailed by Richard Branson and his crew, who took 3 days 8 hr to cross the Atlantic in 1986.

OTHER TRANSATLANTIC RECORDS

In early 1970, Francis Chichester attempted a single-handed passage of 4,000 miles, intending to average 200 miles a day. For this, he commissioned and had built the 15.2-m (50-ft) *Gipsy Moth V*, a fairly conventional boat that did not look particularly light or speedy. To achieve the required distance, Chichester sailed from Bissau in Guinea-Bissau, West Africa, to El Bluff in Nicaragua, Central America. On that passage, he managed 179.1 miles per day at an average speed of 7.46 knots, although for five consecutive days he sailed 1,018 miles, which is 203.5 miles per day at 8.4 knots.

The other Atlantic records are all for the various transatlantic races (see pp 84–91). One, however, should be noted here, for in 1988, Philippe Poupon, sailing the trimaran *Fleury Michon IX* in the single-handed C-STAR race from Plymouth, England, to Newport, Rhode Island, completed the course in 10 days 9 hr, 15 min, breaking the westbound single-handed record by almost six days and coming close to the sort of time set sailing the Atlantic in the easier, eastbound direction: Poupon almost equalled Eric Tabarly's time set in 1980 in *Paul Ricard*.

ONE-STOP CIRCUMNAVIGATIONS

Because the first boats making voyages round the world called in at many ports, their total number of days at sea were interesting but not of any great significance. It was not until 1966 that the first attempt on a speed and endurance record was made. This was by Francis Chichester, sailing around the world with one stop.

Sailing the 16.5-m (54-ft) *Gipsy Moth IV*, designed by Illingworth and Primrose and built by Camper and Nicholsons of Gosport, England, Chichester sailed single-handed from Plymouth, England, on 27 August 1966 via the Cape of Good Hope to Sydney, Australia; after a rest he continued via Cape Horn back to Plymouth, arriving on 28 May 1967. The leg to Sydney had taken 107 days at an average speed of 6.03 knots, the return leg to Plymouth 119 days at an average speed of 5.07 knots; Chichester was at sea for a total of 226 days and averaged 5.99 knots for the

EASTBOUND TRANSATLANTIC RECORDS

	BOAT	SKIPPER	TIME days	hr	min	AV. SPEED IN KNOTS
1905	ATLANTIC	CHARLIE BARR (USA)	12	04	01	10.02
1980	PAUL RICARD	ERIC TABARLY (FR.)	10	05	14	11.93
1981	ELF AQUITAINE	MARC PAJOT (FR.)	9	10	06	12.94
1984	JET SERVICES	PATRICK MORVAN (FR.)	8	16	33	14.03
1986	ROYALE II	LOÏC CARADEC (FR.)	7	21	05	15.47
1987	FLEURY MICHON VIII	PHILIPPE POUPON (FR.)	7	12	50	16.18
1988	JET SERVICES V	SERGE MADEC (FR.)	7	06	30	16.4

whole voyage. No similar feat had previously been attempted.

Soon after Chichester's return to Plymouth, Alec Rose set off in the 11-m (36-ft) sloop *Lively Lady* on a similar voyage. He left Portsmouth, England, on 16 July 1967, and returned on 4 July 1968, having stopped at Melbourne in Australia as intended and Bluff in New Zealand for unplanned repairs. His time was considerably slower than Chichester's, and it was not until 1974 that Chichester's record was broken. The French sailor, Alain Colas, made a single-handed voyage from St. Malo, Brittany, to Sydney via the Cape of Good Hope, and then back again via Cape Horn, in his 20.4-m (67-ft) trimaran *Manureva* (formerly known as *Pen Duick IV* when owned by Eric Tabarly). Colas was at sea for a total of 168 days, and averaged 7.34 knots; his stated best day's run was 326 miles at an average of 13.5 knots.

This appallingly arduous route is not one that is attempted very often, but Colas' record was soon broken by the 23.5-m (77-ft) *Great Britain II*, competing in the FT Clipper Race of 1975-6 (see p81). Sailed by a joint British military services

crew under the command of Roy Mullender, the boat was at sea for a total of 133 days, averaging 8.2 knots. The record was attempted again in 1987, when the 26-year-old Philippe Monnet sailed round the world from Brest in Brittany. Although he originally hoped to circumnavigate the world without stopping, he was forced to stop three times, at Cape Town in South Africa, Bluff in New Zealand and off the Azores, thus disqualifying him from beating the record. Sailing the 23.5-m (77-ft) trimaran *Kriter Brut de Brut*, he left Brest on 10 December 1986 and returned on 19 April 1987, a total of 129 days at sea, averaging 8.63 knots.

NON-STOP CIRCUMNAVIGATIONS

As the exploit of sailing around the world without stopping is even rarer than voyages with one stop, attempts on the record are few. After the first such voyage of 313 days, made single-handedly by Robin Knox-Johnston in *Suhaili* in the Golden Globe Race of 1968-9 (see p78), Chay Blyth single-handedly sailed non-stop around the world 'the wrong way', that is against the prevailing westerly winds in the Southern Ocean, rounding Cape Horn from east to west. In the specially designed 18-m (59-ft) ketch *British Steel*, Blyth left Hamble, England, on 18 October 1970, and returned, 293 days later, on 6 August 1971. His achievement was not so

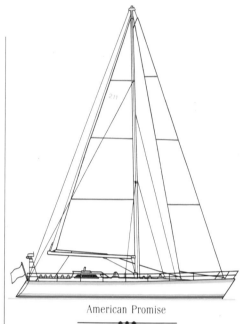

American Promise

much the speed – he averaged 3.85 knots – as the endurance of beating against the prevailing winds, a feat made possible by the strong construction of his steel boat and its windward ability, combined, of course, with the exceptional toughness of the lone sailor himself.

Blyth's record was beaten by David Scott-Cowper in the 12.5-m (41-ft) sloop *Ocean Bound*, who also sailed the same 'wrong way' course as Blyth, leaving Plymouth, England on 22 September 1981, and returning 221 days later, having averaged 5.91 knots. Two years later, this record, too, was broken by John Ridgway and Andy Briggs, who sailed the 17.1-m (56-ft 2-in) ketch *English Rose VI* around the world in 193 days at an average speed of 6.48 knots.

The most recent attempt at the record was made by Dodge Morgan (USA), who left Bermuda in November 1985 on board the 18.3-m (60-ft) *American Promise*, and returned there after 150 days in April 1986, having averaged 7.07 knots. The boat was fitted with every modern aid, and represented an example of the development of the seagoing boat of the 1980s. The speed it achieved, however, should be noted as being slow in relation to most of the records achieved by fully manned monohulls or by multihulls. The endurance factor and lack of progress due to bad weather on a number of days invariably takes its toll on such an endeavor.

AROUND THE WORLD RECORDS

	BOAT	SKIPPER	DAYS	Av. SPEED IN KNOTS
One-stop Circumnavigations				
1966-7	GIPSY MOTH IV	FRANCIS CHICHESTER (UK)	226	5.99
1973-4	MANUREVA	ALAIN COLAS (FR.)	168	7.34
1975-6	GREAT BRITAIN II	ROY MULLENDER & CREW (UK)	133	8.2
Non-stop Circumnavigations				
1968-9	SUHAILI	ROBIN KNOX-JOHNSTON (UK)	313	3.39
1970-1	BRITISH STEEL	CHAY BLYTH (UK)	293	3.85
1981-2	OCEAN BOUND	DAVID SCOTT-COWPER (UK)	221	5.91
1983-4	ENGLISH ROSE VI	JOHN RIDGWAY & ANDY BRIGGS (UK)	193	6.48
1985-6	AMERICAN PROMISE	DODGE MORGAN (USA)	150	7.07

HALF-KILOMETER RUN

It is a fact of speed records of all types, and not just of boats, that the shorter the distance, the faster the speed that can be achieved. This is because the high speed obtained cannot be sustained for long. When measuring speeds of sailing craft over short distances, one half of a kilometer (one-third of a mile) in any direction has become accepted as the standard distance to find the fastest speeds of any type of craft.

The boats used to attempt the half kilometer record for the 'world sailing speed record' have all been specialist craft: when Pascal Maka (France) set the world speed record at 38.86 knots – the highest speed then of any sailing craft – on 21 July 1986, he used a specially built 4-sqm (43-sqft) Gaastra sailboard measuring only 2.6 m (8 ft 7 in) long, 0.3 m (11¾ in) wide, and weighing only 6 kg (13 lbs).

HISTORY OF THE TRIALS

Regular speed trials under sail originated in 1969 from a discussion between Sir Peter Scott, president of the IYRU, and Bernard Hayman, editor of *Yachting World* magazine in England. What resulted was a sponsored speed trial, held in the open waters of Portland Harbor on the south coast of England in 1972.

One aspect of these trials was a negative one: to disprove claims made concerning various existing speed results. In 1955, a US Navy trial, with an experimental 6.1-m (20-ft) sailing sloop on a set of foils, recorded that it lifted out of the water and flew along, but the claim that it reached over 30 knots is dubious, given that her speed was measured by the speedometer in an accompanying motor boat. Similarly, the Little America's Cup British defender, *Lady Helmsman*, was said in the mid 1960s to have sailed at 30 knots, but this speed was based on the speedometer of a car pacing it along the shore! Attempts had been made at Cowes Week in 1954 and 1955 to set up speed trials, on one occasion using the radar of a warship; in these trials, Peter Scott achieved 10.2 knots in a Jollyboat, a conventional planing dinghy. Bernard Hayman had run trials in 1970 for amateur hydrofoil boats with stop-watches; the

THE RULES

Over the years, the rules for establishing a speed record under sail have been kept relatively simple. The records are established under the jurisdiction of the World Sailing Speed Record Committee, an international, autonomous body recognized by the IYRU. The WSSRC numbers about 15 members from different countries, and appoints an official observer for each speed trial.

To enter a speed trial, the craft has to be propelled by the wind; float on water, not ice; carry at least one person; be afloat prior to the attempt; and accelerate from a standing start. The record is established over a half-kilometer distance, and the craft can enter this measured distance at any speed. This half kilometer is measured to one per cent accuracy, and can be indicated by posts and transits ashore, or buoys afloat.

The time is recorded to the nearest one-hundredth of a second, and the speed is calculated to the nearest one-hundredth of a knot, with allowances made for any current or tidal stream on the course. Should either of these exceed 2 knots, any recorded run is invalid and has to be sailed again.

The record in each class stands until it has been exceeded by at least two per cent. There is more than just the overall 'World Sailing Speed Record' at stake, for entrants are divided into classes by sail area, measured confusingly in a mixture of metric and imperial sizes; the hull can be any shape or size.

SPEED CLASSES

UNLIMITED CLASS
300.1 sq ft (27.9 sq m) AND ABOVE
C CLASS
235.1 sq ft (21.8 sq m) – 300 sq ft (27.9 sq m)
B CLASS
150.1 sq ft (13.9 sq m) – 235 sq ft (21.8 sq m)
A CLASS
10.1 sq m (108.7 sq ft) – 150 sq ft (13.9 sq m)
10-SQUARE METER CLASS
UP TO 10 sq m (107.6 sq ft)
WOMEN'S CLASSES
ALL THE ABOVE CLASSES

Pascal Maka, first to break the sailing speed record on a board.

trials were inconclusive but the timing systems came under study.

Portland was chosen for the trials because it is a large harbor over which the wind can blow unimpeded and which has plenty of room for half-kilometer runs, whatever the wind direction.

For the first meeting in 1972, Professor Sam Bradfield, an American academic who had tried out similar trials on Long Island Sound, was present as an adviser. The course was arranged within a circle, enabling boats to be timed on any point of sailing that they wished. Measurement was by a half-kilometer wire which naval divers had placed along the sea bed, and the timing was made by boats alongside the buoys marking the full extent of the course, with the crew holding stopwatches and in contact with each other by radio. Only 12 boats an hour could be processed, a small number compared with the continuous stream of competitors that can be assessed in trials today.

Although in the early years, the trials were held at Portland each October, it was intended that the event become a worldwide competition with rules to enable a world sailing speed record to be established anywhere in the world (see box text on the previous page).

The first week in 1972 saw the establishment of a 26.3-knot record by the specially designed asymmetric proa *Crossbow*, helmed by Tim Colman and designed by Rod Macalpine-Downie. *Crossbow* consisted of a slim hull, 18.2 m (60 ft) long, with an outrigger of 8.2 m (27 ft) on which the crew sat in a pod. It could only sail on starboard tack and had to be rowed into the starting position. Other speeds attained at that first meeting were 21.5 knots by the foil-borne *Icarus*, 19.6 knots by a conventional Tornado catamaran, 16.7 knots by *Trifle*, a heavy offshore trimaran, and 6.3 knots by *Miss Strand Glass*, designed by hydrofoil pioneer Christopher Hook. This monohull was equipped with controllable-angle foils, but the failure of this sound idea by an inventor who had been in the field for many years taught a lesson that became more and more evident as the trials developed: weight was the chief enemy to speed on the water.

Over the years, many extraordinary craft appeared at the annual speed week at Portland. Every kind of small multihull, foil-borne, multi-wing sail and even kite-propelled craft have attempted to beat the record. Many never got off the beach while many others have failed to live up to their designers' expectations, but of those that managed the course, none were able to beat the successively improved speeds of *Crossbow*, which rose to an impressive 31.24 knots by 1975.

In 1976, the same designer and owner built *Crossbow II*, a 18.2-m (60-ft) asymmetric catamaran with a single, huge sail rigged on each hull, although the hulls were staggered so that one had its mast and sail slightly ahead of the other. This new craft improved on its predecessor's record and achieved 31.8 knots, raising that the following year to 33.8 knots. In 1980, *Crossbow II* was timed at 36 knots, a speed it did not exceed again and which remained the world sailing speed record until it was surpassed in 1986.

Crossbow II *With its twin asymmetric hulls and staggered masts, Crossbow II set a new world speed record under sail of 36 knots in 1980 that was to stand until Pascal Maka broke it in 1986.*

— ● ● ● —

THE BOARD CHALLENGE

In 1975, a two-man sailboard was entered in the trials by Mike Todd and Clive Colenso (UK). It was thought of as a bit of a joke, as sailboards had not appeared before at a speed week. However, it hit 13.5 knots on its first attempt.

Sailboards have two important advantages over other boats in terms of speed: they are smaller and lighter, so they create less friction with the water and are, therefore, slowed down less by it. With a boat, the more elaborate the hull, the heavier it is and, therefore, the slower. Since the rules call for at least one crew, it follows that the smallest craft that can support one person is potentially faster than anything. Thus the boards used to challenge the records are the logical outcome of this line of thought.

In 1977, Derek Thijs (Netherlands) sailed a standard Windglider board at Portland at 17.1 knots and took the 10-sqm record. In 1980, off the island Maui in Hawaii, Jaap van der Rest (Netherlands) bettered this result with a speed of 24.45 knots. Later in the year at Portland, Jugen Honscheid (Germany) surpassed this new record with a narrow board, although not by the necessary two per cent to claim the record himself. In 1982, Pascal Maka appeared at Portland and set a new record of 27.82 knots. Each year, the boards were getting smaller and faster.

The following year, Fred Haywood (US) recorded 30.82 knots on a board with a complex rig including a carbon fiber wing mast and rigid airfoil: this complicated line of development was not pursued after 1984, when similar rigs appeared but achieved less speed. In 1985, however, Michael Pucher (Austria) sailed the half-kilometer run at Port St. Louis, France, in a Mistral gusting up to 50 knots, at a recorded speed of 32.35 knots, a time within reach of *Crossbow II*'s record.

Pascal Maka's record breaking speed was achieved at a meeting at Fuerteventura in the Canary Islands. The island's name means 'fire and wind', and indeed this volcanic island does boast strong prevailing winds. The course site was at Sotovento with a beach perfectly angled for broad reaching and allowing boards to sail within 2 m (6 ft) of the shore on flat water. Between 11-22 July 1986, Maka made no less than 20 runs over 36 knots and 3 in excess of 38 knots, so his 38.86 time was no freak result. Maka's record was broken in November 1988 when, during a Mistral, Eric Beale (UK) achieved 40.33 knots on a board at Les Saintes Maries de-la-Mer in the south of France.

LOCATIONS AND TIMING

The number and frequency of speed weeks grew rapidly after the introduction of boards, which are easily transported compared with the big foilers, proas, and other similar craft. In addition to Portland, regular speed weeks are now established at Lethbridge in Canada and Brest, Port Camargue and Port St. Louis in France, while occasional meetings have been held at Safety Bay in Australia, Fos-sur-Mer in France, Sotovento in the Canaries, Port Jefferson and Nantucket in the US, and Hvide Sande in Denmark.

The methods of timing speed trials receive continuous improvement and are supervised by World Sailing Speed Record Committee observers and others. Computers are now used to calculate and store the results, and at trials in the Netherlands in 1980, the old stop-watch and radio system used at Portland was abandoned in favor of filming the run. By replaying the tape, the time can be estimated to one hundredth of a second. Since this method also clearly identifies the boat, a far quicker printout of competitive runs has become possible, a necessary requirement to make use of suitable weather when it occurs. Such is the efficiency of this system that whereas in 1972, 12 boats could be processed an hour, 250 an hour were being processed in 1987. The course needs fixed positions, but the best speeds are now invariably achieved along the edge of a shore with the wind at a favorable angle to the beach.

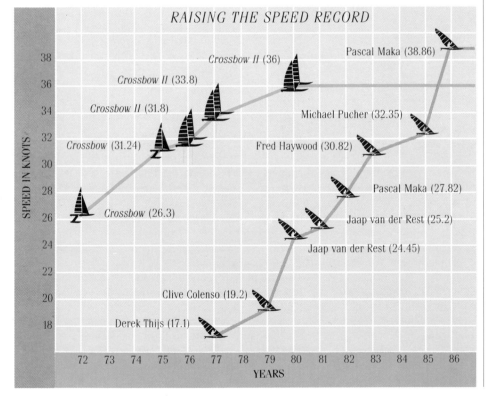

RAISING THE SPEED RECORD

Pascal Maka (38.86)
Crossbow II (36)
Crossbow II (33.8)
Crossbow II (31.8)
Michael Pucher (32.35)
Crossbow (31.24)
Fred Haywood (30.82)
Pascal Maka (27.82)
Crossbow (26.3)
Jaap van der Rest (25.2)
Jaap van der Rest (24.45)
Clive Colenso (19.2)
Derek Thijs (17.1)

SPEED IN KNOTS

YEARS

WORLD SAILING SPEED RECORDS

	RECORD HOLDER	NATIONALITY	KNOTS	VENUE	DATE
OVERALL	ERIC BEALE	UK	40.33	LES SAINTES MARIES	1988
UNLIMITED	TIM COLMAN & CREW	UK	36.0	PORTLAND	1980
C CLASS	JEAN-BERNARD CUNIN & MAURICE GAHAGNON	FRANCE	26.43	PORTLAND	1988
B CLASS	ANDREW GROGONO & JAMES FOWLER	UK	28.15	PORTLAND	1985
A CLASS	SERGE GRIESSEMAN & MANN BERTIN	GERMANY	35.06	SOTOVENTO	1986
10-SQM	ERIC BEALE	UK	AS OVERALL		
WOMEN'S OVERALL	BRIDGETTE GIMINEZ	FRANCE	37.26	LES SAINTES MARIES	1988

BOARDSAILING

Windsurfing, boardsailing or sailboarding – the terms are interchangeable – has added a new dimension to sailing. Thousands of people all over the world sail boards off beaches, on lakes and on stretches of water of all kinds. There are also boards that sail on land, sand and ice.

The appeal of boardsailing is soon apparent: the simplicity of the equipment – which can be carried down to the water, easily transported on the top of a car and stored at home – coupled with physical activity and exciting sailing. Many of those who sail boards do not consider themselves as 'sailors' and would never engage in any other form of sailing. But, like other branches of sailing, indeed like any other new sport, boardsailing has spawned new techniques and designs, special equipment and its own publications.

ORIGINS

The origins of boardsailing are controversial. Like all inventions, there were several people working on the idea at the same time, that idea being a boat steered by moving a sail instead of a rudder.

An article in the American *Popular Science* magazine of August 1965 by S. Newman Darby of Pennsylvania describes a nearly rectangular board on which one stood and held up a diamond-shaped sail; this board was designed mainly for reaching and running. A California sailor, Jim Drake, was also working on the idea and says that he was suddenly inspired, when driving along the Los Angeles Freeway, to install a universal joint at the base of the board's mast. Drake cooperated with a fellow dinghy sailor, Hoyle Schweitzer, to develop the project and make it both sailable and saleable: crucial to these hopes were the use of a simple rope to pull up the mast and a small, stabilizing fin aft. A patent was taken out in 1968 and, having bought out Drake, Schweitzer marketed this new craft.

Schweitzer took out patents in a number of countries, including Australia, Britain, Canada, Germany and Japan; a Dutch textile company, Ten Cate, began importing Schweitzer's boards into Europe. His boards were called Windsurfers and the sport he called windsurfing. However, imitations began to be made in Europe and

Windsurfing in heavy seas

— ◆◆◆ —

it was with these that, in the early 1970s, the sport took off in Western Europe. In America, the Windsurfer patent held up, the result being that in contrast, production and marketing were limited.

Thereafter, Schweitzer initiated a succession of legal battles against boards by other makers, claiming copyright on the terms 'Windsurfer' and 'windsurfing'. Some succeeded, others failed, but generally, Windsurfer has remained a trade name while windsurfing is anyone's term. In a High Court action in Britain in 1982, a man called Peter Chilvers produced and showed to the satisfaction of the court that in 1958, at the age of 12, he had sailed in Chichester Harbor a form of board, using rough materials for a rig and a wishbone made from broomsticks to control the board in the absence of a rudder.

In Britain at least, therefore, no patent was possible, and all over Europe, there are now numerous makers of all patterns of boards. In France, where Windsurfer had not attempted to obtain a patent, there were 60 makes of board at the 1979 Paris Boat Show: not a single board had been on show five years earlier. It is impossible to estimate the number of boards, but in 1980, there were said to be 400,000 boards in Europe and 25,000 in the US.

THE BOARD

Sailing vessels can be steered without a rudder if the rig can be moved fore and aft, but on large boats and most small dinghies, this is impracticable. However, all yacht and dinghy rigs are adjusted to try and 'balance out the helm', that is to make the boat tend to steer one way or the other. On a sailboard, without a rudder, this adjustment is done entirely by the crew, who adjusts the wishbone and therefore the rig, which is connected to the hull by a univeral joint and can move in any direction. A small daggerboard and aft fin provide directional stability, and footstraps allow the sailor to remain securely attached in strong winds.

Before anything else, the sailboard is a beach toy, a first cousin to the surfboard, but it does not need surf, only wind. Other than for simply sailing about, it can be used for racing, for high speed sailing trials on special boards in strong winds, and for stunts like surf jumping and endurance records. The top competitions are in the Olympic Games and speed trials, the sailboard being the fastest sailing craft on water (see pp183-5).

Cheaper boards are made of polyethylene, mid-range boards of ASA and ABS plastics, while expensive boards are formed from the most exotic artificial plastics using Kevlar and foams. The cheap boards are often the most durable, since the special materials have to be treated carefully, being there for outright speed, not for the long life of the board.

Boardsailing will continue to develop rapidly, but the classification of boards has settled down into the following types. Most manufacturers will have each classification in their range, some going under a trade or a class name.

Long boards – over 3.5m (11ft 6in): When these boards have high physical volume, over 200 liters (7 cu ft), they are particularly good in light winds, with enough reserve buoyancy for an average-weight person to race or just to have fun in good weather. When the volume is lower than this, the board is better in medium winds.
Race board A small-volume variation of the long board, used exclusively for racing, the length of this board is used to give a V or concave bottom and pulled-in tail features

to the hull: these produce good windward performance, planing ability and quick turning. The board has several sets of footstraps for different points of sailing.

A sub-category is the Division II open class (see below), which is a long board, but with a very high volume of over 300 liters (10.5 cu ft). When this is combined with a round bottom, they are very unstable and difficult to sail, but fast in light winds. These qualities have made them the choice for the Olympic sailboard class in 1992, which is a one-design supplied by one manufacturer.

Short board – less than 3 m (9 ft 10 in): For strong winds, the shorter the board, the better, but a short board will sink in winds of under about 18 knots (Force 5). Very light materials are therefore used and small variations in design are critical to performance. As the wind becomes stronger, the daggerboard, which stops side slip in moderate winds, actually causes directional instability: one variation of short board, therefore, has no daggerboard. Other than for custom-built boards for special purposes, such as speed records, the minimum size for these boards is 2.65 m (8 ft 8 in) but a more common size is 2.95 m (9 ft 8 in).

Mid-length boards: At 3.3 m (10 ft 10 in) with a volume of 150 liters ($5\frac{1}{4}$ cu ft), these boards are the compromise size. As such, they come somewhere between the long and short boards in all qualities and are therefore popular with the general public in giving fair sailing in all wind strengths.

RACING

The first world championship of the Windsurfer class was held in 1973 in the US, but by 1976, the class was organized enough with sufficient commercial sponsorship to have a world championship in Nassau in the Bahamas. The sponsors supplied all the boards, there were 372 entrants, ranging in age from 11 to 68, and the winner was Robbie Naish, aged 13.

The first board designed especially for racing was the Windglider class, produced in 1977 and subsequently used in the 1984 Olympic Games. By 1988, the IYRU recognized two one-design classes – the Mistral and the Windglider – and three open classes of sailboards:

Division I – Flatboard: This division has rules to ensure that the board is essentially flat. The sail area is restricted to 6 sq m (64.6 sq ft); typical dimensions of the hull are length: 3.9 m (9 ft 6 in); minimum width: 69 cm (2 ft 3 in); weight: 17 kg ($37\frac{1}{2}$ lb). This class is mainly sailed in the UK and had its first world championships in Cornwall in 1987.

Division II – Displacement Division: The main characteristic of a Division II board is that it resembles a log. This is intended as a development class from which the Lechner A390 one-design board was chosen for use in the 1988 Olympic Games. Division II is the main sailboard used for international competition.

Division III – Tandem Class: Classified as such by the IYRU, there is no sign of any international support for this division.

◆◆◆

Windglider *The first board designed for racing, the Windglider was used in the 1984 Olympic Games.*

DIVISION II WORLD CHAMPIONSHIPS

	CLASS	CHAMPION	NATIONALITY
1979	LIGHTWEIGHT	KARL MESSMER	SWITZERLAND
GUADELOUPE	WOMEN	MARIE ANNICK MAUS	FRANCE
1980	LIGHTWEIGHT	KARL MESSMER	SWITZERLAND
NAHARYA	HEAVYWEIGHT	THOMAS STALTMAIER	GERMANY
ISRAEL	WOMEN	MANUELLE GRAVELINE	FRANCE
1981	LIGHTWEIGHT	STEPHAN VAN DEN BERG	NETHERLANDS
ST. PETERSBURG	HEAVYWEIGHT	JAN WANGAARD	NORWAY
USA	WOMEN	MAREN BERNER	NORWAY
1982	LIGHTWEIGHT	ROBERT NAGY	FRANCE
LOREDO	HEAVYWEIGHT	GILDAS GUILLEROT	FRANCE
SPAIN	WOMEN	MARIE ANNICK MAUS	FRANCE
1983	LIGHTWEIGHT	ROBERT NAGY	FRANCE
GUADELOUPE	HEAVYWEIGHT	GILDAS GUILLEROT	FRANCE
	WOMEN	MANUELLE GRAVELINE	FRANCE
1984	LIGHTWEIGHT	ROBERT NAGY	FRANCE
MOMBASA	HEAVYWEIGHT	ANDERS BRINGDAL	SWEDEN
KENYA	WOMEN	MANUELLE GRAVELINE	FRANCE
1985	LIGHTWEIGHT	HERVÉ PIEGELIN	FRANCE
TORBAY	HEAVYWEIGHT	JONAS DAVIDSON	SWEDEN
UK	WOMEN	VALERIE SALLES	FRANCE
1986	LIGHTWEIGHT	ROBERT NAGY	FRANCE
CAGLIARI	HEAVYWEIGHT	HAKEN LING	SWEDEN
SARDINIA	WOMEN	JORUN HORGUN	NORWAY
1987	LIGHTWEIGHT	MICHEL QUINTIN	FRANCE
KINGSTON	HEAVYWEIGHT	GEORGE KENDLER	AUSTRIA
CANADA	WOMEN	JORUN HORGUN	NORWAY
1988	LIGHTWEIGHT	HERVÉ PIEGELIN	FRANCE
HAIFA	HEAVYWEIGHT	LUCA DEPREDRINI	ITALY
ISRAEL	WOMEN	VALERIE CAPART	FRANCE

SAND, LAND AND ICEBOATS

The main attraction of sailing vehicles on land, sand or ice is the high speeds that can be obtained in relation to sailing on water. However, there are relatively few places where landsailing – that is sailing on land or on sand – can take place, for it requires firm, flat surfaces such as on certain beaches, on salt lakes, on disused airfield runways, and in deserts. Iceboating depends even more on suitable conditions, requiring long periods of cold weather, safe ice and a sizeable lake, river or canal. Both land and iceboats require good winds and plenty of courage on the part of the helmsman.

LANDSAILING

The fastest speed recognized by the international authority for the sport, the Fédération Internationale de Sand et Land Yachts, is 107 km per hr (57.81 knots, 66.48 statute miles per hr) achieved by Christian-Yves Nau (France) in the vehicle *Mobil* at Le Touquet, France. At the time of the trial in March 1981, the wind was over Force 12. A speed of 142.26 km per hr (76.86 knots, 88.4 statute miles per hr) is generally recognized to have been achieved by Nord Embroden (USA) in the vehicle *Midnight at the Oasis* at Superior Dry Lake in California, in April 1976.

Certainly, such speeds are not infrequent, but many of them go unrecorded, cars having followed landsailors at over 112.65 km per hr (60.84 knots, 70 statute miles per hr) on a number of occasions. In comparison, the ice speed record stands at 230 km per hr (124 knots, 143 statute miles per hr) achieved by John D. Buckstaff in a Class A stern steerer on Lake Winnebago, Wisconsin in 1938.

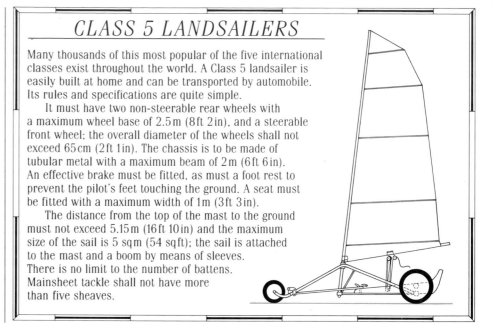

CLASS 5 LANDSAILERS

Many thousands of this most popular of the five international classes exist throughout the world. A Class 5 landsailer is easily built at home and can be transported by automobile. Its rules and specifications are quite simple.

It must have two non-steerable rear wheels with a maximum wheel base of 2.5m (8ft 2in), and a steerable front wheel; the overall diameter of the wheels shall not exceed 65cm (2ft 1in). The chassis is to be made of tubular metal with a maximum beam of 2m (6ft 6in). An effective brake must be fitted, as must a foot rest to prevent the pilot's feet touching the ground. A seat must be fitted with a maximum width of 1m (3ft 3in).

The distance from the top of the mast to the ground must not exceed 5.15m (16ft 10in) and the maximum size of the sail is 5 sqm (54 sqft); the sail is attached to the mast and a boom by means of sleeves. There is no limit to the number of battens. Mainsheet tackle shall not have more than five sheaves.

ORIGINS

The first land vehicles to be driven by sails were probably used in the plains of ancient China, although the first modern land (and ice) boats did not appear until around 1600, in the Netherlands. In the US in the 19th century, Kansas Pacific Railroad repair parties made a sailing car on rails that could average 42.28 km per hr (26 knots, 30 miles per hr) and claimed to have travelled 135.2 km (84 statute miles) in four hours. These early landsailing vehicles, much like early water sailing vessels, could probably only sail downwind. However, at Bruges in Belgium in 1910, Frank and Ben Dumont introduced landsailing as a sport, using bicycle wheels and methods of steering suggested by the newly invented automobile. These ideas enabled the vehicles to tack into the wind, just like a boat.

By 1925, the three-wheel configuration with rigs of gaffs and jibs was adopted (it must be remembered that the bermudan rig did not even get general acceptance in sailing until the late 1920s). The DN iceboat rig of 1937 (see below) had a major influence on cleaning up the rigs of landsailers, which slowly evolved into the single, fully battened sail rigged on a bermudan mast. Today, sand and landsailing is organized in Europe, Argentina, Australia, the Gulf States and the US.

LANDSAILING CLASSES

Classes are rated principally on sail area. The two largest, Classes 1 and 2, seldom seen in Europe, are permitted 17 sqm and 11 sqm of sail respectively (183 sqft and 118 sqft). Both these require a small team to transport and rig them. Class 3 is a popular class and well-developed toward potential speeds of 113-129 km per hr (61-70 knots, 70-80 statute miles per hr); its only restriction is a total mast, boom

Landsailing *In 1809, Captain Molyneaux Shuldham RN and some of his fellow British prisoners of war, held by the French at Verdun, were forbidden from sailing small boats on the River Meuse by their captors. They built two landsailers – one a sloop, the other a schooner – and sailed these instead!*

and sail area of 7.35 sqm (79 sqft). At 6.5 sqm (70 sqft), Class 4 has proved less popular, and racing has tended to polarize towards Classes 3 and 5 (see box text for details of a Class 5 landsailer).

RULES OF RACING

The person steering the landsailer is called the pilot, who needs a special licence before competing in national and international events.

The right of way and sailing rules are very different from those afloat. Landsailers start from a standstill position on a grid, rather like racing cars, and it may be specified on which tack to start. Those approaching each other 'keep right', but on converging courses, the 'boat' on the right side of the course has priority. A sailer being pushed gives way to one under sail, and an overtaking 'boat' keeps clear of the one being overtaken.

Races can last up to about one hour and around several laps of the course. Barging to get an inside advantage at a mark is not allowed, and at the finish, the sailer is timed in when the base of its mast crosses the line. The winner is signalled to have finished by the dipping of a checkered flag.

SAILING TECHNIQUES

In land and iceboating, the speeds in any reasonable breeze are high in comparison with the true wind. Therefore, the apparent wind changes at between 5 and 10 knots by a much bigger angle than when sailing afloat, so that boats are usually closehauled throughout the race. To cope with this, the rigs are designed for beating and there are no arrangements for running sails such as spinnakers. On the single mainsail, the mainsheet is the principal control, although some use is made of a Cunningham hole for loosening the luff in light airs. Sails are invariably fully battened.

The most difficult point of landsailing is downwind: to take advantage of the effect of the apparent wind, landsailers need to tack downwind, a difficult maneuver that can lead to capsizes. These are quite possible, although a side wheel can lift without any loss of balance. If the single front wheel leaves the ground, steering is lost.

The iceboat Icicle, *owned by John A. Roosevelt.*

ICEBOATING

In the 19th century, iceboating flourished every winter on the Hudson River above New York, which froze over for a distance of about 160 km (100 miles). The Hudson River Ice Yacht Club was based at Poughkeepsie, and large and sometimes experimental iceboats were built by wealthy owners. The largest recorded was built for John A. Roosevelt in the 1860s. At 21 m (68 ft 11 in) long, *Icicle* was a gaff-rigged sloop with 99.4 sqm (1,070 sqft) of sail. Somewhat smaller iceboats, and other clubs, prospered then; the classes were rated by sail area. As in sailing afloat in the 19th century, the concept of one-design classes or equal sail area between competitors had not taken hold.

ICEBOAT CLASSES

Today, iceboating takes place mainly in Austria, Canada, the Netherlands, Poland and the US, in two main classes. The E-Skeeter, with its 17 sqm (183 sqft) of sail, is equivalent to the Class 1 landsailer. The DN is the more popular of the two and, as a relatively small craft, was introduced as the old, large iceboats, with their wealthy owners and stern steering, disappeared. It originated from a competition

run by the *Detroit News* paper in 1937. The class spread throughout the US and is now sailed worldwide.

The DN is equivalent to the Class 4 landsailer with the same rig of 6.5 sqm (70 sqft) on a 4.9 m (16 ft) mast. The fuselage is 3.6 m (12 ft) long and weighs about 40.8 kg (90 lbs). Both the DN and the Skeeter are steered by a forward runner or skate. The main runners aft are between 61-91 cm (2-3 ft) long and are of steel, aluminum, wood or carbon fiber: competitive boats carry several sets for different conditions. Masts are usually of aluminum, but wood composite types are also considered advanced, perhaps with carbon fiber added. Some owners have a Class 4 landsailer and interchange the rigs, such is the basic similarity between the structure of land and iceboats.

Races in iceboats begin from a standing start: the pilots run from a 'gate' to the iceboats and begin to push them, leaping on board once about 10 knots is achieved. Since iceboats accelerate even faster than landsailers and sail faster – four to five times the true wind on smooth ice – they rapidly bring the apparent wind forward on all points of sailing and are thus closehauled for most of the time.

Chapter 6

The Olympic Games

*S*ailing is one of the sports in the quad-rennial Olympic Games and the winner of a gold medal holds one of the highest honors in sailing. Yet within the sport, the Olympic Games hold an atypical position. Only eight specialized classes, representative of a few types of boat, are raced today, and they are sailed on specific and unvarying, closed-circuit courses. 'Choosing the right boat' is thus an occupational hazard for competing sailors, and over the years this exercise has been transferred to the international level, resulting in long periods of wrangling over which classes should be sailed in the Games. However, the chosen classes get considerable support from the many nations without a strong sailing tradition; their support for the Olympic Games gives them a chance for their helmsmen to compete in top-level international racing.

THE OLYMPIC GAMES

The first Olympic Games of the modern era were held in Greece in 1896, but it was not until the second Games in 1900, held in Paris, that sailing was included as one of the sports. Since then, sailing has been an Olympic sport at every Games except one, the 1904 Games held in St. Louis, Missouri.

The Olympic regatta takes place in the same country and at the same time as the main events, but is often some way from the principal site of the Games: in 1988, the regatta at Pusan was 350 km (220 miles) from Seoul. The regatta must be held on open waters, usually the sea or on a large inland lake, as was the case in 1976 when the regatta was held on Lake Ontario, Canada. The host country usually takes the opportunity of building a special Olympic harbor and supporting buildings and facilities. When the Games are over, the complex can then be used to further sailing in that country.

The Olympic challenge has always attracted helmsmen and crew of the very highest caliber: the names of medal winners over the years, usually young men, frequently turn up in racing of all kinds, from dinghy championships and inshore races to offshore racing, the America's Cup and long-distance events.

Although the Olympic gold, silver and bronze medallists can be considered the cream of their respective classes and of yacht racing as a whole, the fleets in the Games are often of a lower standard than those in the world championships or in the national trials used to select the Olympic entrants. The reason for this is that in each class, only one boat per nation is allowed in the Games, whereas one or two countries may have a dozen or more helmsmen in a class, all of whom are of a consistently higher standard than the helmsmen selected from the rest of the world.

THE OLYMPIC BOATS

The classes used in the Games have a status of their own. Control is in the hands of the International Yacht Racing Union, which, in cooperation with the Olympic authorities – notably the International Olympic Committee (IOC) – decides which classes are used and the conditions under which they race (see pp 194-7 for details of the individual classes, past and present). Like all the other classes, these classes have annual world championships, except in an Olympic year: these championships are usually regarded as informal Olympic selection trials.

Throughout most of the world, the Olympic classes are usually small in terms of numbers of boats, because sailors believe that they must be of a high standard before they can sail in such classes. This situation does not arise if the class was already widespread before it was selected for Olympic competition, as in the case of the 470, or if it is long established, like the Star. But in Eastern Europe and many Third World nations, the Olympic classes are sometimes numerous in comparison with other boats, or are even the only racing classes. This is because sailing is a relatively new sport, and the government or national sporting body has encouraged competition in the Olympic classes only, training people for future Olympic Games and world championships.

OLYMPIC RECORDS

The record for the countries which have participated in the most sailing Olympics is held by France and Sweden, which have sent boats on every occasion apart from 1980 and 1900 respectively. Britain has missed two Games, 1912 and 1980, while the US competed in 1900 but then not again until 1928, since then it has sent a team every year, except 1980.

The countries to have won the most gold medals up to 1988 are the US, Britain and Norway, all with 15; France and Sweden with 9; Denmark with 8; New Zealand with 5; the Netherlands and the USSR with 4; Australia, Spain and West Germany with 3; Belgium, Brazil, East Germany and Italy with 2; and the Bahamas, pre-war Germany, Finland, Greece and Switzerland, all with 1 each. But only three of the French and Norwegian medals, four of the Swedish and five of the British medals have been gained since 1948: these four countries dominated in the old, heavy keelboats that were used for the earlier Games, but have been less successful in the post-war years.

Of the eight Danish gold medals, four have been won by one man – Paul Elvström. At the time of his fourth victory in 1960, it was unprecedented for any person, in any Olympic sport, to hold four gold medals, although that record has now been superseded in other sports. In sailing, it remains a record. Elvström won his first medal in the single-handed Firefly class in 1948 at the age of 19, going on to win in the single-handed Finn class in 1952, 1956 and 1960. He was 4th in the Star class in 1968, 13th in the Solings in 1972, 4th in the Tornados in 1984, and sailed his last Olympic regatta – his 8th – in a Tornado in 1988, aged 60. In addition, he has won eight world championships in six classes, including the Soling, the Dragon and the 5.5-Meter, and won the Half Ton Cup in a boat of his own design in 1972.

The largest number of boats to compete in any class in the Olympics was 45 in the sailboard class in 1988; among boats with rudders, 36 Finns competed in 1968. 1988 was the record year for entrants, with 370 competitors, 214 boats and 60 countries participating; this was largely due to the popularity of the sailboard class, which had a wider appeal than the other Olympic classes, and the addition of an eighth class, the women's 470.

Paul Elvström *Holder of a record four Olympic gold medals for sailing, Paul Elvström has represented Denmark in eight Olympic Games, the first in 1948.*

THE OLYMPIC COURSE

Much effort is made to make the Olympic Games as fair as possible for all competitors. As a sport, sailing is inevitably full of surprises, usually from the weather, but courses can be chosen, as far as practicable, away from strong tides or currents in order to ensure that there is no noticeable bias on any part of the course.

The Olympic course is triangular, the start and finish invariably to windward. The first leg is a beat, the second leg a reach to a mark on the port side of the course, the third another reach back to the mark at the start of the beat, the fourth another beat, the fifth a dead run, the sixth a final beat to the finish — in effect a triangle, a sausage and a beat. This Olympic course, or variations on it, is used for many other major events, notably the America's Cup and numerous yacht and dinghy championships. If the wind shifts during the race, the points of sailing might not be realized, but the race carries on, the organizers re-laying the final windward mark to give a true beat to the finish.

Each class of boat sails seven races, one a day. The best six races count towards the final result, each helmsman discarding his worst result.

At modern Olympic venues, a circular area is allotted to each class. 'A' circle is for the sailboard class, closest in to the shore, 'B' circle is for the 470 and Finn, 'C' circle for the Flying Dutchman and Star, and 'D' circle for the largest boats, the Soling and the Tornado.

In these circles, the course can be pivoted to suit the wind on the day; thus the diameter of the circle is the length of the windward leg. For the sailboards, the windward leg is 1 mile, for the Finns and 470s, 1.3 miles, for the Solings, Stars, Flying Dutchmen and Tornados, 2 miles. The Finn, Flying Dutchman, 470, Soling and Star classes sail a right-angled triangle with a turning mark of 90° and turns in to and off the beat of 45°.

The Tornado and the sailboard classes have wider turning angles at the reach mark and tighter angles at either end of the beat. This is because they do not set spinnakers and have to develop high speeds in relation to the wind.

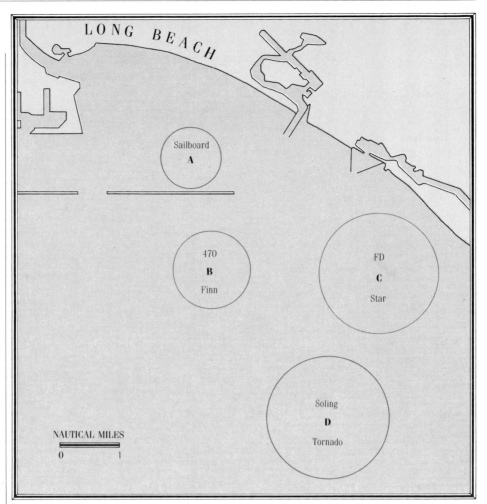

Location of courses at Long Beach Olympic Regatta, 1984

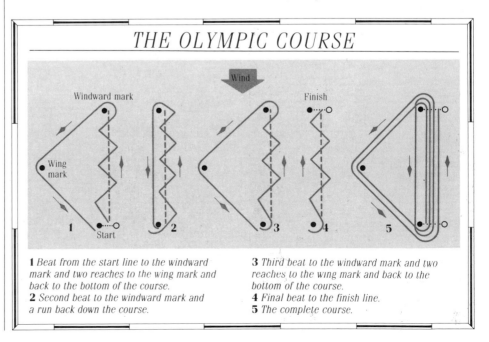

THE OLYMPIC COURSE

1 Beat from the start line to the windward mark and two reaches to the wing mark and back to the bottom of the course.
2 Second beat to the windward mark and a run back down the course.
3 Third beat to the windward mark and two reaches to the wing mark and back to the bottom of the course.
4 Final beat to the finish line.
5 The complete course.

THE OLYMPIC CLASSES

Over the years, the Olympic classes have changed as new ones have gained in popularity and old ones faded away. Throughout the 1960s, the International Yacht Racing Union was involved in wrangling on the choice of classes, but by the 1980s the issue was largely settled.

For the 1988 Games, there were eight classes, including one women-only class. For the 1992 Games in Barcelona, Spain, two further women's classes have been added, making a total of 10 in all. The classes will be: a three-person keelboat, the Soling; a two-person keelboat, the Star; a two-person catamaran, the Tornado; a two-person high-performance dinghy, the Flying Dutchman; a two-man and two-woman, relatively inexpensive dinghy, the 470; a man's single-hander, the Finn; a man's and a woman's sailboard, the Lechner A390; and a woman's single-hander, the Europe.

Women have always been eligible to sail in all classes, but have seldom entered those where physical strength and stamina are at a premium. All the classes have IYRU status; their profiles are given in Chapter Seven (pp 210-49), but their histories are described in detail here.

❖❖❖

The Sailboard Class *The Windglider used in the 1984 Olympics was replaced in 1988 by a Division II Lechner A390 one-design board, shown below.*

FINN

LOA · 4.5 m (14 ft 9 in)
BEAM · 1.5 m (4 ft 11 in)
DRAFT · 0.8 m (2 ft 8 in)
SAIL AREA · 10.2 sq m (110 sq ft)

The Finn is one of the most firmly established of all international racing classes, largely because of its inclusion as the Olympic single-handed class in every Games since 1952. Its status was briefly threatened in 1968 when the IYRU conducted trials for a new single-hander and chose the Contender as a new class. However, despite intensive lobbying on its behalf, the Contender failed to get as far as the Games themselves and the Finn's place was secure.

The first single-handed dinghy class was the Twelve-Voetsjol, also known as the 12-ft International dinghy, sailed in 1924 and 1928. To our eyes today, this boat looks like a simple tender dinghy with a single lugsail. In 1932, the 4-m (13-ft) American Snowbird was sailed, and in 1936 the Olympia-Jolle (see p197). The Firefly (see p197) was used in the first post-war Olympics at Torbay, England, chosen because it happened to be in production in Britain. However, this class was quite unsuitable for single-handed sailing as it sported two sails and was designed for a crew of two, so Finland, host for the 1952 Games at Helsinki, decided to have a new, purpose-designed boat for the single-handed class.

A competition was held in 1949; most design entries were on paper only, but the Swedish designer Rikard Sarby built a new prototype, called the Fin or Fint. The Scandinavian judging committee asked for several rivals to be built, but after final trials in early 1950, the Sarby boat was chosen as a national Finnish class and was renamed the Finn. It was then successfully nominated for the 1952 Games.

From its earliest days, Finns could be built in any country by licensed builders, which necessitated supervised and strict class rules. At first they had wooden hulls and masts, but subsequently all the customary modern materials and equipment have been introduced: plastics hulls, metal masts, dacron sails of various cuts, self-bailers, weighted clothing for crew,

and enough technical rule changes to both hull and rig to cover many pages in any history of the class.

The class also has a rare control called the Lamboley Test, named after the French chairman of the IYRU centerboard boats committee in the 1970s. This consists of suspending the hull and checking its period of oscillation, thus giving a measure of the distribution of weight. This test overcomes a problem in all boat measurement; total weight can be found without difficulty, but not where it is situated in the hull, which makes a marked difference to overall performance.

The wide success of the Finn class has been assisted by the Finn Gold Cup, a major annual trophy presented in 1956 by F.R. Mitchell of the Royal Corinthian Yacht Club, Burnham-on-Crouch, England. Originally it was sailed for every other year in Britain, but after the 1968 event at Whitstable, Kent, when 138 entries from 38 countries came and just about everything on shore and afloat went wrong (few facilities, shallow tidal water, bad weather, and so on), the cup has been held annually in racing ports all over the world. In 1973, the IYRU tried to limit the number of entries to 60, but this was rejected by the class association and members, and the number of competitors has stabilized at around 100 each year.

FLYING DUTCHMAN

LOA · 6.1m (19ft 10in)	
BEAM · 1.8m (5ft 11in)	
DRAFT · 1.1m (3ft 6in)	
SAIL AREA · 18.1sqm (195sqft)	

The Flying Dutchman has participated in every Olympic Games since 1960, when it replaced the 12-Square Meter Sharpie dinghy (see p197). Before 1956, there had been no two-person boat in the Games, despite the immense popularity of such dinghies throughout the world. Being one of the largest and fastest two-person centerboarders in the world, the Dutchman was an obvious choice as an Olympic class, and is likely to stay in the Games for many years to come.

The Dutchman originated from a requirement by the Dutch national authority after World War II for a new European class for inland lakes. A sharpie type was preferred, and the result was a class called the Tornado (no relation to the modern catamaran). This boat proved unsuitable, so in 1951, leading Dutch dinghy sailor Conrad Gulcher and designer Uffa Van Essen constructed a new boat of molded ply, curved in section instead of angular like a sharpie.

Trials were held against what were considered comparable boats in the Netherlands, just before the IYRU meeting of November 1951, and the new prototype sailed rings round the other, mainly prewar, classes. At the IYRU, the name Flying Dutchman became established and it received international status in 1952. The class spread rapidly during the 1950s in Europe, followed by Australia, Canada and South Africa. In 1957, the IYRU made it the Olympic two-person dinghy class.

470

LOA · 4.7m (15ft 5in)	
BEAM · 1.7m (5ft 6in)	
DRAFT · 0.9m (2ft 10in)	
SAIL AREA · 12.7sqm (137sqft)	

The 470, named after its length in centimeters, arrived at the 1976 Games following the decision that the two-person centerboarder, a type of dinghy widely sailed by the thousands across the world, was still not properly represented at the Games. Its main rival to selection was the British-originated Fireball. Since its first production in France in 1963, more than 50,000 of this high-performance, lightweight, fiberglass dinghy have been built. Designed by André Cornu, and with a sailing weight of only 131kg (290lb), the 470 can plane to windward.

Unlike the Flying Dutchman, the 470 is more closely regulated as a one-design: for example, the hull must be made of polyester resin and of nothing more rigid, such as modern foams or epoxy resin. In the effort to concentrate weight in the middle of the hull, the boats can be quite weak; they are thus checked for weight distribution with the Lamboley Test. Such has been its success as an Olympic class that from 1988, the IYRU decided to use the 470 for the new women's class rather than choose yet another class to sail at the Games.

SOLING

LOA · 8.2m (26ft 9in)	
BEAM · 1.9m (6ft 3in)	
DRAFT · 1.3m (4ft 3in)	
SAIL AREA · 21.6sqm (233sqft)	

The Soling was designed by Jan Linge of Norway following the announcement of trials to be held by the IYRU in 1966 and 1967 to find a new international three-person racing keelboat. A prototype was tested in 1966 and subsequently chosen by the IYRU at the trials.

The first European championships for the class were held in 1968, and the boat was nominated for the 1972 Games, taking over from the Dragon (see p197). Several other new boats built for the trials, such as the Etchells E22 and the Trias, have also become established as successful classes in their own right.

The Soling has always been a strict one-design, but there was considerable development in the early years. The IYRU judges envisaged the crew of three sitting inside the cockpit, but a sitting-out method soon developed with two of the crew sitting out of the boat with the inside of their knees on the gunwale and their toes hooked under straps in the cockpit. This requires strength and fitness, for only the helmsman remains in the cockpit.

The Soling hull is made of fiberglass resin, the spars of aluminum and it sports a relatively large spinnaker of 23.1 sqm (248 sqft). Overall numbers are restricted by the high standards of sailing: 1,263 were registered in 1972 but this total had declined to 762 in 1986. The main fleets in 1986 were in the US (203 boats), East Germany (82), Switzerland (65), Sweden (60) and Norway (38).

STAR

LOA · 6.9 m (22 ft 9 in)	
BEAM · 1.7 m (5 ft 8 in)	
DRAFT · 1 m (3 ft 4 in)	
SAIL AREA · 26.1 sq m (281 sq ft)	

The only class to lose Olympic status and then regain it, the Star first sailed as an Olympic class in 1932, one of the first one-designs at a time when all the Olympic classes were formula classes. It sailed in every Games until 1976, when it was dropped in favor of the Tempest two-person keelboat, which officials had chosen in trials for a new boat of this type. But it only missed one Games: the Tempest, although an outstanding boat, did not gain numbers world-wide, and so the strong Star lobby, many of whom had sailed in the class when younger, led by the American delegates, overturned the British-designed and promoted Tempest in the IYRU. Thus the Star was reinstated as an Olympic keelboat class from 1980 onward.

The Star is numerically one of the largest keelboat classes in the world: some 7,000 sail numbers have been issued since the class began, but only about 1,700 are thought to sail now in any one season, with additional, unregistered numbers in the USSR. The hull is a flat scow type, as used on the North American lakes since the beginning of the century.

The Star's predecessor was a 5.5-m (18-ft) sailing scow called the Bug, designed in 1906 by William Gardner (USA). However, this class proved wet to sail, so an improved, larger class was sought. In 1910, the American *Rudder* magazine sponsored a new dinghy design from a colleague of Gardner, Francis Sweisguth, and the first 22 Stars, with low gunter rigs, sailed as a class on Long Island Sound in 1911, all built by Isaac Smith of Port Washington, Long Island. Five raced for the first time from Harlem Yacht Club, New York, on 30 May 1911.

In 1916, some class rules were drawn up, as previously the boats had just been 'built to plans'. A class association was formed during a meeting at the Hotel Astor, New York, on 22 January 1922; it voted in 1926 that the boats must be measured and certified. Although this is commonplace now, it was unusual at the time.

Part of the success of the class has been that its international class association has remained part of the various national authorities, and groups of owners, divided into fleets, run the class themselves. The class has also been updated by allowing innovations under the rules. In 1929, the gunter rig was replaced by the bermudan rig, and several developments – notably bending spars, the use of a kicking strap and self-bailers – were copied by other classes. There is no spinnaker and the hull shape has remained the same: originally of planked wood, it is now made of fiberglass. In about 1930, it became possible to trail the boat behind a car with a four-wheeled trailer; the two-wheeled modern trailer arrived much later. In 1979, the hulls were made buoyant after several people drowned when their boats foundered.

The principles of changing the rules, and thus keeping the class attractive to sailors, are twofold: that the changes must not affect the one-design character of the class, and that the alterations must be readily available to all. The Star has kept true to both these principles. As a class, it has been sailed in more Olympic Games (12 up to 1988) than any other class. Its list of world, North American and European champions reads like a roll-call of 20th-century yacht-racing champions.

TORNADO

LOA · 6.1 m (20 ft)	
BEAM · 3.1 m (10 ft)	
DRAFT · 0.6 m (1 ft 10 in)	
SAIL AREA · 20.4 sq m (220 sq ft)	

When the International Olympic Committee allowed an extra class into the Olympic Games in 1976, the IYRU decided that this should be a multihull. The Tornado, which the IYRU had already chosen in trials as the recognized class of its type, was selected. Originally built of molded plywood, the hulls are now of fiberglass.

The Tornado was intended by its designer, Rodney Marsh, to be a winner under the IYRU B-Division catamaran rules. However, not for the first time among racing classes, owners preferred to stick to a one-design. Therefore, despite improvements, the rig is technologically of the early 1970s, in sharp contrast with the C-class catamaran, where development has continued unabated.

The Tornado is undoubtedly specialized and makes heavy demands on launching facilities and storage areas. In the first Games in which it competed, in 1980, only 14 boats were entered; in 1984, 20 took part; in 1988, 23. There are about 1,000 registered boats sailing at any time, with the main fleets in Australia, Austria, Germany and the US.

EX-OLYMPIC CLASSES

A number of different classes, which are still raced today in various parts of the world, have been used and then dropped from the Olympic Games.

TEMPEST

The Tempest was sailed in the 1972 and 1976 Games, but of all the controversies that raged over which classes to include, that over the Tempest was the greatest. Basically, the Tempest was the victim of different views in the IYRU in the early 1960s: one view was that the Olympic classes should be existing ones that were already well supported; the other was that trials should be set up to find suitable high-performance classes. The problem was that while the first view could be decided reasonably objectively, the second was a matter of judgment, of assessing class against class.

When trials were held by the IYRU in 1965 to find a new two-person keelboat, the Tempest was outstanding in performance and features, having a flexible rig and retractable keel (fixed for sailing but hoisted for easy trailing behind a car). The boat was designed by the British designer, Ian Proctor, then at the height of his success as a small-boat designer and founder of one of the world's most successful mast and spar manufacturers.

The boat made its first appearance at the Games in 1972, but the Star was there as well. In 1976, the Tempest was the only two-person keelboat, the Star having been dropped, but the Star class was widely established and had many adherents in the councils of the IYRU. They lobbied for the return of the Star, and since the Tempest had been badly supported at the Games in 1976, with only 16 entrants, and more countries had people who had sailed Stars at home than had ever seen a Tempest, the new boat was dropped and the Star returned in 1980.

DRAGON

By the time the Dragon was adopted for the 1948 Olympics, it was already sailed by most major sailing nations. The class had originated from a design competition run by the Royal Gothenburg Yacht Club, Swe-den, in 1929, and was designed by Johan Anker, a Norwegian. Rig and class rules have been modernized steadily, and although a small cabin was designed into it, the class came to be used exclusively as a day-racer. The Dragon was dropped in favor of the Soling in 1976. The Dragon Gold Cup is an annual trophy of high standing; it has been competed for in Scandinavia or Scotland every year since 1937, except 1939-46.

SWALLOW AND FIREFLY

Both these classes, for two- and one-person crews respectively, were used only in the first post-war Olympics held in Torbay, England, and were chosen because they were readily available in Britain. The Swallow is still raced locally in Chichester Harbor, while the Firefly has maintained a national popularity, particularly for university team racing.

12-SQUARE METER SHARPIE

Used only in the 1956 Games, before the introduction of the Flying Dutchman in 1960, the 12-Square Meter Sharpie is still sailed, mainly on European lakes and sheltered waters. The term 'sharpie' is used to describe the traditional, European, low freeboard, non-planing type of dinghy with a heavy, metal centerboard that originated in the 1930s. This sharpie was designed in 1931.

OLYMPIA-JOLLE

Another sharpie type, this dinghy, also known as the Olympic Monotype, was designed for the single-handed slot in the 1936 Games by Helmut Stauch, a German designer. A German class was not allowed in the 1948 Games, the first after the war, and German sailors were also excluded, as they had been in 1920. As a result, the Firefly was substituted.

The Olympia-Jolle continues to be sailed in Europe, with a total of around 800 boats in existence throughout Germany, Italy, the Netherlands and Switzerland; its annual world championships attract up to 70 entries.

The hull remains carvel-built and is heavy by modern standards with an all-up weight of 215 kg (474 lb); its old-fashioned rotating centerboard is ideal for the shallow lakes where it sails. It now has a flexible metal mast to support its 10-sqm (108-sqft) mainsail, and various other modifications, which will probably prolong the life of the class.

5.5-METER

Created by the IYRU in 1949 as an 'economical' rated keelboat, the formula of the 5.5-Meter allowed its designer the same scope as with the older meter classes. It proved expensive as a class, partly because of this new formula. The 5.5-Meter rating produced a hull with a waterline length of about 7 m (23 ft) and a length overall of around 10.7 m (35 ft). It was sailed in the Games from 1952 to 1968, and its departure meant that all Olympic classes were henceforward one-designs: a formula class is unthinkable today.

6-METER AND 8-METER

Sailed in the Games from 1908 to 1952 and 1908 to 1936 respectively, these two classes represented yacht racing in the 'traditional style' between the wars. The entries for each class were small, and only a few nations had competitive fleets of either. Scandinavian nations were the experts in the meter boats and their total medals tally in sailing reflects this.

OTHER CLASSES

Seven other formula boats were in use for the Games in 1908, 1912 and 1920: their entries were often the subject of arguments, as were those of the six tonnage classes sailed in 1900. In addition to them, two development-class dinghies – the 12-ft and 18-ft – and two one-design dinghies – the Twelve-Voetsjol and the Snowbird – were sailed between 1920 and 1932.

NON-RUNNERS

There is one final 'class' of boat that was talked about, lobbied, tried and tested, but which never made it through the various IYRU committees into the Games: the non-runner. Some got quite far and were voted on, others were only suggestions on a drawing board. Among such classes are the Snipe and Fireball as two-person dinghies, and the IYRU choice for the single-handed dinghy, the Contender.

1900–1920

1900

The first Olympic Games of the modern era, inspired by Baron Pierre de Coubertin, were held in Greece in 1896, but did not include sailing. The second Games were held in Paris in 1900, but the sailing events were only announced four months before the first race. It was originally intended to have the sailing events on Lake Daumesnil in the Bois de Vincennes – a lake in a park – but sense prevailed and eventually the races took place on the River Seine at Meulan, 32km (20 statute miles) below Paris.

There were six classes with a total of 42 boats participating in the Games, divided by tonnages under the Thames Measurement Rule, a current formula. The divisions were ½ ton, ½ to 1 ton, 1 to 2 tons, 2 to 3 tons, 3 to 10 tons, and a 10 to 20 ton class that raced at Le Havre, since it was too big for the river at Meulan. The half-ton rater *Scotia*, designed by Linton Hope and sailed by Lorne C. Currie and J.H. Gretton of Britain, won both its class and an open prize for all classes, the only time an Olympic boat has won two gold medals at one regatta. There was no restriction on the number of boats representing a country, with the result that France took all three medals in the ½-ton class. Each class sailed four races with no discards allowed, and the places in each race were determined with time allowances. Money prizes were awarded in addition to the customary gold medal for first place, silver for second and bronze for third given to all crew members.

OPEN CLASS	
1 · LORNE C. CURRIE	UK
2 · MARTIN WIESNER	GERMANY
3 · E. MICHELET	FRANCE
½ TON (7 entries)	
1 · TEXIER	FRANCE
2 · PIERRE GERVAIS	FRANCE
3 · HENRI MONNOT	FRANCE
½–1 TON (8)	
1 · LORNE C. CURRIE	UK
2 · JACQUES BAUDRIER	FRANCE
3 · E. MICHELET	FRANCE
1–2 TON (5)	
1 · HERMANN DE POURTALÉS	SWITZ.
3 · F. VILAMITJANA	FRANCE
3 · JACQUES BAUDRIER	FRANCE

2–3 TON (4)	
1 · WILLIAM EXSHAW	UK
2 · SUSSE	FRANCE
3 · AUGUSTE DONNY	FRANCE
3–10 TON (12)	
1 · E. MICHELET	FRANCE
2 · MAURICE GUFFLET	FRANCE
3 · H. SMULDERS	NETH.
10–20 TON (6)	
1 · ÉMILE BILLARD	FRANCE
2 · JEAN DECAZES	FRANCE
3 · EDWARD HORE	UK

1908

The 1904 Games were in St. Louis, Missouri, where there was no sailing. It was too far inland for European sailors to transport boats that they would have had to bring across the Atlantic, and there was no common measurement, class or racing rules between the US and the various European countries (it would be another three years before the IYRU was established).

In 1908, the main Games were in London with the sailing at Ryde on the Isle of Wight, although the 12-Meters raced on the Firth of Clyde in Scotland. The races were in the new meter classes: 6, 7, 8, 12 and 15, although no one turned up for the last. Only one crew competed in the 7-Meter class and both 12-Meters were British. As in 1900, there was no restriction on the number of boats per country, for at this early stage of the Games sailing was not really an Olympic sport. Indeed, it had to compete for attention against races organized for motor boats!

6-METER (5)	
1 · GILBERT LAWS	UK
2 · LÉON HUYBRECHTS	BELGIUM
3 · HENRI ARTHUS	FRANCE
7-METER (1)	
1 · CHARLES RIVETT-CARNAC	UK
8-METER (5)	
1 · BLAIR COCHRANE	UK
2 · CARL HELLSTRÖM	SWEDEN
3 · R. HIMLOKE	UK
12-METER (2)	
1 · THOMAS GLEN-COATS	UK
2 · CHARLES MACIVER	UK
15-METER (0)	
NO ENTRANTS	

Dormy, winner of the 6-Meter class in 1908.

Cobweb, *winner of the 8-Meter class in 1908.* Inset: *the crew.*

1920

Held soon after the end of World War I, the 1920 sailing Olympics were perhaps the strangest of all. The Games were in Antwerp, Belgium, but only 14 nations were represented. Seven of them competed in the sailing events, and seven of the events were uncontested, the sole entrants winning the medal. Four of the classes were duplicated: there were 6-, 8-, 10- and 12-Meters in both old and new rules. The effect of this multiplicity of classes was to encourage a major shift toward one-design classes in future Games. Léon Huybrechts from Belgium won a silver in the new-rule 6-Meter class to add to the silver he won in 1908.

12-FT DINGHY (2)	
1· JOHANNES HIN	NETH.
2· ARNOUD VAN DER BIESEN	NETH.
18-FT DINGHY (1)	
1· FRANCIS RICHARDS	UK
6-METER – new rule (2)	
1· ANDREAS BRECKE	NORWAY
2· LÉON HUYBRECHTS	BELGIUM
6-METER – old rule (4)	
1· ÉMILE CORNELLIE	BELGIUM
2· EINAR TORGERSEN	NORWAY
3· HENRIK AGERSBORG	NORWAY
6.5-METER (2)	
1· JOHAN CARP	NETH.
2· ALBERT WEIL	FRANCE
7-METER (1)	
1· CYRIL WRIGHT	UK
8-METER – new rule (3)	
1· MAGNUS KONOW	NORWAY
2· JENS SALVESEN	NORWAY
3· ALBERT GRISAR	BELGIUM
8-METER – old rule (2)	
1· AUGUST RINGVOLD	NORWAY
2· NIELS MARIUS NIELSEN	NORWAY
10-METER – new rule (1)	
1· ARCHER ARENTZ	NORWAY
10-METER – old rule (1)	
1· ERIK HERSETH	NORWAY
12-METER – new rule (1)	
1· JOHAN FRIELE	NORWAY
12-METER – old rule (1)	
1· HENRIK ÖSTERVOLD	NORWAY
30-SQUARE METER (1)	
1· GÖSTA LUNDQVIST	SWEDEN
40-SQUARE METER (2)	
1· TORE HOLM	SWEDEN
2· GUSTAV SVENSSON	SWEDEN

1912

The sailing Olympics were better organized by 1912, with four International Rule classes sailing and a maximum of two boats per country. The Games themselves were held at Stockholm, with the sailing events taking place at Nynäshamn, 45 miles to the south. Twenty-one boats entered from five nations, an improvement on the poor turnout of only 13 boats from five nations in 1908. Carl Hellström won a gold in the 10-Meter class to add to the silver he won sailing an 8-Meter in 1908.

The 1916 Games were scheduled for Berlin, with the sailing events at Kiel, but they were cancelled because of the war.

6-METER (6)	
1· AMÉDÉE THUBÉ	FRANCE
2· H. MEULENGRACHT-MADSEN	DENMARK
3· HARALD SANDBERG	SWEDEN
8-METER (7)	
1· THORALF GLAD	NORWAY
2· BENGT HEYMAN	SWEDEN
3· BERTIL TALLBERG	FINLAND
10-METER (5)	
1· CARL HELLSTRÖM	SWEDEN
2· HARRY WAHL	FINLAND
3· ESTER BELOSELSKY	RUSSIA
12-METER (3)	
1· JOHAN ANKER	NORWAY
2· NILS PERSSON	SWEDEN
3· ERNST KROGIUS	FINLAND

1924–1932

1924

The 1924 Games were held in Paris and, as in 1900, the sailing took place either at Le Havre on the sea or at Meulan on the River Seine, 32 km (20 statute miles) downstream from Paris. In reaction to the multiplicity of classes in 1920, just three classes raced: the 6- and 8-Meters at Le Havre and the single-handed Twelve-Voetsjol at Meulan, the first time a single-handed dinghy had sailed in the Games. For the first time also, only one entrant per country in each class was allowed, and all three classes were contested, the Twelve-Voetsjol with an impressive 17 entrants. As with the previous Games, there was no such thing as an Olympic course, and at Le Havre, starts were sometimes downwind in an area of strong tides.

The races themselves suffered from the very unsettled weather, with strong winds alternating with flat calms. August Ringvold from Norway won a second gold medal in the 8-Meter class; Léon Huybrechts from Belgium added a gold medal in the Twelve-Voetsjol to the two silvers he had won in 1908 and 1920 in the 6-Meter class; and Johan Carp from the Netherlands added a bronze in the 6-Meter class to the gold he had won in 1920 sailing in the 6.5-Meter class.

TWELVE-VOETSJOL (17)	
1 · LÉON HUYBRECHTS	BELGIUM
2 · HENRIK ROBERT	NORWAY
3 · HANS DITTMAR	FINLAND
6-METER (9)	
1 · EUGENE LUNDE	NORWAY
2 · WILHELM VETT	DENMARK
3 · JOHAN CARP	NETH.
8-METER (5)	
1 · AUGUST RINGVOLD	NORWAY
2 · E.E. JACOB	UK
3 · LOUIS BRÉGUET	FRANCE

• • •

Royal Gold *Crown Prince Olav of Norway (left) – later Olav V – and his crew of three all won gold medals sailing a 6-Meter boat in the 1928 Olympic Games. Thirteen 6-Meters competed in the series of races, held on the Zuiderzee in the Netherlands.*

1928

The main Games were held in Amsterdam in the Netherlands, with the sailing events taking place on the Zuiderzee, now the Ijsselmeer. Once again there were three classes, all with increased entries. Henrik Robert from Norway was once again runner-up in the Twelve-Voetsjol class, while Virginie Hériot from France won a gold medal as one of the crew in the winning 8-Meter boat, the first time a woman had won a yachting medal.

TWELVE-VOETSJOL (23)	
1 · SVEN THORELL	SWEDEN
2 · HENRIK ROBERT	NORWAY
3 · BERTIL BROMAN	FINLAND
6-METER (13)	
1 · CROWN PRINCE OLAV	NORWAY
2 · NIELS OTTO MOLLER	DENMARK
3 · NIKOLAY WEKSCHIN	ESTONIA
8-METER (8)	
1 · DONATIEN BOUCHÉ	FRANCE
2 · LAMBERTUS DOEDES	NETH.
3 · JOHN SANDBLOM	SWEDEN

1932

The sailing events for the Los Angeles, California, Games took place at Newport Beach. Eleven nations competed. The Star was added to the competing classes, and, except for one year, has been sailed in the Olympic Games ever since. The dinghies in the single-handed class – the Snowbird, a sharpie-type boat with a wooden centerboard and a 7.4-sq m (80-sq ft) cat rig – were supplied by the organizers and swapped around between helmsmen after each race. Both these classes had respectable entries, but both the 6- and 8-Meter classes had so few entries that all the entrants won a medal. This was largely because of the problems of transporting keelboats across America from Europe. Tore Holm of Sweden added a gold medal in the 6-Meter class to the gold he had won in 1920 in the 40-Square Meter class. The host country was most successful, winning two golds and one silver medal: only one team member, Charles Lyon in the Snowbird class, failed to win a medal.

SNOWBIRD (11)	
1 · JACQUES LEBRUN	FRANCE
2 · ADRIAAN MAAS	NETH.
3 · SANTIAGO AMAT CANSINO	SPAIN
STAR (7)	
1 · GILBERT GRAY	USA
2 · COLIN RATSEY	UK
3 · GUNNAR ASTHER	SWEDEN
6-METER (3)	
1 · TORE HOLM	SWEDEN
2 · FREDERICK CONANT	USA
3 · PHILIP ROGERS	CANADA
8-METER (2)	
1 · OWEN CHURCHILL	USA
2 · RONALD MAITLAND	CANADA

1932 *The single-handed dinghy at the 1932 Olympic Games, held at Newport Beach, California, was the American Snowbird dinghy. The photograph below shows part of the 11-strong fleet beating to windward. Inset: Edgar Behr, the fourth-placed German entrant. Right: Gilbert Gray, 30-year-old American gold medallist in the Star class. In his dinghy, Jupiter, he won five of the seven races, with only the second-placed British entrant providing him with much competition.*

1936–1952

1936

Berlin, Germany, was the site of the main Olympic Games, with the sailing events taking place at the Baltic port and sailing center of Kiel. Twenty-six nations took part – the biggest number yet – and three of the four classes remained the same. Only the single-handed class was changed, the locally-designed Olympia-Jolle being used. As with the Snowbird in 1932, the boats were supplied by the organizers and swapped around between helmsmen after each race. The entries in both the meter classes were far healthier than in 1932. Magnus Konow from Norway won a silver medal in the 6-Meter class to add to the gold he won sailing an 8-Meter in 1920.

OLYMPIA-JOLLE (25)	
1 · DANIEL KAGCHELLAND	NETH.
2 · WERNER KROGMANN	GERMANY
3 · PETER SCOTT	UK
STAR (12)	
1 · PETER BISCHOFF	GERMANY
2 · ARVID LAURIN	SWEDEN
3 · W. DE VRIES-LENTSCH	NETH.
6-METER (12)	
1 · CHARLES LEAF	UK
2 · MAGNUS KONOW	NORWAY
3 · SVEN SALÉN	SWEDEN
8-METER (12)	
1 · GIOVANNI LEONE-REGGIO	ITALY
2 · OLAV DITLEV-SIMONSEN	NORWAY
3 · HANS HOWALDT	GERMANY

1936 *The Olympic sailing regatta held at Kiel was the best attended yet, with 26 nations taking part. Above: The Star class gold-medal winner* Wannsee, *helmed by Peter Bischoff from Germany. Below: The single-handed Olympia-Jolle fleet prepares to start a race. Daniel Marinus J. Kagchelland from the Netherlands won the gold medal in a fleet of 25 boats, the biggest fleet ever in the Games.*

1948

The first Olympics after a break of 12 years caused by World War II took place in Britain: the main Games were in London with the sailing events taking place in Torbay. Four of the five classes were one-designs, the exception being the 6-Meter, and three – the Dragon, Firefly and Swallow – were making their first appearance in the Games. For the first time, the courses were set according to the wind to give a windward start (see p193 for details of the Olympic course). The races were held in the relative shelter of Torbay in an effort to reduce the influence of any tidal stream on the course, thus making the racing as fair and equitable as possible.

The single-handed class was the Firefly, an unsuitable choice since it has two sails and was designed as a two-person dinghy. But the class gave 19-year-old Paul Elvström from Denmark the first of his four consecutive gold medals. Tore Holm from Sweden added a bronze in the 6-Meter class to his tally of two gold medals won in the 40-Square Meter class in 1920 and the 6-Meter class in 1932, while Adriaan Maas of the Netherlands won a bronze in the Star class to add to the silver he won sailing a Snowbird in 1932. As in 1932, the Americans won a medal in all but one class, the Dragon; they had failed to win a single medal in 1936. The total number of boats competing was 75, a record entry.

FIREFLY (21)	
1 · PAUL ELVSTRÖM	DENMARK
2 · RALPH EVANS	USA
3 · JACOBUS DE JONG	NETH.
DRAGON (12)	
1 · THOR THORVALDSEN	NORWAY
2 · FOLKE BOHLIN	SWEDEN
3 · WILLIAM BERNTSEN	DENMARK
STAR (17)	
1 · HILARY SMART	USA
2 · C. DE CÁRDENAS CULMELL	CUBA
3 · ADRIAAN MAAS	NETH.
SWALLOW (14)	
1 · STEWART MORRIS	UK
2 · D. DE ALMEIDA BELLO	PORTUGAL
3 · LOCKWOOD PIRIE	USA
6-METER (11)	
1 · HERMAN WHITON	USA
2 · ENRIQUE SIEBURGER	ARGENTINA
3 · TORE HOLM	SWEDEN

1952

Held at Harmaja near the main Games at Helsinki, Finland, the number of classes remained at five, with the 5.5-Meter and single-handed Finn class replacing the Swallow and the Firefly. The Finn began its long run that has lasted to the present day: its first winner was Paul Elvström, gaining his second consecutive gold medal. The bronze medal was won by the dinghy's designer, Rikard Sarby. Thor Thorvaldsen from Norway picked up a second consecutive gold medal in the Dragon class, as did Herman Whiton from the US in the 6-Meter class; thus three of the five gold medallists were the same as four years before. The USSR made its debut at the Olympic Games, while teams from Germany and Japan were readmitted for the first time since the war.

FINN (28)	
1 · PAUL ELVSTRÖM	DENMARK
2 · CHARLES CURREY	UK
3 · RIKARD SARBY	SWEDEN
DRAGON (17)	
1 · THOR THORVALDSEN	NORWAY
2 · PER GEDDA	SWEDEN
3 · THEODOR THOMSEN	W. GERMANY
STAR (21)	
1 · AGOSTINO STRAULINO	ITALY
2 · JOHN REID	USA
3 · J. DE MASCARENHAS FIUZA	PORTUGAL
5.5-METER (16)	
1 · BRITTON CHANCE	USA
2 · PEDER LUNDE SR.	NORWAY
3 · FOLKE WASSÉN	SWEDEN
6-METER (11)	
1 · HERMAN WHITON	USA
2 · FINN FERNER	NORWAY
3 · ERNST WESTERLUND	FINLAND

1952 *The Olympic sailing regatta held at Harmaja, near Helsinki in Finland, attracted 93 entries, a record number that was not surpassed until 1960. The 6-Meter class made its last appearance, having sailed in every Games since 1908, and only attracted a small entry of 11 boats. The photograph above shows the fleet beating just after the start. On the right is Llanoria, the American boat which won the series of races, giving the helmsman, Herman Whiton, his second consecutive gold medal in the class. It is followed by the Canadian boat Trickson VI and the Italian boat Ciocca, neither of which finished well enough to win a medal.*

1956–1964

1956

The first Olympics outside Europe or the US were held in Melbourne, Australia, with the sailing events taking place in nearby Port Phillip Bay. The regatta was marked by consistently strong winds, and in these conditions Paul Elvström won his third consecutive gold medal, the second time in a Finn. Folke Bohlin from Sweden improved on his silver medal, won sailing a Dragon in 1948, by winning a gold in the same class, while the 1952 Star gold medallist, Agostino Straulino from Italy, won a silver in the same class. The number of classes remained the same, at five, with four of the classes the same as in 1952, but entries were down on 1952.

DRAGON (16)	
1 · FOLKE BOHLIN	SWEDEN
2 · OLE BERNTSEN	DENMARK
3 · GRAHAM MANN	UK
FINN (20)	
1 · PAUL ELVSTRÖM	DENMARK
2 · ANDRÉ NELIS	BELGIUM
3 · JOHN MARVIN	USA
STAR (12)	
1 · HERBERT WILLIAMS	USA
2 · AGOSTINO STRAULINO	ITALY
3 · DURWARD KNOWLES	BAHAMAS
12-SQUARE METER SHARPIE (13)	
1 · PETER MANDER	NZ
2 · ROLAND TASKER	AUSTRALIA
3 · JASPER BLACKALL	UK
5.5-METER (10)	
1 · LARS THÖRN	SWEDEN
2 · ROBERT PERRY	UK
3 · ALEXANDER STURROCK	AUSTRALIA

1960

With the main Games held in Rome, Italy, the sailing regatta took place in the fickle winds of the Bay of Naples. As before, there were five classes, the Flying Dutchman making its first appearance at the expense of the 12-Square Meter Sharpie; it has been in the Games ever since. However, the mix of two centerboarders and three keelboats meant that the Olympic Games were failing adequately to represent contemporary sailing, which by now was rapidly expanding in popularity, with most people sailing cruiser-racers and dinghies, not keelboats. Forty-eight nations were represented in 138 boats, almost double the entrants sailing in 1956.

Royal Winner *Crown Prince Constantin of Greece won the Dragon gold medal at the 1960 Olympic Games. His country issued a stamp to commemorate the event.*

The Sharpie *The two-person 12-Square Meter Sharpie made its only appearace in the Olympic Games in 1956. In this photo (from left to right), the fourth-placed Italian entry, the second-placed Australian entry, and the third-placed British entry can be seen running down the course in Port Phillip Bay. Thirteen boats competed in the series.*

Both the Flying Dutchman and the Finn attracted over 30 entrants.

Timir Pinegin won the Star class, the first gold medal won for the USSR in sailing; Paul Elvström won his fourth consecutive gold medal, again in a Finn; William Berntsen from Denmark won a silver in the 5.5-Meter class to add to the bronze he won sailing a Dragon in 1948; and André Nelis of Belgium added a bronze in the Finn class to the silver he won in the same class in 1956. Peder Lunde Jr. from Norway won the first gold medal of the Flying Dutchman class: his father had won a silver sailing a 5.5-Meter in 1952, and his grandfather, Eugene, a gold in the 6-Meter class in 1924.

DRAGON (27)	
1 · PRINCE CONSTANTIN	GREECE
2 · JORGE SALAS CHAVES	ARGENTINA
3 · ANTONIO COSENTINO	ITALY
FINN (35)	
1 · PAUL ELVSTRÖM	DENMARK
2 · ALEKSANDR CHUCHELOV	USSR
3 · ANDRÉ NELIS	BELGIUM
FLYING DUTCHMAN (31)	
1 · PEDER LUNDE JR.	NORWAY
2 · HANS FOGH	DENMARK
3 · ROLF MULKA	W. GERMANY
STAR (26)	
1 · TIMIR PINEGIN	USSR
2 · JOSÉ QUINA	PORTUGAL
3 · WILLIAM PARKS	USA
5.5-METER (19)	
1 · GEORGE O'DAY	USA
2 · WILLIAM BERNTSEN	DENMARK
3 · HENRI COPPONEX	SWITZ.

1964

Forty nations competed in the first Olympic Games to take place in Asia. The main events were in Tokyo, Japan, and the sailing regatta off Enoshima Harbor. Because the event was away from the main sailing countries in Europe and America, entries were down from 1960. The US won a medal in every class, and professionalism began to appear as all three places in the Flying Dutchman class were taken by professional sailmakers, racing, of course, as amateur yachtsmen. The rules were changed so that it was no longer necessary to show a rectangular flag at the masthead to indicate when a boat was racing; radios on board competing boats to keep crews in touch with coaches and advisers off the course were banned.

Durward Knowles of the Bahamas won a gold medal in the Star class, improving on the bronze he won in the same class in 1956; he had first sailed in the Games in 1948, and was still competing in 1988; and Lars Thörn from Sweden won a silver in the 5.5-Meter class to add to the gold he won in the same class in 1956.

DRAGON (23)	
1 · OLE BERNTSEN	DENMARK
2 · PETER AHRENDT	E. GERMANY
3 · LOWELL NORTH	USA
FINN (33)	
1 · WILHELM KUHWEIDE	W. GERMANY
2 · PETER BARRETT	USA
3 · HENNING WIND	DENMARK
FLYING DUTCHMAN (21)	
1 · HELMER PEDERSEN	NZ
2 · KEITH MUSTO	UK
3 · BUDDY MELGES	USA
STAR (17)	
1 · DURWARD KNOWLES	BAHAMAS
2 · RICHARD STEARNS	USA
3 · PELLE PETTERSSON	SWEDEN
5.5-METER (15)	
1 · WILLIAM NORTHAM	AUSTRALIA
2 · LARS THÖRN	SWEDEN
3 · JOHN McNAMARA	USA

◆◆◆

Drinking to Success *Although the business of winning a gold medal is a serious affair, the Australian crew of the 5.5-Meter* Barrenjoey *found time to enjoy a can of beer after winning the series and a gold medal in the 1964 Olympic Games. Their skipper was Bill Northam, a 59-year-old former racing-car driver.*

1968–1980

1968

With the main Games held in Mexico City, the sailing regatta took place in Acapulco. The winds were light and the air temperature very hot: to cope with the conditions, many teams arrived with a support team of technicians, coaches and metereologists, a reflection of the increasing sophistication of the sailing Olympics. Rodney Pattison won the first of his gold medals for Britain sailing a Flying Dutchman: in seven races, he won five, was second in one, and was disqualified in another. Lowell North, head of one of the world's leading sailmaking firms, won the Stars for the US; Louis Noverraz from Switzerland took a silver in the 5.5-Meter class at the age of 66; and Peder Lunde Jr. from Norway won a silver medal in the Star class to add to the gold medal he had won sailing a Flying Dutchman in 1960. Paul Elvström, in search of his fifth gold medal, finished fourth in the Star class.

DRAGON (23)	
1 · GEORGE FRIEDRICHS	USA
2 · AAGE BIRCH	DENMARK
3 · PAUL BOROWSKI	E. GERMANY
FINN (36)	
1 · VALENTIN MANKIN	USSR
2 · HUBERT RAUDASCHL	AUSTRIA
3 · FABIO ALBARELLI	ITALY
FLYING DUTCHMAN (30)	
1 · RODNEY PATTISON	UK
2 · ULLRICH LIBOR	W. GERMANY
3 · REINALDO CONRAD	BRAZIL
STAR (20)	
1 · LOWELL NORTH	USA
2 · PEDER LUNDE JR.	NORWAY
3 · FRANCO CAVALLO	ITALY
5.5-METER (14)	
1 · ULF SUNDELIN	SWEDEN
2 · LOUIS NOVERRAZ	SWITZ.
3 · ROBIN AISHER	UK

◆◆◆

Superdocious *One of the most famous dinghies ever, the Flying Dutchman Superdocious is currently preserved at the National Maritime Museum at Greenwich, England. It was helmed by Rodney Pattison and crewed by Iain Macdonald-Smith to a gold medal in the 1968 Olympic Games, also winning the British national championships in 1968, 1969 and 1971, the European championships in 1968 and 1971, and the World championships in 1969, 1970 and 1971. Pattison won a second gold medal in another Flying Dutchman in 1972, and a silver medal in 1976.*

1972

After an interval of 36 years, Germany was once again host country to the Olympic Games. The main events took place at Munich with the sailing regatta held at the traditional center of German sailing – the Baltic Sea port of Kiel. The organization was massive to cope with the 152 boats from 42 nations. A new yacht harbor was built at Schilksee on the west side of Kiel Bay with a specially built administration building for the race committee offices, boat and sail measurement halls, and many other facilities. Accommodation was provided for all competitors and officials in an Olympic village of 34 bungalows and apartment blocks. Entry passes were necessary at all times.

Afloat, there were 26 press boats and 14 other vessels for the several thousand spectators. All the competitors were photographed as they rounded each mark in case of protest. The result of all this was a feeling that officialdom had been overdone, but increasing competition and national aspirations made it necessary to a great extent. The total cost of the Games was about 82 million German marks, then £20 million (US$45 million).

For the first time ever, all six classes were one-designs, but four were keelboats and only two were centerboarders. Rodney Pattison took his second, consecutive gold medal for Britain in the Flying Dutchman class while Paul Elvström, still in search of his fifth gold medal, this time in the Soling class, left half way through the regatta after incidents on the course. Valentin Mankin from the USSR gained his second, consecutive gold medal, this time in a Tempest; Buddy Melges from the US gained a gold medal in the Soling class to add to the bronze he had won sailing a Flying Dutchman in 1964; Paul Borowski from East Germany gained a silver in the Dragon class to add to the bronze he gained in 1968; Pelle Pettersson from Sweden gained a silver in the Star class to add to the bronze he gained in the same class in 1964; and Ullrich Libor from West Germany won a bronze medal in the Flying Dutchman class to add to the silver he had won sailing in the same class in 1968.

DRAGON (23)	
1 · JOHN BRUCE CUNEO	AUSTRALIA
2 · PAUL BOROWSKI	E. GERMANY
3 · DONALD COHAN	USA
FINN (35)	
1 · SERGE MAURY	FRANCE
2 · ILIAS HATZIPAVLIS	GREECE
3 · VICTOR POTAPOV	USSR
FLYING DUTCHMAN (29)	
1 · RODNEY PATTISON	UK
2 · YVES PAJOT	FRANCE
3 · ULLRICH LIBOR	W. GERMANY
SOLING (26)	
1 · BUDDY MELGES	USA
2 · STIG WENNERSTRÖM	SWEDEN
3 · DAVID MILLER	CANADA
STAR (18)	
1 · DAVID FORBES	AUSTRALIA
2 · PELLE PETTERSSON	SWEDEN
3 · WILHELM KUHWEIDE	W. GERMANY
TEMPEST (21)	
1 · VALENTIN MANKIN	USSR
2 · ALAN WARREN	UK
3 · GLEN FOSTER	USA

Reg White from Britain on his way to a gold medal in the Tornado class in 1976.

1976

The main Games were held amid the tightest security at Montreal, with the sailing regatta taking place at Kingston on Lake Ontario. The entry was smaller – 130 boats from 40 countries – and the class line-up at last began to reflect modern sailing. The two-person Tornado catamaran and the 470 dinghy both made their first appearance, while the Star keelboat was temporarily dropped for the first time since its appearance in the Games in 1932. There were now two keelboats, three centerboarders and a catamaran.

Rodney Pattison from Britain and Valentin Mankin from the USSR were each trying to gain their third, consecutive gold medal, but they both only managed the second-placed silver, Pattison in the Flying Dutchman class, Mankin in the Tempest class. Reinaldo Conrad from Brazil added a second bronze medal in the Flying Dutchman class to the one he had won sailing in the same class in 1968.

1980

Held at the Baltic Sea port of Tallinn, the capital city of Estonia, with the main Games in Moscow, the 1980 sailing regatta was seriously affected by the boycott of the entire Olympic Games by many western nations. Australia, Britain, Canada, France, Japan, the US and West Germany all stayed away in protest against the Russian invasion of Afghanistan the previous year, and many top helmsmen were therefore absent. Boat numbers were down to 83, the lowest number since 1956, taking the shine off the level of competition in many classes, notably the 470s and the Solings. As a result of the boycott, the regatta received little publicity outside Russia or Eastern Europe.

Valentin Mankin took the gold medal in the Star class, giving him three gold and one silver in three different classes; Poul Jensen from Denmark took his second consecutive gold medal in the Soling class; Hubert Raudaschl from Austria gained a silver in the Star class to add to the silver he had won sailing a Finn in 1968; and Andrei Balashov of the USSR won a bronze medal in the Finn class, an addition to the silver medal he had won sailing in the same class in 1976.

FINN (28)		
1 · JOCHEN SCHÜMANN	E. GERMANY
2 · ANDREI BALASHOV	USSR
3 · JOHN BERTRAND	AUSTRALIA

FLYING DUTCHMAN (20)		
1 · JÖRG DIESCH	W. GERMANY
2 · RODNEY PATTISON	UK
3 · REINALDO CONRAD	BRAZIL

470 (28)		
1 · FRANK HÜBNER	W. GERMANY
2 · ANTONIO GOROSTEGUI	SPAIN
3 · IAN BROWN	AUSTRALIA

SOLING (24)		
1 · POUL JENSEN	DENMARK
2 · JOHN KOLIUS	USA
3 · DIETER BELOW	E. GERMANY

TEMPEST (16)		
1 · JOHN ALBRECHTSON	SWEDEN
2 · VALENTIN MANKIN	USSR
3 · DENNIS CONNER	USA

TORNADO (14)		
1 · REG WHITE	UK
2 · DAVID MCFAULL	USA
3 · JÖRG SPENGLER	W. GERMANY

FINN (21)		
1 · ESKO RECHARDT	FINLAND
2 · WOLFGANG MAYRHOFER	AUSTRIA
3 · ANDREI BALASHOV	USSR

FLYING DUTCHMAN (15)		
1 · ALESANDRO ABASCAL	SPAIN
2 · DAVID WILKINS	IRELAND
3 · SZABOLCS DETRE	HUNGARY

470 (14)		
1 · MARCOS RIZZO SOARES	BRAZIL
2 · JÖRN BOROWSKI	E. GERMANY
3 · JOUKO LINDGREN	FINLAND

SOLING (9)		
1 · POUL JENSEN	DENMARK
2 · BORIS BUDNIKOV	USSR
3 · ANASTASSIOS BOUDOURIS	GREECE

STAR (13)		
1 · VALENTIN MANKIN	USSR
2 · HUBERT RAUDASCHL	AUSTRIA
3 · GIORGIO GORLA	ITALY

TORNADO (11)		
1 · ALEXANDRE WELTER	BRAZIL
2 · PETER DUE	DENMARK
3 · GÖRAN MARKSTRÖM	SWEDEN

1984-1988

1984

This time it was the turn of the Eastern bloc to impose a sudden boycott of the Games held at Los Angeles. The sailing regatta, held at Long Beach, California, was equally affected, but, nevertheless, there were a record 304 competitors from 62 countries participating in 174 boats. Security was very high: there were more than 100 Coast Guard vessels, almost no spectators, and officials far outnumbered those sailing. It was the first year that a sailboard was allowed; Windgliders were supplied by the host country, increasing the number of classes to seven. Every US team member won a medal in their home waters, a first for a host country.

Because the 1980 Games had suffered from a boycott as well, very few winning medallists had sailed in the Games before. But Gorgio Gorla from Italy won his second successive bronze medal in the Star class, while both father and son Buchan won gold medals, Bill in the Star class, son Carl crewing in the Flying Dutchman class. Paul Elvström came out of retirement at the age of 56 to compete with his daughter in the Tornado class: they finished fourth.

FINN (28)	
1 · RUSSELL COUTTS	NZ
2 · JOHN BERTRAND	USA
3 · TERRY NEILSON	CANADA
FLYING DUTCHMAN (17)	
1 · JONATHAN McKEE	USA
2 · TERRY McLAUGHLIN	CANADA
3 · JO RICHARDS	UK
470 (28)	
1 · JOSÉ-LUIS DORESTE	SPAIN
2 · STEPHAN BENJAMIN	USA
3 · THIERRY PÉPONNET	FRANCE
SOLING (22)	
1 · ROBERT HAINES	USA
2 · TORBEN GRAEL	BRAZIL
3 · HANS FOGH	CANADA
STAR (21)	
1 · BILL BUCHAN	USA
2 · JOACHIM GRIESE	W.GERMANY
3 · GIORGIO GORLA	ITALY
TORNADO (20)	
1 · REX SELLERS	NZ
2 · RANDY SMYTH	USA
3 · CHRIS CAIRNS	AUSTRALIA
WINDGLIDER (38)	
1 · STEPHAN VAN DEN BERG	NETH.
2 · SCOTT STEELE	USA
3 · BRUCE KENDALL	NZ

The New Class *For the first time in the Olympic Games, a sailboard – the Windglider – was used for competition in 1984.*

Veteran Skipper *With his daughter, Trine, as crew, Paul Elvström from Denmark sailed a Tornado in the 1984 and 1988 Games.*

Double Gold *Gold medallist in the Finn class in 1976, Jochen Schümann from East Germany won a second gold medal in the Soling class in 1988.*

Success *Bronze medallists in 1984, Thierry Péponnet and Luc Pillot from France won the 470 gold medal in 1988.*

1988

The main Games were held at Seoul, South Korea, a country with no sailing tradition at all. But despite their inexperience, the South Koreans ran an efficient regatta at Pusan, making the best of the difficult tide and wind conditions. As in previous years, security was tight, but the regatta passed without incident, attracting the biggest Olympic fleet ever, 214 boats.

For the first time, a women-only class was instituted, using the 470 dinghy. The sailboard class used a Division II Lechner A390 one-design board; the host country supplied both these and the Finns.

FINN (33)	
1 · JOSÉ-LUIS DORESTE	SPAIN
2 · PETER HOLMBERG	US VIRGIN IS.
3 · JOHN CUTLER	NZ
FLYING DUTCHMAN (22)	
1 · JORGEN BOJSEN-MOLLER	DENMARK
2 · OLEPETTER POLLEN	NORWAY
3 · FRANK McLAUGHLIN	CANADA

470 – MEN (29)	
1 · THIERRY PÉPONNET	FRANCE
2 · TYNISTE TYNOU	USSR
3 · JOHN SHADDEN	USA
470 – WOMEN (21)	
1 · ALLISON JOLLY	USA
2 · MARIT SOEDERSTROM	SWEDEN
3 · LARISSA MOSCALENKO	USSR
DIVISION II SAILBOARD (45)	
1 · BRUCE KENDALL	NZ
2 · JAN BOERSMA	NETH. ANT.
3 · MIKE GEBHARDT	USA
SOLING (20)	
1 · JOCHEN SCHÜMANN	E. GERMANY
2 · JOHN KOSTECKI	USA
3 · JESPER BANK	DENMARK
STAR (21)	
1 · MIKE McINTYRE	UK
2 · MARK REYNOLDS	USA
3 · TORBEN GRAEL	BRAZIL
TORNADO (23)	
1 · JEAN-YVES LE DEROFF	FRANCE
2 · REX SELLERS	NZ
3 · LARS GRAEL	BRAZIL

Chapter 7

Keelboat & Dinghy Classes

*A*ll sailing boats that race, and many that do not, belong to a class, each with its own set of measurements and rules. There are 216 profiles of different classes from around the world in this chapter. Every active racing class is included, unless very small in number. To qualify for inclusion, the class must have some form of central organization or regular regatta: it may be on any level from club to international. A boat merely offered to the public by a manufacturer and given a name is not listed. Ranging from 2 to 20 meters (7 to 70 feet) in length and dating from 1897 to the present day, the keelboats and dinghies in these profiles present a comprehensive picture of the many different classes of boats that exist around the world today.

SAILING AND RACING CLASSES

Although most sailing boats belong to a 'class,' the word class is very difficult to define and has no single technical meaning. Broadly speaking, a keelboat or a dinghy class is a group of boats sharing an identical design or set of measurements, with a local, national or international organization administering its rules and membership.

The majority of classes dates from either the interwar years or the 1950s. Since then most of the options have been filled and it has become more difficult to establish a new class. There are of course exceptions to this – the single-handed Laser being one of the most notable.

Although it is difficult to classify boats, the ways in which they are designed, built and then kept within their respective rules do suggest seven distinct categories.

ONE-DESIGN CLASSES

Built to an identical design, one-design classes are the most common of keelboat and dinghy classes. When racing, such boats compete among themselves without any handicap, the result of the race depending on the sailing ability of the crew.

The first one-design classes were designed at the end of the 19th century. In Ireland, the Water Wags class first sailed in Dublin Bay in 1887, while in Britain, the Solent One-Design made its appearance in 1895; it was originated by the owners themselves out of frustration with formula classes. In America, the Inland Yachting Association A Scow appeared in 1897.

One-designs proliferated in the US in the first half of this century at the expense of the restricted and formula classes that were favored by the Europeans. The classes used in the Olympic Games typify this trend, with the formula boats used in the early games organized by European countries entirely replaced by 1972 with one-design classes as the Games became more international.

Means of insuring that one-designs are alike vary from class to class. For local classes the simplest method is to have a single builder, but this cannot apply to classes that are spread throughout the world or that allow home construction. In these cases a set of rules lay down a very tight series of measurements within which each boat must be built. Every dimension conforms to a maximum or minimum size or has a plus or minus tolerance. Once constructed, the boat must be inspected by an approved official measurer, who checks hull dimensions, hull and rig fittings, sail material and sizes, the weight of the individual components and the weight of the whole boat, sometimes including its distribution fore and aft.

Some one-design classes succeed in never changing their rules, but most do adapt to allow for new materials, different methods and techniques of building, new fittings and gear, and changing sailing techniques. Classes are forced to change their rules to gain popularity with each new generation of sailors. The art is to change at the correct rate, a continuous preoccupation of all class committees. Many different options are available; some one-design classes allow variety in gear or parts of the rig, while others may or may not have strict rules about rudder edges, toe straps, mainsheet purchase, hull surface and paint, and other technical details, as well as numbers and weight of crew.

For a one-design boat to be recognized as an international class by the International Yacht Racing Union, the IYRU has to be satisfied with the class rules and their enforcement. It requires that a master plug exist for the hull, although molds may be scattered round the world, and that a measurement form is completed for each boat showing that it complies with the class rules.

RESTRICTED CLASS

Sometimes called a development class, a restricted class has a set of rules that lays down maximum and/or minimum dimensions and weight, and various restrictions on material and fittings. The rules allow considerable freedom of design within the parameters set, and encourage designers to experiment by using the latest technology and materials in order to produce faster boats. A restricted class can therefore have many years of life. But while each new boat represents the latest state of the art, by the same token boats a few years old are soon outdated. Examples of restricted class dinghies are the International 14-Foot Dinghy and the International Moth, both highly developed racing boats.

FORMULA CLASS

A formula class goes further along the path of design freedom than the restricted class in having a rating formula within which the designer attempts to produce the fastest boat possible (pp 284-97 explain rating systems and their effect on racing boat design in more detail).

Various rating systems exist. One system produces a rating of, for example, 22ft IOR, on which a time allowance is applied when one boat races against another with a different rating. The level rating system produces such boats as the 6-, 8- and 12-Meters under the International Rule. With this system each boat has a different set of dimensions and therefore a different shape. But because those dimensions combine to give an identical rating, no time allowances are needed when they race together as a fleet.

These and other rating systems consider such items as beam, mast height, amount of jib overlap, construction, hull strength, and fittings and accommodation, in order to arrive at the rating figure.

In the late 1940s, the IYRU introduced formula classes like the 5.5-Meter and the 8-Meter cruiser racer, but although they have a long history, formula classes are seldom if ever introduced today.

HANDICAP CLASS

Although this class often has its own race in a regatta, it does not exist in its own right, the word 'class' in this case merely indicating that miscellaneous boats of different design may race together handicapped by some form of time allowance. This handicapping may well be systematized using one of the many handicap systems in use around the world (see pp 67-9).

PRODUCTION CLASS

Also known as a commercial class, the term implies that this class is produced by one builder. Only those boats organized by an owners' association as a proper class and recognized for racing are included in the profiles that follow. Most production class boats, however, only have an owners' club run by the manufacturer, and it is difficult to discern the borderline between these two types, arrangements varying considerably over the years.

OFFSHORE ONE-DESIGN CLASS

Controlled by the class association rather than the builder, an offshore one-design class boat cannot be modified at the will of the builder for commercial or other considerations, unlike most production class boats. If the class is affiliated to the IYRU or a national authority, then such safeguards are greater. Offshore one-designs are habitable, able to sail offshore and at night, and take part in regular racing. Often they come from a single builder because of the difficulty of manufacturing complex boats in different places, and because numbers are relatively low. There is no single offshore one-design that is internationally accepted.

INTERNATIONAL CLASS

The IYRU reserves for itself the right to add the term 'International' to the name of any class if it is a recognized IYRU class. However many other classes are in fact international in all but name, with boats and class associations spread across the world linked by a central secretariat: the Mirror was one of these, remaining independent for 25 years until 1988.

If a class wishes to become international in the IYRU sense, then conditions for acceptance include class associations in at least six countries and two continents; properly organized class associations of owners; 'adequate' sailing qualities for racing; a written agreement between the IYRU and the copyright owner about their various rights in the class design; and acceptance of a number of IYRU conditions.

IYRU policy is not to accept a new class for international status if this would adversely affect an existing international class, although this rule has not always been applied very strictly. Guidelines also exist concerning the minimum number of boats racing before a class applies for IYRU recognition. These numbers, both in total and per country, vary for centerboard boats, keelboats, multihulls, sailboards and offshore racers.

THE CLASS PROFILES

All the 216 boat profiles illustrated on the following 36 pages are arranged in the same order:

Illustration The color of hull and sails is optional in most cases, but some classes do specify particular colors. The 420 must have a white hull, the Mirror red sails, while it is customary but not compulsory for the Hobie Cat and other 'fun' boats to have striped sails.

Name of the class In many cases, the words national, international, one-design or class have been omitted, even if part of the official class name, unless sense requires their retention.

Symbols See right for explanation.

National origin Although some classes are still local or regional in their distribution, most are now found worldwide. For this reason, only the origin of the boat is indicated: no attempt is made to say where the class headquarters is located.

Designer Either the individual or the company responsible for drawing up the initial plans of the boat is named.

Dimensions Length is length overall, beam is maximum width of the hull, while the sail area is the actual area of the sail plan or the area measured under the rules, without spinnaker. For restricted and formula classes, typical dimensions are given.

Caption Here are given the salient points about the class – its history, location, characteristics and special features. Where numbers are given, this information is frequently open to question, for many class associations have lost count years ago. They may issue sail numbers for boats that have never been built, and issue measurement certificates that are not renewed, while some boats are simply hauled out of the water to rot.

In practice, active classes will have a constant turnover of boats, with newly built ones replacing the old ones. Small local classes tend to be the most accurate with their numbers, while some international classes face the problem that the USSR and other eastern European countries build boats without any reference to international class associations, and without paying royalties to the designer or licensed builder.

 IYRU recognized international class

 Centerboard boat *Open boat relying on the crew for stability*

 Inshore multihull *Catamaran or trimaran restricted to courses within reach of the shore*

 Keelboat *Open-decked day racing boat with a fixed keel to give stability*

 Offshore multihull *Habitable catamaran or trimaran capable of night racing and other self-reliant passages*

 Offshore racer *Habitable monohull capable of night racing and other self-reliant passages*

 Sailboard *Rudderless board that crew steers by jointed rig*

 Number of crew *Either the customary complement or as prescribed by the class rules*

ALBACORE

National origin UK
Designer Uffa Fox **Length** 4.6 m (15 ft)
Beam 1.5 m (5 ft) **Sail area** 11.6 sq m (125 sq ft)
Developed in 1954 as an updated and hot-molded
version of the successful Firefly, this essentially
uncomplicated family, sailing school and racing
dinghy now numbers some 7,500, built mainly
in the UK and US.

AQUA CAT 12.5

National origin USA
Designer American Sale Inc
Length 3.8 m (12 ft 6 in) **Beam** 2 m (6 ft 6 in)
Sail area 8.4 sq m (90 sq ft)
An exciting, lightweight, car-top catamaran, good for
day-sailing or racing. It has a good turn of speed as
well as an ability to point to windward, making it one
of the most popular catamaran classes.

AQUA CAT 14

National origin USA
Designer American Sale Inc
Length 4.3 m (14 ft 4 in) **Beam** 2 m (6 ft 6 in)
Sail area 9.7 sq m (105 sq ft)
A larger version of the 12.5, the 14 sails well with as
many as four people on board. The A-frame
structure and boomless rig gives the lateen-type sail
good pointing ability to windward.

A SCOW

National origin USA
Designer John Johnson **Length** 11.7 m (38 ft 6 in)
Beam 2.6 m (8 ft 6 in) **Sail area** 51.7 sq m (557 sq ft)
The oldest one-design class still sailing, the A is the
largest of all the scows. Light displacement and a
small rudder require skill to maintain proper
balance and sail control; it is also physically
demanding, especially downwind under spinnaker.

ATLANTIC

National origin USA
Designer Starling Burgess **Length** 9.3 m (30 ft 6 in)
Beam 2 m (6 ft 6 in) **Sail area** 35.8 sq m (385 sq ft)
Designed in 1929, one of the largest and best-known
of the day-sailing racing classes. The full keel gives
stability in heavy seas, combining with a turn of
speed in light air. Burgess also worked on the
J-class, with which it has much in common.

BALLYHOLME BAY

National origin Ireland
Designer Colquhoun & Sons **Length** 6.6 m (21 ft 9 in)
Beam 1.8 m (5 ft 9 in) **Sail area** 16.2 sq m (175 sq ft)
Developed from the Coronation One-Design of 1937,
this class first started racing from Ballyholme Bay
on Belfast Lough in 1939. Perfect miniatures of
1930s yachts, the 'Bays' are planked and built in
traditional wooden style.

SYMBOLS KEY
IYRU official class
Centerboard dinghy
Inshore multihull
Keelboat
Offshore multihull
Offshore racer
Sailboard
Number of crew

⊠ ⊞ ⊔ ⊞ ⊞ ⊅ ◁ ╎

CLASSES/A-B

215

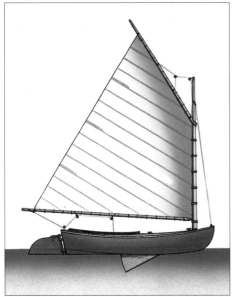

BEETLE CAT
⊞ ⫲ **National origin** USA
Designer John Beetle **Length** 3.8 m (21 ft 4 in)
Beam 1.8 m (6 ft) **Sail area** 9.3 sq m (100 sq ft)
Beamy, traditional, New England dinghy descended
from fishing boats, made of oak and cedar with spars
of fir. Designed in New Bedford in 1921, over 3,000
have been built and it is still popular as a racer,
especially for juniors, and as a training boat.

BEMBRIDGE REDWING
⊔ ⫲ **National origin** UK
Designer Charles Nicholson
Length 8.5 m (27 ft 11 in) **Beam** 1.7 m (5 ft 6 in)
Sail area 18.6 sq m (200 sq ft)
Designed in 1938 to replace the original class, it is
unusual in having a one-design hull but permitting
any sail plan under 18.6 sq m (200 sq ft). Many
variations have been tried with varying success.

BLUE JAY
⊞ ⫲ **National origin** USA
Designer Sparkman & Stephens
Length 4.1 m (13 ft 6 in) **Beam** 1.6 m (5 ft 2 in)
Sail area 8.4 sq m (90 sq ft)
A popular training boat, about 7,000 have been built.
With a relatively wide beam and a flat bottom and
hard chine, the boat has been updated in only minor
ways over the four decades it has been produced.

BRITISH MOTH
⊞ ╎ **National origin** UK
Designer Sidney Cheverton **Length** 3.3 m (11 ft)
Beam 1.2 m (4 ft 1 in) **Sail area** 7.4 sq m (80 sq ft)
First seen in 1935, this British class has proved to
be a fast, racing, single-hander; its unusually tall
mast makes it especially good in light airs. Designs
vary within a basic specification. As a class, it pre-
dates the International Moth.

BUCCANEER
⊞ ⫲ **National origin** USA
Designer J.R. Macalpine-Downie
Length 5.5 m (18 ft) **Beam** 1.8 m (6 ft)
Sail area 16 sq m (175 sq ft)
Designed by one of the most brilliant British
practitioners for Chrysler Corp., the class thrives
after 20 years with 4,000 built. A big dinghy that can
be used for cruising as well as class racing.

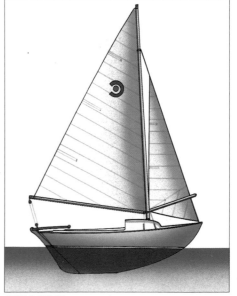

BULLSEYE
⊔ ⫲ **National origin** USA
Designer Nathanael G. Herreshoff
Length 4.8 m (15 ft 9 in) **Beam** 1.8 m (5 ft 10 in)
Sail area 15.2 sq m (164 sq ft)
Designed in 1914 by the old master himself, this is
America's oldest keelboat class, still racing mainly
in Massachusetts, especially Buzzard's Bay, its
original home. Formerly of wood, now in fiberglass.

BUTTERFLY

⊞ ⁛ **National origin** USA
Designer John Barnett **Length** 3.7 m (12 ft 2 in)
Beam 1.4 m (4 ft 6 in) **Sail area** 6.7 sq m (75 sq ft)
One of the best-known of the smaller, inland lake,
scow-type designs, the class has grown steadily to
around 10,000, for the boat provides good speed
especially off the wind, and the cat rig is very
popular with junior sailors.

CADET

⊠ ⊞ ⁛ **National origin** UK
Designer Jack Holt **Length** 3.2 m (10 ft 7 in)
Beam 1.3 m (4 ft 2 in) **Sail area** 4.6 sq m (50 sq ft)
Junior racer designed in 1947 for under-18s. It was
sponsored by *Yachting World* as the ideal child's
boat, complete with spinnaker. Large fleets are in
existence round the world, and many top helmsmen
in Europe began in this class.

CATALINA 22

⊞ ⁛⁛ **National origin** USA
Designer Frank Butler **Length** 6.5 m (21 ft 6 in)
Beam 2.3 m (7 ft 8 in) **Sail area** 21.4 sq m (230 sq ft)
One of the first retractable-keel designs. The boat
has become popular both for racing and as a
cruising boat suitable for family sailing. It can be
transported easily by trailer, which adds to its
widespread popularity.

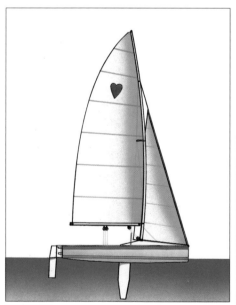

CATAPULT

⊞ ⁛ **National origin** UK
Designers C.R. Ross & R.D. Schuck
Length 5 m (16 ft 5 in) **Beam** 2.3 m (7 ft 5 in)
Sail area 9.9 sq m (107 sq ft)
Unique in having tubular inflatable hull, it is
intended to be fully portable. Over 600 have been
sold since 1981, when the prototype took the 10 sq m
world speed record to 17.3 knots.

CHERUB

⊞ ⁛ **National origin** New Zealand
Designer John Spencer **Length** 3.6 m (12 ft)
Beam 1.5 m (5 ft) **Sail area** 11.6 sq m (125 sq ft)
Very fast, small, two-man racing dinghy with
international distribution. Trapeze for crew and
large spinnaker. Introduced in 1953, it is a restricted
class and a wide variety of designs can be found
among the 3,000 built.

CLASS II DISPLACEMENT SAILBOARD

⊠ ◀ ⁛ **National origin** IYRU origin
Designers Various **Length** 3.9 m (12 ft 9 in)
Beam 0.6 m (2 ft 1 in) **Sail area** 6 sq m (65 sq ft)
Created as a displacement board class by the IYRU
to allow development from which an Olympic class
could be chosen; the above dimensions are the
maximum. The Lechner 390 used for the 1988
Olympics is a design according to the rules.

SYMBOLS KEY
IYRU official class
Centerboard dinghy
Inshore multihull
Keelboat
Offshore multihull
Offshore racer
Sailboard
Number of crew

CLASSES/B-C

217

COMET
National origin USA
Designer Lowndes Johnson **Length** 4.9 m (16 ft)
Beam 1.5 m (5 ft) **Sail area** 13 sq m (140 sq ft)
Originally designed in 1932 to be built in wood, the fiberglass model has gained wider acceptance. With no spinnaker and a large mainsail, it is exciting to sail both upwind and down, its large cockpit and good flotation make it a fast day-sailer.

CONGER
National origin Germany
Designer Uli Libor **Length** 5 m (16 ft 4 in)
Beam 1.8 m (5 ft 10 in) **Sail area** 12 sq m (129 sq ft)
This strongly built boat with ample decking is more often sold for family knock-about sailing than for racing. Although several hundred are registered for racing in the north of Germany, more than a thousand are scattered elsewhere.

CONTENDER
National origin Australia
Designer Bob Miller **Length** 4.9 m (16 ft)
Beam 1.4 m (4 ft 6 in) **Sail area** 10.4 sq m (112 sq ft)
Introduced in 1968 it was originally intended to replace the Finn as a modern, lightweight single-hander for the Olympics. Although this never happened, it is popular and found in around 20 countries, the largest fleet being in Germany.

CONTESSA 32
National origin UK
Designer David Sadler **Length** 9.75 m (32 ft)
Beam 2.9 m (9 ft 6 in) **Sail area** 52.2 sq m (562 sq ft)
Most consistent of the British offshore one-design classes with a deserved reputation for heavy-weather ability. A larger version of the Contessa 26, and a masthead Folkboat, it began as a IOR racer but numbers soared when one-design racing began.

CORONADO 15
National origin USA
Designers Ed Edgar & Frank Butler
Length 4.7 m (15 ft 4 in) **Beam** 1.7 m (5 ft 8 in)
Sail area 12.9 sq m (139 sq ft)
A high-performance racing dinghy that now comes with trapeze, the boat is very popular with family racing crews interested in a maneuverable and durable hull and rig.

C SCOW
National origin USA
Designer John Johnson **Length** 6.1 m (20 ft)
Beam 2 m (6 ft 6 in) **Sail area** 20 sq m (216 sq ft)
Introduced in 1905, the C is one of the most high-powered of the scows. It has a single, large mainsail; to hold the boat down in any kind of wind requires stamina and skill from the skipper and crew to keep the boat in good trim.

DABCHICK

National origin South Africa
Designer Jack Koper **Length** 3.6 m (11 ft 10 in)
Beam 1.1 m (3 ft 8 in) **Sail area** 5.6 sq m (60 sq ft)
The main junior class in South Africa with over
3,300 in use. The strange scow-like effect results
from the original 1955 concept of making the hull
from just three sheets of plywood.

DARING

National origin UK
Designer Arthur Robb **Length** 10.1 m (33 ft)
Beam 1.9 m (6 ft 5 in) **Sail area** 29.7 sq m (320 sq ft)
A strict one-design, this is a 'frozen' 5.5-Meter boat
of 1961. Thirty have been built and it is raced only at
Cowes. Rules insure that sails are ordered in
batches and renewal of them is limited, as are
frequency of haul-outs and type of bottom coating.

DART 18

National origin UK
Designer Rodney Marsh **Length** 5.5 m (18 ft)
Beam 2.3 m (7 ft 6 in) **Sail area** 16.1 sq m (173 sq ft)
With over 4,300 around the world, it is a strict one-
design with no centerboards or boom. Often sailed
single-handed without the jib. Seen as a smaller and
simpler version of the Olympic Tornado catamaran,
by the same designer.

DAY-SAILER

National origin USA
Designer Uffa Fox **Length** 5.1 m (16 ft 9 in)
Beam 2 m (6 ft 6 in) **Sail area** 13.5 sq m (145 sq ft)
With a large cockpit and cuddy cabin, the boat
enjoyed instant success both as a family cruising
boat and racer, with 13,000 built. Its wide beam
and flat sections aft make it stable but able to
move well in light air.

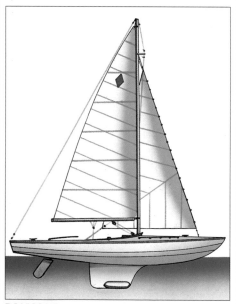

DIAMOND

National origin UK
Designer Jack Holt **Length** 9.2 m (30 ft 2 in)
Beam 2.1 m (6 ft 11 in) **Sail area** 29 sq m (313 sq ft)
In 1961, *Yachting World* added a keelboat to their
many 'build-her-yourself' post-war designs. The
result was this double-chine, plywood, heavily
decked boat, which never grew as a class in the UK,
but has been popular in Australia.

DRAGON

National origin Sweden
Designer Johan Anker **Length** 8.9 m (28 ft 2 in)
Beam 2 m (6 ft 5 in) **Sail area** 26.6 sq m (286 sq ft)
Designed in 1929, it was an Olympic class until
1972, when the Soling was substituted. However,
large fleets still sail in the UK, Australia, Germany,
USA, Scandinavia and elsewhere.

SYMBOLS KEY
IYRU official class
Centerboard dinghy
Inshore multihull
Keelboat
Offshore multihull
Offshore racer
Sailboard
Number of crew

CLASSES/**D-E**

219

DUBLIN BAY 21

National origin Ireland
Designer Alfred Mylne **Length** 9.9 m (32 ft 6 in)
Beam 2.3 m (7 ft 6 in) **Sail area** 58 sq m (630 sq ft)
The first '21's raced in 1903 with a gaff rig and
jackyard tops'l. In 1964, this was replaced with a
bermudan rig, but there are plans to restore the
original rig. 21s have always sailed in Dublin Bay.

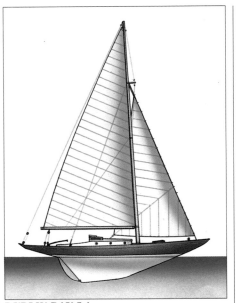

DUBLIN BAY 24

National origin Ireland
Designer Alfred Mylne **Length** 11.4 m (37 ft 6 in)
Beam 2.4 m (8 ft) **Sail area** 49.5 sq m (533 sq ft)
Designed in 1938 as a 24-ft (7.3-m) waterline class,
it was for many years Europe's longest one-design.
Sailing in Dublin Bay and off Ireland's east coast, it
is often used for cruising and offshore racing.

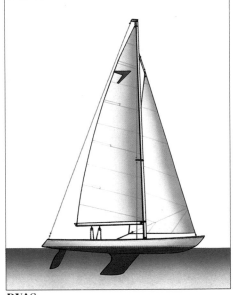

DYAS

National origin Germany
Designer Helmut Stöberl **Length** 7.2 m (23 ft 6 in)
Beam 1.9 m (6 ft 3 in) **Sail area** 21.9 sq m (236 sq ft)
A smaller sister of the Trias, this class, mainly from
central and southern Germany, has a sail area
popular with many other inland racers. About 800
have been built; the crew can use a trapeze.

E 22

National origin USA
Designer E.W. Etchells **Length** 9.3 m (30 ft 6 in)
Beam 2.1 m (7 ft) **Sail area** 27 sq m (291 sq ft)
Originally designed for the 1972 three-man keelboat
competition as an IYRU and Olympic class, although
the Soling was selected for this instead. However
fleets have grown up around the world owing to the
boat's excellent qualities, particularly upwind.

ENDEAVOUR 24

National origin Australia
Designer Len Hedges **Length** 7.4 m (24 ft 4 in)
Beam 2.4 m (7 ft 9 in) **Sail area** 24.5 sq m (264 sq ft)
Australians were already racing cruisers as one-
designs before boats like the J 24s and Laser 28s
changed the sailing scene in the 1980s. Despite the
old-fashioned rig and hull, the 24 is the most
popular of the several Endeavours.

ENTERPRISE

National origin UK
Designer Jack Holt **Length** 4 m (13 ft 3 in)
Beam 1.6 m (5 ft 4 in) **Sail area** 10.5 sq m (113 sq ft)
Launched in 1956 by the London *News Chronicle*, the
newspaper is long since dead but the class has some
22,000 boats all over the world, including the first
one made. A strict one-design hull and sail;
measurements have never been changed.

E SCOW
National origin USA
Designer Arnold Meyer **Length** 8.5 m (28 ft)
Beam 2.1 m (6 ft 9 in) **Sail area** 30 sq m (323 sq ft)
First built in 1923, this is a fast and responsive
racer with twin rudders and bilgeboards. Popular on
inland lakes and coastal estuaries and anywhere
with comparatively smooth water, the small rudders
make steering using the sails critical for speed.

ESTUARY
National origin UK
Designer Morgan Giles **Length** 5.5 m (18 ft)
Beam 1.8 m (6 ft) **Sail area** 19.5 sq m (210 sq ft)
Product of the merger of the Thames Estuary and
Essex One-Designs, designed in 1918. Some 40 have
been built and they have given racing and day-
cruising pleasure for most of the century.

EUROPE
National origin Belgium
Designer Alois Roland **Length** 3.3 m (11 ft)
Beam 1.4 m (4 ft 8 in) **Sail area** 7.4 sq m (80 sq ft)
First built in 1960 as a one-design under the rules of
the International Moth Class, it is a lightweight
single-hander especially suitable for younger
sailors. Many thousands have been built, and are to
be found particularly in central Europe.

FAIRY
National origin Ireland
Designer Linton Hope **Length** 6.9 m (22 ft 6 in)
Beam 1.8 m (6 ft) **Sail area** 21.9 sq m (236 sq ft)
First raced on Belfast Lough in 1902, this class
soon spread to Lough Erne. Built by Hilditch of
Carrickfergus, Belfast Lough boats have changed to
bermudan rig; Lough Erne boats retain the gunter
rig, as shown.

FALCON
National origin UK
Designer Harry P. Dennis **Length** 5.9 m (19 ft 3 in)
Beam 2.2 m (7 ft 3 in) **Sail area** 15 sq m (162 sq ft)
A strongly built centerboarder made for the rugged
conditions of north-west England, where boats have
to dry out on exposed moorings between tides. There
are 37 left from 50 built since 1953, all constructed
of cold-molded wood.

FINN
National origin Finland
Designer Rikard Sarby **Length** 4.5 m (14 ft 9 in)
Beam 1.5 m (4 ft 11 in) **Sail area** 10.2 sq m (110 sq ft)
Single-hander designed specifically for the 1952
Olympic Games and has been used for Olympic
competitions ever since. Used chiefly by Olympic
aspirants as it is taxing to sail. Numbers are
unknown due to a large, undisclosed Soviet fleet.

FIREBALL
National origin UK
Designer Peter Milne **Length** 4.9 m (16 ft 2 in)
Beam 1.4 m (4 ft 6 in) **Sail area** 11.5 sq m (124 sq ft)
One of the main, post-war dinghy classes, with over 14,000 built. Shaped with chines for plywood building when designed, it is now built in fiberglass. Narrowly missed Olympic selection against 470. Crew uses a trapeze.

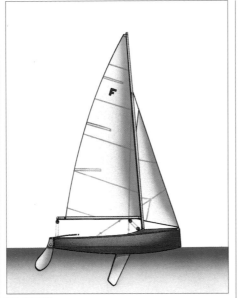

FIREFLY
National origin UK
Designer Uffa Fox **Length** 3.6 m (12 ft)
Beam 1.4 m (4 ft 7 in) **Sail area** 8.4 sq m (90 sq ft)
Basic, two-man dinghy with no trapeze or spinnaker, first built in 1946 of hot-molded wood veneers and used in the 1948 Olympics. Some 550 have been built and they have proved popular anywhere a strong, small, centerboarder is needed.

505
National origin UK/France
Designer John Westell **Length** 5.1 m (16 ft 7 in)
Beam 1.9 m (6 ft 1 in) **Sail area** 13.6 sq m (146 sq ft)
One of the premier, two-man trapeze boats, it was designed for the French Caneton Class Association in 1954, although the largest fleet is now in UK, with others in Australia and the USA. Requires much skill and strength to sail.

FLIPPER
National origin Denmark
Designer Peer Bruun **Length** 4 m (13 ft 4 in)
Beam 1.3 m (4 ft 4 in) **Sail area** 10.3 sq m (110 sq ft)
Designed in 1968, there are around 10,000 of this modern scow-type in Scandinavia. Being light as well as flat, it planes while beating. Class rules allow ample equipment for adjusting the sail plan.

FLYING DUTCHMAN
National origin Netherlands
Designers Conrad Gulcher & Uffa Van Essen
Length 6 m (19 ft 10 in) **Beam** 1.8 m (5 ft 11 in)
Sail area 18.1 sq m (195 sq ft)
Designed in 1951, it was intended for inland waters but soon became popular elsewhere. In 1960, it was chosen as a high-performance Olympic class. Continuous innovations keep it state-of-the-art.

FLYING FIFTEEN
National origin UK
Designer Uffa Fox **Length** 6.1 m (20 ft)
Beam 1.5 m (5 ft) **Sail area** 14 sq m (150 sq ft)
The Flying Fifteen is a planing keelboat designed in 1946 as the smallest of a flying family of similar boats. Over 300 had been built by 1986, spread mainly over the UK, Australasia and South Africa.

FLYING JUNIOR
⊠ ➕ ⫪ **National origin** Netherlands
Designer Uffa Van Essen **Length** 4 m (13 ft 3 in)
Beam 1.5 m (4 ft 11 in) **Sail area** 9.5 sq m (102 sq ft)
Inevitably regarded as a smaller Flying Dutchman since it is by the same designer and is a training boat for the bigger class. High performance tempered with moderate sail area. No major fleet outside the Netherlands.

FLYING SCOTT 19
➕ ⫪ **National origin** USA
Designer Gordon Douglass **Length** 5.8 m (19 ft)
Beam 2.1 m (6 ft 9 in) **Sail area** 17.7 sq m (190 sq ft)
This stable and forgiving design was intended to be used for family sailing and racing. With hard bilges and slightly tunnelled hull, the boat is very stable but can plane easily in a good breeze. Designed in 1958, some 4,400 have since been built.

FOLKBOAT
➕ ⫪⫪⫪ **National origin** Sweden
Designer Tord Sunden **Length** 7.6 m (25 ft)
Beam 2.3 m (7 ft 5 in) **Sail area** 24 sq m (258 sq ft)
The result of a design competition by the Royal Gothenburg YC in 1941, this attractive, open-cockpit, cabin yacht has spread worldwide. Built in wood and fiberglass, there have been numerous variations on its theme.

FORCE 5
➕ ⫪ **National origin** USA
Designer Fred Scott **Length** 4.2 m (13 ft 10 in)
Beam 1.5 m (4 ft 10 in) **Sail area** 8.5 sq m (91 sq ft)
This performance, strict one-design, single-hander is a pleasure to sail in any kind of breeze. The rig with sleeved sail is easily adjusted by means of an outhaul cunningham and vang, and the flat hull sections aft provide speed and stability off the wind.

420
⊠ ➕ ⫪ **National origin** France
Designer Christian Maury **Length** 4.2 m (13 ft 9 in)
Beam 1.9 m (6 ft 1 in) **Sail area** 10.2 sq m (110 sq ft)
Typifies the light, planing dinghy for young crew, and since its launch has become the standard for teenagers and youth sailing world wide, introducing many to the trapeze. It was designed along the same lines as the larger Olympic 470.

470
⊠ ➕ ⫪ **National origin** France
Designer André Cornu **Length** 4.7 m (15 ft 5 in)
Beam 1.7 m (5 ft 6 in) **Sail area** 12.7 sq m (137 sq ft)
Olympic class built in 1963, although not chosen for the games until 1976. Also used for the all-women Olympic class from 1988. 50,000 have been built and can be found in 31 countries. Regarded as the large forerunner to the 420.

SYMBOLS KEY

IYRU official class
Centerboard dinghy
Inshore multihull
Keelboat
Offshore multihull
Offshore racer
Sailboard
Number of crew

CLASSES/*F-G*

223

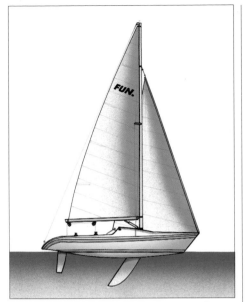

FUN
National origin France
Designer Joubert & Nivelt **Length** 7.5 m (24 ft 7 in)
Beam 2.4 m (8 ft) **Sail area** 24.2 sq m (261 sq ft)
The French answer to the J 24, with rudimentary
accommodation but really used for fast, club, day
racing. Light displacement (750 kg, 1,653 lb) and
lifting keel for trailing. Designed in 1982, with fully
adjustable, modern rig.

GARELOCH
National origin UK
Designer McGruer & Co. **Length** 7.3 m (24 ft)
Beam 1.7 m (5 ft 6 in) **Sail area** 20.8 sq m (224 sq ft)
Designed in 1924 to be built and based in the
sheltered Gare Loch off the Clyde estuary in
Scotland, the class is unusual in having been sold
off, mainly to East Anglia. Boats were regularly
bought back to Gare Loch to rebuild the class.

GLEN
National origin Ireland
Designer Alfred Mylne **Length** 7.6 m (25 ft)
Beam 2 m (6 ft 6 in) **Sail area** 25 sq m (270 sq ft)
Designed in 1945 as an economical, general-purpose
sloop for the austere post-war period, it was
unusual in that the hulls were built upside down
in series production at the Glen Boatyard
on Belfast Lough.

GP 14
National origin UK
Designer Jack Holt **Length** 4.3 m (14 ft)
Beam 1.6 m (5 ft 1 in) **Sail area** 11.3 sq m (122 sq ft)
Robust, family one-design founded by *Yachting
World* in 1951, since when some 25,000 have been
built. Intended for cruising as well as racing, fleets
can be found throughout the English-speaking world.

GRADUATE
National origin UK
Designer Dick Wyche **Length** 3.8 m (12 ft 6 in)
Beam 1.4 m (4 ft 6 in) **Sail area** 8.4 sq m (90 sq ft)
British class introduced in 1952 as a low-cost
version of the National 12. Originally built in wood,
but fiberglass is now also available. The Graduate is
designed for amateur construction and the rules
permit some diversity.

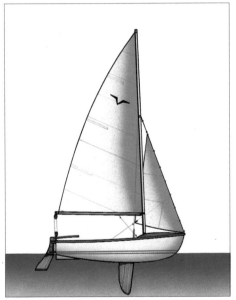

GULL
National origin UK
Designer Ian Proctor **Length** 3.3 m (11 ft)
Beam 1.6 m (5 ft 3 in) **Sail area** 6.5 sq m (70 sq ft)
A versatile, family dinghy that can be sailed and
raced under sloop or cat-rig, rowed, sculled or
outboard-engined. This class has remained popular
since 1956, and the UK fleet of 2,500 is still growing.
First built in wood, now mainly in fiberglass.

HARMONIC 24
National origin New Zealand
Designer Hal Wagstaff **Length** 7.3 m (24 ft)
Beam 3 m (10 ft) **Sail area** 22.3 sq m (240 sq ft)
Designed as a successful quarter tonner in 1974,
this four-berth racer with transom-hung rudder
went on to become a cruiser-racer one-design in
New Zealand's popular sailing waters.

H-BOAT
National origin Finland
Designer Hans Groop **Length** 8.3 m (27 ft 2 in)
Beam 2.2 m (7 ft 2 in) **Sail area** 24 sq m (258 sq ft)
An example of a Folkboat derivative, with moderate
form of separate keel and rudder. After tests, the
class was promoted as a racing boat in 1969. There
are over 1,000 in Scandinavia, as well as further
fleets worldwide.

HIGHLANDER
National origin USA
Designer Gordon Douglass **Length** 6.1 m (20 ft)
Beam 2 m (6 ft 8 in) **Sail area** 20.9 sq m (225 sq ft)
An easily handled, family day-sailer, the boat has
become known for its stable but high-performance
sailing characteristics, particularly its ability to
plane. Its popularity has resulted in fleets in many
areas having different wind and water conditions.

HILBRE
National origin UK
Designer Alan Buchanan **Length** 6 m (19 ft 9 in)
Beam 2.3 m (7 ft 6 in) **Sail area** 18.9 sq m (203 sq ft)
Heavy, mahogany, clinker-planked half-decker built
between 1958 and 1964 for one-design racing on the
River Dee in north-west England. No more can be
built, but 54 owners carefully preserve the class to
race year after year.

H-JOLLE
National origin Germany
Designer Various **Length** 6.2 m (20 ft 3 in)
Beam 2.3 m (6 ft 7 in) **Sail area** 21.9 sq m (236 sq ft)
Typical long, low, German lake-boat with over 900
sailing in the inland waterways, also in Spain and
Switzerland. Long established, it is one of the
world's fastest centerboarders.

HOBIE CAT 14
National origin USA
Designer Hobie Alter **Length** 4.3 m (14 ft)
Beam 2.3 m (7 ft 6 in) **Sail area** 11 sq m (118 sq ft)
The Hobies are the most popular catamarans in the
world. The 14 was introduced in 1968 and uses
asymmetrical 'banana'-hull shapes to develop
hydrodynamic lifts. An excellent beach boat, it can
be sailed single-handed.

SYMBOLS KEY
IYRU official class
Centerboard dinghy
Inshore multihull
Keelboat
Offshore multihull
Offshore racer
Sailboard
Number of crew

CLASSES/*H*

225

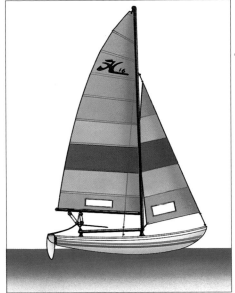

HOBIE CAT 16
National origin USA
Designer Hobie Alter **Length** 4.9 m (16 ft)
Beam 2.4 m (7 ft 9 in) **Sail area** 20.3 sq m (218 sq ft)
Introduced in 1970, this is a larger version of the 14.
It is the best-selling catamaran in the world, with
over 60,000 sold. 17 ft (5.2 m) and 18 ft (5.5 m)
versions also exist in smaller numbers. All for
racing, day-sailing and vacation use.

HORNET
National origin UK
Designer Jack Holt **Length** 4.9 m (16 ft)
Beam 1.4 m (4 ft 7 in) **Sail area** 15 sq m (162 sq ft)
Introduced in 1952 by *Yachting World*, it was
regarded as an innovative design, with sliding seat
and ideal for home construction. Design constraints
have relaxed in recent years and now permit
considerable variation.

HOWMAR 12
National origin USA
Designer Sparkman & Stephens
Length 3.7 m (12 ft 2 in) **Beam** 1.5 m (5 ft)
Sail area 8.4 sq m (90 sq ft)
With dimensions the same as numerous other
12-footers, it is questionable whether there was a
need for yet another in 1981. However, the boat has
established itself in the US.

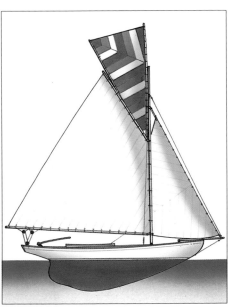

HOWTH 17
National origin Ireland
Designer W.H. Boyd **Length** 6.9 m (22 ft 6 in)
Beam 1.8 m (6 ft) **Sail area** 28.3 sq m (305 sq ft)
The oldest one-design still sailing in the British Isles
in its original, 1898, form, the Howth 17, with its
dramatic jackyard tops'ls, is a miniature of a late-
Victorian cutter.

HUNTER 23
National origin USA
Designer Hunter Design Group
Length 7.1 m (23 ft 3 in) **Beam** 2.4 m (8 ft)
Sail area 21.8 sq m (235 sq ft)
A trailerable boat designed with a shallow, winged
keel. The boat has enjoyed popular success because
of its well thought out accommodation below decks
and its easily handled but powerful sailplan.

HURRICANE CAT
National origin UK
Designers Reg White & Barry Meredith
Length 5.9 m (19 ft 5 in) **Beam** 2.4 m (8 ft)
Sail area 22.1 sq m (238 sq ft)
Twin-trapeze catamaran introduced in 1986 and
built from hi-tech materials, it has proved itself in
several long-distance coastal events to be fast and
durable. By mid-1987, 33 boats had been built.

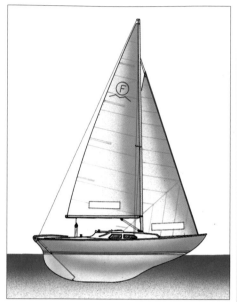

IF

National origin Sweden
Designer Tord Sunden **Length** 7.8 m (25 ft 8 in)
Beam 2.2 m (7 ft 3 in) **Sail area** 31 sq m (334 sq ft)
Originally called the International Folkboat when
designed in 1966, the name was not allowed by the
national authority, but she is one of several Folkboat
derivatives in existence. Very popular, with 4,000
built, 3,000 of which are in Sweden.

ILLUSION MINI 12

National origin UK
Designers Jo Richards & Neil Graham
Length 3.7 m (12 ft) **Beam** 0.7 m (2 ft 3 in)
Sail area 5.9 sq m (64 sq ft)
A unique, miniature version of the 12-Meter, closer
inspection reveals the pilot's head whose feet
stretch under the foredeck! The keel ballast comes
out for transportation and correcting crew weight.

IMPALA OOD 28

National origin UK
Designer David Thomas **Length** 8.5 m (28 ft)
Beam 2.8 m (9 ft 3 in) **Sail area** 26.9 sq m (290 sq ft)
A habitable, strict one-design. One of three offshore
one-designs introduced in the UK in 1979. Used for
class and coastal racing at several centers, its
numbers have decreased in regattas as modern
types have taken over.

INTERNATIONAL 14

National origin UK
Designers Various **Length** 4.3 m (14 ft)
Beam 1.7 m (5 ft 6 in) **Sail area** 17.7 sq m (190 sq ft)
The classic, centerboard, development class was
initiated in 1919 from two existing classes. In 70
years it has changed from a ship's open boat to a
double-trapeze racing machine in the UK, Canada,
Japan, South Africa and the US.

INTERNATIONAL 110

National origin USA
Designer Raymond Hunt **Length** 7.3 m (24 ft)
Beam 1.3 m (4 ft 2 in) **Sail area** 14.6 sq m (157 sq ft)
Its flat-bottomed, narrow-beamed, double-ended,
hull configuration, and deep keel, make it very close-
winded on a beat and give it exhilarating bursts of
speed off the wind. New rules have reduced the crew
to two and allow a trapeze. Only found in the US.

INTERNATIONAL 210

National origin USA
Designer Raymond Hunt **Length** 9.1 m (29 ft 10 in)
Beam 1.8 m (5 ft 10 in) **Sail area** 28.3 sq m (305 sq ft)
A one-design keelboat that has the sailing
characteristics of a 30-footer. Like the 110, the
boat's double-ended hull configuration and large
overlapping genoa make it extremely fast to
windward as well as on a reach.

SYMBOLS KEY
IVRU official class
Centerboard dinghy
Inshore multihull
Keelboat
Offshore multihull
Offshore racer
Sailboard
Number of crew

CLASSES/**I-J**

227

⊗ + ⊞ ⊞ ⊞ ◩ ◁ ♦

INTERNATIONAL CANOE
⊗ + ♦ **National origin** UK/USA
Designer Peter Nethercott **Length** 5.2 m (17 ft)
Beam 1 m (3 ft 3 in) **Sail area** 10.6 sq m (114 sq ft)
Generally considered to be the most challenging of
single-handed dinghies with a sliding seat rather
than a trapeze. Formulated in 1869, some 300 are
still used around the world. The hull is one-design
while the deck and rig are restricted.

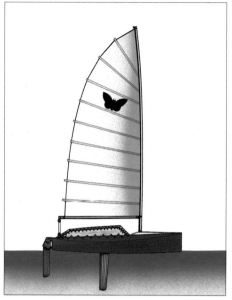

INTERNATIONAL MOTH
⊗ + ♦ **National origin** New Zealand
Designers Various **Length** 3.6 m (11 ft)
Beam 2.2 m (7 ft 4 in) **Sail area** 8 sq m (86 sq ft)
A great variety of designs have evolved since the
first in 1927. A few such as the British Moth and
Europe have survived as one-designs; it can be
characterized as a highly developed single-hander
with wings rather than trapeze; difficult to sail well.

INTERNATIONAL ONE-DESIGN
⊞ ♦♦♦♦ **National origin** Norway
Designer Bjarne Aas **Length** 10.1 m (33 ft 2 in)
Beam 2.1 m (6 ft 9 in) **Sail area** 39.9 sq m (430 sq ft)
Inspired by the 6-Meter class, this strict one-design
puts great emphasis on sailing ability and boat
preparation. Sails are drawn by lot number annually
and several fleets prohibit recutting during a
racing season.

IRISH DINGHY RA 14
+ ♦♦ **National origin** Ireland
Designer O'Brien Kennedy **Length** 4.3 m (14 ft)
Beam 1.5 m (5 ft) **Sail area** 11.1 sq m (120 sq ft)
Introduced by the Irish Dinghy Racing Association
in 1946 as a more rugged version of the
International 14, the IDRA still thrives with the
introduction of newer equipment such as trapezes.

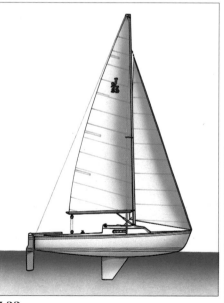

J 22
⊞ ♦♦♦♦ **National origin** USA
Designer Rod Johnstone **Length** 6.9 m (22 ft 6 in)
Beam 2.4 m (8 ft) **Sail area** 21.4 sq m (230 sq ft)
A powerful but easily sailed smaller version of the
popular J 24, this boat has achieved success in the
US as a one-design class as well as a solid
performer in MORC and PHRF events. With a few
additions below, it can also be used as a weekender.

J 24
⊗ ⊞ ♦♦♦♦♦ **National origin** USA
Designer Rod Johnstone **Length** 7.3 m (24 ft)
Beam 2.7 m (8 ft 11 in) **Sail area** 24.2 sq m (261 sq ft)
Designed as a rigid one-design, with careful
monitoring of licensed builders, the J 24 quickly
achieved world-wide fleets as its explosive
downwind speed and seakeeping abilities attracted
a high standard of competition.

J 30
National origin USA
Designer Rod Johnstone **Length** 9.1 m (29 ft 10 in)
Beam 3.4 m (11 ft 2 in) **Sail area** 42.8 sq m (461 sq ft)
A one-design cruiser-racer, the boat appeals to a wide group of sailors, with favorable ratings under most handicap systems as well as a solid class organization in the US. Relatively small headsails allow ease of maneuvering with a family crew.

JAVELIN
National origin USA
Designer Uffa Fox **Length** 4.3 m (14 ft)
Beam 1.7 m (5 ft 8 in) **Sail area** 11.6 sq m (125 sq ft)
A wide beam, full cockpit and comfortable seats spaced on either side of a commodious, 3-m (10-ft) cockpit have made this design enduringly popular. The boat is easily sailed by a novice or expert, and some 5,500 have been built since 1960.

KIELZUGVOGEL
National origin Germany
Designer N. Lehfeld **Length** 5.8 m (19 ft)
Beam 1.9 m (6 ft 1 in) **Sail area** 17 sq m (183 sq ft)
Rather heavy, styled keelboat with 1,100 racing in Germany, it has spread to Chile, Italy, Austria and the Netherlands since 1963. It can be used for coastal cruising; its lifting keel allows trailing.

KNARR
National origin Norway
Designer Erling Kristoffersen
Length 9.3 m (30 ft 5 in) **Beam** 2.1 m (6 ft 11 in)
Sail area 26.6 sq m (286 sq ft)
Designed in 1943 as an economical alternative to the 6-Meter and the Dragon, it became a Norwegian national class in 1948. Built in Denmark from 1973 and now also found on west coast of the US.

KORSAR
National origin Germany
Designer N. Lehfeld **Length** 5 m (16 ft 5 in)
Beam 1.7 m (5 ft 7 in) **Sail area** 11.4 sq m (123 sq ft)
Although 3,000 sail numbers have been issued, this German answer to the Snipe remains at a strength of 800 in Germany, with other fleets in Austria, Chile, Switzerland and the US. A lightweight boat built of fiberglass.

L 26
National origin South Africa
Designer Angelo Lavranos **Length** 8 m (26 ft 3 in)
Beam 2.7 m (8 ft 10 in) **Sail area** 25.6 sq m (276 sq ft)
A South African national class designed in 1980, it was one of the earliest offshore one-designs in the movement against the cost and obsolescence of rated boats. Ninety are in use.

SYMBOLS KEY

IYRU official class
Centerboard dinghy
Inshore multihull
Keelboat
Offshore multihull
Offshore racer
Sailboard
Number of crew

⊗ ✛ ⊡ ⊥ ⊡ ⬠ ◁ ⸢

CLASSES/J-L   *229*

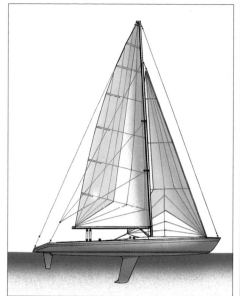

LAKE GARDA SCOW
⊡ ⸢⸢⸢⸢⸢⸢ **National origin** Italy
Designers Various **Length** 13.4 m (44 ft)
Beam 3.7 m (12 ft) **Sail area** 100 sq m (1,070 sq ft)
One of the world's more dramatic classes, sailed
in the sheltered waters of Lake Garda, Italy. High-
speed races of up to 100 miles are sailed with crew
– exceptionally for a boat of this length weighing one
quarter of the 1,820-kg (4,000-lb) hull – all on trapezes.

LARK
✛ ⸢⸢ **National origin** UK
Designer Michael Jackson **Length** 4.1 m (13 ft 4 in)
Beam 1.7 m (5 ft 6 in) **Sail area** 9.8 sq m (105 sq ft)
A strict one-design of lightweight type, with over
2,000 built since 1967, mainly in UK but used for
team racing by MIT, Cambridge, and in Singapore for
SE Asian Games. Benefits by having top builder,
Parker, in UK.

LASER
⊗ ✛ ⸢ **National origin** Canada
Designers Bruce Kirby & Ian Bruce
Length 4.2 m (13 ft 10 in) **Beam** 1.4 m (4 ft 6 in)
Sail area 7.1 sq m (76 sq ft)
Designed in 1969 as a car-top, performance single-
hander with minimum controls. All boats are
identical save for color, and since production began
in 1971, an impressive 127,000 have been built.

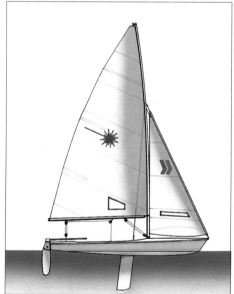

LASER II
✛ ⸢⸢ **National origin** Canada
Designers Frank Bethwaite & Ian Bruce
Length 4.4 m (14 ft 5 in) **Beam** 1.4 m (4 ft 8 in)
Sail area 11.5 sq m (124 sq ft)
A high-performance dinghy light enough to be car-
topped, but which has found acceptance in racing
centers. The spinnaker and trapeze options can
produce extraordinary speeds.

LASER 28
⬠ ⸢⸢⸢⸢⸢ **National origin** Canada
Designer Bruce Farr **Length** 8.7 m (28 ft 5 in)
Beam 2.9 m (9 ft 6 in) **Sail area** 34 sq m (365 sq ft)
A high-performance cruiser-racer with an auxiliary
and a well-appointed cabin area below. Tested for
several years before going into production, it
pioneered several new construction techniques and
has achieved a good racing record.

LEADER II
✛ ⸢⸢ **National origin** UK
Designer Gordon Pollard **Length** 4.8 m (15 ft 10 in)
Beam 1.9 m (6 ft 1 in) **Sail area** 11 sq m (118 sq ft)
First built in 1962, it was redesigned in 1987 in
several aspects, but still forms part of a fleet of 1,100
in UK, Greece and elsewhere. A favorite for training
and vacation use, construction can be all wood, all
fiberglass or a combination of both.

L'ÉQUIPE

National origin France
Designer François Sergent
Length 3.8 m (12 ft 8 in) **Beam** 1.4 m (4 ft 7 in)
Sail area 8 sq m (86 sq ft)
This short, light, low-freeboard boat with small sail area is used in France for junior championships, where the short type of English dinghy is unpopular. One of the smallest two-man dinghies in Europe.

LIGHTNING

National origin USA
Designer Sparkman & Stephens **Length** 5.8 m (19 ft)
Beam 2 m (6 ft 6 in) **Sail area** 16.4 sq m (177 sq ft)
A generous sail area and roomy cockpit have made this 1939 design very popular over the years in numerous US centers. Very responsive to changes in trim and amount of helm, the hard chine and flat bottom make it exciting under a spinnaker.

LIGHTNING 368

National origin UK
Designer Mark Giles **Length** 3.7 m (12 ft)
Beam 1.4 m (4 ft 7 in) **Sail area** 7.1 sq m (76 sq ft)
In the selection of single-handed classes, there is a school which favors something other than massive world-wide designs. The 368 combines the characteristics of the traditional, heavier, reaching type with short length.

LOCH LONG

National origin UK
Designer Charles Nicholson **Length** 6.4 m (21 ft)
Beam 1.7 m (5 ft 6 in) **Sail area** 14.9 sq m (160 sq ft)
In 1936, the Scottish Loch Long Sailing Club requested a design resembling a favored Scandinavian class. Slightly smaller than the Dragon, it has proved suitable for these waters.

MANLY JUNIOR

National origin Australia
Designer Ralph Tobias **Length** 2.6 m (8 ft 7 in)
Beam 4 m (5 ft 5 in) **Sail area** 7 sq m (75 sq ft)
Devised in the 1960s as a training dinghy in Sydney Harbor, it remains a children's class used all over Australia, especially Perth. The simple design can be tweaked up for the enterprising helmsman.

MERLIN ROCKET

National origin UK
Designers Various **Length** 4.3 m (14 ft)
Beam 2.2 m (7 ft 2 in) **Sail area** 10.2 sq m (110 sq ft)
Restricted class formed by the amalgamation of two high-performance 14-footers: the *Yachting World*-sponsored Merlin (1946) and the Rocket (1949). Generally seen to be at the forefront of dinghy innovation, but few found outside the UK.

SYMBOLS KEY
IYRU official class
Centerboard dinghy
Inshore multihull
Keelboat
Offshore multihull
Offshore racer
Sailboard
Number of crew

⊠ ⊞ ⊡ ⊟ ⊞ ▷ ◁ ⸙

CLASSES/**L-M**

231

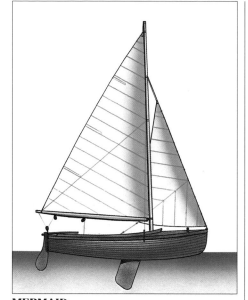

MERMAID
⊞ ⸙⸙⸙ **National origin** Ireland
Designer J.B. Kearney **Length** 5.2 m (17 ft)
Beam 1.8 m (6 ft) **Sail area** 14.9 sq m (160 sq ft)
The creator of some of Ireland's finest cruising
yachts, J.B. Kearney designed this powerful, large
dinghy in 1932. Adopted as a one-design by Dublin
Bay Sailing Club, and still built today.

MICRO MULTIHULL
⊟ ⸙⸙⸙⸙⸙ **National origin** Netherlands
Designers Various **Length** 8 m (22 ft 3 in)
Beam 5.3 m (17 ft) **Sail area** 30.6 sq m (329 sq ft)
A formula class in several European countries, with
8-m (22-ft 3-in) maximum length; the rules allow
catamaran, trimaran or proa configuration. Weight,
measured length, and sail area are used to reckon a
time allowance. Compulsorily trailerable.

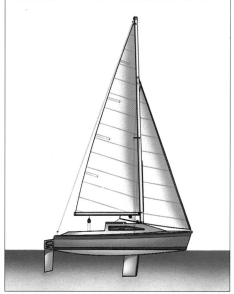

MICRO TONNER
⊟ ⸙⸙ **National origin** France
Designers Various **Length** 5.5 m (18 ft)
Beam 2.4 m (8 ft) **Sail area** 18.6 sq m (200 sq ft)
Dimensions can be varied under the Micro rule
introduced by the magazine *Bateaux* for the
ultimate, small, ton-cup boat, but the rule stands on
its own and is not related to IOR. For coastal racing
but not offshore use.

MINISAIL
⊞ ⸙ **National origin** USA
Designer Ian Proctor **Length** 4 m (13 ft)
Beam 1.1 m (3 ft 8 in) **Sail area** 7.4 sq m (80 sq ft)
An early (1960) beach-boat in modern plastics, it
has been exhibited in New York's Museum of Modern
Art. It was the first boat to have a sail sleeved on to
a jointed metal mast, and with its offspring,
Minisprint, around 15,000 were built.

MIRACLE
⊞ ⸙⸙ **National origin** UK
Designer Jack Holt **Length** 3.9 m (12 ft 9 in)
Beam 1.6 m (5 ft 2 in) **Sail area** 8.8 sq m (95 sq ft)
Seen as the larger version of the Mirror, it was
commissioned in 1974 by the *Daily Mirror* as a
family boat for home construction in wood. Some
3,600 have been built and can be found in the UK,
Cyprus and the US.

MIRROR
⊠ ⊞ ⸙⸙ **National origin** UK
Designer Jack Holt **Length** 3.3 m (10 ft 8 in)
Beam 1.4 m (4 ft 8 in) **Sail area** 6.4 sq m (69 sq ft)
Sponsored by the London *Daily Mirror* in 1963, this
all-purpose boat is of stitch-and-glue wood for home
building. Sails must always be red. Now in sandwich
and composite construction, there are more than
68,000 in 100 countries.

M SCOW
⊕ ⋔ **National origin** USA
Designer Harry Melges Sr **Length** 4.9 m (16 ft)
Beam 1.7 m (5 ft 8 in) **Sail area** 13.6 sq m (146 sq ft)
A fast, very responsive, but smaller version of the
lake-scow designs popular in the mid-western region
of the US. With twin bilgeboards, dual rudders and a
rotating mast, it planes quickly and is very
responsive to helm and sail.

NAPLES SABOT
⊕ ⋅ **National origin** USA
Designers Roy McCullough & R.A. Violette
Length 2.4 m (7 ft 11 in) **Beam** 1.2 m (3 ft 10 in)
Sail area 3.5 sq m (38 sq ft)
Used as a training boat in Southern California,
leeboards are used instead of a centerboard. This
pram dinghy has endured, with some 10,000 built,
because its ease of handling make it fun for all.

NATIONAL 12
⊕ ⋔ **National origin** UK
Designers Various **Length** 3.7 m (12 ft)
Beam 2 m (6 ft 7 in) **Sail area** 8.4 sq m (90 sq ft)
Over 3,000 have been built in this restricted class
but most have been outdated as the original 1936,
all-wood, clinker design has been modified with
hi-tech hull materials, metal spars and mylar sail
cloth. No spinnaker is allowed in this class.

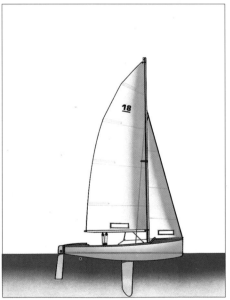

NATIONAL 18
⊕ ⋔⋅ **National origin** UK
Designers Various **Length** 5.5 m (18 ft)
Beam 1.8 m (18 ft) **Sail area** 17.7 sq m (190 sq ft)
Introduced as a restricted class in 1938 by the
national authority in UK to be a big International 14,
the 18, with its small (250) but faithful following, has
advanced from clinker and wood to fiberglass and
single trapeze.

NORFOLK DINGHY
⊕ ⋔ **National origin** UK
Designer Herbert Woods **Length** 4.3 m (14 ft)
Beam 1.6 m (5 ft 4 in) **Sail area** 12.3 sq m (132 sq ft)
Clinker-(lapstrake-)built dinghy first seen in
Norfolk, England in 1931. Eighty-six were built, the
last in 1968. The original gunter rig is still in use.
Typical inland local design unaffected by latest
racing trends.

NORFOLK PUNT
⊕ ⋔ **National origin** UK
Designers Various **Length** 8.2 m (27 ft)
Beam 1.8 m (6 ft) **Sail area** 16.4 sq m (176 sq ft)
Used only on the inland Norfolk Broads of England,
designers can create a very light, large sail area
boat with double-trapeze and unlimited spinnaker. A
one-design from 1952 to 1986, it has reverted
to a restricted class using modern materials.

SYMBOLS KEY
IYRU official class
Centerboard dinghy
Inshore multihull
Keelboat
Offshore multihull
Offshore racer
Sailboard
Number of crew

CLASSES/M-O   233

OK

⊗ 🛥 ⅰ **National origin** Denmark
Designer Knud Olsen **Length** 4 m (13 ft 2 in)
Beam 1.5 m (4 ft 11 in) **Sail area** 8.5 sq m (92 sq ft)
One-design racing dinghy with unstayed rotating
mast. Introduced in 1957, there are some 14,000 in
existence throughout the world. Originally it was
intended as a cheap training boat for the Finn, but is
a strong class in its own right.

OLYMPIA-JOLLE

🛥 ⅰ **National origin** Germany
Designer Helmut Stauch **Length** 5 m (16 ft 5 in)
Beam 1.7 m (5 ft 5 in) **Sail area** 10 sq m (108 sq ft)
Olympic single-hander for 1936 games in Germany,
it has a strange nationalist history, with continued
building in Germany in WWII yet ignored by Britain,
the US and other sailing countries. There are 800
boats in Germany, Holland, Switzerland and Italy.

125

🛥 ⅰⅰ **National origin** Australia
Designer John Blockley **Length** 3.8 m (12 ft 6 in)
Beam 1.3 m (4 ft 5 in) **Sail area** 9.3 sq m (100 sq ft)
Relatively cheap and easily built at home using
stitch-and-glue method. Home construction is
favored in Australia, making the 125 a popular high-
performance class despite a number of other
dinghies this size.

OOD 34

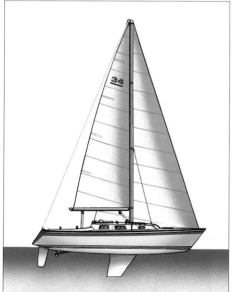

◨ ⅰⅰⅰⅰⅰⅰⅰ **National origin** UK
Designer Douglas Peterson **Length** 10.4 m (34 ft)
Beam 3.5 m (11 ft 6 in) **Sail area** 45 sq m (484 sq ft)
The Offshore One-Design 34 was one of the official
classes chosen for ocean racing in the UK in 1977,
but the collapse of the builders' business meant
numbers remained small (less than 40). Continues
to race in class and in handicap in English Channel.

OPTIMIST

⊗ 🛥 ⅰ **National origin** USA
Designer Clark Mills **Length** 2.3 m (7 ft 7 in)
Beam 1.1 m (3 ft 8 in) **Sail area** 3.5 sq m (38 sq ft)
Conceived in 1947, it is the simplest children's sail
boat and can be found in over 50 countries. It is
estimated that around 250,000 have been built,
many by their owners. Its basic rig and operation
insure its continuing popularity.

OSLO-JOLLE

🛥 ⅰⅰ **National origin** Norway
Designer Erling Kristoffersen **Length** 5.5 m (18 ft)
Beam 1.5 m (5 ft 1 in) **Sail area** 9 sq m (97 sq ft)
A traditional, local, one-design built in 1936 for the
sheltered waters of the Oslo Fjord. There was
originally a lug sail on the double-ended
Scandinavian hull, but both rig and design have
since been updated.

OSPREY
National origin UK
Designer Ian Proctor **Length** 5.3 m (17 ft 6 in)
Beam 1.8 m (5 ft 9 in) **Sail area** 13.9 sq m (150 sq ft)
One of the larger racing dinghies, it was designed in
1952 for the IYRU trials won by the Flying
Dutchman. Since then minor alternations have been
made and a trapeze added. Wood is still preferred to
fiberglass for construction.

P-CLASS
National origin New Zealand
Designer Harry Highet **Length** 2.1 m (7 ft)
Beam 1.1 m (3 ft 6 in) **Sail area** 8.4 sq m (90 sq ft)
Since 1923, this plywood single-hander has been the
training boat for New Zealand helmsmen under the
age of 16; many have gone on to become top sailors.
Sail adjustment and some fine tuning to the rig is
possible and encouraged.

PENGUIN
National origin USA
Designer Philip Rhodes **Length** 3.4 m (11 ft)
Beam 1.4 m (4 ft 6 in) **Sail area** 6.7 sq m (72 sq ft)
First built in wood in 1939, now in fiberglass, an
easily sailed class popular with younger sailors. Its
single sail is adequate for moderate breezes and the
flat sections aft give good stability and planing
potential off the wind.

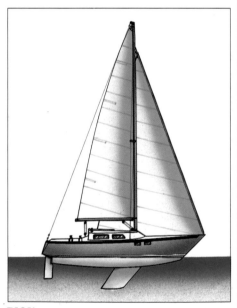

PION
National origin Netherlands
Designer E. Van de Stadt **Length** 9 m (29 ft 6 in)
Beam 2.9 m (9 ft 5 in) **Sail area** 37.5 sq m (404 sq ft)
Notable for serious attempt to establish itself as a
strict, offshore one-design in 1972, when formula
and rated boats were at their peak. Widespread in
the Netherlands, but builders' business failed, so
numbers are static, although boats remain popular.

PIPER OD
National origin UK
Designer David Boyd **Length** 7.4 m (24 ft 5 in)
Beam 1.9 m (6 ft 3 in) **Sail area** 24.3 sq m (262 sq ft)
About 40 of these mini 12-Meter types (as at their
design date of 1966) race on the Clyde estuary,
Scotland. Except for a wooden prototype that was
used as a plug, this conservative design is built to
Lloyd's rules in fiberglass.

PIRAT
National origin Germany
Designer H. Martens **Length** 5 m (16 ft 5 in)
Beam 1.6 m (5 ft 3 in) **Sail area** 10 sq m (108 sq ft)
Strongly built, European, lake type, raced in
Germany, Norway and Switzerland; simple to sail for
less experienced sailors. People can hire them on
small lakes and be left to their own devices. Made in
wood, plywood and fiberglass.

SYMBOLS KEY IYRU official class · Centerboard dinghy · Inshore multihull · Keelboat · Offshore multihull · Offshore racer · Sailboard · Number of crew

PRINDLE 16
National origin USA
Designer Geoff Prindle **Length** 4.9 m (16 ft)
Beam 2.4 m (8 ft) **Sail area** 17.6 sq m (189 sq ft)
The first of the Prindle series of high-performance,
lightweight catamarans for crews weighing less than
136 kg (300 lbs) and without any daggerboard to
prevent damage at high speed. Fleets in the US and
elsewhere total some 10,000.

PRINDLE 18
National origin USA
Designer Geoff Prindle **Length** 5.5 m (18 ft)
Beam 2.4 m (8 ft) **Sail area** 20.3 sq m (218 sq ft)
The largest of a series of Prindle catamarans, there
are 3,000 mainly in the US, but now spreading in
Europe. The powerful design needs a crew of 141 kg
(310 lbs) or more. Like the Prindle 16, the 18 has no
daggerboard.

PUFFER
National origin USA
Designer AMF Corp. **Length** 3.8 m (12 ft 6 in)
Beam 1.7 m (5 ft 9 in) **Sail area** 8.4 sq m (90 sq ft)
Mass-production class used throughout the US as a
general-purpose racer, as it can be rowed or used
with an outboard motor. The mast is simple and
strong and the sail area moderate.

RANDMEER
National origin Netherlands
Designer E. Van de Stadt **Length** 6.5 m (21 ft 4 in)
Beam 2.1 m (6 ft 9 in) **Sail area** 19.1 sq m (206 sq ft)
Strongly built, shallow-draft boat with traditional
sheerline, rubbing strakes and decking making it a
weighty boat. A Dutch national class, this family,
weekend boat has a moderate sail area.

REBEL
National origin USA
Designer Ray Greene **Length** 4.9 m (16 ft)
Beam 2 m (6 ft 6 in) **Sail area** 15.4 sq m (166 sq ft)
First built in 1946, this centerboard sloop, one of the
first ever in fiberglass, has become popular as a
family day-sailer, known for its ease of handling and
stability. A variety of alternative deck and cockpit
arrangements give the class great flexibility.

REDWING
National origin UK
Designer Uffa Fox **Length** 4.3 m (14 ft)
Beam 1.5 m (5 ft) **Sail area** 13.5 sq m (145 sq ft)
Traditional clinker class designed for Looe SC in
1939; the Looe Redwing became West of England
Redwing, then National Redwing. Changes to the
one-design include iron to wood centerboard in
1966, a trapeze in 1976 and alloy mast in 1984.

REGENBOOG

⊥ ††† **National origin** Netherlands
Designer G. De Vries Lentsch **Length** 8 m (26 ft)
Beam 1.9 m (6 ft 5 in) **Sail area** 40 sq m (430 sq ft)
One of the oldest classes still sailing in Europe, it
was designed by a leading architect in 1917; the
wooden-hulled and sparred boats are still built. It
appeals to Dutch enthusiasm for traditional craft; is
used for annual team races between provinces.

REQUIN

⊥ †††† **National origin** France
Designer Gunnar Steinback
Length 9.6 m (31 ft 6 in) **Beam** 1.9 m (6 ft 3 in)
Sail area 25 sq m (269 sq ft)
This French one-design is a frozen version of the
Scandinavian 30-Square Meter, and is still sailed in
a fiberglass version from deep-water ports. It is also
used for club racing by the French Navy.

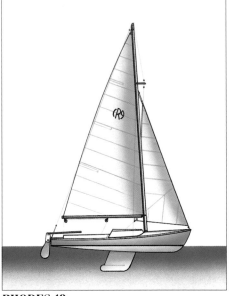

RHODES 19

⊥ ⊥ †††† **National origin** USA
Designer Phillip Rhodes **Length** 5.8 m (19 ft)
Beam 2.1 m (7 ft) **Sail area** 16.3 sq m (176 sq ft)
Available in either a centerboard or keel version, the
boat is an excellent heavy-weather sailer. With a
large cockpit – big enough for six to eight adults –
and dry stowage forward, it is a good day-racer as
well as a popular family day-sailer.

RHODES BANTAM

⊥ †† **National origin** USA
Designer Phillip Rhodes **Length** 4.3 m (14 ft)
Beam 1.7 m (5 ft 6 in) **Sail area** 11.6 sq m (125 sq ft)
Primarily used as a training dinghy for yacht clubs,
the Bantam provides a good-sized sailplan and a
relatively high-performance hull shape. A spinnaker
can produce exciting moments when sailing on a
reach or well off the wind.

RIVER

⊥ †††† **National origin** Ireland
Designer Alfred Mylne **Length** 8.6 m (28 ft 3 in)
Beam 2.1 m (7 ft) **Sail area** 31.6 sq m (340 sq ft)
The hefty River-class sloop was designed in 1919
with racing in the shallow Strangford Lough as a
priority; hence the draft was kept down to
1.1 m (3 ft 9 in). Despite its shoal form, it is an
excellent seaboat.

ROYAL BURNHAM

⊥ †††† **National origin** UK
Designer N. Dallimore **Length** 6.2 m (20 ft 6 in)
Beam 2 m (6 ft 8 in) **Sail area** 22.3 sq m (240 sq ft)
Only 23 have been built since 1933, but 21 remain
and race regularly on the River Crouch, Essex. The
class demonstrates the longevity of a strict one-
design sailed from one location and club, the Royal
Burnham YC, founded in 1895.

SYMBOLS KEY

IYRU official class
Centerboard dinghy
Inshore multihull
Keelboat
Offshore multihull
Offshore racer
Sailboard
Number of crew

⊗ ⊹ ⊡ ⊡ ⊞ ⬗ ◹ ▮

CLASSES/*R-S*

237

ROYAL WINDERMERE 17

⊹▮▮▮ **National origin** UK
Designers Various **Length** 7.9 m (26 ft)
Beam 1.9 m (6 ft 2 in) **Sail area** 37.2 sq m (400 sq ft)
The 17 refers to the waterline footage in this exclusive, restricted class used on Lake Windermere. It represents an older, more elegant type of racing, with craftsman-built boats. Ample sail area and low freeboard for lake conditions.

SABRE

⊹▮ **National origin** Australia
Designer Ron Given **Length** 3.7 m (12 ft)
Beam 1.2 m (4 ft 1 in) **Sail area** 6.4 sq m (69 sq ft)
A strict one-design, single-handed racer, much favored throughout Australian waters because of the stitch-and-glue amateur construction of the hull. A lightweight, high-performance boat, fast and exciting to sail.

SAFIR

⊹▮▮▮ **National origin** Sweden
Designer Gote Berg **Length** 9.8 m (32 ft 3 in)
Beam 1.9 m (6 ft 5 in) **Sail area** 30.9 sq m (333 sq ft)
Like the Daring at Cowes, a one-design frozen from the 5.5-Meter class with modern stern and cabin added, displacing 2,450 kg (5,400 lbs). The narrow hull was designed in fiberglass in 1970.

SAILFISH

⊹▮ **National origin** USA
Designer Alcort Co **Length** 4.1 m (13 ft 7 in)
Beam 0.9 m (3 ft) **Sail area** 7 sq m (75 sq ft)
Originally designed as a fun boat to sail off the beach, it was available in plywood for the home builder. Its simple lateen rig made it very popular. Some 55,000 boats were sold before it was replaced by the Sunfish.

ST MAWES ONE-DESIGN

⊹▮▮▮ **National origin** UK
Designer Frank Peters **Length** 4.9 m (16 ft)
Beam 1.8 m (6 ft) **Sail area** 16.7 sq m (180 sq ft)
Life changes little in the far south-west of England, where this local class, first built in 1923, races regularly in Carrick Roads. Peters built his last boat in 1964; since then nine further boats have been added to the 40-strong fleet.

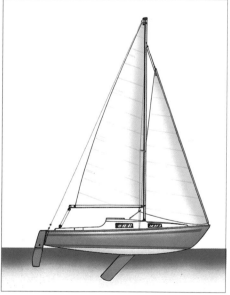

SAN JUAN 21

⊹▮▮▮ **National origin** USA
Designer Don Clark **Length** 6.4 m (21 ft)
Beam 1.5 m (5 ft) **Sail area** 17.7 sq m (190 sq ft)
One of the original, retractable-keel designs, this class is easily trailerable, and its cuddy cabin forward provides overnight accommodation for family cruising. An excellent light-air sailer, this well-organized class races nationally in the US.

SCORPION

⊞ ⵏⵏ **National origin** UK
Designer Uffa Fox **Length** 4.3 m (14 ft)
Beam 1.5 m (4 ft 10 in) **Sail area** 9.9 sq m (107 sq ft)
Designed in 1960 as a basic racing dinghy, there are
now 1,200 throughout the UK. It is used for teaching
and can be constructed by an amateur. Wood is still
the preferred material. Reputation for performance;
mainly suitable for young sailors.

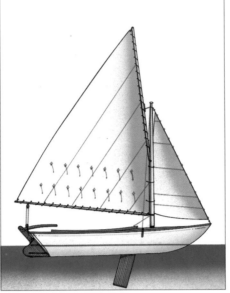

SEABIRD HALF RATER

⊞ ⵏⵏⵏ **National origin** UK
Designers H.G. Baggs & W. Scott Hayward
Length 6.1 m (20 ft) **Beam** 1.8 m (6 ft)
Sail area 18.8 sq m (202 sq ft)
Dating from 1898, it is the oldest, centerboard,
one-design class still racing in the UK. Built in
traditional materials, 69 of the 90 boats constructed
still exist. A distinguished and much-loved class.

SEAFLY

⊞ ⵏⵏⵏ **National origin** UK
Designers S. Herbert & J.O. Kelley
Length 4.5 m (14 ft 9 in) **Beam** 1.8 m (5 ft 9 in)
Sail area 11.1 sq m (120 sq ft)
Developed from the Merlin Rocket and successor to
the smaller but similar Mayfly, it first appeared in
1961. Gradual design evolution has kept this family
boat up to date, and some 650 have been built.

SEAVIEW MERMAID

⊞ ⵏⵏⵏ **National origin** UK
Designer Arthur Robb **Length** 7.8 m (25 ft 9 in)
Beam 1.8 m (6 ft) **Sail area** 19.2 sq m (207 sq ft)
A Seaview Mermaid class based on the Isle of Wight
has existed since 1907; it was redesigned in 1922
(the old boats being scrapped) and again in 1962
(this design). Traditional sit-in keelboat, each a
different color.

SELECTION

◫ ⵏⵏⵏⵏⵏⵏ **National origin** France
Designer Joubert & Nivelt **Length** 10.9 m (36 ft)
Beam 3.2 m (10 ft 8 in) **Sail area** 70 sq m (753 sq ft)
Offshore yacht used for the Tour de France à la
Voile. Intended as a budget racing boat, the
emphasis is on boat speed rather than comfort or
rating. It is built by Jeanneau, one of the world's
largest production-builders.

SHANNON

⊞ ⵏⵏⵏ **National origin** Ireland
Designer Morgan Giles **Length** 5.5 m (18 ft)
Beam 1.4 m (4 ft 9 in) **Sail area** 13 sq m (140 sq ft)
The una-rigged Shannon one-design emerged in 1921
on the great lakes of Ireland's longest river as a
distillation of a type of 18-footer then racing in the
area. Still built and providing excellent sport.

SHARK 24
National origin Canada
Designer George Hinterhoeller **Length** 7.3 m (24 ft)
Beam 2.1 m (6 ft 10 in) **Sail area** 19.5 sq m (210 sq ft)
One of the first light-displacement, fractional-rigged, planing keelboats, the boat is extremely seaworthy and has been successful in offshore racing as well as in closed-course competitions. It has an active international class organization.

SHEARWATER
National origin UK
Designers Francis & Roland Prout
Length 5 m (16 ft 6 in) **Beam** 2.3 m (7 ft 7 in)
Sail area 14.9 sq m (160 sq ft)
Built in 1954, this was one of the first inshore, centerboard catamarans. It has a sloop rig and was unique in Europe in having a spinnaker. The class is still raced in spite of more recent competition.

SHIELDS
National origin USA
Designer Sparkman & Stephens
Length 9.2 m (30 ft 2 in) **Beam** 1.9 m (6 ft 5 in)
Sail area 33.4 sq m (360 sq ft)
One of the earliest fiberglass boats, the design is typical of the handsome, displacement keel-racers that are so popular along the north-east of the US. Strict class rules keep the competition very even.

SIGMA 33
National origin UK
Designer David Thomas **Length** 9.9 m (32 ft 6 in)
Beam 3.2 m (10 ft 6 in) **Sail area** 53 sq m (573 sq ft)
With more than 300 built since 1979, entries of over 50 are not uncommon in racing in the Solent and English Channel in this tightly organized one-design class. The British IOR fleet would look much smaller without this class.

SIGMA 38
National origin UK
Designer David Thomas **Length** 11.6 m (38 ft)
Beam 3.7 m (12 ft 2 in) **Sail area** 61.8 sq m (665 sq ft)
Chosen by the RORC in 1987 as an offshore one-design class, this large OD represents a retreat from formula boats. May take over from other types of offshore racers.

SIGNET
National origin UK
Designer Ian Proctor **Length** 3.8 m (12 ft 6 in)
Beam 1.4 m (4 ft 9 in) **Sail area** 8.1 sq m (88 sq ft)
Originally sponsored by the *Sunday Times* in 1962, it retains a following of about 1,000 in UK, USA and Australia. The construction is still in wood, making it suitable for home building.

SIMOUN 4.85
National origin France
Designer Gouteron SA **Length** 4.8 m (15 ft 11 in)
Beam 1.8 m (5 ft 10 in) **Sail area** 14.1 sq m (152 sq ft)
Large European racing dinghy with fleets in France,
Germany, Netherlands and Switzerland but limited
owing to its size. Relatively light, planing type,
unlike traditional lake-boats in these countries.

6-METER
National origin Europe
Designers Various **Length** 9.8 m (32 ft)
Beam 2.6 m (8 ft 6 in) **Sail area** 34.4 sq m (370 sq ft)
Classic formula class rating six meters under the
International Rule, created in 1906 and successively
updated. The 1930s were their heyday, but they still
provide top international racing. Some new boats
are built for regattas at high, one-off prices.

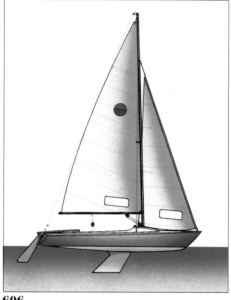

606
National origin Sweden
Designer Pelle Pettersson **Length** 6.1 m (19 ft 11 in)
Beam 1.9 m (6 ft 1 in) **Sail area** 16 sq m (172 sq ft)
About 600 of these racing boats specifically
designed for KSSS (Royal Swedish YC) in 1968 are
sailed in Denmark, Switzerland and southern
Sweden, where there was a revival in the late 1980s.
Popular for club racing.

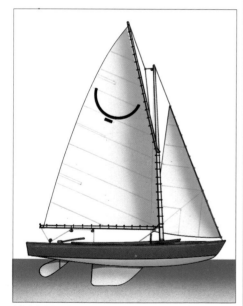

16-SQUARE METER
National origin Netherlands
Designer H. Bulthuis **Length** 6 m (19 ft 9 in)
Beam 1.9 m (6 ft 4 in) **Sail area** 16 sq m (172 sq ft)
Forty-year-old class raced regularly on the
Ijsselmeer and other Dutch waterways. It is built in
traditional wood and is one of a series of Dutch
inland types, graded by sail area, that includes 22-
and 30-Square Meters.

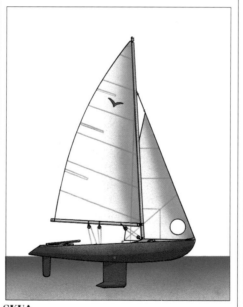

SKUA
National origin UK
Designer Jack Robertson **Length** 5.2 m (17 ft)
Beam 1.5 m (5 ft 2 in) **Sail area** 13 sq m (140 sq ft)
One-design devised in 1964 with stability as main
consideration and so has fin-and-bulb drop keel
weighing 72 kg (160 lb). Fifty have been built – all in
ply – and can be found in the UK and South Africa.

SNIPE
National origin USA
Designer William Crosby **Length** 4.7 m (15 ft 6 in)
Beam 1.5 m (5 ft) **Sail area** 10.8 sq m (116 sq ft)
This design was first published in 1931 in *Rudder*
magazine, and in the late 1940s it was numerically
the largest class in the world. Its simple
construction and gear made it popular in countries
where there was little other sailing.

SYMBOLS KEY
IYRU official class
Centerboard dinghy
Inshore multihull
Keelboat
Offshore multihull
Offshore racer
Sailboard
Number of crew

CLASSES/S

241

SOLING

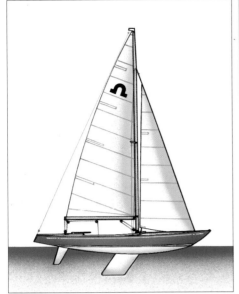

National origin Norway
Designer Jan Linge **Length** 8.2 m (26 ft 9 in)
Beam 1.9 m (6 ft 3 in) **Sail area** 21.6 sq m (233 sq ft)
Chosen by the IYRU in three-man keelboat trials, its
subsequent Olympic status has restricted its general
appeal, although there are numerous small fleets
scattered around the world. It has a moderate sail
plan with spinnaker and self-tacking jib.

SOLO

National origin UK
Designer Jack Holt **Length** 3.8 m (12 ft 5 in)
Beam 1.6 m (5 ft 3 in) **Sail area** 8.4 sq m (90 sq ft)
A single-handed racer introduced by *Yachting World*
magazine in 1955. It is a national class in UK, but
there are also fleets worldwide. It was originally
made of wood for building at home, but is now
commercially produced in fiberglass.

SONAR

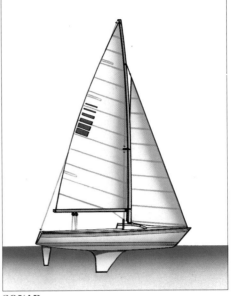

National origin USA
Designer Bruce Kirby **Length** 7 m (23 ft)
Beam 2.4 m (7 ft 10 in) **Sail area** 23 sq m (250 sq ft)
A modern (1980) one-design club racer and day-
sailer with a very large, self-bailing cockpit, a small
cabin forward for two berths and a head. Lively yet
stable enough to ensure popularity with day-sailors
and sailing schools.

SONATA 7

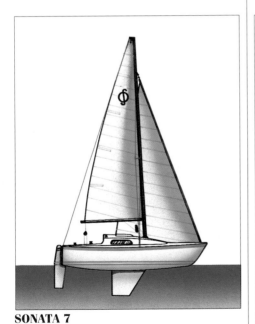

National origin UK
Designer David Thomas **Length** 6.9 m (22 ft 8 in)
Beam 2.5 m (8 ft 2 in) **Sail area** 24.2 sq m (260 sq ft)
Originally built to comply with mini-ton rules in
1976, it soon became a strict one-design class.
Heavy promotion by the builders, a designer well
thought of in Britain, and a gap in the market at that
time, has established many fleets.

SOUTH COAST

National origin UK
Designer Charles Nicholson Jr.
Length 8.4 m (27 ft 6 in) **Beam** 2.5 m (8 ft 3 in)
Sail area 47.4 sq m (510 sq ft)
Also known as a Scod, this is a fine example of a one-
design cruiser-racer. It was introduced in 1956, and
although no new boats have been built for a decade,
the fleet on the south coast of Britain still races.

SOVEREL 33

National origin USA
Designer Mark Soverel **Length** 10.1 m (33 ft)
Beam 3.3 m (11 ft) **Sail area** 49.9 sq m (537 sq ft)
One of the first of the new high-performance, open-
transom, ocean-racers with a 15/16th rig, it has a
wide beam and narrow waterline to achieve stability
when heeled, while keeping wetted surface area to a
minimum. A popular offshore racer in the US.

SPANKER
National origin Netherlands
Designer E. Van de Stadt **Length** 5.8 m (18 ft 11 in)
Beam 1.9 m (6 ft 3 in) **Sail area** 16 sq m (171 sq ft)
First built in the 1960s, it was intended for amateur building in plywood by one of the Netherland's most prolific designers. The 16-sq m (171-sq ft) sail area is typical of European grading by the amount of sail.

SPARK
National origin UK
Designer Rodney Marsh **Length** 4.6 m (15 ft)
Beam 1.8 m (6 ft) **Sail area** 13.2 sq m (142 sq ft)
Developed in 1979 as a recreational version of the Dart, also designed by Rodney Marsh, it has become a racing boat in its own right with over 1,000 sold in Europe and Australia. In 1988 the class was renamed the Dart 15; a trapeze and jib were added.

SPROG
National origin South Africa
Designer Herbert McWilliam **Length** 4.3 m (14 ft)
Beam 1.4 m (4 ft 6 in) **Sail area** 10.2 sq m (110 sq ft)
A major national class of about 1,100 in South Africa with a few in the UK, the dimensions of this 1947 design were classic 14-footer. Strict one-design, good in rough African seas and big lakes.

SQUIB
National origin UK
Designer Oliver J. Lee **Length** 5.8 m (19 ft)
Beam 1.9 m (6 ft 2 in) **Sail area** 16.1 sq m (173 sq ft)
A keelboat designed in 1968 for undemanding family racing, with several fleets around the world, and especially strong in east of England. The small shelter by the mast enables it to be used for day cruising as well as class racing.

STAR
National origin USA
Designer William Gardner **Length** 6.9 m (22 ft 9 in)
Beam 1.7 m (5 ft 8 in) **Sail area** 26.1 sq m (281 sq ft)
The first of these boats was built in 1911; since then it has been updated and has remained an Olympic class for many years. There are fleets worldwide, with the majority in the US and eastern Europe.

STREAKER
National origin UK
Designer Jack Holt **Length** 3.9 m (12 ft 9 in)
Beam 1.4 m (4 ft 7 in) **Sail area** 6.5 sq m (70 sq ft)
Light single-hander, designed in 1975 and intended for home construction. There are fleets of around 1,300 spread round the world. Relatively small numbers are due to competition from subsequent popular single-handers.

SYMBOLS KEY
IYRU official class
Centerboard dinghy
Inshore multihull
Keelboat
Offshore multihull
Offshore racer
Sailboard
Number of crew

CLASSES/S-T

243

SUNBEAM
National origin UK
Designer Alfred Westmacott **Length** 8 m (26 ft 5 in)
Beam 1.8 m (6 ft) **Sail area** 27.9 sq m (300 sq ft)
An open-cockpit, day-racing boat first built in 1922.
Some 43 now exist in two fleets, in the Solent and at
Falmouth. Class rules state that all boats must have
a name which ends in the letter Y.

SUNFISH
National origin USA
Designer Alcort Inc **Length** 4.2 m (13 ft 10 in)
Beam 0.4 m (4 ft 1 in) **Sail area** 8 sq m (86 sq ft)
One of the board boats of the 1950s, it is now
numerically the largest class in the world, with
some 200,000 built. The low-profile lateen rig is
simple to control, which makes it very appealing to
sailors at all levels of skill.

SWALLOW
National origin UK
Designer Tom Thornycroft **Length** 7.9 m (26 ft)
Beam 1.7 m (5 ft 7 in) **Sail area** 18.6 sq m (200 sq ft)
Chosen as a British national class in 1947, it never
achieved more than local support, despite use in the
1948 Olympic Games. Lead keels have been taken
from older wooden boats and used in a fiberglass
fleet of about 30.

SWAN 46
National origin Finland
Designer German Frers **Length** 14.4 m (47 ft 1 in)
Beam 4.4 m (14 ft) **Sail area** 115 sq m (1,240 sq ft)
Cruiser-racer with excellent accommodation
combined with offshore racing performance. The 46
is thought to be the fastest and most seaworthy of all
the Swans, often considered the cruiser-racer type
by which others are judged.

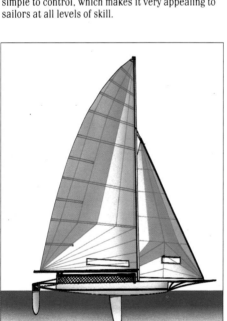

SYDNEY HARBOR 18
National origin Australia
Designers Various **Length** 5.5 m (18 ft)
Beam 2 m (6 ft 6 in) **Sail area** Unrestricted
One of the world's design leaders, it started in 1890
and today has a large sail area, asymmetrical
masthead spinnakers, trapezes for all crew and
latest skimming hulls. The class has always
permitted sponsorship and betting.

TANZER 16
National origin USA
Designer Johann Tanzer **Length** 5 m (16 ft 4 in)
Beam 1.9 m (6 ft 2 in) **Sail area** 13.5 sq m (145 sq ft)
Previously known as the Constellation, 1,500 of this
American answer to the Wayfarer have been built
since 1963. Suitable for one-design racing, it can
also be used for cruising.

TANZER 22
✈ ⊞ ⅄ ⅄ ⅄ ⅄ **National origin** USA
Designer Johann Tanzer **Length** 6.9 m (22 ft 6 in)
Beam 2.4 m (7 ft 10 in) **Sail area** 20.6 sq m (222 sq ft)
Easily trailerable in the centerboard or keel version,
the 22 has a generous cabin arrangement below,
suitable for sleeping four people. A good performer
over a full range of wind conditions, it does well in
class as well as in fleet racing.

TARTAN 10
🄳 ⅄ ⅄ ⅄ ⅄ ⅄ **National origin** USA
Designer Sparkman & Stephens
Length 10.1 m (33 ft 2 in) **Beam** 2.8 m (9 ft 3 in)
Sail area 45.2 sq m (487 sq ft)
One of the first offshore one-designs, it is a
dedicated racing keelboat, with only modest
accommodation below. Its relatively long and
narrow shape give a lively feel on the wind.

TASER
✈ ⅄ ⅄ **National origin** USA
Designer Bruce Kirby **Length** 4.5 m (14 ft 10 in)
Beam 1.57 m (5 ft 2 in) **Sail area** 12.1 sq m (130 sq ft)
One of the Laser derivatives with the same
advantages of car-top transport, total buoyancy and
large sail area. Capacity for extra children, and
though designed for family sailing, is a strict one-
design for racing.

TEMPEST
⊗ ⊞ ⅄ ⅄ **National origin** UK
Designer Ian Proctor **Length** 6.7 m (22 ft)
Beam 2 m (6 ft 6 in) **Sail area** 22.3 sq m (240 sq ft)
Designed for the IYRU two-man keelboat trials in
1965, it was subsequently chosen and sailed in the
Olympic Games, then withdrawn in favor of the Star.
It has a retractable keel and many modern features;
its popularity is confined to a few fleets.

30-SQUARE METER
⊞ ⅄ ⅄ ⅄ ⅄ ⅄ ⅄ **National origin** Sweden
Designers Various **Length** 13.1 m (43 ft)
Beam 2.3 m (7 ft 6 in) **Sail area** 30 sq m (322 sq ft)
A restricted class originating in Sweden in 1908,
since when some 250 have been constructed and
can be found throughout the world. Only the spar
lengths are measured in this class, resulting in the
unusual low freeboard and long overhangs.

THISTLE
✈ ⅄ ⅄ ⅄ **National origin** USA
Designer Gordon Douglass **Length** 5.2 m (17 ft)
Beam 1.8 m (6 ft) **Sail area** 16.3 sq m (175 sq ft)
All-round, one-design, racing class known for its
thrilling speed and planing abilities. Over 3,600
have been built and it remains one of America's
best-known dinghies. The first boat was built in
1945, inspired by British short-ended planing boats.

SYMBOLS KEY
IYRU official class
Centerboard dinghy
Inshore multihull
Keelboat
Offshore multihull
Offshore racer
Sailboard
Number of crew

THUNDERBIRD

National origin USA
Designer Ben Seaborn **Length** 7.9 m (25 ft 11 in)
Beam 2.3 m (7 ft 6 in) **Sail area** 28.6 sq m (308 sq ft)
Designed in 1958 in the Pacific northwest, it was
originally built in plywood. While fiberglass boats
have become popular, wooden boats have won a
number of world championships. Most of the 1,500
boats registered are in the US, Canada and Australia.

TINKER TRAMP

National origin UK
Designer Fred Benyon-Tinker **Length** 2.7 m (9 ft)
Beam 1.4 m (4 ft 6 in) **Sail area** 3.4 sq m (37 sq ft)
One of the few inflatable, centerboard sailing
dinghies; it is safe and stable and can be used as a
tender with outboard or a life-raft (for four persons)
with an inflatable canopy. Various designs have been
in production since 1977.

TOPPER

National origin UK
Designer Ian Proctor **Length** 3.4 m (11 ft 2 in)
Beam 1.2 m (3 ft 10 in) **Sail area** 5.2 sq m (56 sq ft)
A single-handed racing boat that is fun for adults as
well as children. Built of low-priced polypropylene,
there are around 25,000 boats worldwide, and it has
grown in popularity since it was introduced in 1976.
Car-top transportable.

TORNADO

National origin UK
Designer Rodney Marsh **Length** 6.1 m (20 ft)
Beam 3 m (10 ft) **Sail area** 20.4 sq m (220 sq ft)
This is one of the world's fastest, regularly raced
classes and the only multihull in the Olympics. The
sail power given by the wide beam is enhanced by
the crew's trapeze. Strict one-design has left the rig
at 1976 technology, but it has a large following.

TRIAS

National origin Germany
Designer Helmut Stöberl **Length** 9.2 m (30 ft)
Beam 2.1 m (6 ft 11 in) **Sail area** 28.8 sq m (310 sq ft)
Designed in 1968, it was an entry for the IYRU trials
that chose the Soling; like the E 22 it has produced
its own following in Europe. There are 500 of this
classic racer with full buoyancy.

TROY

National origin UK
Designer A.H. Watty **Length** 5.5 m (18 ft)
Beam 1.8 m (6 ft) **Sail area** 26.6 sq m (288 sq ft)
Twelve of these wooden one-designs have sailed for
60 years on the Cornish estuary of the Fowey, with
Fowey Gallants SC. The name, unusually, has a
literary origin from Sir Arthur Quiller Couch's novel
Troy Town. Classic local class, with steady support.

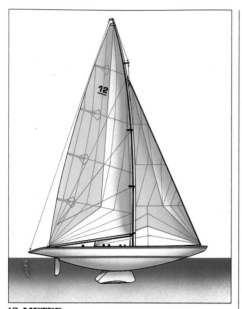

12-METER

National origin Europe
Designers Various **Length** 19.8 m (65 ft)
Beam 3.9 m (13 ft) **Sail area** 167 sq m (1,800 sq ft)
Created by the International Rule in 1906, about 130
have since been built. It was adopted for America's
Cup racing in 1956, resulting in the expensive
development of what is really a heavy, old-fashioned
formula. Unmistakable when sighted at sea.

12-SQUARE METER SHARPIE

National origin Germany
Designer J. Kroger **Length** 6 m (19 ft 7 in)
Beam 1.4 m (4 ft 8 in) **Sail area** 12 sq m (129 sq ft)
Designed in 1931 and used in the 1956 Olympic
Games, this class is still raced today. It has a
special character with a heavy, narrow gunter rig
typical of European lake-sailing boats, but is more
widely used than others of the type.

TWELVE-VOETSJOL

National origin UK
Designer George Cockshott **Length** 3.7 m (12 ft)
Beam 1.4 m (4 ft 7 in) **Sail area** 9.3 sq m (100 sq ft)
Sometimes known as the 12-ft International, this
single-hander was used in the Olympic Games of
1924 and 1928. It typifies the traditional lugsail,
wood-planked, open boat used at the beginning of
the century. Sails inland in Europe.

UNICORN

National origin UK
Designer John Mazzotti **Length** 5.5 m (18 ft)
Beam 2.3 m (7 ft 6 in) **Sail area** 13.9 sq m (150 sq ft)
A racing catamaran introduced in 1967 and usually
home-built in wood or fiberglass. It is virtually a
one-design with mainsail only, and has a trapeze or
sliding seat. Fleets are sailed in the UK, the
Netherlands and Canada.

VALK

National origin Netherlands
Designer E. Van de Stadt **Length** 6.5 m (21 ft 4 in)
Beam 2 m (6 ft 7 in) **Sail area** 18.6 sq m (200 sq ft)
Among the longer, traditional, European, lake types,
this heavy gaff sloop was introduced in 1936. It is
kept moored to fixed jetties and raced on the
Netherlands' many sheltered lakes and waterways.

VAURIEN

National origin France
Designer Jean-Jacques Herbulot
Length 4 m (13 ft 4 in) **Beam** 1.5 m (4 ft 10 in)
Sail area 8.8 sq m (95 sq ft)
The distinctive letter V and wing sail-mark is seen at
nearly every French sailing port and beach. Sheer
numbers keep this popular class going, despite an
outdated design.

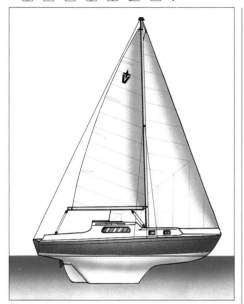

VEGA

⊕ ¡¡¡ **National origin** Sweden
Designer Per Brohäll **Length** 8.3 m (27 ft 1 in)
Beam 2.5 m (8 ft 1 in) **Sail area** 28.3 sq m (305 sq ft)
An ordinary cruiser that demonstrates how a
popular boat with a strong class association and
consistent builder can give good racing in selected
events. Used for passage races of medium length in
the UK and Scandinavia.

VICTORY

⊕ ¡¡ **National origin** UK
Designer Alfred Westmacott **Length** 6.3 m (21 ft)
Beam 1.8 m (6 ft) **Sail area** 18.6 sq m (200 sq ft)
In 1934, Bembridge SC decided to replace their own
class. An association in Portsmouth acquired the
best five of this old class, then built another seven to
the same design. Since then 70 have been built, all
in wood. They race in the Solent and Gibraltar.

VRIJHEID

⊕ ¡¡ **National origin** Netherlands
Designer KNWV (national authority)
Length 5.4 m (17 ft 8 in) **Beam** 1.6 m (4 ft 5 in)
Sail area 16 sq m (172 sq ft)
Designed within the national authority in 1945 to get
sailing started again on the Netherlands' inland
waters. Many thousands race; it has been updated
with crew trapeze and spinnaker.

WANDERER

⊕ ¡¡¡ **National origin** UK
Designer Ian Proctor **Length** 4.3 m (14 ft)
Beam 1.8 m (5 ft 10 in) **Sail area** 10.7 sq m (115 sq ft)
Often described as a smaller version of the highly
seaworthy Wayfarer, this class is also rugged in
concept but, at 45 kg (100 lbs), is lighter than its
predecessor. A strict one-design, suitable for family
sailing and medium-performance racing.

WATER WAG

⊕ ¡¡ **National origin** Ireland
Designer Mamie Doyle **Length** 4.3 m (14 ft 3 in)
Beam 1.6 m (5 ft 3 in) **Sail area** 10.9 sq m (117 sq ft)
The Water Wag was the world's first one-design in
1887; this is the 1900 successor, designed by the
daughter of the original designer. They have raced
ever since, and for 60 years a fleet has sailed in
Madras, India.

WAVERLEY

⊕ ¡¡¡ **National origin** Ireland
Designer John Wylie **Length** 5.5 m (18 ft 3 in)
Beam 1.8 m (6 ft) **Sail area** 22.3 sq m (240 sq ft)
One of the local classes that are virtually a
permanent feature of Belfast Lough. Originally
based at the port of Whitehead, the fleet, all of which
are named after the Waverley novels of Sir Walter
Scott, are now at Ballyholme Bay.

WAYFARER
National origin UK
Designer Ian Proctor **Length** 4.8 m (15 ft 10 in)
Beam 1.8 m (6 ft 1 in) **Sail area** 13.1 sq m (141 sq ft)
A very popular family boat, first built in 1957.
Spacious and rugged, it is a favorite for both
learning and medium-to-long-distance racing and
cruising. Some 15,000 have been sold world-wide.

WEST WIGHT SCOW
National origin UK
Designers Various **Length** 3.4 m (11 ft 3 in)
Beam 1.4 m (4 ft 9 in) **Sail area** 6 sq m (65 sq ft)
Varying slightly in design and name, scows have
been built for racing in different Solent harbors
since 1922. Active fleets continue. Frostbite racing
in the US began when a Lymington Scow was
shipped to Manhasset Bay, Long Island, in 1932.

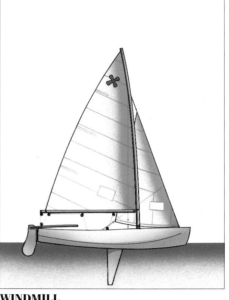

WINDMILL
National origin USA
Designer Clark Mills **Length** 4.7 m (15 ft 6 in)
Beam 1.4 m (4 ft 6 in) **Sail area** 11.1 sq m (119 sq ft)
A light, 90 kg (198 lb), daggerboard sloop built of
closed-cell foam, confined to the US and used as an
advanced trainer for younger sailors as well as
adults. The hard chine allows easy launching from
beaches; it is capable of planing at over 12 knots.

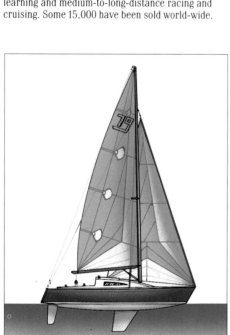

X-79
National origin Denmark
Designer Niels Jeppesen **Length** 8 m (26 ft 1 in)
Beam 2.9 m (9 ft 6 in) **Sail area** 37.9 sq m (408 sq ft)
More than 400 of these light (less than 1,360 kg,
3,000 lbs), habitable day-racers sail in Europe
under local handicap systems or in one-design
fleets. The X-79's designer went on to draw winning
Ton Cup boats.

X-BOAT
National origin UK
Designer J. Westmacott **Length** 6.3 m (20 ft 8 in)
Beam 1.8 m (6 ft) **Sail area** 17.6 sq m (190 sq ft)
Raced every peacetime season since 1909 from six
south-coast ports in Britain and also in Kuwait.
About 170 have been built, of which most still sail;
although the gaff rig has been changed, the planked,
wooden hull has remained unchanged.

X-BOAT
National origin USA
Designer Buddy Melges **Length** 4.9 m (16 ft 1 in)
Beam 1.9 m (6 ft 1 in) **Sail area** 10.2 sq m (110 sq ft)
A well-designed trainer for junior race programs;
the shape is patterned after traditional Great Lake
scows. There are minimum sail controls, a self-
tacking jib and only 0.8 m (2 ft 7 in) draft.

Y-FLYER
National origin USA
Designer Alvin Younquist **Length** 5.5 m (18 ft 2 in)
Beam 1.7 m (5 ft 8 in) **Sail area** 15 sq m (161 sq ft)
With over 2,500 built since it began in 1952, fleets
are well established in south- and mid-USA and
Canada. Its wide beam and flat bottom make it very
stable but quick to accelerate once it is on a reach.
Rig straightforward to assemble.

YNGLING
National origin Norway
Designer Jan Herman Linge
Length 6.3 m (20 ft 10 in) **Beam** 1.7 m (5 ft 8 in)
Sail area 14 sq m (151 sq ft)
This is an international small sister of the Olympic
Soling. One of the many keelboat classes so favored
in Scandinavia, where mooring is easy and racing
unaffected by tide.

YORKSHIRE
National origin UK
Designer J.S. Helyar **Length** 7.8 m (25 ft 6 in)
Beam 2.4 m (7 ft 9 in) **Sail area** 29.7 sq m (320 sq ft)
The oldest one-design keelboat still racing in UK. Six
of the original boats built in 1898 still race in a fleet
of 12 at Royal Yorkshire Yacht Club, Bridlington.
Timbers, deadwood and floors are of English oak;
the gunter rig was converted to bermudan in 1971.

YOUNG 8.8
National origin New Zealand
Designer Jim Young
Length 8.9 m (29 ft 4 in) **Beam** 3.3 m (10 ft 10 in)
Sail area 22.3 sq m (240 sq ft)
Hundreds of this class of family cruiser-racer are
moored within reach of New Zealand's main centers
of population. Many cruise as well as regularly race.
There is also a large fleet in Australia.

YW 14FT DAYBOAT
National origin UK
Designer G. O'Brien Kennedy **Length** 4.3 m (14 ft)
Beam 1.7 m (5 ft 7 in) **Sail area** 12.3 sq m (132 sq ft)
Commissioned by *Yachting World* in 1949, it was
initially without class rules, but the urge to race in
similar boats led to a one-design hull and sail area.
Primarily a family boat; scattered throughout the
British Isles.

YW HERON
National origin UK
Designer Jack Holt **Length** 3.4 m (11 ft 3 in)
Beam 1.4 m (4 ft 6 in) **Sail area** 6.5 sq m (70 sq ft)
Designed in 1951 as a sturdy, build-her-yourself,
family boat for racing or cruising, there are now
around 10,000 throughout the English-speaking
world. Gunter or bermudan rigs are permitted and
home construction from kits is still common.

Chapter 8

Design, Construction & Equipment

*T*he design, production and equipping of a boat is a complex procedure that combines technology with tradition. There is no 'best' material with which to build the hull: wood, plastics and metal in their many variations are all used. Sails used to be made of canvas, flax or cotton, but, since the 1950s, these natural materials have been totally replaced by artificial fibers; the spars that hold these sails up were once of wood but are now almost exclusively of aluminum. Yet despite this use of modern materials, newcomers to sailing declare that it is the most labor intensive of sports. If this is true, there are two constant factors that help to explain why. The first is that those who sail actually like to fuss over, perhaps 'improve', their boats. The second is that sea water and salt air are forever in opposition to the maintenance and good working order of a boat.

HULL CONSTRUCTION

Although every boat hull might look alike at first glance, the similarity is literally skin deep, for boat construction has kept up with and sometimes furthered the technological development of resins, fibers and their many combinations and composites.

The majority of hulls are still made of fiberglass which, combined with polyester resin, results in a strong, impact-resistant, low-cost hull. But this material does have the drawbacks of excessive weight and flexibility; the former is not a liability

for cruising boats, while the latter can be rectified structurally, adding yet more weight to the hull. Faced with such problems, boat builders have continued to experiment with lighter, stronger hull materials.

FIBERGLASS

A variety of fiberglasses can be used by boat builders, of which the four main ones are shown below. They all come in a range of weights, as well as in varying weaves or just as the basic, random, chopped-strand mat.

Chopped-strand mat *has equal strength in all directions but absorbs a high quantity of resin.*

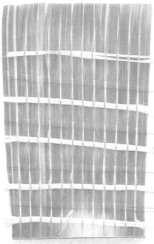

Undirectional E-glass *is used for building high-performance cruising boats on a male mold.*

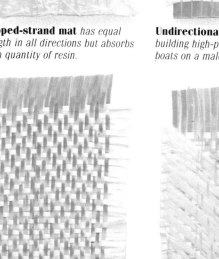

Heavy E-glass *with a flat weave, used for reinforcing internal joinery and other general purposes.*

Multidirectional E-glass, *with its long fibers, is used for craft requiring maximum strength.*

RESIN

The exact properties of resins and their hardeners can be varied according to the type of glass or other reinforcing fibers used, and to suit the conditions of application. Epoxy resin, more expensive than polyester but better in most respects, is invariably used with composites and the higher grades of fiberglass.

Polyester resin

COMPOSITES

Composites, a suitable name for what are otherwise known as hi-tech or exotic materials, include Kevlar and carbon, used either singly or in combination. One limitation on their use is their high cost; many racing classes ban them for that reason.

67% Kevlar, 33% carbon harness weave *(above), used in top-quality hull construction for its qualities of strength, light weight and impact resistance.*

Undirectional Kevlar and carbon *(below) used for local reinforcement of the hull where undirectional properties are called for.*

Carbon fiber *(left), an undirectional, strong but brittle fiber used for an inside skin and reinforcement.*

SANDWICH CONSTRUCTION

Sandwich-constructed hulls use several core materials, notably PVC, polyurethane and acrylics. For decks, end-grain balsa wood is used, as is cedar wood. Most exotic of all cores is honeycomb, in the form of Nomex aramid paper.

End-grain balsa

PVC foam

Honeycomb

Kevlar and carbon weave sandwich *with a foam core is at the top end of hi-tech construction for hulls or decks.*

Balsa sandwich, *in which end-grain balsa wood is sandwiched between two layers of fiberglass, is used for decks because of its light weight and rigidity.*

Honeycomb sandwich *of Nomex paper between layers of Kevlar weave is used where lightness and rigidity are required.*

Foam sandwich *between layers of fiberglass which can be tapered to solid glass at a joint or fitting.*

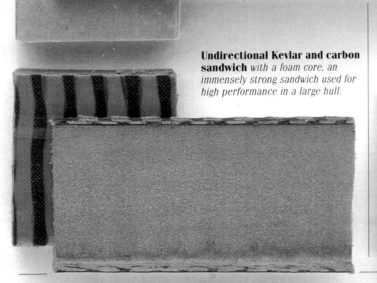

Undirectional Kevlar and carbon sandwich *with a foam core, an immensely strong sandwich used for high performance in a large hull.*

WOOD

The original laminate of all – resin-bonded marine plywood – has changed little in its 50 years of use. Seen today on the decks of wooden-planked boats and in some dinghy hulls, plywood is commonly used for internal joinery and bulkheads in boats of all sizes. Available in various thicknesses, it can be backed up with fiberglass and resin.

KEELBOAT CONSTRUCTION

A senior figure in the boatbuilding trade once gave an opinion on the difficulties faced by his industry. "The problem with boats is that almost anyone with a shed, a can of resin and some fiberglass can start producing boats." Or, to put it another way, boats can be built in the simplest of ways, or can become the most elaborate constructions imaginable, with every trade and craft involved.

For building hulls, there is a wide choice of materials available: plastics, wood, metals and others, including ferrocement. By far the most popular of these over the last 25 years, for all kinds of sailing boats and other small craft, has been plastics. What is generally referred to as glassfibre in the UK, or fiberglass in the US, is more descriptively known as glass-reinforced plastics, or GRP. However, the plastics (which are resins) vary and the reinforcement is not always of glass; these variations and other methods and materials used in boat construction are now reviewed.

FIBERGLASS CONSTRUCTION

A production-boat builder contemplating a long run of the same design of boat will invariably build the hulls in a female mold. First of all, a plug is constructed. This is, in effect, the designer's shape for the hull, accurately shaped in wood and with a perfect surface. From this plug is made the fiberglass female mold, smooth inside and constructed for rigidity and continual use. It is in this mold that the glass and resin are laid up to make a hull. Obviously, the mold can be used more than once to produce a series of hulls, and more than one mold can be produced from the plug to enable production to occur in more than one place. Similarly, in the case of international one-design classes, there is a master plug with female molds in the different countries where the class is sailed, from which hulls can be made as required.

A female mold is also made for the deck and cabin trunk structure, including such details as mountings for fittings and other irregularities in shape. Before the deck structure is fitted on to the hull, light moldings for the cabin interior, including bulkheads to give essential rigidity, are

A modern boatbuilder in operation

dropped into place. Much other work is also done inside the hull before the 'lid' is put on. When this is finally done, there are various methods used to ensure that the hull/deck joint is strong and totally watertight. A major attraction of fiberglass in this context is that, in principle, sealing and attachment are easily possible using further layers of glass and resin, which set strongly and adhere completely.

Another method of construction involves using a male mold. The hull is constructed so that its inner skin is against the mold; the outer skin then goes on last

Working with Kevlar
1 *On this 18-m (60-ft) hull, a first skin of Kevlar is laid over the entire hull.*
2 *The Kevlar is then covered with a layer of E-glass; further glass and filler are put on for the outer skin.*
3 *The hull has been turned right side up, revealing the inner skin of Kevlar. At this stage, the frames are put in.*

1

and requires fairing off. This system contrasts with using a female mold, where the outer skin is laid first against the mold. Boats are built on male molds when they are one-offs, but considerable manual work with sanding machines is always required in rubbing down the rough fiberglass on the outside of the hull in order to achieve a fair surface.

POLYESTER RESIN

The raw materials that have enabled the modern production boat to have so much appeal as a rot-proof, watertight and low maintenance boat come in drums (of resin) and rolls (of fiber). The most commonly used resin is polyester, because it has the lowest price of all the suitable resins and is easy to work with. It does have the disadvantage of weight, which is always an enemy of performance, and for this reason may not be the first choice for racing boats. Polyester, of course, is not confined to sailboats, and is used for hundreds of other types of craft, from minesweepers to the smallest rowboat and every kind of motor boat.

Like all resins in boatbuilding, polyester is a two-part material: when a catalyst is added, the mixture starts to cure. Mixing proportions, temperature in the workshop, and the manner in which it is worked into the fibers to exclude the air bubbles are all very important; yet a finished boat will not reveal if these manufacturing essentials have been ignored. For this reason, boats are frequently classified, that is

given a certificate by the American Bureau of Shipping, Lloyd's Register of Shipping, or other similar classification societies. For production boats, the relevant society cannot oversee every hull, but it will check the facilities in the building shed and make spot checks on the earlier approved resins and mixes.

For a number of years after the introduction of polyester-built boats, it was thought that the material was impervious to water. This has turned out not to be the case, and fiberglass boats can suffer osmosis or blistering due to water penetrating the surface and combining chemically with certain components in the material. These might be traces of undercured resin, the catalyst or other additives; thus the precision of construction determines whether blistering develops or not. There are a number of measures that can be taken to prevent blistering, such as overcoating with water-resistant barriers, but luckily, this problem is restricted to polyester resin only.

Polyester can be painted with two-part polyurethane paint, but this is rarely done on production boats unless to special order. Instead, a pigment, usually white, is added to the gel coat, that is the outer layer of resin in the female mold, making the color integral with the fiberglass. Modern pigments and additives ensure that the outside of the hull remains at a high gloss for many years, requiring only simple cleaning and an occasional waxing to give it an extra shine.

VINYLESTER RESIN

A resin not unlike polyester, vinylester is slightly more expensive and has better tensile and compressive strength. This means that less material can be used for a given hull, saving weight in the process.

EPOXY RESIN

Superior in most respects to polyester, epoxy resin is not used for series production of hulls as it is more expensive. It also had the reputation of being 'difficult to work' at the builders, although techniques have now been developed to handle most resins. A major property of epoxy resin is its excellent adhesion. It is used for reinforcement and for bonding parts of the polyester hull to each other or to wood and metal components, and is therefore extremely useful for repairs. It is also superior to polyester in its resistance to water absorption and to abrasion. A weight saving of 30% in the entire hull can be made, although there are other preferred systems that incorporate the epoxy resin at a lower cost.

BOATBUILDING FIBERS

The concept of reinforcing plastics with strengthening materials can be seen in the use of steel rods in the building industry to reinforce concrete. That comparison is crude, for the reinforcement agents used in boat building are fibers of a fine nature and of many complex designs and arrangements. The fibers are woven in various weights and exist in chopped strands, in

2

3

rovings (rolls of glass-like string) or in numerous weaves.

For standard boats, E-glass is widely used: extruded glass filament with good stiffness, strength and weathering properties. It also has the advantage for production boats of being of relatively low cost and available in a wide range of fabrics. Additionally, there are different qualities of glass: R-glass and S-glass both have better mechanical properties, but once again these are more expensive. However, weight can be saved, if this is necessary, by using less glass, and because the basic strands are finer, the resin can be better absorbed, thus giving more intrinsic strength to the hull.

Other reinforcement fibers include aramid fiber, of which the best known is Kevlar because it is seen in sails: it has a low weight and high tensile strength. Kevlar can be used to make a complete hull or as local strengthening in a polyester or other hull. Carbon fiber, a development of the aerospace industry, has been in existence for many years, but it is expensive, brittle and consists in its raw state of long, extruded, graphite fibers of nearly pure carbon. With high compressive strength, it can be used for additional strength in high-stress areas; unlike Kevlar and fiberglass, which come in mats and multidirectional rovings, carbon is unidirectional and can be used to withstand only a specific directional strain. In the late 1970s, it was used for keelboat rudders, but the numerous failures demonstrated its unsuitability for such applications. Since then, methods have been developed for using it more extensively in hulls, especially as a complete inner skin.

HI-TECH CONSTRUCTION

Hi-tech is a rather loose term in boat construction, but it implies the use of the more expensive artificial resins and fibers in combinations that achieve outstanding strength and lightness: builders have adopted the term composite construction.

The kinds of boat for which hi-tech building takes place will typically be those for which cost is not a major consideration, for which a particular race or series is in prospect, or where the builder specializes in custom building and has little to do with production boats. The hull specification will be by a leading yacht designer advised by the builder and suppliers of the special materials. Among the methods used are sandwich or core construction, the use of pre-preg material, and local hull engineering. A number of the techniques used have been borrowed or adapted from the aerospace industry.

SANDWICH CONSTRUCTION

Sandwich or core construction is nothing very new and, in the case of using end-grain balsa between fiberglass skins, is hardly hi-tech. But this method does give rigidity and some weight saving, and is superior in almost all respects to ordinary fiberglass construction. However, the outer skin is bound to be thinner than that found in a production-boat hull, and so more liable to forms of impact damage. It is, therefore, especially favored for decks and top structures where such damage is unlikely and where flat surfaces need added rigidity and strength.

Lightweight foam cores are an alternative to balsa. These go under various names, such as Airex and Plasticell, both of which are PVC foams, and Klegecell, which is a cross-linked PVC/di-isocyanate mixture. More effective still is Nomex, the trade term for a honeycomb made of aramid paper. However, it is three times the price of balsa or foam.

PRE-PREG MATERIAL

Pre-pregnated material consists of mat, weavings or tape already mixed with the resin and catalyst by the manufacturer but which will not cure until a certain level of heat is applied. The cloth comes with protective coverings on both faces which is stripped off as it is placed in position. The great advantage of this material is that the mix is exactly as determined by the specialist manufacturer.

In order to heat the material, there need to be electrically heated molds and/or heated 'blankets' that cover the surface. This has been difficult for the boatbuilding industry, but development has been along the lines of lower temperatures that are used in the aerospace industry. A typical pre-preg material might be a mixture of carbon fiber, aramid fiber, epoxy resin and additives.

Composite Construction
1 *Carbon fiber is wetted prior to use.*
2 *The carbon is placed in position on the hull.*
3 *A second layer of carbon is laid at an angle to the first layer.*
4 *Kevlar is then added, as is a further layer of fiberglass.*
5 *The hull is cooked in a tent at a high temperature that cures the materials, achieving an immensely strong and stiff hull.*

1

2

LOCAL HULL ENGINEERING

With pre-preg items, it becomes possible to design a boat with different thicknesses of hull, using different pre-pregs to make the ends of the boat lighter and to strengthen such stress areas as the keel and the rigging bases. Because the resin does not cure until heat is applied, the whole process of lay-up can be far more precise than the established ways of rolling resin into cloth. Pieces of material can be positioned exactly, and only then is the heat applied to cure the resin. The use of local hull engineering, pre-preg materials and sandwich construction has contributed to the ability of high-speed, large multihulls to put up increasing speeds on ocean crossings and the high performance of maxi ocean racers.

METAL

Absolute answers as to the best form of hull construction are not possible, since whatever the cost and complication, the preference of the potential owner plays a big part in the choice of hull material.

Until recent years, light alloy or various marine-grade aluminums were favored in racing boats for their lightness, rigidity and strength, but their use has been overtaken by composites. Aluminum has never been inexpensive, and it requires a specialist yard to build to it. Problems encountered during building include the difficulty of achieving a fair surface on the metal hull, corrosion and electrolysis, all of which require preventive measures.

Steel is still favored when strength counts above all. When *Joshua* was sailed thousands of miles around the world by Bernard Moitessier in 1968-9, it suffered no lasting damage to its heavy, steel hull, despite numerous knock-downs in severe storms (see p 78). Similarly *Northern Light*, designed to be taken to the Arctic and Antarctic and into the ice, was constructed of steel (see pp 52-3). Both boats, virtual sister ships, were designed by Jean Knocker (France).

Steel has an appeal for amateur boatbuilders who have welding facilities; for the same reason, it can easily be repaired in most places in the world or where there is a commercial shipyard. The disadvantages of the material are its weight and the potential for corrosion, although these factors have not prevented boats, and ships of all sizes, being constructed from it.

FERRO-CEMENT

Ferro-cement is a mode of construction whereby a framework of steel rods and then mesh is formed to the desired shape of the hull. Layers of fine-consistency cement are then impregnated into the structure. The steel and the cement are relatively cheap, and many amateurs have built boats in this way. The result is a strong hull which can resist impact damage, even hard knocks; it can pulverize locally but is unlikely to split or fracture. The resulting hull is heavy, however, and the finish is bound to look a shade coarse: ferro-cement cannot be concealed.

WOOD

Looking at row upon row of white fiberglass boats moored in the harbors of the world, it is hard to believe that until the 1950s almost every boat was constructed of wood, mostly plank by plank in carvel, that is edge to edge, or in clinker or lapstrake, that is with overlapping planks. These methods of building boats are preserved only in a few places and for some craft in less developed countries. Initial cost, weight, lack of strength, poor resistance to rot and marine borers, swelling and shrinkage with moisture and high maintenance costs all count against wood as a boat-building material.

But there are people who want their boats to be of wood. For them, and for some restricted-class dinghies, wood can be used in conjunction with modern processes to overcome a number of its disadvantages. Some of these have been practiced for very many years, such as the use of molded veneers glued with waterproof glues, a technique known as cold molding. Wood of all kinds is still used for fittings and joinery below deck, and even on occasion for deck fittings such as handholds, toerails and cockpit seats.

For hull construction the most common treatment of wood in order to strengthen it is to saturate veneers of wood with epoxy resin and then to glue them. This can seal the wood against rot and improve its compression strength. This is the best remedy yet against the change of shape caused by sea and air moisture.

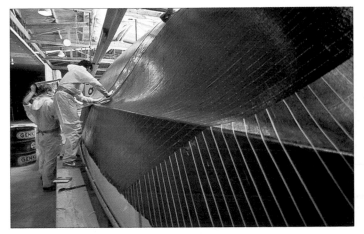

3

4

5

BUILDING A WOODEN BOAT

For more than 2,000 years, the 'natural' look for ships and boats was layer upon layer of wooden planking. In boats, this technique was refined to insure that the planks fitted together well to produce a beautifully finished hull, but the fact remained that what was being constructed was a wooden basket with caulking pushed between the planks to seal the gaps. The onset of riveted steel and then fiberglass at last insured a reasonably watertight hull, but some owners still yearn for a boat that 'looks like a boat', one that is built of wood.

This desire for a 'proper boat' has insured that work has continued on ways to improve wooden boatbuilding, cutting out some of the disadvantages of rot, leaking, bad joints and the difficulty of attaining the correct shape, that come with working in wood. But the fact remains that building a wooden boat is an expensive proposition and is always a one-off construction. There is no possibility of economies with a series production, although a wooden hull, once constructed, can be used as a plug for a series of similar, fiberglass hulls.

The wooden-hulled cruiser-racer, photographed in its various stages of production on the next three pages, was built to a design by Rob Humphreys, a leading designer of IOR and other offshore boats. The builder specialized in one-off boats, but did not consider this commission as particularly hi-tech, although his skills with adhesives and weight saving were no doubt put to good use.

The hull is a combination of different woods, with fiberglass and aluminum for certain items. The keel and stem – the backbone of the boat – are of laminated mahogany; solid members have not been used for more than 30 years, for laminated members are both cheaper and stronger. The hull was built up in 4-mm (0.16-in) strips of ply and wood running in different directions – the first skin of marine plywood, the second and third of western red cedar, and the fourth and final skin of Khaya mahogany, which is what gives the boat its planked look. After this treatment, paint would have disguised such fine work, so the boat was varnished.

In this particular boat, an aluminum frame was made which was fitted inside the hull; this structure takes the strain of the lead keel, the pull of the shrouds, and the pressures from the mast step, where the major strains on the hull can occur. The frame runs aft to support the engine, giving the boat a kind of metal skeleton. The use of a metal frame is not the only method of strengthening available, for additional layers of wood or laminates could well have been used instead.

The 11-m (36-ft) cruiser-racer Apriori *finished, afloat, equipped and ready to sail*

1

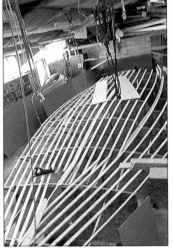

2

3

4

The 15 Stages

1 *The shape of the hull is reproduced by making a frame mold out of soft wood, which is attached to the laminated mahogany stem and keel. The frames, which are derived from the cross-sections of the boat, have been carefully shaped from full-sized patterns drawn on a smooth floor according to the designer's drawings. They are erected upside down at the correct intervals to make an inverted hull shape. Stringers of wood are tacked into place between the frames to give the mold more strength. The entire frame mold is later disposed of as it is not part of the finished boat.*
2 *The deck, to be made of fiberglass sandwich with a core of 12 mm (0.48 in) divinycell foam, is constructed in the same way as the hull, using a frame mold and soft-wood battens.*
3 *The deck superstructure is also made of fiberglass sandwich. Its mold is of carefully shaped plywood. Over this mold will be laid a layer of glass and resin, then one of foam, and then a further layer of impregnated glass, followed by gel coat, which gives the final watertight surface.*
4 *On the hull, the first, inner layer of marine ply is laid athwartships (across the boat) strip by strip. Only that part of the ply that is not covered up inside the boat by a locker or piece of furniture will be visible.*
5 *The hull now has its first, inner, skin of plywood in place.*

5

6 The second skin of wood, this time of western red cedar, has been laid in strips, edge to edge, at a 45° angle to the first skin of ply. It is glued into place with epoxy-based, waterproof adhesives. The third skin, again of cedar, is laid at an acute angle to the second skin and then glued. Because the three skins run in different directions, the hull has immense strength, able to withstand the pressures of stress and tension put on it by the ever-changing surface of the sea, by the sails, by the weight of the keel and the rudder, and by the flexing loads of the rig as the mast pushes down and the shrouds and stays pull up. At this stage, much labor is exerted in fairing off each layer of wood, and this, with other attention to detail, makes the building time of a boat of this type usually about six to eight months.

7 The deck is now finished. Being relatively flat, it does not have the natural rigidity of the curved hull; the use of a sandwich construction compensates for this. Because the deck is on top of the boat, its weight has been kept deliberately low.

8 The fourth and final skin – pieces of Khaya mahogany carefully chosen for their appearance – are glued fore and aft on the hull. Once in position, many hours are spent in fairing the surface; sanding machines are used at first, but toward the end, muscle power and flat sandpaper are best to achieve the required fair and smooth finish. The stem is cut and faired at this stage while, out of sight in this photograph, the mahogany and plywood stern is being fitted and shaped to the hull.

9 With this boat, the surface below the waterline is covered with a layer of fiberglass and epoxy resin. This insures that the permanently immersed part of the hull absorbs no water.

10 After the first coat of polyurethane varnish has been applied, the boat is lifted off its frame mold and turned the right way up. The hull has sufficient rigidity to maintain its shape in the boatyard, but requires more strength before it is fitted out and goes to sea. Therefore, bulkheads of ample marine ply are now inserted inside the hull to give structural integrity. Other work inside the hull is undertaken at this stage, before the deck is put on.

6

7

8

9

10

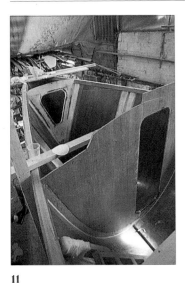

11

12

13

14

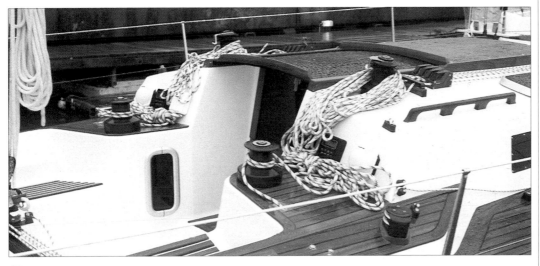

15

11 Two of the forward bulkheads are bonded to the hull by resin and glass. These are shaped to allow access fore and aft inside the hull.

12 The deck is fastened to the hull: the join has to be both strong and completely watertight. Various techniques are used to ensure this, using fiberglass or Kevlar and resin to create a final seal on any join or initial fastening.

13 On this boat, it was decided to have a 9-mm (0.36-in) teak deck laid over the fiberglass sandwich deck, in a traditional planked effect. The deck is sealed and, when the planks are laid, caulking is poured between them. A teak surface gives a good foothold and is easy to maintain, requiring only bleach and a good scrub for it to remain pristine.

14 Considerable work above and below decks remains to be done, with the accommodation, all in wood, to be constructed. In a boat of this type, the furniture has to be strong to withstand heavy treatment, such as the crew grabbing it or being knocked against it while at sea.

15 The positions of the deck fittings were decided at the design stage, for such items as winches and handholds cause heavy, local strains. Where these pieces of equipment are sited in a weak area, the fastenings are bolted through the deck and secured with backing plates; this procedure prevents the deck from crushing, lifting or leaking. During the construction of the boat, large amounts of wood shavings, fiberglass, dust and dirt accumulate in the hull. Time is taken to remove every particle from inside and outside the boat before the varnishes and paints are applied in a dust-free paint shop.

AN OFFSHORE RACING BOAT

Offshore racing boats are designed and equipped to sail at the best possible speed in all weather. Racing under the IOR or other current rating rules, a regional or local handicapping system or as a one-design class, racing boats have evolved from the gradual refinement of cruising boats used for ocean racing and have also borrowed features from both racing dinghies and keelboats.

Although there are some variations, the gear and fittings seen on this 11.5-m (38-ft) cruiser-racer are common to most racing boats of this size. The priorities for fitting out any ocean racer are convenience, and swift and safe handling, for in strong winds or in a rough sea, the deck is an ever-moving platform and everything happens very quickly and very noisily. The rules have always prohibited mechanical or stored power, but loads are too heavy in a boat of this size for unaided human strength: thus an array of winches, tackles and jammers are spread around the deck and rig. The total length of wire and rope involved in rigging and controlling a boat are considerable: care is taken to save weight on the deck and even more in the rig, and all items of equipment must be securely fastened when used at sea.

1 *Headsail foil encloses forestay and is fitted with twin grooves, permitting one headsail to be hoisted before another is lowered; there is thus always one sail working all the time.*
2 *Babystay supports mast about half way up and can be tightened to assist mast bend; it is detached here to enable the spinnaker pole to swing across during a gybe.*
3 *Spinnaker pole fittings and shackles are designed so that the pole is released from the guy during a gybe and the shackles cannot open when the sail is flogging.*
4 *Spinnaker sheets are doubled up on both sides of the boat, with one pair of sheets and guys trimming the spinnaker and one pair not in use until the next gybe. During a gybe, both sets are in use.*
5 *The pole is controlled by the foreguy which stops it flying up, a topping lift which supports its weight when there is no upward pull from the sail, and the spinnaker guy which adjusts the angle of the pole and therefore the sail to the wind. A lazy guy on the windward side receives the pole after a gybe.*
6 *Mainsail reefing is undertaken by pulling the luff down to hooks at the gooseneck and hauling down the leech cringle by a control line that runs via the boom down to the deck. Each line is a different color.*
7 *Color-coded control lines make for quick differentiation, when releasing, hoisting or adjusting lines.*
8 *Ventilators are unobtrusive and low on the deck; essential in heavy weather when all hatches are shut.*
9 *Handholds, which also stop feet sliding, are a major safety device in rough weather or a big swell.*

10 *Aluminum toerail extends right around the boat, stopping feet sliding over the side and enabling gear to be clipped on to its water drainholes. It is a strengthening member where the hull joins the deck.*
11 *Kicking strap for flattening the sail upwind may be of various designs, but must be capable of instant release in order to spill wind from mainsail in event of spinnaker broach.*
12 *Shockcord on the coachroof acts as stowage for the reefing and other lines, which would otherwise slide overboard or trip up the crew.*
13 *Mainhatch must be watertight when closed and also able to open unassisted from inside or out while totally unable to slide open on its own account, even if the boat is inverted.*
14 *Steering compasses on both sides so that the helmsman has optimum reading of them wherever he sits.*

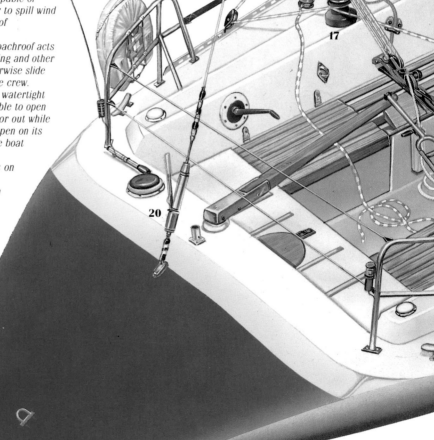

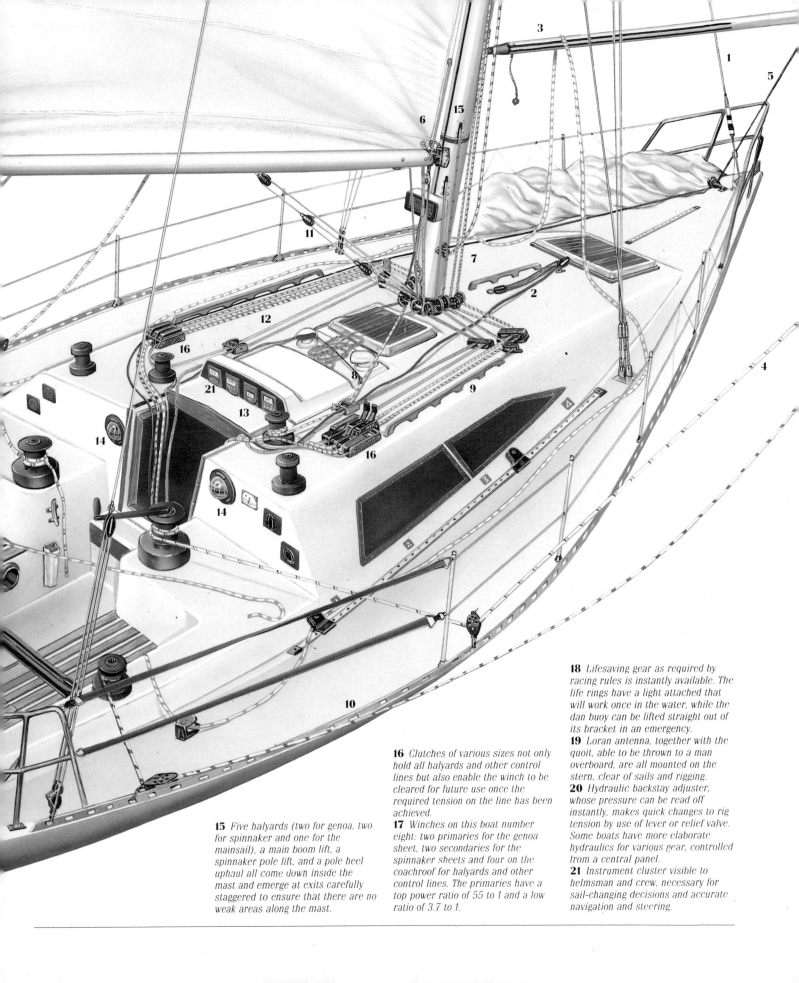

15 Five halyards (two for genoa, two for spinnaker and one for the mainsail), a main boom lift, a spinnaker pole lift, and a pole heel uphaul all come down inside the mast and emerge at exits carefully staggered to ensure that there are no weak areas along the mast.

16 Clutches of various sizes not only hold all halyards and other control lines but also enable the winch to be cleared for future use once the required tension on the line has been achieved.

17 Winches on this boat number eight: two primaries for the genoa sheet, two secondaries for the spinnaker sheets and four on the coachroof for halyards and other control lines. The primaries have a top power ratio of 55 to 1 and a low ratio of 3.7 to 1.

18 Lifesaving gear as required by racing rules is instantly available. The life rings have a light attached that will work once in the water, while the dan buoy can be lifted straight out of its bracket in an emergency.

19 Loran antenna, together with the quoit, able to be thrown to a man overboard, are all mounted on the stern, clear of sails and rigging.

20 Hydraulic backstay adjuster, whose pressure can be read off instantly, makes quick changes to rig tension by use of lever or relief valve. Some boats have more elaborate hydraulics for various gear, controlled from a central panel.

21 Instrument cluster visible to helmsman and crew, necessary for sail-changing decisions and accurate navigation and steering.

A RACING DINGHY

The 505 dinghy is one of the most demanding racing dinghies to sail, requiring considerable skill and agility on the part of its two-man crew in order to obtain race-winning speed. With a large sail area and a fully adjustable rig, this 5.05-m (16-ft 7-in) dinghy has numerous controls, all of which are color-coded in order to avoid confusion. These controls must be easy to handle – ball-bearing blocks and multi-block systems help obtain a good leverage – and within reach of both helm and crew at all times. Where necessary, control lines are led to both sides of the boat so that they can be adjusted on either tack; some, like the genoa and spinnaker sheets, are continuous. Every control is operated manually, with the exception of the compass, used for detecting wind shifts on the long upwind legs of a race course.

1 *One-part rudder and tiller, designed to eradicate any slackness in the steering.*
2 *Transom flaps to remove water from the boat as it sails along.*
3 *Toestraps for helmsman to secure himself inside the boat while sitting out in windy weather.*
4 *Tiller extension to enable helmsman to sit out and steer.*
5 *Continuous spinnaker sheet; continuous sheets avoid rope ends getting caught up or tangled in the boat.*
6 *Multi-part mainsheet to adjust angle of mainsail.*
7 *Continuous spinnaker uphaul and downhaul.*
8 *Continuous line for furling the genoa when coming ashore.*
9 *Control line for raising and lowering the centerboard.*
10 *Self-bailer to remove water from the inside of the boat while sailing.*
11 *Continuous genoa sheet.*
12 *Multi-block system to control the tension of the genoa; because this dinghy has no forestay, the fore and aft tension of the rig is controlled by tightening or loosening the genoa.*
13 *Control line to adjust tension of the shrouds and thus the fore and aft bend of the mast. The line leads to a lever system under the foredeck which connects to wires led through the sidedecks to the shrouds.*
14 *Control line for Cunningham hole to adjust the luff tension of the mainsail. This is tightened to flatten the sail when sailing upwind.*
15 *Control line to move kicking strap, which adjusts the fullness of the mainsail.*
16 *Trimming line to adjust angle of genoa sheet.*
17 *Trimming line to adjust angle of spinnaker sheet.*
18 *Sealed buoyancy tanks to give the hull flotation.*
19 *Inspection hatch to examine inside of buoyancy tank.*
20 *Outhaul for mainsail to control tension along the foot.*
21 *Spinnaker pole downhaul to control angle of pole and thus the fullness of the sail.*

22 *Spinnaker pole to secure spinnaker when sailing downwind.*
23 *Elastic control line to guide spinnaker pole along the boom, where it is stored when not in use.*
24 *Control line to release spinnaker pole from mast when it is no longer needed.*
25 *Compass to detect wind shifts and indicate bearings; an essential aid in starting tactics.*
26 *Trapeze to suspend crew out on the windward side of the boat in order to stabilize it.*
27 *Genoa furling equipment.*
28 *Spinnaker downhaul to guide spinnaker into chute.*
29 *Spinnaker chute to store spinnaker when not in use.*
30 *Transparent windows to enable the crew to see through the sails.*
31 *Mainsail and genoa wire halyards emerge from the mast; the genoa halyard is led to a multi-block system to control genoa tension, while the mainsail halyard is hooked on to a metal rack to secure it.*

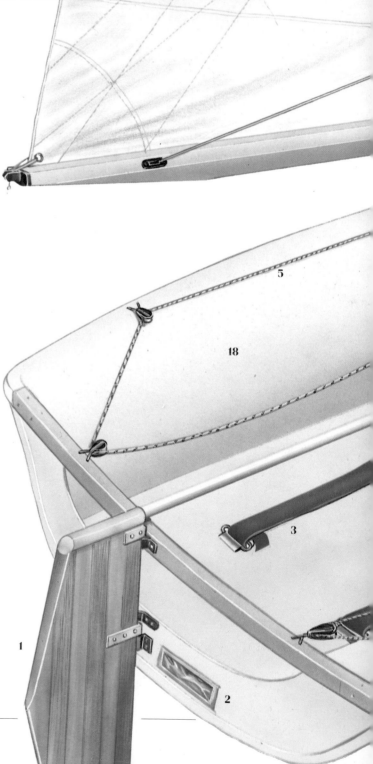

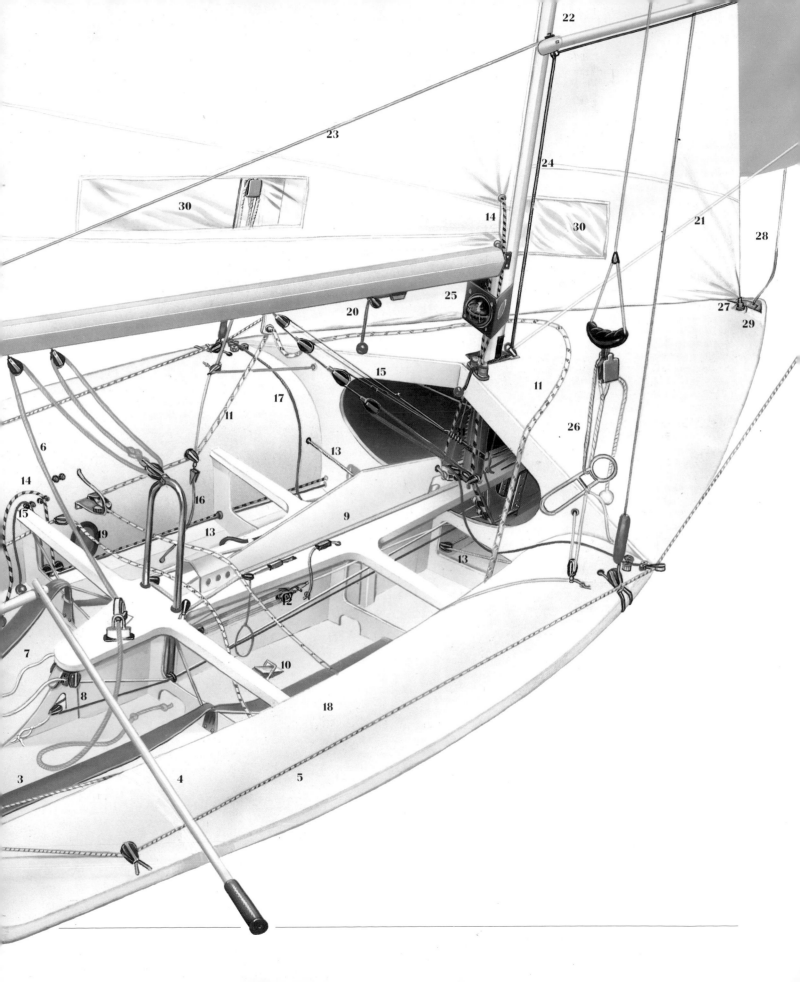

MODERN BOAT EQUIPMENT

The materials used for deck hardware include aluminum, which is usually anodized, marine-grade stainless steel and heavy-duty plastics, including PTFE, nylon and delrin. Moving parts are often eased by stainless-steel bearings.

Because electrical power is a commodity to be conserved on board a boat, most items of deck hardware are manually operated, designed to increase human muscle power and speed in handling sheets, halyards, control lines and sails. In any case, many racing classes, and the racing rules, specify the use of manually operated equipment only.

CONTROL OF SHEETS

Winches are the greatest aid to handling lines and are essential for coping with big loads, particularly mainsail or genoa sheets or spinnaker halyards. Once a line is winched in, jammers or clutches can hold it instantly, thus freeing the winch for use with another line. A number of devices around the deck solve the requirement for releasing sheets or halyards under load.

Blocks *(right) are used to lead sheets, halyards and control lines around the boat. They come in a variety of sizes and numerous variations, depending on the loads they have to carry.*

Single block *(left) with needle bearings to cut friction and stand up to heavy use at sea; for use on a large boat.*

Snap-shackle snatch block *(right) for clipping on to a line already in place.*

Lever jammer *(below) to lock a sheet, enabling one winch to do several jobs in succession. A racing boat will have a number of these grouped together.*

Ratchet block *(below) with one-way movement of control lines for easier hand control.*

Mini-block *(right) for dinghy control lines.*

Cam jammer *(above) for holding a control line; common on keelboats and dinghies.*

Winch *(above) made of aluminum, bronze and stainless steel, for handling sheets, halyards and control lines. Gearing gives the winch at least two speed options by winding the handle in opposite directions.*

Genoa sheet car *(below) with rollers, that moves on a track to the critical position to set the sail.*

Group of sheaves *(above) to separate and organize sheets.*

Top-hinged snap-shackle *(above) for use on spinnaker sheets. Easily released, the shackle will remain firmly shut even when the sail is flogging.*

Clutch *(left) to grip halyard or sheet and release it instantly under load.*

Tiller extension, *the size of which depends on the size of boat. Enables the helmsman to sit out on the windward side.*

FIXED FITTINGS

Every boat carries a number of fittings that are not for sail or rig handling but which remain fixed on deck. Among these are handholds, toe-rails, ventilators, pre-manufactured hatches and chain plates. The demands of the sea do not change, but new materials, which weigh less and have less bulk, alter specific designs from time to time.

PERSONAL SECURITY

In addition to the life preserver and floating light shown below, a boat would also carry a horseshoe life ring, dye marker to color the sea, a drogue and, in certain waters, shark repellent.

Automatic floating light, *invariably attached to a life ring. Carried on board bulb downward, it floats the right way up and switches on when in the water.*

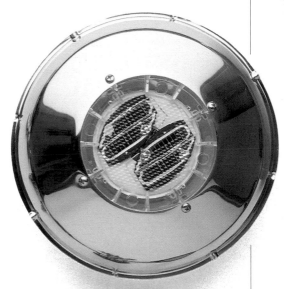

Solar-powered ventilator *(above) driven by the rays of the sun to circulate air through the boat when it is not sailing. In rough weather the ventilator can be plugged to stop water entering the boat.*

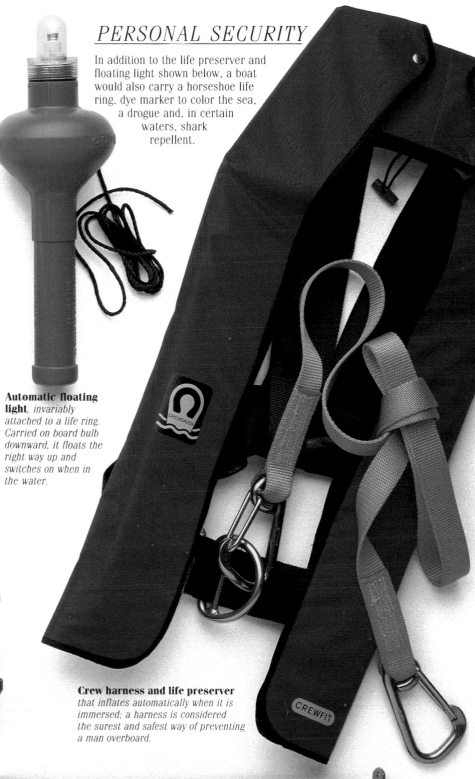

Seacock *to enable an inlet or outlet below the waterline to be shut off as a precaution against flooding.*

Tricolor navigation light *with powerful filament bulb.*

Crew harness and life preserver *that inflates automatically when it is immersed; a harness is considered the surest and safest way of preventing a man overboard.*

ELECTRONIC EQUIPMENT

A vast array of electronic equipment for sailing boats is currently produced across the world, with many new models introduced for both technical and marketing reasons. Since the late 1980s, the read-outs given are usually digital, which makes them easy for the crew to read at a glance. Some instruments have retained the analog (clockface) dials, which are more convenient for an assessment of, for instance, wind angle, where slight changes are better registered by a needle moving position than by a digital reading. Whatever their read-outs, all electronic instruments used at sea must be lightweight, water-resistant, strong enough to resist accidental knocking by the crew, and, above all, absolutely reliable.

PERFORMANCE

There are two pieces of information that are of continuous importance to the helmsman and navigator: apparent wind speed and apparent wind direction. True wind speed and direction can then be calculated from these. In addition, the depth of water and the boat's speed are useful to know.

Digital read-out *(right) giving the navigator below deck numerous sailing data, such as boat speed, distance covered, true and apparent wind direction and speed, depth and battery voltage. The analog dials (below) for specific pieces of data are placed on deck.*

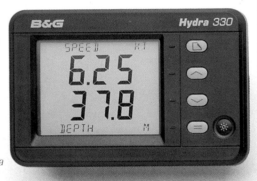

Magnified wind dial

Boat speed dial

Depth-sounding *off the bow of a Dutch sloop, c1630 (above)*

Depth dial (right)

NAVIGATION

Position-finding systems give either continuous or sporadic (timed) readings of latitude and longitude: Loran or Decca transmit the whole time the boat is in the appropriate area. As the sets get smaller and their electrical consumption less, even small boats can now afford to pinpoint their position with accuracy.

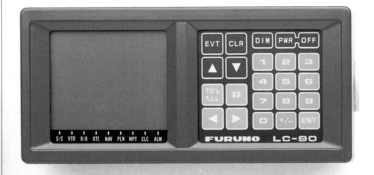

Loran position finder *(above) used especially in US coastal waters. Latitude and longitude readings from land-based radio beacons are recorded, while alternative displays indicate course, bearings and ETA.*

19th-century navigation *by the sun or moon, using a sextant (right)*

Satnav receiver *(below), taking in information from a satellite with additional input from an electronic compass and log.*

DIRECTION

Modern magnetic compasses come in a variety of mountings and suspensions in liquid to suit almost any deck or cockpit layout. Although many boats now carry an electronic compass, a magnetic compass is a prerequisite should the power fail.

Electronic compass *can be placed at an optimum sighting position for the helmsman, regardless of magnetism, since the master unit is protected and isolated below deck from adverse magnetic forces.*

SIGNALLING

For boats close to shore, a VHF radio is virtually standard, while those sailing in mid-ocean use an SSB radio. Numerous radio channels are allotted for specific purposes for all types of shipping.

Emergency position-indicating radio beacon *which sends out a distress call independently of main electrical supply. Can be used on board, in a liferaft or in the water.*

Hand-held radio antenna *connected to the boat's VHF set, to be used if the boat is dismasted and loses its masthead antenna.*

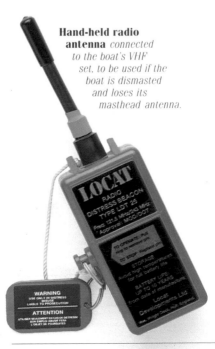

SELF-STEERING

Skippers can choose from a wide variety of self-steering autopilots to relieve them of the chore of steering the boat for the whole duration of the voyage. However, most races ban the use of such equipment.

A self-steering vane *on the stern of Francis Chichester's sloop Gipsy Moth III (left)*

Modern autopilot systems *(below), fitted to thousands of boats, consists of a main control unit with integral compass, and a drive unit, connected to the boat's wheel by a belt. Once the boat's direction is established by the helmsman, the autopilot takes over; small corrections can be made by the button controls on the main unit. In addition, a hand-held control unit enables corrections to be made from anywhere on the boat. The system can work a tiller rather than a wheel, and has the option of a windvane to override the autopilot.*

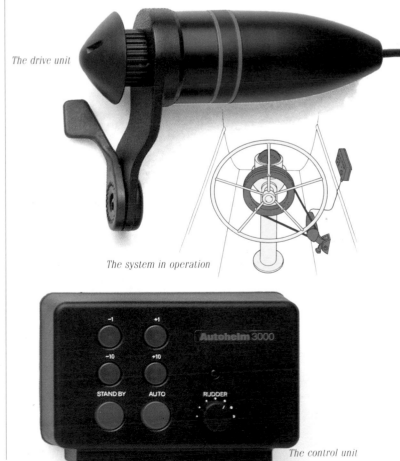

The drive unit

The system in operation

The control unit

SAILING WITH ELECTRONICS

Attitudes to sailing in open water have been profoundly changed in recent years by the wide use of microchip and computer technology on board boats. With the exception of dinghies and day-racing keelboats, modern boats are packed with electronics. The technological development of this equipment has allowed the instruments and hardware to become physically smaller and their current consumption to drop to very low levels. Without these two qualities, it would not be possible for sailboats in particular to be so generously equipped: powerboats, generating electricity all the time, have no such difficulties, but even they would be hard pressed to accommodate the equipment available a few decades ago, the size of which made its installation possible only on commercial vessels. Price has also been a restricting factor, but today's boat generally has the same ears and eyes as a big ship.

It is often forgotten how large the number of wrecks was in the days of sail; according to official records, the number of vessels wrecked "on the coasts and in the seas" off Great Britain and Ireland in 1867 totalled 2,513. Of these, 656 were total wrecks and 97 lost by collision; the rest were stranded and damaged, while 1,333 people lost their lives. As late as the 1950s, before modern aids reached an acceptable level of reliability, there were numerous strandings and many casualties. Apart from the difficulties for all sailing ships in beating off a lee shore, the perpetual problem was not knowing one's exact position.

Until the advent of electronics, sailing vessels were still sailing largely blind, finding their way by dead reckoning and sextant. Dead reckoning, simply explained, is the continuous plotting of the course and the distance run by compass and log, but such a calculation is bedevilled by uncertainty over the course because of the often unknown impact of tides, currents and drift, and having to know exactly which direction the boat has steered. The distance run was also difficult to calculate because of the currents and errors in logs, the distance instruments. If the latter was wrong, a cliff could suddenly appear through the mist or land fail to turn up when expected.

The sextant can give a single position line from a celestial object such as the sun or stars, but not if cloud covers the sky. In rough weather in a small boat, it is difficult to get a sextant sight with any accuracy. An intermediate aid was radio direction finding, which meant tuning to a coastal station or aerobeacon and identifying its morse signal. A miniature directional antenna with attached compass picked up the signal and gave a compass reading to help the navigator plot the boat's position relative to the signal's bearing. Such a system is still used today as a back-up, but reception can be poor and the signal difficult to locate; taking readings also involves physical activity in rough weather and takes time to obtain a satisfactory result.

CONTEMPORARY ELECTRONIC AIDS

Contemporary electronic aids fall into several categories, notably depth sounders, navigational inputs, position fixers, hyperbolic systems, and on-board computers. Most give digital read-outs using light-emitting diodes (LED) or liquid crystal displays (LCD), although some are fitted with incandescent filaments. The power required is ever smaller and all pieces of equipment operate off 12- or 24-volt circuits. The bigger the boat, the more batteries it will carry; they can be recharged from the engine or a generator. Modern alternators and voltage-control systems assist in this necessary recharging.

DEPTH SOUNDERS

Depth sounders to measure the depth of water below a boat are not new and were in use many years before the other systems reviewed below. A wide variety exist, but essential to them all is a transducer in the hull of the boat: this receives an echo of its own signal from the seabed which is then recorded as a depth on a digital read-out at the chart table or in the cockpit.

Digital read-out of depth is probably best, because it is instant and unmistakable, but depths can be read off a display that shows moving traces on charts, traces that show the bottom contour. A simple analog dial uses this information to show the changes in the depth under the boat; analog dials are favored by those who like to observe the speed at which the needle on the dial may be falling. The commonest depth sounder is a circular dial with a rotating neon bulb against which the depth is read off; this can also show minor echoes, such as fish, or produce an extra echo if the bottom is soft mud with more solid ground a little deeper.

INPUT FOR NAVIGATION

Although a boat may well be steered by a magnetic compass, which does not need power of any kind, it can also have an

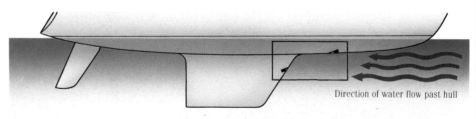

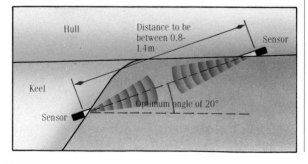

Boat Speed Sensor *A modern electronic log consists of two sensors, one on the leading edge of the keel, the other further forward on the hull. These two transmit sound signals to each other; as the velocity of these signals is affected by the speed of the water between them, a read-out can be obtained as to the exact speed of the boat through the water.*

Direction of water flow past hull

Hull

Distance to be between 0.8–1.4 m

Sensor

Keel

Sensor

Optimum angle of 20°

Sensor

electronic compass, which may be called a heading sensor unit or some such name. Its advantage is that it can provide input concerning the course both to another instrument and, through visual display units in the cockpit and by the chart table, to the helmsman and navigator.

Information about distance and speed come from some form of electronic log. This is often prone to errors, because in its common form it is merely stating what the speed of water is past some form of impeller. Usually, this impeller has a small magnet imbedded in it which then transmits its speed to the log. One more advanced piece of equipment has dispensed with moving parts altogether, since these can catch weed, get damaged and increase hull resistance; instead, two sensors, one on the leading edge of the keel and one further forward on the hull, transmit sound signals between each other. As the velocity of these signals is dependent on the speed of the water between them, the speed of the boat and, therefore, a log (distance) reading is obtained. This log reading is relayed directly to the navigator through a digital display and also serves as input to other items of computerized and electronic equipment on board.

POSITION FIXERS

Position fixing has undergone a major change in present-day navigation, for it is now possible to read off instantly an exact position without taking any special readings at that moment. With the navigator able to do this at any time, the roles of the depth sounder, dead reckoning, celestial or astronomic sightings and position lines, visual bearings, and the identification of marks and lights have been replaced on many occasions or at the least greatly reduced. There are a number of electronic position fixing systems in the world, originated and transmitted by different countries, but the main ones among these are satellite navigation (satnav), Loran and Decca.

What is common to all of these systems is that signals on specified frequencies are picked up by the boat's antenna and relayed via the master set to a digital display, giving a read-out, in latitude and longitude, having considerable accuracy;

WAYPOINT NAVIGATION

Position-finding systems have enabled boats to follow aeronautical practice and use waypoint navigation. Before leaving harbor, or at any time during the voyage, the navigator inputs into the satnav, Loran or Decca set the latitude and longitude of points along the route, usually those at which the boat will have to change direction. Each position gets a number and is known as a waypoint. The series of numbers is known as the sail plan (like a flight plan for aircraft) that can be rearranged or edited at any time; some sets allow the storage of hundreds of waypoints for future reference.

As the boat progresses past each waypoint, the set automatically changes over to indicate the course and distance to the next waypoint. In addition, both Loran and Decca give an 'off-track' reading, showing how far and in which direction the boat has strayed, if at all, from the direct course between the two waypoints. All this information enables the helmsman to see at a glance what is the simplest and fastest course to be steered to the next waypoint, as well as telling him if the boat is being set off course by a current. When tacking, he can tell if the boat is on the most favorable tack.

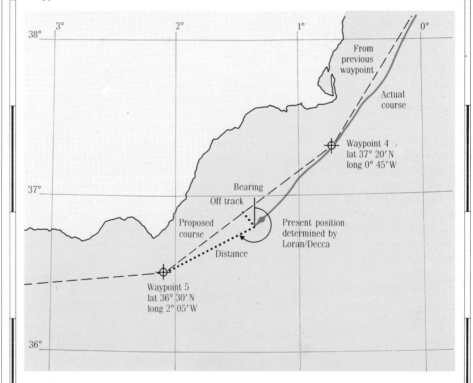

Steering by Waypoints *On the chart above, the boat has passed waypoint 4 and is 53.27 miles from waypoint 5. However, it is 9.13 miles off track and needs to make good a course of 243° to get to the next waypoint. All this information is shown in digital form on the receiving set's visual display unit (right).*

alternatively, a bearing and distance can be given to a chosen object or position.

The satnav system currently in use by boats is the Transit, developed by the US Navy and in use since small receiver sets first became available in 1980. The system receives its information from five satellites orbiting the Earth; when one of them emerges over the horizon, the receiver is alerted and picks up its signals, producing a read-out of the boat's latitude and longitude. As Transit has only five satellites, there can be a gap of up to three hours before the next fix. In the interval, navigation has to be done by dead reckoning, which is where input from the electronic compass and log can be used. These are connected to the satnav and give a continuous update from the last satnav position. The satnav set also informs the navigator when the next satellite is due and reads out any waypoint information (see box text for details). As with all these instruments, different sets vary in their capabilities, but the basics do not alter.

In the early 1990s, an improved satnav system, the American Global Positioning System (GPS), will be available for general use by yachts. Because it will have 18 satellites, there will always be one or more effective over any spot on Earth. When this system is fully operational, satnav will be able to give continuous position read-outs and thus be much more accurate, without the need to use secondary data like dead reckoning. It will also then be possible to use it for piloting, which is not advisable with Transit owing to its intermittent nature. Accuracy is expected to be to within 100 m (328 ft), more than adequate for a sailboat, while military and other special vessels will be able to achieve even

more accurate positioning. When GPS is fully operational, any large or small boat, or any other vehicle on land or sea, will be able to possess an instant position-finding capability at all times.

HYPERBOLIC SYSTEMS

With modern miniaturized equipment, the radio signals from two or more ground radio stations can be picked up and the distance from each transmitter accurately known by means of the time difference or radio phase difference. Whatever the method, the result is that the navigator can constantly read the latitude and longitude at the chart table: as the boat sails along, the tenths and hundreds of a minute of each of these trip over. Alternatively or simultaneously or on a shift mode, he can read the bearings and distance to the next mark or destination point when cruising. These systems are necessary, because satnav does not at the moment have the continuous facility required for navigation anywhere near the coast, or such dangers as shoals and reefs. Satnav is thus for the open ocean, while Loran and Decca are for accuracy nearer the shore. Indeed, both Loran and Decca can be out of range a few hundred miles from the coast. Loran is under the control of the US Coast Guard and covers a number of coasts which are major sailing waters, primarily both coasts of the United States, South-East

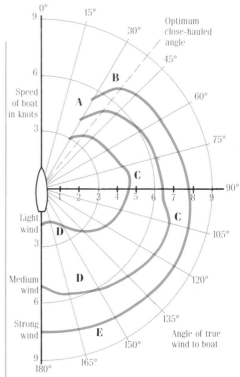

Polar Diagram *(above) Drawn for any boat in which performance is of importance, the polar diagram shows the optimum speed in knots available on all points of sailing for various different wind speeds (in this diagram, three).*

At 30° to the wind (A), a boat will barely move forward, only achieving its best close-hauled performance at 38° (B). Off the wind, a boat obtains its best speed with the spinnaker raised (C) but drops off when running dead before the wind (D). However, in a strong wind, a boat is going at its maximum hull speed, and so is unaffected by such changes (E).

Argos *(right) A transmitting device developed in France, Argos is used to broadcast the position of a boat anywhere in the world. The solar-powered device situated on the deck of the boat transmits a constant signal that is relayed via satellite back to a land base; it is used mainly by race officials keeping track of boats on long transatlantic or around-the-world races. Argos cannot be used to receive any incoming information, nor can its outgoing information be altered by the crew should they wish to falsify their own position to the detriment of their competitors. The system does, however, contain a panic button that the crew can activate in case of emergency.*

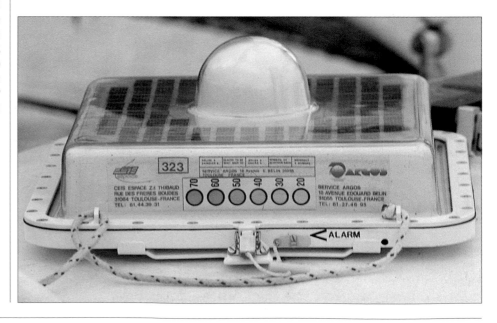

Asia, Japan, the central Mediterranean and the far north of Europe. Decca, which is based on the British Isles, covers virtually the whole western seaboard of Europe, the North Sea and the Baltic.

The compact equipment for these systems is kept at the chart table, with visual displays of information in the cockpit for the helmsman. In addition to position data, time can be shown, with an alarm if necessary, as can the course and speed over the ground, taking into account any current and drift, and the estimated time of arrival. In addition, facilities such as anchor alarms, which warn if the boat at anchor is starting to move, can be incorporated into the system.

ON-BOARD COMPUTERS

Programs exist for computers on board boats using input fed in before the race or voyage and information available as the craft sails along. The input includes information about tidal streams and current, and the boat's known performance across a range of wind speeds, points of sailing and sea state. Such computers, which are relatively expensive, are found on top ocean racers and occasionally on unusually well-equipped cruising boats.

Computer technology for boats is often ahead of the navigator's requirements, but information provided can include apparent wind strength and direction after the next change of course, the course to steer every moment allowing for the current, and whether the boat is at optimum performance for the conditions, compared with previous performances in similar conditions. This information is normally recorded in the form of a polar diagram, a graphic depiction of the vessel's performance and one which, when drawn by hand, was in use well before the onset of modern computers. Software for cruising boats is primarily navigational, with numerous data displayed; some input is then made for each contemplated passage.

OTHER STANDARD ELECTRONIC EQUIPMENT

Scientific development obviously provides the possibility of additional and further-advanced electronics for boats. Among items which are undergoing development

today for all sizes of craft are radar, which is appearing in more and more compact a form, for radar domes of any size are awkward to site in the rigging and cause unacceptable weight and windage aloft; new systems of communication over short and long range and for emergencies; charts on visual display; and alarms for some or all the electronic functions on board a boat that can be set to warn of certain readings, such as approaching a waypoint or the wind rising above a certain figure. Whatever the developments, the demands of light weight and efficiency will remain paramount.

A Navigator's Desk *A well-equipped navigator's desk and chart table carries a wide range of electronic navigation equipment. The digital and analog readings from the various instruments are immediately visible to the navigator. The main position-finding systems of Loran and satnav are alongside the navigational bookshelf. Sailing monitors of various kinds are below, including a compass display and even a simple but very useful clinometer to measure the heeling angle of the boat.*

SAILS

The search for new sailcloth – to increase the speed of racing boats and dinghies and to make cruising easier – has intensified in recent years. Specialist materials – such as dacron, nylon, Kevlar, Mylar and Spectra – are under constant development and are used singly or in combination. In turn, sailmakers experiment with new cuts in order to develop faster sails and increase sales.

The weight of a piece of sailcloth is conventionally stated in American ounces for a piece of cloth measuring 28½ in by 36 in. Where metric systems are in use, the measure is grams per square meter. Such figures are in any case nominal: a 1-oz spinnaker might be made from a piece of cloth weighing 1.2 oz.

SPINNAKER CLOTHS

Spinnakers were once made of cotton or silk, but today nylon is the most popular material, favored for its lightness and strength. In recent years, a lightweight combination of Mylar and woven fibers has been used for light-weather spinnakers.

1oz (40g) nylon *for a moderate-weather spinnaker. This cloth is resinated with silicon to reduce stretch.*

2.2oz (100g) nylon *heavyweight cloth, used as a heavy-weather spinnaker by offshore crews.*

1oz (40g) Mylar *and woven low-stretch cloth for reaching or for fresh winds.*

DACRON

First manufactured in 1953 in the US, dacron was an immediate success. Compared with cotton, which it rapidly replaced, it does not stretch, absorb water or rot, it does not have to be broken in, and it is stronger for its weight and faster.

·*Traditional cotton sails*

Plain woven dacron, *the most common sailcloth today; weights from 2-18oz (80-720g).*

8oz (320g) dacron *soft-woven cloth for working sails of cruising boats; weights from 3-9oz (120-360g).*

Hi-tech dacron *with composite, light yarns to give strength in one direction. Used for mainsails and radially cut genoas; weights from 6½-9½oz (260-380g).*

MYLAR

Made of polyester film, Mylar is invariably combined with woven fibers, sometimes sandwiched between two layers, to give a light cloth with low stretch. It is occasionally used on its own for light-weather sails such as light genoas and floating spinnakers.

0.5 oz (20 g) resinated Mylar *with light, fiber reinforcement, giving a faint square pattern. Used for light spinnakers; when set, appears transparent.*

4.5 oz (180 g) Mylar-dacron, *one side is film, the other woven scrim; used for small-to-medium sized genoas.*

6.5 oz (260 g) triple-layered Mylar-dacron *with undirectional fine weave and heavy film for very large genoas.*

3.3 oz (132 g) Mylar-dacron *with an open scrim on one side, giving equal strength in all directions; used for the front panels in headsails.*

KEVLAR

An artificial fiber from the American firm of Du Pont, Kevlar was developed from research into better automobile tires. It was first used in racing sails in 1980, but most one-design classes ban its use on the grounds of cost. It is conspicuous by its dirty brown color.

Kevlar-Spectra combinations, *typically used in light weights on headsail panels.*

Tx2 Gator Back *with Kevlar warp and dacron fill and an additional Kevlar thread at an angle, giving strength in several directions; weights from 4-9 oz (160-360 g).*

4.8 oz (192 g) Zigzag Kevlar on flex film *with Kevlar warps is in three directions, giving strength over a restricted but useful angle.*

4.2 oz (168 g) plain weave *with Kevlar warp and dacron fill. Used for a big boat genoa.*

2.8 oz (112 g) Kevlar knit *with dacron weft and Kevlar warp, used for big boat genoas.*

Kevlar on film warp and fill, *giving balanced strength in most directions; used experimentally in light weights in the front panels of genoas.*

SAILS

The first sailors – the peoples of the Near and Middle East – made their sails from woven reeds and grass, while the Romans used hemp, which they later sometimes coated with tar. Over the centuries, a wide range of different fibrous materials was used, with flax becoming the most popular by the 19th century. This changed with the success of *America* in its race around the Isle of Wight in 1851: those sails were cotton, and markedly better than the flax sails of its competitors.

The use of cotton in sails lasted for a century or more as a wide variety of weights and grades were developed and different cuts experimented with. But cotton was not that satisfactory, for it stretches under pressure, gains considerable weight when wet, rots, absorbs water, and has to be broken-in slowly.

ARTIFICIAL FIBERS

The first successful challenge to cotton sails came in 1937, when the America's Cup defender, *Ranger*, successfully tried out a suit of rayon, a new artificial fiber.

Another artificial fiber, nylon, was first used for sails in 1940 but did not at first find acceptance owing to its considerable stretch. Improved grades of nylon were used in the US in 1947 for spinnakers, since these sails are not stretched in the same way as fore and aft sails. Nylon has remained the principal spinnaker sailcloth

Cotton Sails *The skilled art of the 19th-century sailmaker is demonstrated by these handmade Egyptian cotton sails rigged on Satanita. Designed by J.M. Soper as a 40-m (131-ft 6-in) racing cutter and built in 1893, the total sail area was 937 sq m (10,094 sq ft); the mainsail alone was 489 sq m (4,919 sq ft), while the boom measured 28 m (92 ft).*

ever since, replacing the highly expensive silk. It is sometimes called ripstop, and appears to be made of small squares, coated and filled to produce a slippery surface. Weights of cloth are much less than for fore and aft sails; indeed, some are so light as to appear almost transparent. Nylon spinnakers have always been multicolored, a contrast to the white sails elsewhere on the boat.

The greatest advance in sailcloth manufacture came in 1953, when fibers of polyethylene tetraphthalate were commercially woven in the US. This polyester fiber, which became known, after its trade name, as dacron – Terylene in the UK, Tergal in France, Tetoron in Japan and Terlenka in the Netherlands – was an immediate success. In the 1954 Star world championships at Cascais, Portugal, Carlos de Cárdenas Culmell from Cuba, who was expected to turn in a result somewhere in the middle of the fleet, arrived with the only suit of dacron sails in the class and won with superior boat speed. The use of dacron spread rapidly as dinghy classes rewrote their rules to allow its use instead of cotton. In ocean racing, there was never any such restriction, and *Carina* won the 1955 Fastnet Race with one of the first complete outfits of dacron sails.

Dacron was attractive to sailmakers, for as a woven cloth, compared with cotton, it hardly stretches at all; it does not have to be slowly broken-in; it does not rot or absorb water; and is stronger for its weight, and faster because it is slippery. But the production quality of dacron was not entirely consistent to begin with, and one of the reasons why American sails were far superior in the 1964 America's Cup was that sailmaker Ted Hood had set up a plant to weave his own cloth. He achieved a weaving process and finish far more suitable for racing sails than the ordinary, commercially produced dacron. Today's sailcloth is made by specialist fabricators and finishers, but to the exacting needs of sailmakers.

MODERN SAILCLOTHS

The search for new materials to improve the performance of sails and the economics of sailmaking is a continuous process. Kevlar, an artificial fiber made by the

American firm of Du Pont, was developed from research into automobile tires, and when used in sails, is conspicuous by its dirty brown color. Used for bullet-proof vests, racing-car bodies and sailboat hulls, it began to be incorporated into racing sails in 1980, and was seen in the America's Cup of that year; most one-design classes banned it, and still do, on the grounds of cost, for a Kevlar sail is about two-and-a-half times that of a dacron one. It suffers from fatigue and is difficult to handle and store. In 1985, the IOR allowed Kevlar to be used in part of the sail only, and the next year without

Sail Reinforcement *Attempts to eliminate all stretch by the use of local panelling and reinforcement are demonstrated on the mainsail and genoa of this 1988 6-Meter registered in Hong Kong. Various Kevlar, Mylar and dacron combinations are in use.*

limit. Unlike dacron, which has found world-wide acceptance in all kinds of boat, Kevlar is almost never used on cruising boats and is rare in all but IOR ocean-racers, 12-Meters, and boats competing in short-handed and various other offshore exotic races.

Sailcloth made of polyester film is now well established and no more costly than dacron. This film is also made by Du Pont under the name of Mylar. It is usually combined with dacron to give a light cloth with low stretch, but when used on its own, is ideal for light-weather sails, such as genoas and floating spinnakers, in which it is colored glassy white. The film itself is quite vulnerable, and so a sandwich cloth can be used, laying the Mylar between two layers of dacron. This produces a more stable sail less liable to damage. Sails are also made combining Mylar with Kevlar or with dacron, Kevlar with dacron, and all three together: this means that the cut of sails and their seaming are no longer conventional and many varieties can be seen, making the best of the individual properties of each cloth in use. Kevlar reinforcement produces a remarkable criss-cross effect and the 'C', or radial cut, of racing sails. Simple, horizontal seaming is thus often restricted to cruising boats or those with older sails.

One sailcloth making a recent appearance on racing boats is Spectra, an artificial fiber developed by the Allied Corporation of the US in 1987. Spectra is used by some sailmakers with a sky-blue color, a tint caused by the glue used to bond it. It can be a substitute for Kevlar, but a general view is that it may have too much creep, that is stretching with time under load. However, it is better when combined with other materials.

PERFORMANCE

The primary requirement for every racing sail is good performance in conditions for which the sail has been made. In cruising boats, all-around performance and longevity are required. Sails are the engine of a boat and a good sail costs little more than a badly made one. The main enemies of performance are stretch and loss of shape. Extra weight is also undesirable, for once the boat heels, the sail adds to the heeling moment: it is not only high up, but also on the leeward side. To avoid these problems, those classes that allow its use display the dirty brown of Kevlar. Although very expensive, Kevlar is light in weight and has negligible stretch.

It has been said that the early attraction of dacron was its lack of stretch, but this was in comparison with cotton. In fact, dacron does stretch, although rarely much on cruising rigs, for it must be remembered that great stresses are demanded of a suit of racing sails by rigid rigs and unyielding hulls.

If a sail does not alter its shape with changes in the force of the wind speed, it can perform well across a greater range of wind speeds. This means that a Kevlar genoa, for instance, can be kept hoisted as the wind increases. The same-sized sail in dacron would be changed for a smaller, flatter sail, with a consequent loss of speed during the time taken to change over, and with reduced speed under the new sail.

LONGEVITY

Sails have got to last, not just for economic reasons, and they must obviously be in a good condition to withstand the stresses of the wind, otherwise sudden failure could endanger the boat. Although Kevlar has improved in quality and sailmakers have learned the best ways to construct a sail out of it, it is still prone to sudden failure, an inescapable fault given its inelasticity. This restricts its use to inshore racing, or those offshore boats with large, replacement sail wardrobes.

Mylar Sails *As many classes either ban or penalize Kevlar on the grounds of cost, considerable ingenuity is used to make dacron-Mylar combinations for racing. The different panels are to prevent the sail losing shape as the wind increases. Mylar is easily recognizable for it is virtually transparent.*

Experimental Cuts *The fleet of IOR boats at a starting mark (above) are all sporting new Kevlar sails of unusual cut. Sailmakers continue to experiment with different ways of making sails in order to best exploit the varieties of cloth and weave available. For these IOR boats, cost and longevity are a secondary consideration to performance.*

Offshore Sails *The cruiser-racer shown on the right sports a mixture of dacron and Kevlar cloths in its sails for best performance offshore. The No 2 genoa in use is for apparent winds of between 20-8 knots.*

Dacron and nylon are both long lasting and cannot rot. About the only threat to them is the effect of the sun's ultra-violet rays in sunny climates, but since the rate of deterioration is slow, they are rarely affected so long as they are kept covered when not in use. However, jibs kept furled on a roller-reef and mainsails furled on a boom will expose the same strip of material each time they are stored, making them particularly vulnerable unless covered with special strips that protect them from the sun.

Sails are not cheap to make because, among other things, of the considerable amount of reinforcement and stitching. These take local stresses and secure fittings for sheets, halyards and the tracks or grooves on mast and boom. It is thus important for boat owners to enhance the effective life of their sails by not allowing them to flog in the wind and by storing them out of direct sunlight.

HANDLING AND STOWAGE

In general, all class rules call for soft sails that can be furled, as do standard IYRU sail regulations; it is only exotic craft like C-class catamarans and other futuristic designs with multiple wings that have solid sails. Such sails may be highly efficient, but they are very difficult to handle and stow and it is not practical to leave such a craft pivoting, fully rigged, head to wind when out of use, for the craft will try to sheer about as stray winds catch the sails at different angles. Whatever the boat, therefore, it is essential that sails are readily reducible in area for security when on a mooring, when in harbor, or when sail has to be reefed in heavy or dangerous weather.

One of the main reasons for designing a boat with two masts rather than one is to split up the sail area, thus making it more manageable. Modern materials and design can support all the sail required to drive a boat of, say, 25 m (80 ft), on one mast, but many people prefer to sail a two-masted design for ease of sail handling, while many older boats have two masts from the days when big sails were less easy to cope with or design effectively.

Ease of handling and stowage are therefore major qualities looked for in a sail, and these are the characteristics of dacron. Kevlar and Mylar can be handled without undue difficulty, so long as there is an active racing crew to do it.

SAILS FOR RACING

Many small classes limit the sails exactly: typically, the rules allow a mainsail, two sizes of jib and a spinnaker. The IOR also has a sail limitation but it is liberal, and an additional number of genoas, jibs and spinnakers can be carried below when racing. Storm sails must also be carried. A large racing boat equipped without regard to expense can carry a big wardrobe of sails, but the size of that wardrobe is necessarily limited by the fact that all the headsails and spinnakers not being used at a given moment are extra weight and therefore have a slowing effect. For this reason, stringent racing rules exist stating that sails stored below cannot be shifted about and used as movable ballast.

A more modestly equipped but nevertheless keenly raced masthead sloop of, say, 12 m (40 ft) will carry a full-size 1.5-oz (60-g) No 1 genoa for use in winds from calm to 10 knots; another full-size 4.5-oz (180-g) No 2 genoa for winds from 8 to 20 knots; a 6-oz (240-g) No 2 genoa for winds from 20 to 28 knots; a 7.5-oz (300-g) No 3 genoa for winds from 25 to 34 knots; an 8-oz (320-g) No 4 genoa, often called a working jib, for winds from 28 to 40 knots; an 8-oz (320-g) heavy-weather jib for winds over 38 knots; and finally an 8-oz (320-g) storm jib for winds over 45 knots. Extra sails designed for reaching or for carrying under a spinnaker are less favored today owing to sail-limitation rules and a belief that the extra speed that they might give is doubtful when set against the extra weight when not being used. They also cause disruption during a race as they are hoisted, lowered and stored. A typical cruiser-racer will only carry four sizes of genoa and a storm jib.

The size of the spinnaker is regulated under IOR and all other racing classes in

SPINNAKERS

Although the 47-ton *Sphinx* was not the first boat to hoist a large triangular sail and boom it out when off the wind, the fact remains that after it used it to remarkable effect in the Royal Victoria Yacht Club regatta of 1866, such a sail was always called a spinnaker. Previously, sailing vessels had used squaresails when running. For many years, the spinnaker was hoisted with its sheet inside the forestay so that the sail had to be taken in before gybing or as soon as the vessel was no longer on a run. Once the sheet was outside the forestay, gybing could be accomplished by disconnecting the spinnaker pole and moving it inside the forestay to connect to the other corner of the sail. The sail could now be carried on a reach or even with the wind ahead of the beam.

A Spinnaker Reach *Three Sigma 33 OODs close-reaching under spinnakers; the tri-radial design of this sail is the most popular one in use today, although many different designs and cuts have been used over the years.*

Sail Furling *Furling sails by rolling them up on their stays or in their spars has a number of attractions for cruising boats and for those participating in short-handed races. Stowage below does not have to be found for headsails, and by using the furler to reduce sail area, fewer sails are needed and all the labor and unpleasantness of the foredeck when changing sail at sea is therefore removed. Rolling a mainsail into the mast has similar advantages but is less popular, as a special, costly spar is required. This spar is heavy aloft and has more windage; there is also the residual problem of the system jamming while at sea, although most systems are now highly effective.*

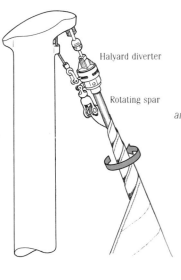

Halyard diverter

Rotating spar

Headsail Reefing *In a headsail reefing system, the sail is hoisted in the normal way by a halyard up a rotating spar fixed around the existing forestay. Once set, the sail can be furled by means of a drum at the base of the spar controlled by a line led aft to the cockpit. In order to unfurl the sail, the control line is released and the sail sheets pulled to unroll the sail. In order to stop the halyard twisting around the forestay, a special halyard diverter is fitted to the top of the spar.*

various ways; within those limits, the sailmaker will cut the seams to provide the best shape for both running and reaching. Spinnakers have evolved in shape through various cuts, but since 1980, are now generally cut with panels in a tri-radial manner. Various specialized spinnakers do exist for different wind strengths and directions, but few class rules allow enough sails for these to be flown. IOR boats are allowed to carry a limited number of spinnakers, for instance, four on a 12-m (40-ft) boat: these might be a light $\frac{1}{2}$ oz (20 g), a heavy $2\frac{1}{2}$ oz (100 g) and two $\frac{3}{4}$ oz (30 g) for most other conditions.

SAILS FOR CRUISING

Specialization in cruising boats has led to a number of features not used on racing boats, although both single- and short-handed racers often use the same techniques. Foremost of these is the roller furling of both genoas and jibs and of mainsails. Effective systems have been devised in the 1980s, making short-handed cruising (and racing) much more practical and safe, for rolling sails have done away with the drawn-out procedure of bringing sails up from below and changing them for others which have been lowered.

From the safety of the cockpit, the genoa can be furled to a smaller area as the wind increases, without stopping or slowing the boat. Modern systems can do this most effectively, insuring that the sail remains flat as it is reduced.

Rolling the mainsail around the boom — roller reefing — to reduce its area was favored in the 1950s and 1960s but has recently been dropped in favor of slab reefing, whereby a piece of the sail is pulled down on to the boom by means of the reefing gear. More elaborate systems now exist whereby the whole mainsail rolls into the mast, the entire operation controlled from the cockpit; thus as the boat enters a harbor or dock, the mainsail conveniently 'disappears.' Since this system requires a special mast, it is not as common as might be. Another way of stowing the mainsail is by using lazy jacks, whereby lines direct the sail down on to the boom when it is furled. Full-length battens help the sail keep its shape when it is partially furled.

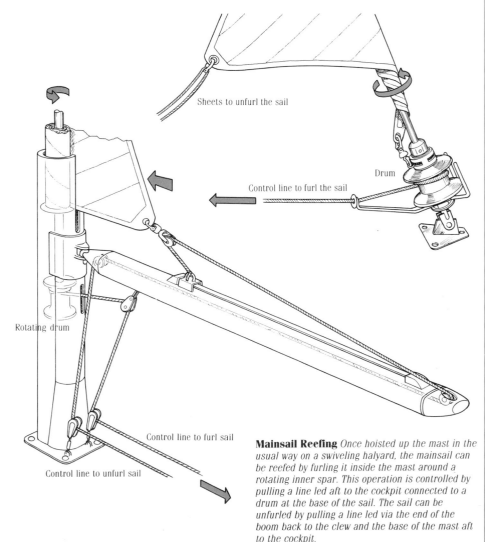

Sheets to unfurl the sail

Control line to furl the sail

Drum

Rotating drum

Control line to furl sail

Control line to unfurl sail

Mainsail Reefing *Once hoisted up the mast in the usual way on a swiveling halyard, the mainsail can be reefed by furling it inside the mast around a rotating inner spar. This operation is controlled by pulling a line led aft to the cockpit connected to a drum at the base of the sail. The sail can be unfurled by pulling a line led via the end of the boom back to the clew and the base of the mast aft to the cockpit.*

ROPE

Almost all sailing operations on deck – except for the turning of the wheel or the moving of the tiller – involve hauling or winching lines, sheets, halyards, tackles, guys, travellers, outhauls, downhauls, lifts, runners, stays, preventers, barber haulers and others. In port, docklines, springs and tow lines may be handled. Yet seldom is the word 'rope' ever heard spoken, although that is, in fact, what all the above are, whether they are of natural or artificial fibers.

Cordage comes in scores of grades, varying in material, construction and thickness, while color variations have been introduced to help identify lines for different purposes. Natural fibers are still available for vintage boats, but artificial fibers, with their immensely longer life and greater strength for a given diameter, are the rule elsewhere.

NATURAL FIBERS

These look fine aboard vintage boats, but have few other assets, being weaker for size and weight than artificial fibers, and more expensive. They swell when damp and therefore jam, and will rot if allowed to remain wet. Among the fibers used are hemp, widely grown in Asia and Italy but in restricted supply because of limited production; flax; manila from a plant grown in the Philippines; and sisal, a low-quality fiber from East Africa.

6 mm (¼ in) *manila for mainsheets on small, old boats*

8 mm (⁵/₁₆ in) *manila for halyards on small, old boats*

12 mm (½ in) *manila for mainsheets on larger, old boats*

10 mm (⁷/₁₆ in) *flax for halyards on larger, old boats*

12 mm (½ in) *flax for mainsheets on larger, old boats*

NYLON

This material will stretch up to 40% before breaking and is ideal for mooring lines and anchor rodes, both of which take shocks. It is useless for halyards and sheets where exact control is required. Nylon is more prone to chafe than polyester, deteriorates in strong sunlight and is slippery – making knots less secure unless special precautions are taken.

10 mm (⁷/₁₆ in) *braided for temporary kedge warps*

14 mm (⁹/₁₆ in) *8-plait (braided) for anchor rodes or tow lines*

POLYETHYLENE & POLYPROPYLENE

These are low-priced materials with numerous uses where long life and ultimate strength are not required, such as for temporary floating marks. They chafe easily and are weakened by strong sunlight, but their floating ability is a major advantage, especially for rescue lines.

4 mm (⅛ in) *for lines below decks*

10 mm (⁷/₁₆ in) *for rescue lines on lifebuoys*

12 mm (½ in) *for pick-up lines to mooring buoys*

POLYESTER

An all-purpose rope which can be used for almost any task on board. The material has low stretch, good resistance to rot and chafe, and a long life. Cable-laid polyester is pre-stretched during manufacture so that it has almost no give when in use.

5 mm (³/₁₆ in) *for light lashings*

6 mm (¼ in) *for general use on small boats*

9 mm (³/₈ in) *8-plait (braided) for genoa and mainsheets on dinghies*

10 mm (⁷/₁₆ in) *16-plait (braided) for genoa sheets on ocean racers*

10 mm (⁷/₁₆ in) *for reef pennants*

10 mm (⁷/₁₆ in) *for reef pennants*

12 mm (½ in) *for mainsheets on boats*

2 mm (¹/₁₆ in) *pre-stretched 8-plait (braided) for flag halyard*

4 mm (¹/₈ in) *pre-stretched, for permanent lashings*

7 mm (⁵/₁₆ in) *pre-stretched, for light-weather spinnaker sheets*

14 mm (⁹/₁₆ in) *pre-stretched, for spinnaker guys on large boats*

KEVLAR

This polyimide was introduced by Du Pont in the early 1980s for car tires and later for bullet-proof vests. It is now used for cordage (as well as in hull and sail construction) because it is 80% lighter than steel wire of equal strength. Compared to polyester, it is more expensive and not very resistant to chafe. Kevlar has virtually no stretch, so lines can be used for special jobs on racing boats: this very property does mean that lines can sometimes part without warning.

10 mm (⁷/₁₆ in) *for halyards on racing boats*

3.5 mm (¹/₈ in) *for control lines in leech of sail*

EARLY SAILING YACHT DESIGN

In the last 150 years, the progress of sailboat design has been influenced by three factors: the availability of materials; rating and measurement; and, to a lesser extent, by the ideas and experiments of designers. How these three have worked together, and what designs have resulted, will be considered in the rest of this chapter.

The first of the three factors has been an enduring influence on design, for when planked wood was the main material for a hull, it strictly limited its shape. It was, for example, extremely difficult to construct a sound wooden hull with a fin keel, even if this was thought desirable, and it was only with the introduction of fiberglass in the 1950s that hulls could be built strongly in any unusual form. Before 1950, the use of wood for spars, which were held up by rigging that stretched, meant that there were limits to the size of sails that could be supported. Sails thus had to be split up into small areas and were less efficient than they might have been.

The second factor, rules and measurement, has had an immense influence on every aspect of design. Logically, such rules should not touch boats designed for cruising, but cruising boats have tended to ape the racers, ex-racers have become cruisers, and designers who thought that they were designing a pure cruiser have incorporated features first used on racing boats. Almost all boats, therefore, whatever their designer's or owner's intentions, show the influence of past and present rating rules.

Of the three factors, the ideas and innovations of designers and owners have been the least influential, for while they have contributed to design, the demanding necessities of seaworthiness and the lack of any serious research and development in design has meant that startling changes have never been that conspicuous. As for any regional or national design features on

◆◆◆

Clara *Designed by William Fife to the British YRA Tonnage Rule and built in 1894, Clara was an extreme type of plank-on-edge cutter, as can be seen from the lines drawings below. Its overall length was 19.6 m (64 ft 4 in), the waterline length 16 m (52 ft 9 in), the beam only 2.8 m (9 ft 2 in), and the draft 2.4 m (8 ft); more than half the displacement of 37 tons was in the ballast keel.*

boats, the internationalization of design and the export and import of boats has wiped out many of the differences. Many dinghy classes originating before, say 1939, have a local character to them and old cruising boats may follow the style of a particular designer in a certain country, but apart from a few types of vessel, design is now seldom national in approach. Exceptions might be the Dutch leeboard craft and the long-ended, narrow 'skerry cruisers' of Scandinavia, but both of these are, in fact, in a minority in their own areas.

EARLY ATTEMPTS AT HANDICAPPING

As the earliest races were matches to challenge the speed of one boat against another, no question of handicapping arose, although every attempt was made to improve the speed of a boat before the next wager was made. As the longest boat was the potential winner, one improvement that could be made was to lengthen the boat and add to its sail area, thus increasing the speed. This happened after the 1827 races at Cowes between Lord Belfast's *Louisa*, Joseph Weld's *Lulworth* and T. Assheton-Smith's *Menai*. At the end of the season, Lord Belfast had his boat cut in half and a new mid-section inserted, raising the tonnage from 139 to 162 tons, and with it the speed.

This sort of modification was expensive and clearly proved nothing, so yachtsmen of the time decided to try some form of time allowances in some races and for some prizes. Not all races used time allowances, whatever the disparity of the

craft: it will be remembered that *America* won its race in 1851 without time allowance, having the best elapsed time of all the entrants. The first time allowance recorded was for the Queen's Cup at the Cowes Regatta of 1838, when a crude three minutes per ton for the entire course was allowed, but by the time of the 1843 season at Cowes, a more systematic time allowance was devised by George Holland Ackers, a member of the Royal Yacht Squadron. He drew up a table showing an allowance for each ton difference between boats of so many seconds per mile of the course. This system could be used for any course, the distance of which was known; similar systems, using seconds per mile, although not related to tons, are in use today, most notably in the USYRU time-on-distance handicap tables.

TONNAGE

Following ship practice, the size of boats was known as so many tons, a figure allocated by the local Customs House under government regulation. It was these tons that were used for the application of time allowances. Once the tonnage rating became a factor in such allowances, it obviously paid to have as low a tonnage as possible, an outcome that led to the strangest of results.

Tonnage was – and still is in some commercial measurements – based not on the weight of the vessel but its cargo capacity. This derived from medieval times when the number of barrels or 'tuns' were counted that could fit into a ship's hold. From this number could be calculated the taxation and duties to be levied

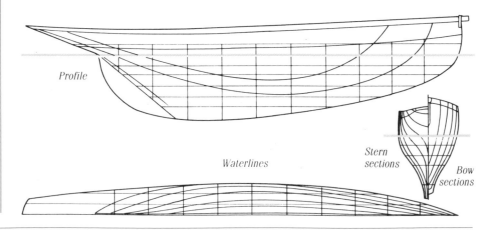

Profile

Waterlines

Stern sections

Bow sections

on the cargo, payload or 'tonnage'. English records from the late 16th century show that it was impracticable to count the actual number of barrels that would fit in the hold; instead, a formula was used, in which L = length, and B = beam:

$$\text{Tonnage} = \frac{L \times B \times \text{depth of hold}}{100}$$

This equalled the 'tonnage' of the vessel; an act of parliament in 1694 changed this formula, defining the length as length along the keel and made the lower factor 94. This new formula was soon modified, owing to the difficulty of measuring into the hold: instead of measuring the depth, half the beam was measured. The result of this change was that for the same capacity, a new ship could be built somewhat narrower and the hold be made deeper. A lesser tonnage resulted, as did less tax and duty. In the case of boats, this was the equivalent of lowering the rating, thus giving a better time allowance against an opponent. Methods to exploit measurement have continued ever since!

The tonnage rule used by the Royal Yacht Squadron in the early 19th century originated in 1773 and was known by the name of Builder's Old Measurement (BOM). The formula was:

$$\text{BOM} = \frac{(L - \frac{3}{5}B) \times B \times \frac{1}{2}B}{85}$$

The strange $\frac{3}{5}B$ allowed for the rake of the stem. As L was the length along the keel, a rule-cheating device was to shorten this length yet keep the boat virtually the same size. With so much emphasis on beam, it was not surprising that if low

tonnage was wanted, the boats the formula produced were narrow. It should also be noted that in this simple formula, there is nothing about sail area, freeboard or draft. Therefore, boats designed for speed had masses of sail area, low freeboard and a deep draft.

In the United States, tonnage was by Customs House Measurement: this was much the same as BOM, but without the final $\frac{1}{2}B$. Instead, some form of real depth was measured, resulting in boats that were less deep and had more beam than their English counterparts. Partly because of rules, partly tradition, American designs had greater beam for their length until the early 1960s, when new rules

ended the contrast. With yacht racing expanding in Britain in the mid 19th century, BOM became inadequate as a rating. Therefore, in 1854, the Royal Thames Yacht Club introduced a new formula, known as Thames Tonnage. This still penalized beam, but the length was now to be measured between perpendiculars, that is between the stem and stern post:

$$\text{Thames Tonnage} = \frac{(L - B) \times B \times \frac{1}{2}B}{94}$$

COLLAPSE OF THE TONNAGE RULES

In the 1860s and 1870s, the Victorian sailors agonized over the tonnage rating rules. The correspondence columns of the sailing magazines were full of suggested solutions, for all the while, boats were becoming narrower and carrying increasing amounts of sail. If this sounds unseaworthy, the impact of this evolution

Mohawk, *built to the American Cubic Contents Rule in 1875.*

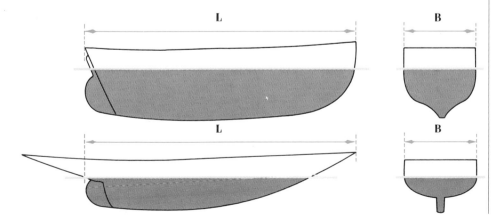

L

B

L

B

Thames Tonnage *The Thames Tonnage formula of 1854 measured only the beam (**B**) and the length (**L**) between perpendiculars, that is between the stem and the stern post. This allowed designers considerable leniency in designing boats to benefit from the formula. The two boats illustrated here both rated the same tonnage, yet the one on the bottom is half the weight of the one on top, and is radically different in overall length and hull profile.*

was somewhat hidden because races only took place in protected waters, often in quite small boats, and with professional crews. The vessels of over 100 tons that cruised in open waters followed conservative designs and all boats in Britain still used inside ballast, which had the effect of retarding the spread of extreme designs. Yet for some reason, British rule makers of the time felt that any formula had to be simple and seemed reluctant to use in it more than the simplest dimensions of a boat. In America, there were similar debates, with at least one trial of a pure sail-area rule, although, as in Britain, formulas measured only length (as defined in various ways) and beam.

One rule that did have a few years of life in the 1870s and 1880s was the Cubic Contents Rule of the New York Yacht Club. This rule took three cross-sections of a boat below the waterline, added them together, and multiplied the result by four! Whatever the rule was intended to do, it was an attempt to give a rating in tons by the displacement, or true weight, of the boat. The rule was used for the 1876 and 1881 America's Cup races, but in the words of W.P. Stephens, an American designer and yachting commentator of the early 20th century: "While the New York YC tried rules of measurement, all of which proved eventual failures, the smaller clubs blundered on from year to year with no better results."

The Cubic Contents Rule encouraged low freeboard, high sail area and shallow hulls. One boat built to the rule was *Mohawk*, a 45.7-m (150-ft) schooner with a beam of 9.2 m (30 ft 4 in), a draft of only 1.8 m (6 ft), a deep centerboard and a huge sail area. In July 1876, it was hoisting sail and weighing anchor off Staten Island, New York, when a puff of wind capsized it, drowning the owner, the publishing millionaire, William T. Garner, and all his invited guests as they sat below. This well-publicized disaster, and the capsize

Puritan *A compromise between the deep cutter, such as Clara, and the shallow-draft boat, such as the extreme Mohawk. Puritan was designed by Edward Burgess with an external keel and a displacement of 105 tons. It successfully defended the America's Cup in 1885. Its lines are shown to the right.*

THE EFFECT OF THE TONNAGE RULES

	BOAT	LWL	BEAM	DRAFT	SAIL AREA – WITHOUT TOPSAILS
1873	DIAMOND	7.7 m (25 ft 3 in)	2.2 m (7 ft 2 in)	1.4 m (4 ft 6 in)	62.3 sq m (671 sq ft)
1876	VRIL	8.6 m (28 ft 4 in)	2.0 m (6 ft 7 in)	1.6 m (5 ft 2 in)	77.1 sq m (830 sq ft)
1879	TRIDENT	9.8 m (32 ft)	1.8 m (6 ft)	1.9 m (6 ft 3 in)	84.7 sq m (912 sq ft)
1883	OLGA	10.1 m (33 ft)	1.7 m (5 ft 9 in)	1.9 m (6 ft 4 in)	91.5 sq m (985 sq ft)
1885	DORIS	10.3 m (33 ft 8 in)	1.7 m (5 ft 7 in)	2.1 m (7 ft)	103.7 sq m (1,116 sq ft)
1886	OONA	10.4 m (34 ft)	1.6 m (5 ft 6 in)	2.5 m (8 ft)	111.9 sq m (1,205 sq ft)
For comparison:					
1988	X-372 DANISH CRUISER-RACER	9 m (29 ft 6 in)	3.6 m (11 ft 8 in)	2 m (6 ft 7 in)	75.9 sq m (817 sq ft)

The Tonnage Rules
The effect of the Tonnage Rules on hull shape can be seen in the four hull profiles to the right, dating from 1873 to 1886. As the length increased and the draft deepened, the beam became narrower.

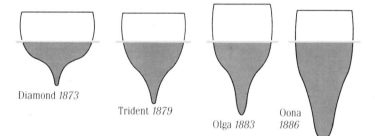

Diamond *1873*

Trident *1879*

Olga *1883*

Oona *1886*

of several other centerboard boats of basically shallow draft, spelled the end of tonnage rules in the US.

In Britain, there was one last attempt to find a better tonnage rule. The newly formed Yacht Racing Association promulgated a rule in 1882, whereby:

$$\text{Tonnage} = \frac{(L + B)^2 \times B}{1730}$$

By this date, the British had adopted outside ballast to enable some stability to be found in boats of ever narrower beam, deeper draft and increasing sail area. But this rule contributed to a period which was the most disastrous in the history of yacht design, for the boats were built to even

more extreme measurements, as demonstrated in the table above.

One of the most extreme boats was *Oona*, with a very narrow beam, deep draft and 12,700-kg (28,000-lb) displacement, of which 9,752 kg (21,500 lb) was in lead ballast; even contemporary sailors recognized it as a freak. On its first voyage from the Solent to the Clyde, it was driven ashore on the Irish coast in a gale and the heavy keel was torn from its lightweight, although apparently well-built, hull. All hands were lost, including the designer William Evans Paton. *Oona* was among the last of the 'plank-on-edge' boats which had demonstrated that the measurement rule must be changed.

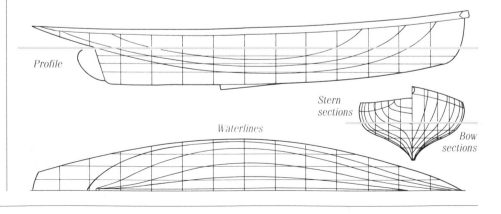

Profile

Waterlines

Stern sections

Bow sections

THE FIRST MODERN RULES

Dixon Kemp was the secretary of the Yacht Racing Association in Britain, the author of a number of influential books on the design and handling of boats, and a yacht designer himself. His influence was paramount in the adoption of a new rating rule in 1886. Beam was left out altogether, and sail area(S) was at last brought in:

$$\text{Rating} = \frac{L \times S}{6000}$$

The length was the load waterline of the boat, and the figure resulting from this formula was made roughly to equate to the old tonnage rules. In other words, what used to be a 5 tonner was now a 5-rater. There were thus half-raters, 2-raters, 20-raters and so on.

At around the same time as this rating was being devised, the Seawanhaka Corinthian Yacht Club, one of the leading clubs on Long Island, New York, adopted a similar formula in 1883, only stating the final rating in feet:

$$\text{Rating in feet} = \frac{L + \sqrt{S}}{2}$$

This rule was used for the first 10 races for the Seawanhaka Cup (p172) and the first race for the Canada's Cup (pp128-9).

The effect of both these rules was much the same, producing racing boats in the 1890s that were popularly known as 'skimming dishes'. These big-class boats were flat, low-freeboard craft with long, overhanging, U-shaped ends at both bow and stern, so shaped because only the waterline length was measured and the U-shaped ends gave extra waterline length when the boat was heeled over. The boats were fun to sail but not that seaworthy, although this was scarcely necessary for the inshore races of the time. The America's Cup boats in the eight matches from 1885 to 1903 were all built to this length-and-sail-area rule, culminating in the extreme *Reliance*, the American defender in 1903 (p147), while one of the most successful designs under the rule was *Gloriana*, designed by Herreshoff in 1890.

The same direction in design was also evident in the smaller classes of boats, which were also skimming dishes of a shorter overall size. Some had centerboards, others fin keels, and each year the

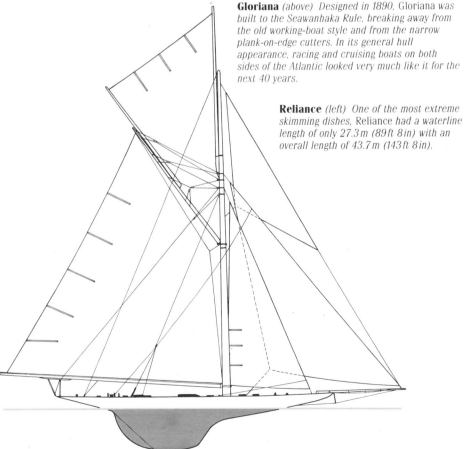

Gloriana *(above) Designed in 1890, Gloriana was built to the Seawanhaka Rule, breaking away from the old working-boat style and from the narrow plank-on-edge cutters. In its general hull appearance, racing and cruising boats on both sides of the Atlantic looked very much like it for the next 40 years.*

Reliance *(left) One of the most extreme skimming dishes, Reliance had a waterline length of only 27.3 m (89 ft 8 in) with an overall length of 43.7 m (143 ft 8 in).*

boats got slightly longer for the same rating, outclassing their predecessors. A successful 5-rater of 1883 was 6m (20ft) on the waterline, but a 5-rater of 1892 had a waterline length of 10.4m (36ft)! The overhangs would have been a massive 5m (15ft) or more, half as much as the waterline length. The American designer, Nathanael Herreshoff, designed raters to the British rule, with long overhangs fore and aft, and bronze centerboards with bulbs on the end. In 1891, two of his designs, the half-rater *Wee Win* and the 2½-rater *Wenonah*, both with such a configuration, swept all before them in the races they entered.

The campaign against skimming dishes was led in Britain by R.E. Froude, a writer and yacht designer. At his suggestion, the YRA brought beam and a new concept, girth (G), into the rating formula in 1896, expressing the final rating in feet:

$$\text{Rating in feet} = \frac{L + B + 0.75G + 0.5\sqrt{S}}{2}$$

The rating looks like the Seawanhaka Rule with the addition of girth, a measurement around the cross section including the

The Herreshoff-designed Wee Win *– the most successful half-rater of its day.*

keel, so that the more pronounced the fin, the more G would be. However, the new rule had little effect on the skimming dishes: in the small-sized classes, each new boat still outclassed the older ones, while in the big-sized classes, the rule had the effect of discouraging big-class racing altogether. It was no coincidence that this

was the period when one-design classes began, in reaction to the rating rules.

Revival came to the big classes in Britain in 1893, when the Prince of Wales commissioned *Britannia*, a new big-class racing cutter. Although the designer, G.L. Watson, had the length-and-sail-area rule in mind and the new boat was by measurement a 151-ft rater, it was essentially a seaworthy vessel, with an LOA of 37m (121ft 6in), an LWL of 26.7m (87ft 7in), a beam of 7.1m (23ft 4in) and a sail area of 959.4sqm (10,327sqft). Despite the rating rule, the royal patronage revived big-class racing, although it should be remembered that when speaking of a revival, half-a-dozen boats were considered a big fleet at that time.

In 1901, the YRA made a further modification of the rule by inserting a measurement of the difference between the girth G, which was taken by a taut chain or cord around the cross section of the boat, and the skin girth, which was a measurement around the actual skin of the hull and keel. This difference was expressed as d, and the more extreme the fin, the bigger was d, and the bigger the rating:

Britannia *Designed by G.L. Watson for the Prince of Wales, later Edward VII, in 1893, the Royal Yacht underwent numerous changes to its racing rig during its 43 years. Although first measured to the length-and-sail-area rule, its all-around ability helped revive the fortunes of the big classes after the failures of the 1880s.*

$$\text{Rating in feet} = \frac{L + B + 0.75G + 4d + 0.5\sqrt{S}}{2.1}$$

This final length-and-sail-area rule, although introducing some more factors, still failed to solve the problem of outclassed and light boats. As the new century began, the search was on in Europe and America for a new rule altogether.

THE UNIVERSAL RULE

Even as *Reliance* was winning the America's Cup in 1903, its designer, Nathanael Herreshoff, was working on a sounder rating rule. This was adopted in 1903 by the New York Yacht Club as the Universal Rule, which brought back displacement on the lower line and measured L, one quarter of maximum beam from the centerline. Together, these two measurements eliminated the scow-like ends and extra-light weight. In other words, it killed the skimming dish at last. The Universal Rule was:

$$\text{Rating in feet} = 0.2\,\frac{L \times \sqrt{S}}{\sqrt[3]{\text{displacement}}}$$

Amendments and limitations were introduced into the rule about freeboard, draft and the relationship between S and L in the formula, in order to prevent big sail areas at the expense of length in the light-weather areas of North America. With these alterations, the Universal Rule was used in the US for many successful inshore classes until 1924. It also spawned a number of classes itself – for instance, the R-class at 20ft-rating and the M-class at 46-ft rating – and American sailors tended to use the rule to settle a design as a one-design, with the result that for a short time, from roughly 1900 to 1941, there existed New York Thirties, Forties and even Seventies, the numbers referring to their Universal Rule rating in feet.

After 1924, the rule was only used for the big classes, in effect the J-class, which rated 76ft under the rule (see p149 for a photograph of *Ranger*, the successful American defender of the America's Cup in 1934 and the ultimate in J-class boats). Under agreement with the Europeans, the smaller classes were promoted under the International Rule (see next page). Today the Universal Rule is dead, its formula hidden among the complexities of the IOR.

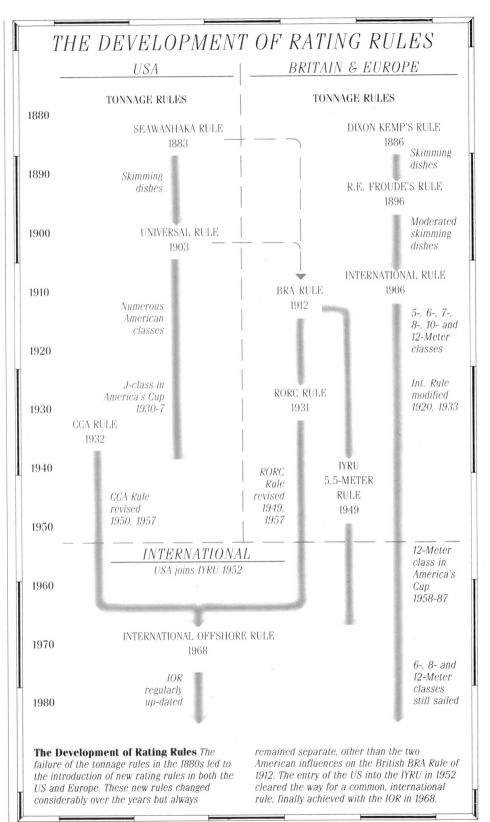

THE DEVELOPMENT OF RATING RULES

	USA	BRITAIN & EUROPE
	TONNAGE RULES	**TONNAGE RULES**
1880		
	SEAWANHAKA RULE 1883	DIXON KEMP'S RULE 1886
		Skimming dishes
1890	*Skimming dishes*	R.E. FROUDE'S RULE 1896
1900	UNIVERSAL RULE 1903	*Moderated skimming dishes*
		INTERNATIONAL RULE 1906
1910	BRA RULE 1912	*5-, 6-, 7-, 8-, 10- and 12-Meter classes*
	Numerous American classes	
1920		*Int. Rule modified 1920, 1933*
1930	*J-class in America's Cup 1930-7*	RORC RULE 1931
	CCA RULE 1932	
1940		*RORC Rule revised 1949, 1957* — IYRU 5.5-METER RULE 1949
1950	*CCA Rule revised 1950, 1957*	
	INTERNATIONAL *USA joins IYRU 1952*	*12-Meter class in America's Cup 1958-87*
1960		
1970	INTERNATIONAL OFFSHORE RULE 1968	
	IOR regularly up-dated	*6-, 8- and 12-Meter classes still sailed*
1980		

The Development of Rating Rules *The failure of the tonnage rules in the 1880s led to the introduction of new rating rules in both the US and Europe. These new rules changed considerably over the years but always remained separate, other than the two American influences on the British BRA Rule of 1912. The entry of the US into the IYRU in 1952 cleared the way for a common, international rule, finally achieved with the IOR in 1968.*

THE INTERNATIONAL RULE

At the turn of the century, several clubs in various European countries had their own series of rating rules based on length and sail area, not unlike that of the YRA in Britain. One such rule was that of the Yacht Club de France:

$$\text{Tonnage} = \frac{^{5}/_{4} \times (L - ^{1}/_{2}B)}{5.5}$$

This rule produced 1, 2½, 5, 10 and 20 tonners, all of which were sailed in the first Olympic sailing regatta, held in France in 1900 (p198). The first five races for the One Ton Cup were sailed in One Tonners (p73), while the 10 and 20 tonners were used for the Coupe de France in its early days (p172).

In an effort to co-ordinate the various rating rules, a conference was called in London in April 1906 (p161). The New York Yacht Club, having only recently drawn up the Universal Rule, declined to attend, but the European countries present decided on a new International Rule. It was intended to produce desirable and seaworthy boats and therefore did not just contain a formula. The scantlings – that is the set of standard dimensions for the hull and its components – were to be laid down by Lloyd's Register of Shipping in London for

A fleet of 6-Meters in 1911; note the gaff rigs and small jibs.

each size of boat, and, at last, a measurement of freeboard (F) was inserted, so that low freeboard would be penalized. In order to prevent low, flat, U-shaped ends, length was assessed by measuring the waterline length and considering the girth at the overhanging bow and stern; if the latter were long and wide, the apparent length would be longer and thus penalized. The measurements were to be taken in meters or feet, but the rating would always be quoted in meters:

$$\text{Rating in meters} = \frac{L + B + \frac{1}{2}G + 3d + \frac{1}{3}\sqrt{S} - F}{2}$$

The rating could be used on a time allowance system, but it was recommended that boats were built to exact ratings and sailed level against each other, in other words, without any handicaps.

Thus were born the famous 6-Meter, 8-Meter and 12-Meter classes, which have raced on and off from 1906 to the present day. In the early days of the rule, however, it was not clear which ratings would be most popular. Thus between 1906 and 1914, 771 meter designs measuring to 10 different ratings were built to the International Rule in Europe, as listed below, although only the 6-, 8- and 12-Meters survived after 1918 to race in any numbers:

5-Meter	41	10-Meter	54
6-Meter	328	12-Meter	35
7-Meter	86	15-Meter	19
8-Meter	174	19-Meter	6
9-Meter	25	23-Meter	3

In 1920, the International Rule was modified and simplified:

$$\text{Rating in meters} = \frac{L + \frac{1}{4}G + 2d + \sqrt{S} - F}{2.5}$$

From then until 1939, the meter boats were considered to be at the top in inshore racing and attracted the best helmsmen and the cleverest designers to squeeze the most out of the rule. The meter classes

Early, gaff-rigged 8-Meters racing downwind.

Bermudan-rigged 6-Meters racing at Cowes in 1923.

were first sailed in the Olympic Games in 1908, with the 6-Meter class remaining until 1952 (pp198-203), while the 12-Meter class was sailed in the America's Cup from 1958 to 1987 (pp150-7). The 10-Meter and then the 8-Meter class was used for the Coupe de France between 1911 and 1938, as was the 6-Meter class from 1984, while the Seawanhaka, British-American, Australian-American (all pp172-3) and the One Ton cups (p73) were all competed for at one time or another up to the present day in 6-Meters. Between 1930 and 1954, the Canada's Cup was sailed for in 8-Meters (p128-9).

American sailors soon became attached to the 'sixes' and 'eights' but only began building 12-Meters in 1928, by which time the British had already built 26. The first American 12-Meter was not launched until 1935, but in 1938-9, Sparkman and Stephens designed four 12s for American owners, the last of which, *Vim*, came over to England and showed her superiority over the British 12-Meter fleet.

By the early 1930s, American clubs had all but abandoned the Universal Rule as a rating rule, favoring instead the classes of the International Rule. The exception was the J-class, 76ft under the International Rule, which still sailed in the America's Cup in the 1930s. The 19- and 23-Meter classes soon died out, as the Europeans declined to continue with them; on both sides of the Atlantic, only a handful of wealthy owners and syndicates had been interested in them.

In 1933, the International Rule was simplified still further:

$$\text{Rating in meters} = \frac{L + 2d + \sqrt{S} - F}{2.37}$$

This is what the rule still looks like today. However, much of the rule does not show in the formula as such, for over the years, numerous sub-regulations have been added, limiting the maximum and minimum dimensions of such measurements as the height of the jibstay up the mast and controlling how the measurements are taken. These sub-regulations have the effect of making the boats look similar, although they may be designed with slightly different dimensions. At any one time, there also tends to be a consensus of the best dimensions and shape within the tolerances for the length, beam, sail area and weights of all kinds.

Up until 1987, the maximum design effort in the International Rule was for the 12-Meters intended for the America's Cup. As pictures of meter boats taken at different times in the 20th century show, there is a strong family resemblance within each class, which is a credit to the rule. Unlike ocean racers, the changes have not been startling, for it has remained in the interests of owners that design changes to boats only occur slowly.

The first boats to the rule tended to copy what had been practiced under other rules, only with longer waterlines compared with overall length. A major change occurred after 1918, with the replacement of the gaff rigs with bermudan rigs. Freeboard increased as the rule penalized low freeboard more after 1920. In the later 1930s, the 6- and 12-Meters had mainsails with inboard booms – in other words, not extending beyond the stern – and had developed the genoa. This sail was first seen at the 6-Meter regatta at Genoa in Italy in 1927. The Swedish skipper, Sven Salén, already had a balloon staysail on his

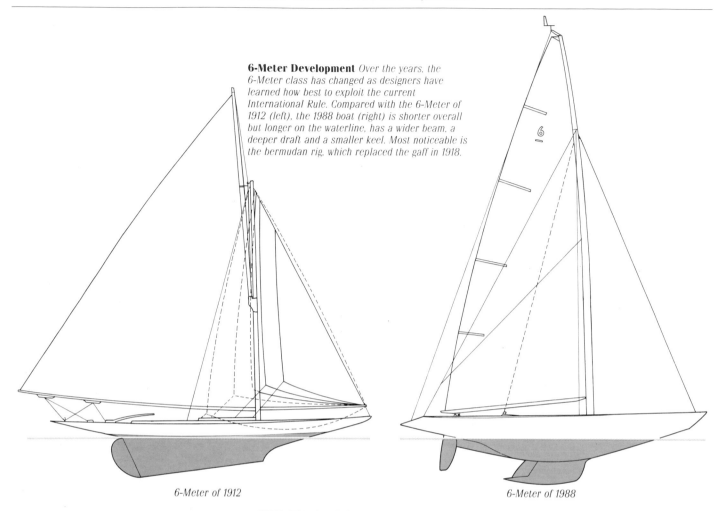

6-Meter Development *Over the years, the 6-Meter class has changed as designers have learned how best to exploit the current International Rule. Compared with the 6-Meter of 1912 (left), the 1988 boat (right) is shorter overall but longer on the waterline, has a wider beam, a deeper draft and a smaller keel. Most noticeable is the bermudan rig, which replaced the gaff in 1918.*

6-Meter of 1912

6-Meter of 1988

yacht *Lilian*, which he hoisted when reaching, as did several other craft. But in this regatta, he had the staysail cut flat and sheeted it in when he came on the wind. From then on, the 6-Meter class was allowed the overlapping genoa, and it spread rapidly to other classes. The convention in the meter classes is to measure the foretriangle, that is the area between the mast, the forestay and the deck, and then limit the overlap in genoa in relation to the deck length. In other words, the actual sail is not measured for area.

Today's meter boats have shortened their ends, cut away as much surface of the hull as the rule allows, and utilized the many modern materials available. Accommodation was built in to the early 8- and 12-Meter boats, but this gradually became minimal to meet the rule, as the classes were used for racing only, and the crews slept elsewhere. In 1974, the 12-Meter class formally abolished the requirement for minimum accommodation.

THE FINAL FORMULA CLASSES

After 1945, the IYRU realized that the 6- and 8-Meter classes were expensive for their size and showed few signs of popularity. A new Meter-class rule was therefore formulated in 1949 based simply on length and sail area, a formulation looking quite like the old Universal Rule. The subregulations on dimensions, however, had the intended effect of making the boats very similar. There was a fixed rating at 5.5 Meters; compared with the 6-Meter, the 5.5-Meter was lighter in displacement and no genoas were allowed, since it was thought that this would reduce costs in the austerity of the post-war years.

$$5.5\text{-Meter rating} = 0.9 \frac{L \times \sqrt{S}}{12 \times \sqrt[3]{\text{displacement}}} + 0.25L + 0.25S$$

The 5.5-Meter class was used in the Olympic Games from 1952 until 1968, when it was dropped in favor of the one-design Soling (see p 205 for a photograph of the 5.5-Meter boat). It was the last formula class to be in the Olympic regatta, and never achieved widespread popularity. Today, a few small fleets remain in Scandinavia and Switzerland.

In 1949, the IYRU also tried to replace the meter boats with a cruiser-racer on a formula and dimensional rule. Levels were set up at 7 Meters, 8 Meters, 9 Meters, 12 Meters and others, and a small number of 7- and 8-Meter cruiser-racers were built and raced in Scandinavia, Scotland and elsewhere. However, if in the 1950s, an owner wanted a cruiser-racer, it was to the ocean-racing rules (see pp 293-5) that he or she would turn, not the International Rule, and the experiment was not a success. It now seems very unlikely that the IYRU will attempt to introduce an inshore formula class; its active commitment remains to one-design classes, and only small numbers of 6- and 12-Meter boats, and a very few 8-Meters, have been built in recent years.

RULES AND DESIGN OFFSHORE

Since 1945, it has been the rating rules for ocean racers that have most influenced all kinds of seagoing craft, be they cruisers, production boats or ocean racers themselves, built to a particular rating rule. Unlike the various formulas designed for inshore racing, the offshore rating rules started from quite a different premise, being intended merely to handicap the disparate set of boats that made up the fleets in the early days of ocean racing. A good example of just how mixed the early ocean racers were in origin is provided by *Jolie Brise*, winner of the first Fastnet Race in 1925. It was a modified Le Havre pilot cutter, in origin therefore a work boat, and it competed against basically cruising boats (for a photograph of *Jolie Brise*, see p63).

THE FIRST OFFSHORE RULES

In 1912, when the new International Rule was prospering, a group of sailors in Bri-

tain were unhappy with the rule and wanted cheaper, smaller, boats to race. They formed the Boat Racing Association and for a while, a mixed bag of boats used the BRA formula with some form of time allowance. After 1918, an inshore 18-ft rating class was raced to this rule, but with the 6-Meters doing well, the BRA was absorbed by the YRA and the International Rule prevailed in Britain. The only interest in this diversion lies in the rule itself, which was a direct combination of the Seawanhaka and the Universal Rules, both of which were American:

$$\text{Rating} = \tfrac{1}{3}\,\frac{L \times \sqrt{S}}{\sqrt[3]{\text{displacement}}} + 0.25L + 0.25\sqrt{S}$$

When the first Fastnet Race was about to be run in 1925, the organizers looked about for a rating on which to base the time allowance. One of the organizers, Malden Heckstall-Smith, who had been involved

with the creation of BRA, recommended using an adaption of it, in which F was a freeboard calculation:

$$\text{Rating} = 0.1\,\frac{L \times \sqrt{S}}{\sqrt[3]{\text{displacement}}} + 0.2L + 0.2\sqrt{S} - 0.2F$$

The displacement, that is the actual weight of the entire boat, was taken from the designer's drawings, but this proved unsatisfactory, for boats seldom weigh as designed, and some boats had no plans on file. A new formula was devised in 1931, therefore, by the Royal Ocean Racing Club, in which displacement was replaced in the rating by a measurement of the beam multiplied by the draft (D) of the boat:

$$\text{Rating} = 0.15\,\frac{L \times \sqrt{S}}{\sqrt{B} \times D} + 0.2L + 0.2\sqrt{S}$$

This was the exact form of the RORC Rule until it was finally abandoned in favor of its successor, the IOR, in 1970. Tacked on to it by then were 'stability allowance,' 'propeller allowance,' 'draft penalty' and many other modifications. But what always resulted was a rating in feet that could come out at any number, for instance 24.3ft or 61.8ft, and to which a time allowance was applied. It was to this rule that many hundreds of ocean racers were built throughout the world in the later 1930s and after 1945.

THE CCA RULE

In the United States, the organizers of the Bermuda Race, the Cruising Club of America, used from 1923 to 1926 a time-allowance system based simply on length, which worked because the boats in the race were roughly similar. From 1928 to 1932, a slight variant of the Universal Rule

Nina *Designed in 1928 by Starling Burgess and owned by Paul Hammond (USA), the schooner Nina was 18 m (59 ft) long and had a bermudan sail on one mast, the first such sail to be used to cross the Atlantic. It was designed to rate well under the handicapping system to be used in the 1928 Transatlantic Race, while the schooner rig benefited from the Universal Rule. With its low weight and sparse accommodation below decks, it attracted complaints that it was 'against the spirit of modern racing' and 'too racy.' Under different ownership, Nina won the 1962 Bermuda Race, the oldest boat ever to have done so.*

was used, with the result that the CCA Rule looked much like that of the RORC.

One boat that rated well under both rules was *Dorade*, designed by Olin Stephens. Winner of the 1931 and 1933 Fastnet and the 1931 Transatlantic races, it began the trend to design and build boats to suit both rules. *Dorade* was 15.8 m (52 ft) long with a narrow beam of 3.1 m (10 ft 3 in) and a bermudan yawl, which put an end to gaff rigs for ocean racers. For speed, it owed something to the meter boats in its fair lines and moderate ends, but the freeboard, moderate sail area and yawl rig were to become a mark of boats built to the RORC rule in this period (for a photograph, see p 84).

In 1932, the CCA decided to try a different formula for the 1934 Bermuda Race, based on the Seawanhaka Rule, with plus or minus factors for beam, draft and freeboard. The new CCA Rule was:

$$\frac{\text{Rating}}{\text{in feet}} = 0.6\sqrt{S} \times \text{rig allowance} + 0.4L$$

Not only was the structure different from the British RORC Rule, but the method of measuring length had the effect of producing different shaped boats. The RORC used girth stations in the manner of the meter boats, so that fuller ends were penalized. The CCA considered the profile only and measured at four per cent of the waterline length above the waterline plane; thus they retained full sterns. Additionally, the American rule was a 'base boat rule,' the figures being regularly adjusted to try to keep the design of boats 'desirable.' The British, although making adjustments to their rule from time to time, did not tune the rule with the same frequency.

Since designers were able to evolve any shape that they thought would benefit from whichever rule they were designing to, from 1932 until 1970, the British and American offshore rules produced different boats. It became obvious to any sailor looking at a boat which rule it had been built under. Ironically, boats which competed on the opposite side of the Atlantic using the 'wrong' rule often met with success. One such example was the highly successful *Carina*, owned by Richard Nye and designed by Philip Rhodes. A typical CCA boat of the period, it was a 16.3-m

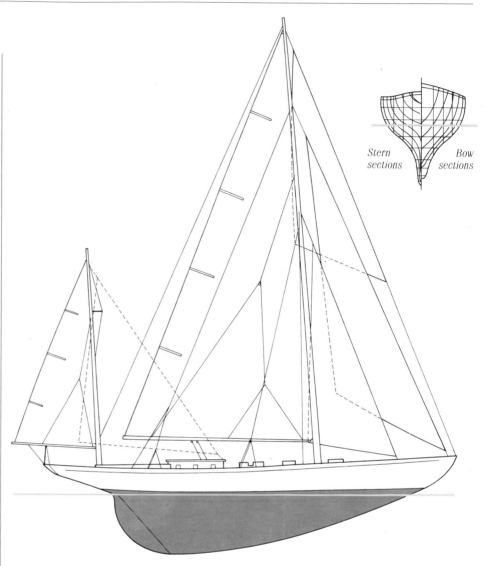

Stern sections Bow sections

(53-ft 6-in) yawl with a wide stern, a draft of only 1.8 m (6 ft), and a 4-m (13-ft) wide beam which carried along much of its length (see p 96 for a photograph). For a time, the CCA Rule favored centerboards, although *Carina* had a fixed keel, but it was in strong contrast to a typical RORC boat with its pinched ends, narrow stern and small sail area. In 1957, it won both the Transatlantic and Fastnet races in heavy weather.

The RORC Rule was revised in 1949 and 1957, reflecting new ideas in design. One of these was that light displacement would be an advantage. In the first postwar races in Britain, success went to two boats, sailed by Blondie Hasler and Adlard Coles respectively. Both were lightweight Scandinavian designs, Hasler's actually a 30-Square Meter boat, but neither were

Dorade *Designed in 1930 by Olin Stephens and built by his brother Rod, Dorade rated well under both the CCA and RORC Rules. By the standards of the day, Dorade was a small boat, with a narrow beam (see bow and stern sections top right) and a weight-saving interior, but it was one of the most successful ocean racers of the 1930s.*

◆◆◆

originally designed for offshore races although both did well under the RORC Rule. The boat which changed European ocean-racing thought was *Myth of Malham*, designed in 1947 by Laurent Giles to a concept and detail as required by its owner, John Illingworth. With very short ends, a high freeboard and a cutter rig in the center of the boat, it was a light-displacement craft, 11.5 m (37 ft 9 in) long with a 2.8-m (9-ft 4-in) beam and 2.1-m (7-ft) draft. Its successes outdated the rest of the fleet and inspired a new breed of

Clarionet *Boats designed to the RORC Rule in the late 1960s, like* Clarionet *(above), were beamier than their predecessors, with fin keels and separate rudders. In this respect, they became more like those boats designed to the CCA Rule.*

boats that dominated British ocean racing into the 1950s.

The RORC Rule was followed in Europe, Australia and New Zealand, while the few ocean-racing boats in South American countries followed the CCA Rule, as did most, but not all, parts of the United States, there being other kinds of rating in use by various clubs and associations. The final form of the CCA Rule, as revised in 1950 and 1957, was a pure 'base boat' formula with the measured length, L, adjusted by factors found by measurement and definition:

$$\text{Rating in feet} = \frac{0.95 \, (\text{L} \pm \text{D} \pm \text{displacement} \pm \text{S} \pm \text{F} + \text{iron keel factor})}{\times \text{ballast ratio} \times \text{propeller factor}}$$

In the final days of both this and the RORC Rule, boats began to be designed with fin keels and separate rudders. The British boats began to get more beam at last, which made them sail better and which was actually an advantage under their rule. Strangely, the American boats became progressively narrower for their length by the late 1960s.

Myth of Malham *One of the most successful post-war ocean racers,* Myth of Malham *changed the face of European yacht design with its light displacement, short ends and high freeboard. The lines are shown to the right.*

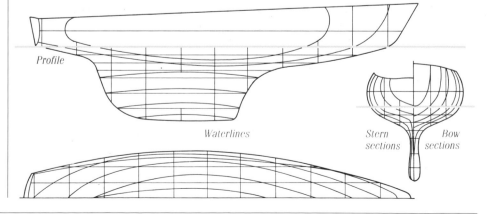

Profile

Waterlines

Stern sections

Bow sections

THE INTERNATIONAL OFFSHORE RULE

From the mid-1930s, there was considerable talk of merging the CCA and RORC Rules. In particular, German and Scandinavian yachtsmen felt that the 'Anglo-Saxon' rules should cease being divided, so that they could design new boats for international competition with some confidence of success. A meeting was held in Bremen, West Germany, in June 1961, at which leading offshore sailors requested the creation of a single, uniform, international, rating rule for ocean racing boats. It was noted that despite its title, the old International Rule for inshore racing had never been agreed to by the Americans and only used by some of their sailors some time after it had been in use. The result of the meeting was the formation of the Offshore Rules Coordinating Committee, which matched some minor methods and regulations under the two rules. The formulas, however, remained far apart, as did their management.

Matters took a further step forward in 1967 when the Offshore Rules Coordinating Committee formed an 'international technical committee' under the chairmanship of Olin J. Stephens to merge the two rules. By November 1968, the draft of the new rule was ready, based on the best points of the CCA and RORC Rules. After revision, the new rule – the International Offshore Rule or IOR – became fully effective from 1 January 1971 (pp 64-5 for the full history of the creation of the IOR).

The CCA abolished its own rule and began racing under the IOR in the 1970 season. The RORC did the same to its rule, while the British, Australian and European boats previously rated under the RORC were rated to the IOR for the 1971 season. It must be realized that it was existing CCA and RORC boats that were first measured to the IOR, but it was not long before new designs were being built to the new formula itself.

The IOR looked more like the RORC Rule than the CCA, but the RORC Rule itself had evolved via the BRA Rule from two American rules, the Seawanhaka and the Universal Rule. The rule included DC, a correction for draft; FC, a freeboard correction; EPF, an engine and propeller factor; and CGF, the center of gravity, found by inclining the boat and seeing how it

IOR Fleet *A fleet of One Tonners (27.5 ft IOR) line up at the start of a race for the One Ton Cup, held in Torbay, England, in 1974. Note the masthead rigs of the period and the moderate to high freeboard.*

---

heeled at small angles. This detected whether the hull was light in comparison with the ballast.

Rating in meters or feet =

$$\left(0.13 \frac{L \times \sqrt{S}}{\sqrt{B \times D}} + 0.25L + 0.2\sqrt{S} + DC + FC \right)$$
$$\times EPF \times CGF$$

PRESSURES ON THE IOR

The euphoria with which the introduction of a single, international, ocean-racing rule was greeted proved to be short lived. Owners of existing boats designed to previous rules found that their boats did not do so well against boats specially designed and built to the IOR. In other words, thousands of boats were outclassed, particularly in the US, where the CCA type of boat was even less favored by the new rule. Because the new rule was established and international, designers put considerable effort into designs which might well now be marketed everywhere; in doing this, they took advantage of the 'small print' of the formula, aided by computers which could give an almost instant

answer on the rating effect of small changes to aspects of a new design.

Despite a running battle with critics, and continuous small, and some quite large changes to the IOR, racing under the rule prospered, with many major events using it. The fact that it was possible to contemplate a race around the world – the first Whitbread Race from 1973-4 – using the IOR was surely a vindication of it; it is unlikely that such a race could have been arranged under the old national rules.

The maximum number of boats rated to the rule occurred in the 1978 season, when 10,500 were certified. Thereafter, a slow decline began, with a rather faster decline in the US, reflecting that country's tradition of regional and club rules. The Europeans, Australians and New Zealanders were more used to centralized national authorities administering a current and generally acceptable rule. By 1989, the total number of IOR boats was about 6,400 world-wide. But, for all its problems, the

◆◆◆

L'Esprit d'Equipe *The winner of the fourth Whitbread Around-The-World Race in 1985-6, L'Esprit d'Equipe is an example of a very seaworthy IOR design of the period. At 17.6 m (57 ft 9 in) LOA, it had a big sail area, fractional rig, minimum profile and a contemporary keel shape.*

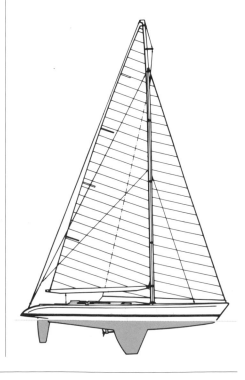

State of the Art *The design thinking of 1987 under the IOR can be seen in the Three-Quarter Tonner Decosol. A light-displacement boat with a complex fractional rig and sail control, its cabin has been reduced to the minimum dimension under the Three-Quarter Ton Rule. The wide, almost flared, stern is intended to give a lever for crew weight; all seven crew are seen here as far to windward as allowed. Their weight is around one sixth of total displacement.*

IOR has created by far the largest fleet of keeled boats ever known.

The fact remains that the rule is both complicated and expensive to measure to. Computers have long been in use by 'both sides' — the rating authorities and the designers. The intensity of competition at the top means that designs are soon out-dated, but this issue is clouded because the very best crews invariably climb into the newest boats. As for the rating rule itself, it probably represents the last stage in the evolution of rating rules, since embedded in it are the Seawanhaka and Universal Rules, the Boat Racing Association formula and the resulting RORC Rule. It may sometimes be difficult to recognize these, with so many additions, modifications and tortuous means of arriving at the basic factors. In 1988, the book setting out the Rule ran to 84 pages of fine print. For instance, the methods of arriving at the sail area took up 16 pages.

A number of factors now show in the formula, so that the basic formula, previously detailed within the parentheses, is now known as the 'measured rating' (MR); the total rating today is:

$$\text{Rating in meters or feet} =$$
$$MR \times DLF \times EPF \times CGF \times MAF \times SMF \times LRP \times CBF \times TPF$$

Of those factors not previously mentioned, DLF is the displacement length factor; MAF, multiple appendage factor; SMF, spar material factor; LRP, low rigging penalty; CBF, centerboard factor; and TPF, trim penalty. All these are means of adjusting the rating of a boat, depending on its supposed speed-producing or decreasing features.

With many thousands of boats built or converted to the rule, there have been numerous changes of detail and attempts at hull and rig design, some of which succeeded and progressed, others of which were quietly dropped. In general, over the years, displacement has become lighter, sail area larger, rigs more delicate and accommodation almost non-existent. Wetted surface has been reduced by cutting down on the keel profile. Except in the larger boats, wheels for steering have given way to tillers, and cockpits have been opened at the stern to save weight and drain off water quickly. Hulls have become more beamy and more reliant on the weight of the crew for performance, an aspect which has caused alarm from the point of view of safety and stability.

MEASUREMENT RULES AND MULTIHULLS

A multihull first raced in the Seawanhaka Cup in 1898, but this type of boat did not become part of ocean racing until the 1960s. At that time, the protagonists were eager to prove that they could manage faster speeds and passages than conventional monohulls. Once this was established, it seemed logical to have a rating rule and a time scale so that multihulls of various designs could race together offshore. The racing practices of multihulls have, however, turned out rather differently to other boats and they tend to go in for special events, notably single-handed, long-distance races. Among the reasons for this is that they are weight sensitive, so that a big crew, their food and equipment would be detrimental to performance and safety. Berthing these wide hulls also causes problems in certain harbors, so they berth at selected centers only.

In the 1980s, a few, new formula rules have been created for specific classes racing level without handicap, notably the Formula 40 (see p167) and the Micro Multihull (see p231). There have also been efforts to introduce a wider measurement rule for various offshore multihulls. The RYA introduced a multihull rule in 1960 based on length, beam and sail area, since weight was considered too complex to measure. However, since weight is critical to these craft, the rule did not prosper. Then Vic Stern, a Californian, proposed the Stern Rule, which weighed the boat and had a computer program to allow for numerous measurements. This rule was adopted by the IYRU as the International Offshore Multihull Rating (IOMR) Rule. Some enthusiasts used it in the 1970s in Australia and California, but in Britain, the Multihull Cruiser Racing Association (MOCRA) found it complex to administer and instead used the Portsmouth Yardstick (see p68). Currently, it appears that multihull racing thrives without a conventional measurement rule.

THE EFFECT OF RACING BOAT DESIGN

Scores of features first tried in racing boats have found their way into the design and building of all kinds of boats never intended for racing, such as daysailers, cruisers and production boats.

MATERIALS

A vast number of improvements have occurred in sail, spar and hull materials over the years, a number of which were first tried out on ocean racers. Artificial fibers for sails have been in general use since the 1950s, but first appeared in racing spinnakers and light sails in the 1930s. Almost all spars are now in aluminum, a material first used in 1947 to improve the strength and lightness of offshore racing-boat rigs. Large boats, such as the J-class, had often had steel masts many years before. Development continues in racing rigs, with such mast fittings as spreaders and their attachments, masthead equipment, halyard sheaves and other items first introduced as a way of reducing overall mast weight and then gradually adopted by other, non-racing boats as standard equipment over the years.

In recent years, there has been an increase in the use of 'exotic' materials for hulls, carbon fiber for some spars and foils, and titanium for metal fittings on deck. Few of these have been copied by non-racing craft because they offer only marginal improvement in performance for very high cost and in some cases are suspect over a long period of use and need renewal or constant monitoring.

MEASUREMENT RULE EFFECTS

In the 19th century, working boats had low freeboard, a characteristic inherited from the need of fishermen to handle nets over the side of the deck. Yacht designers copied this until the ocean-racing rules of the late 1930s gave a bonus to freeboard. Under the RORC Rule of the early 1950s, there was a move towards 'reverse sheer,' giving a humpback effect. Other sheers were straight and high, and cruising boats have copied this with ample freeboard, improving accommodation and keeping decks dryer.

The profiles of both bow and stern have invariably aped contemporary racers, for nothing gives away the age of a boat quite like these two features. The overhanging spoon bows and counters caused by the length-and-sail-area rules stayed with the cruising boat through the first half of the 20th century, albeit in modified form. The planked wood construction of the period lent itself to ends which drew out in this way, but really it was fashion, copying the rated ocean racers. When the IOR became established in the early 1970s and short, straight ends came in, ordinary sailing boats followed this trend. Today, stems are a straight line with just a slight rake forward. The detrimental weight of the overhanging counter has gone.

A major innovation in yacht design, although now historic, was ballast on the outside of the keel. Once, ballast was all inside in the form of pigs of lead or iron, although in working boats, stones, shingle and copper ore were used. The plank-on-edge boats depended entirely on ballast for their stability, having no form of stability in their hull shape. The idea thus occurred to boat builders to fasten lead to the outside of the hull, thereby getting it low enough to be effective. A Scotsman, John Inglis, is said to have been the first to add an outer ballasted keel to a 5-tonner in 1877. Today, all ballast, either iron or lead, is on the outside, although it is still possible to use inside ballast for trimming the boat and adjusting the total displacement. It is possible to cut into the lead itself if adjustment is needed.

IMPROVEMENTS IN SPEED

For a number of years, the almost universal bermudan rig – a triangular mainsail fastened along the mast and boom – was considered a rather dangerous innovation, for inshore racing only, and hoary debates on the merits of gaff versus bermudan rigs for cruising continued into the 1950s. In the US, the rig was once called the Marconi rig, after early radio towers, or leg o' mutton, being triangular.

The rig originated on the Atlantic island of Bermuda, where as early as 1808,

Nyria *Originally a 23-Meter under the International Rule, Nyria was rerigged with a bermudan rig for the 1920 racing season, the first big-class boat to be so rigged. The rig shown here is a simplification of its first bermudan rig.*

a local schooner was reported with a triangular sail on a single mast. Local, unballasted racing boats had big triangular sails, laced to a single mast, that could not be lowered, which made for exciting racing in regattas.

When the big cutters were fitted out after World War I for the 1920 season, one of them, *Nyria*, which had been built to the 23-Meter rating under the International

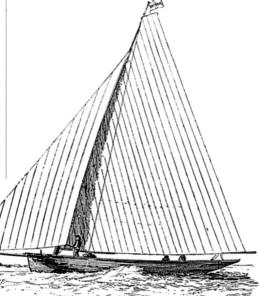

The Bermudan Rig *Locally designed boats raced in Bermuda in the 19th century with triangular sails rigged on a single mast. This bermudan rig was not widely adopted for sailing boats until the 1920s.*

Rule of 1906, and which was owned by Mrs. R.E. Workman, was fitted out with a single tall mast and a new rig designed by C.E. Nicholson. Its opponents at the time all kept the gaff rig and topsails. The 1920 America's Cup races were the last to see gaff mainsails and topsails; by the time of the next race in 1930, the bermudan rig was well established for racing boats. At the same time, the first Fastnet races were being competed for by gaff-rigged boats, although by the late 1930s, a mixture of rigs was evident, with the new ocean racers such as *Dorade* sporting the bermudan rig. In the US, the Seawanhaka Cup winner of 1895 had a bermudan rig, but the gaff rig remained popular, with a new one-design class, the 13.7-m (45-ft) Larchmont, fitted out with a gaff rig and a topsail in 1917, although there was one boat in the fleet with an experimental bermudan rig. The Star class, originally gaff rigged, changed to bermudan rig in 1922.

As teething troubles were overcome in the rig, it was universally adopted for cruising, being simpler and lighter and, for the reason that it was first adopted, immensely more efficient to windward.

After the genoa jib originated in the 6-Meter class in 1927, it soon spread to ocean racers. In due course, it appeared on racing boats in the form of the masthead genoa, as the sail was less highly rated per area than the mainsail. What was once considered as an excessive sail has now become standard in most cruisers, again because of its simplicity; ironically, many ocean racers have reverted to fractional rigs, in which the forestay and genoa are attached a slight distance below the top of the mast.

HULL CONFIGURATION

A major contribution to improving speed, and a conspicuous feature transferred from ocean racers to many standard and cruising boats, is the fin keel with separate rudder. This is not a matter of any rating rule as such, rather the eventual result of reducing the area of the keel for minimum skin friction. Separate keels and rudders are nothing new, as the lines of skimming dishes show, but for the offshore racer and all cruising boats, this profile was not generally acceptable. The Dutch designer, E.

Conquistador *Winner of the SORC in 1964, this Cal 40 was one of the first successful ocean racers equipped with a separate fin keel and rudder. This new configuration marked the end of keels with attached rudders on racing boats.*

Van de Stadt, first produced boats with this configuration in the 1950s, while the British yachtsman, John Illingworth, designed and sailed *Wista*, a miniature ocean racer, with this configuration in 1954. Other designers of the time copied him, but most successful boats continued with shorter and shorter keels with the rudder attached to them. The result of this was that the rudder became closer and closer to the center of the boat, causing severe steering difficulties.

In 1964, the Cal 40 *Conquistador*, designed by Bill Lapworth, won the SORC; it had a minimal fin keel with a quite separate rudder aft, balanced without any skeg or structure attached. For the 1966 RORC season in Britain, Sparkman and Stephens designed *Roundabout* and *Clarionet* with the same configuration, and both swept all before them, while Dick Carter's *Rabbit*, again with a separate keel and rudder, won the 1965 Fastnet Race. From then on,

the separate rudder was used for all new ocean racers and was increasingly adopted for production boats; it was probably the biggest change of any accepted hull shape since *Britannia* and *Gloriana* in the 1890s.

For one reason or another, some cruising boat designs have compromised with medium-length keels, but the option is there and the fin keel has proved itself racing and cruising across the oceans of the world. Some ocean racers may have quite extreme keels of a smaller area than ever, but there is a limit to this, for if the boat has too small a lateral area, it will tend to drift sideways. This slows it down through an effect called induced drag.

Chapter 9

Sailing Waters of the World

Few seas and oceans are closed for sailing, but there are certain coasts and waters that are deservedly popular, whether for cruising, racing or just berthing a boat. In these areas, it is impossible to count the vast number of anchorages, ranging from open roadsteads to enclosed basins, where boats can moor. Some are utterly delightful, others quite appalling, but a number of them stand out as being almost synonymous with boats and sailing. In this chapter, 40 such places are described in detail, with sketch maps to illustrate the topography of the area. In addition, a few introductory words give a feel for the regional sailing waters in which these ports are located.

SAILING WATERS OF THE WORLD

Few of the world's waters are actually inaccessible to sailing boats; at the right time of the year and with a suitable vessel, an adventurous sailor can explore anywhere in the world, including such seemingly inhospitable waters as those of the Antarctic or the Red Sea. If some waters are out of bounds or are inadvisable destinations, it is for political or military reasons or because they are frequented by drug-runners or local pirates.

There are certain coasts, though, which are deservedly popular for cruising, racing or just berthing a boat. These vary tremendously in style and atmosphere – from a crowded Mediterranean resort to a deserted Caribbean cay, from the rocky, tree-lined coast of New England to the coral paradise of the Great Barrier Reef. Each sailor will have his or her own preferences: some will praise one harbor or stretch of water for the very reasons that another dislikes it.

Any selection of specific ports and coasts must, of necessity, be somewhat arbitrary. Thus the waters and ports covered in this chapter are, on the whole, those that are synonymous with sailing, whether racing or cruising, or those that are representative of the facilities and atmosphere in a particular part of the world. Some ports are particularly associated with cruising, their marinas, facilities and ambience all relating to a leisured, relaxed way of life. Others are the venues for inshore races and have a very different atmosphere; a visiting class championship or the start or finish of a major, long-distance, ocean race imparts a feeling of excitement and activity to such a port.

FACILITIES

The growth of both cruising and racing has meant a vast increase in the standard and range of facilities available in a port. Marinas are now found in most places around the world; many ports that were once predominantly fishing or commercial centers now have a sailboat basin or have been entirely transformed into sailing harbors. Many well-established sailboat havens have been expanded by dredging and blasting or the construction of moles and new harbor walls.

The facilities available vary from port to port. They may be as sophisticated as those found at Fort Lauderdale, Florida, where it is possible to obtain a maid, laundry and valet service, as well as a full range of sailing, commercial and other ancillary services. Or it could be as basic as those in many Caribbean ports where new equipment or spare parts for a boat have to be ordered from America.

THE CHARTER INDUSTRY

The growth in sailing since the 1960s is in a large part due to the charter industry. In 1947, a retired British navy commander, Vernon Nicholson, set off from England on a cruise to Australia. One of his ports of call was English Harbor on the West Indian island of Antigua. He so liked the town that he decided to stay. Aware that the location was ideal for a resort, Nicholson decided to set up his own company, Nicholson Yacht Charters, in 1948, to develop the potentially lucrative charter business in the Caribbean.

Prior to this date, there had been some private chartering, but Nicholson's was the first firm to concentrate solely on chartering as a commercial business. It was the beginning of a revolution in sailing; subsequently, the charter industry has spread to virtually every popular cruising area in the world.

There are three basic types of charter: crewed, bareboat, and flotilla. Depending on the size of the vessel, a crewed charter can vary from a full ship's crew to various combinations of skipper, cook and deckhand, according to the needs of the charterers. Such a charter is ideal for those with limited sailing experience.

Bareboat chartering is for those with sailing experience and, rather like renting a self-drive car, means that a fully equipped boat can be chartered and sailed without a hired crew. The half-way house between those two extremes is flotilla or fleet-cruise sailing. Each boat in the flotilla is sailed by the charterers, but one of the boats has an experienced skipper and crew on board, employed by the charter company. Every day the fleet meets up at appointed ports and the experienced skipper is always in radio contact in case of an emergency.

PROFILES AND MAPS

On the next 35 pages is a series of profiles of major sailing waters and ports of the world, chosen because of their popularity with yachtsmen. The latitudes and longitudes given in the text are those of the approximate center of the port or sailing water. All miles are nautical miles unless specifically stated otherwise. The descriptions of facilities available are written in general terms, for such facilities, of course, are subject to constant change. These profiles are intended to give an idea of what is available in each port or anchorage, and are not definitive in their information. Those who intend to sail to any of these destinations will obviously need to acquire and consult the relevant charts and pilot books.

The following symbols are used on the accompanying maps:

 Mean high-water line
Mean low-water line

 Steep cliffs

 Rocks exposed at low water

 Coral reefs

 Fairway, usually marked with buoys or directed by leading lights

 Yacht club

 Yacht marina or onshore mooring

 Offshore mooring

 Significant lights: lighthouse, beacon, leading light

Conspicuous monument, fort or castle

THE BALTIC

In 1888, one of the most enduring sailing tales, *The Falcon on the Baltic* by Frank Knight, was published. The *Falcon* was an 8.5-m (28-ft) converted lifeboat and its voyage, covering only a small part of the Baltic, was, in fact, a trip through the waterways of the Netherlands, the Frisian Islands and Germany, then, via some of the Danish islands, to Copenhagen. Nevertheless, although the big-crewed yachts of the 19th century had often visited the main ports, it was the *Falcon*'s voyage that established the tideless Baltic as a classic cruising ground.

The Baltic's southern shore is about 54°N and the main sailing waters extend to 60°, although the Gulf of Bothnia extends even further north, to one degree short of the Arctic Circle. The location means that summers are short – there can still be ice in places at the beginning of May – but daylight lasts almost around the clock in June and July. The climate from June to August is usually temperate, but there can be gales, fog, or just cold weather. On the other hand, anticyclonic spells tend to last longer. An added attraction is that the air seems free of pollution and the harbors are kept cleaner than anywhere else in the world. The rocky islets and myriad channels of the northern Baltic; the flatter, but no less attractive, Danish landscape; and the universal friendliness, give the area a continuing appeal.

The Scandinavian countries have always made a substantial contribution to the world of sailing in terms of builders, designers, racing organizations and cruising of every sort. While production boats all over the world become more and more similar, there remains a distinctive Baltic boat, one with light displacement, long ends and a small overnight cabin, typified perhaps by the 30-Square Meter. In recent years, the Scandinavians have also produced the best in sailboat electronics and quality equipment. In addition, their helmsmen are held in high regard within racing circles.

The Baltic's sailing fraternity generally take long vacations in mid-summer. Their boats can be found moored in the thousands of protected inlets in the lee of islands, on many of which stand little vacation houses. Although a large number of people actually live on their boats, the host of possible anchorages means that few night passages are necessary. In the archipelagos, it is also possible to sail in sheltered water for miles on end. This means that sailing appeals to a wide number of people, a fact enhanced by the general prosperity of the region, together with its seafaring and sailing tradition (the Royal Swedish Yacht Club, for instance, dates back to 1830).

DANISH ISLANDS
LAT · 55°30′N   LONG · 11°00′E (STORE BAELT)

Much of Denmark is made up of islands. Copenhagen, the capital, is on the largest island, Sjaelland, the other main ones being Fyn, Lolland and Falster. Between these and the mainland (Jylland) run the Store Baelt (Great Belt) and Lille Baelt (Little Belt), main waterways dotted with numerous smaller islands. Öresund (the Sound) is the narrow waterway between Denmark and Sweden. Thus Denmark is blessed with a mass of water, protected from almost all directions. Because the Danes are great sailing enthusiasts, among the waterways are many small marinas and havens, in all sorts of bays and villages. Although the waters are tideless, currents can be quite strong in some of the narrows. However, this varies with the weather and time of year.

In the Great and Little Belts, many of the waters and the smaller harbors are shallow to an extent that restricts cruising to small or shallow-draft boats.

The Little Belt, at its narrowest near Fredericia, has two road and rail bridges over it, but these are high enough for boats with tall masts to pass under. South of the bridges, the narrow channel, for boats of any draft, is like a voyage on an inland waterway. Forty miles north of Sjaelland is the island of Anholt, a popular destination for many cruisers. As a result, it is invariably crowded, if not full up, in the season. Indeed, the whole area can reach saturation point for boats needing berths.

Night sailing is not necessary in the area, as distances between harbors are invariably just a few hours' sail. This part of the world is extremely well covered by pilot books and charts, which describe every haven and anchorage in detail. In contrast to the skerries (rocky islands) of the popular parts of the Baltic, such as the Stockholm Archipelago, the area is low-lying with fields, woods and attractive buildings.

The quayside at Fåborg, on the island of Fyn

The Kongelig Dansk Yachtklub (KDY) – the Royal Danish Yacht Club – has its clubhouse at the Landgelinie in the center of the port of Copenhagen; it has been based there since 1866. Its second clubhouse was destroyed in 1944, and the present building dates from 1960. The club's summer station, and racing base, is at Skovshoved, a few miles further north, where it has acquired a large and prestigious sailboat harbor.

KIEL

LAT · 54°20' N   LONG · 10°10' E

Kiel is Germany's longest-established port for salt-water sailing and a base for the German navy. Situated in the south-west Baltic, Kiel's V-shaped bay gives protection to racing courses from the prevailing south-westerly winds, while for cruising boats and ocean racers, it offers immediate access to the more open Baltic, or to the sheltered passages of the Danish islands and cruising grounds of the Swedish coast.

The 53-mile Nord-Ostsee Kanal (Kiel Canal) connects Kiel's Baltic sailing waters to the North Sea. The canal is continuously used by commercial shipping, but sailboats simply motor on the starboard side close to the bank. They are allowed to sail, but must not tack! Along the canal there are specific permitted stopping points for boats, including the pleasant town of Rendsburg and the Gieselau Canal, which connects with the Eider River to the west, where there are berths in rural surroundings. At the western end of the Nord-Ostsee Kanal is the berthing at Brünsbuttel and, beyond it, the Elbe estuary.

The annual Kiel Week was established in July 1882 by Germany's first yacht club, the Norddeutscher Regatta Verein (see pp170–1). Kaiser Wilhelm II planned it in imitation of Cowes Week, where his grandmother Queen Victoria presided. Kiel Week is now held in June and has ocean-racing, keelboat and dinghy classes. Kiel was host to the Olympics in both 1936 and 1972. The Kiel Yacht Club was formerly known as the Marine Regatta Verein.

There are a number of havens on both shores of the bay; it has been estimated that two-thirds of all German seagoing boats are based in them. The most northerly haven on the west shore is Strande, where most of the boats are moored stern to

post, with access via the bow to a float – a sure sign for those who have come from the North Sea that they are no longer in tidal waters. This is a large, well-protected haven, but all the others, even if they are small, give secure berths.

The largest haven of all is· Schilksee Olympic Haven, built for the 1972 Games. Part of this is used regularly as a marina, but it is also commandeered for the occasional dinghy championship and Kiel Week.

All the havens are a long way from Kiel and its facilities, and their rather suburban surroundings are in sharp contrast to the Baltic waters to the north and the deserted North Sea shores, but the area is a useful staging post for cruising, and the sailing base for Germany's very short coastline.

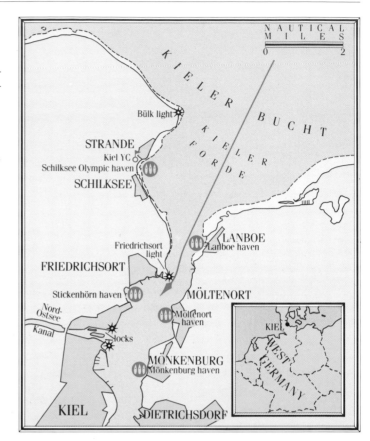

The Schilksee Olympic Haven, built for the 1972 Games.

MARSTRAND

LAT · 57°53′N   LONG · 11°35′E

The major Swedish racing and cruising port of Marstrand, on the island of Koon, faces west into the Skagerrak, but is protected by a ring of rocks and small islands which form Marstrand Fjorden, a perfect bay for a race course of about two miles diameter, regardless of the wind's direction. Permanent buoys are laid in the summer for racing purposes. Because the entrance is possible in all weather, offshore races also start and end here, including the Skaw Race when it is Sweden's turn to run this annual event (see pp 112–13). Every year there are several major championships held at Marstrand, including at least one world championship for meter boats, Olympic classes or Ton Cup boats.

On the small island of Marstrandson is the summer station of the Göteborg Kungliga Segel Sallskapet (GKSS) – the Royal Gothenburg Yacht Club – which has its own racing boat haven. Cruising boats and other visitors, including ferries from

Koon, the larger island opposite, are packed along a waterfront that is backed by stores and houses, all in spotless condition, as are the streets of the town and waters of the harbor. Sailing traffic is continuous in the height of the summer, but boats can be accommodated in large numbers by being berthed bow-on (as in the skerries) with stern lines to buoys – there is always room for one more!

Up and down the coast lie sheltered waters behind islands and skerries, although they are not quite as deep and numerous as those on the east coast of Sweden. The prevailing westerly weather and open Skagerrak also make Marstrand comparatively exposed, but it has an advantage in that, for boats sailing from Kiel and the Danish islands, it is nearer than the east coast of Sweden. From Marstrand, Copenhagen and the Little Belt are both 150 miles away to the south; Kristiansand in southern Norway 120 miles to the west; and Oslo 130 miles to the north.

SANDHAMN

LAT · 59°17′N   LONG · 18°54′E

Sandhamn, on the outer edge of the Stockholm Archipelago on the east coast of Sweden, is the country's most important racing harbor. The Archipelago itself consists of more than 30,000 islands and skerries. The outer skerries are barren boulders, open to the sea and salt air, but the nearer they are to mainland the more vegetation they support. Where permitted by planning, summer cottages have been built on skerries and islands, but the dominant feature remains the characteristic rounded rocks, worn smooth by glaciers and weathered by ice.

Off these rocks, staging and landing places are built wherever it is convenient, while the surrounding water is immediately deep. As a result, a standard Swedish manner of mooring, with the bow almost touching the rock and an anchor or permanent buoy astern, has evolved. As there is no tide, nor tidal stream, a boat can lie at right angles across the channel if necessary. This manner of mooring has had a permanent effect on the design of Swedish boats: the bow pulpit has either an open gate or wooden foot platform to facilitate stepping on and off the boat.

The Kungelig Svenska Segel Sallskapet (KSSS) – the Royal Swedish Yacht Club – besides its permanent clubhouse in Stockholm, has had a summer station on Sandhamn since 1897. The KSSS owns three islands opposite Sandhamn and the group make a perfect harbor, with courses for inshore and offshore racing out to the east and south-east. (When cruising among the channels to the west it is possible to get lost.) The KSSS clubhouse has plentiful permanent accommodation and an excellent restaurant, as well as race offices.

Innumerable local, national and international championships have been held at Sandhamn, including those for various meter and Ton Cup boats.

To get to this island where sailing is king, one has to come by sea, but there is a ferry from Sandhamn to Saltsjöbaden, an outpost of the mainland connected by a nine-km (six-statute mile) road to Stockholm. The distance south to Malmö in south Sweden is 310 miles; north-east to Mariehamn on the Finnish Åland Islands 55 miles; and south to Saltsjöbaden, through the skerries, 23 miles.

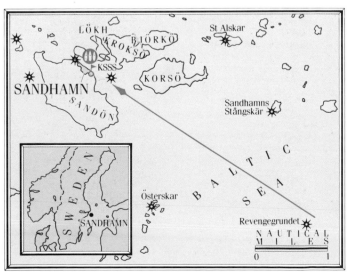

WESTERN EUROPE

This part of the world was the cradle of sailing and has been the scene of its continued expansion for 300 years. Even during the two world wars, building, designing and sailing continued inland, on the German and Swiss lakes and the River Thames in England, for example. The temperate climate generally restricts sailing to the months of April to October, but there are an increasing number of events, especially for dinghies, that take place in sheltered waters all the year round. Winter days are short, often with gales or fog, while mid-summer days are much longer. But the weather still remains somewhat unpredictable, and gales or strong winds can occur at any time. The most frequent winds are from the west, as far south as Cape Finisterre in north-west Spain, where the Portuguese trades from the north are generally more prevalent.

Excellent access to sailing areas means that there are thousands of sailors active on all of western Europe's usable coasts, whether on weekends or on longer vacations and extended voyages. Cultural and topographical differences mean there is immense variety in harbors and coastlines, so sailors can make different-style cruises within the area, year after year. Contrast, for example, the wild but sheltered islands of western Scotland, with their particularly uncertain climate, but many sheltered and uncrowded anchorages; the civilized harbors and deep rivers of north-west France, with tides as high and fast as any in the world (mean spring tides are 11.8m, 38ft 8in); the Channel Islands, with the same tidal regime, a mass of rocks and small harbors, though suffering from over-popularity; and the warmer waters off the Atlantic coasts of Spain and Portugal, not immune to bad weather, but sunny and relaxed.

Racing in north-west Europe is highly organized and plentiful, encompassing all types of sailing. As a result, in many other parts of the world (except the United States), the European systems regarding yacht and dinghy racing are almost slavishly followed. The institution of the yacht club, which originated in Ireland in the early 18th century, is everywhere, although exact customs and functions vary from culture to culture. Spanish clubs tend to have big buildings and few boats, most French clubs have active sailors but little club life, while Britain has no fewer than 1,350 yacht and sailing clubs of all types and varieties.

A multiplicity of harbors exist, from isolated creeks to tidal fishing ports with locks and big commercial-shipping ports. Marinas are established in traditional sailing centers and, increasingly, in restored, once-commercial ports. Facilities are excellent for the most part, and are backed up by a highly developed and commercialized sailing industry.

THE IJSSELMEER

LAT · 52°45′N   LONG · 5°20′E

The largest freshwater lake in Europe that can be entered by seagoing boats, the Ijsselmeer is significant in that it is the center of Dutch sailing, most of which takes place on inland waters. This is because the Dutch coastline is generally low and inhospitable, being a lee shore (for the prevailing wind) in an often bleak North Sea. As a result, the Netherlands is a leading sailing country, but one with a definite difference.

The Ijsselmeer was created out of the Zuiderzee, a gulf of the North Sea. Work began in 1920 on major dikes to exclude the sea, reclaim land, and create the freshwater lake. The main dike, the Afsluitdijk, was completed in 1932 and the final canal in 1956. Entrance from the North Sea is now through locks at either end of the Afsluitdijk, or along the Nordzeekanaal, via Amsterdam, and through a further lock either at Enkhuizen or to the south at Lelystad.

The lake's flat surroundings have a character of their own: attractive towns and villages form small ports with yacht clubs and numerous marinas, which are invariably very crowded. The lake is a mass of sail at the height of the season. A major yacht and dinghy racing base is Medemblik, with its important marina and beautiful old houses. In the days of the Zuiderzee, Enkhuizen was a fishing port, but it now has numerous sailboat berths and a reconstructed open-air fishing village with a sea wall, once needed to withstand the North Sea. The compact town of Hoorn is another major sailing port. The notorious Cape Horn, at the tip of South America, was named after the town when Willem Schouten, a native of Hoorn, rounded the Cape.

There are a number of other ports in the Ijsselmeer, all with marinas and berthing. Amsterdam, for the sailing world one of the great commercial centers for boat builders, equipment makers, insurers and financiers, is also easily accessible. In most harbors there are important docks used by the many commercial barges.

Traditional Dutch barges sailing on the Ijsselmeer.

THE WEST COAST OF SCOTLAND
LAT · 56°05′N   LONG · 5°15′W (CLYDE ESTUARY)

The west coast of Scotland has been a cruising ground since the earliest days of yachting, and it remains a fascinating and unique sailing area. Although it is windy and wet, there is ample sailing under the protection of numerous capes and islands. The unspoiled, mountainous scenery makes the coastline one of the most attractive in Europe, and sometimes, in the mid-summer months, high pressure can settle over the area, providing the additional bonus of good weather.

Most boats and the major yacht clubs are based in the Firth of Clyde. It is from here that the Clyde Yacht Clubs Association, the Clyde Cruising Club, the Royal Northern Yacht Club, the Royal Gourock Yacht Club, and the Royal Western Yacht Club (of Scotland) organize a full racing program. Until 1970, Clyde Fortnight was an established equivalent to Cowes Week, but in recent years Scottish Week (under one sponsor or another) has taken its place. Based at Tarbert, Loch Fyne, it is held in the last week in May. The competition is for offshore, one-design and handicap classes, but many Scottish ports have their own local, long-established, one-design classes, for which there are races in Scottish Week. Away from the Clyde, other clubs include the Oban Sailing Club, the Royal Highland Yacht Club, Oban, and the Western Isles Yacht Club, Tobermory.

For cruising boats, 'inner routes', avoiding the Atlantic seas and weather, tend to be most popular. One such route is from Loch Fyne, through the Crinan Canal (which saves the long journey round the Mull of Kintyre) and then across the Firth of Lorn and on to Tobermory, the last stop before the Minches and Hebrides. Beyond the more distant Hebrides there are even more remote islands, such as St. Kilda to the north-west, once inhabited by people who depended on sheep and some fishing. Life became insupportable on the island in the 1930s, and now only the army occupies it as part of a rocket range. St. Kilda boasts the highest sheer cliffs in Britain at 183m (600ft). It lies 55 miles west of the Outer Hebrides.

Tarbert on Loch Fyne is home to the Scottish Week, held in May.

CROSSHAVEN
LAT · 51°48′N   LONG · 8°17′W

Crosshaven is the sailing harbor of the port of Cóbh, Ireland's chief naval base and a ferry port. It is known as the place where the oldest yacht club in the world is situated. The Royal Cork Yacht Club dates back to at least 1720, being the descendant of the Water Club of the harbor of Cork. Cork Harbor is big enough for sheltered dinghy and keelboat sailing, and every year it hosts national and international championships. Occasionally, a medium-length ocean race is held from Cowes (320 miles), or another English or Scottish port, to Crosshaven. A regular fixture, on even years in July, is Cork Week, a major European regatta for offshore boats of all classes. Crosshaven is also a port of call for the Two-handed Around Britain and Ireland Race, held every four years (see pp102–3).

Transatlantic races have also ended here.

Although a moderate tidal stream sets across the entrance, Cork Harbor is one of the world's most accessible ports in all weathers. Crosshaven itself is up a deep estuary with ample, although unlit, moorings and shelter. There are two marinas, one at the Royal Cork Yacht Club and one off the boatyard. Crosshaven's sailing facilities are probably the best in Ireland, with builders, repair yards, slips, lifts and sailmakers. The Crosshaven Boatyard Ltd has built many famous boats, including *Gipsy Moth V* for Sir Francis Chichester. One yacht designer of world renown, Ron Holland (NZ), has set up his drawing office here.

Extensive waters suitable for cruising lie beyond Fastnet Rock, which is 60 miles to the west.

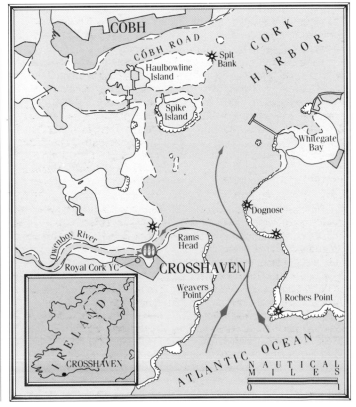

THE THAMES ESTUARY
LAT · 51°40′N   LONG · 1°00′E

During the 19th century, industrialization pushed yachting away from London and the Thames Estuary. In recent years, the improved environment of the river, but more especially the decline of the London docks, has led to the reappearance of moorings and brought a marina to St. Katharine's Dock, near Tower Bridge. But the nearest established bases for cruising and racing remain the ports on the East Anglian coast of Essex and Suffolk, on the northern side of the Thames Estuary. These towns have access to the North Sea and to the ports of the Netherlands. On the south side of the estuary lie less popular, more industrialized ports, such as those on the Medway.

The major racing center of Burnham-on-Crouch is just 72km (45 statute miles) from the center of London. The relatively narrow mouth of the River Crouch and the nearby sandbanks in the Thames Estuary itself are the base of three active racing clubs: the Royal Corinthian Yacht Club, the Royal Burnham Yacht Club and the Crouch Yacht Club. Thanks to these clubs, numerous one-design classes are based at Burnham, and the annual Burnham Week, at the end of August and beginning of September, attracts large fleets of IOR, local handicap, one-design and dinghy classes.

The mouths of the Blackwater and Colne rivers form the next tidal inlet north, with towns along them such as West Mersea, Brightlingsea, Tollesbury, Bradwell Quay and Maldon being synonymous with sailing. They are packed not only with marinas and moorings, but also with sailmakers, boatbuilders, chandleries, brokerages and repair yards. In the early part of this century, it was from these ports that the professional crews of the big cutters were, for the most part, recruited. In the winter months, the same men earned a living by fishing in the estuary waters.

The featureless coast, with its sea walls, flat land and prevailing offshore wind has a reputed tradition of producing a tougher breed of sailor than some of the more popular sailing ports. Further north are the modern container port of Felixstowe and the ferry port of Parkeston Quay, at the entrance to the Stour and Orwell rivers, which are sailing grounds themselves for smaller boats. From Pin Mill in the Orwell, Flushing in Holland is 95 miles east; Dover 50 miles south; and the Solent 160 miles south and then west.

West Mersea on the Essex coast

THE SOLENT AREA
LAT · 50°48′N   LONG · 1°15′W

The principal sailing waters of Britain in terms of actual activity, numbers of boats moored, regular races, and proportion of harbors given up entirely to the sailing industry, the Solent area has long been associated with sailing. It has not always dominated the scene in the way it does in the 1980s – East Anglia, the Clyde and Ireland were as active until the 1930s – but after World War II the Solent ports emerged as the center for sporting and commercial activities. However, with the over-crowding of the Solent sites, better transport to other parts of Britain and the building of marinas elsewhere, the trend is now being reversed.

Strictly speaking, the Solent is the water between the Isle of Wight and the English mainland. It is not a large area, being 20 miles from the western entrance of the Solent to a point in the middle of Spithead, the name for its eastern entrance. The inlet to the north is known as Southampton Water, while the large and rather shallow harbors to the east – Portsmouth, Langstone and Chichester – are not actually on the Solent, but house several thousand boats and are part of the same cruising and commercial area. Although the western Solent averages a little under two miles in width, a prevailing south-west wind produces a fine beat for a race. However, if the winds are northerly, it is difficult to set courses which do not involve extensive reaching.

The Solent's proximity to London means that thousands of Londoners berth their boats in all the harbors. Marinas and marina villages are being created either on new sites, or in Southampton (still a container port) and Portsmouth (a naval base and major ferry port), industrial areas that were lost to boating in the last century. Major sailing bases are Lymington, Hamble,

The River Hamble

❖❖❖

Southampton, Cowes, and the eastern harbors already mentioned. Quieter harbors are Yarmouth, Newtown, Wootton Creek, Bembridge, Seaview, Keyhaven, Beaulieu and Hill Head. Manufacturing, design, maintenance and servicing of every conceivable type of boat are excellent in the area.

From the western end of the Solent, Cherbourg, France, is 65 miles south, Falmouth, 145 miles south-west and the Strait of Dover, 110 miles east.

❖❖❖

Bosham, Chichester Harbor

COWES

LAT · 50°45′N   LONG · 1°18′W

Cowes is famed as a starting and finishing port for innumerable races, long and short, as well as for its role as the social center of British sailing for nearly two centuries. Lying on the north shore of the Isle of Wight, it faces the protected waters of the Solent, where many racing courses can be set. The prevailing south-westerly wind gives a typical windward first leg to a race westward down the Solent, with rural landscapes on either side. Large numbers of starts can be set, as the classes follow each other westward. The anchorages of Cowes Roads and the north of the River Medina are conveniently sheltered from the prevailing wind. There are swinging moorings and marinas further up the river, so almost limitless numbers of boats can be packed in.

The first record of racing at Cowes was in 1813, although there may have been earlier races, as a program of 1814 refers to "the Isle of Wight Annual Regatta." From 1826, a regular regatta was held in early August and run by the Royal Yacht Club (which in 1833 became the Royal Yacht Squadron) and this has continued ever since. Cowes Week is now run by 'the combined clubs' – the Royal London Yacht Club, the Royal Corinthian Yacht Club, the Island Sailing Club, the Royal Yacht Squadron, the Royal Thames Yacht Club, the Royal Southern Yacht Club, the Royal Southampton Yacht Club and the Royal Ocean Racing Club.

Apart from Cowes Week, there are numerous class championships, local races and starts for offshore events. The most popular course is the Island Sailing Club's annual Round-the-Island Race. The starting lines from the Royal Yacht Squadron and other clubs are idiosyncratic: tide-swept, constrained by commercial traffic and in the channel for cruising boats, although the prevailing wind can give a start approximately to windward.

At Cowes there are a number of leading boatbuilders, repairers, sailmakers and equipment manufacturers.

Famous names, past and present, include Uffa Fox's yard, sailmakers Ratsey and Lapthorn, who made sails for 18th-century warships, Marvin's yard, which fitted out King George V's *Britannia*, and Ancasta yard and marina, used for Cowes Week.

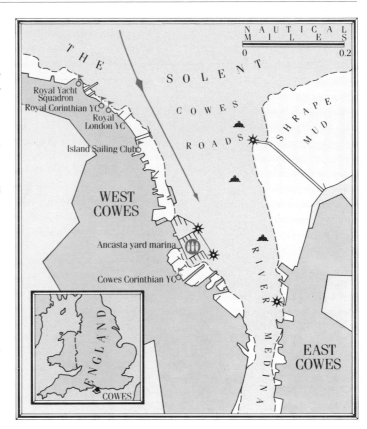

The Royal Yacht Squadron, Cowes

DARTMOUTH

LAT · 50°21′N   LONG · 3°35′W

Dartmouth, with its natural deep-water harbor, has long been important to maritime England. In the *Canterbury Tales*, written in the 14th century, Chaucer tells of "A shipman ... For aught I woote, he was of Dertemouthe ... He new alle the havenes, as they were, fro Gootlond to the cape of Fynystere." Today, the symbols of the maritime tradition are the old custom house quay and the ancient forts guarding the entrance to the port.

In keeping with its historical importance, Dartmouth in the 20th century is the ideal English sailing harbor. Crowded berthing is endemic; visitors are crammed side by side on outer floats, but there always seems to be room for one more! Its beautiful scenery and position in the mildest, southern part of the country make it attractive to cruising boats, and it also caters for racing boats.

On the east side of the estuary, across from the medium-sized town, stands the village of Kingswear. Upstream from them, the river winds between steep banks covered in trees to Totnes, with various landings and hamlets on the way. There are sizeable marinas at both Dartmouth and Kingswear, where cruising traffic is busy in the season. The area is one where tourism rules, but not in detrimental fashion, as Dartmouth's good restaurants and bookshop illustrate.

The marina at Kingswear
◆ ◆ ◆

The Royal Dart Yacht Club, founded in 1866, is across the river from the Dartmouth Yacht Club on the Kingswear waterfront; from there, regular dinghy racing is conducted on courses up and down the river, although the wind is often confusing and squally. Numerous passage races start and finish at Dartmouth, but the climax of the season is the Dartmouth Royal Regatta (its approved title, since the big cutters of earlier days, including *Britannia*, made it a regular port of call). This is invariably held at the end of August. In the days when the racing season was shorter, it was always the last regatta, and the saying was "when Dartmouth Regatta's o'er, there's only Christmas to look forward to."

Dartmouth is commonly thought of as one of a group of sailing ports that make the south-west coast of England a sought-after cruising ground, all ports being within a day's sail. From Dartmouth, it is 65 miles to Guernsey and 90 miles to the nearest point on the north Brittany coast — Perros Guirec. Torbay is just around two headlands, 6 miles to the north-east; to the west lie the other deep-water harbors of Devon and those of Cornwall — the nearest, Salcombe, is around the exposed headland of Start Point 15 miles away. England's most westerly outpost, the Isles of Scilly, is 110 miles away to the south-west.

THE CHANNEL ISLANDS

LAT · 49°10′N   LONG · 2°05′W
(JERSEY)

Politically part of the United Kingdom, the Channel Islands, known in France as Les Îles Anglo-Normandes, have their own parliaments and taxation system. Their place names are a strange mixture of English, French and old Norman words. The islands of Jersey, Guernsey, Alderney, Sark, Herm, Jethou, the rocky outcrop of the Casquets and the vast reef of Les Minquiers, are all popular destinations for cruising boats and are very crowded in season. Alcohol and tobacco have a very low tax rate, which is an added attraction. Financial laws differ from those on the British mainland, so there are numerous offshore financial houses and banks. Boats registered here under the British ensign are outside many British laws.

The strong tides and crowded harbors make cruising more popular than racing, although there are a number of annual races to the islands from British and French ports. The Royal Channel Islands Yacht Club is based at St. Peter Port, Guernsey, and St. Helier, Jersey, where extensive marinas, developed since the 1970s, accommodate hundreds of boats.

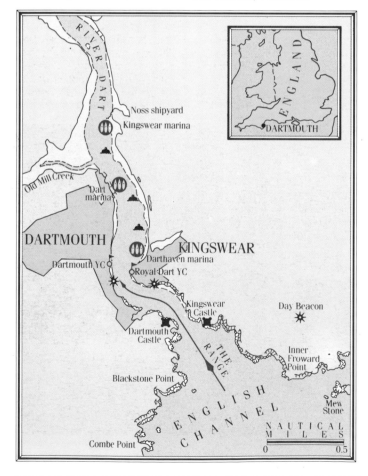

Inner harbor, St. Peter Port

St. Aubin, Jersey

• • •

Guernsey, in particular, has made a major effort to attract racing events. Its new marina, completed in 1988, has been built out over what had been just exposed rocky shore. This has been reserved for residents, leaving the inner harbor for cruising and racing visitors. The 11m (36ft) rise and fall of the tide means that the inner harbor has a dam, enabling boats to stay afloat regardless of the tides. However, it is only possible to leave harbor for 6 hours out of every 12.

The many rocky capes and bays of the Channel Islands provide numerous minor anchorages. In addition, the rocky scenery and clear water are particularly attractive to cruising boats.

Between Alderney and Cap de la Hague on the French mainland, the tidal stream – known as the Race of Alderney – runs to a maximum of 10 knots when north-going at spring tides. Although there are some overfalls, it is safe to pass through, except in heavy weather. When wind and tide are in opposition in strong or gale force winds, boats are strongly advised to avoid this particular route.

Distances from St. Peter Port are: Weymouth, on the English coast, 65 miles north; St. Malo, France, 50 miles south; Needles, Isle of Wight, 85 miles north-east; and Ushant, France, 120 miles south-west.

ST. MALO AND DINARD

LAT · 48°39′N   LONG · 2°01′W

With a rock-strewn entrance, massive rise and fall of tides, and a grandeur well suited to its position on the Côte d'Émeraude, St. Malo is one of France's great sailing centers. The walled town is part of France's maritime heritage: from here sailed privateers and explorers including Jacques Cartier, the first European to sail up the St. Lawrence River, Canada, in 1535. In 1944, many of St. Malo's old buildings were destroyed when the American army besieged the occupying German troops, but the town has been lovingly and thoughtfully restored.

Because of the huge rise and fall of tide, second only in the world to the Bay of Fundy, Canada, the harbor is enclosed by massive locks. Mean high water during spring tides is a remarkable 12m (39ft 4in). Boats lie in basins alongside floating docks, but a newer marina, Port des Sablons, has a sill which allows entrance above a certain height of tide without having to wait for gates to open and shut. Opposite St. Malo, on the west side of the River Rance, lies the town of Dinard, where the bay has been dredged to take boats on moorings at all states of the tide. One mile upriver is one of Europe's few tidal barrages, which makes use of the huge rise and fall of tide to generate electricity. A lock enables boats to pass through the barrage and sail on up the Rance to various anchorages and, eventually, to the town of Dinan, from where a canal goes further inland.

Both the Yacht Club de Dinard and the Société Nautique de la Baie de St. Malo (SNBSM) are active and the area has a full racing program. It is also a major port of call for the annual Tour de France à la Voile (see pp 108-9). The annual Cowes to St. Malo race is usually held at the time of 'le quatorze' (14 July), a national holiday in France that marks the beginning of the main vacation season. The race invariably attracts hundreds of starters from both Britain and France. Additionally, every four years, the Route de Rhum to Guadeloupe (see pp 90-1), starts from St. Malo.

West of St. Malo is the Brittany coast, which is one of the world's great cruising grounds and gourmet areas. Only 130 miles away, just beyond the coastline's western tip, is the island of Ushant, south of which are the harbors of south Brittany and the Bay of Biscay.

The inner basin, St. Malo

LA ROCHELLE

LAT · 46°09′N   LONG · 1°09′W

La Rochelle was a leading French seaport until the end of the 16th century, after which it became a stronghold of the Huguenots. Its trade declined substantially with the loss of France's Canadian colonies in 1763, and no further commercialization took place. Later, installations for transatlantic ships were concentrated at La Pallice, a few miles to the west. Because it was never developed for commercial use, La Rochelle makes an ideal port for sailing.

The entrance to the sheltered harbor is marked by medieval towers, which are part of a city wall. Inside, it is clearly divided into areas for fishing boats and areas for sailboats, as is now the case in many French ports, with resultant advantage to both. Around the harbor, which consists of tidal and non-tidal basins, are some of the finest seafood restaurants in Europe.

La Rochelle's climate is an improvement on Brittany and the English Channel, without the high summer heat of the Mediterranean. The configuration of the land and two large islands, Île d'Oléron and Île de Ré, the latter about 24 km (15 statute miles) long, give semi-sheltered waters for all types of racing boat. This makes it possible to set inshore and Olympic courses, as well as offshore courses of almost any length into the Atlantic and up and down the coast. La Rochelle has been used for Ton Cup and other major ocean-racing events.

During the season, there are regattas for successive classes on most weekends, with a regular spring regatta for dinghy classes, mainly the 470, 420, L'Équipe, Europe and Laser. To cope with the increased numbers of cruisers and offshore racers, a basin has been excavated south-west of the old harbor; known as the Port des Minimes, it has capacity for 2,800 boats, 300 berths being kept solely for visitors.

One of France's major clubs, the Société des Régates Rochelaises (SRR), founded in 1860, is situated by the new sailboat basin marina in a large, modern clubhouse.

Further south, the Atlantic coast of France – with the exception of the Gironde and Arcachon Basin, both of which can be difficult to enter – is without shelter and therefore unsuitable for coastal sailing.

BAYONA

LAT · 42°08′N   LONG · 8°50′W

The north-west coast of Spain, and Bayona in particular, is a natural destination for boats from northern Europe seeking a two-to-three-week return cruise. It is also on the route from the north to the Mediterranean and for Atlantic crossings making use of the trade winds.

Bayona also has historical significance: after Christopher Columbus discovered America, the first of his ships to return, the *Pinta*, arrived here with the news in the spring of 1493; an impressive memorial near the water commemorates this. Bayona's latitude may be the same as that of Boston, Massachusetts and the French Riviera, but the Atlantic Ocean can bring gales at any time and fog is common on the exposed headlands.

Bayona is the best port for boats in the region because it is at the entrance of Vigo Bay, and has good berthing and a large yacht club. If the port were in Sweden, Britain or France, its sheltered waters would be alive with sailing boats and marinas, and boatyards would abound, but because Spain has a longer coastline on the Mediterranean, the development of sailing

Bayona, at the entrance to Vigo Bay

facilities and racing regattas has taken place there. However, an uncrowded sailing area makes a pleasant change.

Bayona's Monte Real Club de Yates runs local class racing and occasionally organizes an offshore series. The port has been the finishing point for transatlantic races and for races organized from Cowes by the Royal Ocean Racing Club, to give a distance of about 630 miles.

For an even bigger yacht club and more facilities, one must travel to the large town of Vigo, further east. Here the Real Club Náutico has boats on moorings all the year around. From Bayona, Ushant is 420 miles to the north-west, Lisbon 200 miles to the south-west, and the Azores 1,200 miles to the west.

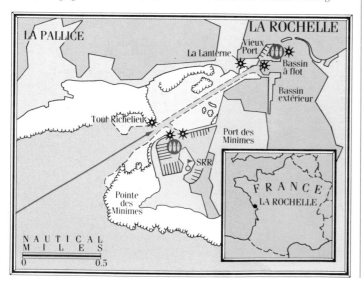

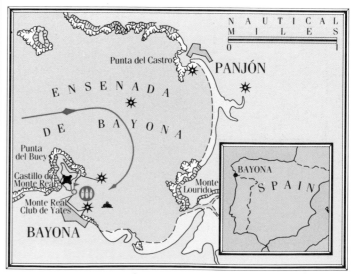

VILAMOURA
LAT · 37°04′N   LONG · 8°07′W

Vilamoura Marina

Unlike many other European ports, with their historical associations and long traditions, Vilamoura is a product of modern sailing and air travel. In the center of Portugal's south coast, the Algarve, it is both on the route from northern Europe to the Mediterranean and a vacation and cruising center in its own right. However, few boats in Vilamoura are Portuguese. Instead, every northern European ensign and flag of convenience is evident. Many owners and crews fly in and out of Faro airport, only 20km (12 statute miles) away to the east.

In sailing terms, Portugal's south coast has grown because its western, Atlantic coast is not ideal for sailing – the harbors are few and have been adapted to suit cruising and racing needs. In addition, an almost continuous north wind, the Portuguese trades, blows down the coast, itself often covered in fog – so boats bound south have an incentive to sail on. Around Cape St. Vincent, south of Lisbon, several harbors have been developed from old fishing villages and anchorages: Sagres, Lagos, Portimão and Vilamoura. With specially built jetties and a totally protected inner harbor, 1,500 full-time berths and a further 300 for visitors, Vilamoura has lifting and yard facilities, a permanent haul-out area, and shops and hotels close by. The entire complex is considered to be a successful answer to the problem of meeting the demand for berthing.

The local yacht club, Club Internaçional da Marina de Vilamoura (CIMAV), promotes at least one international regatta annually, in April, for IOR, CHS, local handicap and Olympic dinghy classes.

The average temperature here is 28°C (82°F) in August and 16°C (61°F) in February. From Vilamoura it is 45 miles west to Cape St. Vincent, and 130 miles south-east to Gibraltar.

GIBRALTAR
LAT · 36°08′N   LONG · 5°22′W

Gibraltar is the gateway to the Mediterranean for boats from northern and western Europe and from across the Atlantic. It also serves as a departure point for boats leaving the Mediterranean for the Caribbean in the fall.

To boats from Britain, Gibraltar is a particularly attractive port of call. Local equipment can be ordered and obtained with ease, along with British Admiralty charts (thanks to the presence of the Royal Navy), while there are marine engineers, lifts, agents of most makes of engine and electronics, sailmakers and boatyards.

In the 19th century, Gibraltar was just as welcoming. On 4 August 1896, a single-handed boat arrived there. Such craft were previously unheard of in the port. Admiral Bruce, the senior naval officer, arranged for *Spray* to be towed by steam launch to a secure berth; then Joshua Slocum recorded in his log, "Not even HMS *Collingwood* was better looked after than *Spray* at Gibraltar ... The governor, with other high officers of the garrison and all the commanders of the battleships, came on board and signed their names in *Spray's* log book ... how could one help loving so hospitable a place? Vegetables twice a week and milk every morning came from the palatial grounds of the admiralty."

Small boats, even single-handed ones, are more commonplace today. Established marinas (Sheppard's and Marina Bay) are ever more crowded, and there is a third marina, Queensway, in the sheltered part of the harbor. Along the neighboring Malaga coast the number of ports with yacht harbors is growing.

The Royal Gibraltar Yacht Club, which was founded in 1829, is one of the oldest in the world and organizes regular racing for local classes.

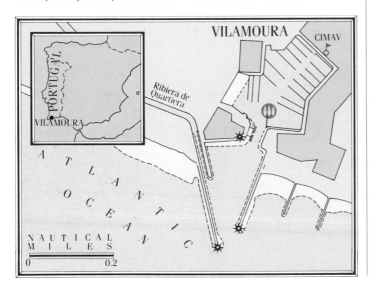

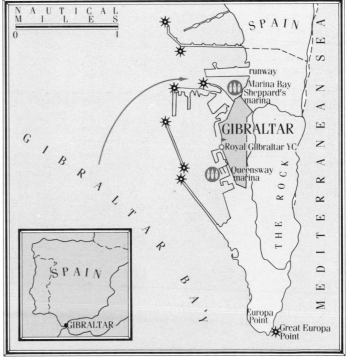

THE MEDITERRANEAN

Europeans expect to find consistent summer sunshine and fair weather in the Mediterranean, unlike the changeable conditions on their Atlantic and Baltic coasts. The 2,300-mile-long inland sea is also virtually tideless, but the winter is unsettled, so the season runs from April to late October in most areas.

Spain, France, Italy, Yugoslavia, Albania, Greece and Turkey line the Mediterranean's northern coasts. These countries and the islands renowned as vacation destinations – the Balearics, Sardinia, Sicily, Crete, the Greek Islands, Malta and Cyprus – are the sailing centers. Africa, to the south, has relatively few ports and long coastlines of desert. Through the Strait of Gibraltar, at the western end of the Mediterranean, boats come and go from northern Europe and America, but at the eastern end only a few staunch cruisers use the sometimes perilous Suez Canal and Red Sea route.

The cities and harbors of the European shore are – with the exception of those in Albania – easily accessible and welcoming to the visitor. Throughout the Mediterranean, the way to moor has traditionally been to secure stern to quay, with an anchor over the bow, but in the last two decades marinas have emerged on a widespread scale. Some have grown from scratch or from sheltered beaches that were once used just by local fishing boats. Despite this growth, the range of harbors does still vary, from the established ones of the French Riviera, which cater to very large boats, especially motor yachts, to the still unspoilt inlets of Yugoslavia and Turkey, where smaller bareboat charters venture. In the west particularly, pollution, aggravated by increased building for shoreside vacationers and the non-tidal nature of the sea, has become a serious problem.

Because it is a vast, tideless sea surrounded by land, the Mediterranean has a unique climate. In the summer, when high pressure predominates, there are long periods of calm under a cloudless sky, so it is advisable to have an engine capable of making long passages when cruising. However, near some coasts the hot sun can generate a sea breeze up to 35 knots by late afternoon. On the other hand, at any time of year depressions can upset this pattern and give rise to cyclonic winds, and also more localized winds common to particular areas. Some of these, such as the Mistral in the south of France, the Levanter in the Strait of Gibraltar and the Meltemi in the Greek Islands, can develop into strong gales over prolonged periods.

PALMA

LAT · 39°33'N   LONG · 2°38'E

On the southern edge of the island of Majorca, the largest of the Balearic Islands, Palma is a sophisticated yet attractive resort about 150 miles from Alicante on the Spanish mainland, and 300 miles from Cannes on the French Riviera. One of Spain's most important sailing centers, it is significant for its role in both cruising and racing in the western Mediterranean. With regard to the former, Palma is commonly used as a final stopping point in the Mediterranean for boats leaving to cross the Atlantic, and so in the fall is full of vessels of all sizes undergoing their final repairs and provisioning before starting the crossing. For the less adventurous, its position makes it a convenient point from which to explore the coasts of Spain, France and Italy, as well as the islands of Sicily, Sardinia and Corsica. Palma is thus an ideal base for those wishing to see the western half of the Mediterranean.

In terms of racing, Palma is important in that it hosts a variety of international events, including the One Ton Cup in 1986, plus local regattas in the summer months.

There are two major marinas in Palma, adjacent to the two yacht clubs, the Real Club Náutico and the Club de Mar. They are situated at opposite ends of the harbor, and both have full yard facilities. In between the two, smaller boats can lie alongside the town quay. Palma's commercial port is capable of catering for the largest sailing and motor vessels. The climate is mild, even in the winter, although the Mistral, known locally as the Tramontana, is to be respected. There is also a south-easterly/ easterly current all around the Balearic Islands, running at one knot.

The Real Club Náutico, Palma

THE RIVIERA
LAT · 43°35′N   LONG · 7°08′E (ANTIBES)

In the first week of March 1894 the royal yacht *Britannia*, under the command of His Royal Highness the Prince of Wales, attended the local regattas in Cannes and Nice and won seven races out of seven entered. As the arbiter of good taste in English society, the prince brought the spectacular coastline, with its numerous rocky harbors and sandy bays, to the attention of the English upper classes. The area rapidly became fashionable and the aura of wealth and high society persists in it to this day. The largest and most expensive boats in the Mediterranean are to be found on the Riviera.

The coastline has two distinct identities. From Cap Roux to Nice it is basically flat, with wide sandy beaches, while from Nice to the Italian border it is mountainous, as the foothills of the Alpes Maritimes come down to the sea. These foothills protect the shore from the worst of the Mistral and make the climate more predictable than it is further west.

The major ports on the Riviera are world-famous. Places such as Cannes, Antibes, Nice and Monaco are internationally known for the activities of the jet-set and boating fraternities. The main boating centers are at Cannes, with 1,700 berths, and Antibes, with 1,125. Other ports, such as Hyères, St. Tropez, St. Raphaël and Beaulieu are almost as well known.

Racing takes place almost continuously during the season, with a succession of local regattas. Hyères, St. Raphaël and Toulon are the principal harbors, with Hyères hosting an annual Olympic-class regatta and other international events. Toulon caters to ocean-going boats, and is a stop for the Course de l'Europe (see pp 108-9). Each October, St. Tropez hosts the Nioulargue – a gathering of both large and classic vessels.

The fashionable port of Cannes

LANGUEDOC-ROUSSILLON
LAT · 42°50′N   LONG · 3°05′E

Stretching from the Spanish border to the mouth of the River Rhône, Languedoc-Roussillon is a 200-km (125-statute mile) stretch of the French coast. It is remarkable in being the first product of a massive project, initiated by the government, aimed at turning an essentially barren, often marshy and unproductive coastline into a giant tourist resort. Begun in 1965, the Coastal Development Plan was a sympathetic but comprehensive program designed to transform the region, steep and rocky in the south, flat and monotonous in the north, into a cosmopolitan playground.

Existing towns, notably Port-Vendres, Sète and Aigues Mortes, were smartened up and enlarged, and a number of entirely new settlements, such as Cap d'Agde, were created out of the marshlands. Of the 31 major harbors along the coast, the largest is Port-Camargue, at the mouth of the Rhône, constructed around what is virtually an inland lake. It has berths for 1,800 boats. Other ports of note are St. Cyprien-Plage, Port-Vendres, Canet-en-Roussillon, St-Nazaire, Port-Barcarès, Port-Leucate, Gruissan, Valras, Cap d'Agde, and Palavas-les-Flots. Canals connect this coast to the Atlantic, via Toulouse and Bordeaux (the Canal du Midi), and the Rhône.

Languedoc-Roussillon was one of the first areas to utilize the marina-village concept, the interposing of housing and berthing facilities that is now so popular in Europe. As a result, there are numerous marina-villages along the coast and a relaxed atmosphere prevails. There are regular racing regattas at La Grande-Motte, Port-Camargue and Cap d'Agde.

The Golfe du Lion is somewhat notorious for its bad weather: the Mistral can rise from nothing to gale force in under an hour.

Port-Leucate, with its modern apartments and berthing

PORTO CERVO
LAT · 40°55′N   LONG · 9°34′E

One of the most remarkable ports in the Mediterranean, Porto Cervo was transformed in 1962 from a local fishing village into a millionaire's resort by a small group of property developers led by the Aga Khan. This new Sardinian resort remains highly exclusive.

The town itself is beautiful, having been constructed on a master plan designed to make it environmentally harmonious. The harbor is excellent: built like a large creek, it extends one km (half a statute mile) inland and is open to the east. Harbor facilities are more than adequate, with a 600-berth marina taking boats up to 55m (180ft) long, a town quay and good holding ground off the northern shore. There is, in addition, a large repair yard that can take vessels weighing up to 350 tons.

Porto Cervo is a center of international importance for racing, with a number of events organized by the Costa Smerelda Yacht Club. Chief among these is the Sardinia Cup, held biennially in even years (see pp 110-11). The Sardinia Cup

The yacht marina at Porto Cervo

◆ ◆ ◆

is held concurrently with the Swan Worlds, organized by the class builders and now a major championship event in itself. In addition, the One Ton Cup was competed for at Porto Cervo in 1973, the Two Ton Cup in 1981 and the 12-Meter Worlds in 1985.

The port is well situated not only for exploring the rugged and mountainous coastline of Sardinia, but also because it is within easy reach of the south coast of France and the west coast of Italy. Despite these advantages, it remains to be seen whether the center's very high profile can be maintained; prices of food, drink and facilities are exceptionally high.

PORTOFINO
LAT · 44°18′N   LONG · 9°12′E

The Gulf of Genoa is an important center for Italian sailing and racing, and the small harbor of Portofino is probably the most glamorous and attractive port in its waters. Surrounded by high, wooded slopes and with an imposing castle dominating one headland, the harbor itself is like a film set, with a host of sailboats and small craft moored stern-to, broad quaysides and characteristic Mediterranean buildings. The atmosphere is warm and relaxed, giving the place an almost escapist feel. Of course, the first floors of the houses tend to have shops for the tourist (rather than the sailor), at appropriate prices. The same applies to the restaurants, which have menus that are second to none throughout Europe.

Approaching the town by land is difficult, for it involves driving along a winding coast road with sharp corners and, in places, a sheer precipice to one side. It seems preferable, therefore, to come by sea. In the harbor, there is some swell at times because

Portofino is entirely open to the north-east. In addition, it faces Golfo Tigullio, which, in turn, faces to the south and the open sea. Ocean racers and performance cruisers normally berthed at Genoa come for race weeks here, although racing boats are kept at Santa Margherita, three miles to the east. The latter harbor has facilities that are totally lacking in Portofino, but this shortage of facilities adds to the charm and 'romance' of Portofino's atmosphere.

Genoa has given its name to the most-used sail – after the mainsail – and Beppe Croce, former long-serving president of the IYRU, lived near Portofino. The area therefore has a well-established place in both the history and the administration of sailing.

From Portofino, Genoa is 12 miles to the west; Porto San Stéfano is 130 miles south-east; and San Remo is 65 miles south-west. Milan is 125km (75 statute miles) due north inland.

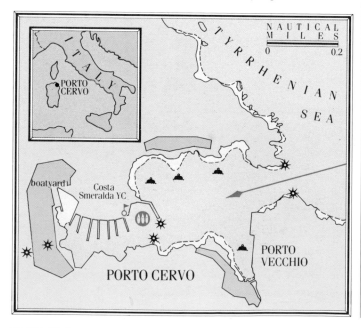

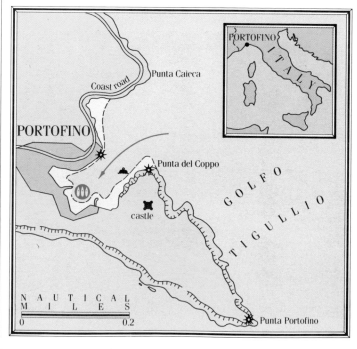

PORTO ERCOLE
LAT · 42°23′N   LONG · 11°13′E

The shores of Tuscany, on the long western coastline of mainland Italy, provide several important sailing areas. The scattered islands off Tuscany are known as the Tuscan Archipelago: Gorgona, Capraia, Elba, Pianosa, Montecristo, Giglio and Giannutri all have popular, crowded harbors. Portoferráio on Elba is a particular favorite for visitors.

Jutting from the mainland, is an almost circular, mountainous outcrop, the Argentario Promontory. There are several ports nearby, including, on the east side, Porto Ercole and, less than one mile to the north of it, Marina Cala Galera. The latter has over 700 berths for boats, excellent shelter and boatyard facilities, including haul-out and dry storage. Boats winter here afloat.

Traditionally, Porto Ercole is a fishing port, but boats moor all around the southern section. Surrounded by mountains, Porto Ercole is attractive, as well as being the last major anchorage for 150 miles for those heading toward the south.

Ten miles' sail around the Argentario is Porto San Stéfano, which has a strong sailing presence and one of the best yards in Italy for custom boats, Cantiere Nevala d'Argentario.

The summer climate along the west coast provides moderate west to north-west winds, but as is common in the Mediterranean, there can be long periods of calm. Sometimes depressions enter the Gulf of Genoa and intensify, causing strong south-westerlies, the Libeccio. When there is a low in the Adriatic and a high to the west, a strong north or north-east wind blows, the Tramontana. There is a weak northerly current on the north side of Elba, but there is no noticeable tide anywhere in the area (predicted range 0.3 m, 1 ft).

Italy has long played an important part in the sailing scene. By the late 1980s, Italy had more IOR boats than any other nation; the decline of this class has not affected the Italians' desire to have the latest type of racing boat. In addition, Italy has some of the best boat builders in Europe.

DUBROVNIK
LAT · 42°38′N   LONG · 18°07′E

Yugoslavia's Adriatic coastline is considered to be one of the most unspoilt in the Mediterranean. It is mountainous and, on the whole, covered in trees, with chains of islands running down its length. Dubrovnik, situated about two thirds of the way down the coast, is the principal tourist and sailing center in the country. This status is enhanced by the town's spectacular medieval walls and architecture, and the range and quality of facilities available. The old city has changed little in the last 400 years; new developments have been kept outside its walls.

For cruising boats, there are two marinas outside the town (the harbor itself is kept for the fishing boats and craft used for tourist trips). The nearest marina, at Gruž, only has stern-to mooring, but good access to the town and comprehensive shopping facilities. Dubrovnik Marina itself is several miles outside the town at Komolac; it has 450 berths, full dockyard facilities, and is therefore a favored wintering place for foreign boats.

The marina at Komolac

◆◆◆

Dubrovnik is an ideal starting point from which to explore the Yugoslavian coast, with its cultural and historical heritage and hundreds of deserted coves and beaches, and the Adriatic coast of Italy. Sailing is still a relatively new industry in the country and, apart from in the main centers, facilities are basic where they exist at all; boats sailing in the area need to be largely self-sufficient. However, charter boats, both bare and crewed, are now arriving in ever-increasing numbers, along with private boats; the region, like Turkey, seems set to be one of sailing's major growth areas in the 1990s.

The enclosed anchorage of Porto Ercole

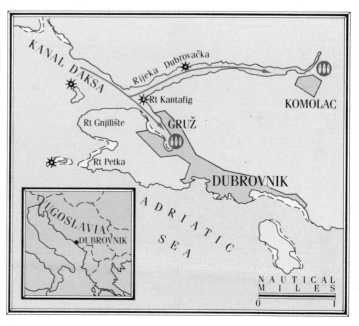

CORFU
LAT · 39°38′N   LONG · 19°55′E

A sickle-shaped island just off the western coasts of Greece and Albania, Corfu was one of the first Greek Islands to become a popular destination for tourists from north-west Europe. Despite the annual influx of visitors, it is still surprisingly easy for the sailor to find a multitude of deserted coves and beaches. The Ionian Islands, of which Corfu is the largest, are also attractive because they are forested and generally more fertile than the islands in the Aegean. This is due in part to their more northerly position and the correspondingly higher rainfall.

The town of Corfu reflects the wide variety of influences that have touched the island over the centuries. The Venetian citadel is most notable, standing out on the northern promontory, but Byzantine churches, French houses, an English palace and Roman ruins can all be seen. The marina is about 13 km (8 statute miles) outside the town at Gouvia, and can take 500 boats of all sizes. However, boats can moor at the town quay to gain easy access to the shops and restaurants in the old town and the hotels in the new. The outer

One of Corfu's quiet anchorages

◆◆◆

breakwater is recommended for stays of more than a few hours because it provides protection from the swell that rises when the afternoon breeze comes up from the north-west; from the breakwater it is then a short trip in a dinghy to the shore. Corfu has an active charter fleet, with bareboat and flotilla cruises particularly popular, and the varied coastline, with its many bays and ports, makes the island ideal for short day trips.

Access to the Aegean is through the Corinth Canal, almost 200 miles away, while Italy is only 70 miles away at its nearest point. Corfu therefore is more centrally placed in the Mediterranean than any other Greek Island.

RHODES
LAT · 36°27′N   LONG · 28°14′E

The largest and most south-westerly island of the Dodecanese, Rhodes has the hot summers and mild winters so typical of the southern Mediterranean. The island's main town, also called Rhodes, is a chaotic mix of ancient history and modern tourist development. Dominated by the massive fortifications originally constructed by the Knights of St John in the 14th and 15th centuries, the town also shows much evidence of the various invaders who have trod its shores since; from the Ottoman Turks to the Germans.

The harbor – called Mandraki – is similarly steeped in history, for it is thought that the Colossus of Rhodes – a legendary statue over 30 m (100 ft) tall and made of bronze – straddled the narrow entrance until an earthquake destroyed it in 224 BC. While

Mandraki is totally secure, it becomes somewhat crowded during the summer months, when there are boats moored stern-to three or more deep around the entire harbor.

Yard facilities are excellent, so are the shops, and the night life is both loud and varied. The old town, with its small tavernas and quieter atmosphere, is favored by the regular visitors who wish to avoid the hectic pace set by the package-tour vacationers.

Rhodes can be used as a base to explore both the nearby Turkish coast and the local Greek islands: it has excellent facilities and a large international airport. However, while some people enjoy these readily available trappings of civilization, many find the hordes of tourists too much and subsequently leave to find quieter waters.

Corfu, where vessels moor at the town quay for easy access to stores

Rhodes, where stern-to mooring is general practice

MARMARIS

LAT · 36°51'N   LONG · 28°16'E

A corner of the port of Marmaris

◆◆◆

A typical example of a modern Turkish tourist resort, Marmaris is a small, white-washed town on the north side of an almost totally enclosed bay, some two-and-a-half by three-and-a-half miles wide. The bay has only two narrow entrances on either side of a small island to the south. Built on a promontory, Marmaris has extensive quays that provide for stern-to mooring; and at the time of writing, a 1,750-berth marina is nearing completion on the eastern edge of the town. On the whole, it is a well-protected harbor and is normally an ideal anchorage. But in strong southerlies a swell can develop in the bay that renders the quays untenable. In the summer months the Meltemi, a north-westerly local wind, can arise rapidly and then blow up to 35 knots for several days.

Marmaris' popularity as a port stems not so much from its facilities, for both Bodrum and Kuşadasi to the north are better equipped, but from its central position on the beautiful south-west coast of Turkey, and its proximity to a number of the Greek islands, particularly Rhodes. Thus Marmaris is frequented by both private boats and a wide variety of both crewed and flotilla charter boats. It also has a direct ferry service to Rhodes, one of the few between Turkey and Greece.

The surrounding area is attractive: above numerous inlets are mountains covered by heavy woods or maquis (scrub). Towns are relatively scarce. However, while the region is comparatively undeveloped, the rapid increase in tourist traffic promises to bring extensive and far-reaching changes in the near future.

LARNACA

LAT · 34°55'N   LONG · 33°39'E

Larnaca, on the south coast of Cyprus, has the island's only specially-built marina; it contains only 210 berths. However, there are a number of other harbors that can take boats on comfortable moorings. Larnaca has limited facilities, but one can find engineers and boat repair shops, as well as hotels, restaurants and an airport.

As in much of the Mediterranean, the months from April to November are most suitable for sailing, for the winter months have a high proportion of disturbed weather, including gales caused by depressions travelling along the Mediterranean.

The coasts are characterized by diurnal winds: a typical summer's day dawns calm, or with a light offshore land breeze; by midday, the onshore breeze is stirring, and by mid-afternoon, it is likely to be up to 20 knots. However, on some days it can rise to Force 7 (32-8 knots). In the evenings, the wind dies down again. The sea breeze does not blow onshore throughout the Mediterranean: at Larnaca, for instance, the prevailing wind is from the south-west. The generally settled weather makes dinghy sailing off the ocean beaches practical, while numerous bays provide excellent anchorages overnight when the breeze drops.

For political reasons, parts of the eastern Mediterranean are unsuitable for voyaging, notably the nearby coasts of Syria and Lebanon. Cyprus thus makes a secure haven for cruising boats in the area. From Larnaca, the coast of Israel is 200 miles to the south-east and the cruising ground of south-west Turkey is about 300 miles to the north-west. For those who prefer not to sail such distances, day cruising around the island is feasible; there are harbors at Limassol (45 miles south-west) and Paphos (65 miles west).

However, the northern ports of Famagusta, on its large, sheltered bay, and the attractive old port of Kyrenia, with its Crusader castle guarding the entrance, are occupied by Turkey. At the time of writing, it is not possible for boats to sail to them from the Greek ports on the south coast.

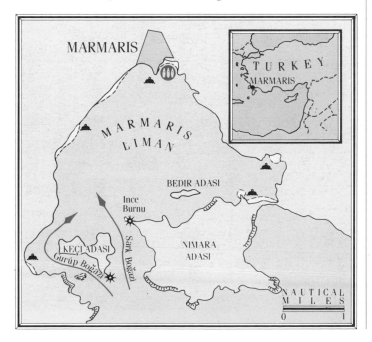

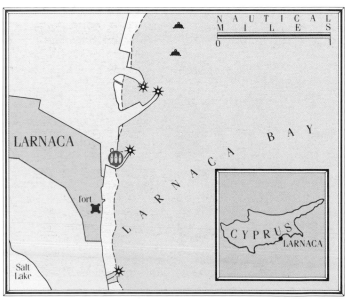

NORTH AMERICA – EAST COAST

Stretching from Maine to Florida, and around to Texas, the East Coast of North America comprises a mass of famous ports and shores, from the some-times cold and foggy inlets of Maine in the north to the sub-tropical beaches of Florida in the south. The popular, attractive areas are not necessarily evenly spaced, nor continuous, but their very names have become synonymous with sailing. The main sailing areas in the east are all in the United States: the Maine coast, Boston and Massachusetts Bay, Nantucket Sound and Buzzards Bay, Rhode Island Sound and Block Island, Long Island Sound, Delaware Bay, Chesapeake Bay, the Carolinas and south-east Florida. In addition, in the Gulf of Mexico are the ports and anchorages of west Florida, Lake Pontchartrain and Corpus Christi. Inland, there are the Great Lakes and innumerable other lakes and waterways.

Many of the established clubs, boat-builders, designers and equipment manu-facturers are to be found in this region.

The United States has remained far ahead of Europe in most technical aspects of sailing, partly due to the effect of two world wars on the European sailing scene. In America, many large population centers are situated near the water and this, com-bined with a relatively high standard of living, means that the sheer number of boats is greater than elsewhere. However, in spite of this, sailing waters are not overly crowded because of the vast and varied choice of ports, inlets and anchorages along the coastline, as well as on the inland waterways and lakes.

In the famous, northern cruising grounds and racing courses stretching from Chesapeake Bay up to New England, there is usually a sudden change from win-ter to summer in early May. Boats are then prepared for a season that generally con-sists of long periods of settled weather; certainly the weather is much less changeable than that experienced by European sailors. In winter, boats in the northern harbors are hauled out of the

water to protect them from the hazards of winter, which include ice.

The climate further south is more trop-ical; the ports and harbors around Miami enjoy large amounts of winter sunshine. As a result, a number of boats head south in the fall to escape the severe continental winter. The long trip south, however, is not without its perils; there are numerous tales of boats that left too late and were caught offshore in severe weather. The waters around Cape Hatteras have a noto-riously bad reputation in this respect.

The offshore passage can be avoided by using the remarkable Intracoastal Waterway, a mixture of canals, natural waterways, lakes and estuaries which have been linked together. The Waterway runs from Trenton, New Jersey, to Brownsville, Texas, with open water extensions from Trenton to Boston and along the west coast of Florida. Originally for commercial vessels, it now allows boats to travel up and down the East Coast in relative safety.

MAINE

LAT · 44°20′N   LONG · 69°10′W (CAMDEN)

In the far north-eastern corner of the United States is the state of Maine. Sailors find its coastline quite different from any other part of the US; Europeans will be reminded of Scandinavia. Coves, bays, rivers and channels are set in rocky scenery, covered in conifers. Buildings are sparse in number and rugged in appearance, their steep roofs designed for the severe winters.

This 200-mile-long coast is only lat 45°N, the same as the wine-producing area of Bordeaux in southern France, but the Labrador Current ensures cold water all the year around. In summer, when these cold waters combine with the prevailing, moisture-laden, south-west winds blowing off the hot continent, the result is fog. This is a frequent occurrence; Petit Manan Point in the far east of the region averages 75 days of fog a year. Although fog can occur anywhere

in Maine, the records show that the further east one travels, the higher the incidence of fog. The worst month is August, which is also the peak of the recommended cruising season, which lasts from June to September. During this time it is possible, for instance, to have only four hours' clear visibility in a full week of cruising.

This possibility serves to heighten the confirmed attractions of Maine; despite the fog, sailors continue to seek out its refreshing scenery. Its waters are generally uncrowded and free from the marinas and power boats of warmer climates. There are exceptions: Camden is the base for numerous boats, as well as for large charter schooners. In addition, the traditional New York Yacht Club cruise (see p 28) sometimes makes Camden its final port of call before the fleet disperses.

The picturesque harbor of Rockport, Maine

Mount Desert Island, the largest of the scores of off-lying islands, is only 11 miles north to south. A fiord, Somes Sound, almost splits the island in half and contains numerous anchorages, while Cadillac Mountain rises to 467m (1,532ft). The proliferation of little harbors around this island is typical of Maine waters. Bass

Harbor, in one inlet, is frequently quite crowded, but there are creeks a few miles further along the coast where the crew of a cruising boat might expect to be the only visitors.

The nature of this north-east coast means that cruising predominates; racing tends to take place in small boats close to the chief ports.

MARBLEHEAD

LAT · 42°30′N   LONG · 70°50′W

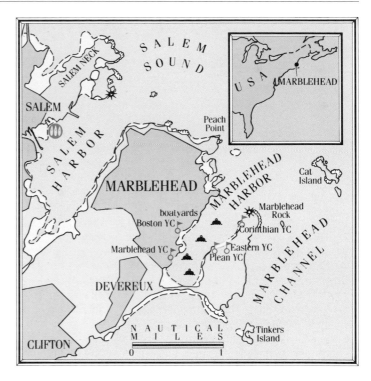

Imagine high summer in this latitude, a temperate sea breeze off the Atlantic, an inlet full of boats on moorings, and the white sails of fleets on the horizon. It is perhaps not surprising that boat owners here take great pride in the maintenance of their craft; they are under the direct scrutiny of club members from no less than five yacht clubs.

This is Marblehead, its attractive clapboard houses contrasting pleasantly with the background greenery and the occasional granite outcrop. Its name is one of those which have become synonymous with racing (along with Annapolis, Cowes and Sandhamn). It has also given its name to several racing classes, including a model boat class which is raced worldwide by radio-control enthusiasts.

As with most New England harbors, there is also a fishing fleet, which was, of course, the chief reason for the establishment of the port. Today, such fleets maintain New England's reputation for lobsters, clams and other shellfish, which in turn enhances the area's appeal as a cruising ground.

Strictly speaking, Marblehead is situated on Salem Sound, which is itself within Massachusetts Bay. It is one of four historic harbors along this coast, the other three being Beverly, Manchester and Salem. However, Marblehead is on a separate inlet within the Sound; a causeway leading to Marblehead neck turns the inlet into a bay.

Marblehead is just outside the suburbs of Boston; 12 miles north by sea. Although parts of Boston's big harbor does accommodate pleasure boats, there are inevitable industrial and shipping pressures that make Marblehead and its neighboring ports very attractive to sailors. As a result, Marblehead is invariably crowded in season; in addition, various offshore events start here, including the race from Marblehead to Halifax.

The closest Marblehead comes to a marina are docks located on the north side of the inlet. Here, too, is the main town of Marblehead, containing the Boston Yacht Club, the Marblehead Yacht Club, boatyards, chandlers, brokers, yacht designers and the headquarters of Doyle Sails, and Hood Sailmakers. Ted Hood, in his time one of America's best helmsmen, was the first sail-maker to weave his own cloth. Hood sails were in the forefront of sailmaking for many years, and the US still leads the field.

Over on the south side of the inlet lie the residential areas, along with the large clubhouse of two of the USA's oldest clubs – the Eastern and the Corinthian yacht clubs.

From Marblehead, Camden in Maine, is 140 miles north; Newport, Rhode Island, is 135 miles south if one sails outside Cape Cod, but only 75 miles via the Cape Cod Canal.

The busy harbor of Marblehead, with its attractive clapboard houses

LONG ISLAND SOUND
LAT · 41°00′N   LONG · 73°48′W

A great body of sheltered water, 90 miles long and up to 20 miles wide in the center, narrowing at the ends; a hot summer climate; close proximity to huge population centers: this is Long Island Sound. With a host of attractive boat harbors on its mainland shore and Long Island itself to protect its waters from the Atlantic Ocean, it is not surprising that this is an extremely popular area; vast numbers of boats are based here and sail regularly in its waters all summer.

Summers are hot and fine in this latitude, although even here fog occurs on some summer days. If an area of high pressure is centered on Bermuda, calms can be prolonged; thus the Sound has a reputation for light weather and lack of wind. Thunderstorms are a summer feature but give warning of their approach: often they pass with some shifting wind and a shower of rain, but sometimes they result in a prolonged squall which can produce potentially dangerous high wind conditions.

Some of the most prominent racing courses and clubs in the

world are found here, notably at Larchmont (Larchmont YC), Manhasset Bay (Manhasset YC) and Oyster Bay (Seawanhaka Corinthian YC). Courses for inshore and offshore boats can be set inside the Sound; in fact, some boat owners never feel the need to take their boats outside. The relatively sheltered waters of the Sound provide many opportunities for cruising along the north shore of Long Island as well as the south coast of New York and Connecticut.

At the western end of the Sound, it is possible to enter New York's harbor via the East River. Until recent times, boats kept well away from its waters because of the intense commercial activity and pollution. However in recent years the environment has improved greatly and the result has been that there is a revival of sailing interest and activity around the island of Manhattan.

Harbors along the New York and Connecticut shores all have the marinas, clubs, yards and facilities to be expected in such a

Mystic Seaport

sophisticated area. From west to east these include City Island, Larchmont and Mamaroneck in New York; and Darien, Norwalk, Bridgeport, West Haven, Old Saybrook, New London, Mystic and Stonington in Connecticut. Mystic Seaport, which adjoins Mystic, is a remarkable outdoor museum of New England's nautical and sailing history. On Long Island, are the harbors of Manhasset, Great Neck, Sea Cliff, Glen Cove, Bayville, Oyster Bay, Cold Spring Harbor, Huntington Harbor, Port Jefferson, Orient and Montauk.

At the eastern end of the Sound, tidal streams run fast through The Race and Plum Gut out into the Atlantic Ocean.

NEWPORT
LAT · 41°48′N   LONG · 71°15′W

Newport's harbor is within excellent, sheltered sailing waters on the coast of Rhode Island. The climate is hot in summer with reliable breezes, but fog is not uncommon; the winters can be hard and boats are therefore usually hauled out. Many local regattas are held in Narragansett Bay, while, for cruising boats, some of the best cruising grounds in North America are within range.

The port was a naval base from the 18th century up to the end of World War II, but now the old quays and docks have been replaced with sailboat harbors and repair yards, hotels and restaurants. At the turn of the century, many of the wealthiest families in New York built huge mansions, known as 'summer cottages,' just inland from the town. The annual New York Yacht Club cruise would carry the Vanderbilts, Astors, Morgans and Whitneys to Newport each July.

In this century, Newport has hosted the America's Cup on 12 occasions. The first races for the Cup were held here in 1930, having been moved from New York, where the waters had become too commercial. The last races were held in 1983: they took place in open water, at the America's Cup buoy lying positioned nine miles south-east of Brenton Reef Tower.

Newport is also the starting point for the biennial Newport to Bermuda Race (see pp121-2) and the finishing point for the biennial race from Annapolis (see pp123-4), as well as the finishing point for the single-handed and two-handed transatlantic races from Plymouth, England (see pp86-91) and the BOC Challenge Around-Alone race (see pp78-9).

In addition to these major events, Newport is a base for hundreds of cruising boats berthed on moorings and in ships off the town at Goat Island Marina. Here the United States

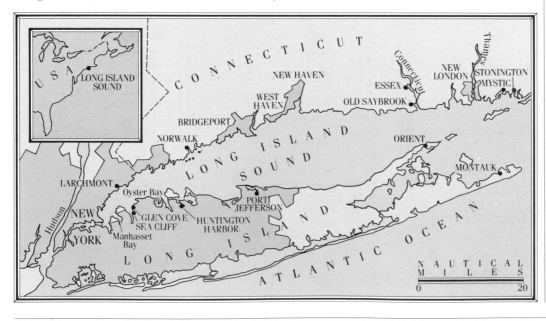

The harbor at Newport, Rhode Island

CHICAGO

LAT · 41°50′N   LONG · 87°38′W

Chicago's waterfront

Yacht Racing Union has its headquarters. Further up Narragansett Bay, in places such as Bristol, where yacht designer Nathanael Herreshoff lived, there are additional yards, marinas and moorings. Within a day's sail from Newport are Buzzard's Bay and Nantucket Sound to the east, and Block Island and Long Island Sound to the south and west.

The five inland seas of the Great Lakes comprise one fifth of the earth's freshwater surface. The lakes extend more than 700 miles from east to west and boast more than 7,200 miles of coastline.

In such a vast area, the scenery and climate are bound to be extremely varied. In some parts, pollution and lakeside industrial decay are prevalent; in others, there are unspoilt dunes and rocky shores. Cruising and racing are therefore popular in some places and completely unknown in others.

The canals and locks between some of the lakes are mainly for commercial shipping, but also can be used by pleasure craft. The water levels of the lakes have changed over the years: in the 1980s, for reasons not entirely understood, they are at their highest for 120 years. Although there are no tides, winds from one direction or another cause currents and temporary changes in water level of as much as 2.5 m (8 ft).

The winter climate can be severe, with prolonged ice and snow; the summer can be unsettled, with depressions forming that race eastward. Interestingly, the depression that brought disaster to the 1979 Fastnet Race (see pp 96-7) formed west of Lake Michigan on 9 August, depositing 37 mm (1½ in) of rain. The low then passed across Lake Michigan and Lake Huron to the east coast, bringing severe storms to Rhode Island and south-eastern Massachusetts, before crossing the Atlantic and hitting the largely unprepared Fastnet fleet on 14 August.

There are large population centers around the lakes: 13% of the American population and 32% of the Canadian live here. Large cities such as Chicago, Detroit and Toronto are situated on the shores of the lakes. Such cities often have clubs which encourage major regattas or race weeks. For example, the city of Cleveland on Lake Erie, 260 miles by land to the east of Chicago, runs such an annual event, attracting over 300 boats.

Chicago, despite industrialization, has kept its waterfront available for public use and leisure activities. It runs for several miles along the lake shore, backed by impressive skyscrapers. There are seven harbors, all publicly owned, but with private clubs and facilities. In addition, a string of harbors runs north along the western shore: Winnekta, Waukegan, Kenosha, Racine, Milwaukee, Port Washington, Sheboygan and Manitowoc. Waukegan, 35 miles to the north of Chicago, has some 1,500 marina berths, while 30 miles further on, Racine's capacity for berthing has recently been expanded. Farther up the coast is Sturgeon Bay, site of Palmer Johnson, a well-known boatbuilder. Mackinac Island, in the Strait of Mackinac, is about 180 miles north-east from Manitowoc.

The Chicago Yacht Club, founded in 1875, boasts two clubhouses and 1,750 members; it entered a 12-Meter in the 1987 America's Cup trials and is the starting point for the annual Chicago-Mackinac race (see p 125). Lake Ontario, 420 miles to the east, is the setting for the long-established Canada's Cup (see pp 128-9).

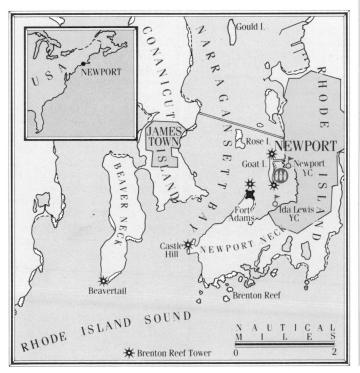

Gould I.

USA

NEWPORT

CONANICUT ISLAND

NARRAGANSETT BAY

RHODE ISLAND

JAMES TOWN

Rose I.

NEWPORT

Goat I.   Newport YC

BEAVER NECK

Fort Adams   Ida Lewis YC

Castle Hill

NEWPORT NECK

Beavertail

Brenton Reef

RHODE ISLAND SOUND

Brenton Reef Tower

N A U T I C A L
M I L E S
0   2

ANNAPOLIS
LAT · 39°00'N   LONG · 76°35'W

This major yachting center is yet another example of the vast areas of semi-sheltered waters that exist in the United States. It contains marinas, boatbuilders, sailmakers, designers and hundreds of cruising and racing boats. The Annapolis Sailboat Show and its power-boat show are held on successive weeks in October every year, and are among the most important 'in-the-water' shows in the US.

Although it is the principal small boat harbor in Chesapeake Bay, Annapolis is only one of many fine ports here. The Chesapeake is not a bay in the usual sense of the word, but more a huge inlet with hundreds of creeks and anchorages. It measures 170 miles from the Delaware Canal in the north to the Bay's Atlantic exit near Norfolk, Virginia. Nearly 40 rivers, including the Potomac, flow into it, as well as their many tributaries.

The Bay's lower latitude produces a sailing season that is longer than in the north-east, extending from early May to mid-November. Summer, however, can be very hot, with thunderstorms and calms;

because of the Bay's inland nature, a strong sea breeze does not develop. Despite this, the Chesapeake Bay Yacht Racing Association manages to hold races successfully all through the season. The vast number of boats is guaranteed by the proximity of Washington DC, Baltimore, Philadelphia, and other population centers.

Annapolis was named after Princess Anne, daughter of the English king, James I; it is an historic city and was, for a few years, the capital of the US. The US Naval Academy is based here; here, also, the schooner *America* was destroyed in the winter of 1945.

The Annapolis Yacht Club was given its present name in 1937; before that, from 1886, it was known as the Severn Boat Club. The present clubhouse on Spa Creek was built in 1962. The Club runs the biennial Annapolis to Newport race (see pp123-4); its Wednesday evening races attract large entries every week.

A number of other sailing clubs organize one-design and handicap racing. Annapolis Sailing School is situated on the south side of Spa Creek.

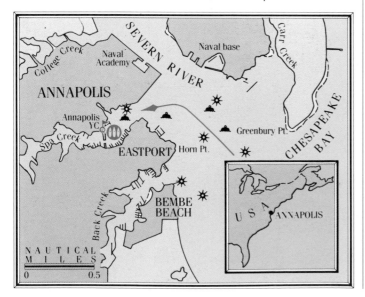

CAROLINA SOUNDS
LAT · 31°31'N   LONG · 80°53'W (BLUFFTON)

Few boats pause in the Carolinas on their way down the Intracoastal Waterway from the northern ports to Florida and the Caribbean. The Waterway markers guide them through North and South Carolina and most skippers aim to make mileage quickly. Some sailors, however, decide to linger, attracted by the deep creeks, wooded islands and hidden waterways on, or rather behind, the coast.

Several sections of these waters are protected from the open Atlantic by a strip of beach, or a necklace of islands, making attractive cruising for those who like relative solitude and out-of-the-way places.

The Carolinas are in low latitudes between 32° and 36.30°N, and the best sailing season is between March and December. However, January and February, although relatively cool and subject to unsettled weather, are still quite possible

cruising months. The prevailing winds in the area are south-east.

The waters behind Cape Hatteras, which has the tallest lighthouse in North America, are particularly appealing to the increasing numbers of sailors seeking anchorages away from marinas. Isolation, however, on most of the East Coast is a relative term; facilities are seldom far away from most sailing waters. Towns close to the Sounds are New Bern, with an airport, and Oriental, with marinas and moorings. The latter is a small, quiet town with some attractive houses and shops. It should be noted that there are no public bars in North Carolina. Prices are mostly lower than those in New England or Florida.

The distance from Oriental to the main channel leading to the open Atlantic at Cape Lookout is 50 miles, which gives some idea of the extent of these protected waters. For exploring both these and the other Carolina Sounds to

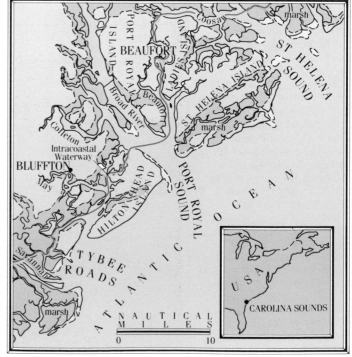

Cape Hatteras lighthouse

the south, a boat with a draft of less than 1.25m (4ft 2in) is preferable.

About 240 miles south down the Intracoastal is the beginning of another strip of islands and creeks, both broad and narrow. This stretch covers the southern coast of South Carolina, as well as the coast of Georgia.

This southern area is one of those parts of the world where an active history has given way to a more relaxed present. These coasts and islands were once massive rice plantations worked by slaves until the Civil War. After the war, they fell into disuse and the wetlands have reverted to swamp and forest.

In contrast to the northern Sounds, this stretch contains two large coastal cities – Charleston, South Carolina, and Savannah, Georgia. Between Charleston and the Florida border are more than 60 islands, and the boating season is virtually all year around. The historic areas in towns such as Bluffton and Beaufort (shown on the map to the left), are generally well-preserved and reflect the architecture of the old south.

There is a tidal range up to 2.75m (9ft) and some tidal streams. Because of the large mileage of waterways, there is no feeling of overcrowding, despite the fact that boating continues to increase in popularity. There are now at least two charter firms based at Hilton Head Island, 16 miles from Savannah.

LAKE PONTCHARTRAIN
LAT · 30°04′N   LONG · 90°05′W

A maze of waterways runs north and east from the Mississippi Delta, some of them leading into Lake Ponchartrain. New Orleans, situated on this lake, is the largest population center in the area, as well as being the last city on the Mississippi before the river reaches the sea.

Lake Ponchartrain is yet another of the large stretches of sheltered water in the US that is eminently suited to sailing. Such waters, so seldom found in other parts of the world, allow sailors to perfect their class-racing skills on closed courses, and are far preferable to the more exposed waters of the Gulf of Mexico. This ideal boating lake measures 30 miles by 18 miles. There is a negligible tidal range, but if the wind blows from one direction for any length of time, the water level can change by up to 1.2m (4ft), a substantial amount considering that the depth mid-lake is only 4.9m (16ft). Where the lake opens to the sea, at its eastern end, there are some shoal waters.

In addition to all the boats, there are numerous shrimp boats, both professional and amateur, fishing in the brackish waters. In spring, the sluice gates may be opened to release the Mississippi floodwater, allowing mud and debris into the lake. However, local sailors are always forewarned, and these conditions last for a finite period only.

The Intracoastal Waterway from the east bypasses Lake Pontchartrain to the south, connecting with the Mississippi River gulf outlet, continuing through Louisiana to Galveston, Texas, and ending at Brownsville. Boats not continuing along the Waterway can sail through The Rigolets, a channel leading into Lake Pontchartrain.

Once in Lake Pontchartrain, there are some berths in New Orleans, famous for its French Quarter, horse racing, holiday festivals and Mississippi River boats. There are also a number of marinas on the north shore of the lake near the resort towns of

French Quarter, New Orleans

Lewisburg, Madisonville and Mandeville.

The second-oldest yacht club in the US, founded in 1859, the Southern Yacht Club, is in New Orleans. The clubhouse is now at West End, along with the New Orleans Yacht Club, new marinas, condominiums and boat services of many kinds.

The lake is crossed by an automobile causeway which is one of the longest in the world. The distance to St. Petersburg, Florida, is 400 miles to the south-east; while Corpus Christi, Texas, is 420 miles to the south-west.

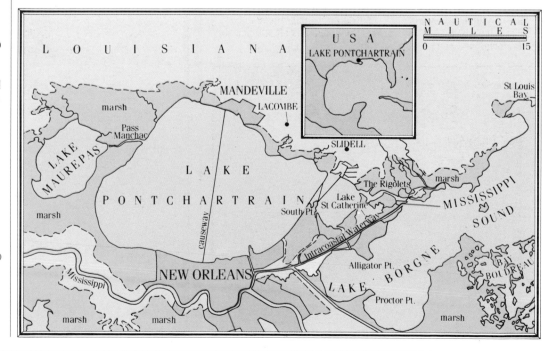

FORT LAUDERDALE
LAT · 26°06′N   LONG · 80°08′W

Less than three degrees north of the Tropic of Cancer, Fort Lauderdale is a mass of channels, waterways, canals, docks and large marinas. Often referred to as the 'Venice of America,' Fort Lauderdale is a year-round resort and marine center for yachts both power and sail.

The port was named after Major William Lauderdale, who arrived in 1838 with his Tennessee Volunteers to quell an Indian mutiny and built a fort on the site. It is now part of a large built-up area; the adjoining Port Everglades serves commercial and freight interests. Boat and yacht building, chandlers and boat servicing combine to form the city's third-largest industry. In addition to the direct servicing of boats, there is a considerable supporting structure of restaurants, banks and stores of all kinds. Many are on the water, so that boats can berth alongside or nearly alongside, enabling crews to step off their boats virtually straight into them.

Among the many super-marinas is one of the first in the world to be constructed, the Bahia Mar. This includes a 300-room hotel and 350 berths, plus, it is claimed, "200 yachts in the half-million dollar category and seven miles of beach adjacent."

Before Bahia Mar, marina berthing barely existed, even in the US. Now a mass of other complexes have appeared, particularly along the Miracle Mile, which is more like two nautical miles. Here marinas and boat services are jammed together side by side offering unmatched services, from a golf course for sailors to drive-on piers and a valet and maid service for boats.

Fort Lauderdale is on the Intracoastal Waterway, which means that traffic is heavy in places. Crews can avoid long sea passages by using the Waterway to reach Florida, or else have the boat delivered to Fort Lauderdale by a professional delivery crew.

The Waterway is a mixture of natural and specially-constructed features; an annual *Waterway Guide* is published to assist navigation in this vast and lengthy system.

Fort Lauderdale is the jumping off point for the Bahamas — Nassau is 175 miles away — and thence for the rest of the Caribbean. The best season, therefore, is November to May; the summers are quite hot and from July to October, hurricanes are a possibility.

One of the races for the major ocean-racing series, the SORC, ends at Fort Lauderdale (see pp126-7), and the city has been chosen as a stop for the 1989-90 Whitbread Race (see p80).

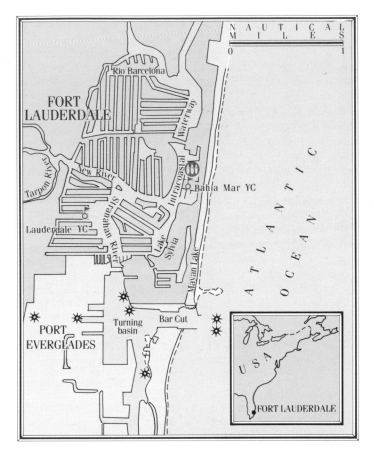

Fort Lauderdale, the 'Venice of America'

NORTH AMERICA – WEST COAST

The Pacific coast of the United States (excluding Alaska) extends from about 49°N, just south of Vancouver, to San Diego, California, and is shorter than the East Coast, particularly if indentations are taken into account. There are fewer ports and suitable boating areas than in the east, though as always in the US, large, sheltered tracts of inland water are never far away. The best-known areas for boating are in the extreme north, the extreme south and the 'middle,' the port and major city of San Francisco; in between are large, exposed stretches of coast which are not as intensively utilized for sailing purposes.

In the north are the waters around the big, busy ports of Vancouver and Seattle, partly Canadian and partly American. Sheltered, with many inlets, islands and towns, the area is popular for both racing and cruising.

Southward stretches a long tract of Pacific Coast without any major sailing ports until San Francisco, with its virtually landlocked bay. Unlike most of this coast, San Francisco also boasts a hinterland of waterways.

In the south, from Point Conception south-eastward lie a string of major sailing areas such as Long Beach and Newport Harbor, ending at San Diego, which was catapulted into the headlines when it hosted the 1988 America's Cup, long the preserve of New York and Newport, Rhode Island.

The West Coast has vast numbers of boats, many of them large by European standards. The world's largest marina in terms of berths, the Marina del Rey in greater Los Angeles, has over 5,700 berths. In terms of tonnage, the West Coast ports far outstrip any European boating center.

The climate along the West Coast is seasonal, although in the far south the winter is extremely mild. None of this western seaboard is within the traditional hurricane paths; in fact, San Diego has a reputation for light winds. Further north, San Francisco Bay has prevailing fresh winds, due to being in the path of prevailing westerlies that are accelerated by the sea breeze. At the Canadian border, the climate is still temperate, with westerly winds and seas that reflect the fact that they have rolled across the entire breadth of the Pacific. Offshore are the north winds of the Pacific High, as well as the northeast trades that take the offshore racers from Los Angeles to Hawaii.

All the Pacific ports are a long way from any lands to the west; yet this does not deter the many cruising boats that set sail to the many appealing islands of the South Pacific Ocean.

VANCOUVER

LAT · 49°17′N   LONG · 123°07′W

In the summer of 1794, Captain George Vancouver explored both sides of what is now Vancouver Island and the mainland opposite. He found mountainous country, sometimes plunging directly to the sea, rocky shores covered in firs, and waters that were unusually deep close in to land. The Spanish captain, Quadra, was exploring at the same time, hence the mixture of Spanish and English names in the area.

Vancouver is Canada's largest western city and its principal Pacific port. Its spectacular mountain backdrop, large parks and mild climate, make it an attractive city to visit.

Boats wishing to venture further than the waters around Vancouver have several alternatives. Queen Charlotte Strait, 200 miles north of the city, is one such option, but its weather tends to be more unsettled than that of Vancouver.

For those with more time and a suitable vessel, cruising further

north to Alaska is quite possible in summer. The southernmost point of the Alaskan coast is only 55°N and mild weather prevails. The port of Ketchikan, with its unspoilt scenery, conifers and wildlife – ranging from deer to bears – is a popular destination.

However, for most sailors with limited time, Princess Louisa Inlet, 130 miles north of Vancouver Island, is their northernmost port of call.

Forty miles south of Vancouver, between the city and Puget Sound, the San Juan Islands are a popular cruising destination. Known as the 'sunny San Juans', because their climate is supposed to be better than that of the mainland, they range from large islands to rocks. The largest island, Oreas, boasts a peak of 731m (2,400ft) and has a number of summer homes and small-craft moorings.

Racing is popular and the yacht clubs in the area organize both offshore and inshore events. The Royal Victoria Yacht Club

organizes a variety of races including one to Maui, Hawaii, and the annual Swiftsure Lightship Race; the West Vancouver Yacht Club runs the Southern Straits Race.

An exhibit at Victoria of interest to sailors is *Tilikum*, the

strange canoe of Captain Voss. In the days when few people ventured on long voyages, Voss' exploits in his canoe and his writings about his voyages were viewed as being almost as remarkable as Joshua Slocum's circumnavigation.

PUGET SOUND

LAT · 47°20′N   LONG · 122°32′W

Spectacular scenery, sheltered waters and a profusion of harbors make Puget Sound and the approaches to it a popular area for American and Canadian sailors.

The Pacific coast in general does not have as many harbors as does the East Coast, and this is particularly true of this area. However this coast is formed by Vancouver Island, which is some 240 nautical miles long. As a result, there are many miles of sheltered cruising to be had in the Strait of Juan de Fuca and the Strait of Georgia, quite aside from Puget Sound itself. It is quite possible, therefore, to sail the 110 miles between Seattle and Vancouver in relatively sheltered water.

To enter Puget Sound, one sails through Admiralty Inlet; Seattle is 30 miles from Port Townshend at the entrance to the Inlet. From Seattle, the Sound extends 45 miles south, ending in a mass of small inlets and winding creeks.

Seattle is the largest city in Washington State, the main commercial port for the area, and the base for most of the boats in the Sound. It is situated on a narrow, hilly stretch of land, with Puget Sound on its west side and the 18-mile-long, freshwater Lake Washington bordering its east side.

The popularity of these sailing waters is demonstrated by the number and quality of the marinas, such as that in Shilshole Bay, one of Seattle's many bays. Here, too, is the ship canal through to Lake Washington, the site of the largest marina in the area; it contains berths for 1,500 boats, some of which are up to 40 m (130 ft) long, a control tower, a boatyard and related facilities, plus a large area of dry storage. Toward the head of the Sound, 30 miles south of Seattle, there are other marinas at Tacoma.

The summer climate on this coast is said to be somewhat similar to north-west Europe in that it lacks wind and has a high rainfall. The winters are mild and wet, with the possibility of fog and gales at times. Seattle and the inner Sound are sheltered from excessive rainfall and extremes of climate by high mountain ranges, both to the east and west.

The Sound is distinctly tidal, with a spring tide range of 3.4 m (11½ ft) and streams that reach 7 knots at some points near the coast and in the narrows.

Seattle is the base for considerable racing activity: the Seattle, Queen City, Shilshole

Puget Sound

and Maydenbauer yacht clubs run races throughout the season. The 6-Meter class is still raced regularly here, despite the fact that in most other parts of the world it was all but abandoned some time ago.

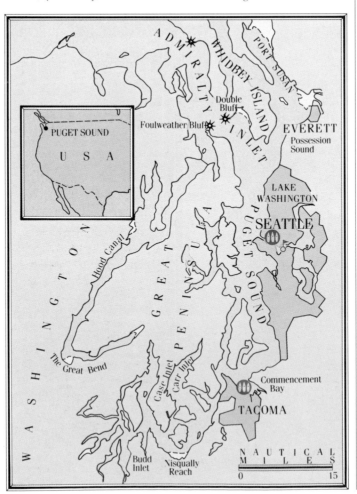

SAN FRANCISCO

LAT · 37°48′N   LONG · 122°25′W

For 100 years, from 1850 to 1950, San Francisco was, with the exception of the established East Coast ports, the most important sailing center in the US. Since 1950, Seattle and Southern California have moved close to San Francisco, in terms of sailing activities, although the city and its almost completely landlocked bay remain a major boating area for all sizes of craft.

The first racing boats to reach San Francisco were shipped from New England ports in 1850. In 1869, only 19 years after California became a state, the San Francisco Yacht Club was formed. In 1871, the club went bankrupt, but it was soon followed by numerous others. In the 1870s and 1880s, men who had made fortunes from mining and railroading began building large boats of up to 24 m (80 ft) in length and entering them in races down the coast to Santa Cruz or Monterey.

For many years, sailors discussed the possibility of racing from San Francisco to Hawaii, but they were always deterred by the prospect of sailing back against the north-east trade wind. Finally, in 1906, an Hawaii resident set out in his schooner for the race and arrived in San Francisco a month later, only to discover the city had been devastated by a great earthquake three weeks earlier. He sailed south to Los Angeles, which is where the classic Transpac race has started ever since (see pp 134–5).

From its junction with San Pablo Bay, San Francisco Bay extends south-eastward for 39 miles. When combined with San Pablo Bay, the Sacramento River and adjacent waterways, the result is a sheltered cruising area covering 400 sq nautical miles. The Sacramento River is navigable to Sacramento and its tributary, the San Joaquin River, is navigable to Stockton.

San Francisco's skyline

Many large towns border the shores of the Bay, including Oakland, Emeryville, Richmond, Berkeley, San Leandro, Sausalito, Redwood City and South San Francisco. Many of them contain yacht clubs, boatyards and marinas.

To enter the Bay from the sea, vessels pass under the Golden Gate Bridge. Two miles east of the Bridge is Marina Yacht Harbor, the city's main berthing area for boats. Here too, is the St. Francis Yacht Club. Further east along the waterfront is the famous Fisherman's Wharf; adjoining it are most of San Francisco's historic buildings.

Two miles north of the Golden Gate Bridge, on the other side of the Bay, is Sausalito. This attractive town has several marinas, including Clipper Yacht Harbor with 700 berths, and is quieter than the city itself.

NEWPORT HARBOR

LAT · 33° 40′ N   LONG · 118° 05′ W

The area within easy reach of Los Angeles and the densely populated areas around it sports a number of large harbors with massive marinas that have been enlarged specifically for small boats. These include Santa Monica, Long Beach (the venue for the 1984 Olympic Games), Marina del Rey (the world's largest marina) and Newport Harbor.

Newport Harbor is really part of the town of Newport Beach. Originally, the harbor site was a lagoon, with a small town nearby called Balboa. Dredging began about the same time as the Newport Harbor Yacht Club was founded in 1917. As a result of the dredging, the Santa Ana river, which had meandered through the area, now exits to the sea five miles to the west and the little town became Balboa Island. Gradually, more and more of the area has been dredged out and developed. The harbor now has approximately 4,000 berths, as well as every possible boating facility, including hotels, restaurants, shopping areas, a helicopter port, charter companies, boat yards and sailmakers. The Balboa Yacht Club is near the entrance.

The Newport Harbor Yacht Club is an important organizer of racing events, among them, the Newport Harbor Challenge Cup. The famous Newport to Ensenada, Mexico, Race also starts here (see pp134-5). A number of other coastal races also start and finish at Newport Harbor. In addition, the 1932 Olympic Games were based here, with sailing in Newport Bay.

The prevailing winds are westerly, but moderate. When combined with a sea breeze, the result is a good sailing wind of 8-15 knots. A severe wind called the Santa Ana blows off the desert, but is usually of relatively short duration. Fog is a possibility in the spring, but winters are quite pleasantly warm.

Santa Catalina Island, one of the large islands belonging to the Channel Islands group, is only 26 miles offshore. Many of the other islands in this scattered group, some as far as 60 miles offshore, have neither harbors nor landings. To the north-west, the port of Santa Barbara is 95 miles from Newport; beyond it lies Point Conception and a rugged coastline. San Diego lies 85 miles to the south-east.

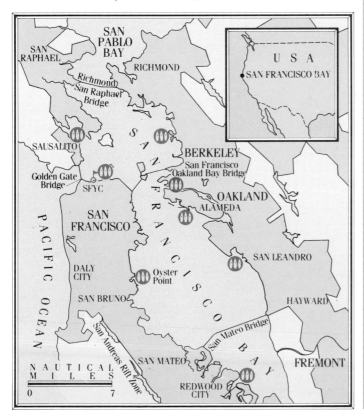

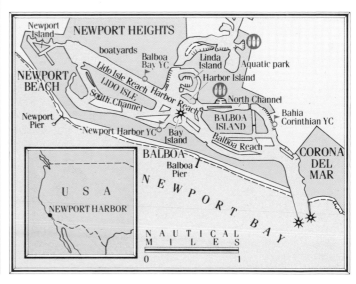

THE WEST INDIES

The chain of islands that extends east and south from Florida to just north of the Venezuelan coast, curving around the Caribbean, makes up one of the world's great sailing grounds. To the large sailing population of the United States the islands are conveniently close, and for the European sailing community they are on the tradewind route. Except for the northern Bahamas, all the islands are within the tropical zone, so the generally sunny climate is attractive. The steady north-east trade wind, and the position of the islands in relation to it, also mean that most trips include some good reaching.

As the chain of islands is over 2,500 miles long, there are hundreds of small ports and anchorages among them. This ideal combination of anchorages, settled weather, warm sea averaging about 24°C (75°F), and the many beaches mean that sailing life is very different from that in northern Europe, the United States, and the Mediterranean. From anchorage to anchorage, it is usually under a day's sail.

For political reasons, some potential sailing areas, such as those around Cuba and Haiti in the Greater Antilles, are not sailing territory. Apart from the Bahamas, the remaining islands can be divided into smaller, more specific sailing groupings, such as the Turks and Caicos Islands; the Virgin Islands (American and British); the Windward Islands and the Leeward Islands, which together make up the Lesser Antilles. Among these groups, sailors familiar with the area would no doubt name innumerable different places as their favorites, but in a book such as this, there is only space to focus on three major centers. Outside these, facilities are generally sparse, so boats need to be self-reliant and well equipped with spare parts. Otherwise these may have to be sent from the United States or Europe.

Crewed and bareboat charter operations are central to the sailing scene in the Caribbean, because only a minority of people have the time or the inclination to sail their own boats there. A new capital of the bareboat charter industry is Roadtown, on Tortola, one of the British Virgin Islands. This is really only a base, rather than a port of any size.

NASSAU

LAT · 25°4′N   LONG · 77°21′W

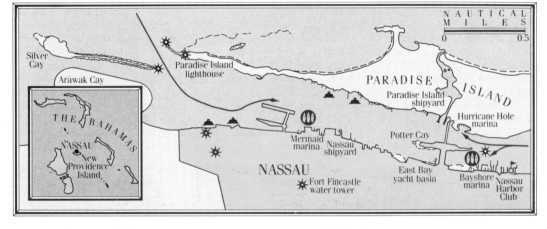

Only 130 miles from Miami and the big American harbors of Florida, Nassau is the capital of the Bahamas, a group of over 600 islands set in one hundred thousand square miles of tropical and sub-tropical sea. The area is an obvious draw for American boats, not only as a cruising center, but also as a stop-off point on the way to the Virgin Islands in the popular eastern Caribbean. About 20 of the islands, outcrops and cays (low islets) are inhabited. Unlike other West Indian islands, all are low-lying, none exceeding 500 ft (152 m) in height. San Salvador, one of the islands, is generally considered to have been where Christopher Columbus first landed, on 12 October 1492, in the New World. British possession of the islands was confirmed by the Treaty of Paris in 1763. The islands have been independent since 1973.

Throughout the islands, there is regular racing for one-designs and local sailing boats, while for many years Nassau was the finish for the last race of the Southern Ocean Racing Conference (see pp126-7). The leading clubs are the Nassau Yacht Club (established 1931) and the Royal Nassau Sailing Club.

Nassau has a number of fully equipped marinas, mostly at the eastern end of the harbor. Because the city is also a major cruise-liner port and a commercial harbor, facilities are excellent. The so-called Hurricane Hole on Paradise Island has about 50 berths, but most are rented full-time. East Bay Yacht Basin, near Paradise Island bridge, has a major shopping center called East Bay. It is a crowded and somewhat haphazard marina, with a mixture of locally owned boats and Nassau-based charter boats. Next to East Bay Yacht Basin is Potter's Cay, where the local sloops unload fish and take on inter-island cargo. Throughout the surrounding waters there are also many anchorages outside marinas, such as the one off Paradise Island, west of the docks. Smugglers and drug runners use some islands and local law enforcement advice should be taken before cruising.

The Gulf Stream flows north between Florida and the Bahamas at between two- and four-and-a-half knots, but it does not intrude into island waters.

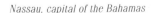

Nassau, capital of the Bahamas

CHARLOTTE AMALIE

LAT · 18°23′N   LONG · 64°56′W

The harbor at Charlotte Amalie

Otherwise known as St. Thomas Harbor, Charlotte Amalie is the principal town on St. Thomas, one of the American Virgin Islands. It is certainly the most important port between the Bahamas and Antigua. A favorite haunt of pirates in the 17th and 18th centuries, the harbor is well protected from all but strong southerlies, and thus provides a large anchorage in 4m to 11m (14ft to 35ft) of water.

A port for cruise-ships as well as boats, Charlotte Amalie's chief attractions lie in the facilities available to cruisers, and the sophistication of shops and restaurants for the tourist. There are a number of marinas, the largest being the St. Thomas Hotel and Marina to the east of the town, but there is also an anchorage at Prince Rupert dockyard on the eastern side of Hassel Island.

The town itself demonstrates an interesting combination of old world elegance – the original colonists were the Danes, who sold the islands to the US in 1917 – and the modern, post-war developments that have mushroomed to cater to the ever-increasing tourist trade. Despite the mix of old and new, Charlotte Amalie is one of the more attractive Caribbean towns.

While its fame lies firmly in its significance to the cruising scene, for some years the harbor has hosted the Rolex Cup, a series of short day races, which is the climax of the Caribbean Ocean Racing Triangle, and as such attracts a significant international entry.

ENGLISH HARBOR

LAT · 17°07′N   LONG · 61°52′W

The island of Antigua, which became independent from Britain in 1981, lies in a central position in the Leeward Islands, and is therefore an ideal base from which to explore the surrounding islands. As a result, it is a major base for charter boats, mainly crewed, as well as being the favorite meeting place for private boats cruising around Antigua and the various neighboring islands.

Unusual for the Caribbean, the main port on the island (English Harbor) is different from the chief center of population (St. John's). The harbor's name goes back to the 17th century, when it was an important base for British naval operations in the Caribbean. A superb natural harbor, it is virtually land-locked owing to a series of interlocking capes and bays that provide protection from all quarters. Its development dates back to 1948, when Commander V.E.B. Nicholson began a tiny charter operation that is still run by his family in considerably expanded form. The port now boasts a boatyard, chandlery, electronic supplier, surveyors and brokerage at Nelson's Dockyard on the west side and another boatyard on the east side. Purposely, there are no marina berths, but some boats lie stern-to off Nelson's Dockyard and in Ordnance Bay.

Many cruising boats from both Europe and the US plan their Caribbean cruises to arrive at English Harbor; the Canary Islands are only 2,400 miles away and boats can expect a fair wind. The anchorage is always crowded with boats, particularly during Antigua Sailing Week, held annually in the last week of April. This event has become one of the area's most important regattas with serious racing for all sizes, including maxis and larger vessels, and a non-stop party on shore. The 60-mile coastline of Antigua has numerous good anchorages and bays, hence there are passage races to these as well as courses off English Harbor.

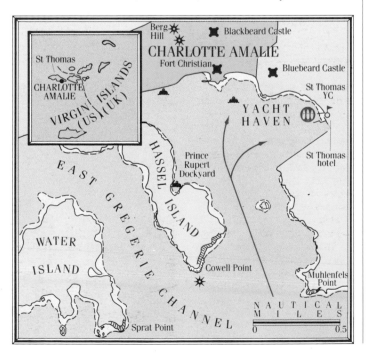

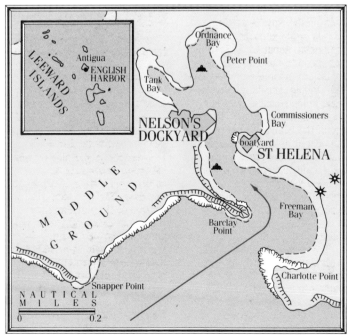

AUSTRALIA

Australia can undoubtedly be ranked among the top sailing nations in the world; Australian crews can be found on cruising boats all over the world and, whether racing or cruising, Australian crew members and yacht hands have a particularly high reputation, especially in heavy weather. In 1967, Australia became the first country, other than Britain and the US, to win the Admiral's Cup, winning again in 1979, the year of the notoriously stormy Fastnet Race.

The success of Australian ocean and small-boat racing, and the prowess of its designers, were crowned by the America's Cup victory of 1983. Whatever the future of the Cup, that exciting first victory over the New York Yacht Club can never be taken away. Certainly, it had a major impact upon the entire nation, and was celebrated by Australians around the world.

The shores of Australia's southern states have a sub-tropical climate, but there is always the threat of severe gales and storms as the prevailing Roaring Forties edge northward. In the far north, the sailing is tropical, but between December and April, there is the possibility of tropical cyclones. The popular sailing centers, however, tend to be in areas with a less extreme climate, where summer breezes provide balanced, predictable sailing conditions. In all parts, sea breezes blow onshore as Australia's great landmass heats up. The prevailing winds are south-west in the west and south, and north-east to south-east along the eastern coastline. Most of the time the wind strength is 10 to 15 knots. However, in the Fremantle area to the west, the summer wind, known as the Fremantle Doctor, increases in strength to 20 to 25 knots.

The most popular areas for racing, aside from Fremantle in the west, are Sydney Harbor, Broken Bay, Botany Bay and Lake Macquarie in New South Wales; Port Phillip Bay in Victoria; Gulf St. Vincent and Port Lincoln in South Australia; and the Derwent and Tamar rivers in Tasmania.

Cruising boats favor the hotter north, where it is possible to sail within the Great Barrier Reef and the other island groups outside the cyclone season.

Despite the size and variety of the country and its coast, its sailors seem to feel a certain sense of isolation from the northern hemisphere. This perhaps explains the high proportion of voyages undertaken by cruising boats from Australia to other seas. The usual route starts by heading for the Great Barrier Reef, then strikes across the Pacific Ocean.

Remarkable voyages by Australian sailors include Kay Cottee's 1987-8 single-handed voyage around the world from Sydney and back again in a time of 189 days, and, perhaps most amazing of them all, Jon Sanders' 1986-8 non-stop voyage three times around the world (see p 57).

MELBOURNE

LAT · 37°51′S   LONG · 144°56′E

Melbourne, one of Australia's principal cities and the state capital of Victoria, appears at first glance to enjoy the immense advantage of being situated on a land-locked bay. Port Phillip Bay measures about 37 miles from the narrow Bass Strait entrance to Melbourne, and about 27 miles from north-west to south-east; it covers an area of no less than 725 square miles. The Bay's eastern arm extends into Corio Bay, where the town of Geelong is situated. In fact, Port Phillip Bay's lack of indentation and low shoreline make it unsuitable for cruising. Commercial marinas are scarce, and there is a general lack of berths, apart from some sheltered moorings in state-made boat harbors.

This lack of moorings means that off-the-beach dinghy and catamaran sailing is popular. Another alternative is 'trailer sailing,' where centerboard boats between 5 m to 9 m (16 ft to 30 ft), with accommodation, are towed from other parts of the state and launched off trailers.

The Bay's low shore does mean, however, that there are steady winds, while the deep water in the northern part has no significant current. As a result, the Bay is particularly suited to inshore racing. Because its entrance is only just under two miles wide, with tidal streams of up to eight knots at times and dangerous overfalls known as The Rip, offshore races into the Bass Strait are arranged so that boats pass through at slack tide and finish elsewhere.

The clubs are concentrated on the northern shores of the Bay. They include the Royal Yacht Club of Victoria, founded in 1853 at Williamstown, where the earliest recorded regatta was held in 1838; the Royal Brighton Yacht Club (1875); the Royal Melbourne Yacht Squadron at St. Kilda (1876), Sandringham Yacht Club (1910) and the more recently formed Hobson's Bay Yacht Club.

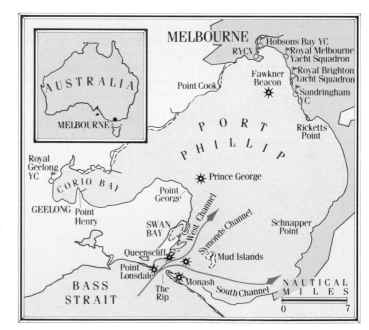

At Geelong is the Royal Geelong Yacht Club, which is an important center for the Dragon class and the venue for several world championships.

The waters off Melbourne were also the venue of the 1956 Olympic Games; the only time they have been held in the Southern Hemisphere. This demonstrates the particular suitability of the area for inshore, closed-course racing. Another event that has been held here is the C-class catamaran Little America's Cup (see pp176-7).

SYDNEY HARBOR

LAT · 33°49'S   LONG · 151°18'E

Australia's financial and business capital, Sydney, boasts the world's largest natural harbor and a near-perfect climate for sailing. As a result, the harbor is crowded at weekends with tourist ferries, general shipping and cruising or charter boats, as well as being the regular venue for the racing courses of several clubs, including the Royal Prince Edward, Middle Harbor and Sydney Amateur Sailing yacht clubs.

During the week, however, there is much less congestion and, with 188 miles of foreshore and many deep inlets, there is immense scope for cruising in sheltered waters and for learning to sail. Facilities at club bases, as well as in and around the city, are of a high standard, and include boat repair yards, sailmakers and chandlers.

Yachting in Sydney got off to a conventional start in 1862 with the founding of the Royal Sydney Yacht Squadron, in an unashamed imitation of the English yachting tradition. Sailing activities split into two main groups: conventional racing and locally developed small skiffs with a large sail area and high performance.

The Sydney Harbor skiffs and derived classes are still thriving and have had an important influence on yacht design. In addition, in 1867, the Prince Alfred Yacht Club was formed to cater for smaller craft. By the turn of the century, the Club had expanded to spacious rooms in the city and boasted a fleet of 30-raters. Today, the Royal Prince Alfred has a large marina and dry storage for scores of dinghies and keelboats. It also runs many championships, including world championships for various classes on its Palm Beach circle course.

The Cruising Yacht Club of Australia, founded in 1944, fosters long-distance and offshore cruising. It also has an offshore racing program that includes the Sydney-Hobart Race (see pp114-16).

Sydney sailors have long been known for innovative designs and experiments, but it is the skiffs that for more than a century have symbolized Sydney sailing.

THE GREAT BARRIER REEF

LAT · 20°18'S   LONG · 149°00'E (WHITSUNDAY IS.)

The Great Barrier Reef runs along the north-east coast of Queensland, protecting a 1,200-mile length of the coast; in some places it is 140 miles away from the mainland, and in others only 12 miles. The Reef is formed from living coral, growing beneath the surface of the sea and creating considerable hazards for any visiting boats.

The official guide says, "a few feet rise and fall of the tide will, on a smooth day, completely alter the appearance of the reefs". As a result, cruising and charter boats tend to avoid visiting the Reef itself. Instead, it is usual for those who wish to dive and explore the Barrier Reef to travel out there in motorized catamarans or in helicopters. Sailing, therefore, is based on the islands between the mainland and the Reef and protected by the Reef itself.

Captain James Cook first entered the channels between the Reef and the mainland in March 1770. The remoteness of this area, however, has meant that few but the adventurous were able to follow him. In the last decade, jet flights and modern sailboats have transformed this tropical rarity into a sought-after cruising area.

Because of its remoteness, charter cruising predominates, although there is nothing to prevent those with enough time from sailing their own boats there. In fact, it is possible to voyage the entire length of the Reef in the protected channels. The traditional route is from south to north, because in winter, from June to September, there is no danger of cyclones; instead, there is a daily sea breeze, typical of most coasts in this sub-tropical belt, reinforced by the south-east trade winds.

There are hundreds of islands with possible anchorages, but the most popular are the Cumberland and Whitsunday groups; it is on these that the charter industry is based. Its headquarters is at Hamilton on the Whitsundays, where there is an airfield serviced by domestic flights. Inshore from the islands, on the mainland, the two most important harbors are Airlie Beach and Shute Harbor.

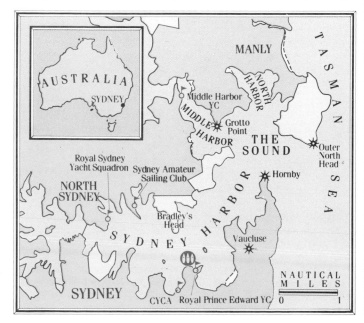

Challies Beach, Whitehaven Bay, Whitsunday Island

NEW ZEALAND

Since the 1970s, New Zealand has been considered to have a highly sophisticated sailing scene relative to its size. It boasts advanced yacht design and racing techniques and a remarkable number of international race successes.

Many of the world's top yacht designers are, or were, New Zealanders, including Bruce Farr, Ron Holland, John Ligard, John Spencer, Hal Wagstaff, Paul Whiting and the late Arthur Robb. Their boats have been instrumental in New Zealand's success in the Admiral's Cup, which they won in 1987, and in the 1987 America's Cup challenger trials, in which they finished second to the Americans. New Zealanders have won numerous Olympic medals, world championships and other prestigious events, and are sought after as crew members on many foreign boats.

This national success owes much to the temperate climate and geography of the country, which has many fine sailing waters. Although conditions can be very rugged off the South Island and in the Cook Strait, restricting the sailing season to summer, the North Island sports many safe anchorages and sheltered harbors, especially along its eastern coast near Auckland, the main center of population. In these more hospitable waters, it is possible to sail all the year around. All New Zealand's sailing waters are uncrowded and unpolluted, and thus present a pleasant contrast to the sailing grounds of the Northern Hemisphere.

Almost every New Zealand sailor begins sailing in the P-Class one-design dinghy, although the Optimist is increasing in popularity. Unlike many parts of the world, there is a high proportion of moderate to fresh winds, which seems to breed toughness in the New Zealand sailor.

Yacht racing was taking place before New Zealand became a British colony in 1841; the Auckland Anniversary Day regatta was first held in September 1840, when the British flag was "hoisted on a promontory commanding a view of the harbor" and the first European settlement was declared. From 1842 onward, the regatta was held every January. By early in the next century, locally built and designed craft were appearing, including the Mullet class. This was a flat-bottomed craft with a large spread of sail, and its hull was based on a boat used for netting the fish of that name. These boats still race as a class today, although they now have bowsprits, metal masts and dacron sails.

The Auckland Yacht Club was founded in 1871, and from 1902 has been known as the Royal New Zealand Yacht Squadron. The North Shore Sailing Club started in 1894, becoming the Royal Akarana Yacht Club in 1937. Both these clubs organize many leading events; the Akarana being particularly active offshore.

Such is the strength of sailing in a country of just over 3 million people that when a national team competes in the Admiral's Cup, or the Whitbread Race fleet arrives in Auckland, the event is front-page news and featured prominently on radio and television. New Zealanders cannot understand why far less notice is given in the American or British media to such important sporting events.

HAURAKI GULF

LAT · 36°50′S   LONG · 175°20′E

When Auckland sailors leave harbor, they sail out into the Hauraki Gulf. Enclosed on three sides in its southern waters, the Gulf is some 60 miles from north to south. The whole area, including 40 islands and some mainland, is preserved as Hauraki Gulf Maritime Park. Some of the islands have been designated as nature reserves to ensure that the Gulf and its scenery are preserved.

The map shows only that part of the Gulf near to Auckland, which is the area most visited by boats on weekends and vacations. Its size, however, allows for much more extensive cruising and racing.

The largest island, Waiheke, is 10 miles east of Auckland, and sports numerous inlets and bays. When the prevailing south-west wind is blowing, popular anchorages are Omaru, Little

Muddy and Man o'War Bays at the eastern end of the island. On the northern end, a typical small anchorage is Garden Cove. A large gannet colony nests on part of the island, as well as on Gannet Rock to the north.

Nearby, Ponui Island possesses several sheltered bays and sandy beaches. When the weather deteriorates, Islington Bay, also known as Drunken Bay, is a much-used anchorage. Half a mile wide and more than a mile long, it separates Rangitoto and Motutapu islands and is about four miles from the entrance to Waitemata Harbor, Auckland. The secure holding ground is thick, black mud. Other anchorages in the Gulf vary in suitability from day to day, depending on the direction of the wind. Among these are Rakino Island, Maori Garden, Sandy Bay, Station Bay and Home Bay on

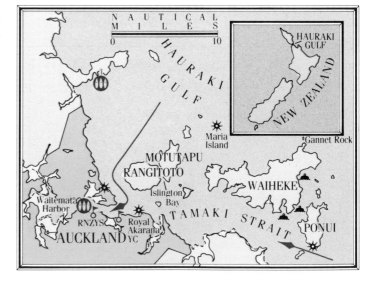

Motutapu: the very names seem to symbolize leisurely sailing.

Numerous races criss-cross the Gulf, organized by the clubs in Auckland and neighboring areas. Westhaven Marina in Auckland has berths for some 1,500 boats, but when the Whitbread Race (see pp 80-3) arrives in port once every four years, the visitors are berthed at a commercial wharf cleared for the purpose. Some 6,000 boats and 300,000 people on shore watched the departure of the fleet for Cape Horn in 1986.

BAY OF ISLANDS

LAT · 34°50′ S   LONG · 174°15′ E

The Bay of Islands is nearly 120 miles to the north of Auckland, on a north-east-facing coast. The Bay contains about 150 islands in a sub-tropical setting. Invariably, the water is clear, and blue-green in color, and the Bay's position as one of the most northerly cruising grounds in New Zealand means that the weather is frequently pleasantly sub-tropical.

The harbors of Russell and Paihia on the mainland are the headquarters for the charter fleets. The area is also noted for big-game fishing, which, to some extent, takes precedence over sailing activities.

Since most boats are based near Auckland, cruisers or overnight racers are most likely to make the passage up the coast to the Bay, with the port of Tutukaka providing a suitable stop-off point.

To the north of Tutukaka are the Poor Knights Islands, situated in the path of a tropical current that flows southward along the coast. The warm water in this marine reserve supports coral and a host of tropical fish and fauna. The islands were the site of one of the last of the Maori massacres, and a reputed hide-out for a German U-boat during World War II.

Even further north of the Bay of Islands are the Cavalli Islands and the perfect harbor of Whangaroa. The entrance to the latter is tricky in onshore (easterly) winds, but, once inside, the harbor typifies New Zealand's sailing scene – changeable on the open coast, but with an abundance of beautiful, secure anchorages. Whangaroa has a waterfront of shops and houses, but otherwise its shores are bush-clad banks. There is a freshwater stream which can be reached by dinghy.

If continuing further north, the next major harbor is Mangonui, but to venture far beyond it takes the cruising boat out toward the tropical waters of the Pacific Ocean.

OTHER NEW ZEALAND WATERS

The Bay of Plenty is a wide bay, about 100 miles in extent, on the north-east of North Island. Boats from Auckland reach the Bay by sailing out of the Hauraki Gulf via the Colville Channel and then heading south-east past the Mercury Islands. Although these are small, with rocky outcrops, they provide several anchorages. The Bay's first mainland port is Whitianga, on its north-west extremity. This is a general coastal resort, better known for offshore fishing than for sailing.

Out in the Bay, some 20 miles offshore, are Mayor and White Islands. Both are of volcanic origin; White Island is still active, but boats have been known to anchor there when ash has been spewing out of the crater. Such sights are not uncommon in some of New Zealand's sailing waters.

The Marlborough Sounds are deep inlets on the South Island which lead into Cook Strait. The waters here are not unlike those of Scandinavia and the water is colder than that off Auckland. The climate is more unsettled than the north. Boats anchor by leading warps out to trees, or to secure points on steep, rocky shores. The large cities of Wellington and Nelson are in this area. The latter is the base for a number of cruising boats, as is the town of Picton.

In the far south-west of South Island is the Fiordland National Park. The country and its coast are altogether more rugged; high mountains come down to the sea and there is snow on some peaks all year round. A number of the many inlets are named and charted, but others are not. The entire area includes thousands of miles of foreshore, and provides New Zealand's sailors with a very special cruising experience. However, katabatic winds (blowing down from the mountains), and full exposure to the Roaring Forties, make this a very different world from the ideal cruising waters off the North Island.

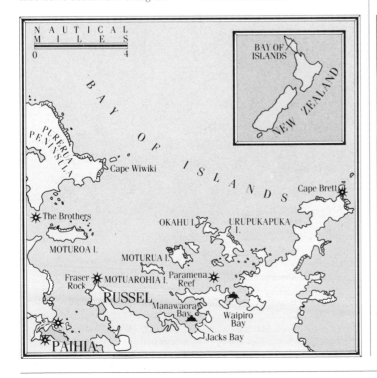

Queen Charlotte Sound

THE FAR EAST AND PACIFIC

The Far East and the Pacific are comparative newcomers to the yachting scene, although the Royal Hong Kong Yacht Club was founded in 1889 and the Royal Suva Yacht Club in 1931. Both areas, however, are gradually increasing in importance and their future potential is more significant than their present status. The Pacific islands, in particular, have benefitted from improvements in communication and increasing wealth. When combined with idyllic weather and scenery, the result has been a rapid growth in sailing activities.

Phuket, in Thailand has taken the lead in the promotion of sailing along the mainland of south-east Asia, but Hong Kong, Singapore and Manila are all planning to enlarge their marinas and to enlist government and sponsored support for promoting sailboat racing.

It is probable that at least 1,000 boats cruise the South Pacific each season. They come mainly from Australia, New Zealand and the West Coast of the US, but lately many more are from Europe. This may not sound very impressive to those who are used to the busy waters of Europe and America, but consider how long it takes to sail to the Pacific and the vast distances within the area; the distance between London and Leningrad, for example is 530 nautical miles less than that between Sydney, Australia and Suva, Fiji.

It is impossible to do more than mention a few of the islands in the West and South Pacific. The romantic Tahiti of Gauguin now suffers from high prices, although it is still popular with many Europeans and Americans. The Cook Islands possess one surge-prone harbor on Rarotonga, with limited facilities but no other safe anchorages except the lagoons of Penrhyn and Suwarrow 500 miles to the north. Apia and Pago Pago in the Samoas offer comparatively good facilities, but little cruising. Tonga is making an effort to cater to cruisers: Nuku'alofa has a new small-boat basin; 'Uta Vava'u, a charter center 150 miles to the north, is a beautiful island with safe anchorages, but very limited facilities.

Fiji's central position in the Southern Pacific is largely responsible for its popularity. In addition, it offers more varied cruising than the other island groups and has the best facilities at the best prices.

Vanuatu, which inspired Michener's *Tales of the South Pacific*, has charm, safe anchorages and a fascinating cultural mix, but few marine facilities. Nevertheless, it is a popular stopping off point for those en route to Fiji and neighboring islands. The Solomon Islands are said to be a largely unexplored delight, with safe but rarely visited coves and no facilities at all. Noumea in New Caledonia is popular, less expensive than Tahiti, but lacking its cruising variety.

It is particularly essential to possess adequate charts when travelling in the Pacific; coral abounds in all the island groups, as well as between islands. Some two-thirds of Fiji's local craft, few of which have charts, run aground every year. The cyclone season varies from group to group, but in general cyclones are a risk from mid-November to early March.

PHUKET

LAT · 7°58′N   LONG · 98°24′E

The largest island off the coast of Thailand, Phuket is the size of Singapore and typical of the coastline in the area. Covered in tropical rain forest, the island is indented with numerous bays and inlets with sandy beaches, many of which are accessible only from the sea, and is itself surrounded by rocks and islands of varying sizes. The climate is naturally tropical, so the sailing season is from October to April when the north-west monsoon averages Force 3 to 4, although it can occasionally reach Force 6 to 7. During the summer months there is the threat of typhoons.

Phuket town still has something of a colonial flavor, although the development of hotel and tourist facilities is continuing apace. While there is a quay in the town, most boats choose to lie off the beaches around the island, notably those at Patong, Karon and Kata. Various charter outfits operate from these beaches, offering cruises to local destinations.

Phuket's main racing event is the Pansea Cup, first held in January 1987; it is an annual series of passage races to Pangkor Laut, in Malaysia, and in its first year attracted 42 participants from all over the Far East. Apart from this competition, Phuket is a somewhat isolated sailing area, with the nearest other major sailing center – Hong Kong – over 1,500 miles away!

While it is still an area generally frequented by those with much time or money, it is becoming ever more popular with the more mainstream European and American vacation markets. It seems set to become a major charter region by the end of this century.

NUKU'ALOFA, TONGA
LAT · 21°10'S   LONG · 175°10'W

Many cruisers regard Nuku'alofa as one of the most important ports in the Pacific; it has all the facilities of Tahiti, without the expense. These include slips, building and repair facilities and limited spares. The compact town has its commercial area, royal palace, and main wharf all close together. Among them is a small-craft basin. Set back from this is the Nuku'alofa Yacht Club. Despite the fact that it is small in size, with no actual waterfront facilities, the Club's friendliness and warmth provide ample compensation.

The port is the capital of Tonga and is situated on its main island, Tongatapu. Although the island is flat, without any scenic features, sailors can visit sites of local interest, such as the Ha'amonga Trilithon, a mysterious stone circle, reputedly dating from 1000BC, or just enjoy the fresh fruit and vegetables, inexpensive restaurants and the overwhelming friendliness of the locals.

Most visiting boats are on their way to or from the north. From Nuku'alofa, it is one day's sail northwards to the Ha'apai Group, a cluster of low atolls, set in protective coral reefs. A further day's sail north is 'Uta Vava'u, the base for the South Pacific's major charter operator. The steep, forested hills on either side of the narrow entrance channel provide a spectacular approach to the Port of Refuge; almost every cove on the island offers safe, sheltered anchorage. Facilities are limited, but the sandy beaches on the surrounding islands, sights such as Swallow's Cave and the hospitality of local villages make this a popular cruising area.

The harbor at Neiafu on 'Uta Vava'u, Tonga

SUVA, FIJI
LAT · 18°8'S   LONG · 178°25'E

Suva is the capital and the largest city of the most populous nation in the South Pacific, Fiji. It is also the region's largest and busiest port. The city is situated on Fiji's only natural harbor, its open southern end protected by a reef with a safe, easy passage for ships of any size. It offers the best facilities in the region and the only cruising club, the Royal Suva Yacht Club. There are two marinas, four slipways, a lift, boatbuilding and repair yards, sailmakers and chandlers. The area known as the Bay of Islands in the north-west corner of the harbor is considered to be the Pacific's safest hurricane hole, although in a real blow it is safe for only about 20 craft.

The harbor is the venue for short-course keelboat and dinghy racing, while further racing takes place outside the reef. A biennial race is run from Auckland, New Zealand to Suva (see p119), while Fiji is also one of the ports of call in the Auckland-Fiji-Vila (or Noumea)-Auckland event. This unique cruise-race stops at Musket Cove on Malolo Lailai island, a day's sail west of Suva. From here, local races through the Yasawa and Maranuca islands take place. Racing rules include obligatory use of engines, a major prize for the last boat home and bonus points for pot plants or old sails!

Cruisers visiting Fiji must register first at one of the following ports: Suva on the east coast of Viti Levu, Lautoka on its western coast, Levuka on the island of Ovalu to the east, or at Musket Cove during race time. They must also formally apply for permission to visit most outer islands. Entry and clearance are routine; island permits are not, and they are strictly enforced.

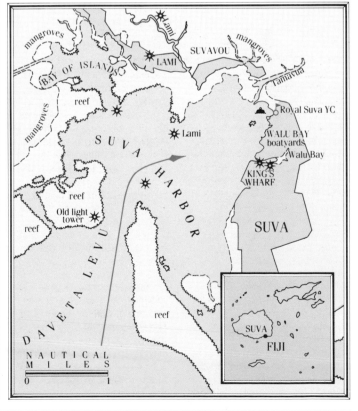

GLOSSARY

All terms in italic are cross-referenced.

Almanac Annual book containing information on the sun, stars, tides, pilotage, radio signals, etc.

Angle of heel Angle of mast from vertical when sailing, measured by clinometer. Excessive heel reduces speed; rectified by reducing sail.

Anti-fouling Paint compound containing toxins which repel marine growth. Used to protect underwater area of hull; recently the object of environmental concern.

Autopilot Device for steering boat on pre-set course, either to a compass bearing or at an angle to the wind. Operates tiller, wheel or auxiliary rudder.

Auxiliary Old-fashioned term for sailboat with engine, also refers to motor itself. Today, boats without engines are the exception.

Back Wind backs when it moves counterclockwise. Opposite of *Veer*.

Ballast Dead weight to lower boat's center of gravity, usually in the form of a lead or cast-iron keel, but can also be in pieces in the hull, provided it is secured.

Beaufort Scale Scale of wind speed ranging from 0 (calm) to 12 (hurricane).

Best corrected time Lowest *corrected time* of a boat in all classes in a race.

Bilgeboard Instead of a single centerboard or deep keel; this is a board on each side of the centerline, one of which is lowered to leeward. Penalized in IOR.

Blanket Racing technique whereby one boat deliberately blocks the wind of another boat.

Boat speed Actual speed of hull through the water, regardless of speed over the bottom.

Bowman Also known as bow. Crew member responsible for foredeck, particularly spinnaker work.

Brig Two-masted sailing ship with *gaff* mainsail and square sails on both masts.

Brigantine Two-masted sailing ship, schooner-rigged on main mast and square-rigged on foremast.

Broach Inadvertently slewing round when running before a big sea; also losing control under spinnaker and rounding into the wind. An unwanted gybe is apt to result in a leeward broach away from the wind.

Buoyage Attempts to agree a standardized system worldwide have resulted in two main systems – A, used mainly in European waters, and B, used mainly in American and Canadian waters.

Cabin trunk In UK: coach roof.

Cable One-tenth of a nautical mile; 185.2 m or 202.5 yd (commonly thought of as 200 m or yd).

Calm Wind strength of less than 1 knot; Force 0 on *Beaufort Scale*.

Carvel Form of wooden hull construction in which planking is laid edge to edge.

Cat boat One-masted boat carrying a single *gaff* sail. Cat-ketch has two main masts, each with a single sail. No connection with 'cat' as abbreviation for catamaran.

Cheat the tide Sail against tidal stream where it is weakest, usually close to shore.

Clinker Form of wooden hull construction in which planks overlap; also known as lapstrake.

Cold molded Construction of ply veneers glued together to produce a strong, light hull.

Colregs International Regulations for Prevention of Collision at Sea, sometimes known as IRPCS.

Compressive strength Ability of material to withstand a crushing force, measured in gms per sq cm or lbs per sq in.

Congressional Cup racing System of match racing in which successive pairs of boats are started at regular intervals; each boat eventually sails against every other boat to find an overall winner.

Corrected time Time after application of *time allowance* to the *elapsed time*. Used to place boats in a race.

Cunningham hole Eye in *luff* of sail above *tack* which allows tension of luff to be adjusted.

Cutter Single-masted vessel that can set two *foresails* at any one time.

Death roll Steadily increasing roll when running nearly dead before the wind under spinnaker. Alleviated by taking spinnaker sheet well forward and steering toward spinnaker.

Displacement Any floating object displaces its own weight. Displacement is used to calculate actual weight of boat; builder's figures are notoriously inaccurate.

Dock Jetty or staging where boat is moored. Originally US term, it is now widely used.

Draft Vertical distance from waterline to bottom of keel.

Drift Wind, current and tide push a boat off its presumed course and, unless taken into account, can cause navigational error.

Drogue Tapered tube on a line which, when towed, prevents the *drift* of a boat.

Elapsed time The actual time of a boat over the race course.

Fairlead Bolt, ring or other fitting through which rope is run to guide it in required direction.

Fetch Sailing a leg to a windward mark without having to tack; also distance between a boat and windward shore.

Fiberglass In UK: glassfibre. See *GRP*.

Fleet position When racing, a boat's placing in relation to entire fleet, rather than individual classes. The term IOR or CHS or PHRF fleet is current list of rated boats to the respective rule.

Foot Sailing quickly to windward as the result of high *boat speed* rather than *pointing* very close; also, the lower edge of a sail.

Foreguy Line leading forward from end of spinnaker pole, boom, etc. to keep it in position. Sometimes known as downhaul.

Foresail Principal sail set on forward mast, not to be confused with *headsail*.

Fractional rig Rig in which forestay and genoa are attached a slight distance below top of mast.

Free A boat is freed when the wind angle from the bow increases. Such a wind is known as a freer. Opposite of *Head*.

Gaff Spar which extends a four-sided fore-and-aft mainsail, or triangular topsail.

Gale Refers specifically to mean wind speed: 30 knots is near gale or moderate gale, 37 knots is gale or fresh gale.

Gnomonic Projection Form of chart projection in which lines of latitude are curved; in less frequent use than *Mercator Projection*.

Great Circle route Ocean crossing along the shortest distance between two points on the Earth's surface. On a *gnomonic* chart, the great circle appears as a straight line.

GRP Glass-reinforced plastics, used in hull construction; confusingly plastics vary and reinforcement is not always of glass. Also known as glassfibre and fiberglass.

Guns Used in talking of race starts. The 10-minute gun is the preparatory signal. The 5-minute gun is the warning signal. The gun is the start. Custom is to give a finishing gun to first three boats to complete course. Guns also draw attention to other important signals.

Gybe-set Gybing round mark and immediately hoisting spinnaker.

Hand To lower and stow a sail.

Handicapping Adjustment of times between unequal boats in a race according to a system of rated or allocated figures.

Harden up Sail closer to the wind.

Hardware Bolted-on or loose deck fittings.

Head Wind moves toward the bow. Known as a header. Opposite of *Free*.

Headsail Sail set forward of a mast. Usually does not include spinnaker or *running sails*.

Heave to Trim sails or use engine to keep boat almost stationary.

Heavy weather General term for conditions with wind at level of strong breeze (Force 6) or above.

Helm Used to refer to tiller, wheel or helmsperson.

Hi-tech Loose term for technically advanced materials and construction in sails, hull and spars.

Hurricane Tropical revolving storm in west Atlantic, or wind speed of 64 knots and over. Force 12 on *Beaufort Scale*.

Jackstay A wire along which a *traveller* or slider runs.

Jockey pole Holds spinnaker guy out from shrouds and stanchions; also reaching strut.

Jury Emergency or temporary repair, as in jury rig, jury rudder.

Keelboat Many boats have keels, but in this book the term is confined to day-racing boats that are neither centerboarders nor multihulls.

Ketch Two-masted boat, the taller mast stepped forward, and the smaller *mizzen* mast before the rudder post. Modern two-masters are almost all ketches.

Kicking strap Tackle or rod that prevents boom from lifting. Also known as boom vang or kicker.

Knock-down Boat pressed horizontally, or nearly so, by sudden squall. A B2 knock-down became notorious as term used in official inquiry into 1979 Fastnet Race for being hove down beyond 90°.

Land breeze Wind from land on to sea. Opposite of *Sea breeze*.

Layline Line along which a boat can *fetch* a mark when sailing close hauled; very important in racing tactics.

Lazy Rope not in use at the moment, such as lazy guy, lazy sheet.

Leading lights and beacons Two or more lights or beacons to keep in line when entering harbor. The line made by these is called a transit line or range.

Leeboard Device fitted instead of centerboard which drops down lee side of vessel, as on traditional Dutch sailing craft; also board fitted to side of bunk to prevent occupant falling out.

Leech After edge of fore-and-aft sail; both edges of square sail.

Lie a-hull Allow boat to drift sideways in a gale with no sails up. Dangerous in winds of 50 knots or above because of possible *knock-down* or capsize.

Lifeline Wires, usually double and 0.6 m (2 ft) high, around edge of deck for safety; also known as guardrail.

Life preserver Flotation device; also known as lifejacket.

Liferaft Inflatable craft carried on board for emergency use.

Light air Mean wind speed of 2 knots; Force 1 on *Beaufort Scale*.

Light breeze Mean wind speed of 5 knots; Force 2 on *Beaufort Scale*.

Light list List of fixed lights on rocks, seabed or coast, with descriptions of their structures by day as well as lights by night.

Light weather General term for wind below about 13 knots (Force 4).

Line honors In some races, awarded to boat which finishes first.

Log Instrument for measuring boat's speed through water; also book for recording weather, navigation, etc.

Luff Steer into the wind; also forward edge of sail.

Measurement rule Method of rating a boat by taking numerous dimensions of hull and rig to arrive at a single rating figure.

Mercator Projection Principal form of chart projection in sea navigation, in which lines of latitude and longitude are straight.

Messenger Light line passing via leads, blocks, etc. which pulls the working line into position.

Millibar Unit of pressure measured by barometer.

Mizzen Aft mast of various rigs; the fore-and-aft sail hoisted on the mizzen mast.

Overhaul To loosen ropes in a tackle or over any block. Also, to overtake.

Overstand To arrive at a mark close hauled further to windward than necessary. Undesirable as it means extra distance covered.

Pilot charts Issued by US Hydrographic Office, showing wind direction expected during each month in numerous sub-divided sea areas.

Pitchpole Boat tipped stern over bow, usually in very high seas, resulting in capsize and almost certain damage.

Point To sail as close to the wind as possible. Points of sailing are the different directions of the boat's heading to the wind.

Pushpit Stern pulpit.

Rating Single figure in a linear dimension (meters or feet) allocated to a boat or class as a measure of potential speed.

Rhumb line Course that cuts all meridians at the same angle. On a *Mercator* chart, the straight line between two points.

Rode In UK: anchor cable.

Rules Principal rules for racing are: racing rules of the IYRU; measurement or rating rule applicable or rules of the class; and sailing instructions of the race.

Runner Standard term for running backstay, a movable support for the mast, adjusted on each tack to allow boom to swing.

Running sails Sails to be used with wind aft, including square sails, spinnakers and *mizzen* staysails.

Sail area Important indication of boat's character. May be actual or in accordance with *measurement rule*.

Sailing directions Book of pilotage.

Sailing instructions Written rules for a race issued by organizers, additional to established racing and class rules, covering course to be sailed and other matters. Verbal instructions have no legality.

Sail plan Designer's vertical profile of entire rig. Also means series of *waypoints*.

Schooner Two-masted boat with aft mast equal or taller than the other.

Sea anchor Any type of *drogue* used as floating anchor, especially during a gale.

Sea breeze Wind from sea on to land. Opposite of *Land breeze*.

Self-bailer Device through bottom of hull that sucks out bilgewater; it only works if the boat has more than minimal speed.

Self-tacking Jib that does not need to be hauled round on each tack.

Ship's papers Varies from nation to nation. However, any boat voyaging beyond its own country's waters is advised to carry proper documentation.

Sloop Single-masted boat with one *headsail*, either gaff or bermudan rigged.

Spreaders Struts on either side of mast, connected to shrouds, to strengthen it.

Stable Ability to return to upright position from any given angle of heel. Not to be confused with *stiff*.

Stiff Resistance to heeling due to boat's shape and low center of gravity. Opposite is *tender*.

Storm Mean wind speed of 59 knots; Force 11 on *Beaufort Scale*.

Stripped out Implies racing boat with poor accommodation; aim is to save weight and increase speed.

Tack The foreward lower corner of a fore-and-aft sail; also to turn the bows of a boat through the wind.

Tactician Crew member who assists helmsman plan racing tactics in response to positions of other boats, marks and obstructions.

Tender Boat which heels easily. Opposite to *stiff*; also, the dinghy belonging to a sailboat.

Tensile strength Strength of a material when pulled apart. Measured in gms per sq cm or lbs per sq in, it is an important quality in hull and rig construction.

Time allowance Number of seconds per mile or seconds per hour allocated between one boat and another in *handicapping*.

Tonnage Term used to describe size of boat. Originally number of casks (tuns) hold would carry; now many factors involved in calculation.

Traveller Slider on a wire or track; also known as car or fairlead. Alters sheeting angles of sail.

Trimmer Crew member who tends the set of a sail.

Trip Release line instantly, usually with device intended for such action.

Trysail Triangular loose-footed sail aft of mast, used to replace mainsail in heavy weather.

Tuning Adjusting deck equipment and rig for best performance.

Turnbuckle Also known as rigging screw.

Veer Wind veers when it shifts clockwise. Opposite of *Back*.

VMG Velocity-made-good is progress made directly into the wind.

Waypoint Latitude and longitude of points at which proposed track alters on a passage. These are fed into position-fixing equipment and helmsman then follows electronically deduced course.

Wetted surface Area of hull in contact with the water. This is the major cause of resistance at low speeds, so the area must be kept as smooth as possible.

Wind Described as true when measured from stationary position; apparent when boat is moving; and tidal or current induced, when applicable.

Wind speed Measured at sea in knots, meters per second or *Beaufort Scale* (Forces 0 to 12).

Windward leg Section of race course directly into the wind to a windward mark.

Wing keel Hydrodynamically shaped bulbous section along bottom edge of keel to lower center of gravity and improve performance.

Working sails Mainsail and *headsails*.

Yawl Two-masted boat with her *mizzen* mounted aft of rudder post; now obsolescent because rudders are invariably right aft.

INDEX

J

H

ACKNOWLEDGMENTS

Chapter 7 illustrations Ray Harvey
Other illustrations Peter Bull – except
                          pp 7, 64, 163, 185, by
                          Thomas Keenes, and
                          pp 148-9, 152, 155, by
                          Kevin Molloy
Original photography Peter Chadwick
Cartography Lovell Johns Ltd, Oxford
Index David Linton
Production Jeanette Graham

Dorling Kindersley would like to thank James Allen and Sarah Godowski for their help with the text, and Hannah Moore, Mark Regardsoe, Bryan Sayers (Diamond Arts) and Christian Sévigny for their help with the design and artwork.

AUTHOR'S ACKNOWLEDGMENTS

This record of world sailing could never have been compiled without the help of many people. I particularly wish to thank: Ray Harvey for the color illustrations for Chapter 7; Charles E. Mason III, executive editor of *Sail*, for the major contributions of information and facts from the US; Svante Domizlaff, racing and classes in Germany; Matt Johnson, research in the Mediterranean and UK; Winkie Nixon, for providing the basis of Chapter 2 and information on Irish classes; Simon Forbes of the IYRU; Bengt O. Hult, racing and classes in Sweden; and D.H. Clarke, © records of ocean voyaging, pp 54-7.

The following people also supplied me with information and I would like to thank them for their time and effort: Eivind Amble, Norway; Mike Balmforth, Scotland; Grete Bierring, Denmark; Tony Blachford, boat equipment; François Carn, Yacht Club de France; H.S. Cocks, New Zealand; Martin Cowell, sailmaking; David Cox, South Africa; Bruce Farr & Associates Inc, development designs; Alan Green & Janet Grosvenor, RORC; Mike Hampton, landsailers; Roger Hill, New Zealand; Philip Jenkins, South America; Peter Kay, sailmaking; Aedgard Koekebakker, Dutch classes; David Lines, 505 dinghy; Ian A. McCurdy, Seawanhaka Corinthian YC; James McVie, Canada; Murray Masterton, Fiji and the Far East; Joan Matthewson, ORC; Arthur Middleton, Victorian navigation equipment; Kenneth L. Morrison, Royal Hawaian Ocean RC; John Nicholls, the Far East; North Sails UK, sailcloth; John Roberson, Australia; Bob Ross, Australia; SP Systems, boat construction; Gilbert Scheuss, German classes; Gaither Scott, Annapolis YC; Diane Sloma, Gibraltar; Sandy Taggart, Clyde CC; Telesonic Marine Ltd, electronic equipment; Tom Vaughan, International 14; Hal Wagstaff, New Zealand; Penny Way, boardsailing; West Custom Marine, boat construction.

It is not possible to mention individually the numerous people from the different classes in Chapter 7: builders, designers, class chairmen, secretaries and class bulletin editors supplied more details than I could use. Thanks are also due to several others who assisted me in tracking down some important, but elusive, classes of sailing boat.

A work of this kind needs considerable professional support and guidance, and I wish to thank all those at Dorling Kindersley with whom I have worked, especially Vicky Davenport, Simon Adams, Mark Richards and Angela Murphy.

PHOTOGRAPHIC ACKNOWLEDGMENTS

Prelims: 2-3 Peter Neuman, Yacht Photo Service, Hamburg; 6tl Nederlandsch Historisch Scheepvaart Museum, Amsterdam; 6tr From *The Sunbeam* by Lord Brassey (1917); 6bl Roger Lean-Vercoe; 6br Garrard, London; 7tr Bob Fisher/Pickthall Picture Library.
Chapter 1: 8-9, 10b,t, 11t Nederlandsch Historisch Scheepvaart Museum, Amsterdam; 11b National Maritime Museum, London; 12t Oliver Swann Marine Paintings, London; 12-13, 14, 15 National Maritime Museum, London; 16 From Vol II of the Badminton edition of *Yachting* (1894); 17 Royal Thames YC, London; 18, 19t Royal Yacht Squadron, Cowes; 19b Royal Dart YC, Devon; 20 Royal Yacht Squadron, Cowes; 21 Section IV of a 'View of New York' by William Burgis, 1717/Courtesy The New York Historical Society; 22t Peabody Museum, Salem, Mass.; 22b Stevens Institute of Technology, Hoboken, NJ; 23t Mystic Seaport Museum; 23b J. Clarence Davies Collection, Museum of City of New York.
Chapter 2: 26-7 Tilman Collection/Courtesy of Pam Davis; 28t From *Down Channel* by R.T. McMullen (1869); 28b The Parker Gallery, London; 29t From *Down Channel*; 29b Beken of Cowes; 30l From *The Voyage alone in the Yawl Rob Roy* by J. Macgregor (1864); 30tr From *The Sunbeam* by Lord Brassey (1917); 30tr (inset) Beken of Cowes; 30br National Maritime Museum, London; 32l Courtesy of Maldwin Drummond; 32br, 32t Royal Cruising Club; 33t West & Son/Courtesy of Peter Johnson; 33b From *The Falcon on the Baltic* by F. Knight (1888); 34t, 34b William le Fanu/Courtesy of Mrs Lucie Christie; 35t From *Sailing Alone Around the World* by Captain J. Slocum (1900); 36t Rosenfeld Collection, Mystic Seaport Museum; 36b From *Rudder* magazine (1901)/National Maritime Museum, London; 37t Royal Cruising Club; 37b The Cruising Association, London; 38b From *The Cruise of the Amaryllis* by Lt. G. Mulhauser (1924); 39t Rosenfeld Collection, Mystic Seaport Museum; 39b Beken of Cowes; 40t Rosenfeld Collection, Mystic Seaport Museum; 41t From *The Flight of the Firecrest* by Alain Gerbault (1930); 41b Courtesy of Peter Johnson; 42t From *Around the World Singlehanded* by H. Pidgeon (1951); 42b Robin Bryer; 43t Beken of Cowes; 43b Courtesy of Peter Johnson; 44t Courtesy of Peter Johnson; 44b, 45t Jonathan Eastland; 45b David Lewis; 46 Royal Cruising Club; 47t From *Rough Passage* by R.D. Graham (1934); 48 From *The Macpherson Voyages* by A. Macpherson (1939); 48 (inset) Royal Cruising Club; 49t From *Alone through the Roaring Forties* by V. Dumas (1960); 49b Joe Rooney; 50l W.G. Lee/Courtesy of Peter Johnson; 50t Tilman Collection/Courtesy of Pam Davis; 50-1b Tom Lawlor; 51t Major Willie Ker; 52l Gerry Clark; 52-3 Deborah Shapiro & Rolf Bjelke; 54 Beken of Cowes; 56b Jonathan Eastland; 56t Courtesy of Miles Clark.
Chapter 3: 58-9 Peter Neuman, Yacht Photo Service, Hamburg; 60-1b, 61t, 62, 63 Rosenfeld Collection, Mystic Seaport Museum; 67 Peter Johnson; 70-1bl Jonathan Eastland; 71 Patrick Roach; 73br Brian Manby; 74 Colin Jarman, Eyeline Photos; 75 Rick Tomlinson; 78t Pickthall Picture Library; 79b Christian Février, Paris; 81 Peter Neuman, Yacht Photo Service, Hamburg; 82t Jonathan Eastland; 82b Peter Neuman, Yacht Photo Service, Hamburg; 83t, 83b Colin Jarman, Eyeline Photos; 84 Rosenfeld Collection, Mystic Seaport Museum; 86-7b Bob Fisher/Pickthall Picture Library; 87t Pickthall Picture Library; 88 Patrick Roach; 89 Christian Février, Paris; 90 Pierre Lenormand/Christian Février; 91 Christian Février, Paris; 92 Irish Times; 94 Roger Lean-Vercoe; 95 Rick Tomlinson; 96 Beken of Cowes; 97 Greg Shires, Chicago; 98bl Roger Lean-Vercoe; 98t Rick Tomlinson; 99 Roger Lean-Vercoe; 100-1t Jonathan Eastland; 101r Champagne Mumm; 103 Jonathan Eastland; 106 Times Newspapers; 107t Patrick Roach; 107b Colin Jarman, Eyeline Photos; 109 Patrick Roach; 110t,b Colin Jarman, Eyeline Photos; 113 Nordisk Pressefoto, Copenhagen; 114 Pickthall Picture Library; 115 Australian Picture Library; 119 *New Zealand Yachting Magazine*; 121, 122 Rosenfeld Collection, Mystic Seaport Museum; 123 Bob Fisher, Pickthall Picture Library; 124 Pickthall Picture Library; 127 Neil Rabinowitz; 128b Rosenfeld Collection, Mystic Seaport Museum; 128t Royal Canadian YC; 129 Guy Gurney; 131t Neil Rabinowitz; 131b Royal Hawaiian ORC; 132, 133 James McVie; 134 Casarell/Pickthall Picture Library; 136 Agencia JB/Peter Siemens; 137 Alberto Ferreira/Peter Siemens.
Chapter 4: 138-9 Kos; 140 National Maritime Museum, London; 141 Garrard, London; 142 Library of Congress; 143 National Maritime Museum, London; 144 Photo by Allen & Co/From *British Yachts and Yachtsmen* (1907); 145 Beken of Cowes; 146bl From *Judge* magazine (1901)/British Library; 146 Rosenfeld Collection, Mystic Seaport Museum; 147, 149t Beken of Cowes; 149b Rosenfeld Collection, Mystic Seaport Museum; 150 Australian Picture Library; 151 Rosenfeld Collection, Mystic Seaport Museum; 152 Australian Picture Library; 153 Beken of Cowes; 154 Kos; 155t Barbara Pyle/Contact/Colorific; 155b Benoit/AP; 156t Colin Jarman, Eyeline Photos; 156b Christian Février, Paris; 157 Colorsport.
Chapter 5: 158-9, 160 Roger Lean-Vercoe; 162 Alastair Black; 165l Richard Sadler; 165r *Yachting World*; 166-7 Roger Lean-Vercoe; 167r Christian Février, Paris; 170 Carlo Borlenghi, Milan; 171t Roger Lean-Vercoe; 171b Kos; 172 Christian Février, Paris; 173 Beken of Cowes; 174-5, 175 Pickthall Picture Library; 177 Christian Février, Paris; 178 The Mariner's Museum, Newport News, Va; 179 Christian Février, Paris; 180 Rosenfeld Collection, Mystic Seaport Museum; 181t Jonathan Eastland; 181b Peter Howell; 182l Courtesy of the Post Office; 183 Jon Nicholson; 184 Guy Gurney; 186 Jonathan Eastland; 187 Roger Lean-Vercoe; 188 From *The Sailing Boat* by Henry Folkard (1901); 189 Courtesy of Peter Johnson.
Chapter 6: 190-1, 192 Bob Fisher/Pickthall Picture Library; 194l Roger Lean-Vercoe; 194r Colin Jarman, Eyeline Photos; 195l,r Roger Lean-Vercoe; 195c Colin Jarman, Eyeline Photos; 196l,r Roger Lean-Vercoe; 198, 199 From *The Yachting and Boating Monthly* (Sept 1908); 200 Keystone/Hulton Deutsch Collection; 201t, 201b From *Die Olympischen Spiele, 1932*; 202t,b From *Die Olympischen Spiele, 1936* (Vol II); 203, 204b Popperfoto; 205 Keystone/Hulton Deutsch Collection; 206 Kos; 207 Colorsport; 208t Pickthall Picture Library; 208b Kos; 209t Roger Lean-Vercoe; 209b Popperfoto.
Chapter 7: 210-11 Theo Kampa.
Chapter 8: 254t Pertti Puranen/SP Systems; 254b, 255 Bild Euro Seeina/SP Systems; 256-7 SP Systems; 258-261 Peter Johnson; 268 Lady Annie Brassey/Courtesy of East Sussex County Library; 268 Nederlandsch Historisch Scheepvaart Museum, Amsterdam; 269 Beken of Cowes; 272 Christian Février, Paris; 273 Roger Lean-Vercoe; 274 From *Small Yachts* by C.P. Kunhardt (1891); 276 Beken of Cowes; 277, 278b, 278-9t, 279r; Rick Tomlinson; 280 Patrick Roach; 285 Charles Parsons; 287 Rosenfeld Collection, Mystic Seaport Museum; 288t,b, 290t,b, 291 Beken of Cowes; 293 Rosenfeld Collection, Mystic Seaport Museum; 295r,l, Beken of Cowes; 296t Peter Johnson; 297 Courtesy of Peter Johnson; 298b From *The Sailing Boat* by Henry Folkard (1901); 299 Rosenfeld Collection, Mystic Seaport Museum.
Chapter 9: 300-1 Roger Lean-Vercoe; 303, 304 Peter Neuman, Yacht Photo Service, Hamburg; 306 Paul van Riel/Robert Harding Picture Library; 307 Patrick Roach; 308l Nick Glanvill; 308-9, 309t Patrick Roach; 309b Jonathan Eastland; 310t, b Patrick Roach; 311t Robert Harding Picture Library; 311b French Government Tourist Office; 312 Jonathan Eastland; 313 Portuguese National Tourist Office; 314 Patrick Roach; 315 French Government Tourist Office; 316 Kos; 317b Italian State Tourist Office; 317t Roger Lean-Vercoe; 318t Angela Murphy; 318bl Robert Harding Picture Library; 318br Patrick Roach; 319, 320 Angela Murphy; 321 Ulrike Welsch; 322 Robert Harding Picture Library; 323l Rick Tomlinson; 323r, 325l Picturepoint; 325r Robert Harding Picture Library; 326 Picturepoint; 328 Geoff Pack; 329 Pickthall Picture Library; 330 Kos; 331 Robert Harding; 333 Miles Clark; 335 Angela Murphy; 337 Picturepoint.

The publishers would also like to thank Maldwin Drummond, Christopher Buckley and Simon Butler of the Royal Cruising Club, Paul Miller of the Cruising Association and Charles Vilas of the Cruising Club of America for additional help with illustrations.